ABRAHAM LINCOLN

This book
belongs to

David Scott

ABRAHAM LINCOLN

A Biography

By BENJAMIN P. THOMAS

BARNES
&NOBLE
BOOKS
NEW YORK

This edition published by Barnes & Noble, Inc.,
by arrangement with Alfred A. Knopf, Inc.

1994 Barnes & Noble Books

ISBN 1-56619-360-5 *casebound*
ISBN 1-56619-802-X *paperback*

Printed and bound in the United States of America

MC 9 8 7 6 5 4 3
MP 9 8 7 6 5 4 3 2

To Martha, Sarah, and George

PREFACE

NOTWITHSTANDING the great number of books that have been written about Abraham Lincoln during our generation, a major need, perhaps *the* major need so far as most persons are concerned, has long remained unfilled. There has been no accurate, readable one-volume biography for the Lincoln beginner, for the person who can devote only a small portion of his time to learning about Lincoln, or for the high-school teacher or college professor who wishes to include a reasonably short life of Lincoln on his students' reading list.

The last satisfactory life of Lincoln within the covers of a single volume was written by Lord Charnwood, an Englishman, and published thirty-five years ago. That is still an excellent book; but we have learned much more about Lincoln during those thirty-five years. Indeed, the very intensity of Lincoln study during that period, with the publication of the work of Barton, Beveridge, Sandburg, and Randall, the research done by the Abraham Lincoln Association, and the investigations of a host of other students into one phase or another of Lincoln's life, makes the correlation and condensation of our findings all the more imperative.

Perhaps the principal reason why no one has attempted to write a one-volume life of Lincoln in recent years is the students' knowledge that, with the opening of the Robert Todd Lincoln Collection in the Library of Congress and the publication of the

Preface

forthcoming *Collected Works of Abraham Lincoln* by the Abraham Lincoln Association, any such biography would immediately become obsolete, unless rewritten. The first of these great source collections became available to us in 1947; I have fully explored it. And as an editorial adviser in the preparation of the *Collected Works*, I have also been able to make full use of them in advance of their publication.

So it is my hope and purpose that this book will fill a long-felt want. It is intended primarily for the reading public rather than for the expert, though I hope that the experts will approve of it. And I believe that even they will discover that it offers new interpretations and reveals many unknown facts.

BENJAMIN P. THOMAS

ACKNOWLEDGMENTS

———————•••———————

I WISH to extend my sincere thanks to Roy P. Basler, Mrs. Harry E. Pratt, Lloyd Dunlap, and George W. Bunn, Jr., of the Abraham Lincoln Association, to Allan Nevins, of Columbia University, and to Harry E. Pratt, Illinois State Historian, for reading my entire manuscript, offering valuable suggestions and criticism, and calling my attention to letters and documents. Mrs. Pratt also checked my Lincoln quotations. Paul M. Angle, Director of the Chicago Historical Society, likewise suggested improvements in those parts of the manuscript which time enabled me to have him read.

Ralph Newman pointed out the whereabouts of material. Alfred W. Stern and Foreman M. Lebold, of Chicago, loaned me manuscripts from their collections. Earl Schenck Miers offered constant counsel and encouragement.

Margaret Flint, James N. Adams, and S. A. Wetherbee, of the Illinois State Historical Library, rendered gracious assistance. David C. Mearns and Percy Powell, of the Library of Congress, and Bert Sheldon, of Washington, D.C., were helpful and hospitable. The poem "Ann Rutledge" is quoted with the permission of Mrs. Ellen C. Masters, and General Stephen D. Ramseur's letters to his wife are quoted by the permission of David Schenck.

Hirst Dillon Milhollen and Milton Kaplan, of the Library of Congress, Josephine Cobb, of the National Archives, H. Maxson Holloway, of the Chicago Historical Society, and Mrs. Mary

Acknowledgments

Handy Evans and Mrs. Alice Handy Cox, of the L. C. Handy Studios, Washington, D.C., aided in my search. My wife gave her usual unfailing encouragement all the while I was at work. The helpfulness of Alfred A. Knopf, Roger Shugg, Harold Strauss, and others of the house of Knopf far exceeded their obligations to an author.

BENJAMIN P. THOMAS

CONTENTS

Contents

ABRAHAM LINCOLN

CHAPTER I

"The Short and Simple Annals
of the Poor"

AS O N E travels south from Louisville, Kentucky, one comes, after some forty miles, to a high, steep, craggy elevation known as Muldraugh's Hill, through which Knob Creek, a clear, swift-flowing stream, has gouged a pass to make its way to the Rolling Fork. Branches of Knob Creek have cut deep gorges into the escarpment on either side, eroding out and washing down the limestone to form small, delta-like patches of rich silt at intervals along the stream.

On one of these fertile patches two and one-half miles above the Rolling Fork, Thomas Lincoln had established a homestead, where he lived with his wife, Nancy, and their young son and daughter. His farm contained 230 acres, but only thirty acres along the creek bottom were tillable; the rest was scarred by deep ravines and overgrown with scrub trees and tangled underbrush.

Spring had brought a warm softness to the air, and the surrounding hills, which had loomed so bleakly sinister all winter, seemed to enfold the valley with new friendliness. It was corn-planting time. Tom Lincoln was out in the bottom land plying a crude hoe, and behind him toddled his small son, dropping two pumpkin seeds into every other hill of corn in alternate rows. The planting finished, the whole family rested on the Sabbath, when up in the hills a terrific cloudburst came. No rain fell in the valley,

but down the gorges rushed a swirling flood, washing out corn
and pumpkin seeds and carrying them along with much of the
loose topsoil down the creek to the Rolling Fork. It was the first
home and the first incident of his life that Abraham Lincoln could
remember when he had grown to be a man.

Of Lincoln's childhood in Kentucky we know little more than
he. Born on February 12, 1809, in a backwoods cabin three miles
south of Hodgenville, he was brought to the Knob Creek place
when he was two years old, and lived there more than five years.
A neighbor boy saved him from drowning in the creek; otherwise
his childhood years in Kentucky were uneventful. He knew the
numbing cold of winter that seeped through the chinks of the
rude cabin and defied the efforts of the roaring fire to force it out.
He knew the friendly warmth of the Kentucky sun, the touch of
cool, soft earth against bare feet. His food was coarse and plain.
His clothes were such as his mother spun and wove or fashioned
from the skins of animals brought down by his father's gun. He
did the simple tasks of a small boy—running errands, bringing in
wood and water, weeding the garden, picking grapes and wild
berries on the surrounding bluffs, dropping the seeds at planting-
time.

In later years, when Abraham Lincoln was a candidate for
President of the United States, and John Locke Scripps, a campaign biographer, asked him about his boyhood years, he replied:
"Why, Scripps, it is a great piece of folly to attempt to make
anything out of my early life. It can all be condensed into a
single sentence and that sentence you will find in Gray's Elegy—
'The short and simple annals of the poor.'"

Abraham's father, Thomas Lincoln, was born in Rockingham
County, Virginia, on January 6, 1778, the youngest son of a
prosperous pioneer farmer, also named Abraham Lincoln, who
brought his family from Virginia to Kentucky about 1782 and
settled near Hughes Station, in Jefferson County, some twenty
miles east of Louisville. A few years afterward this grandfather of
young Abraham was killed from ambush by a skulking Indian,
and the eldest son, Mordecai, witnessing the murder from the

family cabin, shot the savage just as he was making off into the forest with the younger brother, Thomas, who had accompanied his father to the woods.

After Abraham Lincoln came to manhood, he tried to trace his Lincoln ancestry, but could never follow it beyond his grandfather and namesake. After Lincoln achieved greatness, biographers, seeking an explanation of his capacities in terms of heredity, traced the Lincolns in unbroken line back through Virginia, Pennsylvania, and New Jersey to Samuel Lincoln, a weaver's apprentice, who emigrated from England to Hingham, Massachusetts, in 1637. Without exception Lincoln's forebears proved to be self-reliant, upright men of moderate or even comfortable means, who earned the respect of their neighbors. Some Lincolns in collateral lines achieved distinction, but nowhere in the lineage of Abraham were qualities foretelling greatness to be found.

In the father, Thomas, there seemed to be a falling off in the general level of Abraham's ancestry. Soon after the death of Abraham's grandfather, Thomas moved with his widowed mother to Nelson County, Kentucky. Then, after his sixteenth year, he roved about, living for a time with an uncle and aunt in Tennessee, and settling eventually in Hardin County, Kentucky. In 1803 he bought a farm of 238 acres located on Mill Creek about eight miles north of Elizabethtown, the county seat. On this farm, the first of three that he owned in Kentucky, Thomas Lincoln probably lived until a few months after his marriage to Nancy Hanks, on June 12, 1806.

Although Thomas is often represented as a shiftless man, the fact that he could pay 118 pounds cash for this farm is evidence of thrift and enterprise. True, the money may have come to him as a share of his father's estate; still, in so far as the years of his young manhood are concerned, the picture of Thomas Lincoln as a lazy ne'er-do-well has been unfairly overdrawn. From the time he reached manhood he always owned one or more horses; once he paid taxes on four. He had good credit, and no unpaid debts incurred by him have ever been discovered. A tax book of the year 1814 lists him as fifteenth in property values out of the ninety-eight persons enumerated, so that in worldly goods he stood well among his neighbors. He served on the county patrol and as a guard of prisoners. He sat on juries several times. He acted as appraiser of an estate, and while living on the Knob Creek farm he was supervisor of a few miles of road "between the Bigg Hill and the Rolling Fork." The cabins he built for his family compared favorably with those of other pioneer settlers in the region. He never learned to read, however, and his sole accomplishment in writing was to be able, with painful concentration, to scrawl his name.

Thomas Lincoln was of no more than average height, with sturdy arms and legs and heavy chest. Only his leathery complexion and coarse black hair seem to have been inherited by his son; otherwise they differed so strikingly in appearance as to support the suspicion—entertained by many persons at one time or another, but utterly discredited now—that Abraham was not Thomas's son.

Their development was even more incongruous. Abraham's most striking characteristic was a capacity for moral and mental growth, whereas steady retrogression marked Thomas's later years. Whatever energy and ambition Thomas displayed in early manhood soon abated, and eventually he seems even to have forgotten how to write his name.

Little is known about Lincoln's mother, Nancy Hanks, and the Hanks genealogy becomes a confusing wilderness that most scholars despair of ever penetrating. Lincoln himself seems to have believed that his mother was born out of wedlock to Lucy Hanks, who later married Henry Sparrow. According to his notation in the family Bible, his mother was born on February 5, 1784, so she married Thomas Lincoln at the age of twenty-two. Traditions differ as to her height, her build, the color of her eyes and hair. Whenever she signed a legal document she made her mark. Acquaintances agreed that she was intelligent, deeply religious, kindly, and affectionate.

Soon after their marriage Thomas and Nancy Hanks Lincoln moved to Elizabethtown, where Thomas purchased two lots and built a log cabin for their home. He made his living by carpentry, in which he had considerable skill, and by doing odd jobs. Their first child, Sarah, was born in Elizabethtown on February 10, 1807. In December 1808 Thomas purchased a second farm, a tract of 348½ acres on the South Fork of Nolin Creek, eighteen miles southeast of town, paying $200 cash and assuming a small obligation due a former titleholder. The soil was poor and covered with a thick mat of tall, coarse grass. Few trees grew on the land. The only attractive feature of the place was a great spring that, flowing through a cavelike channel in a hill, dropped precipitately into a deep basin in the rock, where it disappeared.

On a high point above the spring Thomas Lincoln built another rude log cabin of one room, with dirt floor, roughhewn door and window, and a big fireplace of logs and sticks lined with clay. Here Abraham was born. Thomas Lincoln still owned the Mill Creek farm that he had bought before his marriage, as well as the farm on Nolin, so that at the birth of his son he had 586½ acres of land, two town lots in Elizabethtown, some livestock, and the usual personal possessions of the pioneer farmer.

Some time in the spring of 1811 the Lincolns moved from the birthplace farm to Knob Creek, the first home that Abraham remembered. The land proved more productive, and the region was more thickly settled. The old Cumberland Trail from Louisville to Nashville passed close to their door, and along it moved a restless, eager cavalcade: pioneers with rumbling wagons and driven livestock, heading for the Northwest, peddlers who brought wares from the outside world, itinerant preachers, now and then a coffle of slaves, trudging behind a mounted overseer or slave-trader. Few slaves lived in the immediate neighborhood, however, for the landholdings were small, and sentiment among the local Methodists and especially the Baptists, with whom the Lincolns had affiliated, was decidedly antislavery.

Occasionally, when Tom Lincoln thought he could spare his children from their chores, they walked two miles to a log schoolhouse, where they learned their A B C's and the rudiments of reading, writing, and arithmetic from Zachariah Riney, a Catholic, and Caleb Hazel, who succeeded him as teacher. But this privilege came at rare intervals and never continued for long. A third child, named Thomas, was born to the Lincolns on Knob Creek, but he died in infancy.

In 1814 Tom Lincoln sold his Mill Creek farm for 100 pounds, eighteen pounds less than he had paid for it. His loss resulted from a flaw in title; the farm contained thirty-eight acres less than he supposed. Kentucky land titles in general caused constant trouble, for patents had been granted carelessly, private companies had made purchases from the Indians in defiance of colonial claims and then resold the land, and surveys were often inaccurate and overlapping. Thomas Lincoln, besides losing thirty-eight acres of his Mill Creek farm, became involved in litigation over his farm on Nolin Creek. Then title to his third farm, the Knob Creek place, came under question when a suit was filed to dispossess him. Utterly discouraged, the elder Lincoln decided to move north to Indiana, where the land had been laid off by government survey, and title could be purchased from the government. Tradition has it that he made a preliminary trip to look over the land. Then, in December 1816, the Lincolns, with all their personal possessions, set out for Indiana. Abraham was seven years old.

*

THE FAMILY's method of travel to Indiana is not known, but they probably journeyed on horseback. Passing through Elizabethtown, they made their way northwestward in order to reach the Ohio at a point opposite Troy, where a makeshift ferry took them to the Indiana shore. Now their route lay through an untracked wilderness, very sparsely settled and largely unexplored. The rolling, broken country was heavily wooded with giant oaks and elms, with maples, hackberry, sycamores, and birches. Wild grapevines laced the trees, and the undergrowth had become so densely intertwined that Thomas Lincoln had to go ahead and hack a path. Leaf-mold lay dank and heavy on the ground. Thick fog sometimes enshrouded the land, giving the gloomy forest an added mystery. One settler described the country as "woods, woods, woods, as far as the world extends!"

Wild animals abounded—raccoons, squirrels, deer, wolves, panthers, wildcats, bears. Wild turkeys, quail, and grouse nested in the underbrush. Ducks, geese—wildfowl of many sorts— whirred up from the marshes and watercourses to soar and glide and dip in honking flights. A multitude of pigeons roosted in the trees. Mosquitoes, flies, and other insects buzzed and swarmed in summer. In a poem that Lincoln composed some twenty years later he wrote:

> *When first my father settled here,*
> *'Twas then the frontier line:*
> *The panther's scream filled night with fear*
> *And bears preyed on the swine.*

The few settlers who had penetrated the region, about one family to every four square miles, were the roving half-hunter, half-farmer type. Indiana as a whole had acquired sufficient population, however, to be ready for admission to the Union as a state.

At a point some sixteen miles north of where the Lincolns had landed, Thomas Lincoln chose a homesite. Situated in what is now Spencer County, it stood on a knoll, where the trees and undergrowth were thinner. Winter already gripped the country, and Thomas must make haste to provide a shelter. Lacking time to build a cabin, he threw up a "half-faced camp," a rude shelter of logs and boughs, enclosed on three sides, with the fourth side protected only by a roaring fire, which must be kept blazing constantly to assure even a minimum of comfort. Strangely enough, he did not think of water. The nearest supply was almost a mile away, unless the family used melted snow, and young Abraham trudged to the spring whenever water was needed for drinking and cooking. During this first winter in Indiana the family subsisted almost entirely on game, which also furnished skins and furs to keep them warm. It was the low point in the Lincolns' fortunes.

In a short autobiography that he wrote in the third person in 1860, Lincoln recalled that "the clearing away of surplus wood was the great task ahead. Abraham, though very young, was large of his age, and had an axe put into his hands at once; and from that till within his twentythird year, he was almost constantly handling that most useful instrument—less, of course, in plowing and harvesting seasons." Almost every biographer of Lincoln has stated that the family lived in the half-faced camp almost a year, and cites this as evidence of Thomas's shiftlessness. Actually, Thomas built a better home at once, for Abraham recalled that a few days before his eighth birthday, when a flock of wild turkeys came over "the new log-cabin," he stood inside with a rifle and, sighting through a crack, brought one of them down. "He has never since," he added, "pulled a trigger on any larger game." With the necessity of providing food by hunting and fishing, and in view of Thomas Lincoln's fondness for those sports, it is strange that Abraham never developed any liking for either of them.

By spring Thomas, with what help young Abe could give him, had hacked out a small clearing for a crop. Year by year the forest yielded grudgingly to their axes until they had planted some seventeen acres in corn, wheat, and oats. They raised some sheep and hogs, and acquired a few head of cattle. Their diet became more varied as farm products supplemented the game and fowl brought down by the father's gun. The children helped gather berries and nuts. When they found a bee tree, Thomas would smoke out the swarming denizens, bring the tree down with his axe, and add the honey to their scanty larder.

For almost a year after coming to Spencer County, Thomas Lincoln "squatted" on the land. On October 15, 1817 he entered his farm at the government office at Vincennes and made a preliminary payment of sixteen dollars on 160 acres. Two months later he paid sixty-four dollars more, to complete the first installment of eighty dollars, a fourth of the purchase price.

About this time Thomas Sparrow and his wife, Elizabeth, Nancy Hanks's uncle and aunt, who had cared for Nancy in childhood, migrated from Kentucky to join the Lincolns. With them came Dennis Hanks, an illegitimate son of another of Nancy's aunts, a cheerful and energetic waif of nineteen, who became Abraham's close companion. During the winter of 1817–18, the newcomers lived in the half-faced camp vacated by the Lincolns.

In the late summer of 1818 a dread disease swept through southwestern Indiana. Known as the "milk-sick," it is now believed to have been caused by cattle eating white snakeroot or rayless goldenrod and passing on the poison in their milk. All that the pioneers knew about it, however, was that it struck quickly and usually brought death. In September both Thomas Sparrow and his wife came down with it. The nearest doctor lived thirty miles away; even if his services had been available, he could have offered little help. Within a few days both sufferers died. Thomas Lincoln knocked together two crude coffins and buried the Sparrows on a near-by knoll. Soon afterward Nancy Hanks Lincoln became ill and died on October 5. Again Thomas put together a rude coffin, and again the awfulness of death afflicted the little group in the wilderness cabin. The body lay in the same room where they ate and slept. The family made all the preparations for burial, and conducted the simple funeral service, for no minister resided in the neighborhood. The woods were radiant with autumn's colors as they buried Nancy Lincoln beside the Sparrows.

Once again the Lincolns had hard times. Twelve-year-old Sarah cooked, swept, and mended, while Thomas, Abraham, and Dennis Hanks hewed away at the forest and tended the meager crops. Their fortunes ebbed. Deprived of the influence of a woman, they sank almost into squalor.

In the early winter of 1819 Thomas Lincoln returned to Elizabethtown, Kentucky, where, on December 2, he took a second wife, Sarah Bush Johnston, a tall, attractive widow with three children. She owned some household goods, a modest dowry, but better than anything to which the Lincolns were accustomed. Loading these goods, together with his bride and her children, into a borrowed wagon drawn by a four-horse team, Thomas set out once more for Indiana.

Now eight persons occupied the roughhewn Lincoln cabin: Thomas, Abraham, and Sarah; Dennis Hanks; the new stepmother; and her children—Elizabeth, Matilda, and John D. Johnston, aged twelve, eight, and five, respectively. Despite the overcrowding, the condition of the Lincolns became better as the kindly, hard-working stepmother brought order out of the chaos and took the motherless children to her heart. The boy Abraham adored her. Recollection of his own mother dimmed. And in later years he called this woman, who filled her place so well, "my angel mother."

That winter the stepmother saw to it that Abe obtained a few more weeks of schooling under the instruction of Andrew Crawford. Public education was still unknown in Indiana, and the teachers, none too well educated themselves, derived an uncertain livelihood from the small tuition fees the parents paid them. Schoolmasters seldom stayed long in that neighborhood, and the school soon closed. Two years later, however, Abe attended another school, about four miles from home, taught by James Swaney. Again, after a year's interval, he picked up a few more weeks of instruction under a man named Azel Dorsey. These were all "blab" schools, so called because the pupils studied aloud in order that the master might measure their diligence from the volume of the babel. Both discipline and learning were promoted by the rod. These short intervals of instruction marked the end of Lincoln's formal education. All told, he attended school less than a year.

The Record Book of the Pigeon Creek Baptist Church shows that Thomas Lincoln joined by letter on June 7, 1823. He was an active member, serving as trustee for several years, attending a church conference as a representative, and acting on a number of committees. His benefactions included one gift to the church of twenty-four pounds of corn meal. Sarah Bush Lincoln also became a member of the church, but Abe never joined.

*

As time passed, the region became more thickly settled, mostly by people of Southern antecedents. But conditions remained primitive. Farming with iron-shod plows, crude sickles, spades, and hoes required back-breaking labor. Wheat was threshed with a flail, fanned by tossing it in a sheet, and ground at a horse or water mill. The rough-mannered, superstitious settlers believed in ghosts, witches, and charms. Faith healers plied their art. Signs and portents played an important part in life; planting, harvesting, and weeding must be correlated with the stages of the moon. Sanitation was ill-understood and often unattainable, what with the overcrowding in the cabins, where families usually cooked, ate, and slept in a single room. Humor was boisterous and bawdy, pungent and close to nature.

Almost everyone drank heavily, even women and some preachers gulping their dram of raw whisky. Yet it was a democratic way of life, with no class distinctions, a pervading sense of justice and fair dealing, and sometimes a yearning for economic and even intellectual betterment. Religion, though primitive and emotional, with vociferous preaching strongly tinctured with hell-fire, nevertheless provided the most potent influence in the taming of the raw frontier.

People still lived far apart, but would come a long way for a frolic. Their social functions were the sort they could combine with work—corn-shuckings, logrollings, "raisings," wool-shearings, hog-killings, quilting bees—with an occasional dance. Boots or moccasins were much more often seen than shoes, which graced only the most formal occasions. A great deal of the time the women and children went barefoot. Clothing was homemade of fur, linsey-woolsey, buckskin, or jean. Money was scarce and of uncertain value, so that trade was usually by barter; hogs, coonskins, deerskins, and other pelts being exchanged for powder, shot, coffee, sugar, and cloth.

The richest man in the neighborhood was James Gentry, a North Carolinian who brought his large family from Kentucky about the same time the Lincolns migrated. Entering 1,000 acres of land, he continued to buy more, and established a store at his farmhouse. Soon his place became a trading center, which grew to be the village of Gentryville, a mile and a half from where the Lincolns lived. There young Abe spent much of his spare time. He craved companionship, and as soon as he had finished his chores he would set out for the village, often accompanied by Dennis Hanks. Here, hour after hour, he entertained with quips and yarns, bringing loud guffaws from the farmer boys, lingering so late at night that Dennis would grow tired, want to go home, and, as he recollected, "cuss Abe most heartily."

Abe grew tall, angular, rawboned. He developed terrific strength in the lean, flat muscles of his legs and chest, and especially in his arm muscles, so that he could grasp an axe by the handle and, raising his arm to the horizontal, hold the axe out straight. His long body, those long arms, could exert tremendous leverage on an axe. Young Lincoln, strong, dexterous, and fleet of foot, won recognition as the best all-round athlete in the Gentryville neighborhood.

Abe had talent as a mimic, and often imitated the preachers and politicians he had heard. Sometimes he mounted a stump to orate, bringing belly-laughs from the other laborers and causing them to slight their work, thereby evoking a sharp rebuke or cuff from his father for such nonsense. The traditions of the community affirm his kindliness, his sense of fair play, his helpfulness to others, his love of dumb animals, his ambition to excel. His neighbors remembered his laconic speech. They also remembered that plowing, hoeing, grubbing, and making fence held little attraction for him. The Lincoln farm was small, and Thomas often hired out the boy to work for neighbors. Abe did what was expected of him, but he showed no zeal about it, for he much preferred to read. One man recalled how he would take a book to the fields, so that at the end of each plow furrow he could read while allowing the horse to "breathe."

Abe was generally accounted lazy except for his desire to learn. But his progress in education was amazing for one who had such meager opportunities. He could spell down all the other pupils in school. He did all the writing for his family and much of it for their neighbors. At home he ciphered on boards when he had no paper or slate, shaving off the ciphering with a hunting-knife to start afresh. In a copybook in the smooth round script that became so easily distinguishable in his later years, he composed a bit of boyish doggerel, the earliest known specimen of his handwriting:

> *Abraham Lincoln, his hand and pen,*
> *He will be good but God knows when.*

From Abe's reading, scanty as it was, he had already acquired a sincere respect for the founders of the American Republic and for the precepts of the Declaration of Independence. Reading Parson Weems's *Life of Washington*, he thrilled to the accounts of the battles of the Revolutionary War. The hardships and determination of the soldiers so impressed him that even as a boy he thought "there must have been something more than common that those men struggled for."

Neighbors remembered how young Lincoln ranged the countryside for books, yet their recollection of his great desire for learning is difficult to reconcile with his own statement that his boyhood home offered "absolutely nothing to excite ambition for education. Of course when I came of age I did not know much. Still somehow, I could read, write, and cipher to the Rule of Three; but that was all."

While Lincoln did not read many books, since few were to be had, those that he read he devoured. Among these, besides Weems's *Washington* were *Robinson Crusoe*, *Pilgrim's Progress*, Æsop's *Fables*, Grimshaw's *History of the United States*, and *The Kentucky Preceptor*. Yet his very limitations held some advantages, for more benefit may be derived from assimilation of a few worth-while works of literature than from gorging a full fare of trash and mediocrity. Lincoln's consciousness of his educational shortcomings in later life shows a total lack of that complacency and smug assurance too often evinced by one who has successfully made his own way.

Testimony differs about the place of the Bible in Lincoln's

reading; some old acquaintances affirmed that he studied it assiduously, while others declared that it held little interest for him. But the Bible was probably the only book the Lincolns owned, and he must have acquired at an early age that easy familiarity with the Scriptures which flavors his speeches and writings.

*

SIXTEEN miles from the Lincoln cabin, where the family landed when they came to Indiana, Anderson Creek comes down through high banks to join the Ohio, making the junction through a wide flat near the town of Troy. Here river boats often tied up at night and took on fuel from the big woodyard. Sometimes the passengers and crewmen came ashore. A traveler told of such an occurrence on one of his Ohio trips when the passengers built a great fire and roasted a beef, and as climax of their frolic burned down a tree! The people of Troy enjoyed a thriving business with the river steamers.

James Taylor operated a ferry at the mouth of Anderson Creek, and Abe got a job as his helper. At the age of seventeen he had the physique of a man, but he was not paid a man's wages, receiving only thirty-seven cents a day for what he remembered as the roughest work a young man could be made to do. In his few leisure moments he built a small scow. One day two travelers rushed down to the riverbank, crying for transportation to a steamboat lying off the creek-mouth. Sculling his cumbersome scow with all his might, young Lincoln brought them alongside the steamer just as it took off, and as the two men clambered aboard he pitched their carpetbags after them. Leaning over the rail, each man tossed a silver half-dollar into his boat, much to the astonishment of the youngster, who "could scarcely credit that I, a poor boy, had earned a dollar in less than a day."

The river at Anderson Creek makes a sweeping, graceful bend, the water slipping along slowly and quietly. A constant stream of travel passed up and down—steamboats, keelboats, scows, flatboats, and rafts, carrying all sorts of cargoes. All manner of people traveled the great waterway—pioneers, traders, circuit riders, gamblers—the motley advance guard of a pulsating civilization. Young Lincoln's spirits lifted as he watched the pageant go by—the stately steamboats trailing their plumes of smoke, the rafts gliding silently as the roustabouts kept them on course with their long sweeps, at night the twinkling lights, the songs and oaths and laughter carrying across the water on the still air. Lincoln felt the wanderlust and, at the age of nineteen, contracted with James Gentry to take a cargo to New Orleans.

Constructing a crude flatboat, young Lincoln and Gentry's son Allen loaded it with farm produce and glided down the Ohio to the Mississippi, then on to the bustling city that was the emporium of the West. Lolling on the low deck, giving an occasional tug on the slender sweeps to avoid the snags and sandbars, gossiping with Gentry, watching the river traffic passing by, Lincoln realized how vast and magnificent was his country. While trading on the Louisiana sugar coast, the boatmen were attacked one night by a band of thieving Negroes who surprised them while they slept along the shore. The young giant and his companion fought them off at the cost of a few minor injuries, then went on to New Orleans, a thousand miles from the mouth of the Ohio, where they sold the flatboat and the balance of the cargo, and took passage on a steamboat for home.

The three months' trip opened new vistas to young Lincoln. Roaming the city, he encountered for the first time an urban way of life. The waterfront bustled with activity. Often as many as fifteen hundred flatboats and keelboats, lashed four or five abreast, extended along the levee as far as one could see, disgorging the products of the Western country, which were then carried off by wagons, carts, and drays to the bursting warehouses to await transshipment on the square-rigged sailing vessels bound for the marts of the world.

The cobblestone streets along the great levee were thronged with planters, venders, clerks, boatmen, and stevedores. Near the spacious market place were moored a multitude of skiffs and scows loaded with poultry and vegetables to feed the city. River

steamers maneuvered to a landing against the sullen current,
crewmen and passengers lining their rails. The levee and the
neighboring streets were piled high with bales of cotton, hogs-
heads of sugar and tobacco. Wealth such as young Lincoln never
imagined confronted him on every side.

A confusion of strange tongues came to his ears, for among
the city's population of some forty thousand were French,
Spanish, Portuguese, Irish, half-breeds, and crossbreeds, proud
Creoles, a host of laboring Negro slaves—altogether an inter-
mixture and commingling of peoples bespeaking the whole great
family of mankind.

Close by the city superb plantations displayed brilliant
gardens and well-kept lawns. Near its center the cathedral rose
in quiet grandeur. Houses of white and yellow stucco, exotic
with iron grillwork, enclosed courtyards, and second-story
porches, crowded upon the narrow thoroughfares of the French
and Spanish quarters. Spanish moss festooned the trees. The
humid climate soon overlaid even modern buildings with an
aspect of age, so different from the newness and rawness of the
frontier young Lincoln knew.

There was something fantastic and unique about the city,
with its Old World background and traditions, its European Sabbath, enlivened with balls, festivities, and theater-going, its gay,
vivacious people of cultivated manners and urbane sophistication.
And behind its sleek façade lurked flagrant wickedness; it was
renowned for its gilded gambling palaces and ravishing women of
frivolous virtue, and notorious by reason of the noisome dives
that catered to the lusts of the rivermen and roustabouts. In
the famed slave market, which drew its wares and custom from
the whole great South, men, women, and children were auctioned
to the highest bidder.

Young Lincoln returned to the crude simplicity of backwoods Indiana excited and aroused, soon to sink back, however,
into the dull routine of farm work and odd jobs. The twenty-four
dollars he had earned were turned over to his father, according
to the law and custom of that day.

*

M E A N W H I L E , shortly before Abe left for New Orleans, death had struck his family once again. On January 20, 1828 his sister Sarah died in childbirth. She had married a young farmer of the community, Aaron Grigsby, and either because Abraham held her husband responsible for her death or for other reasons undisclosed, a sort of feud broke out between young Lincoln and the Grigsbys. When two other Grigsby brothers married sisters in a joint wedding, young Abraham became the moving spirit in a plot that resulted in maneuvering the brides into the wrong bedchambers on their wedding night. The mistake was rectified before too late, but not without considerable chagrin to those involved, a state of mind not assuaged when Lincoln publicized the incident throughout the countryside by writing an account of it in Biblical language. Titled "The Chronicles of Reuben," Lincoln's lampoon was eventually forgotten by almost everyone, until years later, when William H. Herndon, his former law partner, combed the Indiana countryside for biographical data, and an old lady recited it to him from memory. Both the incident and Lincoln's literary efforts in connection with it typified the Rabelaisian humor of the frontier. Lincoln also made other literary gestures in the form of doggerel verse, most of them satirical in character.

*

O n A p r i l 30, 1827 Thomas Lincoln completed payment on the west eighty acres of his farm, relinquishing his title to the east eighty acres. Then, on February 20, 1830, he and his wife sold their farm to Charles Grigsby for $125. The years in Indiana had fallen short of Thomas's expectations. The family was frightened by another outbreak of the milk-sick. And John Hanks, a cousin of Nancy Hanks Lincoln, who, after living with the Lincolns and Johnstons for about four years, had moved to central Illinois, was sending them the usual glowing reports about the new country. So on March 1, 1830 the whole family set out for Illinois, themselves and their possessions jouncing on three wagons, one drawn by a four-horse team, the others each pulled by two yoke of plodding oxen. Mounted on one of the ox-drawn wagons, urging the sluggish animals forward with voice and goad, sat Abraham, just come of age.

Crossing icy creeks and rivers still unbridged, stopping at suitable spots to cook their meals, sleeping at night wherever darkness found them, they came at last, after a journey of more than two hundred miles, to a place on the north bank of the Sangamon River, a few miles west of Decatur, which John Hanks had chosen for their home. Again they must build a cabin, but Hanks had cut and trimmed the logs, and the structure went up quickly. The Lincolns found conditions almost as primitive as those in Indiana when they first settled there, though the new country was mostly open prairie rather than a wooded wilderness, with trees growing most abundantly along the watercourses.

During the spring and early summer the men cleared about fifteen acres of ground and split enough rails to fence it. They planted corn. Then, with John Hanks, his cousin, Abe hired out to split three thousand rails for William Warnick, the county sheriff, and helped split an additional thousand for two other neighbors. He also aided Charles Hanks, John's brother, at breaking prairie sod, driving "a joint team of his and ours, which in turn, broke some on the new place we were improving."

Although Lincoln had become a man, he still showed no noteworthy initiative. He seemed to be drifting into the same unimaginative life of a pioneer farmer or hired hand that had become the lot of his father and those about him.

In the autumn almost all the Lincoln family came down with fever and ague, common afflictions of the Illinois country in the pioneer days. They became so discouraged that again they decided to move. But they stayed on through the winter—a hard winter. In December a raging blizzard set in. For days it showed no letup, until the snow piled three feet deep on the level, with heavy drifts. Then came rain, which froze. More snow. When the weather cleared at last, a lashing northwest wind drove the sharp crystals across the prairie in blinding, choking swirls. Tracks made one day were wiped out by the next. The crust would support a man, but cows and horses broke through. Deer became an easy prey for wolves as their sharp hoofs penetrated the icy surface and imprisoned them. Much fodder still stood in the fields, and feed for stock ran low. Day after day the temperature rose no higher than twelve below zero. For nine weeks the snow lay deep. When the spring thaw came, floods overspread the country.

Now the Lincoln family moved once more, to Coles County, Illinois. But Abe did not accompany them. During the "Winter of the Deep Snow" he, his stepbrother John Johnston, and John Hanks had agreed to make another trip to New Orleans with a cargo belonging to Denton Offutt. When the snow went off the ground, the three men bought a large canoe. Riding the crest of the spring flood, they paddled down the Sangamon River to a point near Springfield, where they had arranged to meet Offutt. "This is the time and the manner of Abraham's first entrance into Sangamon County," Lincoln wrote. And while he may not have realized it then, the event marked a turning-point in his life. Never more would he be trammeled by his family. Having reached an age when his father could no longer command his earnings, he struck out on his own.

*

So LINCOLN came to manhood, a product of the American frontier. Already he bore its impress, for the frontier was inexorable, breaking some men as it broke his father, but infusing qualities of courage, perseverance, and self-confidence, and a capacity and determination to order one's own destiny, into those who had the hardihood to take its discipline.

Just as the West became a major determining factor in American national life, so it exerted a compelling influence on Lincoln. More strikingly than anyone else he would exemplify its power and what it could do in fashioning a man. Nor was the frontier through with him, for he would live in a frontier climate for another score of years. To the end of his days his rural background colored his writings and speech. The horse, the dog, the ox, the plow, the hog became interpreters of his meaning when he tried to make simple people understand him. Many of the similes and metaphors that enrich his literary style smack of the countryside. A crossroads twang was in his anecdotes. He would learn to put a point across by means of homespun analogies.

Hard work left him with a body tough and strong, assuring good health when his occupations became sedentary. Physically he was always a powerful man whose body, like his mind, moved slowly, as is likely to be the way with country people. He walked firmly, but with a sort of caution, putting his whole foot on the ground at once instead of landing on the heel, in the manner of one whose feet have known plowed ground. His ways and manner would always be somewhat rustic.

CHAPTER II

———◆•◆———

Young Man on His Own

PADDLING downstream with the current and disembarking at Judy's Ferry, where the village of Riverton now stands, Lincoln, Hanks, and Johnston walked to Springfield to find Offutt. A frontier promoter of grandiose designs and hearty personality, Offutt liked to talk and drink. The most likely place to look for him was Andrew Elliott's Buckhorn Tavern, and there they found him, regaling the customers with his large-scale plans for quick riches. But in the gush of his enthusiasm he had failed to provide a boat, so the three men contracted to construct their own at wages of ten dollars a month.

At the point where Spring Creek empties its waters into the Sangamon River they built a shanty for lodging, chose Lincoln as cook, and cut timber for their craft from the government land. Bringing the big trees down, they sawed them into logs, which they rafted downriver to Kirkpatrick's mill to be ripped into planks. A visitor remembered seeing Lincoln, stripped to his undershirt and pants and begrimed with sweat, pushing back his clotted hair as he pounded away on the boat.

The construction took a month. Then, loading their cargo of barreled pork, corn, and live hogs, they cast off downstream, fending off the overhanging branches and steering their clumsy vessel around the snags and shallows. The spring floodwater had receded and the river was low. At the little hamlet of New Salem a mill dam obstructed the stream. The water still flowed over it, however, and the boatmen believed they could force their craft across. But halfway over it stuck, shipping water at the stern. A crowd of villagers assembled on the shore, generous with advice, but the utmost efforts of the crewmen could not budge the heavy craft. Finally, under Lincoln's direction, the men carried part of the cargo to the riverbank and pushed the rest of it forward to balance the boat. Lincoln went ashore and, borrowing an auger, bored a hole in the overhanging bow to let the water out. Then, having plugged the hole, the boatmen eased their craft across the dam.

Offutt, who had accompanied his crewmen on this first stage of their journey, was impressed with Lincoln's ingenuity. He appraised him as a promising young man. The little settlement on the bluff above the mill dam also seemed destined for growth, so Offutt planned to rent the mill and open a store, and he engaged young Lincoln to operate these enterprises when he returned.

John Hanks said that on this second visit to New Orleans Lincoln was so distressed by a slave auction that he declared: "If I ever get a chance to hit that thing, I'll hit it hard." But Hanks's testimony is questionable because he left the party at St. Louis. The deep compassion that Lincoln revealed in later life had not become evident yet. Nor did he suppose himself to be a man of destiny. Doubtless what he saw of slavery repelled him, but we must doubt that he gave such dramatic expression to his distaste at this time of life.

Lincoln arrived back in New Salem in late July 1831, "a piece of floating driftwood," as he described himself. On August 1 an election took place in the village, and for the first time Lincoln exercised his right to vote, announcing his choices orally to the clerks of election, who sat behind a table marking their tally sheets. Offutt's stock of goods did not arrive until September, so for a month or more Lincoln helped at the mill and did odd jobs.

The village where Lincoln found himself was a thriving place, situated on a high bluff above the Sangamon River. Two little streams had cut deep ravines on each side of the townsite, making access difficult from north and south, but to the west the bluff broadened and flattened to merge with the level prairie. Across the river to the east, thick woods covered hills and bottom land.

At the height of New Salem's prosperity, which came two years after Lincoln's arrival, the village had a population of about twenty-five families. It boasted a cooper, a cobbler, a wheelwright and cabinetmaker, a blacksmith, a hatter, two physicians, a tavern, a carding machine for wool, two stores, and two saloons. A post office handled mail, and a ferry operated across the river. It had a fluid growth, however, characterized by change and shift, as men drifted into town, then moved along to try their fortunes elsewhere. Local business enterprises changed hands frequently. Settlement in early Illinois progressed from the south northward, so that most of the residents were Southerners. Once again Lincoln found the life about him conditioned by Southern influences.

A typical pioneer community, the place, with its surrounding farming area, was largely self-sufficient. Most persons made their living from the soil, using hand tools or crude farm implements, though the presence of craftsmen indicates some division of labor. In some respects the women worked harder than the men, and usually died younger; a man often outlived two wives, and sometimes three, or even four. An English traveler described central Illinois as a hard country for women and cattle. Families were large and babies came in annual crops. "The fittest survived and the rest the Lord seen fittin' to take away," a settler said.

Lincoln found the same community pastimes he had known in Indiana—square dances, house-raisings, wolf hunts, quilting bees, shooting for a beef. The village had no church, but the Reverend John M. Berry preached and prayed, and circuit-riding parsons, notably the celebrated Peter Cartwright, often visited the neighborhood. Preaching reeked of brimstone and bristled with dogma and doctrine. Sects were jealous and intolerant of one another. At the camp meetings, which were held almost every year in the village or close by, emotionalism ran rampant.

*

OFFUTT'S goods having arrived at last, his store opened for business, with Lincoln as clerk at wages of fifteen dollars a month plus the privilege of sleeping in the room behind the store. Close by, Clary's grocery, or saloon, served as a hangout for a clannish group of young roisterers from west of town known as the Clary's Grove boys. They continually engaged in rough mischief of some sort—cropping the manes and tails of horses, putting stones under saddles to make horses pitch, rolling sodden drunkards down the bluff in a barrel. Their favorite sports were wrestling, cockfighting, and gander-pulling, a pastime in which they hung a tough old gander, its neck thoroughly greased, head down from the limb of a tree, and a rider, dashing past at full speed, tried to snap off the head of the fowl.

Lincoln soon attracted the attention of the Clary's Grove boys because of Offutt's boasts; according to his employer, the young clerk and millhand had no equal at running, jumping, wrestling, or in rough-and-tumble combat. But at New Salem such supremacy was never conceded; Jack Armstrong, leader of the Clary's Grove boys, challenged Lincoln to a wrestling match.

On the frontier, courage was the first essential to success. Nothing could more quickly doom a man to ostracism than evidence of cowardice. Lincoln accepted Armstrong's challenge at once. Physical combat offered a welcome diversion, and on the appointed day an excited crowd of men and boys gathered on the bluff above the river, wagering money, knives, keepsakes, and trinkets, as the contestants stripped for combat.

The two men circled cautiously, came to grips, broke, pawed for a hold again. They closed, twisted, wrenched, and tugged. Lincoln gained the hold he wanted, and as they went down he flopped on top. Relentless pressure forced Armstrong's shoulders toward the ground; then his companions, unwilling to see their leader whipped, joined the scuffle. Lincoln freed himself and backed against a wall, voicing defiance as he offered to fight, race, or wrestle any or all of them singly. None saw fit to take him on, and Armstrong, appraising him admiringly, slouched forward to offer his hand. He and Lincoln became fast friends, and Armstrong's cronies not only admitted the newcomer to their fellowship but acknowledged him their leader. During Lincoln's sojourn at New Salem their unswerving loyalty proved invaluable to him.

*

T H U S   L I N C O L N not only won acceptance at New Salem, but also gained a place of leadership among the rougher element. To many young men of his sterile background this would have been completely satisfying. Since Lincoln had left his family, however, his latent ambition for self-advancement had begun to assert itself. Freed for the first time from the necessity of hard physical toil, he aspired to improve his education. "After he was twenty-three, and had separated from his father," he explained, "he studied English grammar, imperfectly of course, but so as to speak and write as well as he now does." He also studied mathematics. For the most part, he taught himself, but whenever he needed help he consulted Mentor Graham, a local schoolmaster. Through Jack Kelso, an aimless village character who spent most of his time fishing and hunting and yet had certain intellectual attainments, Lincoln developed a lasting fondness for the writings of Shakespeare and Robert Burns.

During the winter of 1831–2 young Lincoln became a regular attendant of the New Salem Debating Society. Here he met a more intelligent group of people, for New Salem had a budding intellectuality, inspired largely by Dr. John Allen, a graduate of Dartmouth who came west to improve his health. Besides starting the debating society, Allen also organized a temperance society and a Sunday school.

The New Salem "intellectuals" welcomed young Lincoln to their gatherings with some surprise. What reputation he enjoyed up to this time derived from physical prowess and robust humor. As he rose to speak for the first time, an observer noted that "a perceptible smile at once lit up the faces of the audience, for all anticipated the relation of some humorous story, but he opened up the discussion in splendid style, to the infinite astonishment of his friends. As he warmed to his subject, his hands would forsake his pockets, and would enforce his ideas by awkward gestures; but would very soon seek their resting place. He pursued the question with reason and argument so pithy and forcible that all were amazed. The president, at his fireside after the meeting, remarked to his wife that there was more than wit and fun in Abe's head; that he was already a fine speaker; that all he lacked was culture."

*

ENCOURAGED by the general commendation of his neighbors, Lincoln decided to take a turn at politics, for politics offered an avenue of quick advancement in a frontier settlement. The popular young store clerk might easily have won a local office, but he aimed high, announcing himself as a candidate for the State Legislature.

With the demise of the Federalist Party, old political alignments had broken down, and politics, especially of the frontier sort, was in a state of flux, men grouping themselves behind individual leaders like Andrew Jackson, Henry Clay, and John Quincy Adams. With matters in this inchoate state, candidates could obtain no party backing and simply announced themselves as aspirants for office by means of handbills or in the newspapers. Personal popularity or influential connections were the chief requisites for success. Andrew Jackson had won the adulation of the frontier, but Lincoln's favorite, Henry Clay, had many admirers, too.

Lincoln's platform, which appeared in the *Sangamo Journal* of Springfield on March 9, 1832, declared for internal improvements, better educational facilities, and a law to limit interest rates. With respect to internal improvements, he considered the navigation of the Sangamon River most vital to his own community, and from personal knowledge asserted that simply by cutting through some of its bends the stream could be made to cut a deeper and straighter channel that would not clog with driftwood. Railroads provided a more dependable means of travel than rivers, he conceded, but their cost was prohibitive. Education seemed to him the most important question a people could consider, for every man should have sufficient education to enable him to read the history of his own and of other countries, "by which he may duly appreciate the value of our free institutions . . . to say nothing of the advantages and satisfaction to be derived from all being able to read the scriptures and other works, both of a religious and moral nature, for themselves." He believed that a law prohibiting usurious interest rates was most essential to a new country, where most settlers needed capital. Such a law would not materially injure any class of people, he thought, for in extreme cases, where excessive interest might be justified, means could always be found to evade the law!

"Every man," Lincoln concluded, "is said to have his peculiar ambition. Whether it be true or not, I can say for one that I have no other so great as that of being truly esteemed of my fellow men, by rendering myself worthy of their esteem. How far I shall succeed in gratifying this ambition, is yet to be developed. I am young and unknown to many of you. I was born and have ever remained in the most humble walks of life. I have no wealthy or popular relations to recommend me. My case is thrown exclusively upon the independent voters of this county, and if elected they will have conferred a favor upon me, for which I shall be unremitting in my labors to compensate. But if the good people in their wisdom shall see fit to keep me in the background, I have been too familiar with disappointments to be very much chagrined."

Lincoln acted wisely in chosing internal improvements as a campaign issue, for the fate of the Western country depended on better transportation. The soil was rich, but the cost of getting the abundance of agricultural products to market consumed the profit. Similarly, the price of manufactured goods mounted with the distance from the major river ports. Lincoln's choice was also timely, because for several weeks the Sangamo country had thrilled to the prospect of steamboat transportation on the river. Even now a small, light-draft steamer, the *Talisman*, lay at

Beardstown, on the Illinois River, ready to hazard the Sangamon as soon as the ice went off.

To assure the success of this venture, Lincoln and several other men, equipped with crowbars and axes, went down the river to clear the channel of snags and overhanging limbs. Four days were spent in breaking the ice jam at the river's mouth, and then, accompanied by a cheering crowd of men and boys, the little steamer chugged triumphantly upstream, tooting its whistle as it passed the settlements, to tie up at Portland Landing, seven miles from Springfield. Here, in the county seat of five hundred people, everyone was jubilant as the hope of cheap and steady transportation seemed about to be fulfilled. But the river level, raised by the spring thaw, was falling fast; the boat must leave at once or risk stranding. Rowan Herndon, an experienced boatman, agreed to pilot her back, with Lincoln as his assistant. At New Salem part of the mill dam had to be torn down so that she might pass. But the pilot and his helper took her through to Beardstown; then, each pocketing forty dollars, they tramped back home across country.

*

H A R D L Y had Lincoln arrived home when New Salem throbbed with new excitement. The village stood on the northern fringe of settlement. Beyond it, except for scattered cabins here and there, the only settlements were at Peoria, Dixon's Ferry on Rock River, and in the Galena lead-mining region along the Mississippi. Where the great city of Chicago would rise, a few cabins clustered around Fort Dearborn. Most of northern Illinois was trackless woods or prairie still roamed by treacherous Indians.

Now real trouble threatened, for Black Hawk, war leader of the Sauks and Foxes, dissatisfied with the lands allotted to him west of the Mississippi, had recrossed the river with five hundred braves. They came ostensibly to plant corn, but they were well mounted and well armed, and a detachment of U.S. regulars at Fort Armstrong watched them suspiciously. Panic spread over the frontier until at last some nervous shooting brought savage, flaming war.

Governor John Reynolds immediately called for volunteers from the state militia, a loose organization embracing all males between eighteen and forty-five except conscientious objectors and those physically unfit, who could escape the annual musters upon payment of seventy-five cents a year. The men supplied their own arms and elected their own officers.

When the Governor's messenger came spurring down the main street of New Salem, Lincoln was out of a job, or about to be. Storekeeping proved too tame for Offutt; he preferred to speculate in seed corn and cottonseed, which he shipped in from Tennessee, three or four thousand bushels at a time. Now he found himself financially hard pressed, and, as Lincoln expressed it, the store was about to "wink out." With no job and no family ties, Lincoln enlisted at once. Borrowing a horse, he hastened to the rendezvous at Richland Creek, nine miles southwest of New Salem. His company consisted mainly of his friends and neighbors, with the Clary's Grove boys prominent in voice and numbers. Their support elected Lincoln captain, with Jack Armstrong as first sergeant. Even after Lincoln's nomination for the Presidency he remembered this as the most satisfying honor of his life.

The volunteer contingent assembled at Beardstown, where Lincoln's company became part of a mounted brigade. While the civilian soldiers waited for marching orders their patriotism distilled into a holiday mood, and in the intervals between drilling they sang, roistered, wrestled, and played rough pranks. Lincoln spun his yarns around the campfires. In a wrestling match to decide whether his or another company should have a certain campground, the young captain met his match in Lorenzo D. Thompson, who threw him in two straight falls.

The volunteers did not like discipline, and Lincoln's first order brought a retort to go to the devil. His ingenuity made up for his lack of military knowledge. Leading his company across a field one morning, twenty abreast, he saw ahead a narrow gate

through which his men must pass. But he could not remember
the command to "turn the company endwise," and as a desperate
expedient, at the last moment he wheeled suddenly to face his
men and shouted: "Halt. This company will break ranks and reform immediately on the other side of that gate." The movement
was successfully executed.

Getting under way at last, the volunteers marched to the
mouth of Rock River, where they joined a detachment of U.S.
regulars and were sworn into Federal service. The regulars under
Colonel Zachary Taylor embarked in keelboats to ascend the
river, but the volunteers began to experience some of the hardships of war as they slogged along on shore. Baggage wagons
mired down in the swamps, and the militiamen floundered knee-
deep in the black muck and tangled roots as they pushed and
hauled to get them through. Shoddy tents leaked copiously in the
spring rains. Soldiers and horses became exhausted. Men talked of
deserting.

Lincoln needed all his resourcefulness to maintain order
among his grumbling men. When some members of his company
raided the quartermaster's stores of liquor and indulged in a
roaring spree, Lincoln as the responsible officer was placed under
arrest and ordered to carry a wooden sword for two days. Another time he was arrested for shooting a gun in camp.

One day the young captain showed his innate kindness by
saving the life of an old Indian who ventured into camp bearing
a safe-conduct from General Lewis Cass. Regardless of the red-
skin's credentials, the men threatened to kill him, for they subscribed to the frontier dogma that the only good Indian was a
dead one. But Lincoln, "swarthy with rage," avowed himself the
Indian's protector and dared anyone to lay a hand on him. The
incident has all the qualities of legend, but when it was printed in
a campaign biography, which Lincoln corrected carefully for a
friend, he allowed it to stand as written.

At Ottawa, where Lincoln's thirty days' enlistment expired,
his company disbanded. Some of the men went home, but Lincoln
enlisted for twenty days' additional service as a private in the

mounted company of Elijah Iles, a command made up largely of former colonels, captains, lieutenants, and even one general from disbanded units. Lieutenant Robert Anderson, later to command Fort Sumter, mustered Lincoln in.

Iles's company rushed to the relief of Galena when the Indians threatened to cut off that isolated mining settlement. The danger proved to be exaggerated, however, and they encountered no redskins. Returning from this expedition, Lincoln re-enlisted for another thirty days, this time in a spy battalion commanded by Jacob M. Early, a Methodist preacher and physician from Springfield. Again he saw no action, but at Kellogg's Grove he helped bury five of General Isaiah Stillman's men just killed in a sharp skirmish. For a long time he remembered how "the red light of the morning sun was streaming upon them as they lay heads toward us on the ground. And every man had a round, red spot on top of his head, about as big as a dollar where the redskins had taken his scalp. It was frightful, but it was grotesque; and the red sunlight seemed to paint everything all over. I remember that one man had on buckskin breeches."

Lincoln spent the last days of his enlistment in a futile search for Black Hawk and his warriors in the swamps around Lake Koshkonong in southern Wisconsin. He was mustered out of service at White Water River, four miles above its junction with the Rock, on July 10. Someone stole his horse and the mount of one of his companions the night before, but the other men of the company came to their aid, all walking and riding by turns, everyone in a jovial mood as soldiers just released from service usually are. At Peoria the men scattered to their homes. Lincoln and his companion bought a canoe and paddled to Havana, then trudged cross-country to New Salem. Six months later, when the army paymaster arrived in Springfield, Lincoln received about $125 for his eighty days of service.

In later years Lincoln made light of this, his only military experience. In a speech in Congress in which he ridiculed the efforts of the Democrats to magnify the military record of Lewis Cass, their candidate for President, he said: "By the way, Mr.

Speaker, did you know I am a military hero? Yes sir; in the days
of the Black Hawk War, I fought, bled, and came away. Speaking
of Gen. Cass' career, reminds me of my own. I was not at Stillman's defeat, but I was about as near it, as Cass was to Hull's
surrender; and, like him, I saw the place very soon afterwards. It
is quite certain I did not break my sword, for I had none to break;
but I bent a musket pretty badly on one occasion. If Cass broke
his sword, the idea is, he broke it in desperation; I bent the musket
by accident. If Gen. Cass went in advance of me in picking huckle-
berries, I guess I surpassed him in charges upon the wild onions.
If he saw any live, fighting Indians, it was more than I did; but I
had a good many bloody struggles with the musquitoes [sic]; and,
although I never fainted from loss of blood, I can truly say I was
often very hungry. Mr. Speaker, if I should ever conclude to doff
whatever our democratic friends may suppose there is of black
cockade federalism about me, and therefore, they shall take me
up as their candidate for the Presidency, I protest they shall
not make fun of me, as they have of Gen. Cass, by attempting to
write me into a military hero."

In many ways, however, it proved a valuable experience for
young Lincoln. He learned something of soldiers and the soldier's
life, the value of morale and discipline. He acquired a new fund of
stories. He learned the elements of handling men. He made new
friends, some of whom would be most helpful to him, for many
future leaders in Illinois served in the Black Hawk War. And
in spite of Lincoln's bantering attitude toward his military
service, William H. Herndon, his law partner of later years,
believed he was rather proud of it after all.

*

LINCOLN arrived in New Salem late in July, just two weeks
before election day. Immediately he started his belated campaign
for the Legislature, traveling through the countryside to introduce
himself to farmers working in the fields, often seizing a pitchfork
or scythe to lend a hand. He exchanged quips with the loungers
at the country stores or joined them at pitching horseshoes. He

made few formal speeches, but at Pappsville a crowd that had gathered for an auction called upon him to talk. As he rose to speak, a fight broke out in the audience when his friend Rowan Herndon was set upon by cronies of a man Herndon had recently whipped. Lincoln, interrupting his remarks, strode through the crowd, grabbed the principal assailant by the neck and the seat of the trousers, and tossed him several feet. Hostilities stopped. Lincoln mounted a box and resumed his speech. Persons who remembered him during this campaign remarked how tall and awkward he looked in his calico shirt and old straw hat without a band, and with six inches of blue yarn sock revealed between his thick-soled brogans and the bottoms of his pantaloons, which, besides being much too short for him, hung from a single suspender. But he made a good impression on almost everyone he met.

Lincoln lost the election, running eighth among thirteen candidates. He remembered it as the only time he was defeated on a direct vote of the people. But defeat did not discourage him, for in the New Salem precinct he received 277 of the 300 votes, although he had lived there only a little more than a year. His defeat resulted from his being unknown elsewhere in the county. The campaign broadened his acquaintance, however, and also gave him needed experience in public speaking as well as greater confidence in himself. And he found such zest in politics that rarely throughout the remainder of his life was he free from political ambition.

*

MEANWHILE he had no job and wondered what to do. He thought of becoming a blacksmith, but saw no future in it. He thought of studying law, but decided that was impossible with his meager preparation. In any small community the local storekeeper enjoys a certain celebrity. Everywhere that Lincoln had lived the village merchant was looked up to as a leading citizen. His place of business provided a focus of community life, a political forum, and a social club, where loungers whiled away the empty hours, clustered about the stove in winter or on the porch in summer, a place to meet friends and exchange news and gossip.

Three general stores operated in New Salem at this time; Samuel Hill's, the best established and most prosperous; Reuben Radford's; and one owned by Rowan Herndon and William F. Berry. And now, with Lincoln at loose ends, a chance to become a merchant on his own account presented itself when Herndon offered to sell out to him.

The deal was closed, Lincoln, in accordance with the easy financial practices of the frontier, merely giving Herndon his note and becoming Berry's partner. Then as a new opportunity confronted them, Lincoln and Berry bought out Reuben Radford.

But selling lard, bacon, and firearms, trading muslin and calico for eggs, beeswax, and honey did not prove to be the easy way to success that Lincoln expected. He had little aptitude for business; he was not a shrewd bargainer. And whenever he went to the whisky barrel to fill a jug for a customer, he noted that inroads had been made on the liquor. The culprit turned out to be his partner Berry, a heavy drinker. The partnership, as Lincoln said, "did nothing but get deeper and deeper in debt."

Unquestionably Lincoln dispensed liquor at his store; every general store on the frontier sold whisky. Later, however, when Stephen A. Douglas publicly accused Lincoln of having kept a "grocery," the frontier name for a saloon, Lincoln replied truthfully that he never kept a grocery anywhere in the world. The distinction lies in the fact that every store could sell liquor in quantities greater than a quart, for consumption off the premises, without taking out a license, whereas a license was required to sell liquor on the premises by the drink. No stigma attached to the former practice; only when one was licensed to permit drinking on his premises did one engage in the questionable occupation of grocerykeeper.

The tavern license issued to Lincoln & Berry seemingly contradicts Lincoln's positive denial of ever having kept a grocery. Issued by the County Commissioners' Court of Sangamon County on March 6, 1833, it authorized them to sell wines and spirituous liquors in quantities less than a quart, and beer, ale, and cider in quantities less than two gallons. But the license was taken out by Berry, and neither of the signatures of Lincoln and Berry, appearing on the bond required, is in Lincoln's handwriting. Local tradition maintained that disagreement over the sale of liquor caused the dissolution of the Lincoln-Berry partnership soon after they obtained the liquor license.

Lincoln was never known to make a willful misstatement about himself. When he denied that he ever kept a grocery, he admitted that he did "work the latter part of one winter in a little stillhouse up at the head of a hollow." But he never liked liquor. It always left him "flabby and undone," he said. Since this statement indicates that he knew the effects of alcohol, he must have sampled liquor, probably in Indiana, where he lived among hard drinkers. In New Salem, too, hard drinking prevailed, with camp meetings, funerals, weddings, and house-raisings often enlivened by the antics of men in their cups. Few even of the better class of citizens abstained, for Dr. Allen, in his temperance endeavors, "found his worst opponents among the church members, most of whom had their barrels of whiskey at home." Whatever Lincoln's experiences were in Indiana, however, by the time he came to New Salem he was a confirmed teetotaler, and never touched liquor thereafter.

William F. Berry died on January 10, 1835, leaving an estate of $60.87½, half of which went to pay the three physicians who attended his last illness. Lincoln, unable to collect whatever Berry owed him in the termination of their joint venture, now became solely liable for all the obligations contracted by the partnership. These, together with his own liabilities, put him in debt about $1,100, a burden so enormous for one of his small resources that he called it "the National Debt." Almost without exception, Lincoln's biographers assert that he was not able fully to pay off this debt until he went to Congress in 1847. But a careful student of his personal finances is convinced he paid it off much sooner.

That Lincoln paid his debt at all attests his character. Many men in similar circumstances would simply have moved away, left their debts unpaid, and blamed the town for their failure. But Lincoln not only had no intention of evading his obligations; he believed that if he could succeed anywhere, he could do so at New Salem, where he had made so many friends. His straight-forward conduct in this and other dealings earned him the nick-name "Honest Abe."

*

But Lincoln's immediate prospects were discouraging. With his strength and reputation for honesty, he could always find work, but he faced a time of austerity while discharging his obligations. Besides, he hoped to advance beyond the status of a common laborer.

At last, on May 7, 1833, he realized this ambition in small degree when he was appointed postmaster at New Salem, suc-ceeding Samuel Hill. Still an adherent of Henry Clay, he thought President Jackson gave him the job because it was not sufficiently important to make his politics an objection. He retained the position until the removal of the post office to Petersburg, on May 30, 1836.

During the first year of Lincoln's tenure mail came to New Salem by post rider, but in 1834 a stage route was established through the village. Stamps and envelopes had not come into use; letters were simply folded and sealed with wax. The number of pages in a letter and the distance it was carried determined the postal charges, which were paid by the addressee. So whenever a mail arrived, Lincoln estimated the number of pages in each letter, noted the postmark to determine how far it had traveled, then calculated the charge and marked it in the upper right-hand corner of the sealed and folded letter. If the recipient questioned Lincoln's figures, he could open the letter in his presence and count the sheets to prove the overcharge.

Lincoln's remuneration, based on the receipts at his office, averaged about fifty-five dollars a year. As other perquisites he enjoyed exemption from militia and jury duty, could send and receive letters free, and receive one newspaper daily without postal charge. Franking letters for others made him liable to a ten-dollar fine. He seems to have taken the postal regulations lightly, however, for Matthew S. Marsh, writing to his brother from New Salem in 1835, observed: "The Post Master (Mr. Lincoln) is very careless about leaving his office open & unlocked during the day—half the time I go & get my papers etc. without any one being there as was the case yesterday. The letter was only marked 25 & even if he had been there & known it was double, he would not have charged me any more—luckily he is a very clever fellow & a particular friend of mine. If he is there when I carry this to the office—I will get him to 'Frank' it. . . ." On the outside of this folded sheet is written: "Free—A. Lincoln P. M. New Salem Ills. Sept. 22."

A letter to George Spears also reveals Lincoln's indifference to postal regulations. "At your request," Lincoln wrote, "I send you a receipt for the postage on your paper. I am some what surprised at your request. I will however comply with it. The law requires News paper postage to be paid in advance and now that I have waited a full year you choose to wound my feelings by insinuating that unless you get a receipt I will probably make you pay it again."

But Lincoln's carelessness did not extend to the handling of government money that came into his hands. With this he used scrupulous care. Government mail contractors obtained their pay by means of warrants drawn on the postmasters along their routes, and Harvey Ross, who rode the New Salem post route, recalled that when he attempted to collect upon these orders, many of the postmasters were not prepared to pay. But Lincoln always had his money ready, kept separate from his personal funds in an old blue sock in a wooden chest beneath the counter.

Lincoln was always eager to accommodate his neighbors; whenever business took him to the country he carried letters in his hat to distribute along the way. This marked the beginning of his lifelong habit of using his headgear as a depository of letters and documents. His position gave him a chance to read every

newspaper that came to the office, and he began the practice of
regular newspaper-reading, which later helped him to interpret
the people's thinking. He became acquainted with every person
in the neighborhood—no mean advantage to an aspiring politician.

Unable to survive on the slender commissions the job provided, and utterly free from false pride, Lincoln welcomed every
chance to earn an extra dollar by splitting rails, helping at the
mill, working as a farmhand, and serving as local agent for the
Sangamo Journal, a newspaper published in Springfield. Frequently he served as clerk at elections, and gratefully pocketed
the two dollars and a half paid for carrying the tally sheets to
Springfield.

*

S E T T L E R S crowding into the Sangamo country created heavy
demand for running boundary lines on farms, for locating roads
and surveying townsites. John Calhoun, the county surveyor and
a prominent Jacksonian politician, finding himself encumbered
with more work than he could attend to, offered to appoint
Lincoln his deputy to work in the northwestern part of his
territory, in what is now Menard and the southern part of Mason
County. Making sure that the job entailed no political obligations,
Lincoln accepted, and, as he said, "procured a compass and chain,
studied Flint, and Gibson a little, and went at it." One of his
first surveys was made for Russell Godbey, who paid him two
buckskins, which Hannah Armstrong, wife of his friend Jack,
"foxed" on his pants to protect them from briers.

Most of the county surveyor's records for Lincoln's three-
year tenure have been lost, but several roads that he located are
still in use, and he surveyed the towns of Petersburg, Bath, New
Boston, Albany, and Huron.

But he found it hard to get ahead, plagued as he was by debt.
To carry on his surveying duties he bought a horse, saddle, and
bridle on credit for $57.86. When this debt fell due and he was
unable to pay, his creditor sued and levied on his personal pos-

sessions to satisfy the judgment. To be deprived of his horse and his surveying instruments meant loss of his means of livelihood, but friends came to his aid. Bill Greene, a young, enterprising New Salem businessman, turned in a horse against the judgment, and a friendly farmer, "Uncle Jimmy" Short, bid in Lincoln's other possessions when they were sold on execution, and returned them to him.

*

I N T H E spring of 1834, with another election for state legislators impending, Lincoln determined to run again. Party lines had become more definite now, and the Whig and Democratic organizations were beginning to take form. Support of or opposition to President Jackson and his policies determined political alignments, with the Jacksonians more cohesive than the opposition. But even among the Jacksonians shades of loyalty ranged from "whole-hog" stalwarts, who supported the President unswervingly, to "milk-and-cider" Democrats, who would not always go along with him. No presidential election occurred in 1834, however, and with national issues subordinated, personal popularity and factional maneuvering were most likely to determine the outcome of the contest for the Legislature.

In Lincoln's own community he enjoyed bipartisan support when his friend Bowling Green, the local justice of the peace, persuaded his fellow Democrats to back the young surveyor. Elsewhere in the county, in a campaign of subtle strategy, each side sought to outmaneuver the other. Lincoln had his first experience with tricky political tactics when Democratic emissaries came to him with a proposal to drop two of their own men and support him, in an effort to squeeze out John T. Stuart, of Springfield, the Whig leader in the county. Lincoln immediately informed Stuart of this chicanery, but Stuart, confident of his own invulnerability, told Lincoln to go ahead and dicker with the Democrats. Then Stuart directed the Whig strategy against a lone Democrat, Richard Quinton, with the result that Lincoln and John Dawson, another Whig, won handily; William Carpenter, a Democrat, ran third; and Stuart nosed out Quinton for the fourth and last winning place.

Probably because of Lincoln's bipartisan candidacy, he issued no declaration of principles and made few speeches, but campaigned quietly at the post office and on surveying trips. His friend Rowan Herndon remembered that Lincoln came to his house at harvest time, when some thirty men were working in the fields, and after eating his dinner went out and won their unanimous vote by surpassing them all at cradling wheat.

*

D uring this campaign Stuart, who had taken a great liking to Lincoln, encouraged him to study law. Kentucky-born, a graduate of Centre College, at Danville, Stuart had enjoyed all the advantages denied to Lincoln. His father, a Presbyterian minister, was professor of classical languages at Transylvania College. Widely read, with Southern grace and charm of manner, Stuart had studied law in Kentucky and began practice in Springfield in 1828. Only two years older than Lincoln, he had won election to the Legislature in 1832 and already enjoyed a position of leadership not only in state and county politics but also in his profession. Six feet tall, handsome, with a mild and amiable expression, he was open and friendly in his personal relationships and at the same time uncommunicative and inscrutable in party management.

Lincoln had always liked the law. Back in Spencer County he had not only read the *Revised Statutes of Indiana* but also lounged around the county courthouse, listening to the trials. He thought of becoming a lawyer as early as 1832, but put the idea aside, although he bought a book of legal forms from which he drew up deeds, mortgages, and other legal instruments for his neighbors. He even argued minor cases before Squire Bowling Green, taking no pay for any of these services, since that would have violated the law.

Lincoln's election to the Legislature and Stuart's faith in his ability buttressed his self-confidence, and now he applied himself in grim earnest to becoming a lawyer. Borrowing books from Stuart, he took them to New Salem, and whenever a respite from work permitted he would seek a secluded spot where he might study, often lying on his back in the shade of a tree, with his long legs aloft against its trunk. At an auction in Springfield he bought a copy of Blackstone's *Commentaries* and mastered it, as well as Chitty's *Pleadings*. Abe's New Salem acquaintances thought he was becoming lazy, for few of them could comprehend the utility of mental as opposed to physical labor. Russell Godbey, seeing Lincoln stretched out on a woodpile with an open book before him, asked what he was reading. "I'm not reading," replied Lincoln, "I am studying law." "Law," gasped Godbey, "Good God A'mighty!" and passed on in bewilderment.

Henry E. Dummer, Stuart's law partner from 1833 to 1837, told how Lincoln came to the office to borrow books. "Sometimes he walked," Dummer recalled, "but generally rode. He was the most uncouth looking young man I ever saw. He seemed to have but little to say; seemed to feel timid, with a tinge of sadness visible in the countenance, but when he did talk all this disappeared for the time and he demonstrated that he was both strong and acute. He surprised us more and more at every visit."

Lincoln spent the remainder of the summer and the autumn of 1834 surveying, performing his duties at the post office, piecing out his income with odd jobs, studying law whenever time permitted. Then, as the opening of the legislative session drew near, he borrowed two hundred dollars from his friend Coleman Smoot, and in keeping with his new eminence spent sixty dollars for a tailor-made suit of clothes. In late November he took the stage for Springfield, where he changed coaches, and where Stuart, William Carpenter, and John Dawson, the other representatives from Sangamon County, also clambered aboard. Together the four men made the two-day trip to Vandalia, the capital of Illinois. Excited by his prospects, eager to make his mark, young Lincoln was entering a field in which competence, resourcefulness, and integrity might take a man a long way.

—◆—

CHAPTER III

Frontier Legislator:
His Love Affairs

ABOUT a mile from Vandalia the lumbering stage coach picked up speed as the driver cracked his whip and urged the horses forward to make his customary spectacular entrance into town. Thundering down the main street, he let out a blast on his horn, swung sharply round a corner, and hauled back hard on the reins to pull up in front of the post office. Stuart, Dawson, Carpenter, and Lincoln swung stiffly to the ground, picked up their bags, and made their way through the inquisitive crowd to seek lodgings at one of Vandalia's several taverns.

Looking about, Lincoln saw an overgrown prairie village of eight or nine hundred inhabitants built around a spacious public square, its wide streets, now rutted and muddy from autumn rains, dotted with frame houses and log cabins. Across the street from the square, the two-story brick State Capitol and another brick building used for state offices rose above the business buildings. The unfinished Cumberland Road, coming from Terre Haute, far to the east, passed through the town, dipped down some sixty feet to cross the Kaskaskia River on a new bridge, and stretched westward toward St. Louis. Intersecting it near the center of the town, another highway came from Tennessee and Kentucky and traversed the state from north to south. The whole place looked ramshackle and slattern.

The size and aspect of the seat of government did not impress young Lincoln; Springfield was larger and more imposing. But he thrilled to the excitement, for, with the Legislature and the State Supreme Court in session, Vandalia pulsated with restless energy. Arriving on horseback and by stage and carriage, legislators, jurists, and lobbyists taxed the taverns and boarding-houses to the bursting-point. Crowds milled along the sidewalks. The hum of conversation in the taprooms was punctuated with the clink of glasses, the sharp pop of unloosed corks, backslaps, loud laughs, and hearty greetings. Strong drink and picturesque language gave place to courtly graciousness when ladies alighted daintily from the stage or, after sorting their finery in their hotel rooms, tripped lightly downstairs to join the men; for many visitors brought their wives and daughters to enjoy the social season at the capital.

By reason of Stuart's standing in his party, the room that he and Lincoln shared at once became a sort of Whig head-quarters. As lawyers, legislators, and favor-seekers came in, Stuart introduced his protégé, the towering young giant with the deep-lined face thrusting out his huge, gnarled, work-worn hand in steady grip, appraising these new acquaintances as they in their turn measured him.

At this session of the Legislature Lincoln became acquainted with a young Democrat four years his junior, Stephen Arnold Douglas from Morgan County. Only slightly more than five feet tall, he was sturdily built, and his massive shoulders, deep chest, and bulging neck, together with his hard-clamped jaws and heavy brows projecting over piercing eyes, gave him a stern, almost belligerent appearance. His dark-brown hair grew thick. His voice had depth and resonance; his manner was quick and alert. Like Lincoln, he had a faculty for making friends. Born in Vermont, he had moved to Morgan County to teach school and practice law, and had come to the state capital to promote his candidacy for state's attorney of the first judicial district.

*

W I T H   T H E opening of the legislative session, Stuart and Lincoln entered the State Capitol, only ten years old, but already in such disrepair that flights of frontier eloquence were sometimes interrupted by the crash of falling plaster. The hall of the House of Representatives occupied most of the first floor; upstairs were the Senate chamber and rooms for offices. Members sat in movable chairs at long tables, each accommodating three men. The Speaker, on a small platform, also sat behind a table. On each table stood a cork inkstand. Sandboxes, distributed about the room, not only furnished sand for blotting but also served as cuspidors. A fireplace and a stove provided warmth. Over the water pail hung three tin dippers. Candles in tall holders shed dim light on evening sessions.

Notwithstanding this unpretentious background, the scene became impressive when members congregated in the chamber, dressed in long coats with wide lapels, with tight trousers overhanging their boots and wide stocks wound round their necks, and here and there a farmer in rustic garb. The visitors' gallery shimmered with the gay dresses of the ladies.

Fifty-five representatives and twenty-six senators made up the General Assembly. In the House seven men besides Lincoln had been captains in the Black Hawk War, two had been majors and one a colonel; others had served in the ranks. More than half the members were farmers, about a fourth were lawyers, and the remainder was made up of merchants, mechanics, doctors, and men of miscellaneous callings. Almost all of them were young. Very few had been born in Illinois. Many proved capable and a few would distinguish themselves. Lincoln was probably surprised to find himself at about the general level.

Illinois, enjoying statehood for sixteen years, had a history going back more than a century. Like Lincoln, it was large, strong, and still unpolished, with possibilities of great development. Its population, already exceeding 200,000, was still heaviest in the south, but was extending rapidly northward.

Agriculture, the state's chief occupation, made for a decentralized economy. Each community provided largely for its own needs. But wheat that brought fifty cents in Illinois would sell for a dollar and a half in Buffalo, so that better transportation became of first importance. While community needs were similar throughout the state, few general laws had been enacted. Special acts of the Legislature must be obtained to open roads, build bridges, incorporate manufacturing companies or banks, establish educational institutions, and in some instances even for a divorce. Consequently, each member felt responsible to his own constituents rather than to the people of the state at large, a condition not only conducive to logrolling and pork-barrel legislation but also too apt to bring political success to those adept in bargaining rather than to men of statesmanship.

The members having come to order and drawn for seats, James Semple, a Jacksonian, was elected Speaker, Stuart and Lincoln voting against him. The Democrats had control, and the Whigs must present a united front behind Stuart, whom they chose as their floorleader. Some members were appointed to as many as three committees—Stuart served on two—but Lincoln, as a new member, drew only one unimportant assignment: to the committee on public accounts and expenditures.

On the fifth day of the session the new member from Sangamon gathered his long legs under him, rose deliberately, and, addressing the House for the first time, announced his intention to introduce a bill limiting the jurisdiction of justices of the peace. In the course of the session he introduced two other minor bills: one authorizing his friend Samuel Musick to build a toll bridge across Salt Creek, a tributary of the Sangamon, northeast of New Salem; the other naming three other friends, Reuben Harrison, John Clary, and Tandy James, "to view, mark and permanently locate a road from Springfield to Miller's Ferry" on the Sangamon River, twelve miles northwest of New Salem.

Lincoln listened to a long debate on President Jackson's attack on the United States Bank, the first issue of national importance to come before the legislators, and on a vote upholding the President's action voted with the Whig minority. Soon afterward he introduced and spoke on a resolution directing the Illinois senators and representatives in Washington to obtain Congressional legislation assigning to Illinois not less than twenty per cent of the proceeds of the sale of public lands within the state.

The House devoted about half its time to two important measures: one to construct the Illinois and Michigan Canal connecting the Illinois River with Lake Michigan in order to provide a continuous waterway from the interior of Illinois to the Atlantic coast via the Great Lakes and the Erie Canal, the other to charter a state bank. Illinois had had a bank previously, but it proved a fiasco. Now, however, because of President Jackson's attack on the United States Bank, many Whigs believed that state institutions must take its place. Both measures became law, and both received Lincoln's vote.

Stuart was often absent from the chamber because of committee work, but whenever Stuart missed a session, Lincoln was on hand. They worked as a team. Stuart had ambitions to go to Congress, and apparently was grooming Lincoln to take his place as Whig floorleader. A number of bills written by Lincoln but introduced by other members indicate either that members utilized his legible penmanship or that he exerted more influence than the House Journal shows.

As Lincoln left for home at the end of the session, he pocketed $258 for his services and traveling expenses—more than enough to pay his debt to Coleman Smoot. He had had a rewarding experience. Absorbing his first lessons in parliamentary procedure and political maneuver, he learned that legislation comes about through give-and-take. He noted that personal influence and popularity, rather than the merits of a measure, often determined its fate. Broadening his outlook, he polished off some of his rough edges in his contacts with leaders of the state.

*

BACK in New Salem after a bitter ride in sub-zero weather, Lincoln entertained the villagers with stories of the legislative session. Taking up his work as postmaster and surveyor, he also resumed his law studies, for he was now assured that he could become a lawyer. Years later, in advising a young law student, he gave an insight into his methods of study. "If you are resolutely determined to make a lawyer of yourself, the thing is more than half done already," he explained. "It is but a small matter whether you read *with* any body or not. I did not read with any one. Get the books, and read and study them till you understand them in their principal features; and that is the main thing. It is of no consequence to be in a large town while you are reading. I read at New Salem, which never had three hundred people living in it. The *books*, and your *capacity* for understanding them, are just the same in all places. . . . Always bear in mind that your own resolution to succeed, is more important than any other one thing."

*

I N T H E   summer of 1835 the New Salem community was saddened by the death of a young lady, Ann Rutledge, daughter of the former tavernkeeper. A pretty, unaffected girl of twenty-two, with blue eyes and auburn hair, she contracted a disease, probably typhoid fever, that baffled the frontier doctors, and died after a brief illness. Lincoln took her death unusually hard. He had boarded at her father's tavern during his first months in the village and knew the family well. After the Rutledges moved to a farm on Sand Ridge, seven miles north of the village, Lincoln often visited them on his surveying trips.

These are all the proved facts about Lincoln's relations with Ann Rutledge, yet this frail frame of reality supports a legendary romance known to people everywhere.

By the time Lincoln became President, Ann Rutledge and Lincoln's relations with her, whatever they may have been, had been forgotten by almost everyone. Then, on February 15, 1862, John Hill, son of the former New Salem merchant Samuel Hill, published in his *Menard Axis*, of Petersburg, Illinois, under the title "A Romance of Reality," an unflattering account of an ungainly youth who, known to his neighbors at New Salem as a store clerk, soldier, day laborer, hog-drover, surveyor, and lovelorn swain, was then President of the United States. On the theme of the lovelorn swain, Hill told how the awkward young man had met and wooed a young belle of the village and won her heart. They planned to be married, but the maiden died, and her lover became so melancholy that friends feared he might attempt suicide. Hill did not mention the young lady's name, but it could easily be discovered by anyone who cared to investigate the story.

Hill's article attracted little attention. Only in 1944 did Lincoln students learn about it when a copy turned up among William H. Herndon's manuscripts. This clue, however, had inspired Herndon to search for additional evidence. Interviewing old settlers or their children, thirty years after the alleged event took place, he found that they disagreed. Some claimed to recall the incident, while others, equally competent as witnesses, remembered nothing about it. What remained clearest in the memories of most of them was Ann's engagement to John McNamar, partner of Samuel Hill, who had assumed the name McNeil while seeking his fortune in the West. Some time before Ann became ill, McNamar left on a visit to his family in New York State, where he remained so long that his betrothed wondered if he might have left for good.

Through interviews and correspondence, Herndon collected a mass of contradictory evidence, from which he prepared a lecture delivered at Springfield on November 16, 1866. From this the world first learned that Lincoln loved Ann Rutledge with "all his soul, mind and strength," that her love for him was equally strong, but that, finding herself engaged to Lincoln and McNamar at the same time, and wishing to be perfectly honest with both, Ann became so torn in spirit that she could neither eat nor sleep. Racked with fever, she became weak and emaciated to the point of death. Lincoln visited her sickroom. "The meeting was quite as much as either could bear," asserted Herndon, "and more than Lincoln, with all his coolness and philosophy, could endure. The voice, the face, the features of her; the love, sympathy and interview fastened themselves on his heart and soul forever." On August 25, 1835 Ann died.

According to Herndon, Lincoln's heart was buried with her in the grave. The bereaved lover talked wildly and incoherently, and friends took measures for his safety. After a visit with Bowling Green and his family, however, Lincoln regained his mental balance. But he had changed, and the change endured. Later he married, but Ann Rutledge was the only woman he ever really loved. Her memory exerted a mystic, guiding influence throughout his life. Repeated by Ward Hill Lamon, who obtained materials for his biography of Lincoln from Herndon, and later by Herndon in his own biography of Lincoln, the story caught the popular fancy. Embellished by sentimental fiction-writers and dramatists, it became enshrined in American folklore.

In 1890 Ann's body, or one that passed for it, was taken from the humble Concord Cemetery, where it was originally buried, and reinterred in the more easily accessible Oakland Cemetery, on the southwest edge of Petersburg. In a new tombstone were engraved the immortalizing words of Edgar Lee Masters:

> *Out of me unworthy and unknown*
> *The vibrations of deathless music;*
> *"With malice toward none, with charity for all."*
> *Out of me forgiveness of millions toward millions,*
> *And the beneficent face of a nation*
> *Shining with justice and truth.*
> *I am Ann Rutledge who sleep beneath these weeds,*
> *Beloved of Abraham Lincoln,*
> *Wedded to him, not through union,*
> *But through separation.*
> *Bloom forever, O Republic,*
> *From the dust of my bosom.*

Thus came to culmination a legend for which no shred of contemporary evidence has been found. Nothing in Lincoln's writings supports it. In the face of affirmative reminiscences, Lincoln students can scarcely declare with certainty that no such romance took place. But most of them regard it as improbable, and reject utterly its supposed enduring influence upon Lincoln.

*

In December 1835 Lincoln returned to Vandalia for a special session of the Legislature, called by Governor Joseph Duncan to speed up construction of the Illinois and Michigan Canal and to reapportion legislative representation on the basis of a recent state census.

The business of the session was not limited to matters mentioned in the Governor's call, as is the case today, and the legislators introduced a flood of bills—139 in the House and 106 in the Senate. Ninety-nine of these related to roads, eighty-one to railroads, seven to bridges, three to canals, and five to navigation, the remainder pertaining mostly to private relief and benefit.

Lincoln himself had a pet project that he guided through the Legislature: the incorporation of the Beardstown and Sangamon Canal, with its eastern terminus at Huron, a townsite at Miller's Ferry, near New Salem. Several of his friends had financial interests in the paper town of Huron, and the young legislator himself owned several lots, acquired as payment for surveying it. He also purchased a forty-seven-acre tract of land close by the projected town, and in a speech at Petersburg he urged the people to subscribe for stock in the canal, a few shares of which he may have purchased himself. This was one of the few times when he speculated in either land or stock, and his ability to do so, even in a modest way, indicates that he was paying off his debts—an assumption that is further supported by his purchase of two town lots in Springfield.

With a presidential election coming up in 1836, the Legislature debated lengthily on national affairs. Martin Van Buren, Vice President and heir apparent to President Jackson, was the Democratic candidate for President, while the Whig strategy called for support of Daniel Webster, William Henry Harrison, or Hugh L. White of Tennessee, whichever seemed strongest in each particular state, in order to prevent Van Buren's attaining a majority in the electoral college. In Illinois the favored candidate was White, who had long been a follower of Jackson, but had recently broken with him. Personally and because of his political record, Van Buren was unpopular, and the Democrats, facing a hard fight, resorted to every expedient to hold their wavering followers in line. Prompted by Douglas and others, they turned to a political device that had proved effective in assuring party regularity in the East: the nominating convention.

Up to this time anyone could run for office, but under the convention system a man's claim must be passed upon by party representatives. Moreover, once a candidate had been chosen, all members of the party must support him or risk expulsion. Noting with foreboding the probable effectiveness of this device, the Whigs immediately denounced it, some from party expediency, some from conviction. "Heretofore the voters of this County have been accustomed to vote as they please . . . but this will no longer be permitted to the Van Buren men," complained the *Sangamo Journal*. "They must give up their private judgment—and be led up to the polls by a twine through the gristle of the proboscis." Illinoisans of the frontier days would not readily sacrifice their independence of thought and action even to promote their party's interests.

Nevertheless, the Democratic leaders forced their program through, and on the first day of the legislative session a Democratic state convention met at Vandalia and endorsed Van Buren. Two days later the Whigs countered with a resolution in the House condemning the convention system as undemocratic and dictatorial. All through the session the rival parties skirmished, with Lincoln in the forefront of the battle, and even serving as Whig floorleader when Stuart was otherwise engaged.

*

THE SESSION soon ended, and Lincoln returned to New Salem. On March 24, 1836 he satisfied the first requirement for admission to the bar when the Sangamon Circuit Court certified him as a person of good moral character. Shortly afterward he announced that he would run for re-election to the Legislature.

The Whigs were aided by a revolt of "milk-and-cider" Democrats, who resented the adoption of the convention system, and

the whole Whig county ticket swept to victory, with Lincoln leading all the candidates. The reapportionment act passed by the last
Legislature gave Sangamon County seven representatives in the
lower house, an increase of three and the largest number awarded
to any county. Elected to the House of Representatives with
Lincoln were six other Whigs. A seventh Whig won election to
the Senate, and since the holdover senator also belonged to that
party, Sangamon County would be represented in the Legislature
by a solid phalanx of Whigs. The average height of this delegation
was slightly over six feet, and at the next session they would
become celebrated as the "Long Nine." The only Whig disappointment was Stuart's defeat for Congress.

*

AT LAST Lincoln mustered courage for his bar examination.
It proved easier than he expected. After answering some more
or less perfunctory questions, he followed the practice of treating
his examiners to dinner. On September 9, 1836 he received his
license.

One further step remained to make him a full-fledged lawyer:
enrollment by the clerk of the Supreme Court. This must have
been a mere formality, however, for two days after Lincoln received his license he participated in his first law case, in Springfield. Actually it consisted of three related suits, docketed as
Hawthorn v. *Wooldridge*, and involved failure of the defendant to
furnish the plaintiff with two yoke of oxen to break prairie, and
refusal to permit access to a tract of land on which he had granted
the right to raise a crop. The plaintiff claimed one hundred dollars
damages, and other claims and counterclaims were filed. Stuart
had begun proceedings some time before, but when the case came
to trial Lincoln appeared in Stuart's place, losing on one count
and settling the others out of court. Stephen T. Logan, later to be
Lincoln's second law partner, sat on the bench. An Eastern lawyer
who visited the Sangamon County courthouse about this time
recalled: "To us, just from the city of New York with the sleek
lawyers and the prim dignified judges, with audiences to cor-

respond, there was a contrast so great, that it was almost impossible to repress a burst of laughter. Upon the bench was seated the judge, with his chair tilted back and his heels as high as his head, and in his mouth a veritable corn-cob pipe; his hair standing nine ways for Sunday, while his clothing was more like that worn by a woodchopper than anybody else. There was a rail that divided the audience; outside of which smoking and chewing and spitting tobacco seemed to be the principal employment."

Lincoln's appearance in this case in place of Stuart indicates that the two men had already agreed to practice law in partnership. The relationship had not yet become official, but Henry E. Dummer, Stuart's partner, had decided to move to Beardstown, and Stuart was giving the young man who had so impressed him in the Legislature a chance to familiarize himself with court procedure.

*

THE TENTH General Assembly of the State of Illinois convened on December 5, 1836 and remained in session for three months. Not only was this the longest session held up to that time, but it also became the most notable. And in the brilliance of its membership this Legislature ranked foremost in the history of the state. The Democrats again had a majority in both houses, but the discontent of many "milk-and-cider" men made their control uncertain. James Semple was re-elected Speaker of the House, with Lincoln recognized as Whig floorleader. Solidly behind him stood the Long Nine, all able, dependable men.

As population pushed northward in Illinois, many persons wanted the seat of government moved north. For several years Springfield had coveted being the capital. Little could be done about relocation during Lincoln's first two sessions in the Legislature. The south was still too strong, and further efforts must wait until legislative seats were reapportioned according to the census of 1835. Now the time for action had arrived. Boasting the largest delegation of any county in the state, the Long Nine came to Vandalia with predetermined purpose to remove the seat of government to Springfield.

The citizens of Vandalia were forewarned, and as a counter-move they had torn down the decrepit state buildings and erected a new statehouse at their own expense, trusting to the Legislature to reimburse them. When the members of the General Assembly drifted into town, they peered with interest at the new Capitol, its interior unfinished and its grounds still littered with tool sheds, discarded lumber, and piles of brick and sand. As the House settled down to work, the chamber was dank and acrid from the drying plaster.

*

DURING the early days of the session Lincoln became ill, perhaps because of the clammy atmosphere inside the statehouse, and his illness tapered off into an attack of that baffling melancholy which oppressed him throughout his life. As puzzling to his friends and acquaintances as to his biographers, it afflicted him even as a young man, becoming more pronounced as he grew older, seeming to well up from something deep within him, and creating intermittent mental tensions, which he was sometimes able to thrust off with indulgence in humor.

Shortly before this session of the Legislature, Lincoln had become infatuated with Mary Owens, an amiable, attractive Kentucky girl of considerable culture. He had met her three years before, when she had visited her sister, Mrs. Bennett Abell, of New Salem; and recently when Mrs. Abell left to visit the Owens family, she had told Lincoln jestingly that she would bring Mary back with her if he would marry the girl. Not to be outdone in banter, Lincoln laughingly agreed. He was surprised, however, when Mary did return with her sister. She was far superior to the young surveyor and legislator in background and breeding, but the two enjoyed each other's company and soon struck up a courtship.

Perhaps Lincoln's brooding during the first days of the legislative session came from loneliness and fear of unrequited love, for Mary did not write to him. Under date of December 13, he addressed her as follows:

Mary

I have been sick ever since my arrival here, or I should have written sooner. It is but little difference, however, as I have very little even yet to write. And more, the longer I can avoid the mortification of looking in the Post Office for your letter and not finding it, the better. You see I am mad about that *old letter* yet. I dont like very well to risk you again. I'll try you once more any how.

The new State House is not yet finished, and consequently the legislature is doing little or nothing. The Governor delivered an inflamitory [*sic*] political Message, and it is expected there will be some sparring between the parties about it as soon as the two Houses get to bussiness [*sic*]. . . .

Our chance to take the seat of Government to Springfield is better than I expected. An Internal Improvement Convention was held here since we met, which recommended a loan of several millions of dollars on the faith of the State to construct Rail Roads. Some of the legislature are for it and some against it: which have the majority I can not tell. There is great strife and struggling for the office of U. S. Senator here at this time. It is probable we shall ease their pains in a few days. The opposition men have no candidate of their own, and consequently they smile as complacently at the angry snarls of the contending Van Buren candidates and their respective friends, as the christain [*sic*] does at Satan's rage. You recollect I mentioned in the outset of this letter that I had been unwell. That is the fact, though I believe I am about well now; but that, with other things I can not account for, have conspired and have gotten my spirits so low, that I feel that I would rather be any place in the world than here. I really can not endure the thought of staying here ten weeks. Write back as soon as you get this, and if possible say something that will please me, for really I have not been pleased since I left you. This letter is so dry and stupid that I am ashamed to send it, but with my present feelings I can not do any better. Give my respects to Mr. and Mrs. Abell and family.

Your friend
Lincoln

*

A L T H O U G H seventeen railroad charters had been granted at the last session of the Legislature, none of these projects had advanced beyond the paper stage. Promoters hoped to borrow Eastern capital, but found money hard to obtain; so they turned to the state as the only source of funds. When the State Internal Improvement Convention, to which Lincoln alluded in his letter to Miss Owens, convened at Vandalia, it recommended a vast program of improvements at state expense.

A few days after the session opened, Douglas, now a member of the Legislature, brought these proposals before the House, and the committee on internal improvements approved a gigantic omnibus bill designed to crosshatch the state with railroads, turnpikes, and canals to be built on the credit of the state. All this, moreover, at a time when Lincoln, as chairman of the finance committee of the House, reported that the state's income—derived from taxes on non-resident landowners and dividends from the State Bank—amounted to $57,891.15, with expenditures of $55,151.91, leaving a surplus of $2,739.24!

The proposed measure gave the Sangamon delegation a welcome opportunity. Every county wanted a slice of this luscious pie, and legislators, mindful of election day, wished to please the folks back home. The situation became ideal for logrolling, and Lincoln and his colleagues from Sangamon made the most of it to promote their own design, promising support for a railroad here, a canal there, and an improved road or a deepened river somewhere else, in return for pledges of votes for Springfield as the future capital. Lincoln's friendly manner and ingratiating personality proved effective aids as he circulated through the chamber and the taverns, joking, backslapping, consummating a bargain with a handclasp, coming to regard himself as "the DeWitt Clinton of Illinois" in emulation of the New York statesman who had built the famous Erie Canal.

Supporters of Vandalia and Alton attempted to counteract Lincoln's designs by similar tactics, but they lacked the power of the Long Nine, who, acting as a unit under Lincoln's leadership, could exert tremendous pressure.

*

As an interlude to all this bargaining the Senate and House
met together to elect a United States senator. On all three ballots
the Long Nine cast their votes for Archibald Williams, of Quincy,
who would become Lincoln's firm friend. A self-made lawyer from
Kentucky, a backsliding Democrat, he had a physical resemblance
to Lincoln, and rivaled him in homeliness. Williams dressed so
shabbily that once a hotel clerk, noting his disreputable appearance as he slouched in a chair in the lobby, had taken him for a
loafer and, approaching him, inquired: "Pardon me, sir, but are
you a guest of this hotel?" Whereupon Williams fastened him
with an icy stare and snarled: "Hell, no! I am one of its victims. I
am paying five dollars a day!"

Williams finished third in the balloting for U.S. senator, with
Richard M. Young, former representative, circuit judge, and an
independent Democrat, the winner.

Young's election called for a celebration at one of the local
hostelries. The usual diet of wild game gave place to more
sumptuous fare, and, as the spirits of the lawmakers became
enlivened under a copious flow of liquor, Douglas and James
Shields, another legislator, climbed upon one of the cluttered
tables and performed a lively dance, pirouetting with mock
grace amid the clouds of smoke, prancing and jigging with
such gusto that crockery and glassware flew in all directions, to
crash and smash on the floor, as the crowd, in utter abandon,
roared encouragement. The next morning Judge Young paid six
hundred dollars for supplies and breakage, and a visiting clergy-
man wrote home that Vandalia was a scandalous place, much in
need of reform, and that church members should be more circumspect in their choice of legislators.

*

As the House met in committee of the whole to discuss the
internal-improvement bill, petitions from all sections flooded in,
praying for railroads, canals, and turnpikes. Bargaining ran riot
as the lawmakers made certain that their districts would not be
slighted. A few cautious spirits tried to stem the avalanche,

warning of state bankruptcy. Absurd, replied the spenders; the
Illinois projects, like the Erie Canal, would soon pay for themselves. The Rothschilds and the Barings would compete strenuously for the state bonds, bidding them up to such a figure that
the premium alone might pay for the cost of the works.

About this time Lincoln was embarrassed by the arrival in
Vandalia of John Taylor, of Springfield, land speculator, re-
ceiver of the Land Office, and promoter of the town of Petersburg,
close by New Salem. For Taylor brought with him a petition for
a new county to be created out of the northern part of Sangamon.
Opposition to the proposal on the part of the Sangamon delegation might bring retaliation from voters in the affected area,
whereas division of the county would so reduce Sangamon's
strength in future legislatures that opponents of capital relocation
would be encouraged to fight a delaying action. To meet the
emergency, the Long Nine revised the petition to include a
portion of Morgan County in the proposed new county, thus
assuring the opposition of the Morgan delegation. In this form it
went to Douglas's committee on petitions, where it languished
long enough for Lincoln to build backfires. Remonstrances
against division began to come in, until at last Douglas reported
that the remonstrants outnumbered the petitioners. A motion to
print the minority report from Douglas's committee brought a
sharp exchange of repartee between Lincoln and Usher F.
Linder, a tall, loose-jointed lawyer from Coles County, who
favored retention of the capital at Vandalia. Linder cared
nothing about division, one way or the other, but he seized every
opportunity to blunt the Sangamon attack. A division bill
eventually passed the House, but Archer G. Herndon, of Sangamon, took care that it perished in the Senate. The Long Nine had
stood together to beat back a serious threat.

But Linder attacked from another angle when he introduced
a resolution calling for an examination of the State Bank at
Springfield by a House committee. On any such committee a
majority would be Democrats, unfriendly to the bank, and
Linder hoped to put the institution in such jeopardy that Spring-

field would yield her claim to the capital rather than lose the bank. Sparring between Linder and Lincoln continued for several days, until Lincoln, primed with facts and arguments furnished by friends of the bank who had hastened down from Springfield, delivered a prepared address. The controversy resulted in a limited investigation rather than the sweeping examination proposed by Linder, and the bank gained a clean bill of health.

*

D u r i n g the bank squabble another matter came before the House when Governor Duncan called the attention of the General Assembly to memorials from certain Southern state legislatures decrying agitation for the abolition of slavery, a movement which had assumed such formidable proportions in some sections of the North that the complaining states demanded that Northern legislatures prohibit the sending of inflammatory literature into the South.

A joint committee of the House and Senate recommended the adoption of a series of resolutions condemning the abolitionists, declaring that the Constitution sanctified the right of property in slaves, that slavery was wholly within the jurisdiction of the states, and that the Federal government had no right to abolish it in the District of Columbia. Lincoln moved to add: "Unless the people of the said District petition for the same," but his amendment failed.

The resolutions did not accord with Lincoln's thinking on the slavery question. He would have liked to express his views, but to do so at this juncture might engender antagonism perilous to his political plans. So, for the moment, he kept silent, and the resolutions passed, 77 to 6, Lincoln, Dan Stone, and Andrew McCormick of the Sangamon delegation voting nay.

*

W i t h   a l l threats repelled and the strength of the Long Nine unimpaired, the internal-improvement bill came out of committee. It called for the expenditure of $7,000,000 for a north-south railroad and two east-west lines, $100,000 for road improvements, and $400,000 for dredging rivers. Pressure was exerted to enlarge the program, and after much debate the bill was recommitted. The Long Nine went to work again, placating neglected counties and garnering more votes for Springfield as the capital. Lincoln spent so much time discussing amendments with the committee that years afterward one legislator erroneously recalled him as a member of it. Finally the bill came before the House again, amended to provide for $10,000,000 of expenditures. The three trunk railroads were now consolidated into two, with six spurs to important towns; road appropriations were doubled; and a sort of grab-bag appropriation for those counties not otherwise benefited totaled $200,000.

Fighting off restrictive amendments, the spenders pushed the bill to passage, 61 to 25. When the Senate approved it, bonfires lighted the streets. Speculators rushed to enter land along prospective rights-of-way, and the *Illinois State Register* declared: "We have no doubt the passage of the bill has already increased the value of the land in the State more than 100 per cent, and every day is adding to its value. We have the utmost confidence that every acre of the public land will, in a few years, be settled by immigrants, who will add to the population of the State, will increase its wealth, its influence and power among the other States of the confederacy. If the present Legislature had done no more, they would have deserved the thanks of the People for the passage of this law."

*

WITH THE internal-improvement project out of the way, the question of relocation of the capital became the chief business before the House. Already a bill to "permanently locate the seat of government of the State of Illinois" had passed the Senate; Lincoln decided that it should be initiated in the upper chamber, since the House would look with greater favor on a bill approved by the Senate. Now, as the threat to Vandalia became imminent, little John Dement, of Fayette County, where Vandalia was

located, smaller even than Douglas and equally fiery, led the fight
for the defense, resorting to every parliamentary tactic he could
bring to bear. Lincoln faced a formidable and desperate opposition, and his resourcefulness in countering every move attests his
political sagacity and the skill he had attained in parliamentary
procedure during his short experience as a lawmaker.

As the debate became more furious, Alexander P. Dunbar, of
Coles County, moved, at Lincoln's suggestion, that no less than
$50,000 and two acres of land must be donated by the city chosen
for the capitol site on penalty of voiding the act. This was
adopted, 56 to 25, with the aid of a solid Sangamon vote. It
proved a skillful move, for few competitors of Springfield could
meet such a condition. But the opposition countered with a
motion to table the whole subject until July 4, a date well beyond the life expectancy of the session, and the motion passed
by one vote, all of Sangamon's representatives voting nay.
Lincoln refused to concede defeat by such a scanty margin.
Calling his colleagues together at his lodgings, he gave each of
them a specific job to do. They rounded up absent members and
pledged them to be present the next morning. They persuaded
five men to change their votes by reminding them of their debt
of gratitude to Sangamon for internal improvements granted to
their districts. When persuasion failed, they used threats. The
relocation measure was brought back to the floor and approved.

With that the House and Senate met in joint session to
choose the new capital. Springfield led on the first ballot with
35 votes, with 16 for Vandalia, 15 for Alton, 14 for Jacksonville,
and the remainder scattering. On the next two ballots Springfield's lead increased as men who could not help Lincoln on the
first ballot came over to him after casting complimentary first-
ballot votes for their home communities. On the fourth ballot
Springfield had 73 votes against 50 for all other places. Only the
Vandalia men still held together, but they were powerless against
the Sangamon spearhead.

Back in Springfield wild rejoicing culminated in a huge
bonfire built around the whipping-post on the public square.

Leading citizens quickly pledged the $50,000 required as a condition of the removal of the capital. In the town that Lincoln had already planned to make his home, he was the man of the hour.

*

THREE DAYS before the end of the session Lincoln, his legislative program safely enacted into law, expressed himself on the slavery resolutions passed six weeks earlier. Writing a protest, which he and Dan Stone subscribed, he spread it upon the Journal of the House. Declaring that they believed the institution of slavery to be founded on both injustice and bad policy, the protestants deplored the promulgation of abolition doctrines as calculated to increase rather than abate the evils of slavery. Congress had no power under the Constitution to interfere with slavery in the states, they said, but it did have power to abolish slavery in the District of Columbia, though it should not do so except at the request of the people of the District. The "difference between these opinions and those contained in the said resolutions, is their reason for entering this protest," they explained.

Thus, at the age of twenty-eight, Lincoln made public avowal of his dislike of slavery, basing his position on moral grounds when he characterized the institution as an injustice attended with evils, while conceding the sanctity of Southern rights. In 1860, in his autobiography, he stated that the protest "briefly defined his position on the slavery question; and so far as it goes, it was then the same that it is now."

Near the end of the session Lincoln satisfied the last requirement for practicing law when the clerk of the Supreme Court enrolled his name as an attorney. As Lincoln packed his bags to leave for home, he could look back on the achievements of the past thirteen weeks with great personal satisfaction. Three years before, he had been an unknown political novice of uncertain future. Now he was a qualified lawyer and a power in state politics.

*

W I T H   T H E close of the legislative session Lincoln returned to New Salem, but only to prepare to move, for he saw no future in the town. It had begun to decline a year before, and already the post office had been transferred to Petersburg, which was rapidly superseding the older village as a trading center. Within three years New Salem would be a ghost town.

But during its brief span of life the village on the bluff meant much to Lincoln. With less than a year of formal schooling, he learned mostly by mingling with people and discussing things with them, by observation of their ways and their reactions. At New Salem, as had been true in lesser degree in Indiana, many of his neighbors helped give direction to his actions or his thinking, while the humblest of the villagers touched his life at one point or another, exerting an intangible influence in the making of the later, greater Lincoln. Lincoln knew the common people because he sprang from them.

Coming to New Salem an irresolute pioneer youth, he had found himself and learned to make a living with his brain instead of his hands. He could do this more easily at New Salem than in an older established community, because humble origin and lack of schooling did not handicap him. They were common deficiencies. No social castes existed and none of the residents enjoyed distinctive wealth, so that democracy was an actuality as well as an ideal. With no formal obstacles to check him, Lincoln forged ahead. The individuality that became so marked in later life already set him apart. Yet, as he became a leader of his fellows, Lincoln never lost touch with them. He would grow beyond his old associates but not away from them.

In a manner, the frontier environment of the place had been his school, amplifying what he learned from books. Rural living developed a talent for inventiveness, for resorting to expedients when ordinary practices were unavailable or unavailing. Cherishing personal independence in thought and action, he also learned to value friendship and unselfish neighborliness. In a region where one constantly met strangers, he discovered the uses and virtues of the good-tempered approach.

The Westerner, primarily a realist, was speculative too. In Lincoln's case, the conditions of rural living intensified a natural bent for philosophic thinking. The vastness of the country gave him breadth of outlook. A sevenfold increase in the population of Illinois during the three decades that he lived there impressed him with the nation's buoyant virility. The traits of birds and farmyard animals, the majesty of forests, plains, and rivers, the beauty, the mystery, the bounty, and the dreadfulness of nature quickened his imagination, bestirred his reflections, and increasingly adorned his speech.

Most important of all, perhaps, everywhere about him Lincoln saw grass-roots democracy successfully at work. James Hall, editor of the *Western Monthly Magazine*, noted that throughout the Western country everything was done in popular assemblies, by popular vote, through public argument and discussion. Robert Dale Owen, founder of the famous New Harmony colony, declared that in many a backwoods cabin, lighted only by a blazing heap of logs, he had heard arguments on government, views of national policy, and judgments of men and things expounded with a sound sense and practical wisdom that would have done credit to any legislative body in the world. Thus Lincoln saw men come together in equality and mutual respect, not only in the State Legislature but also in private homes and humble crossroads meeting-houses to voice their free opinions. And at the same time he saw judge and doctor each doing his own stable work, preachers turning to the plow to supplement their livelihood, established lawyers serving in the ranks of the militia.

So Lincoln drew into himself the raw, rich strength of the frontier. But at the same time he avoided the most flagrant of the frontier's faults, or learned to overcome them. His self-reliance was unspoiled by boastfulness. His ardent nationalism held no contempt for foreign lands and foreign people. His robust jocularity remained untamed; but an early impulsiveness would give place in time to calm analysis. He realized the value of law and became respectful of law and tradition in a region where men sometimes took the law into their own hands and where people were concerned with the present and the future rather than with the past. One profound student of his life believes that he early came to think that he was odd, that, being odd, he must learn to stand alone, and that standing alone would make him strong.

*

T A K I N G leave of New Salem on April 15, 1837, Lincoln rode into Springfield with all his personal possessions in his saddlebags, and took lodgings in a room above a store kept by Joshua F. Speed, who charged him no rent and soon became his closest friend. That same day the *Journal* announced that "J. T. Stuart and A. Lincoln, Attorneys and Counsellors at Law, will practice conjointly, in the courts of this Judicial Circuit." The young lawyer just beginning practice had a stroke of rare good fortune in his partnership with Stuart, for Stuart and Dummer had built up the largest business of any law firm in Springfield, and Lincoln, stepping into Dummer's position, did not have to wait for clients.

Yet Lincoln's first weeks in his new home depressed him. Perhaps he had expected a more enthusiastic welcome in Springfield because of the part he had played in making it the capital. Perhaps he became more conscious of his poverty and social shortcomings amid more affluent and cultured surroundings. Three weeks after his arrival he wrote to Mary Owens: "This thing of living in Springfield is rather a dull business, after all; at least it is so to me. I am quite as lonesome here as [I] ever was anywhere in my life. I have been spoken to by but one woman since I've been here, and should not have been by her, if she could have avoided it. I've never been to church yet, nor probably shall not be soon. I stay away because I am conscious I should not know how to behave myself."

Lincoln's mention of churchgoing is noteworthy, for up to this point he had manifested no religious convictions. Although his parents joined the church in Indiana, he did not. And at New Salem the religious emotionalism and bitter sectarianism

repelled him. He had become something of a skeptic or deist, for
he always experienced a sense of frustration when dealing with
abstractions, and many years would pass before he came to
understand how the incomprehensible might still be true.

*

H o w e v e r disappointed Lincoln may have been with his new
home, he soon became too deeply immersed in politics to repine.
During the struggle to obtain the capital, Springfield politicians
had declared a sort of truce, but pent-up partisan energies could
be suppressed no longer. The county election on August 1 centered
on the contest for probate judge between Lincoln's friend Dr. Anson G. Henry, Whig, and General James Adams, Democrat.
About seven weeks before the election Lincoln and Stephen T.
Logan had sued Adams to recover title to ten acres of land held by
the general under assignment of a judgment from the deceased
husband of a Mrs. Mary Anderson. The widow claimed that the
land rightfully belonged to her, and Lincoln, upon investigation,
became convinced that Adams had obtained it by fraud.

Immediately after the filing of this suit, the Whigs, intent on
defeating Adams, began a mud-slinging campaign by insinuating
in a series of anonymous letters in the *Sangamo Journal* that
Adams's title to the land on which he lived—not the same land at
issue in the suit—rested on a forgery, and that the rightful owners
were the heirs of a man named Sampson. These letters, signed by
"Sampson's Ghost," have been attributed to Lincoln. Whether he
composed them or not, he had a hand in their production.

Adams replied to the accusations with a series of letters in
the *Republican*, a local Democratic journal, maintaining his
innocence and protesting the conspiracy of "a knot of Whig
lawyers" to ruin him. Two days before the election an anonymous
handbill was widely circulated, giving a detailed account of
Adams's alleged fraud and the manner of its discovery. It was
later acknowledged by Lincoln to be his work.

Public sympathy seemed to regard Adams as a victim of

persecution, for he was elected by a large majority. His accusers were relentless, however, and the newspaper controversy continued. But nothing ever came of it. Adams was twice re-elected and the suit against him never came to trial.

If Lincoln deserved commendation for wishing to unmask Adams's alleged dishonesty, his tactics did him no credit. The place to try Adams was in the courts, not the newspapers, and resort to anonymous letters was reprehensible. Lincoln acted with the frontiersman's reckless urgency. Here was a crudity attaching to him from his environment, a manifestation of the impulsiveness that would be restrained as he became scrupulous in his methods and more careful in his judgments and taught himself to respect an opponent's feelings and point of view. But these lessons he had still to learn.

*

D U R I N G the Adams controversy Lincoln wriggled out of his entanglement with Mary Owens. The courtship had continued after he moved to Springfield, but seemingly without enthusiasm on either side. To the lady it seemed that Lincoln lacked those small habits of courtesy which indicate good breeding. On an outing at New Salem, Mary noted that her swain allowed Mrs. Greene to struggle along with a heavy baby in her arms without once offering his aid. When a group of young folk went horseback-riding, all the other gentlemen solicitously helped their partners ford a stream, but Lincoln rode across without even looking back, leaving Mary to get over as best she could. Lincoln, on his part, became conscious of Mary's portliness: her charms seemed less alluring than at first.

On August 16, 1837 Lincoln wrote a curious letter to Miss Owens in which he declared that he would leave the future course of their relations entirely to her. He wanted to do right in all cases, he assured her, and particularly in all cases involving women. He suspected that her happiness would be best served by his leaving her alone, and if she agreed, she could ignore his letter.

If she felt in any degree bound to him, he would release her if she wished. But if he could add to her happiness, he avowed himself willing, even anxious, to bind her faster.

Evidently Lincoln wished to escape gracefully from a romance now gone stale. If so, the lady obliged him. She ignored his letter, and they never met again.

Up to this point Lincoln acted with strict correctness. But about eight months later he wrote a flippant account of the whole affair to Mrs. Orville Hickman Browning, wife of a state senator from Quincy, with whom Lincoln exchanged banter and small talk. Adverting to his erstwhile sweetheart's "want of teeth" and "weather-beaten appearance in general," Lincoln pictured her as "a fair match for Falstaff." She could scarcely "have commenced at the size of infancy, and reached her present bulk in less than thirtyfive or forty years," he thought, "and, in short, I was not [at] all pleased with her." Repenting his romantic rashness, he puzzled how to extricate himself; and now, he exulted to Mrs. Browning, he was completely free without violation of word, honor, or conscience, for the lady would not have him on any terms. To his surprise, however, he now found himself somewhat put out when he realized "that she whom I had taught myself to believe no body else would have, had actually rejected me with all my fancied greatness; and to cap the whole, I then, for the first time, began to suspect that I was really a little in love with her." He confessed to making a complete fool of himself. Never again would he think of marriage, he declared, for he could never be satisfied with any woman who would be such a "block-head" as to accept him.

Written on April Fool's Day, 1838, and undoubtedly intended to be humorous, the letter furnishes another instance of Lincoln's penchant for merciless satire, which had evinced itself in the "Chronicles of Reuben" and would only be curbed later when it brought him a challenge to a duel. Lincoln did not divulge Miss Owens's name, and he made himself the scapegoat, but his letter exhibited such bad taste as to confirm Miss Owens's judgment regarding his lack of gallantry. Mrs. Browning and her husband looked on the story as a witty fiction. Not until years afterward did they learn from Lincoln that he had related an actual experience.

*

M E A N W H I L E broader problems commanded Lincoln's attention. The internal-improvement program that he had done so much to foster was just getting under way when panic struck. Business ground to a stop. Financial houses closed; loans became unobtainable. "One loud, deep, uninterrupted groan of hard times is echoed from one end of the country to another," the *Sangamo Journal* reported. The State Bank at Springfield suspended specie payments, a measure that would bring automatic forfeiture of its charter if continued for sixty days; and the Bank of Illinois at Shawneetown, whose charter had been renewed in 1835, took similar action.

Governor Duncan called a special session of the Legislature in July, blaming Jackson for all the troubles. "Never was wisdom from above to direct your counsels more to be implored than at this moment," he informed the legislators. He could offer no alternative to legalizing the suspension of the banks, but he recommended abandonment of the internal-improvement project, a scheme "so fraught with evil" that it was eating up the resources of the state. The legislators approved the action of the banks, but reproved the Governor for his timidity about internal improvements, and directed the improvement commissioners to proceed with surveys and construction.

*

W H I L E Lincoln developed his law practice and wrestled with state problems, his mind, stimulated by discussions of national affairs in the Legislature, took on a broader cast. The abolition agitation, which seemed so menacing to the South, also stirred up such hot resentment in the North that it sometimes resulted in mob violence; and the mob spirit, once aroused, vented itself against others besides the antislavery agitators. In St. Louis a free mulatto who stabbed an officer while resisting arrest was burned at the stake by outraged citizens, and a local judge condoned their action. At Vicksburg, Mississippi, three white men, professional gamblers, were strung up by a mob. Closest to home, however, occurred the murder of Elijah P. Lovejoy, killed at Alton, Illinois, while attempting to defend his abolition press. Eleven weeks after the Alton outrage Lincoln spoke before the Young Men's Lyceum of Springfield, taking as his theme the danger and wickedness of mobs and the value and necessity of law and order.

Mentioning the Mississippi and St. Louis outrages specifically, Lincoln adverted only indirectly to the Lovejoy incident, though it was more pertinent to his argument. Lincoln never moved too far in advance of public opinion, and his avoidance of any direct mention of Lovejoy has been taken as an early example of his caution in this respect, for Springfield, with its Southern background, disliked antislavery agitation.

But neither did Lincoln hesitate to influence public opinion when he thought he could, and he did mention anti-abolition disorder specifically when he said: "There is no grievance that is a fit object of redress by mob law. In any case that arises, as for instance, the promulgation of abolitionism, one of two positions is necessarily true; that is, the thing is right within itself, and therefore deserves the protection of all law and all good citizens; or it is wrong, and therefore proper to be prohibited by legal enactments; and in neither case, is the interposition of mob law, either necessary, justifiable, or excusable." Lincoln did not shrink from possible public condemnation. His reason for not expatiating on the Lovejoy matter was probably the fact that his listeners were fully familiar with it.

*

IN THE legislative campaign of 1838 Lincoln stood as a candidate for a third term. He did little speaking on his own account, but worked vigorously for Stuart, who again sought election to Congress with Douglas as his opponent. Early in the campaign Lincoln wrote to a friend that the Whig strategy aimed to ignore

Douglas. "Isn't that the best mode of treating so small a matter?" he asked.

But Douglas was not a man to be ignored, and as the campaign wore along, it became almost malevolent. On one occasion Stuart and Douglas fought like wildcats in the rear of Herndon's store over a floor drenched with slops. A few days before the election, in a speech in front of the Market House in Springfield, Douglas so angered Stuart that the latter seized his undersized opponent by the neck and dragged him around the Market House; and Douglas, fighting furiously to free himself, bit Stuart's thumb so viciously that the dignified Kentuckian bore the imprint of the Little Giant's teeth for life. When Stuart fell ill, Lincoln debated the issues with Douglas at Bloomington and perhaps at other places. Stuart won, but his margin was only 36 votes in a total of 36,495.

*

W H E N   T H E Legislature convened for the last time at Vandalia in December 1838, Lincoln, as the outstanding Whig in the House, was put forward for speaker. But the Whig majority split, and Lincoln lost, again becoming Whig floorleader. Duncan, the outgoing Governor, again recommended abandonment of the internal-improvement plan; nearly two million dollars had been spent with nothing to show for it.

While the most levelheaded of the legislators realized by this time that the whole internal-improvement scheme was impractical and must eventually be repudiated, Lincoln and many others were reluctant to renounce a project on which so much had been spent, and Lincoln also felt in honor bound to those counties that had voted for Springfield as the capital in return for promised benefits. With economic conditions what they were, however, more state bonds simply could not be sold; so Lincoln, seeking a way out of the difficulty, offered a resolution from the finance committee urging the Federal government to allow the state to purchase the unsold public lands within its borders, estimated at some twenty million acres, at twenty-five cents an acre. The state would issue another five million dollars' worth of bonds to pay for them, then resell the lands to individuals at the government price of a dollar and a quarter an acre, and thus realize over a period of time profit not only enough to pay off its debt and provide for the interest on it, but to complete the internal-improvement project as well. The resolution passed, but nothing ever came of it in Congress.

To provide additional revenue immediately, the legislators at last brought themselves to levy a general tax of twenty-five cents per one hundred dollars of assessed valuation on all property within the state, a measure they had fought shy of heretofore by taxing only the property of nonresidents. The bill's passage brought immediate complaints. Lincoln comforted one worried politician by assuring him that the new law was not only necessary but equitable, in that it took from the *"wealthy few"* rather than the *"many poor"* by taxing land according to its value. If the wealthy few thought it unfair, "it is still to be remembered, that *they* are not sufficiently numerous to carry the elections," he offered in consolation.

*

RETURNING to Springfield at the end of the session, Lincoln soon found himself caught up again in the political whirl. Mindful of the approaching presidential election of 1840, he and other Whig leaders, impressed by the unity achieved by the Democrats through the convention system, called the first Whig state convention. Not too well attended, it endorsed William Henry Harrison for President and laid plans to bring out the vote. Lincoln served on the state central committee of five, and also as a Whig presidential elector.

The campaign opened in Springfield with the convening of the Circuit Court. One night during a vigorous argument in the rear of Speed's store Douglas protested that this was no place to wrangle over the issues, and challenged the Whigs to public discussion. The resulting debates continued for a week in an oratorical free-for-all. Lincoln spoke twice. His second speech refuted Douglas's defense of President Van Buren's Subtreasury, which had replaced the United States Bank as a repository of government money. Douglas defended the recent Democratic administration from Whig charges of extravagance by pleading the necessity of unusual expenditures; but Lincoln, quoting irrefutable statistics from government documents, pointed out so many factual errors in the Little Giant's statement that he reduced it to absurdity. This resort to documents marked a new departure for Lincoln, and he found it so effective that more and more, as he faced sterner problems, he would ground his arguments firmly on documentary evidence.

Throughout the presidential campaign Lincoln worked assiduously in helping to direct Whig strategy. He saw more clearly than other Whig leaders that the party needed to develop its strength throughout the state, especially in the south, instead of relying on a few Whig strongholds. Twice he went south on speaking tours. His second trip lasted four weeks and took him to Shawneetown, far down on the Ohio, then north through the counties bordering the Wabash River. Harrison won the election, but Van Buren carried Illinois.

*

MEANWHILE Governor Thomas Carlin had proclaimed Springfield the new capital of Illinois as of July 4, 1839. Wagons loaded with the state archives, packed in boxes, set out from Vandalia in a driving rain. As state officials moved to Springfield, Lincoln's home town took over Vandalia's place as the political, judicial, and social center of the state.

Developing along the pattern of most Midwestern towns, the new capital of some 2,500 residents sprawled off in all directions from a public square, where the unfinished statehouse reared its classical columns. The four sides of the square and the adjacent blocks contained the business houses, some, like the State Bank, adequate and imposing, others, like those on "Chicken Row," no better than eyesores. Girdling the business district, the residential areas also offered striking contrasts, with homes of architectural elegance mingled with crude log cabins. Magnificent trees embowered the whole town, and a small stream, the Town Branch flowed through an especially beautiful grove just south of the business district.

The worst features of the place were the mud, which soon became notorious, and the hogs, which roamed the streets as scavengers. Street crossings became abominable in wet weather and presented hazards to ladies in long skirts. Lincoln, watching from his office window one day as a matron, adorned in a great hat bedecked with long plumes, picked her precarious way across the street, could not restrain his penchant for salty humor; for as she slipped and went down in the mud he turned to another watcher and remarked: "Reminds me of a duck." "How is that?" his companion asked. "Feathers on her head and down on her behind," Lincoln explained.

Even the wooden sidewalks soon became overlaid with a thick coating of treacherous slime, when the prowling swine did not root out the boards altogether. The editor of the *Journal*, warning that visitors would not tolerate such conditions much longer and that the town's apathy toward its shortcomings might bring agitation for removal of the capital, commented that " 'Chicken Row' was highly perfumed yesterday by opening the hog wallows in front of the stores," and on another occasion he recommended the planting of wild rice as a civic project. Being an aquatic plant, capable of growing in six to twelve inches of water, it was well adapted to the town's terrain, and a sufficient quantity might be grown in the statehouse grounds alone to provide an adequate ration for state officers.

But Springfield offered more pleasing aspects, too. Six churches boasted resident ministers, and an academy and several private schools had been established. The Thespian Society, the Young Men's Lyceum, and the Temperance Society promoted moral and cultural uplift. Traveling theatrical companies visited the town. Lecturers like Colonel Lehmanowski, formerly an officer under Napoleon, and celebrities like Daniel Webster and ex-President Van Buren included it in their itineraries. The Swiss Bell Ringers stopped off for a concert, and local singing societies performed.

Leaders of the social set were Ninian W. Edwards, son of a former Governor, and his wife, Elizabeth, a member of the prominent Todd family of Kentucky; Mr. and Mrs. Lawrason Levering, the Nicholas Ridgelys, the James Conklings, and the Gersham Jaynes. Other Todds and Edwardses also enjoyed social prominence—Frances Todd, who married Dr. William Wallace; Elizabeth, daughter of Dr. John Todd; and John Todd Stuart, cousin of the Todd sisters.

Picnics, sleighrides, parties, and dances furnished diversion for the younger social circle, a group to which Lincoln won ready admission by reason of his political alignment with Edwards and his partnership with Stuart. The first session of the Legislature to be held in Springfield had scarcely opened when invitations to a cotillion bore among others the names of Douglas, Edwards, Shields, Lincoln, and Speed.

Most impressive to visitors was Springfield's hospitality. Persons fortunate enough to have relatives in the capital—especially those with marriageable daughters—contrived for invitations for the social season and found them easy to obtain. Out-of-town lawyers, judges, legislators, and their families were splendidly entertained. Years afterward a Chicago lawyer who often visited Springfield remembered "the old-fashioned, generous hospitality . . . hospitality proverbial to this day throughout the State. We read much of 'Merrie England,' but I doubt if there was ever anything more 'merrie' than Springfield in those days."

On June 24, 1839 Lincoln was elected a trustee of the town. He served until April 1840, when Springfield began to operate under a new city charter, which he helped to obtain from the Legislature.

*

E L E C T E D to the General Assembly for the fourth time in 1840, Lincoln once again came to the aid of the State Bank at a special session in November. The Senate occupied its new chamber in the statehouse, but the House met in the Methodist church while waiting for its quarters to be finished. Defeated a second time for speaker, Lincoln again served as Whig floorleader.

Hard times had again forced the State Bank to suspend the redemption of its notes in specie, and an act granting it temporary relief specified that this suspension must not extend beyond the adjournment of the Legislature. To postpone this contingency, Lincoln and other Whigs planned to prevent adjournment of the special session until the regular session began, so that there would be no official adjournment until it ended. To thwart the Democratic majority, which wished to end the session in order to embarrass the bank, enough Whig members stayed away each day to prevent a quorum from acting.

Two days before the regular session would begin, Lincoln and two Whig friends took seats in the House to enjoy the frustration of their opponents. Failing to note how many members were present, they voted against a motion to adjourn, only to find to their consternation that their votes made a quorum, and the Speaker adjourned the House. In a futile attempt to avoid being counted in the tally the three Whigs jumped out the window of the church—a gymnastic feat that made Lincoln a target for Democratic ridicule for a long time afterward.

For three weeks during the regular session, which convened in the new statehouse, Lincoln was seriously ill. But he recovered in time to oppose a Democratic attempt to pack the State Supreme Court by increasing the number of justices from four to nine. The measure passed, however, and Stephen A. Douglas took a seat on the supreme bench as one of the new appointees.

Thus ended Lincoln's service as a state legislator. But what of the internal improvement program? And what of the resulting debt, amounting now to more than seventeen million dollars, which Lincoln had helped to saddle upon the state?

The state paid interest on its debt through July 1841; then it defaulted. Work on improvements stopped, and thrifty farmers planted crops on the abandoned railroad gradings. The state's credit was almost destroyed. Finally, in 1845, Governor Thomas Ford persuaded those English investors who held most of the Illinois and Michigan Canal bonds to advance enough additional money to complete the canal; and tolls from the canal, together with an increase in the general property levy and the sale of all lands and properties acquired in connection with the other internal-improvement projects, eventually brought solvency. At the same time Governor Ford dissolved the State Bank at Springfield and the Bank of Illinois at Shawneetown, thus ending the stormy history of those institutions.

*

IF LINCOLN's four terms in the Legislature proved not altogether happy for the state, they were an invaluable experience for him. The techniques of politics—appeal, persuasion, compromise, maneuver—became thoroughly familiar to him; he learned the ways and nature of politicians. He found how best to use his personal attributes and discovered that moral convictions must sometimes be temporarily subordinated if a man is to work effectively in politics.

If Lincoln had proved himself an able politician, however, it was in a rather narrow meaning of the word. In his methods and his outlook, he was still a man of expediency and limited vision.

One may well wonder why Lincoln, with his humble pioneer background and strong feeling for the common man, associated himself with the Whigs, who were generally accounted the party of wealth and privilege, instead of casting his fortunes with the Jacksonian Democrats. Actually, political divisions in his part of the country were not primarily along class lines, and Jackson himself had many of the attributes of the aristocrat. Clay, with his "American system" of using the powers of the national government to develop the country's resources through conservative banking, a stable currency, internal improvements, and a protective tariff for infant industries, appealed as strongly to the frontiersman as did Jackson; and since Lincoln had taken Clay as his ideal at a time when party lines were undefined, it was quite natural that he should follow him when they solidified. Moreover, Stuart and others who befriended Lincoln during his first ventures into politics became Whigs and undoubtedly helped to shape his thinking. Nor was Jackson's irascible personality of the sort to appeal to Lincoln. There was much of the autocrat in Jackson, notwithstanding his hatred of pelf and privilege. Quite likely Lincoln suspected that the waspish old general's policies too often originated in personal animosities rather than political convictions.

Always respectful of tradition, Lincoln believed in the economic doctrines of the Founding Fathers. He revered established institutions and adhered to Alexander Hamilton's ideas of utilizing banks as fiscal agencies of government. As a man who had risen from poverty by his own efforts he had no quarrel with the existing economic order. Essentially the Jacksonian movement aimed to divorce government from business by eliminating monopolistic and other special privileges originating in acts of government, to the end that the opportunities of the small businessman and wage-earner might be enlarged. Lincoln's conception of the government's relation to the economic welfare of the people went beyond this laissez-faire philosophy; he favored direct government expenditures for public improvements, as well as grants in aid to states, and help to private enterprise. "The legitimate object of government," he would one day declare, "is to do for a community of people whatever they need to have done, but cannot do at all, or cannot do so well for themselves, in their separate and individual capacities."

Lincoln knew the crying need of bank credit to develop the resources of his state. He believed that only the State Bank could meet this need as the Bank of the United States succumbed before Jackson's assault. So Lincoln served the interests of the State Bank at a time when Old Hickory and his followers were making war on the moneyed interests of the country in the name of the people.

CHAPTER IV

———◆•◆———

Courtship and Marriage

FOR SEVERAL years after the panic of 1837 the state of Illinois remained in a precarious condition. It had incurred obligations out of all proportion to its resources, and a period of low prices retarded tax collections. With the State Bank unable to redeem in specie, the negotiable value of its notes slipped to forty-four cents on the dollar. To avoid acceptance of tax payments in this depreciated currency, James Shields, the state auditor, ordered the collectors of revenue to take State Bank paper at no more than its actual value—an action that evoked a roar of protest.

Since Shields was a Democrat, the Whigs lost no time in capitalizing on the popular discontent, and a series of letters from the "Lost Townships," expounding Whig doctrine in rural idiom, appeared in the *Sangamo Journal*. The third of these letters, dated August 27, 1842, dealt with Shields and his proclamation. Purporting to be written by a widow named Rebecca, it told the editor about a friend of hers, a Democratic farmer, who, when informed of Shields's abhorrent conduct, insisted that the auditor must be a Whig and not a Democrat, since no Democrat would be so faithless with the people.

"I seed him when I was down in Springfield last winter," the pseudonymous farmer maintained. "They had a sort of a gathering there one night, among the grandees, they called a fair. All the gals about town was there, and all the handsome widows, and

married women, finickin about, trying to look like gals, tied as
tight in the middle, and puffed out at both ends like bundles of
fodder that hadn't been stacked yet, but wanted stackin pretty
bad. . . . I looked in at the window, and there was this same
fellow Shields. . . . He was paying his money to this one and
that one, and tother one, and sufferin great loss because it wasn't
silver instead of State paper; and the sweet distress he seemed to
be in,—his very features, in the exstatic agony of his soul, spoke
audibly and distinctly 'Dear girls, *it is distressing*, but I cannot
marry you all. Too well I know how much you suffer; but do, *do*
remember, it is not my fault that I am *so* handsome and *so*
interesting.' . . . He a democrat! Fiddle-sticks! I tell you, aunt
Becca, he's a whig, and no mistake: nobody but a whig could
make such a conceity dunce of himself."

A promising attorney and politician, Shields was Lincoln's
junior by two years. A native of Ireland, quick-tempered in the
manner of the men of Eire, he became infuriated by the slurs and
aspersions in the anonymous letter. Demanding the name of his
detractor from the editor of the *Journal*, he learned that it was
Lincoln. Before he could take action, however, he was called out
of town on business. During his absence another letter from Aunt
Becca offered him her hand in marriage to solace his anger. "I
know he's a fightin man," Aunt Becca said, "and would rather
fight than eat; but isn't marrying better than fightin, though it
does sometimes run into it?" If Shields insisted on fighting,
however, Aunt Becca demanded fair play, which could be
assured either by her donning breeches or by Shields wearing
petticoats. "I presume that change is sufficient to place us on an
equality," she concluded.

Although dueling was contrary to law in Illinois, Shields,
on his return to Springfield, sought Lincoln in order to challenge
him, only to find that he had left for court at Tremont. Selecting
John D. Whiteside as his second, Shields started in pursuit; but
Elias H. Merryman and William Butler, friends of Lincoln,
learning of Shields's intentions, also started for Tremont and
by riding all night reached Lincoln in time to warn him. Lin-

coln, though opposed to dueling, had got himself into a plight. He would avoid a meeting if he could do so without dishonor, he decided; otherwise he would fight.

The next morning Shields and Whiteside galloped into town, and Whiteside immediately presented Lincoln with Shields's demand for a confession of his authorship of the offensive letters and a complete retraction on pain of "consequences which no one will regret more than myself." Lincoln replied that Shields's note contained "so much assumption of facts, and so much of menace as to consequences," that he would submit no further answer.

Arriving in Springfield, Lincoln found the town in such a high state of excitement that he slipped away to avoid arrest, instructing his friend Merryman that if Shields would submit another note devoid of "menace or dictation," he would admit the authorship of the letter of August 27 and assure Shields that what he had written was intended to be wholly political in effect and without design to harm Shields's character. If this did not prove satisfactory, Lincoln would accept Shields's challenge, and his choice of weapons would be cavalry broadswords of the largest size. These were to be wielded across a plank set edgewise in the ground, each man to be allowed to retreat no farther than a line drawn some eight feet behind the plank on either side and parallel to it.

These conditions contained a touch of the ridiculous, for Shields would scarcely be able to reach his long-armed adversary. Lincoln never showed physical cowardice throughout his life, and his terms may have been intended to bring home to his opponent the absurdity of the whole affair.

From this point on, however, the seconds took over and managed further negotiations with such meticulous conformity to the code of honor that a meeting seemed unavoidable. Both principals, accompanied by a retinue of seconds, hastened to the rendezvous across the Mississippi from Alton, but there all differences were reconciled and everyone returned to Springfield. Such rancor had been generated, however, that as an aftermath

Shields challenged Butler, who chose rifles at one hundred yards, the affray to take place in a near-by meadow at dawn. Whiteside, acting for Shields, refused because of the certainty of arrest. Then Whiteside requested Merryman to meet him in St. Louis so that he could challenge him at a place where they would have no trouble with the law. Prolonged disputes over punctilio finally ended the matter.

But it remained a source of embarrassment to Lincoln throughout his life. He would never talk about it, even with close friends, and the mere mention of it caused him the keenest vexation. It taught him a needed lesson, however, for never again did he write anonymous letters. Lincoln exhibited a contradiction in character when, with his deep human sympathy, he failed to appreciate the pain and humiliation his scathing satire inflicted on its victims. This remissness was another of those crudities originating in his rough-and-tumble background and the tough school in which he learned his politics. But the near-duel with Shields made him reflect; and thereafter, if he did not reject satire and ridicule altogether as political weapons, he became more circumspect in using them and ceased giving them too personal an application.

That it was Lincoln's true nature to compose rather than to foment quarrels had been demonstrated three years before the Shields affair. For when William Butler and Edward D. Baker, another of his closest acquaintances, became involved in a political dispute that threatened to disrupt their friendship, Lincoln had written to Butler: "There is no necessity for any bad feeling between Baker & yourself. Your first letter to him was written while you were in a state of high excitement, and therefore ought not to have been construed as an emanation of deliberate malice. Unfortunately however it reached Baker while he was writhing under a severe toothache, and therefore he was incapable of exercising that patience and reflection which the case required. The note he sent you was written while in that state of feeling, and for that reason I think you ought not to pay any serious regard to it. It is always magnanamous [sic] to recant whatever

we may have said in passion, and when you and Baker shall have
done this, I am sure there will be no difficulty left between you.
I write this without Baker's knowledge; and I do it because
nothing would be more painful to me than to see a difficulty
between two of my most particular friends."

*

NEITHER Lincoln nor the *Journal* editor ever revealed the
fact that Lincoln did not write the second of the two letters from
the "Lost Townships" which so offended Shields. That letter was
the handiwork of two young ladies of the social set, Mary Todd
and Julia Jayne, with the first of whom Lincoln was having a
somewhat tumultuous romance.

The daughter of Robert S. Todd and Eliza Parker Todd, of
Lexington, Kentucky, Mary had come to Springfield in 1837 to
visit her sister, Mrs. Ninian W. Edwards. Two years later, at the
age of twenty-one, she returned to make her home with the
Edwardses, probably because she could not get along with her
stepmother. Brought up in the cultured atmosphere of Lexington,
she had been educated at a private academy and the exclusive
school of Madame Mentelle, where she learned French, music,
dancing, drama, and all the other genteel social graces.

Her great-grandfather was a Revolutionary general; a great-
uncle served as an officer under George Rogers Clark in the
conquest of Illinois; and her grandfather, Levi Todd, who lived
in a commodious mansion called Ellerslie near the home of Henry
Clay, had helped wrest Kentucky from the Indians as a major
general of militia. Her father was a businessman and politician
of broad interests and high social standing. No one knew yet
that of the six children of Robert Todd and Eliza Parker who
reached maturity, four would have "abnormal personalities."

A rather short young lady with clear blue eyes shaded by
long lashes, Mary had a rosy-tinted skin and light-brown hair
that glinted with a touch of bronze. A tendency to plumpness
made her face too full, but also gave her a beautiful neck and
arms. "A very creature of excitement," high-strung, impulsive,

vivacious, she was witty and warmhearted and could be unusually charming when she chose. But she was willful and demanding, too, and a hair-trigger temper sometimes caused her to lash out in cutting sarcasm.

Making her home with the Edwardses, Mary soon spun blithely in the Springfield social whirl. With men like Douglas, Shields, and other young gallants of the capital about, it was strange that she should be attracted to Lincoln, who was described by a man who became acquainted with him about this time as "very tall, awkward, homely, and badly dressed. . . . Although he then had considerable ambition to rise in the world, he had, or seemed to have, done very little to improve his manners, or appearance, or conversation. He generally wore an old rusty hat; his pantaloons were often too short and his coat and vest too loose. His features were rugged, his hair coarse and rebellious, and he was, when in repose, by nature and habit a man of sad countenance."

In spite of their incongruities, some time in 1840 Lincoln and Mary Todd became engaged. What followed has never been made completely clear. Lincoln's affair with Mary Owens showed that he was unsure of himself with women. He disliked loose ends in his thinking and found romantic notions hard to systematize. And he was reluctant to commit himself to marriage until sure he was in love. William H. Herndon, trying to unravel the mystery of what happened between Lincoln and Mary, concluded that they planned to be married on January 1, 1841, and that Lincoln, in desperate indecision, failed to appear. But Herndon's explanation does not fit the facts. More likely, they broke their engagement.

Lincoln had a moody temperament. At times his melancholy became so acute as to be an actual mental ailment known as hypochondria, which is described in the medical literature of that day as a remarkable lowness of spirits or a desponding habit of mind brought on gradually and imperceptibly by too intent or long-continued application, or by anxieties or disappointments. The symptoms and their causes fit Lincoln's case exactly, for he had been working hard and long, and he was worried about his true feelings respecting Miss Todd. Wretchedly despondent and uncertain of himself, he explained his condition to her, and she, realizing that his perplexity and dejection were beyond his control, released him from his engagement, but at the same time hoped he would renew the courtship when he had recovered.

This is the only explanation consistent with the documentary evidence and with Mary's personality. Had Lincoln failed to appear for a wedding, the proud and high-spirited Mary would never have forgiven him; and if he had broken their engagement merely by expressing the same sort of doubts about which he had written Mary Owens, she would have put him out of her thoughts.

Friends of the couple thought Lincoln had been jilted and was taking it awfully hard. Contemporary letters describe him as a rejected suitor. "Poor L!" wrote James C. Conkling to Mary's friend Mercy Levering, "how are the mighty fallen! He was confined about a week, but though he now appears again he is reduced and emaciated in appearance and seems scarcely to possess strength enough to speak above a whisper"; and in a later letter Conkling referred to Lincoln as a "poor, hapless, simple swain who loved most true but was not loved again."

Fearful of having ruined Mary's happiness, Lincoln became even more confused and morbid. For a week or more he did not attend the Legislature. One of his acquaintances wrote to a friend: "We have been very much distressed on Mr. Lincoln's account; hearing that he had two Cat fits and a Duck fit since we left."

On January 20, 1841 Lincoln wrote to John T. Stuart, in Washington, urging him to obtain the Springfield postmastership for Dr. Anson G. Henry. "I have, within the last few days, been making a most discreditable exhibition of myself in the way of hypochondriaism," he explained, "and thereby got an impression that Dr. Henry is necessary to my existence. Unless he gets that place he leaves Springfield. You therefore see how much I am interested in the matter." Three days later he wrote again to tell Stuart: "I am now the most miserable man living. If what I feel were equally distributed to the whole human family, there would not be one cheerful face on the earth. Whether I shall ever be better I can not tell; I awfully forebode I shall not. To remain as I am is impossible; I must die or be better, it appears to me."

Gradually Lincoln came out of it, but he avoided Mary. Edwin B. Webb, a middle-aged widower with two children, who had been cutting quite a figure in local society, had been squiring her about, and rumor had them "*dearer* to each other than friends." Mary wrote to Mercy Levering that such unfounded gossip came "merely through the folly & belief of another, who strangely imagined we were attached to each other." She regretted Webb's constant attentions and was trying to discourage him. Lincoln, she confided, "deems me unworthy of notice, as I have not met *him* in the gay world for months. With the usual comfort of misery, [I] imagine that others were as seldom gladdened by his presence as my humble self, yet I would that the case were different, that he would once more resume his station in Society, that 'Richard should be himself again,' much, much happiness would it afford me."

Early in 1841 Joshua F. Speed, who befriended Lincoln when he moved to Springfield, and became his closest friend, sold his store and moved to Kentucky. In August, Lincoln visited him and rested in the big Speed home near Louisville, where he met Fanny Henning, Speed's fiancée. Speed was racked by the same doubts that haunted Lincoln, and on his return to Springfield Lincoln wrote him several letters in which he tried to explain away Speed's apprehensions and to assure him that only true love could bring such misery. "I tell you, Speed, our *forebodings*, for which you and I are rather peculiar, are all the worst sort of nonsense," he wrote. In bringing comfort to Speed, Lincoln began to resolve his own misgivings.

Convinced by Lincoln's arguments, Speed married, and wrote Lincoln that he was happy—what Lincoln had said was true. "The short space it took me to read your last letter, gave me more pleasure than the total sum of all I have enjoyed since that fatal first of Jan'y. '41," Lincoln replied. "Since then, it seems to me, I should have been entirely happy, but for the never-absent idea, that there is *one* still unhappy whom I have contributed to make so. That still kills my soul. I can not but reproach myself, for even wishing to be happy while she is otherwise."

Speed now took over the role of counselor. Lincoln must either make up his mind to marry Mary or put her forever out of his thoughts, he warned. Lincoln replied that he realized this was so. "But before I resolve to do the one thing or the other, I must regain my confidence in my own ability to keep my resolves when they are made. . . . Until I do, I can not trust myself in any matter of much importance."

Somehow Lincoln and Mary were brought together unexpectedly by Mrs. Simeon Francis, wife of the *Journal* editor. Both were agreeably surprised. Other meetings followed in the Francis home. Only Mary's friend Julia Jayne knew of their rendezvous, and perhaps in the Francis parlor the two girls showed Lincoln the Aunt Becca screed they had written to tantalize Shields. Lincoln and Mary shared a common adventure when he took the responsibility for writing the piece, even at the risk of a duel with Shields. This appealed to Mary's strong sense of chivalry and melodrama; the two drew closer together. Lincoln asked Speed for one final reassurance. "Are you now, in *feeling* as well as *judgment*, glad you are married as you are? From any body but me, this would be an impudent question not to be tolerated; but I know you will pardon it in me. Please answer it quickly, as I feel impatient to know."

Speed's answer put Lincoln's mind at rest. What he felt must really be love. On November 4, 1842 he and Mary Todd stood up together in the Edwards parlor and spoke the marriage vows before a small group of friends. Five days later Lincoln concluded a letter to a Shawneetown lawyer: "Nothing new here, except my marrying, which to me, is matter of profound wonder."

*

T H E   Y E A R S   of marriage that followed offer contrasts as striking as those between the bride and groom, who were opposites in almost every way. She was short and inclined to corpulence, he was tall and lean. He was slow-moving, easygoing, she precipitate and volatile. He had the humblest of backgrounds, hers was aristocratic. He was a man of simple tastes, she liked fine clothes and jewelry. His personality and mind were the sort that grow continuously, hers remained essentially in a set mold. Both had ambitions, but her determination was so much more intense than his that it would be like a relentless prod, impelling him onward whenever he might be disposed to lag.

She willingly made sacrifices. Their first home was the Globe Tavern, a modest place, where they lived simply. Here their first child, Robert Todd Lincoln, was born on August 1, 1843. About five months later they paid fifteen hundred dollars for a plain frame residence of a story and a half, a few blocks southeast of the business district, where they lived until they went to Washington. Lincoln curried his own horse, milked his own cow, cut and carried in the firewood. Three more babies came: Edward Baker, William Wallace, and Thomas, whom they called Tad. Eddie died when he was four; Tad had a cleft palate and lisped, handicaps that endeared him all the more to his father.

Lincoln was not an easy man to live with. His careless ways and dowdy dress, and his interludes of abstraction and dejection, must have annoyed his wife. But Mary learned to overlook his shortcomings. Their letters, written when they were apart, reveal sincere affection. They went to parties together and they entertained. Together they met defeats and rejoiced in victories.

Lincoln was indulgent as a father and left the upbringing of the children largely to "Mother," who was forbearing and overstrict by turns. Her whole nature took on a sort of instability as time went on. Devoted, even possessive toward her husband, she was eager to make him happy. But small matters upset her and brought on fits of temper. Servants found her difficult to please; she quarreled with tradesmen and neighbors. She suffered violent headaches, known now to have been warnings of mental illness, and these sometimes made her utterly unreasonable. Lincoln bore it all as best he could, taking her tongue-lashings, yielding to her whims whenever possible, offering excuses to the neighbors, trying to make allowances for the affectionate wife and mother he knew she was at heart. When her upbraidings became unbearable he would not talk back or censure her, but simply slip off quietly to his office.

Gossips have overstressed these unpleasant aspects of their life together; they were not always present by any means. For the most part Lincoln and Mary were happy with each other. Yet there was the other side, nor can it be ignored. It was unquestionably a factor in shaping Lincoln's character. For over the slow fires of misery that he learned to keep banked and under heavy pressure deep within him, his innate qualities of patience, tolerance, forbearance, and forgiveness were tempered and refined.

CHAPTER V

Lawyer — Politician

AT T H E time of Lincoln's marriage his earnings amounted to twelve or fifteen hundred dollars a year, a gratifying income compared with the Governor's salary of $1,200 and the $750 received by circuit judges. But it required hard work, for fees were small, usually ranging from $2.50 to $50 and averaging about $5 a case, and they were often paid in groceries, vegetables, produce, poultry, or clothes.

Cases were usually simple, however, and required little preparation, since they dealt mostly with such commonplace matters as damage to growing crops from marauding livestock, the ownership of hogs, horses, cows, and sheep, small debts, libel, slander, or assault and battery, with an occasional action for divorce or a murder trial to enliven the stuffy courtroom atmosphere. Jurisprudence was still in infancy, so that no intricate accumulation of precedent need be mastered, and issues were usually decided according to fundamental precepts of right and wrong. Since lawyers tried even the pettiest cases before a jury, a winning personality, common sense, ready wit, the ability to reason clearly and succinctly, and a reputation for honesty were a lawyer's most effective weapons.

With the Springfield courts in session only a few weeks out of the year, most lawyers were obliged to follow the circuit in order to make a living. Stuart had built up an extensive circuit practice, and when he went to Washington in 1839, Lincoln took over, setting out from Springfield every spring and fall to supplement the income of the partnership.

The Eighth Circuit, to which Sangamon County was assigned about that time and in which it remained for almost twenty years, was an imperial domain of some 12,000 square miles, 120 miles long and 160 miles wide at its extreme limits, extending from Springfield to the eastern border of the state and embracing most of the Sangamon River valley and the territory between that river and the Illinois.

A large part of this area remained so sparsely settled that a man might ride or drive for hours or even a day without encountering a human habitation. The county seats were mere hamlets, some of them little more than crossroads settlements. The rate of travel depended on the roads. Under favorable conditions six or seven miles an hour was good time; when roads were muddy, a horse could average only three or four. Thirty-five miles made a long day's ride. Traveling the long, slow miles on horseback with a volume of the *Revised Statutes* and well-worn copies of Blackstone and Chitty in his saddlebags, along with an extra shirt and a change of underwear, Lincoln had ample time for contemplation.

Frequently he must rise before dawn and ride all day in order to reach the next court on time. The blustery winds that swept the open prairie in early spring and late autumn, sometimes bringing sleet or snow flurries, caused the young lawyer to hunch his shoulders, lower his head, and pull his heavy shawl closer about him as his horse plodded on against the blast. Sticking his long legs out of the covers in a farmhouse bedroom where he had put up for the night, and clambering out of bed in his short, homemade, yellow flannel nightshirt, he might find the water pitcher filled with ice. Heavy showers overtook him on the prairie far from shelter; he might ride all day in drizzling rain. When floods swept away the bridges, he had to swim his horse across the swollen streams.

Judge and lawyers visited each county in rotation. Court terms lasted from three days to a week. Arriving in the little county towns, the lawyers were sought out by litigants, or by local attorneys wishing to employ additional counsel. Court week provided a gala time for the inhabitants of the sleepy settlements and the farmers of the back country; the latter flocked to town by scores to purchase supplies, renew acquaintances, and enjoy the court proceedings. Judge and lawyers became celebrities. "The leading advocates had their partizans," an old lawyer recalled, "and the merits of each were canvassed in every cabin, schoolhouse, and at every horse-race, bee and raising." During political campaigns, in the late afternoon when court had adjourned, or at "early candle-light," the lawyers entertained and edified the citizenry with speeches or debates. A popular lawyer like Lincoln, bent on a political career, could acquire a formidable following among acquaintances and admirers on the circuit.

Notwithstanding the long absences from home, the difficulties of travel, and the poor accommodations, most of the lawyers enjoyed this nomadic way of life, with the excitement of court week, the adulation of the simple people, the easy camaraderie at night when work was finished, the jokes, the pranks, the steadfast friendships they formed. To Lincoln, with his variable cravings for companionship and solitude, it was like an elixir.

It was an educational process, too. No profession offers such insights into human nature as does the law, while in the give-and-take of discussion in these rural forums Lincoln observed the development of political issues and the formation of public opinion on men and measures. Here was a training-ground on which he further developed his political astuteness, learning the thought-processes of the people and how they might be guided, when to speak and when to maintain silence, what to say and how to say it.

But Lincoln was not advancing much in his profession. At

this time both he and Stuart regarded the law primarily as a springboard to political preferment, and neither of them was studiously inclined. Stuart was either in Washington or away campaigning much of the time; in the office he paid little attention to Lincoln. Each man was more or less slipshod; and in the courtroom each relied more on native ability than on careful preparation. This did not handicap them seriously in circuit work, but they now found their most lucrative employment in the State Supreme Court and the United States circuit and district courts, all of which met in Springfield. Many capable lawyers practiced in these courts, and as the state developed and litigation became more complex, sound legal learning was needed in order to cope with them. Even circuit work became more demanding as time went on.

Perhaps Lincoln realized that he was not learning much from Stuart; perhaps each man recognized that to continue in politics he should be associated with someone who would devote more time to law practice. In the spring of 1841 they reached an amicable parting of the ways, and Lincoln formed a new partnership with Stephen T. Logan.

*

THE ASSOCIATION with Logan became one of the most constructive influences in Lincoln's life, for Logan would not tolerate haphazard methods. Methodical, industrious, painstaking, and precise, he had not only grounded himself in precedents and method, but was a student of the philosophy of the law as well. Ten years older than Lincoln, a Kentuckian of Scotch-Irish ancestry, he was small, thin, and wiry, with thick, frizzy red hair. Utterly careless in his dress, he wore an unbleached cotton shirt, an oversized, rumpled coat, and baggy pants. He was never known to don a tie. In winter he made his way to court or office in a shabby fur cap; his summer headgear was a fifty-cent straw hat. Handicapped by a thin, shrill voice, he was no orator, but he argued with convincing power. He had come to Springfield in 1833 with a reputation already established through ten years of practice in his native state, and from 1835 to 1837 had served as judge of the First Circuit. Now he stood as undisputed head of the Sangamon bar.

The Logan-Lincoln partnership developed into one of the leading firms of the state as Lincoln became more studious and painstaking under Logan's tutelage. While Lincoln was not a student by nature, he would work unremittingly to attain a particular end, and as Logan showed him the value of exactitude and thorough preparation as opposed to mere cleverness and high-flown rhetoric, the young man became recognized as a resourceful and powerful opponent in any type of case. Reinforcing his natural talents with a readiness to meet any argument the opposition might propound, and learning to write and speak briefly, clearly, and directly to the point, Lincoln advanced steadily in his profession.

Logan served in the State Legislature from 1842 to 1848, and rumor had it that his political ambitions and those of his partner clashed. Moreover, Lincoln may have been dissatisfied with one third of the income of the firm after sharing equally with Stuart, especially since such a division made him a subordinate. Logan was often demanding and irritable, too, so when he expressed a wish to take his son as a partner, Lincoln willingly agreed to dissolve the firm. In December 1844 Lincoln opened his own office and took as partner William H. Herndon, a young man just licensed to practice. This last partnership terminated only with Lincoln's death.

*

LINCOLN's junior by nine years, Herndon was a son of Archer G. Herndon, with whom Lincoln had served in the Legislature. Educated in elementary schools in Springfield, young Herndon had entered the preparatory department of Illinois College at Jacksonville, where his lively antics often brought him trouble. His father believed firmly in slavery, and when he suspected Billy of absorbing the "rank poison" of abolitionism from his New England teachers, he became mightily displeased. For this reason, or because William could not maintain the academic pace, the youth returned home, obtained a job at Speed's store, and roomed upstairs with Lincoln and Speed. At night he joined the gatherings around the potbellied stove to listen to the political discussions and laugh at Lincoln's yarns. Married in 1840, he aspired to more remunerative employment and began to study law in his spare time. Later, at Lincoln's suggestion, he became a student in the Logan-Lincoln office.

Springfield people were surprised when Lincoln chose Herndon for a partner—any number of experienced lawyers would have welcomed such an alliance. But Lincoln regarded Herndon as a promising young man. Perhaps he would bring order to the untidy office, and surely he would be a political asset by reason of his influence with the "shrewd, wild boys about town." Moreover, Lincoln could train him according to his own methods and would no longer be dominated by an older man.

For a while the firm kept books, but Herndon turned out to be no more systematic than Lincoln, so they discontinued the practice and divided their fees equally as they were paid. The office windows were never washed; papers piled up on desk tops and worktables and overflowed the pigeonholes of the battered secretary that adorned one of the walls. Lincoln stuck letters and papers in his stovepipe hat—once when he bought a new one the contents of the discarded headpiece were lost—and Herndon often took notes and letters home and then forgot them; the partners sometimes searched frantically for correspondence. An envelope bore the injunction in Lincoln's hand: "When you can't find *it* any where else, look into this."

Herndon was something of a dandy in his younger years, affecting a tall silk hat, kid gloves, and patent-leather shoes. Five feet nine inches in height, thin, angular, erect, he moved and walked quickly with a superabundance of nervous energy. Dark-skinned, with raven hair, he had sharp black eyes set deep in crater-like circles. His nature was contradictory; a good lawyer, he never acquired any fondness for the law; a temperance advocate, he frequently got drunk. Although he was an earnest student of philosophy, he never learned to systematize his thoughts. His literary style was verbose and often pompous. Time and again Lincoln would counsel: "Billy, don't shoot too high. Aim lower and the common people will understand you." An amateur psychologist, Herndon prided himself on a "mud instinct" or "dog sagacity," which he credited with enabling him to fathom men's secret thoughts and purposes.

Lincoln and Herndon were the antithesis of each other in many respects. Whereas Lincoln was deliberate, easygoing, cautious, and conservative, Herndon was quick-tempered, rash, and unpredictable. Although devoid of social aspirations and lacking in social graces, Lincoln moved in Springfield's most respectable circles, while Herndon, by reason of his misadventures, never made the social grade.

But the two men worked well in double harness. While Lincoln traveled the circuit, Herndon stayed at home and did the office work, and when the Eighth Circuit underwent reorganization from time to time, the junior partner tended to business in those counties cut off from the circuit where Lincoln had built up a clientele. Each man tried cases in the Illinois Supreme Court, though Lincoln handled the cases in the Federal courts. Herndon sometimes checked authorities for Lincoln and gathered material for his briefs, but for the most part each man not only pleaded his own cases but also did his own preparation and underwent the necessary drudgery of paper work. In some respects it was as though two lawyers worked in the same office independently of one another.

Their courtroom tactics differed. Herndon was high-strung, determined, humorless. He battled for every point. Playing to the jury, he might be purposely careless in his dress, dramatic, sometimes so heated that he would break out with an oath or fling his coat on the floor. He used every technicality to win. He played on the jury's emotions. "When you get tears on the jury, you win your case," he told his nephew.

Lincoln could use pathos and emotion quite as well as Herndon, but more often he appealed to reason. His manner was casual, almost negligent at times, as he questioned witnesses in friendly tones, threw in a witticism now and then, and good-naturedly conceded point after point until he seemed to be giving away his case. But on the crucial point he was relentless, trying to put it clearly before the jury, bringing the argument around to it again and again until the dullest mind on the jury understood it. For lucidity of statement and ability to clarify by means of homely analogies he had no equal. He was almost unbeatable when simple right and justice were involved.

Herndon had a wide-questing intellectuality, whereas Lincoln's interests were somewhat circumscribed. The junior partner read a great deal and tried to interest Lincoln in good books, but usually, after glancing through a page or two, Lincoln tossed them aside and asked Herndon to brief him on their contents. Philosophy and metaphysics, which Herndon thought so fascinating, Lincoln found too abstruse. Nor did he share Herndon's love of nature, though he had grown up in the woods. In one respect, however, he read more than his partner, for he conned every newspaper that came to the office from the first page to the last, spilling himself out on the old frayed sofa and perusing the contents aloud, a practice, he explained, that enabled him to bring two senses to bear at once, but which irritated Herndon almost beyond endurance.

But while Herndon read, Lincoln thought, slowly, method-ically, deeply, as he tried to find the "nub" of a question and strip it of irrelevancies. Herndon believed his partner thought more than any man in America, for he was little influenced by others and must work out his own conclusions. He was "pitiless and persistent in pursuit of truth," separating it from dross and sham. He took nothing on faith; to believe, he must be able to try, test, demonstrate, and prove, as Herndon saw him.

Herndon sometimes wearied of Lincoln's stories, some of which he had heard again and again; but most annoying to him were the Lincoln "brats," whom the father brought to the office on Sunday mornings and immediately forgot as he became

absorbed in work, whereupon they "soon gutted the room—
gutted the shelves of books—rifled the drawers and riddled
boxes—battered the points . . . of gold pens against the stove—
turned over the ink stands on the papers—scattered letters over
the office and danced over them," until Herndon yearned to
wring their necks, while Lincoln worked on, unconcerned.

The Herndons and the Lincolns never met socially, for
Herndon and Mrs. Lincoln loathed each other. Herndon attributed her dislike to his use of an ill-chosen word; when he first
met her at a ball he became so fascinated by her pliant grace
that he likened her to a serpent. Mrs. Lincoln took his intended
compliment as an insult and never forgave him.

All in all, however, Lincoln and Herndon got along unusually
well. As the years passed, their relationship became more than
a mere business arrangement and took on something of the
nature of that between father and son. With Lincoln, it was
"Billy"; with Herndon, it was always "Mr. Lincoln." And if, in
time, Lincoln grew somewhat beyond his junior partner's comprehension, no diminution of trust, faithfulness, and affection showed
on either side.

*

T H E Y E A R before the formation of the Lincoln-Herndon partnership Lincoln had suffered a disappointment. After four terms
in the Legislature, during two of which he was the Whig candidate for speaker and served as his party's floorleader, he believed
himself entitled to advancement and had aspired to run for
Congress, since Stuart had announced that he would not seek
re-election. Early in 1843 Lincoln began to write confidentially to
Whig friends throughout the Congressional district somewhat as
he did to Richard S. Thomas, of Cass County, to whom he wrote:
"Now if you should hear any one say that Lincoln don't want to
go to Congress, I wish you as a personal friend of mine, would
tell him you have reason to believe he is mistaken. The truth is,
I would like to go very much. Still, circumstances may happen
which may prevent my being a candidate."

The greatest concentration of Whig strength in Illinois was in Lincoln's own Seventh Congressional District, which comprised eleven counties: Sangamon, Scott, Morgan, Cass, Menard, Logan, Mason, Tazewell, Woodford, Marshall, and Putnam. While some of these counties normally voted Democratic, the district as a whole was so predominantly Whig that the Whig nomination practically assured election. This very fact, however, brought strong Whig leaders to the fore, and two of them, John J. Hardin of Jacksonville, in Morgan County, and Edward D. Baker of Springfield, having come up in party affairs as rapidly as Lincoln, rivaled him for preferment.

All three men were young: Lincoln thirty-four, Hardin thirty-three, and Baker thirty-two. All were able lawyers and veterans of the Black Hawk War. Each had served in the Legislature, and Baker was then a state senator. All were capable speakers and good campaigners; Hardin, though handicapped by a slight speech impediment, spoke as logically and convincingly as Lincoln, and Baker was unexcelled as an orator of the flag-waving, spread-eagle type. In fact, an eagle, used as a stage property at a Whig rally, had done not a little to bring Baker his reputation. Chained to a ring in the platform as Baker spoke, it had moped in dejection as he compared it to the American Republic, tied and manacled under Democratic misrule. Then, as Baker reached his peroration and told how, with Whig victory, the Republic would cast off its chains and soar free into the blue of heaven, the drooping eagle, according to a Whig account, "reared its head, expanded its eyes, and gave a loud cry."

Like Lincoln, Hardin and Baker craved political distinction—the latter so much so, according to one story, that he wept when he learned that his foreign birth made him ineligible for the Presidency. Born in London, Baker had lived in Philadelphia, New Harmony, Indiana, and Belleville, Illinois, before moving to Springfield in 1835. Like Lincoln, he was self-educated. Although the two men were political rivals, they became such close friends that Lincoln named his second child for Baker. The same close feeling did not exist between Lincoln and Hardin, for, while they respected and perhaps liked each other, their rivalry engendered some asperity.

Of the three, Hardin was best qualified by background and formal training. Born in Kentucky, the son of a United States Senator, he was graduated from Transylvania University and had studied law under Chief Justice John Boyle of the Kentucky Supreme Court. Coming to Illinois about the same time as Lincoln, he built up a lucrative practice.

As the Congressional campaign got under way in early March 1843, Lincoln, as a result of a Whig conclave in Springfield, wrote an "Address to the People of Illinois," in which he explained Whig principles and sought to overcome two party weaknesses: first, the failure to run candidates throughout the state, no matter what their chances of election; and second, dislike of party conventions. On the latter point, he said, the party must either bow to necessity or see "the spoils chucklingly borne off by the common enemy." Party unity was the first essential to victory, he urged, for "a house divided against itself cannot stand"—employing a metaphor that would become a political catchword when he used it again fifteen years later.

As the Whigs fell into line and began to elect delegates to a district convention, Lincoln's first objective in promoting his own candidacy was to have the Sangamon delegation pledged to him. But this plum went to Baker; and to make Lincoln's portion more bitter, he was selected as a delegate to the district convention, notwithstanding his efforts to decline. In thus being pledged to support Baker, he wrote to his friend Speed: "I shall be 'fixed' a good deal like a fellow who is made groomsman to the man what has cut him out, and is marrying his own dear 'gal.'"

Lincoln's defeat galled him all the more because of the way it came about. Writing to a friend in Petersburg, the county seat of Menard County, which had been formed from the northern part of Sangamon and embraced the New Salem area, Lincoln explained: "It would astonish if not amuse, the older citizens of your County who twelve years ago knew me a strange, friendless, uneducated, penniless boy, working on a flat boat at ten dollars per month to learn that I have been put down here as the candidate of pride, wealth, and arristocratic [*sic*] family distinction. Yet so chiefly it was." A strange combination of religious influences also opposed him, and "it was every where contended that no ch[r]istian ought to go for me, because I belonged to no church, was suspected of being a deist, and had talked about fighting a duel." He might have added that he had also offended several people when, speaking before the Washington Society, an organization of reformed drunkards, he had extolled the victims of strong drink for being as kind and generous at heart as any class in the community, and had chided their more fortunate neighbors for want of sympathy and helpfulness.

Having argued for the convention system and party regularity, Lincoln had no choice but to abide by his instructions and vote for Baker at the district meeting. But he clung to one last hope: his name might be put forward by some other county, perhaps Menard. When Martin S. Morris, a Menard delegate, wrote to Lincoln that this county favored him, Lincoln expressed gratification "that while the people of Sangamon have cast me off, my old friends of Menard who have known me longest and best, of any still retain there [*sic*] confidence in me."

"You say you shall instruct your delegates to go for me unless I object," Lincoln continued. "I certainly shall not object. . . . And besides if any thing should hap[p]en (which however is not probable) by which Baker should be thrown out of the fight, I would be at liberty to accept the nomination if I could get it." Desperately anxious for the nomination, Lincoln saw no reason why his friends should not put him forward if they chose to do so. Yet, in order to play absolutely fair with Baker, he felt that he must not hinder him in any way. "I should dispise [*sic*] myself were I to attempt it," he wrote to Morris. But conventions sometimes take unexpected turns, and Lincoln was disinclined to lower his lightning-rod so long as there remained a chance of its attracting a charge.

When the district convention met, at Pekin, in Tazewell County, on May 1, Hardin had the necessary votes, however, and

in order to swing a solid party vote behind Hardin's candidacy
Lincoln moved to make his nomination unanimous. With the
adoption of this motion, Lincoln offered a resolution naming
Baker as the choice of the party two years thence, subject to the
decision of a convention. This was adopted 18 to 14.

While Lincoln willingly subordinated his own ambitions to
party harmony, he had no intention of remaining permanently in
the background. What he had in mind was to establish a principle
of rotation in office, whereby Baker would succeed Hardin after
one term and Lincoln would succeed Baker in 1846. Lincoln
later reminded Hardin of "the proposition made by me to you and
Baker, that we should take a turn a piece," and several delegates
came out of the convention convinced that the three rivals had
agreed on this means of reconciling their ambitions.

The contest left Lincoln and Baker as friendly as ever, but a
suppressed hostility between Lincoln and Hardin intensified as
time went on. Hardin suspected that Sangamon and Menard
counties did not intend to support him wholeheartedly, but Lincoln assured him that every effort would be made to give him even
a larger majority than that in his own county. "In relation to
our congress matter here," Lincoln wrote to his friend Speed,
"you were right in supposing I would support the nominee. Neither Baker or I, however, is the man; but *Hardin*. . . . We shall
have no split or trouble about the matter; all will be harmony."

Yet on election day Lincoln did a strange thing. He went
to the polls and voted—but only for candidates for constable and
justice of the peace. He not only cast no vote either for or
against Hardin, but also refrained from voting either for or
against any of the Whig candidates for county offices. Voters
still balloted by word of mouth, so Lincoln's action was no secret,
but the reason for it remains a mystery. Was he showing his
displeasure at Hardin, or at the county organization that had
thrown him over, or both? Hardin did not need Lincoln's vote,
however, for he won easily. Sangamon County gave him a
majority of 504 votes, more than twice the majority he polled in
Morgan.

During the autumn of 1843 Lincoln was mentioned as the Whig candidate for governor, but gave the movement no encouragement. In the summer of 1844, as a presidential elector for Henry Clay, he took to the stump, speaking continually as he traveled the circuit and even neglecting his circuit duties to fill outside appointments. Wholeheartedly enlisted in the cause of his political idol, in mid-October he journeyed into southwestern Indiana to speak at Vincennes, Rockport, and Gentryville, where he visited the scenes of his youth and renewed acquaintances with former neighbors. But he faced another disappointment. Sangamon and several other central Illinois counties went for Clay, but James K. Polk carried Illinois and the nation.

*

M E A N W H I L E Lincoln's aspiration to go to Congress went forward according to plan when Baker, nominated by acclamation, succeeded Hardin. Now Lincoln began efforts in his own behalf, writing letters to influential party workers and cultivating Whig editors throughout the district. When Baker came home from Washington in the summer of 1845, Lincoln questioned him about the next Congressional campaign. Would Baker stand aside and give Lincoln his turn? Having had a taste of office, Baker was not eager to comply. He would do so, he agreed, except that Hardin might run again, defeat Lincoln, and snatch the prize from both of them. So Lincoln had an interview with Hardin, and, to his dismay, found the Morgan County leader not at all disposed to stand aside. Lincoln renewed his letter-writing, urging potential supporters that "Turn about is fair play," and insisting that since he had deferred to both Hardin and Baker, it would be palpably unjust to refuse him his opportunity now. As he made the rounds of the circuit, he overlooked no chance to promote his candidacy.

Before Baker returned to Congress in November, he assured Lincoln that he would not seek re-election, and promised to announce his decision publicly whenever Lincoln wished. But with Baker off the track, Hardin was definitely on it, rumbling

up fast behind Lincoln. To sidetrack him, the editor of the
Tazewell Whig, a friend of Lincoln's, proposed Hardin for governor, and other editors friendly to Lincoln fell in with the idea.
While Lincoln had no foreknowledge of this movement—though
he surely did not object—Hardin accused him of inspiring it to
get him out of the way. Angrily declining the honor, Hardin
announced that he preferred to re-enter politics as a Congressional
candidate and declared that the Whigs of the district should
decide the contest "in some acceptable manner."

Hardin and other Morgan County Whig leaders had never
favored the convention system, and in this instance, with so
many delegations already pledged to Lincoln, Hardin stood no
chance whatever if a convention picked the candidate. So Hardin
proposed to Lincoln that the convention be called off and that
the nominee be chosen in a district party primary, no candidate
being permitted to electioneer outside his own county or to
allow his friends to do so.

Hardin advanced his idea in the name of party harmony,
but Lincoln saw at once that it would put him at a disadvantage.
Not only would his prospective delegates be released, but Hardin,
having served in Congress, would enjoy greater prestige than
Lincoln among the rank-and-file voters. So Lincoln declined,
stating that he was satisfied with the convention system under
which Hardin and Baker had been nominated and elected and
that he saw no reason to change.

Lincoln was seriously concerned, however, for he saw Hardin
as "a man of desperate energy and perseverance; and one that
never backs out." "If Hardin and I stood precisely equal," he
wrote to Dr. Robert Boal, a friend and party worker in Marshall
County,"—that is, if *neither* of us had been to congress, of if we
both had—it would only accord with what I have always done,
for the sake of peace, to give way to him; and I expect I should
do it. That I *can* voluntarily postpone my pretensions, when they
are no more than equal to those to which they are postponed, you
have yourself seen. But to yield to Hardin under present circumstances seems to me as nothing else than yielding to one who

would gladly sacrifice me altogether." Lincoln determined to "go it thoroughly, and to the bottom."

As Hardin found himself outmaneuvered in every stratagem, he became chagrined and peevish. "It will be *just all we can do*, to keep out of a quarrel," Lincoln wrote to B. F. James, a friendly editor. Hardin's letters became caustic as he charged Lincoln with "management," "maneuvering," and "combination," and expressed mortification that those whom he had accounted his friends were resorting to such means to thwart him. Lincoln, summoning his last reserves of patience, replied that "if there is cause for mortification any where, it is in the readiness with which you believe, and make such charges, against one with whom you truly say you have long acted; and in whose conduct, you have heretofore marked nothing as dishonorable. I believe you do not mean to be unjust, or ungenerous; and I, therefore am slow to believe that you will not yet think *better* and think *differently* of this matter."

On February 16, 1846 Hardin, with what grace he could command, withdrew from the race, leaving Lincoln a free field. In the district convention at Petersburg on May 1, Lincoln was nominated by acclamation.

*

LESS THAN two weeks later, war broke out with Mexico. Hardin, a major general of state militia, immediately volunteered and was commissioned colonel of the First Illinois Volunteers. Baker also hastened to enlist, and delivered an impassioned speech in Congress in full military panoply before resigning his seat to take command of the Fourth Illinois Regiment. Volunteers across the country rushed to join up. Illinois speedily filled its quota of three regiments, and thousands more begged to go. Cannon grumbled on the border as Lincoln squared off against the circuit-riding Methodist parson Peter Cartwright, his Democratic opponent in the Congressional race.

From the beginning, Lincoln had some inner doubts about the justness and necessity of the war, but he voiced no opposition to it. The *Sangamo Journal*, which usually reflected his views, denounced President Polk for pusillanimity toward Mexico and demanded that he assert American rights. At a great mass meeting in Springfield on May 30, Governor Thomas Ford, Lincoln, and other orators urged prompt and united action against the enemy, and some seventy men volunteered.

Illinois farm boys who had marched off so jauntily were stopping lead in Mexico as Lincoln and Cartwright made the rounds of the towns and villages. The prairies flamed with martial spirit. Against the throbbing of the war drums the Congressional campaign proved unexciting. Lincoln took conservative Whig ground, and Cartwright, while persuasive as a revivalist, was a poor campaigner. The Democrats soon gave up. Lincoln polled 6,340 votes to Cartwright's 4,829.

*

D U R I N G the later stages of the contest, Cartwright furtively spread charges of infidelity against Lincoln, and, while Lincoln's friends advised him to disregard these canards during the campaign, soon afterward he set the record straight with a public statement. Printed in the *Illinois Gazette* of Lacon on August 15, 1846, it provides the only public and personal expression of religious convictions ever vouchsafed by Lincoln. "A charge having got into circulation in some of the neighborhoods of this District, in substance that I am an open scoffer at Christianity," he explained, "I have by the advice of some friends concluded to notice the subject in this form. That I am not a member of any Christian Church, is true; but I have never denied the truth of the Scriptures; and I have never spoken with intentional disrespect of religion in general, or of any denomination of Christians in particular. It is true that in early life I was inclined to believe in what I understand is called the 'Doctrine of Necessity'—that is, that the human mind is impelled to action, or held in rest by some power, over which the mind itself has no control; and I have some-times (with one, two or three, but never publicly) tried to main-tain this opinion in argument. The habit of arguing thus however, I have, entirely left off for more than five years. And I add here, I have always understood this same opinion to be held by several of the Christian denominations. The foregoing, is the whole truth, briefly stated, in relation to myself, upon this subject.

"I do not think I could myself, be brought to support a man for office, whom I knew to be an open enemy of, and scoffer at, religion. Leaving the higher matter of eternal consequences, between him and his Maker, I still do not think any man has the right thus to insult ᵗthe feelings, and injure the morals, of the community in which he may live. If, then, I was guilty of such conduct, I should blame no man who should condemn me for it; but I do blame those, whoever they may be, who falsely put such a charge in circulation against me."

*

W I T H H I S mind eased by Hardin's withdrawal from the Congressional contest, Lincoln had given expression to that poetic impulse which always hovered near the surface of his nature. The visit to his old home in Indiana during the campaign of 1844 had moved him deeply, and in an effort to express the nostalgia evoked by memories of old friends and places he wrote three poems, one depicting his emotions at the sight of his boyhood home, another telling of a youth he had known who suddenly went mad, and the third describing a bear hunt. Sending his rhymes to a fellow lawyer, Andrew Johnston, of Quincy, Lincoln explained that the Indiana region where he grew up was "as unpoetical as any spot of the earth," but the recollection of his mother, his sister, and old friends and times had "aroused feelings in me which were certainly poetry; though whether my expression of those feelings is poetry is quite another question." In return, Johnston sent Lincoln a parody of Poe's "Raven," in which an experience with a polecat replaced Poe's conversation with his feathered midnight visitor. Lincoln got several hearty laughs and sought out Poe's original poem, which had been written the previous year.

Lincoln sent Johnston a copy of the poem "Mortality," better known by its first line: "Oh, why should the spirit of

mortal be proud?" written by William Knox, the Scotsman. Its
tone of melancholy resignation appealed strongly to the strain of
doleful fatalism in Lincoln, and it remained one of his favorite
works of literature. When Johnston asked if Lincoln had written
it, he replied: "I would give all I am worth, and go in debt, to be
able to write so fine a piece as I think that is. Neither do I know
who is the author. I met it in a straggling form in a newspaper
last summer, and I remember to have seen it once before, about
fifteen years ago, and this is all I know about it." Lincoln sent
Johnston one effort in prose, an account of the Fisher murder
case in Springfield, in which, after a confession by one of three
brothers named Trailer, who had allegedly committed the crime,
the supposed victim turned up alive.

As Lincoln prepared to step forth on the national stage in
Washington, he was far different from the uncouth young man
who had come to Springfield almost ten years earlier. He had
established himself as a successful lawyer. He had been dis-
ciplined by marriage and family responsibilities and by four years
of association with Stephen T. Logan. He had regained his
mental balance after the fiasco of "the fatal first of January."
Home life and political disappointments had taught him patience
and self-control. He had come to the front in politics against
strong and determined rivals. He had been honest with opponents,
giving others their opportunity and demanding for himself only
what he held to be his due. Not satisfied with such forcefulness
and clarity of expression as might be demanded by politics and
the law, he was yearning and striving for beauty in the cadenced
use of words.

CHAPTER VI

———•◦•———

The Gentleman from Illinois

THE FIRST session of the Thirtieth Congress would not convene until December 1847, almost seventeen months after Lincoln's election, and in the interim he followed his usual routine of court work. He helped to promote two railroads, one from Alton to Springfield and the other from Springfield to Meredosia, on the Illinois River. In July 1847 he made his first visit to the fast-growing city of Chicago, a place of 16,000 inhabitants, to attend a great convention called to protest against President Polk's veto of an appropriation for river and harbor development and to promote internal improvements. The trip by stagecoach took four days; when Lincoln arrived he found persons from all over the United States assembled. Horace Greeley had come to report the proceedings for his *New York Tribune*. Thurlow Weed represented the *Albany Evening Journal*. Daniel Webster, Thomas Hart Benton, Thomas Corwin, Edward Bates, and other national leaders spoke. When David Dudley Field criticized one resolution as too radical, Lincoln made a brief reply that won favorable comment from Greeley. It was Lincoln's first close contact with men of national repute.

Except for three temperance speeches, Lincoln took no part in the manifold social and reform movements that swept the country in the forties. Neither the Liberty Party, the political manifestation of the abolition movement, nor the extreme anti-slavery doctrines of such agitators as William Lloyd Garrison held any appeal for him. The abolitionists, to his way of thinking, were doing more harm than good. Had not the Whig abolitionists of New York State brought about the defeat of Henry Clay and thus made certain the annexation of Texas, another slave state, by voting for James G. Birney, the Liberty Party candidate? For Clay would have carried New York and won the Presidency with their votes. They should have overlooked the fact that Clay was a slaveholder; the evil of voting for a slaveholder would have been offset by the possibility of preventing the extension of slavery. As a matter of fact, however, Lincoln had no strong feelings one way or the other about the annexation of Texas. He could not see how annexation would "augment the evil of slavery," since slavery already existed there. One must be realistic about this slavery issue, Lincoln thought. At the fall term of the Coles County Circuit Court he represented Robert Matson, a slave-owner, in a suit to regain possession of a slave family who had escaped and claimed their freedom because they had been brought to the free state of Illinois. He showed no zeal in such a cause and lost the case, but the slavery issue had not yet seared itself into his conscience to the point of inducing him to place the plight of a few hapless Negroes above the abstract legal aspects of the question. He took slave cases, like other business, as they came; six years before, he had won freedom for a slave girl sold in Illinois.

While Lincoln made the rounds of the circuit and tended to his office work in Springfield, the war in Mexico brought glory to American arms. General Zachary Taylor won a desperate battle at Buena Vista, where death came to John J. Hardin as he withstood a frenzied charge of Mexican horsemen. General Winfield Scott, landing at Vera Cruz, defeated the Mexicans at Cerro Gordo, where James Shields took a bullet through the lungs while charging a battery. Then, in a campaign marked by brilliant generalship, Scott took his army up 7,400 feet from sea level through rugged country and fought his way into Mexico City on September 14, 1847. President Polk tried to make peace on the basis of assumption of American claims against Mexico by the United States in return for the cession of California and New Mexico (including the present Arizona, Utah, and Nevada), but the Mexican government repulsed his overtures.

At the beginning of the war many persons besides Lincoln had doubted its justness and necessity, but few of them cared to risk an accusation of disloyalty by objecting openly. In Congress only two members of the Senate and fourteen in the House had voted against the bill authorizing the President to call volunteers, appropriating ten million dollars for the conduct of the war, and declaring in its preamble that war existed "by the act of the Republic of Mexico." With subsidence of the first surge of enthusiasm, however, opposition to the war became outspoken. Looking to the presidential election of 1848, Whig leaders found it difficult to resist the political opportunities in a situation where they could place the war guilt on the President, find fault with the way the Democratic administration waged the war, and at the same time demonstrate their own patriotism by voting supplies to see it through.

Added to the Whig criticism was that of abolitionists and Liberty Party men, who looked on the war as a conspiracy to extend slavery. Even within the ranks of the Democracy the austere Polk met opposition. He was unpopular, and personal rivalries and sectional animosity rent his party into factions. The strongest support of the administration came from the Democrats of the Northwest and Southwest, where nationalism and the idea of "manifest destiny" were rampant, and where the abandonment of the American claim to 54° 40' and settlement of the Oregon boundary dispute with Great Britain on the basis of the extension of the 49th parallel simply served to whet the appetite for expansion elsewhere. As Mexico rejected offers of peace, demand for more territory to defray the costs of prolonging the war, even to the absorption of all of Mexico, was voiced increasingly.

During the first session of the Twenty-ninth Congress, David Wilmot, a Pennsylvania Democrat, proposed to add to an appropriation bill a proviso prohibiting slavery in all territory

to be acquired from Mexico. The proviso passed the House, but
the session ended before the Senate could take action on it.
Again in the second session opponents of the administration
added the proviso to an appropriation bill, only to see it stricken
out on the last day of the session. But the resulting debates
aroused both North and South to fever pitch, widened the rifts
in the Democratic Party, and threatened to split the Whigs as
well.

By the time Lincoln prepared to leave for Washington, the
fighting had stopped, and the questions at issue were the justness
of the American cause, which the Whigs continued to deny; the
amount of spoils to be demanded; and the vexing issue of slavery
in the territories to be acquired. Hitherto alignments had been
chiefly partisan or factional, but with the slavery issue assuming
increasing prominence, cleavages developed more and more on
sectional lines. In the South, Whigs and Democrats alike resolved
to oppose on principle the Wilmot Proviso or any other measure
denying the South equal rights in the new territories; whereas in
the North, while many Democrats preferred to keep the slavery
issue out of politics, conviction that the spread of slavery must be
resisted tended more and more to cut through party lines.

*

ON OCTOBER 23, 1847 Lincoln leased his house for one year
for ninety dollars; and two days later, with Mrs. Lincoln and their
sons Robert and Eddie, he started for Lexington, Kentucky,
where they planned to visit Mrs. Lincoln's relatives en route to
the capital. After a three weeks' sojourn they were on their way
again, traveling by stagecoach to Winchester, Virginia, from there
on stuffy, jerky steam cars to Harpers Ferry, thence down the
Potomac gorge. Arriving in Washington at last and taking an
omnibus to Brown's Hotel, they looked out on a patchy, sprawling
town, whose population of 40,000 included 8,000 free Negroes and
2,000 slaves. The city was "a collection of neighborhoods,"
separated by undeveloped areas held by pinch-penny owners
against an expected rise in land values. Elegance and squalor

existed side by side; mansions and government buildings were flanked by shanties. Pigsties, cowsheds, and privies cluttered the back yards, and the garbage that littered streets and alleys provided forage for the pigs, geese, and chickens that roamed at will. Wells supplied the city's water. Produce was brought in from Maryland and Virginia farms in carts driven by slaves in tattered clothes. Damp and cold in winter, the city became so humid and malarial in summer that high government officials and the wealthier citizens deserted it as soon as hot weather came.

As Lincoln ambled along the brick sidewalk on the north side of Pennsylvania Avenue, which was the city's promenade, carts, wagons, and carriages clattered noisily over the rough cobblestones that paved the street. Off Pennsylvania Avenue few streets were surfaced at all, and sidewalks consisted of gravel or ashes. Oil lamps gleamed murkily along the Avenue at night, but even these, the only street lights in the city, were turned off when Congress was not in session.

The new Congressman from Illinois peered appreciatively at the White House in its spacious grounds, with a great marsh stretching to the Potomac in the rear. Far down the Avenue the Capitol stood out against the skyline, minus the wings that were added later, and surmounted by a wooden dome. Only the front of the Treasury had been completed, and the foundation of the Smithsonian Institution had just been laid. Two-story brick dwellings housed the State, War, and Navy departments.

The city had thirty-seven churches of eight denominations, though no record exists of Lincoln's attending any of them during his Congressional term. Passing along Pennsylvania Avenue, he could hear sounds of conviviality issuing from the numerous saloons—they enjoyed large custom during Congressional sessions. Forsaken in daytime, affluent gambling-houses came quietly alive at night.

Near the Capitol, Lincoln saw the "sort of negro livery-stable" where, as he remarked, "droves of negroes were collected, temporarily kept, and finally taken to Southern markets, precisely like droves of horses." The place had been an affront to

Northerners for years, but Washington was a center of the domestic slave trade, and efforts to be rid of it had failed.

After a few days at the hotel, Lincoln moved his family to cheaper quarters at Mrs. Sprigg's boarding-house, on the site of the present Library of Congress and overlooking the Capitol park with its gravel walks, summerhouses, and fountains. Mrs. Sprigg's place had been so popular with antislavery Whigs in years gone by that it had been called "the Abolition House," and doughty old Joshua R. Giddings, the Ohio abolitionist, still had lodgings there. Several other Whig legislators roomed or boarded at Mrs. Sprigg's, and Lincoln soon became a general favorite because of his simple manners and fund of jokes. A young doctor, Samuel C. Busey, recalled that when about to tell an anecdote at mealtime, Lincoln "would lay down his knife and fork, place his elbows upon the table, rest his face between his hands, and begin with the words, 'that reminds me,' and proceed. Everybody prepared for the explosions sure to follow."

Since most of the legislators roomed in boarding-houses or hotels, few of them brought their wives to Washington. Mrs. Lincoln soon became lonesome, the more so because she did not get along well with the few women whom she met. She kept to her room except at mealtime, and after three months she and the boys returned to Lexington.

The transient nature of Washington's population left entertainment largely in the hands of cabinet members, foreign diplomats, and local business and social leaders. The White House, usually the social Mecca of the capital, took on such an air of stern simplicity under Polk, with no dancing or refreshment of any kind at the levees, that one Senator declared: "I had rather be whipped than go," though he went none the less. Balls, receptions, and dinners, at which, according to a diarist, some of the Southwestern Congressmen "got fearfully drunk," provided most of the formal social recreation. In this sort of diversion a simple Western small-town lawyer of temperate habits scarcely had a place, and Lincoln limited his social activities to an occasional dinner or public ceremony and the concerts given by the

Marine Band on Wednesday and Sunday afternoons on the White House lawn. Favorite recreations of Congressmen were whist and bowling, and while Lincoln had no liking for cards, he often bowled with other members of Mrs. Sprigg's "mess." Enthusiastic but unskilled as a player, he excelled at repartee, and a crowd usually gathered to enjoy his witticisms.

*

IN INTELLIGENCE and ability the Thirtieth Congress ranked high. Lincoln drew one of the poorest seats in the House, in the center of the back row on the Whig side, and as he looked about him he saw men already known to him by reputation, and others destined for distinction. A few rows ahead of him, near Giddings, sat George Ashmun of Massachusetts, never suspecting that thirteen years later he would preside over a Republican national convention that would nominate for the Presidency the long-legged, sallow-faced Westerner who sat behind him. In the middle of the Whig section was a thin, sickly-looking little man from Georgia, Alexander H. Stephens, later to be Vice President of the Confederacy, whose intellect and moving eloquence impressed Lincoln tremendously. Near Stephens sat his colleague from Georgia, florid-faced Robert Toombs, a future Confederate Secretary of State and brigadier general. Close to Toombs, Caleb B. Smith of Indiana, one day to be Secretary of the Interior in Lincoln's cabinet, had his seat. Conspicuous by reason of his age and talents was former President John Quincy Adams, eighty years old, honest, experienced, shrewd, and fearlessly uncompromising on moral issues.

On the Democratic side sat blond, nervous David Wilmot of Pennsylvania, lately thrust into prominence because of the proviso that bore his name and would continue to exert as powerful a disruptive force throughout this session as it had during the preceding one. The tall, slender, bearded man near him was Robert Barnwell Rhett of South Carolina, able and distinguished, an intransigent defender of slavery and state rights, who would soon take over John C. Calhoun's role in the Senate. Heavy-

browed Andrew Johnson of Tennessee, who had come up the hard
way like Lincoln, would one day be Vice President under him.

The Senate boasted a galaxy of famous men or men to whom
fame would come—John J. Crittenden, Hannibal Hamlin, Daniel
Webster, Lewis Cass, Jefferson Davis, Thomas Hart Benton,
David R. Atchison, John P. Hale, John A. Dix, Simon Cameron,
John Bell, Sam Houston, James Mason, Robert M. T. Hunter,
and William L. Dayton, among others. Stephen A. Douglas,
after two terms in the House, had just been elevated to the upper
chamber by the Illinois Legislature. The Senate was predominantly Democratic, while the Whigs controlled the House by a
slim margin.

*

UNTIL LINCOLN took his seat in Congress he had kept his
doubts about the justness of the Mexican War to himself. In
Lexington, however, he had listened to a rousing speech in which
his political favorite, Henry Clay, flayed Polk for starting
hostilities. "This is no war of defence," Clay cried, "but one of
unnecessary and of offensive aggression. It is Mexico that is
defending her firesides, her castles and her altars, not we." In
Washington Lincoln heard the same sentiments expressed by
other Whig leaders.

On the second day of the session, Polk's message reasserted
that Mexico had caused the war by shedding the blood of American citizens on American soil. Two weeks later William A.
Richardson, one of Lincoln's colleagues from Illinois and an
aggressive administration-supporter, introduced a resolution
declaring the war to be just and necessary, and asserting that the
amount of indemnity should be determined by the degree of
Mexico's obstinacy in prolonging it. Lincoln could no longer remain passively acquiescent even if he wished, and he joined with
virtually all the other Whig members in voting the resolution
down. As a practical politician Lincoln would scarcely have opposed the Whig majority in any event, but by this time his doubts
had ripened into certainty that the war guilt rested upon Polk. A

few days after Richardson's resolution was defeated, Lincoln entered the Whig lists by introducing a series of resolutions calculated to embarrass the President by forcing him to admit that Mexico and not the United States had jurisdiction over the "spot" where the first blood was shed. Three weeks later Lincoln followed up with his first important speech, amplifying his charges, clarifying his argument, and challenging the harassed Polk to answer him. The speech contained nothing original—Whigs had been saying the same things for months—and the President gave no heed to it whatever.

Throughout the session, until the treaty of peace was ratified on May 30, 1848, Lincoln voted with the Whigs on all resolutions designed to put the administration in the wrong on the origin of the war, and to capitalize on its mistakes in waging it. When George Ashmun moved to add the amendment: "in a war unconstitutionally and unnecessarily begun by the President," to a resolution of thanks to General Taylor for his victory at Buena Vista, Lincoln's vote helped to force its adoption. But whenever supply bills for the army came before the House, Lincoln, like most other Whigs, supported them. Furthermore, he took a realistic attitude toward annexation of territory by refusing to vote for a resolution, sponsored by the extreme anti-expansionist group, which demanded that our army be withdrawn to the east bank of the Rio Grande and that peace be made without indemnity.

*

B ACK IN Illinois, where patriotic fervor and hunger for new lands extinguished any doubts the people may have entertained about the righteousness of the American cause, Lincoln's "spot" resolutions, his anti-administration speech, and his attitude on war guilt created surprise and resentment. What will the "gallant heroes" from the Seventh District say when they learn that their representative in Congress has voted that the war is "infamous and wicked," asked the Democratic *State Register*, as it warned that obstructionists in Congress "will find that the masses—the honest and patriotic citizens of Illinois—will mark their course and condemn them to infamy. . . . Thank Heaven, Illinois has eight representatives who will stand by the honor of the nation. Would that we could find Mr. Lincoln in their ranks doing battle on the side of the country as valiantly as did the Illinois volunteers on the battle fields of Buena Vista and Cerro Gordo. He will have a fearful account to settle with them, should he lend his aid in an effort to neutralize their efforts and blast their fame."

All over central Illinois the Democrats excoriated Lincoln as a disgrace to his state. One Democratic paper labeled him a modern Benedict Arnold; another dubbed him "the Ranchero Spotty," who would be retired at the end of his term. Adverting to a peculiar disease called "spotted fever," which was prevalent in Michigan, the *State Register* remarked: "This fever does not prevail to any very alarming extent in Illinois. The only case we have heard of that is likely to prove fatal, is that of 'spotty Lincoln,' of this state. This 'spotty' gentleman had a severe attack of 'spotted fever' in Washington city not long since, and fears were entertained that the disease would 'strike in,' and carry him off. We have not heard of any other person in Washington being on the 'spotted list'—and it is probable that the disease died with the patient.—What an epitaph: 'Died of Spotted Fever.' Poor Lincoln."

Against such gleefully remorseful ridicule the *Journal* and other Whig papers, in view of the general approbation of the war, could present only a weak defense. The appellation "Spotty Lincoln" stuck, with calamitous consequences to Lincoln's political aspirations.

Frightened by the outcry against Lincoln, Billy Herndon warned his partner not to flout popular sentiment. "I will stake my life, that if you had been in my place, you would have voted just as I did," Lincoln replied. "Would you have voted what you felt you knew to be a lie? I know you would not. Would you have gone out of the House—skulked the vote? I expect not. If you had skulked one vote, you would have had to skulk many more, before the end of the session. Richardson's resolutions, introduced before

I made any move, or gave any vote upon the subject, make the direct question of the justice of the war; so that no man can be silent if he would. You are compelled to speak; and your only alternative is to tell the *truth* or tell a *lie*. . . . The Locos are untiring in their effort to make the impression that all who vote supplies, or take part in the war, do, of necessity, approve the President's conduct in the beginning of it; but the whigs have, from the beginning, made and kept the distinction between the two."

While the Whig attack on the administration centered upon the origin of the war, other issues, such as Polk's opposition to internal improvements, reduction of the tariff, and especially the question of slavery in the new territories, offered other salients for attack. On these issues Lincoln reflected more accurately the views of his constituents. On the tariff and internal improvements he took traditional Whig ground. One of his speeches reproved Polk for vetoing the river and harbor appropriation bill, and in two other speeches he upheld the policy of internal improvements at government expense. Admitting that such a program was subject to abuses, still, he declared, "The true rule, in determining to embrace, or reject any thing, is not whether it have *any* evil in it; but whether it have more of evil, than of good. There are few things *wholly* evil, or *wholly* good."

Lincoln was diligent in the routine work of the House. He rarely missed a roll call and performed his full share of labor on his two committees—that on the Post Office and Post Roads and the Committee on Expenditures in the War Department. Few first-term members have been more active, yet his colleagues generally appraised him as a droll Westerner of average talents.

*

D u r i n g the first session of the Congress the chief concern of both parties was the presidential election of 1848. No sooner had General Taylor's victories brought him acclaim than the Whig leaders canvassed his availability. A professional soldier whose ability to inspire confidence made up for his meager military knowledge, "Old Rough and Ready" had never voted for President, was a man of prejudices rather than opinions, a slave-owner, an advocate of annexation of Mexican territory, and an exponent of the military spirit that the Whigs denounced. But his vote-getting potential was tremendous. And he appealed all the more to the Whig leaders because they so well remembered that their sole presidential triumph came in 1840, when they turned their backs on Henry Clay, their recognized leader, and rode to victory on the military reputation of William Henry Harrison. Now, with their opponents plagued by factionalism and a great opportunity bidding them make the most of it, they again relegated Clay to the background and rallied around the candidacy of the intrepid but unseasoned Taylor.

Since Lincoln's entry into politics he had hoped to see Henry Clay elected President. But he knew Clay stood no chance. Throughout the early months of 1848 Lincoln gauged the direction of the political currents, particularly in Illinois, and did what he could to rally support to Taylor, "not because I think he would make a better president than Clay," he explained in numerous letters, "but because I think he would make a better one than Polk, or Cass, or Buchanan, or any such creatures, one of whom is sure to be elected, if he is not." Largely under Lincoln's urging, prominent Illinois Whigs climbed on the Taylor bandwagon.

Early in June Lincoln went to Philadelphia to attend the Whig national convention, where he witnessed Taylor's nomination and saw the Illinois delegates help to bring it about. On the first three ballots the votes of his state were split—three for Clay, one for General Scott, and four for Taylor. But on the fourth and final ballot the whole Illinois delegation swung to Taylor.

From June until election day Lincoln worked unceasingly in the general's cause, trying to convince doubters of Taylor's capabilities. Perceiving that the tide was running toward the general, he exulted to Herndon: "By many, and often, it had been said they would not abide the nomination of Taylor; but since the deed has been done, they are fast falling in, and in my opinion we shall have a most overwhelming, glorious, triumph. One unmistakable sign is, that all the odds and ends are with us. . . . This is important, if in nothing else, in showing which way the wind blows. Some of the sanguine men here set down all the states as certain for Taylor, but Illinois, and it as doubtful. Can not something be done, even in Illinois?"

Lincoln felt gravely concerned as to how Illinois would go. He was not a candidate for re-election; according to the policy of "turn about is fair play," the Whigs had chosen Logan to succeed him. But the result would be important to Lincoln's political prospects, and he worked hard to bring out the vote. Deluging doubtful voters with Whig documents, he urged the pessimistic Herndon to rally the young men in a "Rough & Ready club." Recruit everyone that will come in, he implored his partner, and assign each one the sort of job he can do best—"some speak, some sing, and all 'holler.' "

But Herndon was not easily warmed up, for he knew of the discouragement throughout the district. Many young men, he reported, were dissatisfied "at the stubbornness and bad judgment of the old fossils in the party," who were holding the young men back. This was a cruel thrust, but Lincoln replied with fatherly kindness that he knew of no effort on the part of the old men, of whom he supposed he was one—he was thirty-nine, but already referred to himself as an old man—to act ungenerously toward younger members of the party. "The way for a young man to rise," he patiently advised, "is to improve himself every way he can, never suspecting that any body wishes to hinder him. Allow me to assure you, that suspicion and jealousy never did help any man in any situation."

Herndon was mollified. He and others went to work. But the results proved disappointing. In the Congressional election on August 6, Logan went down before Thomas L Harris, Democrat of Petersburg, 7,095 to 7,201. Lincoln tried to bolster Herndon's spirits by explaining that Logan was unpopular with many Whigs, whereas Harris's war record had made him a hero. "That there is any political change against us in the district I cannot believe," he wrote.

But the *Register's* explanation came closer to fact. "The whigs about Springfield are attributing their defeat to Judge Logan solely," it commented, "alleging that the Judge's unpopularity brought about the result. This will not do, gentlemen, you must put the saddle on the right horse. It was the crushing load Logan had to carry in the shape of whig principles, and the course of the whig party for the past two years. Besides his own dead weight, Logan had to carry the votes of the whig party, including Lincoln, that the war was unconstitutional and unnecessary. . . . 'Acknowledge the corn,' whiggery is getting in bad odor." Lincoln could scarcely underestimate the ominous tidings, but he still labored unremittingly to save his district for Taylor.

On July 27 Lincoln made a speech in the House in which he ridiculed the efforts of the Democrats to make a military hero out of their presidential candidate, Lewis Cass, by comparing Cass's military accomplishments with his own experiences in the Black Hawk War. Those who were trying to tie Cass to a military coat-tail were "like so many mischievous boys tying a dog to a bladder of beans." In his subservience to the slave power, declared Lincoln, Cass was like a listless ox backing off from the farmer's goad. Cass had seemed willing to support the Wilmot Proviso at first, but as the voice of his master warned him back, he slunk meekly into his stall.

When the first session of Congress ended, Lincoln did not return to Springfield but remained in Washington to write letters and frank documents. In the latter part of August and the first week of September he made a few speeches in Washington and in near-by towns in Maryland. Then, probably under the sponsorship of the Whig National Committee, he set off for Massachusetts on a speaking tour. There his efforts were directed at the Free-Soilers, who had nominated Martin Van Buren for President on a third-party ticket, and at wavering antislavery Whigs who were tempted to join them. The burden of Lincoln's argument was that the Whigs and Free-Soilers occupied similar ground with respect to the spread of slavery, and that a vote for Van Buren would simply benefit Cass by splitting the anti-Democratic ballots. Lincoln concluded his tour at a huge meeting at Tremont Temple in Boston, where he and William H. Seward, former Governor of New York, spoke from the same platform. Seward's remarks against the extension of slavery impressed Lincoln mightily; his experience in Congress and the presidential contest awakened him to the urgency of the problem.

From Boston Lincoln started home, stopping off at Albany for conferences with the Whig vice-presidential candidate, Millard Fillmore, and with Thurlow Weed, Whig boss of New York State, and at Buffalo for a view of Niagara Falls. At Chicago he addressed a large Whig rally. Home at last, for two weeks he stumped the northern part of the Congressional district, appealing for Free-Soil votes for Taylor as he had done in New England. But whenever an opposition speaker appeared on the same platform, he put Lincoln on the defensive by bringing up his record on the war. A correspondent of the *State Register* opined that "Lincoln has made nothing by coming to this part of the country to make speeches. He had better have stayed away." Nevertheless, on election day Taylor carried the district by fifteen hundred votes, a result for which Lincoln claimed a large measure of credit.

*

I n D e c e m b e r, after a much needed rest, Lincoln returned to Washington for the second session of Congress, in which he continued his diligent but unspectacular role. As the only Whig Congressman from Illinois, he recommended several candidates for office under the incoming Taylor administration, and tried unsuccessfully to obtain a cabinet appointment for his friend Edward D. Baker, who, moving to Galena, had been elected to the Thirty-first Congress.

The last months of Polk's administration were turbulent, for no sooner had Congress reconvened than agitation of the slavery question recommenced. Usually the most salutary effect of a war is to unify a country in common purpose, but this was not true of our conflict with Mexico. No sooner had Polk in his an-

nual message recommended the establishment of territorial
governments for New Mexico and California than sectional
animosities became more virulent than ever. As an indication of
the turmoil in the country, resolutions of state legislatures
cascaded upon Congress, those from the North supporting the
Wilmot Proviso, and those from the South protesting against the
exclusion of slavery from the new territories and threatening a
dissolution of the Union if Southern rights were denied.

There were several points at issue in the controversy.
California urgently needed state government as men flocked to
the gold-fields, but since she would inevitably become a free
state, some Southerners opposed her admission altogether, while
others determined to obtain some offsetting concession. The
boundary between New Mexico and Texas was in dispute, and
since New Mexico also seemed likely to become a free state,
Northerners wished to push its boundary as far east as possible,
while Southerners supported the Texan claim to more westerly
limits. The slave trade in the District of Columbia came under
heavy attack from the North, whereas the South, exasperated by
the action of Northern legislatures in passing personal-liberty
laws, which impeded the recapture of fugitive slaves, demanded a
more effective fugitive-slave law.

Opposed to unnecessary agitation of the slavery question,
Lincoln remained silent during the discordant debates that shook
the House. But he voted consistently for legislation designed to
establish free governments in California and New Mexico and
would claim later that he voted for the Wilmot Proviso in one
form or another no less than forty times. When Joshua Giddings
attacked slavery as the most heinous of crimes and brought up a
proposal to abolish it in the District of Columbia, Lincoln gave
notice of his intention to introduce a bill of his own designed to
effect the same end. His measure would have liberated and placed
under apprenticeship all children born to slave mothers of the
District after January 1, 1850, and also provided for voluntary
compensated emancipation of other slaves within the District,
the whole project to be contingent on the consent of the people

of the District. When Lincoln became convinced that his plan had no chance of adoption, however, he never introduced it as a bill. He supported a bill prohibiting the slave trade in the District, but as usual it failed to pass.

Sensitive to any threat to their peculiar institution, or to denial of what they considered equal rights in the new territories, the more militant Southerners, led by John C. Calhoun, met in caucus to organize a Southern party to resist Northern "aggression." The manifesto they issued warned of imminent peril to the South; the ultimate design of the free-soil forces was to abolish slavery. To Calhoun and other Southern radicals this was a mad design, for they had evolved a new philosophy of slavery as a positive good, a blessing to master and slave alike since it afforded the white man leisure for cultivation of the highest talents while bringing the black man out of savagery. The only system under which the two races could live together peaceably and to their mutual benefit, it had endowed the South with a superior civilization, and those who would disturb this way of life were evil bigots. By what right did these fanatics seek to exclude slavery from the territories? Slaves were property, just as cows and sheep and walking-sticks were property, and as such Congress not only had no power to discriminate against them, but was obligated to protect the master in his right to take slaves anywhere within the national domain. Unless the South were granted equal rights in the territories, and unless the North hushed its antislavery agitation, the South's proper course was secession.

Here was the voice of the new South, expressing a philosophy rooted in something deeper than a mere determination to perpetuate slavery, a philosophy nurtured by a passionate state pride, by a haunting fear of an insoluble race problem if the slaves were freed, by a fierce determination to keep the South a white man's country, and to preserve the easy, cultured, cordial Southern way of life.

Near the end of the session the proslavery bloc supported the so-called Walker Amendment, which would have extended the Constitution, with its recognition of slavery, over all the new territory. Northern Whigs and free-soil Democrats girded to meet the challenge. The session closed amid exchanges of threats and epithets, with one lively but short-lived fist fight. None of the conflicting issues was decided. But Lincoln, witnessing the intensity of sectional hostility, realized its sinister implications.

*

A s   t h e session ended, Lincoln, having had a taste of Federal office, was reluctant to return to the less eventful life of Springfield. Moreover, with his own party soon to be in power, he hoped to share with Baker the control of Federal patronage in Illinois. On March 9, 1849 he wrote to William M. Meredith, Secretary of the Treasury, requesting that he and Baker be consulted about appointments for or from Illinois, since the Whigs of the state held them responsible for such appointments. But the conclusion of his letter would seem to indicate the extent of his influence. "We do not know you personally," he wrote, "and our efforts to see you have, so far, been unavailing."

For almost three weeks after Taylor's inauguration Lincoln lingered in Washington. He tried his first and only case before the U.S. Supreme Court, losing an appeal from the U.S. Circuit Court of Illinois; and he took steps to obtain a patent on a device he had worked out for lifting boats over shoals and sandbars by means of expansible air chambers.

Returning at last to Springfield, Lincoln found that his most perplexing problem concerned the appointment of the commissioner of the General Land Office at Washington, an office that had been virtually promised to Illinois. The difficulty came from the fact that two candidates were in the field, Cyrus Edwards, of Edwardsville, to whom Lincoln was committed, and J. L. D. Morrison, of St. Clair County, to whom Baker had promised support. Lincoln tried to persuade one or the other of the aspirants to withdraw so that he and Baker could unite on a recommendation, but neither man would do so. Lincoln's friends urged him to become a candidate himself as the only means of breaking the deadlock and saving the office for Illinois, but he refused. "I must not only be chaste but above suspicion," he explained. "If the office shall be tendered to me, I must be permitted to say 'Give it to Mr. Edwards, or, if so agreed by them, to Col. Morrison, and I decline it; if not, I accept.'"

Meanwhile the contest was intensified by the entry of a dark horse in the person of Justin Butterfield, of Chicago. "Of the quite one hundred Illinoisians, equally well qualified," Lincoln complained, "I do not know one with less claims to it." For Butterfield had worked for Clay against Taylor "to the bitter end," and had done nothing for the Whig ticket during the campaign. In desperation Lincoln rushed off letters to friends in Washington, urging: "Try to defeat B[utterfield]; and in doing so, use Mr. Edwards, J. L. D. Morrison, or myself, whichever you can to best advantage."

By June 1 the contest had narrowed down to Butterfield and Lincoln. Thomas Ewing, Secretary of the Interior, favored Butterfield, but Taylor, at the request of Lincoln's friends, agreed to delay the appointment for three weeks. Lincoln pitched in frantically, requesting recommendations from anyone who might have influence at the Federal capital. Both candidates circulated petitions, and finally both set off in haste for Washington. But all Lincoln's efforts proved unavailing; on June 21 Butterfield received the prize.

Lincoln returned to Springfield thoroughly disheartened. He continued to recommend appointments to the administration, but as his lack of influence became increasingly evident, his political enthusiasm cooled. When the Sangamon Circuit Court convened in the summer of 1849, Lincoln had no choice but to return to the practice of law.

CHAPTER VII

Echoes of National Conflict

AS GOLD-SEEKERS rushed to the new Eldorado in California and trains of covered wagons toiled through snow-capped mountain ranges and across forbidding deserts to the land of promise in the West, Lincoln took to the dusty roads of the Eighth Circuit to regain the friends and clients who had slipped away from him while he was gone. He had no wish to join the westward migration, and when the administration at Washington tried to appease him with an offer of the governorship or secretaryship of Oregon Territory, he turned both offices down.

Apprehending that he had no future in politics, Lincoln did not repine. He began at once to make himself a better lawyer and a more enlightened man, and the decision made the years of his political retirement, from 1849 to 1854, among the most fruitful of his life. For as he put aside all thought of political advancement and devoted himself to personal improvement, he grew tremendously in mind and character.

Outwardly Lincoln remained unchanged as he moved among his townsmen and the rural folk of the county towns, still wearing the familiar tall hat with the nap rubbed off, an ill-fitting swallow-tail coat bulging at the elbows, "high-water" pantaloons, and unblacked boots. When seated he did not look taller than the average man, but as he rose and his long legs unfolded, he towered six feet four inches. He was proud of his height and liked to measure back-to-back with other tall men. He was lean, sinewy, rawboned, thin through the chest, and somewhat stooped. He weighed about one hundred and eighty pounds. His skin was wrinkled, dark, and leathery. His unruly dark hair was scarcely touched with gray. When he walked, his huge hands dangled at the ends of his long arms. His head was long, his forehead high and narrow, his cheekbones prominent, and his gray eyes deep-set below jutting brows. His chin was sharp, his ears large and out-standing, and his thick lower lip protruded. He had a mole on his right cheek.

*

O B S E R V I N G what went on in Washington at long range, Lincoln seemed satisfied when, in 1850, the aging Henry Clay worked out a series of measures designed to quiet the sectional hostility, and with the aid of Webster and Douglas forced them through Congress in the face of opposition from radical free-soilers on the one hand and Southern secessionists on the other. California was admitted as a free state. The territories of New Mexico and Utah were organized without mention of slavery, and with its fate to be determined by the people when they were ready for statehood. The Texas boundary dispute was composed by paying Texas $10,000,000 to renounce her claim to the eastern portion of New Mexico. The slave trade was abolished in the District of Columbia. And finally, to placate the Southern "fire-eaters," the Federal courts were given jurisdiction over cases of fugitive slaves, so that personal-liberty laws enacted by Northern legislatures would no longer impede the capture and return of runaways.

The South as a whole accepted the Compromise heartily, and those extremists who had preached disunion found their followers melting away. In the North, too, almost everyone except the abolitionists acceded to the settlement. The controversies that had threatened to split the nation seemed ended—except for the Fugitive Slave Law.

One would have expected the abolitionists to denounce any statute intended to return a fugitive to bondage, but the provisions of the new enactment were odious even to moderates. No jury trial was allowed a Negro claimed as a fugitive, nor was he permitted to testify in his own defense. A master or his agent simply made affidavit of ownership before a Federal commissioner, whose fee was fixed at five dollars if he decided for the Negro and ten dollars if he decided for the master. The difference in fees was defended on the ground that a decision for rendition involved more paper work, but to antislavery men it seemed a bribe. Furthermore, everyone was made a potential slave-catcher; to aid a runaway or refuse to assist a Federal marshal in catching him made one liable to a heavy fine and imprisonment. And, finally, the law was *ex post facto*—it applied to slaves who had escaped at any time, even years before its passage.

Despite these distasteful aspects of the law and the ranting of extremists on both sides, most persons accepted the Compromise measures as a final settlement of all outstanding issues of the slavery controversy. Like other Union-loving moderates, Lincoln felt relieved to see the tension ease. For the danger to the nation had been critical—threats of disunion were more than bombast, and the controversy might well have caused civil war. On the death of Henry Clay, in 1852, Lincoln eulogized the author of the Compromise as a man of moderation and humanitarianism. Although himself a slaveholder, Clay had always opposed slavery "on principle and in feeling," Lincoln declared; but "he did not perceive, as I think no wise man has perceived, how it could be at *once* eradicated, without producing a greater evil, even to the cause of human liberty itself." Assailing the abolitionists who would "shiver into fragments the Union of these States; tear to tatters its now venerated constitution; and even burn the last copy of the Bible, rather than slavery should continue a single hour," Lincoln also stigmatized those Southern hotheads who, in their idolatry of slavery, denied the assertion of the Declaration of Independence that "all men are created equal."

*

THE GREATER attention that Lincoln bestowed on the law rewarded him with an increasing practice. As he felt a larger responsibility in his calling he resolved to stay out of politics. In October 1852, when his name was presented to a county convention as a prospective nominee for the State Legislature, Herndon, doubtless acting under instructions, informed the convention that business claimed all his partner's time. Mention of Lincoln as a candidate for governor failed to evoke his interest. The presidential campaign of 1852, in which the Whigs again turned to a military hero, General Winfield Scott, aroused him only mildly. He served as a national committeeman and made a few speeches, but compared with his activity in other presidential contests his efforts were perfunctory.

He watched what went on about him, however, and did a great deal of thinking. In his leisure time at home and on the circuit he read the newspapers assiduously. Mulling over his enforced retirement to private life, he realized more acutely that a politician who hopes to be successful in a democracy can go no farther in any direction than public opinion will allow.

Fellow lawyers observed that desire for understanding had become almost a passion with Lincoln. He was never satisfied in handling a thought until, as he said, he had bounded it east, west, north, and south and could express it in the simplest, clearest language. He had always had a bent for mathematics, and now, as a mental discipline, he mastered the first six books of Euclid, conning their pages in the cheerless hotel rooms or on the lonely prairie as he lolled in his buggy while his horse plodded on unguided from town to town. He also read books on astronomy and renewed his study of Shakespeare.

The abysmal gloom that had afflicted him periodically did not again become acute, as it had at the time of his engagement to Mary Todd; instead it became a chronic malady. "Melancholy dripped from him as he walked," Herndon observed; it was a constant torment that he had to learn to live with. At times he threw off his dejection and found relief in boisterous merriment.

Among the many contradictions in Lincoln's personality was a belief in dreams. With a mind otherwise precise and practical, he accepted things that came to him in sleep as warnings and portents. A fatalist, he regarded man as the pawn of some over-ruling power, able only in small measure to control the larger aspects of his destiny.

Notwithstanding Lincoln's easy ways and genial camaraderie, he had a certain remoteness that repelled familiarity. Most persons addressed him as Mr. Lincoln or Lincoln; not even his best friends called him Abe. He had personal magnetism, a quality of open friendliness that attracted people and impelled them to confide in him, and yet he was a close-mouthed man himself and seldom revealed his plans or purposes to anyone. His closest friends were baffled by his reticence; there were things about him they would have liked to learn but never did. They confessed they never fully understood him.

He was simple yet complex—natural, unostentatious, humble, but at the same time self-reliant and self-assured. Keen-minded, analytical, and practical, still he was something of a visionary. Undemonstrative on the surface, he had unfathomed depths of tenderness and pity. By nature conservative and cautious, he never took unnecessary risks. While several of his fellow lawyers were laying the basis of fortunes by speculation in farm land and city real estate, he was content to confine his investments to safer commitments in notes and mortgages.

On January 15, 1851 Thomas Lincoln died in Coles County. Lincoln did not attend his father's funeral, and the letter of reassurance that he sent during the old man's last illness has an unconvincing tone. One cannot escape the feeling that Lincoln had no real affection for his father and could not dissimulate about it; Tom Lincoln had offered him scant encouragement in his efforts to make something of himself. But Lincoln loved his stepmother and carefully safeguarded her small inheritance from his lazy, grasping stepbrother.

Lincoln's inability to make even a pretense of affection for his father was in keeping with his fundamental honesty; for frankness, candor, and truthfulness were second nature with him. There was simply no deception in him; he was not only honest as most men are honest, but integrity became so much a part of his nature that acquaintances and observers who wrote about him invariably mention it. This quality helped him both professionally and politically—people believed him.

And if the people trusted Lincoln, he also trusted them. He had supreme faith in their right-mindedness, provided they could be made to understand, and he never questioned their powers of comprehension when the facts were presented to them simply and honestly. When he credited the farmer boys with originating most of the aphoristic stories he told, he affirmed his faith in the grass-roots philosophy of the plain people. And while his utterance of the epigram: "You can fool some of the people all the time, and all the people some of the time, but you can't fool all the people all the time," has never been verified, it can be taken as a characteristic avowal of his democratic faith.

More and more his discourse took an axiomatic turn. Familiarity with Shakespeare and the Bible, proficiency in story-telling, a craving for exactitude, a talent for the quick association of ideas, a continued striving for literary excellence, all these were infusing his diction with a distinctive, hard-muscled grace.

*

A s t h e year 1853 came to a close, with Lincoln busy at his law practice, the country was calm. Except for a few extremists without important influence, most people, North and South, had accepted the Compromise of 1850. And yet there was a static tingle in the air, and every now and then a flash of far-off lightning warned of a lurking storm.

Now it was news that the California Legislature had for the third time moved back the deadline when slaves brought into the state before the adoption of its constitution must be removed, so that Horace Greeley of the *New York Tribune* muttered that slavery threatened to fasten itself upon the state. Now it was an inconspicuous newspaper notice that a slave, Dred Scott, who claimed his freedom on the ground that his master had taken him into Illinois and then into Wisconsin Territory, in both of which slavery was illegal, had been remanded to slavery by the Supreme

Court of Missouri because he had voluntarily returned to a slave state. Now it was an attempt to thwart the operation of the new Fugitive Slave Law by men who could not stand idly by while a cringing Negro was snatched back into bondage before their eyes. Again it was some act of brutality against a slave which found its way into the newspapers. Or it might be rumors of intrigues of the "slave power" to seize the Spanish island of Cuba.

Uncle Tom's Cabin, a plaintive, sentimental novel written by a little plain-faced woman, Harriet Beecher Stowe, put slavery in a very different light from that of the benevolent institution pictured by Southern apologists. In its representation of the Negro as a human being, with the same mental and emotional qualities as others of God's creatures, it struck a thudding blow at the very keystone of the arch of slavery: the generally accepted notion of the Negro as an inferior being, destined by reason of his mental and moral insufficiency to remain fixed in the order of nature only slightly above the brute.

As Lincoln conned the newspapers, he could scarcely have been heedless of these tremors at the base of the national structure. If the demon of sectional discord was somnolent, it slept only fitfully. The thinking of the country had diverged so sharply as to make the slavery question irrepressible. No longer was it primarily a social, constitutional, or economic problem to be adjusted through the give-and-take of compromise. More and more it tended to become a moral issue, with the opposing forces increasingly convinced that right and justice lay altogether on their side.

The times demanded cautious leadership, but talented leadership was lacking. The shallow, spineless Franklin Pierce was a weak President, dominated by hard-minded advisers like Jefferson Davis of Mississippi and Caleb Cushing of Massachusetts. The great senatorial triumvirate of Clay, Webster, and Calhoun were dead, and younger men of incautious ambition vied for power. The Whig Party had all but foundered on the slavery issue. The Democratic Party lacked guidance and a focal principle. The situation held all the elements of catastrophe if some rash man should make an unwise move.

Several ambitious young senators loomed as potential trouble-makers. There was tall, handsome Salmon P. Chase, an antislavery zealot who concealed a calculating ambition beneath an aloof exterior. An abstemious, prayerful, carefully precise Ohioan, his humorless solemnity moved Tom Corwin to mark him as surely destined for distinction, since, in Corwin's estimation, "If you would succeed in life you must be solemn, solemn as an ass. All the great monuments of earth have been built over solemn asses." Regardless of Constitution or statutes, Chase believed that slavery was condemned by "that law of sublime origin and more awful sanction than any human code"—the law that enjoined every man "to do unto others as we would that others should do to us."

Representing New York was thin, beak-nosed William H. Seward, brilliant, erratic, and devious, with his quizzical alertness and keen, wide-questing mind. Like Chase, he expounded the doctrine that a "higher law" than the Constitution demanded men's obedience. Grave, egotistical Charles Sumner of Massachusetts was another Senator who might get out of bounds. Severely self-disciplined in tastes and mental habits, with a commanding figure and haughty, frigid manners, he displayed a stodgy pedantry as he interlarded his speeches with classical allusions and quotations. Irritatingly assured of his own rectitude, he had taken the oath of office with a mental reservation: he held the Fugitive Slave Law to be unconstitutional and had no intention of upholding it.

And finally there was Stephen A. Douglas, from Lincoln's own state of Illinois, who, while Lincoln moved ahead politically and then fell back in frustration, had advanced steadily under the spur of a relentless determination. Now forty years old and in his second term as a Senator, he had become a national figure— chairman of the powerful Committee on Territories, which controlled the destiny of the undeveloped regions of the country. Bold to the point of recklessness, often inscrutable, incessantly active in politics, business, and Washington social life, a brilliant improviser rather than a reflective, far-seeing planner, Douglas presented a spectacular figure with his undersized but vigorously compact body, his great head crowned with a dark mane of hair, and his scowling visage. A sincere patriot, a fervent nationalist, eager for expansion and the development of the West, he displayed an affability and charm that won him a host of loyal followers among the younger and more vigorous members of his party. Well versed in governmental and political lore, scornful of opposition, he was an overpowering orator when in the right, and a skillful and sometimes unscrupulous dissembler when arguing a bad cause. Douglas was the ablest of all the eager young senators, and yet it was Douglas who precipitated trouble when, with the country seemingly pacified, he suddenly moved to repeal the slavery-restriction clause of the Missouri Compromise.

At once the dispersed static collected in a rending, crashing charge!

What prompted Douglas to his reckless course has never been adequately explained, though a variety of reasons has been offered. Douglas wanted to further the construction of a transcontinental railroad by a northern route through Nebraska. Unless that territory was organized speedily, however, the road might take a southern route. And quick organization could be brought about only by winning the support of certain Southern senators who regarded the prohibition of slavery north of the Missouri Compromise line of 36° 30′ as an affront to the South. Important in Douglas's calculations was a reinvigoration of the Democratic Party. Perhaps its Northern and Southern factions could be united in support of the new principle of popular sovereignty, already applied to New Mexico and Utah in the Compromise of 1850, which allowed the people of those territories to determine the fate of slavery for themselves.

The political maneuvering that ended with the repeal of the Missouri Compromise began during the Congressional session of 1852–3, when a bill for the organization of Nebraska Territory, with no mention whatever of repeal of the Compromise, had been passed by the House of Representatives against strong Southern opposition. The Senate calendar was crowded, and the measure was tabled in the upper house. When Congress reconvened, however, Senator Augustus C. Dodge of Iowa introduced the identical bill. It was referred to Douglas's Committee on Territories. But when this committee reported it out, a new section had been added allowing the people of Nebraska to admit or exclude slavery as they chose. The Missouri Compromise was not mentioned, but its prohibition of slavery north of 36° 30' was impliedly overridden by this provision. The amendment foretokened a mighty victory for the partisans of slavery—an acceptance of the South's claim to equal rights in all the national domain.

But even this implied concurrence in the Southern view did not go far enough to satisfy some radical Southern leaders. Archibald Dixon, Senator from Kentucky, pointed out to Douglas that unless the Missouri Compromise were expressly repealed, no slaveholder would dare take his slaves to the new territory. To assure Southerners of an equal chance, the Missouri Compromise must be repealed explicitly.

Douglas was somewhat shocked at the suggestion. Less than five years earlier he had told his constituents at Springfield that the Missouri Compromise had "become canonized in the hearts of the American people as a sacred thing, which no ruthless hand would ever be reckless enough to disturb." Now, however, he admitted the validity of Dixon's argument. Once more the bill went back to committee. When it was reported out the next time, it provided for the division of the affected area into two territories, Kansas and Nebraska—because of certain exigencies of Iowa and Missouri politics—and expressly repealed the restrictive feature of the Missouri Compromise. Douglas correctly predicted that "it will raise a hell of a storm," when it came before the Senate on January 23, 1854.

*

As news of this ominous skirmishing in Congress reached the quiet towns of central Illinois, Lincoln's companions on the circuit noted that he kept more and more to himself. His thoughts seemed far away. Many a time he sat in reverie while all the others slept; waking in the morning, they found him sitting lost in thought before the fire.

The most mystifying feature of Douglas's action was his seemingly callous indifference to free-soil opinion in the North. He must know, thought Lincoln, that he would raise a storm. Yet he did not seem to care. Did he think only the radical extremists would object? Did he think the storm would soon subside? Or did he scorn the free-soil opposition?

Probably, since Douglas had no moral repugnance to slavery himself, he could neither foresee nor understand the depths of Northern resentment. Douglas's attitude toward slavery was utterly materialistic. He had little humanitarian sympathy for the Negro. "Whenever a territory has a climate, soil and productions making it the interest of the inhabitants to encourage slave property," he declared, "they will pass a slave code and give it encouragement. Whenever the climate, soil, and productions preclude the possibility of slavery being profitable, they will not permit it. You come right back to the principle of dollars and cents." Douglas repeatedly asserted that he did not care whether slavery was voted up or voted down. The decision should rest solely with the white people of the affected area. As between the white man and the Negro, he declared, he favored the white man every time; and as between the Negro and the crocodile, he favored the Negro.

Lacking any moral sensitivity about slavery, Douglas could never comprehend why millions at the North should be so vitally concerned about the status of the Negro in far-off New Mexico, Utah, or Kansas. Nor could he see anything shocking in scrapping the Missouri Compromise. What if it was part of a compact—or that it had become hallowed in Northern hearts? Why should it be held so sacrosanct when he had adduced a fairer and better principle: the principle of popular sovereignty? Northern concern was merely academic anyhow. His principle would not extend the area of slavery. Physical and economic factors dictated that slavery could never exist in one additional square mile of the national territory, according to Douglas's view.

Besides, said Douglas, the people themselves had already repudiated the Missouri Compromise. In allowing the people of Utah and New Mexico to admit or exclude slavery as they chose, they had adopted a principle of general application. But Lincoln knew that this claim did not square with the facts. When the people of the North accepted the Compromise of 1850, they thought the popular sovereignty feature had a specific application, just as the Missouri Compromise applied to a specific region.

As Lincoln carefully analyzed the Little Giant's reasoning, he perceived that the new principle of popular sovereignty contained a fundamental ambiguity. When could the people of a territory decide whether they would have slavery or not? When the population reached 1,000? or 10,000? or 30,000? or when the territory became a state? And could the nation as a whole be unconcerned in the decision? Was it fair for a handful of settlers in an outpost territory to decide for slavery or freedom while millions equally interested in the outcome stood by in helplessness? Douglas himself was indefinite as to the exact point in a territory's development when the decision should be made, though he favored an early time. Not so the proslavery radicals, however. They maintained with grim tenacity that the settlers could make no decision until a territory was ready for statehood—slavery entering freely in the meantime. The history of many commonwealths had proved that if slavery once got a foothold, it became extremely difficult to eradicate.

Lincoln must have wondered if Douglas appreciated the determination of Northern free-soil sympathizers to make the philosophy of freedom dominant. In the minds of many people the important conflict now was one of ideologies. "Every day's experience convinces me that matters are approaching a crisis in this country on the subject of slavery," wrote Edward Everett in his diary. "The differences, not of interest but of opinion and feeling are irreconcilable." "The slavery agitation you deprecate so much," Seward told his Southern colleagues in the Senate, "is an eternal struggle between conservatism and progress, between truth and error, between right and wrong." Slavery had become an anachronism, according to the Northern point of view, contrary to the principles of the Declaration of Independence as well as the spirit of the age. If the nation could not be rid of it at once, at least it should be put in course of ultimate extinction.

*

No sooner had Douglas introduced his bill in the Senate than two battles began to rage—one in Congress, the other throughout the country, each fought with the bitterness of desperation. In an "Appeal of the Independent Democrats in Congress to the People of the United States," Chase blasted the Kansas-Nebraska Bill as "a gross violation of a sacred pledge," "a criminal betrayal of precious rights," and a part of "an atrocious plot to exclude from a vast unoccupied region immigrants from the Old World and free laborers from our own States, and convert it into a dreary region of despotism, inhabited by masters and slaves." Chase accused the Little Giant of selling out to the South to further his ambition to become President.

Free-soil editors dipped their pens in acid. The Northern clergy, hitherto mostly cautious or apathetic, now spoke for freedom with new unity in the name of Almighty God. German-Americans and other racial groups who intended to move west excoriated Douglas for "Africanizing" their prospective homeland. Even businessmen whose interests linked them with the South held meetings to voice their moral indignation and to flay Douglas for imperiling the national prosperity by reopening a sectional conflict abated by the Compromise of 1850. For four months the debates in Congress raged, while the usually discordant chorus of Northern opinion boomed out in thundering and wrathful harmony.

Since the new principle of popular sovereignty granted the proslavery interests that equality of opportunity in the territories for which Calhoun and others had contended, the South rallied to Douglas's bill on principle. But the Southern states had little real enthusiasm for it, since few Southerners were convinced that it offered anything of practical value. The claim of Chase and Sumner that the bill was the fruit of a conspiracy of the "slave power" had no foundation in fact. But with the Pierce administration determined to support it as the embodiment of the new Democratic faith, party recalcitrants were whipped and jostled into line.

The indomitable Douglas led the fight. The incarnation of combativeness and tenacious determination, he loved a rough-and-tumble bout. If irrational impulse had taken him farther than he meant to go, he was not the man to draw back. Summoning all his parliamentary skill, all the power of his incisive oratory, all the ripping fury of his invective, he pressed the measure toward passage. He battled against time, for his greatest fear was that pliant Democrats would bend before the Northern blasts. Instead, they quailed before the Little Giant's raw belligerence. After six weeks of debate, culminating in a continuous session of seventeen hours during much of which Douglas held the floor, the bill passed the Senate at daybreak on March 4. Eleven weeks more were needed to force it through the House.

Abraham Lincoln heard about its passage at Urbana, where he was attending court. The news roused him, he said, "as he had never been before." Three months later we shall find him back in politics. But he will emerge as a different Lincoln from the ambitious politician whose hopes were seemingly blighted in 1849. His ambition, reawakened, will become as compelling as before, but it will be restrained now by devotion to a cause. When he speaks again, it will be with a new seriousness, a new explicitness, a new authority. From his young manhood a lucid thinker and a clever man before a crowd, he will stand forth hereafter as a political analyst and debater of surpassing power. The impact of a moral challenge, purging Lincoln of narrow partisanship and unsure purpose, is about to transform an honest, capable, but essentially self-centered small-town politician of self-developed but largely unsuspected talents into a statesman who will grow to world dimensions.

CHAPTER VIII

———◆●◆———

Lincoln Re-enters Politics

IMMEDIATELY upon the passage of the Kansas-Nebraska Act, frayed party ties began to snap. Thousands of Northern Democrats withdrew in indignation from their party. The Whig Party, already split along sectional lines, ceased to function as an effective national organization though it managed to maintain itself a little longer in some Northern states.

Inevitably, the antislavery castoffs came together. As early as February 28, 1854 a group of Whigs, Democrats, and Free-Soilers, meeting at Ripon, Wisconsin, resolved to organize a new party to resist the extension of slavery if the Kansas-Nebraska Bill became law. On May 9 several antislavery Congressmen, meeting in a Washington boarding-house, advocated the same course. On July 6 a great fusion mass meeting at Jackson, Michigan, adopted the name Republican in emulation of the Democratic-Republican Party of Thomas Jefferson. Thereafter hundreds of gatherings in the North took similar action. The fact that seven states later claimed to have been the birthplace of the Republican Party proves the spontaneity of the movement.

In some states fusion of the various free-soil elements into the new Republican Party was accomplished quickly; elsewhere it took a year or more. In Illinois the fusion movement began as early as March 18, 1854, when a mass meeting at Rockford voted for the formation of a new party. On August 1 a gathering at Ottawa adopted the name Republican. But both Whigs and

Democrats held back. Many free-soil Democrats still hoped to control their state organization instead of leaving it. And among old-line Whigs like Lincoln, an ingrained party loyalty, a reluctance to sacrifice prestige and position won through years of party service, and above all a hesitancy about identifying themselves with antislavery radicals, inspired a final effort to maintain their organization and quicken its feeble pulse. Consequently, the Republican Party in Illinois was originally composed almost exclusively of former Free-Soilers and abolitionists.

If the embryonic Republican Party looked to the principles of Jefferson for its ideals, the American or Know-Nothing Party, likewise an outgrowth of the political derangement of the times, was nurtured in intolerance and prejudice. Revolutions in continental Europe and famine in Ireland induced a swelling tide of emigration to America, and while many of the newcomers displayed energy and ambition and brought cultural enrichment to the land of their adoption, many others were ill-educated, improvident, and troublesome. Most of the Irish and large numbers of the Germans were Catholics. The Irish were often disorderly. Settling mostly in cities and remaining largely unassimilated, the new arrivals were regarded with hostility by many of the native-born.

As early as the 1840's numerous anti-foreign and anti-Catholic secret societies had sprung up in opposition to what their members ardently believed to be a threat to the Republic and its ideal of religious freedom. In the early fifties these dispersed units came together to form the American Party, popularly known as the Know-Nothings because members, when questioned about their organization, professed utter ignorance. With old party structures crumbling, many lovers of the Union, especially conservative Whigs both North and South, were attracted to the new party by its fervent nationalism. But if many persons joined from honest convictions, the rank and file were bigoted and ignorant. The tenets of the party were pernicious, and as the venom of intolerance seeped through the party organism and found outlet in provocative demonstrations, bloody riots broke out in several cities. Nevertheless, in the elections of 1854 the Know-Nothings swept New England, would have carried New York except for the opposition of Seward and Greeley, won a number of municipal elections, and rolled up impressive totals almost everywhere.

*

WHEN LINCOLN re-entered politics in 1854, he had no thought of a new political career for himself. His sole purpose was to assure the re-election of Richard Yates, of Jacksonville, who, as representative of the Seventh Congressional District, had been a staunch opponent of the Nebraska Bill. In late August, Lincoln took the stump in Yates's behalf, and, in an effort to rally the Whig forces, he and Stephen T. Logan agreed to run for the State Legislature.

From the time Douglas introduced the Nebraska Bill in the Senate, Lincoln, while pondering deeply on the slavery issue, had also studied the debates in Congress, pored over books in the State Library, and jotted down memoranda for future use. Now, as he toured the Congressional district in Yates's behalf, his speeches attracted more attention than ever before as men sensed his new-found power. Soon he received invitations to speak beyond the bounds of the district.

Meanwhile, with the adjournment of Congress, Douglas returned to Illinois to defend his record and inspirit his flagging followers. On the way he met denunciation everywhere. As his train rolled through the cities, he looked out to see his effigy in flames. In Chicago, where he now made his home, he was met with sullen hostility. So ugly was the public temper that friends feared for his safety, but the intrepid Douglas, resolved to meet his calumniators face to face, announced that he would speak at North Market Hall, in the heart of the Irish district, on the night of September 1.

Rumors of anticipated violence spread through the city. In a speech at Philadelphia, Douglas had denounced the Know-Nothings as a foul, subversive element and promised that all good Democrats would stand fast against the "allied forces of Abolitionism, Whiggism, Nativism, and religious intolerance, under whatever name and on whatever field they may present themselves." Wrathfully, the Know-Nothings bided their time. As preparations for Douglas's meeting went forward and Democratic wheelhorses let it be known that the embattled Irish would deal roughly with anyone who tried to badger Douglas, the Know-Nothings were said to be arming themselves with guns and knives. Less belligerent but no less determined were the anti-Nebraska forces, whipped up to hot resentment by reports that Douglas planned to obtain endorsement of his principles from a packed meeting and then claim that it spoke for Chicago.

Eight thousand people jammed Market House Square on the appointed night, so the meeting was held outdoors. Hundreds looked on from windows, balconies, and rooftops. The air was still and hot. Ominous silence greeted Douglas as he rose to speak, and as he proceeded, groans, catcalls, and hisses answered him. Douglas's temper flared. As hecklers interrupted him he laid aside his manuscript and began to bandy retorts. When he tried to continue speaking, the crowd drowned him out with jeers until at last he shook his fist at them and angrily strode from the platform.

But Douglas did not give up; antagonism always roused his fighting spirit. He began to tour the state, while opposition speakers dogged his trail. On September 26, when he arrived in Bloomington to speak, Lincoln was on hand to answer him. Jesse W. Fell, a friend of Lincoln's, proposed a joint debate. "No," Douglas replied, "I won't do it. I come to Chicago, I am met by an Abolitionist; I come to the center of the State and am met by an Old-Line Whig; I come to the South and am met by a Democrat. I can't hold the Whig responsible for what the Abolitionist says; I can't hold either responsible for what the Democrat says. . . . This is my meeting. The people came here to hear me, and I want to talk to them." So after listening to Douglas in the afternoon, Lincoln spoke that night.

On October 3 the State Fair opened in Springfield. For

weeks Douglas had been advertised to speak, and five thousand seats had been set up in a grove north of town. But it rained, and the meeting was held in the hall of the House of Representatives, which was packed to suffocation. Douglas gave essentially the same speech he had been making everywhere, a speech that was winning back large numbers of those who had lost faith in him. He began with the development of the West and explained the national problems it had raised. He recited the history of the Missouri Compromise. He claimed that his efforts to carry the Compromise line to the Pacific had been defeated by a combination of Northern Whigs, Free-Soilers, and abolitionists. Then came the Compromise of 1850, which, according to his assertion, substituted the principle of popular sovereignty for a geographical line delimiting slave and free territory. This new principle he had applied in good faith to the Kansas-Nebraska area, only to be assailed for wishing to extend slavery, when soil and climatic conditions had already determined that slavery could never exist there. He ended with an arraignment of the Know-Nothings.

Outside in the lobby Lincoln paced nervously back and forth while Douglas spoke, and as the meeting broke up he stood on the landing of the stairway to announce that next day he would reply to Senator Douglas. There was no relief from the stifling heat, but again the hall was packed as Lincoln, in his shirt-sleeves and without collar and tie, mounted the platform. Douglas sat in the front row; Lincoln had invited him to be present and to answer if he chose.

Lincoln was fully prepared, for he had written his speech, but it was not reported in its entirety until he repeated it twelve days later at Peoria, where he and Douglas met again. Thus it is known as his Peoria address. Lincoln began haltingly, and his voice was shrill, but as he proceeded his hesitancy disappeared and his tones became better modulated, earnestness and conviction making him forget himself. Soon he was wet with sweat, and his matted hair became tousled as he flung back his head. Time and again the hall rang with applause.

Lincoln began by showing how the founders of the Republic,

formulating a policy designed to put slavery in course of ultimate extinction, had excluded it from the national domain and assured the cutting off of the source of supply by providing for the eventual abolition of the slave trade. Then, as the nation acquired new land, a series of compromises had preserved as much territory as possible to freedom. Lincoln described the Kansas-Nebraska Act as a direct violation of one of these sacred compacts and as a grievous wrong. "Wrong in its direct effect," he asserted, "letting slavery into Kansas and Nebraska—and wrong in its prospective principle, allowing it to spread to every other part of the wide world, where men can be found inclined to take it. This *declared* indifference, but as I must think, covert *real* zeal for the spread of slavery, I can not but hate. I hate it because of the monstrous injustice of slavery itself. I hate it because it deprives our republican example of its just influence in the world—enables the enemies of free institutions, with plausibility, to taunt us as hypocrites— causes the real friends of freedom to doubt our sincerity and especially because it forces so many really good men amongst ourselves into an open war with the very fundamental principles of civil liberty—criticising the Declaration of Independence, and insisting that there is no right principle of action but *self-interest.*"

This high moral note that Lincoln sounded early in his speech re-echoed to the end of it. He showed no prejudice against the Southern people. "They are just what we would be in their situation," he declared. They were no more responsible for the existence of slavery than Northerners. He acknowledged fully and ungrudgingly their constitutional right to own slaves, and would give them any legislation for reclaiming fugitives "which should not, in its stringency, be more likely to carry a free man into slavery, than our ordinary criminal laws are to hang an innocent one."

Lincoln wished to distinguish clearly between his attitude toward the extension of slavery and his position with respect to slavery where it already existed. If all earthly power were given to him, he would not know what to do with slavery as an established institution. His first impulse would be to free the slaves and send them to Liberia, where the American Colonization Society had established a Negro republic. But he granted that whatever of hope this might offer as a long-range solution, its immediate accomplishment was physically impossible. "I think I would not hold one in slavery, at any rate," he said, as though he were thinking out the problem before his audience, "yet the point is not clear enough for me to denounce people upon. . . . It does seem to me that some system of gradual emancipation might be adopted; but for their tardiness in this, I will not undertake to judge our brethren of the south."

Taking up Douglas's arguments in justification of the repeal of the Missouri Compromise, Lincoln pointed out their fallacies. The chief argument—that the "sacred right of self-government" demanded that the people of a territory determine the slavery question for themselves—ignored the fact that the whole nation was concerned that the best use be made of the territories. The North wanted them for homes for free white people, which they would never be if slavery were allowed to enter them. Moreover, because five slaves were counted as the equal of three white persons in determining representation in Congress and in fixing the number of presidential electors, every increase in slave territory tended to augment this unfair inequality against the free states. "When I am told that I must leave it altogether to other people to say whether new partners are to be bred up and brought into the firm, on the same degrading terms against me," Lincoln insisted, "I respectfully demur."

"The doctrine of self government is right," Lincoln agreed, "absolutely and eternally right—but it has no just application, as here attempted. Or perhaps I should rather say that whether it has such just application depends upon whether a negro is *not* or *is* a man. If he is *not* a man, why in that case he who *is* a man may, as a matter of self-government, do just as he pleases with him. But if the negro *is* a man, is it not to that extent, a total destruction of self-government, to say that he too shall not govern *himself*? When the white man governs himself, that is self-government; but when he governs himself, and also governs

another man, that is *more* than self-government—that is despotism. If the negro is a *man*, why then my ancient faith teaches
me that 'all men are created equal,' and that there can be no
moral right in connection with one man's making a slave of
another."

As Lincoln probed, dissected, and dissevered in an effort to
find the very heart of the issue while the Nebraska Bill was under
discussion in Congress, he had concluded that the struggle for
human freedom was simply one aspect of the endless and world-
wide conflict between right and wrong. "Slavery is founded in
the selfishness of man's nature," he affirmed, "opposition to it
in his love of justice. These principles are an eternal antagonism,
and when brought into collision so fiercely as slavery extension
brings them, shocks, and throes, and convulsions must ceaselessly follow. Repeal the Missouri Compromise—repeal all
compromises—repeal the declaration of independence—repeal all
past history, you still can not repeal human nature. It still will be
the abundance of man's heart, that slavery extension is wrong,
and out of the abundance of his heart, his mouth will continue to
speak."

The proper course, in Lincoln's view, was to return to the old
faith in the equality of men voiced in the Declaration of Independence, and to restore the Missouri Compromise. "We thereby
restore the national faith, the national confidence, the national
feeling of brotherhood," he pleaded. To accomplish the restoration of the Compromise, Whigs, Free-Soilers, and abolitionists
must act together, even though the alliance might be distasteful
to some old-line Whigs. "Stand with anyone that stands *right*,"
Lincoln urged his fellow party members. "Stand with him while
he is right and *part* with him when he goes wrong. . . . Stand
with the Abolitionist in restoring the Missouri Compromise; and
stand *against* him when he attempts to repeal the fugitive slave
law. In the latter case you stand with the southern disunionist.
What of that? you are still right. In both cases you are right. In
both you stand on middle ground, and hold the ship level and
steady. . . . In both you are national and nothing less than

national. . . . To desert such ground, because of any company, is to be less than a whig—less than a man—less than an American."

*

ON THE same day that Lincoln spoke, the antislavery radicals, having taken the name Republican, had scheduled a meeting in Springfield to form a state organization. In order that they might hear Lincoln, however, they postponed their meeting till the next day. Herndon, who was in close touch with Ichabod Codding and Owen Lovejoy, leaders of the abolition forces, learned that they hoped to persuade Lincoln to join them because of his willingness to stand with them in restoring the Missouri Compromise. Herndon knew, however, that while Lincoln would co-operate with them to certain ends, he was unalterably opposed to anything suggesting a permanent alliance. He also knew that in view of the coming election Lincoln could not afford to offend the antislavery radicals. As an escape from the dilemma, Herndon suggested to Lincoln that he find business out of town. So early the next morning Lincoln hitched up Old Bob to his ramshackle buggy and started for court at Tremont. After listening to several fiery speeches, the Republicans adopted resolutions, several of which Lincoln disapproved, and elected him a member of their state central committee, an office he speedily declined.

*

WHILE the Springfield and Peoria addresses were high points in Lincoln's career, to Douglas they were merely part of the daily grind of speechmaking in what seemed more and more a lost cause. In the October elections the Democrats lost thirty-one Congressional seats in Pennsylvania, Ohio, and Indiana. The Know-Nothings cut in heavily in New England. And when Illinois voted on November 7, the Democrats elected only four of the nine Congressmen. More than that, the new Illinois Legislature, which would choose a United States senator to succeed James Shields, would contain forty-one regular Democrats and fifty-nine anti-Nebraska men of various affiliations. If the latter stuck together, they could elect a senator. Both Logan and Lincoln were elected to the Legislature, but Yates lost his seat in Congress by a narrow margin.

After meeting Douglas at Peoria, Lincoln spoke at several other places in central Illinois and once in Chicago. The strength of his argument, his fairness and moderation, projected him into a prominent place throughout the state and made him an obvious candidate for Shields's place. Nor was he loath to accept the honor. "That man who thinks Lincoln calmly sat down and gathered his robes about him, waiting for the people to call him," wrote Herndon, "has a very erroneous knowledge of Lincoln. He was always calculating, and always planning ahead. His ambition was a little engine that knew no rest. . . . His canvass . . . was marked by his characteristic activity and vigilance. During the anxious moments that intervened between the general election and the assembling of the Legislature he slept, like Napoleon, with one eye open."

Shortly after the make-up of the Legislature became known, Lincoln wrote from Clinton to Charles Hoyt, of Aurora, that "some friends here are really for me, for the U.S. Senate; and I should be very grateful if you could make a mark for me among your members. Please write me at all events, giving me the names, postoffices and '*political position*' of all members round about you. Direct to Springfield. Let this be confidential."

In the weeks that followed, Lincoln wrote many letters in the same vein. As quietly as possible he tried to learn the intentions of other possible candidates. He concluded that his chances were good. "I understand myself as having 26 commitals," he wrote to Elihu Washburne, Congressman from the Galena district, "and I do not think any other man has ten." But, he added, "I do not know that it is much advantage to have the largest number of votes at the start."

Actually, the situation was complex. While the anti-Nebraska men had a majority of thirteen in the Legislature, they were only loosely held together, with their ranks made up of old-line

Whigs like Lincoln, revolting Democrats, and a few Republicans. Their only common bond was aversion to the Kansas-Nebraska Act and a determination to chastise those who favored it. Old party loyalties remained strong; both Whigs and antislavery Democrats wanted to elect a senator from their own ranks.

Regarding Douglas's home state as crucial territory, the regular Democrats prepared to make a last-ditch fight, even though they were outnumbered in the Legislature. Convinced that Shields could never be re-elected, they planned to use him as a stalking-horse for their real candidate, Governor Joel A. Matteson, a wealthy man with a large personal following, who had taken no position on the Kansas question and might win back some of the revolting Democrats or attract certain of the Whigs, especially if one or the other of those factions should lose faith in the chances of its own candidate.

Lincoln was the undisputed champion of the Whigs, and he resigned from the Legislature in order to be eligible for the Senate race. But he faced a formidable opponent in Lyman Trumbull, lawyer, former state legislator, one-time Illinois secretary of state and Supreme Court justice, who had just been elected to the lower house of Congress as an anti-Nebraska Democrat. Trumbull had married Julia Jayne, Mary Lincoln's friend. Although he had far less support than Lincoln, his backers resolved to stay with him to the end and never to go for a Whig. Hating him for bolting the organization, the regular Democrats had marked him for destruction.

At three o'clock on Thursday, February 8, 1855, every inch of space was jammed as House and Senate convened in joint session. Mrs. Lincoln looked on from the gallery, along with Mrs. Matteson and her daughters. On the first ballot Lincoln had 44 votes, Shields 41, and Trumbull 5, with the remainder scattering. Five more ballots showed no significant change. Then suddenly, on the seventh ballot, the Democrats unmasked their strategy as Shields's votes went to Matteson. On the next two ballots Lincoln's vote dropped to 15, Trumbull climbed to 35, and Matteson had 47, only four short of election. Lincoln was clearly out of the running, and the next ballot might see Matteson victorious. At this juncture Lincoln instructed his remaining supporters to go for Trumbull; and on the next ballot the anti-Nebraska Democrat, picking up one additional supporter, was elected by just sufficient votes. Again Lincoln had come close to realizing an ambition, only to fail.

"I regret my defeat moderately," he confided to Elihu Washburne when he wrote the next day to explain what had taken place, "but I am not nervous about it. I could have headed off every combination and been elected, had it not been for Matteson's double game—and his defeat now gives me more pleasure than my own gives me pain. On the whole, it is perhaps as well for the general cause that Trumbull is elected. The Neb[raska] men confess that they hate it worse than any thing that could have happened. It is a great consolation to see them worse whipped than I am." To another friend Lincoln wrote that "a less good humored" man might have held out to the end. "I could not, however, let the whole political result go to ruin, on a point merely personal to myself." But he suffered deep disappointment as he turned once again to the law.

*

F O R   F I V E more years Lincoln made his living as a lawyer, but in his profession, as in politics, he found that he must adapt himself to changing times. By the decade of the fifties the West began to capitalize on those revolutionary industrial developments which had already brought such notable advancement in manufacturing, farming, communication, and transport to the New England and Middle Atlantic states. Telegraph lines, already extended from the seaboard to Chicago, Springfield, and St. Louis, would soon form a network linking every town of any size in Illinois. Labor-saving machinery was introduced on farms. New businesses were established, old ones expanded. Steamboats, ever more palatial, plied the Western rivers and the Great Lakes. As science and invention altered the pattern of American life, they also affected the law, making it more complex, demanding broader and more expert knowledge of its practitioners, bringing them larger fees.

The improved means of transportation for which Lincoln himself had striven became a reality as the iron tentacles of the railroad, reaching out to bind the Northwest to the cities of the North Atlantic seaboard, opened up new areas to settlement, changed the course of trade, and stimulated a mutually profitable exchange of goods between prairie farms and Eastern factories. From 1849 to 1857 nearly seventeen thousand miles of track were laid, mostly north of the Ohio River; by the latter year Lincoln could reach every town on the circuit by train. Farmers and businessmen of Ohio, Indiana, and Illinois now looked toward Boston, New York, and Philadelphia rather than New Orleans.

Running counter to the general east-west trend, the Illinois Central Railroad reached south from Chicago. Made possible largely through the efforts of Douglas, who obtained a large Federal grant of land to the states of Illinois, Mississippi, and Alabama to aid construction, by 1854 it operated from Chicago to Cairo, with a branch line pushing westward toward Galena. Had the entire road been completed sooner, it might have partially counteracted the influence of the Erie, the Pennsylvania, the New York Central, and the Baltimore & Ohio, which were drawing the Northwest away from the South and attaching it to the East, a development fraught with momentous political as well as economic consequences. But construction south of the Ohio River lagged, so that the road, instead of binding North and South, drew southern Illinois away from St. Louis, a city of Southern sympathies, into Chicago's orbit—likewise a development of extreme political importance.

In so far as Lincoln was concerned, the coming of the railroads not only made circuit travel quicker and easier, but brought him a new type of business. The Illinois Central employed him as a lobbyist to help obtain its charter from the State Legislature and retained him as an attorney for several years. He and Herndon also handled cases for the Ohio & Mississippi, the Rock Island, the Tonica & Petersburg, and the Chicago & Alton.

The largest fee Lincoln ever earned—five thousand dollars—was paid by the Illinois Central when he won a case involving the right of McLean County to tax the railroad's property. A provision of the company's charter exempted it from taxation for six years, in lieu of which it agreed to pay seven per cent of its gross earnings to the state. But officials of McLean County claimed that the exemption applied only to state taxes and proceeded to levy upon the road. Had the state Supreme Court upheld their action, every other county and every school district and township in which the road owned property would have levied against it, causing inevitable bankruptcy. In view of the crucial nature of the case and the work involved, Lincoln charged a reasonable fee, but he was obliged to sue to prove this to the company.

Another of Lincoln's cases held transcendent importance in the rivalry between the railroads and the river interests. On May 6, 1856 the steamboat *Effie Afton* crashed into a pier of the newly completed railroad bridge across the Mississippi at Rock Island and burned and sank with its cargo. A year later the owners of the vessel filed suit in the U.S. District Court at Chicago, claiming that the bridge obstructed navigation. Norman B. Judd, of Chicago, general counsel for the Rock Island Railroad, employed Lincoln to represent the bridge company.

The case had significance far beyond the property loss involved—it was a conflict of sections, economies, and eras. It arrayed the east-west railroad axis against the north-south river axis; New Orleans and St. Louis against Chicago and New York; the steamboat age against the new era of railroads. And it involved highly technical problems of mechanical engineering, bridge construction, river currents, and navigation. After listening to two weeks of testimony and four days of argument by counsel, the jury disagreed—a virtual victory for the railroad interests.

Many of Lincoln's railroad cases established general principles of law. With railroading in its pioneer stage, numerous decisions based upon his reasoning became precedents in future litigation.

In addition to Lincoln's railroad business, he handled cases for other types of corporations: banks, insurance companies, gas companies, large mercantile and manufacturing concerns. He was retained in a number of patent cases. Yet he was not a corporation lawyer in the sense of specializing in corporate practice. He still took business as it came, and opposed the corporate interests as often as he represented them.

Most important of Lincoln's patent cases was the suit of Cyrus H. McCormick of Chicago against John H. Manny of Rockford for $400,000 for alleged infringement of patent rights in a mechanical reaper. Several other manufacturers were making machines similar to McCormick's, and the litigation held such fateful consequences for these companies that they pooled their funds to fight to the limit. Each side retained eminent counsel: Edward M. Dickerson, of New York, and Reverdy Johnson, of Baltimore, appeared for McCormick, and George Harding, of Philadelphia, and Edwin M. Stanton, of Pittsburgh, for Manny. Suit was brought in the U.S. District Court at Chicago, and in keeping with the usual corporation practice of employing some local lawyer in good standing with the court, the Manny interests retained Lincoln, with a five-hundred-dollar advance. Since 1853, when rail connection was established, Lincoln had been practicing regularly before the Chicago District Court.

Finding himself arrayed with some of the outstanding legal talent of the country, Lincoln prepared a careful argument. By agreement, however, the litigants removed the case to Cincinnati, so that Lincoln was no longer essential to the defense. When he arrived at the Burnet House in Cincinnati, dressed in his usual careless manner and carrying a blue cotton umbrella with a ball on the end of the handle, Harding was scarcely courteous, and the irascible, churlish Stanton acted downright rude.

Naïvely assuming that he would have an important part in the trial, Lincoln felt mortified and hurt when his associates brusquely informed him that he would not be needed. Not the least resentful, however, he remained in Cincinnati through the trial, admiring the skill of the rival attorneys, marveling at their mastery of technical data, their close-knit arguments and easy speech.

In May 1858 word came to Lincoln while he was busy on the circuit that Hannah Armstrong, who had often welcomed him at mealtime and mended his socks and breeches, direly needed help. Her husband, Jack, Lincoln's rival and then friend of the New Salem days, was dead, and her son William, known as Duff, whom, as a baby, Lincoln had dandled on his knee, turning out to be a hard-drinking, harum-scarum youth, had been jailed on a charge of murder.

Near a camp meeting, drinking bouts had led to fights, and one witness claimed that by moonlight he had seen young Armstrong and another youth, James Norris, waylay one James Metzger on his way home, Norris striking him on the back of the head with a heavy stick and Armstrong whirling a slung-shot, a piece of metal fastened to a strap, against his right eye. Three days later Metzger died. Norris was immediately tried, convicted of manslaughter, and sentenced to eight years in the penitentiary. Armstrong's lawyers obtained a change of venue to Beardstown.

Lincoln dropped everything to hasten to the little river town. Hannah had no money for expensive lawyers, she warned Lincoln; she needed none, he told her. By means of an almanac he proved that the moon had almost set and the night was dark at the time the witness claimed to have seen Duff strike his alleged victim. Then Lincoln produced the owner of the slung-shot, who declared that he had thrown it away the day after the supposed murder at the spot where it had been found. Further testimony brought out the fact that Metzger, weaving drunk, had fallen off his horse several times on his way home.

With that, Lincoln went to the jury, speaking slowly, carefully, sincerely, reviewing the testimony, and concluding with a frank plea for the sympathy of the twelve men who held Duff's fate in their hands, as he told of his acquaintance with the Armstrongs, and of rocking Duff in his cradle. These were good people, he maintained—the boy Duff wild perhaps, like his father in his younger days, but incapable of murder. A lawyer who assisted the prosecution noted that tears brimmed Lincoln's eyes. "But they were genuine. . . . His terrible sincerity could not help but arouse the same passion in the jury." While Lincoln comforted Hannah, his arm around her shoulders, the jury brought in a verdict of acquittal.

*

As LINCOLN enhanced his reputation on the circuit, as his practice in the Federal courts increased in volume, and as practice in Chicago became part of his routine, his business in the state Supreme Court grew commensurately. By any standard of measurement—the number and significance of his cases, percentage of cases won and lost, the estimate of his fellow lawyers and the judges before whom he appeared—he ranked as a distinguished lawyer in a state that boasted an unusual array of outstanding legal talent.

CHAPTER IX

———•—————

A Political Plunge

WHEN Lincoln returned to his law practice after his defeat in 1855, he did not turn his back on politics as he had done before. His interest became more acute than ever. But with the party situation in a state of flux, he remained inactive. "Just now," he wrote to Owen Lovejoy, "I fear to do anything, lest I do wrong." This was his mood for several months, while he tried to gauge the capricious political currents, and watched events in Kansas, where popular sovereignty, undergoing its first practical test, was working out in a manner unforeseen by Douglas.

Before Kansas was opened to settlement, an Emigrant Aid Society had been organized in Massachusetts with the twofold purpose of filling Kansas with antislavery settlers and making a profit on the enterprise. Similar societies were formed in other Northern states, and as exaggerated rumors of the magnitude of the movement reached Missouri, proslavery men planned counter-action. Even before the passage of the Kansas-Nebraska Act several Missourians had slipped across the border to stake out claims to land. As the first trickle of Northern settlers made its way toward Kansas, secret societies, known variously as the Blue Lodge, the Social Band, the Sons of the South, sprang up in northwestern Missouri.

At first, proslavery settlers in Kansas outnumbered the free-soilers, but the Missourians were taking no chances. If fanatics and demagogues a thousand miles off proposed to abolitionize Kansas, the Missourians saw no reason why they should not take a hand too. In late November 1854, when a territorial delegate to Congress was to be elected, hundreds of Missourians swarmed across the border, stuffed the ballot boxes, and made certain of the election of the proslavery candidate.

As time passed, men from the Northern states, mostly from the Midwest, came in increasing numbers. Nor could threats or intimidation keep them back. For the most part these men had no antipathy toward the South, nor were they strongly antislavery. They wanted land. And they wanted no competition from Negroes, either slave or free. Had the settlement of Kansas proceeded peaceably, it would probably have come into the Union as a free state of moderate Southern sympathies.

By March 1855 the territory had a population of 8,500, of whom only 242 were slaves, and Governor Andrew H. Reeder set a date for the election of a territorial legislature. Again the Missourians swarmed in, this time in loose military formation, with cannon, guns, and banners and a commissary plentifully supplied with liquor. Of the 6,310 votes cast, 4,908 proved upon investigation to be fraudulent.

As in the previous election the Southern-rights men would probably have won without imposture. With a few exceptions Governor Reeder certified the results of the election, and the Pierce administration recognized the legality of the proslavery Legislature. Not so the free-soilers, however. They defied the "bogus" body and began to organize themselves into military companies. When the Legislature chose Lecompton as the capital of the territory, adopted the civil and criminal code of Missouri, and added drastic provisions making it a felony to deny the right to hold slaves and prescribing the death penalty for aiding a slave to escape, the free-state men set up an extra-legal government of their own. Tinder for a civil war was ready for the match in Kansas.

*

"CAN WE as a nation continue together permanently—forever—half slave and half free?" Lincoln asked George Robertson, professor of law at Transylvania University in Lexington, Kentucky, as he watched the ominous developments in Kansas. "The problem is too mighty for me," he admitted; "may God, in his mercy, superintend the solution."

Lincoln's old friend Joshua Speed wrote from Kentucky that, while he admitted the abstract wrong of slavery, yet as a Southerner he would see the Union dissolved before yielding his legal right to the slave, especially at the bidding of those who had no interest in the matter. Who bade him yield that right, Lincoln asked in reply. Surely Lincoln did not. Every time he touched the Ohio River or some other slave border he saw sights that horrified him. Yet he bit his lip and kept silent, just as he did when he saw a fugitive hunted down and taken back to bondage. Speed and other Southerners should appreciate how much the great body of Northern people crucified their feelings in order to maintain their loyalty to the Constitution and the Union.

Speed said that while he would hang the trouble-makers in Kansas, yet if that territory fairly voted for slavery, she must be admitted or the South would secede. That was not the point, Lincoln replied. Suppose Kansas should vote herself a slave state illegally? That would be the practical aspect of the question, the way it was working out. And if that happened, Lincoln had no intention of trying to dissolve the Union. He would oppose the admission of Kansas, but he would accept the result.

Lincoln confessed to Speed that he did not know just where he stood in party politics. "I think I am a whig," he wrote, "but others say there are no whigs, and that I am an abolitionist. When I was at Washington I voted for the Wilmot Proviso as good as forty times and I never heard of any one attempting to unwhig me for that. I now do no more than oppose the *extension* of slavery. I am not a Know-nothing. That is certain. How could I be? How can any one who abhors the oppression of negroes, be in favor of degrading classes of white people? Our progress in degeneracy appears to me to be pretty rapid. As a nation, we began by declaring that *'all men are created equal.'* We now practically read it 'all men are created equal, *except negroes.'* When the Know-Nothings get control, it will read 'all men are created equal, except negroes, *and foreigners and Catholics.'* When it comes to this I should prefer emigrating to some country where they make no pretense of loving liberty—to Russia, for instance, where despotism can be taken pure, and without the base alloy of hypocracy [*sic*]."

*

B Y T H E beginning of 1856, a presidential election year, Lincoln, his indecision ended, was ready to translate his thinking into action. On February 22, while a meeting of Republican leaders at Pittsburgh laid plans for the party's first national convention, he took the train to Decatur, where a group of anti-Nebraska editors were trying to organize the state for the coming election. As Lincoln had anticipated, several Republican editors appeared in the gathering. But Lincoln no longer shunned the radicals as he had done in 1854. His purpose now was to try to work with them —to unify the anti-Nebraska elements in Illinois. This demanded moderation. Through Lincoln's efforts extreme statements were kept out of the call for an anti-Nebraska state convention to meet at Bloomington on May 29.

When a Sangamon County convention met to select delegates to the Bloomington convention, Lincoln was away on the circuit. Most Illinoisans thought the Bloomington meeting would be dominated by abolitionists and that few moderates would attend. But Herndon, knowing Lincoln's desire for co-operative action, put his partner's name at the head of the list of 129 persons who signed the call. This shocked the old-line Whigs. Rushing to Herndon, Stuart asked if Lincoln had signed "that Abolition call." No, replied Herndon; he had taken the responsibility himself.

"Then you have ruined him," exclaimed Stuart angrily.

Somewhat frightened, Herndon wrote to Lincoln explaining

what he had done and informing him that the matter was causing
"a stir." Did Lincoln approve his action?

"All right; go ahead," came the reply. "Will meet you,
radicals and all."

While preparations for the Bloomington meeting went
forward, telegraph and newspapers reported fresh outrages in
Kansas. "Border ruffians," serving as a sheriff's posse, had invaded the free-soil "capital" of Lawrence, burned down the Free
State Hotel, which was built more like a fortress than a hostelry,
wrecked the presses of the *Herald of Freedom*, and pillaged private houses.

The week before the Bloomington meeting, Northern newspapers were lurid with accounts of the vicious beating administered to Senator Charles Sumner of Massachusetts by Congressman Preston Brooks of South Carolina as chastisement for a
ferocious antislavery speech in which Sumner had abused a Southern Senator and the state of South Carolina. Affairs were at a crisis
stage as delegates converged on Bloomington.

Lincoln feared that few moderates would show up, but he
found all shades of antislavery opinion represented—old-line
Whigs, bolting Democrats, Free-Soilers, Know-Nothings, and
abolitionists. As he walked to the Alton depot with a fellow delegate to see who was coming from Chicago, he stopped in a jewelry
store and bought his first pair of spectacles. When Norman B.
Judd, an anti-Nebraska Democrat, stepped off the train, Lincoln
whispered to his companion: "That is the best sign yet. Judd is a
trimmer."

The convention assembled in Major's Hall, over a store
near the courthouse square. The platform was the work of the
conservatives and accorded with Lincoln's views. He was influential in the selection of William H. Bissell, an anti-Nebraska
Democrat, as the candidate for Governor, and in drawing up the
remainder of the slate. Then came the usual oratory, and calls
for Lincoln to speak.

Lincoln knew what was needed—a speech that would weld

the discordant factions into a vigorous party. Outwardly calm,
inside he was on fire. The audience sat enthralled. Men listened
as though transfixed. Reporters forgot to use the pencils in their
hands, so that no complete and authentic record of what may
have been his greatest speech has ever been found. At the end
the hall rocked with applause. The Republican Party was reborn
in Illinois, even though, because of its radical origin, Lincoln and
most of the other delegates still avoided the use of that name.

*

F IVE D AYS after the Bloomington convention the Democrats
met at Cincinnati in the first national convention ever held in
the West. Declaring that the Kansas-Nebraska Act embodied
the "only sound solution of the slavery question," the platform
made popular sovereignty the party faith. James Buchanan, of
Pennsylvania, an august party wheelhorse whose absence from
the country as Minister to England during the recent trying times
made him a noncontroversial figure, won the nomination for President, with John C. Breckinridge, of Kentucky, as his running
mate.

The Republicans met at Philadelphia on June 17 to choose
their first national ticket and call for a political new deal. The
same elements that came together at Bloomington were present,
but radicals of the stripe of Giddings, Codding, and Lovejoy
exerted a stronger influence than they did in Illinois. Blaming
the Democrats for the fraud and violence in Kansas, the platform
branded slavery a relic of barbarism and opposed its extension
to the territories. Colorful John C. Frémont, of California,
known as "the Pathfinder" because of his explorations in the
West, was selected to head the ticket. He was not Lincoln's
choice. The Illinoisan wanted a more conservative candidate who
could attract the old-line Whigs, and preferred Justice John
McLean of the United States Supreme Court, before whom he
practiced in the Circuit Court at Chicago.

In the balloting for Vice President the Illinois delegation

promoted Lincoln strongly as a favorite son. He received 110
votes on the initial ballot. But he was not sufficiently well
known. On the second ballot the convention swung to William L.
Dayton, of New Jersey.

The Know-Nothings split. An anti-Nebraska Northern group
seceded when they were unable to control the party convention,
and went over to Frémont. The regulars nominated ex-President
Millard Fillmore and Andrew J. Donelson, of Tennessee. As a
former Whig, Fillmore appealed to cautious, Union-loving people
of moderate antislavery inclinations. His candidacy was certain
to split the free-soil vote. As a party, however, the Know-
Nothings were definitely on the wane.

*

"IT WOULD have been easier for us, I think, had we got
McLean," Lincoln wrote to Lyman Trumbull soon after the
Republican convention. Publicly, however, he endorsed Frémont
and threw himself wholeheartedly into the contest. During the
next three months he made more than fifty speeches in all parts
of Illinois, devoting his most strenuous efforts to the critical
central counties.

It was a feverish campaign, reminiscent of the Log Cabin
and Hard Cider contest of 1840, with bands, fireworks, rallies,
parades, and banners. Thousands came together to hear the
rival orators. Yet through all the fanfare rolled a solemn overtone
of earnestness. The issues were momentous for the nation.

Accentuating the high pitch of excitement came stridently
discordant notes from Kansas. Up to this time, notwithstanding
all the lawlessness, few lives had been lost in that territory. Now,
however, murder stalked the plains. The trouble was not due
altogether to proslavery and free-soil hostility. Some of it was the
usual frontier turbulence. Much of it involved cupidity for land.
Neither side was guiltless, but the chief trouble-maker was old
John Brown, an abolitionist fanatic of doubtful sanity. In a
sudden foray he and his sons killed five unarmed men in cold

blood, and as the proslavery men retaliated, Kansas experienced a reign of terror. Crops were burned, horses stolen, men cut down from ambush in venomous small-scale warfare.

Partisan editors, glorying in new power as they entered the modern age of journalism and began to take over the role of the preachers as molders of public opinion, played up the Kansas troubles with everything at their command. Special correspondents shocked the country with exaggerated news reports. Horace Greeley, Joseph Medill, William Cullen Bryant, and James Gordon Bennett touched off inflammatory editorials. The guerrilla warfare in Kansas was bad enough, but far worse was the hysterical war of words.

Rabble-rousing politicians quickly turned the situation to account. But this was not true of Lincoln. He did not play the agitator. His purpose was to win the antislavery Fillmore men to Frémont by convincing them that Fillmore had no chance. The choice must lie between Buchanan and Frémont, and every anti-Democratic vote for Fillmore helped Buchanan.

It was not an easy task. The Democrats denounced the Republicans as a sectional party, and Southern hotheads threatened secession if Frémont won. This was by no means the prevailing Southern sentiment; most Southerners were still loyal Unionists. But when James M. Mason, of Virginia, shouted that "immediate, absolute, eternal separation" must be the Southern answer to Frémont's election, and when Governor Henry A. Wise of Virginia proposed an emergency conference of Southern governors, peace-loving men became cautious.

Forced to the defensive, Lincoln tried to refute the charge of sectionalism and to make light of the threat to the Union. "We don't want to dissolve it, and if you attempt it, *we won't let you,*" he warned the Southern disunionists in a speech at Galena. "With the purse and the sword, the army and navy and treasury in our hands and at our command, you couldn't do it. . . . All this talk about the dissolution of the Union is humbug—nothing but folly. We won't dissolve the Union, and you shan't."

But many of Lincoln's Northern listeners were not convinced. If they could not go for Buchanan, it seemed safer to vote for Fillmore.

In a memorandum on sectionalism, which Lincoln unquestionably used in his speeches, few of which were fully reported, he pointed up the naked issue that was to be decisive of peace or war, though he did not yet expect to see armed conflict. Granting that slavery had become a sectional question, how could the issue be resolved, he asked. Only by one side or the other yielding. Who should yield? There could be only one answer. The side that was morally wrong. Right could never yield to wrong.

Yet Lincoln blamed the South for the existence of slavery no more than he blamed the North. Slavery was a national evil. And a national admission of guilt would open the way to a long-range solution, acceptable to both North and South. Without such an admission, he feared that war might come.

*

B Y L A T E summer it became evident that Buchanan would carry the South and that Frémont would win in New England and New York. The pivotal states were Pennsylvania, Indiana, and Illinois. Douglas rushed out to help save Illinois, and after weeks of speechmaking reported to Buchanan that while he was in the midst of the most exciting contest ever witnessed in his home state, the Democrats were now assured of victory.

The result confirmed his prediction. Buchanan carried Illinois two to one over Frémont, the latter trailing Fillmore by 500 votes. He also carried Pennsylvania, Indiana, and New Jersey. Frémont won all the other Northern states. The border state of Maryland went to Fillmore. The electoral vote tallied Buchanan 174, Frémont 114, and Fillmore 8. If Frémont could have attracted the old-line Whigs he would have won in Illinois, for Bissell was elected Governor by 5,000 majority. The Republicans captured all the state offices, but because of an outdated apportionment of seats, the Democrats regained control of the Legislature.

The Republicans showed surprising strength throughout the

North. If they could have carried Pennsylvania and either Illinois or Indiana, they would have won. Speaking at Chicago about a month after the election, Lincoln pointed out that Buchanan's popular vote was 400,000 less than the combined total for Frémont and Fillmore, and pleaded for unity in 1860. That should be less difficult to attain, for the Know-Nothings were not likely to prove a factor any more. Like locusts, one observer commented, "They came out of the dark ground, crawled up the sides of the trees, ate their foliage in the night, chattered with a croaking harshness, split open their backs and died."

As for Lincoln, two years had seen him make tremendous strides. At the time of his emergence from retirement in 1854, his influence scarcely extended beyond Sangamon County. Now he was the foremost Republican in Illinois, with a reputation spreading to neighboring states. During the campaign he received invitations to speak in Wisconsin, Iowa, and Indiana, and did deliver one out-of-state address at Kalamazoo, Michigan. As a result of the vice-presidential vote at Philadelphia, his name became known to thousands. Outside of Illinois, however, he was still little more than a name.

CHAPTER X

———◄•►———

Defeated for the Senate

BY THE TIME of James Buchanan's inauguration, on March 4, 1857, a strong Governor, John W. Geary of Pennsylvania, backed by United States troops, had quelled the disorders in Kansas. With these troubles and the election excitement ended, the country became relatively calm once more.

As Buchanan saw his problem, it was to unite and invigorate the Democratic Party in order to meet the challenge of the virile young Republicans. But popular sovereignty, chief tenet of the party faith, was itself a divisive factor. Northern Democrats, adopting Douglas's view, maintained that the first settlers in a territory, acting through their first legislature or any subsequent one, could admit or exclude slavery as they chose. Southerners, on the other hand, denied this. Neither Congress nor a territorial legislature, according to their contention, could keep slavery out of a territory. Only when the people were ready for statehood and framed their state constitution could slavery be prohibited, if the people so decided. Both sides demanded that Buchanan pronounce on this question in his inaugural address. For the sake of party harmony, however, he wished to avoid it if possible, though he inclined to the Southern opinion.

At this very time the question was before the United States Supreme Court in the case of the slave Dred Scott, who, under secret abolition auspices, was suing for his freedom on the ground that he had been taken to and had resided in a territory where slavery was prohibited by the Missouri Compromise. Learning through correspondence with members of the Court that they intended to pronounce on the powers of Congress and territorial legislatures over slavery in the territories, Buchanan simply stated in his inaugural that the question was now, "happily, a matter of little practical importance" because it would soon be "speedily and finally" decided by the Court. "To their decision," he promised, "in common with all good citizens, I shall cheerfully submit, whatever this may be." President Pierce had made a similar statement in his last annual message.

Two days after the inauguration Chief Justice Roger B. Taney, gaunt and sepulchral in appearance, gentle and composed in manner, read his opinion before a packed courtroom. It was a five-to-four decision. The first part of Taney's opinion was a historical survey, designed to demonstrate that, while the position of the Negro had been much improved in recent years, before and at the time of the adoption of the Constitution Negroes were looked on as such inferior beings that "they had no rights which the white man was bound to respect." They were not included within the meaning of the pronouncement of the Declaration of Independence that "all men are created equal," asserted Taney, in contradiction of Lincoln's belief, nor were they recognized as having any standing under the Constitution. They were not citizens of any state, and hence not citizens of the United States. Therefore, not being a citizen, Scott had no right to sue in a Federal court. The case must be dismissed.

Taney might have ended there. Anticipating a contrary opinion from certain of the justices who had declared their intention of pronouncing on the territorial question, however, he went on to declare that the Missouri Compromise was void. The only power of Congress over the territories was to prepare them for statehood. It must act strictly within the Constitution, which guaranteed citizens the right to property. Slaves were property, and Congress had no power to exclude them from a territory. Consequently, that part of the Missouri Compromise prohibiting slavery north of 36° 30' was of no effect. If Congress could not prohibit slavery in a territory, it followed that a territorial legislature, created by act of Congress, likewise had no power to do so. The decision opened all the national domain to slavery.

The Republicans broke out in wrathful uproar, for the decision cut the ground from under their feet. Of what use now was a platform opposing the extension of slavery to the territories? How could slavery be kept out? Horace Greeley sneered at the decision as no more entitled to respect than if it had emanated from some Washington barroom. Other Republican editors called it "infamous," "a judicial lie." All over the North resounded the charge that the decision was a conspiracy of the slave power—another step in a well-planned plot to legalize slavery everywhere.

Most virulent were the abolitionists of the Garrisonian school. Enraged at the Court's pronouncement, they clamored for disunion more noisily than had the Southern fire-eaters. "No Union with slaveholders," cried Garrison; while Wendell Phillips declared the Union to be "accursed of God—away with it." Secession meetings were held in New England and elsewhere in the free states. Lincoln and other moderate Republicans who had been denouncing the secession spirit in the South were embarrassed to have it voiced so fiercely in the North.

The decision also troubled Douglas and the Northern Democrats. What became of popular sovereignty if settlers had no means of excluding slavery from a territory? Under this decision, as Lincoln hastened to point out, popular sovereignty could not be exercised until the statehood stage. Since no one had ever denied the people of a territory the right to frame the sort of constitution they wanted when they formed a state government, what did popular sovereignty give them that they had not always enjoyed? In a later speech Lincoln declared that the Dred Scott decision made popular sovereignty as thin as a homeopathic soup made by boiling the shadow of a pigeon that had starved to death.

But Douglas quickly adjusted his reasoning to conform to the Court's decision. In a speech at Springfield on June 7, 1857, he commended the high tribunal. By pronouncing the Missouri

Compromise unconstitutional, the Court had vindicated his action in repealing it and had confirmed the principle of popular sovereignty. For the decision did not debar the people from excluding slavery. The right of a slaveowner to bring slaves into a territory became a "barren and a worthless right, unless sustained, protected and enforced by appropriate police regulations and local legislation." By refusing to give slavery such local protection, the people could effectually exclude it, Douglas claimed.

Douglas agreed with Taney that the signers of the Declaration of Independence had not meant to include Negroes in their equalitarian pronouncement. Under Lincoln's interpretation of that document, said Douglas, complete political and social equality for Negroes, including the right to intermarry with whites, must be the end result. Douglas conceded that the Negro was entitled to certain rights and privileges. But, he asserted, in the manner of some persons of our own time, these must be determined by the white people of each state and territory, according to the Negro's capabilities, instead of being prescribed by a policy of general application such as Lincoln advocated.

On the night of June 26 Lincoln replied to Douglas in a speech at Springfield. He did not hold with those who would resist the Dred Scott decision; the Supreme Court must be respected and obeyed. But this decision was erroneous. The Court had reversed itself before, and the Republicans would do what they could to have it do so in this case. Meanwhile they would offer no resistance. Lincoln defended his interpretation of the Declaration of Independence. Of course the Fathers had not meant to assert "the obvious untruth" that everyone is equal in all respects. "They meant to set up a standard maxim for free society, which should be familiar to all, and revered by all; constantly looked to, constantly labored for, and even though never perfectly attained, constantly approximated, and thereby constantly spreading and deepening its influence and augmenting the happiness and value of life to all people of all colors everywhere." Lincoln protested the "counterfeit logic" of Douglas's claim that Republicans stood for complete racial equality. Because Lincoln did not want a black woman for a slave, it did not follow that he wanted her for a wife. "In some respects she certainly is not my equal," Lincoln conceded; "but in her natural right to eat the bread she earns with her own hands without asking leave of any one else, she is my equal, and the equal of all others."

Since 1857 was an off year in politics in Illinois, this was Lincoln's only speech, but he looked ahead and planned constantly. Not only did he believe that Douglas's defeat in the senatorial contest of the coming year would be the most effective rebuff to the wrongful national policy Douglas had sponsored, but, as the logical man to oppose the Little Giant, he was intensely anxious for the senatorship. While he carried on his court work he never overlooked a chance to promote his candidacy.

But events took an ominous turn. Again Kansas intruded. For a time the political situation became so deranged that it seemed that Douglas, rather than Lincoln, might carry the Republican banner in Illinois.

*

O N J U N E 15, 1857 an election of delegates to frame a state constitution took place in Kansas. The antislavery men could easily have won. But they doubted the good faith of the territorial Legislature that had called the election, and did not wish to recognize it. Most of them refused to be registered. The proslavery party elected all the delegates.

President Buchanan had promised that when the Kansas constitution was drafted it should be submitted to a vote of the people. Robert J. Walker, of Mississippi, had accepted the governorship of the territory expressly on that condition. Now, however, with the proslavery party in absolute control of the constitutional convention, radical Southern politicians in Washington and proslavery leaders in Kansas determined to push their advantage to the limit. Meeting at Lecompton, the Kansas convention inserted a proslavery provision in the constitution, and proposed to submit, not the constitution as a whole, as Buchanan and Walker had pledged, but simply the provision respecting slavery. On the remainder of the document, including a clause protecting the right of property in slaves already in the territory, the people were not to be allowed to vote.

Under Southern pressure, Buchanan weakened. After all, according to the President's way of thinking, submission of the slavery clause would essentially fulfill his promise. He had become weary of the subject and thought the country must be, too. It threatened the unity of his party and the peace of the nation. Here might be a way to be rid of it quickly. Deciding that the Lecompton plan must be carried through, Buchanan endorsed it in the annual message he was preparing, and, without consulting Douglas, who as chairman of the Senate Committee on Territories would have to bear the responsibility for the party's policy, telegraphed his decision to party leaders in Kansas.

Resolved to see fair play in Kansas, Douglas hastened from Chicago to Washington and went immediately to the White House, where an angry clash took place. Determined to end the Kansas controversy and to make support of his Lecompton policy a test of party loyalty, Buchanan threatened to purge Douglas if he rebelled. Douglas implied that he would break Buchanan if he tried it. As titular head of the party, with the patronage under his control, Buchanan exercised vast power. But Douglas was powerful, too. In the Democratic nominating convention of the previous year Douglas, as Buchanan's most formidable rival for the Presidency, had withdrawn his name in order to break a deadlock and allow Buchanan to obtain the honor. But Buchanan, jealous of his rival's influence in party affairs, had rewarded Douglas by slighting him in patronage. The Little Giant resented this. The suppressed hostility between the two now flared into open flame. It would be a battle to the death.

*

WHEN THE free-state men in Kansas refused to vote in the referendum, the slavery provision of the constitution was adopted overwhelmingly. A fortnight later, however, the free-soilers voted solidly for legislative and state officials and elected most of their candidates. Also—without authority of law—they voted down the whole Lecompton constitution by ten thousand majority. But when Kansas applied for statehood under that pro-slavery instrument, Buchanan not only urged Congress to accept it as the legal expression of the people's will, but used all the pressure at his command to push it through. Douglas angrily opposed the "fraud" as a travesty on popular sovereignty. "If this Constitution is to be thrust down our throats," he threatened in a Senate speech, ". . . I will resist it to the last. . . . I will stand on the great principle of Popular Sovereignty, which declares the right of all people to be left perfectly free to form and regulate their domestic institutions in their own way. I will follow that principle wherever its logical consequences may take me, and I will defend it against assault from any and all quarters."

The Democracy split behind the rival leaders. During the Congressional session of 1857–8 Douglas, aligning himself with the Republicans, made such a valiant fight and became so embittered against the administration that certain influential Republican leaders in the East thought their party should support him in his campaign for re-election.

Buchanan could not push his program through, and finally gave way to the extent of endorsing a face-saving measure known as the English bill. This called for the immediate admission of Kansas as a state provided the people voted to approve the Lecompton constitution, including the slavery provision, but put off admission until such time as Kansas had the usual population required for statehood—some 93,000 as compared with its actual number of 35,000—if they rejected it. Douglas did not relax his opposition in the slightest, but the measure passed. Whereupon the people of Kansas rejected the Lecompton constitution decisively.

*

As early as January 1858 Lyman Trumbull reported to Lincoln that Senator Seward was friendly to the Little Giant's candidacy for re-election. Later, rumor had it that Douglas and Seward had struck a bargain to re-elect Douglas to the Senate and make the shrewd New Yorker President in 1860. Republicans like Anson Burlingame and Henry Wilson of Massachusetts were reported to be courting Douglas; and at Douglas's own dinner table, so it was said, Simon Cameron, Republican boss of Pennsylvania, had promised to persuade the Illinois Republicans not to oppose him. Horace Greeley, whose *New York Tribune* circulated widely in Illinois, pleaded that Douglas had earned Republican support. The movement became so formidable that Lincoln seemed about to be side-tracked again.

In Illinois, however, outside "interference" was resented. The *Chicago Tribune* commented that there "seems to be a considerable notion pervading the brains of the political wet nurses at the East, that the barbarians of Illinois cannot take care of themselves." To support Douglas would be to destroy the Republican Party in Illinois. The *Chicago Journal* warned Easterners to keep hands off; Illinoisans would "deal with Senator Douglas in their own way." Other editors throughout the state voiced similar sentiments.

Even Illinois Republican politicians who admired Douglas for his splendid stand against the administration did not want him for their leader. They had been fighting him too long. The Republican Party in Illinois was an anti-Douglas party; opposition to Douglas formed the strongest tie uniting its diverse elements. "It is asking too much of human nature to bear," State Auditor Jesse K. Dubois wrote to Trumbull, "to now surrender to Judge Douglas after having driven him by force of public opinion to what he has done, to quickly let him step foremost in our ranks now and make us all take back seats."

Lincoln regarded the Douglas movement not only as a menace to his own candidacy, but as a threat to Republican integrity as well. What if Douglas had acted with the Republicans in opposing the Lecompton constitution, he asked in numerous letters to party leaders. He was still the chief advocate of popular sovereignty and still approved the Dred Scott decision, both of which were hateful to Republicans. Douglas and Buchanan were both wrong, and the fact that Buchanan was "a little farther wrong of the two" did not call for Republican support of Douglas. Such a course would be a surrender of the fundamental principles of the party. "As yet I have heard of no republican here going over to Douglas," Lincoln wrote to Trumbull, "but if the [New York] *'Tribune'* continues to din his praises into the ears of its five or ten thousand republican readers in Illinois, it is more than can be hoped that all will stand firm."

Although busy with professional work, in February 1858 Lincoln took time for a hurried trip to Chicago to consult Norman B. Judd, chairman of the state central committee, who had just returned from Washington. Herndon went east to talk with Republican leaders and report their sentiments to Lincoln.

Even if Easterners, with only superficial acquaintance with the situation in Illinois, were willing to sacrifice Lincoln, the Republican leaders of his state remained staunchly loyal to him. Trumbull reminded former antislavery Democrats of how Lincoln had stepped aside for him in 1855, and party editors descanted on the same theme. With one senatorship held by Trumbull, a former Democrat, it was generally conceded that the other rightfully belonged to an ex-Whig. Lincoln had worked faithfully for the party without reward; he was Douglas's most troublesome antagonist on the stump. If Douglas wished to come over openly to the Republicans, declared the *Chicago Tribune*, they would give him a place in the cabinet of their next President—but not the senatorship. Lincoln had earned that.

During the early summer ninety-five Republican county conventions named Lincoln as their choice for senator. And when the state convention met at Springfield on June 16, a resolution, unanimously adopted and framed as a rebuff to pro-Douglas sentiment in the East, declared that "Abraham Lincoln is the first and only choice of the Republicans of Illinois for the United States Senate as the successor of Stephen A. Douglas."

This did not constitute a nomination. Senators were still elected by state legislatures and nominated in legislative party caucus. But with the party speaking with such certainty, Lincoln's nomination was assured.

*

LINCOLN had expected the convention to endorse him and was ready with a speech. He had prepared it carefully. Some friends whom he favored with a preview warned that it went too far; but, relying on his own judgment, as he usually did, he decided to deliver it as written.

"If we could first know *where* we are, and *whither* we are tending," he began, "we could then better judge *what* to do, and *how* to do it. We are now far into the *fifth* year, since a policy was initiated, with the *avowed* object, and *confident* promise, of putting an end to slavery agitation. Under the operation of that policy, that agitation has not only, *not ceased*, but has *constantly augmented*. In *my* opinion, it *will* not cease, until a *crisis* shall have been reached, and passed. 'A house divided against itself cannot stand.' I believe this government cannot endure permanently half *slave* and half *free*. I do not expect the Union to be dissolved— I do not expect the house to *fall*—but I do expect it will cease to be divided. It will become *all* one thing, or *all* the other. Either the *opponents* of slavery, will arrest the further spread of it, and place it where the public mind shall rest in the belief that it is in course of ultimate extinction; or its *advocates* will push it forward, till it shall become alike lawful in *all* the States, *old* as well as *new*, North as well as *South*."

"Have we no *tendency* to the latter condition?" Lincoln asked; and then proceeded to trace the alarming advance of slavery in the last four years. Up to this time he had not joined the clamor about the existence of a proslavery conspiracy. Now, however, noting how nicely everything was working out—Douglas's repeal of the Missouri Compromise, Franklin Pierce's and James Buchanan's adjurations that the people accept the Supreme Court's decision respecting the power of Congress over slavery in the territories, and finally Roger Taney's opinion itself—he was inclined to believe the whole process had been planned.

"We can not absolutely *know* that all these exact adaptations are the result of preconcert," he granted. "But when we see a lot of framed timbers, different portions of which we know have been gotten out at different times and different places and by different workmen—Stephen, Franklin, Roger and James, for instance—and when we see these timbers joined together, and see they exactly make the frame of a house or a mill, all the tenons and mortices exactly fitting, and all the lengths and proportions of the different pieces exactly adapted to their respective places, and not a piece too many or too few—not omitting even scaffolding—or, if a single piece be lacking, we can see the place in the frame exactly fitted and prepared to yet bring such piece in—in *such* a case, we find it impossible to not *believe* that Stephen and Franklin and Roger and James all understood one another from the beginning, and all worked upon a common *plan* or *draft* drawn up before the first lick was struck."

The missing piece, Lincoln suggested, the one thing needed to make slavery legal everywhere, was another Supreme Court decision declaring that the Constitution did not allow a state to exclude slavery. "Welcome or unwelcome," Lincoln foreboded, "such decision *is* probably coming, and will soon be upon us, unless the power of the present political dynasty shall be met and overthrown."

Although Lincoln could count on the support of the state Republican leaders, he was gravely concerned lest Douglas make inroads on the rank and file. The last part of his speech asserted Douglas's unfitness as an antislavery leader. How could Douglas oppose the advance of slavery when he had said repeatedly that he cared not whether it was voted up or voted down? How ineffective his principle of popular sovereignty had proved to be! Douglas was a great man—a lion, in fact—but for this sort of work "a *caged* and *toothless* one." "A *living dog* is better than a *dead lion*," declared Lincoln in a none too felicitous phrase. Stand firm, he pleaded in closing. The Republican cause must be entrusted to its friends. Sooner or later, victory would surely come.

While this was one of Lincoln's most historic speeches,

owing largely to his use of the Biblical phrase, it was not altogether wise or just. As his friends foresaw, it marked him as a radical in certain quarters when in fact he was conservative. In implying a conspiracy for the extension of slavery he went beyond the facts. And in giving the impression that Douglas's popular-sovereignty principle had been intended to help spread slavery he was unfair. But this is to judge him in the light of present knowledge. To him the advance of slavery seemed resistless and well planned.

*

IN WASHINGTON, when Senator Douglas heard of Lincoln's nomination, he predicted: "I shall have my hands full. He is the strong man of his party—full of wit, facts, dates—and the best stump speaker, with his droll ways and dry jokes, in the West." And, to make Douglas's task more difficult, the Buchanan administration, intent on destroying him politically, was setting up a rival organization in Illinois. Democratic legislative candidates pledged to oppose Douglas were put forward in every district. Douglas men were ousted from Federal jobs. Postmasters, United States marshals, and editors of Democratic papers were dragooned into the assault. Money poured into the state. The Little Giant faced a battle for survival.

But Douglas had never been more popular with his constituents, who were fired by his fight for fair play. When he opened his campaign in Chicago on July 8, 1858, a frenzied demonstration greeted him. Speaking from the balcony of the Tremont House, he looked out on a sea of eager faces. Lincoln was on hand to listen.

Douglas took immediate issue with Lincoln's "house-divided" doctrine. It invited a war of sections, he declared. Why could the nation not continue part slave and part free, as it had for eighty-two years? Uniformity of local institutions was neither essential nor desirable. Autonomy in domestic concerns was the fundamental principle of our Federal system. It constituted the nation's strength.

The American government had been founded on the white basis, Douglas asserted once again. "It was made by the white man, for the white man, to be administered by the white man." To be sure, the Negro was entitled to all the rights he could exercise consistently with the safety of society, but each state must determine what those rights should be. So, concluded Douglas, the issues between him and Lincoln were "direct, unequivocal, and irreconcilable. He goes for uniformity in our domestic institutions, for a war of sections, until one or the other shall be subdued. I go for the principle of the Kansas-Nebraska bill, the right of the people to decide for themselves."

The following night Lincoln spoke in Chicago before a crowd he estimated to be as large as that which welcomed Douglas and "five times as enthusiastic." Once more he pointed out the ineffectual nature of popular sovereignty in the face of the Dred Scott decision. He denied Douglas's claim to the major credit for defeating the Lecompton constitution; the Little Giant and his followers had furnished a mere three votes against it in the Senate compared with the Republicans' twenty, and only twenty in the House to the Republicans' ninety or more.

Lincoln insisted that Douglas drew wrong inferences from his "house-divided" passage. Lincoln had merely offered a prediction, "it may have been a foolish one"; he had not expressed a wish. He had said a hundred times that the people of the North should not meddle with slavery in the states where it existed. He did not favor enforced uniformity in local institutions. But slavery must be put in course of ultimate extinction by confining it where it existed. The philosophy of freedom or the philosophy of slavery must prevail. "Let us then turn this government back into the channel in which the framers of the Constitution originally placed it," he urged. "Let us discard all this quibbling about this man and the other man—this race and that race and the other race being inferior . . . and unite as one people throughout this land, until we shall once more stand up declaring that all men are created equal."

*

WITH THESE two eloquent addresses by the rival candidates, the campaign got under way. Lincoln and Douglas both remained in Chicago for a few days to consult advisers and complete their plans. Then Douglas started downstate, with Lincoln on his trail, for the strategy devised by the Republican state central committee called for Lincoln to follow Douglas and answer him wherever possible in order to take advantage of the crowds he drew.

Douglas traveled in a private car, gaily decorated with banners and signs. Accompanying him were his beautiful wife, his secretaries, stenographers, and an ever changing retinue of henchmen. Coupled to his train was a flatcar mounting a brass cannon served by two young men in semimilitary dress; and as the train approached the prairie towns the gun crashed out to inform the local citizenry that Douglas was on his way. Often traveling on the same train that drew the Little Giant's private car sat Lincoln, riding as an ordinary passenger.

At Bloomington, Lincoln listened while Douglas repeated the arguments of his Chicago speech. At Springfield, Douglas spoke in the afternoon and Lincoln in the evening. The Douglas press ridiculed Lincoln for following his adversary. He could obtain a crowd in no other way, they scoffed. So, on the advice of his managers, Lincoln challenged Douglas to a series of debates. The Senator was reluctant; he had nothing to gain. A list of his speaking engagements, covering the entire state, had already been announced. Joint meetings would serve simply to give Lincoln a share of the publicity he was attracting. But he could scarcely refuse. He consented to meet Lincoln once in each Congressional district except those of Chicago and Springfield, where both had already spoken, and named as the most convenient towns Ottawa, Freeport, Jonesboro, Charleston, Galesburg, Quincy, and Alton, in that order. Lincoln agreed.

These joint debates marked the highlights of a spectacular campaign, but they represented only a small part of the effort put forth by the rival candidates. Between the debates each man spoke almost every day for four months to large crowds in the open air, and traveled incessantly between engagements, by railroad, steamboat, or horse and buggy, putting up with the scanty comforts and poor food of country inns, and never, so far as the record shows, missing a single engagement. At the end Douglas's voice was a hoarse croak, but Lincoln's seemed as strong as ever.

Both men knew that the contest would be decided in the central tier of counties. The northern counties were heavily Republican, with an infusion of abolitionists, while "Egypt," as southern Illinois was called, where people took their Democracy and liquor straight, was sure to go for Douglas. Although the forces of the Buchanan administration labored lustily, they diverted few votes from Douglas.

The campaign set the prairies in a blaze. Ten thousand persons turned out for the first debate at Ottawa and listened for three hours under a blazing sun. Fifteen thousand were on hand at Freeport in a chilly drizzle. Reporters estimated the crowd at Charleston at twelve to fifteen thousand. Turnouts of five and six thousand were not unusual in smaller towns where the candidates spoke singly. Almost every debate was served by special trains. Dust clouds rising from parched country roads signaled that farmers and their families in wagons, hayracks, buggies, on horseback, or afoot were converging on a place where either or both of the rivals were scheduled to speak. At Jonesboro, far south in "Egypt," where Illinois thrusts like a wedge between Kentucky and Missouri, a newspaper correspondent noted that the country folk "came into the little town with ox teams mostly, and a very stunted breed of oxen, too. Their wagons were old-fashioned and looked as though they were ready to fall to pieces."

Bands, military companies, and cavalcades of horsemen headed long processions escorting the speakers to the stand. Glee clubs gave forth with harmony. Serenaders woke the candidates at night. Fireworks, rockets, and cannon flared and boomed. At one place Lincoln rode in a Conestoga wagon drawn by six white horses. In the Lincoln parade at Charleston a huge wagon festooned with bunting and flowers carried thirty-two pretty girls, each with a banner inscribed with the name of a state, while thirty-two young horsemen caracoled behind it.

Towns were brilliant with mottoes, flags, and banners, hung from buildings and suspended across streets. At Galesburg a whipping wind worked havoc with the decorations. Crayon drawings depicted the Living Dog and the Dead Lion; displayed a rushing locomotive labeled "Freedom" bearing down on Douglas's oxcart, while his Negro driver shouted: " 'Fore God, Massa, I b'leves we's in danger"; represented Douglas riding for a fall as he tried to straddle two horses designated "Dred Scott" and "Popular Sovereignty."

Each candidate had his own shorthand reporter to keep the record straight. Speeches of both candidates were widely published from the reports of special correspondents; some papers printed some or all of the debates in full. The press was violently partisan. According to Republican journals, Lincoln virtually destroyed the Little Giant every time they met; Democratic papers had Lincoln blanching under Douglas's onslaught. When Lincoln's friends carried him off the platform on their shoulders at the conclusion of the Ottawa debate, opposition papers reported him too weak to walk.

Thus through the torrid summer, while the corn grew tall, tasseled, and formed its golden ears, Lincoln and Douglas battled it out, while Illinois listened and the nation read about it. Neither man said anything strikingly new. Each had already defined his position; each knew how the other stood. Now each sought to win the people to his side. They respected one another and were personal friends of a sort. For the most part they observed the amenities. But Douglas lost his temper once or twice and used such words as "slanderer," "wretch," and "sneak," while Lincoln, holding his anger in tight check, applied "fraud," "forgery," "perversion," "falsehood" to some of Douglas's arguments.

A young German immigrant, Carl Schurz, brought into Illinois from Wisconsin by the Republican central committee to make speeches in Lincoln's behalf, listened to the two men at Quincy and was struck by the contrast in their looks and mannerisms. Lincoln's high-pitched voice became shrill in moments of excitement. It did not sound disagreeable, however, and carried to the farthest edge of the crowd. His gestures were awkward. Now and then, to give a point special emphasis, he would bend his knees, crouch slightly, and then shoot upward to his tiptoes. Beside him Douglas looked like a pygmy, but a belligerent and forceful one. His dress was natty and he wore a wide-brimmed white felt hat. Schurz thought his face seemed puffy. His expression was arrogant. He shook his head defiantly, waved clenched fists, and stamped his feet. Worn with long-continued speaking, his voice was rough, sometimes almost a bark.

*

D E S I G N I N G to rouse the latent antagonisms within the Republican Party and capture conservative Republican votes, Douglas opened upon Lincoln with a charge of abolitionism. In 1854, he said, Lincoln and Trumbull entered into a plot whereby the former would abolitionize the old-line Whigs while the latter abolitionized the antislavery Democrats, thereby seducing both groups into the Republican Party. Lincoln was to be elected to the Senate, but Trumbull had double-crossed him and obtained the place for himself. Now the Republicans were salving Lincoln's feelings by making him their candidate for senator.

As has been noted, Lincoln shunned the abolitionists in 1854, and only reluctantly joined the Republicans in 1856. Trumbull's integrity in the senatorial contest was unimpeachable. But if Douglas's charges were easily disproved, he would not be silenced on this point. Admitting that he might have been inaccurate in historical details, he insisted that this was immaterial—that Lincoln was pledged to abolition doctrines. So persistent was the Senator that Lincoln, in desperation, asked how he could stop his opponent's deliberate reiteration of an untruth. Must he put his denial in the form of a corncob and stuff it in Douglas's mouth?

Lincoln, on the other hand, was just as tenacious in his allusions to the alleged proslavery conspiracy on the part of

Douglas, Pierce, Buchanan, and Taney, even after Douglas
branded it a lie. Not content to denounce the Dred Scott decision
for what it was, Lincoln repeatedly predicted another decision
declaring that a state could not exclude slavery if the Democrats
retained control of the government. Douglas, with his doctrine
of "don't care," was doing more than anyone else to prepare the
public mind to accept such a decision. When it came, would
Douglas acquiesce in it?

Douglas regarded such a possibility as ridiculous. It was
"an insult to man's understanding." He would not discuss it.

Douglas hammered relentlessly at Lincoln's "house-divided"
doctrine. It was destructive of the American scheme of government. It invited a sectional war. It insisted on uniformity in
domestic institutions. Why not preserve the government as the
Fathers made it, part free and part slave?

Lincoln replied that Douglas utterly misrepresented his
position. Lincoln would allow the people of a state to determine
their domestic concerns for themselves, just as Douglas would,
even as to slavery. And when Douglas called for a restoration
of the slavery question to the status in which the Fathers put it,
Lincoln agreed with him. That was exactly what Lincoln wanted.
But Douglas distorted history. The Fathers did not make the
nation part free and part slave. They recognized an existing
situation as to slavery, and took measures to prevent its spread
and put it in course of extinction. Lincoln asked for nothing more
than that.

Douglas belabored Lincoln on the question of Negro equality
until, in the debate at Charleston, Lincoln, sorely pressed,
declared that "I am not, nor ever have been in favor of bringing
about in any way the social and political equality of the white and
black races—that I am not nor ever have been in favor of making
voters or jurors of negroes, nor of qualifying them to hold office,
nor to intermarry with white people; and I will say in addition to
this that there is a physical difference between the white and black
races which I believe will for ever forbid the two races living together on terms of social and political equality. And inasmuch as

they cannot so live, while they do remain together there must be the position of superior and inferior, and I as much as any other man am in favor of having the superior position assigned to the white race." Douglas quickly pointed out that this scarcely squared with Lincoln's previous exhortation "to discard all this quibbling about this man and the other man—this race and the other race being inferior."

Douglas could scarcely have been expected to overlook Lincoln's record on the Mexican War. And his repeated mention of it so exasperated his tall opponent that at Charleston Lincoln reached out his long arm, grabbed Orlando B. Ficklin, who had served with him in Congress, pulled him toward the stand, and made the reluctant Ficklin confirm Lincoln's assertion that, while he had regarded the war as unjust and unnecessary, he had consistently voted supplies to sustain the troops.

At Freeport, Lincoln asked Douglas if, in view of the Dred Scott decision, the people of a territory could, in any lawful manner, exclude slavery from that territory prior to the formation of a state constitution. This has often been represented as a master stroke of strategy, designed to force Douglas to alienate the South and to render impossible his nomination for the Presidency in 1860. But Douglas had already given his answer several times. The South knew his position, and so did Lincoln. It is doubtful if Lincoln was looking ahead to 1860. Probably his purpose in forcing Douglas to restate his position was to widen the breach between Douglas and the Buchanan forces that were working to defeat him.

As expected, Douglas replied that slavery could be excluded from a territory, notwithstanding the Supreme Court's attitude, by the people's refusal to enact protective legislation. In reply Lincoln denied that friendly legislation was essential to the establishment of slavery. Slavery had been established in the American colonies against the wishes of the colonists. Moreover, Lincoln asked, how could a member of a territorial legislature, sworn to uphold the Constitution, deny slave property that protection which the Constitution, according to Taney's opinion, guaranteed to it? Even more to the point, how could a territorial legislator vote for unfriendly legislation in the face of his oath to support the Constitution? And lastly, was not Congress itself bound to pass protective legislation? If Douglas's argument that a legislature could nullify a constitutional guarantee by means of unfriendly legislation was valid, would it not apply to the Fugitive Slave Law? Would it not justify a state legislature in passing laws designed to impede the recovery of fugitive slaves? Even a large majority of men of antislavery sympathies granted that the Constitution required Congress to give the South an effective fugitive-slave law. Yet, said Lincoln, "I defy any man to make an argument that will justify unfriendly legislation to deprive a slaveholder of his right to hold his slave in a Territory, that will not equally, in all its length, breadth and thickness furnish an argument for nullifying the fugitive slave law."

Profiting from experience as he always did, shaping himself against events and people, evincing that capacity to rise to the occasion which became so marked a feature of his character, Lincoln, under Douglas's pounding, formulated his thoughts more clearly as the campaign wore on. Uncertain and forced to the defensive at the beginning, he appeared at his best toward the end. In the fifth debate, at Galesburg, he began to stress the moral issue. The Republicans regarded slavery as a wrong and were charting their course accordingly, whereas Democratic policies took no account of the rightfulness or wrongfulness of slavery. Was this not their basic difference?

In the sixth debate, at Quincy, Lincoln bore down strongly on this point. Douglas responded that the people of the slaveholding states were no less civilized than their brethren in the North. It did not become Lincoln or anyone else to tell them they had no conscience, that they were living in iniquity and in violation of the laws of God. It were better for Lincoln not to judge lest he be judged. Plenty of wrongs needed righting in the free states, without Lincoln's going south to look for them.

But Lincoln had his teeth in the issue now. Here was the "nub" or "kernel" of the question, for which he always sought.

"The real issue in this controversy—the one pressing upon every mind," he reiterated in the last debate, at Alton, "is the sentiment on the part of one class that looks upon the institution of slavery *as a wrong,* and of another class that *does not* look upon it as a wrong. The sentiment that contemplates the institution of slavery in this country as a wrong is the sentiment of the Republican party. . . . They look upon it as being a moral, social and political wrong; and while they contemplate it as such, they nevertheless have due regard for its actual existence among us, and the difficulties of getting rid of it in any satisfactory way and to all the constitutional obligations thrown about it. Yet having a due regard for these, they desire a policy in regard to it that looks to its not creating any more danger. They insist that it should as far as may be, *be treated* as a wrong, and one of the methods of treating it as a wrong is to *make provision that it shall grow no larger.* They also desire a policy that looks to a peaceful end of slavery sometime, as being wrong. . . . If there be a man amongst us who does not think that the institution of slavery is wrong in any one of the aspects of which I have spoken, he is misplaced and ought not to be with us. And if there be a man amongst us who is so impatient of it as a wrong as to disregard its actual presence among us and the difficulty of getting rid of it suddenly in a satisfactory way, and to disregard the constitutional obligations thrown about it, that man is misplaced if he is on our platform. We disclaim sympathy with him in practical action. He is not placed properly with us. . . .

"On the other hand, I have said there is a sentiment which treats it as *not* being wrong. That is the Democratic sentiment of this day. I do not mean to say that every man who stands within that range positively asserts that it is right. That class will include all men who positively assert that it is right, and all who like Judge Douglas treat it as indifferent and do not say it is either right or wrong. . . . He contends that whatever community wants slaves has a right to have them. So they have if it is not a wrong. But if it is a wrong, he cannot say people have a right to do wrong." Repeating an assertion of his Peoria address, Lincoln declared that the slavery controversy was simply a phase of that eternal and world-wide struggle between right and wrong that runs through all human history.

When we note the similarities in Lincoln's and Douglas's thinking, the accuracy of Lincoln's analysis becomes evident. Neither man favored Negro equality, though Lincoln was more liberal, as well as more uncertain, than Douglas on this point. Both deplored sectionalism. Both wanted to quiet the slavery agitation. Neither wished to see slavery extended. Both desired fervently to preserve the Union of the states. Their fundamental difference was ethical. Slavery being what it was, Lincoln knew that men of moral sensitivities would inevitably take their stand against it. Douglas thought these sensitivities could and should be suppressed.

*

E L E C T I O N day in Illinois dawned wet and raw. And though the Republican legislative candidates polled four thousand more votes than their opponents, it soon became evident that the out-dated apportionment law, which favored the Democratic southern districts of the state, would assure Douglas's re-election by the Legislature. The vote there was 54 for Douglas to 46 for Lincoln.

*

H I S T O R I C A L L Y the great debates had two important results. First, by publicizing Douglas's position at Freeport in answer to Lincoln's question, they made it easier for Southern extremists to bring about a fateful schism in the Democratic Party in 1860, and this in turn would defeat Douglas for the Presidency. The result was not due to any adroitness on Lincoln's part, however, but rather to Douglas's forthrightness in expounding an interpretation of popular sovereignty favorable to free-soil interests in the territories, but distasteful to proslavery radicals. Secondly, the debates made Lincoln a national figure and put the Presidency within his reach. Any man who could hold his own with Douglas had proved his qualifications for high office. Moreover, Lincoln handled himself so skillfully that while taking a moderate position he had not antagonized the abolition element in his party. And his language, purged of the floridity that had occasionally marred his pre-Nebraska speeches, had taken on a simple eloquence.

Lincoln felt keenly disappointed but not disheartened by defeat. Six years later he recalled how, on election night, he walked home through the gloomy streets. "The path had been worn pig-backed and was slippery. My foot slipped from under me, knocking the other out of the way; but I recovered and said to myself, '*It's a slip and not a fall.*' "

Two days after the election Lincoln wrote to Senator John J. Crittenden, an old-line Whig of Kentucky who had used his influence for Douglas: "The emotions of defeat, at the close of a struggle in which I felt more than a merely selfish interest, and to which defeat the use of your name contributed largely are fresh upon me; but, even in this mood, I can not for a moment suspect you of anything dishonorable."

"I am glad I made the late race," Lincoln wrote to Dr. A. G. Henry, a personal friend. "It gave me a hearing on the great and durable question of the age, which I could have had in no other way; and though I now sink out of view, and shall be forgotten, I believe I have made some marks which will tell for the cause of civil liberty long after I am gone."

Consoling Norman Judd, his campaign manager, who was more dispirited than he, Lincoln urged that the fight must go on. Republican organization and morale must be maintained. Trumbull, who had labored hard for Lincoln, must be re-elected when his term expired in 1860. To arrest any suspicion that he might seek Trumbull's Senate seat in the next election, Lincoln assured Judd: "I shall be in no one's way for any of the places." The next campaign would find him fighting in the ranks.

But fate would order otherwise.

CHAPTER XI

The Making of a President

I HAVE been on expenses so long without earning any-thing that I am absolutely without money now for even house-hold purposes," Lincoln lamented to Norman Judd in reply to a plea for help in making up the campaign deficit. Yet, since he had held the place of honor on the ticket, he felt obliged to give what he could spare, and contributed $250 more, bringing his total outlay to well over $500. Then, weary in mind and body, he returned once again to his law practice.

Scarcely had the outcome of the campaign become known when small-town newspapers in Illinois, and even a few Republi-can journals in other states, began to mention Lincoln as a worthy presidential candidate. At dusk one day, when Lincoln left the courthouse at Bloomington, Jesse Fell took him by the arm and guided him to his brother's law office. Founder of the *Bloomington Pantagraph*, a large landowner, a canny politician, and a man of wide-ranging intellect, Fell had just returned from the East, where, time and again, persons had asked him: "Who is this man Lincoln, who is opposing Douglas?" Lincoln was acquiring a national reputation, Fell would have him know, and if his background and opinions were sufficiently brought before the people, Fell believed he could become a formidable presiden-tial candidate.

Lincoln was not impressed. What was the use of talking about him for the Presidency, he replied, when such men as Seward, Chase, and others of almost equal prominence were in the running? Everyone knew them. Scarcely anyone outside of Illinois knew Lincoln. Besides, such men were more deserving of the honor; they had fought for Republican principles from the beginning on the national level in the face of opposition and abuse.

Fell conceded the truth of Lincoln's argument. But personal service and merit did not always signify a winning candidate. Both Seward and Chase had made enemies and uttered radical statements. Perhaps they could not be elected, even if nominated. The Republican candidate in 1860 must be a man of the people, conservatively antislavery, with no tincture of radicalism about him. Lincoln was such a man. Fell wanted Lincoln to write a short autobiographical sketch suitable for publicity purposes.

But Lincoln did not warm to the idea. Fell paid him a great compliment, he said, and he confessed he would like to be President. But he would try to keep his ambition within attainable limits. What he wanted was Douglas's Senate seat in 1864.

Three months later, when Thomas J. Pickett, editor of the *Rock Island Register*, proposed to come out publicly for him, Lincoln begged him not to do it. "I must, in candor, say I do not think I am fit for the Presidency," he wrote. And when Pickett insisted that he planned to consult other Illinois Republican editors with a view to a simultaneous endorsement of Lincoln, the latter again protested his unfitness and assured Pickett: "I really think it best for our cause that no concerted effort, such as you suggest, should be made."

Wittingly or unwittingly, and whatever Lincoln's secret feelings may have been, he acted wisely in declining the overtures of those who wished to push him forward. Premature announcement of his candidacy would immediately have brought him under rival fire. A presidential candidate is often in a stronger position when he seems not to seek the office.

Lincoln's correspondence shows that his influence in party affairs now extended beyond the borders of his state. He proffered

advice regarding the Republican platform in Kansas. He coun-
seled Chase that the plank in the Ohio platform calling for
repeal of the Fugitive Slave Law endangered the party's fortunes
in more conservative regions and must by all means be kept out
of the national convention. Lincoln advised Schuyler Colfax, an
Indiana party leader, that every local convocation of Republicans
must be careful to do nothing calculated to alienate voters elsewhere. "In a word," he cautioned, "in every locality we should
look beyond our noses, and at least say *nothing* on points where
it is probable we shall disagree." Aware of the importance of the
cohesive and increasing German vote, in late May 1859 Lincoln
through his friend John Bunn purchased from Theodore Canisius
the type and other equipment of the *Illinois Staats Anzeiger*, a
German-language newspaper published in Springfield, and
granted Canisius full control of it so long as it should support the
Republican Party. The consideration was $400, which Bunn
may have advanced. After the election Lincoln resold the paper
to Canisius for the same price he paid for it.

If Lincoln refused to allow himself to be projected into the
presidential arena, he overlooked no opportunity to influence
his party's policies. On a business and pleasure trip to Iowa in
August, he accepted an invitation to speak at Council Bluffs.
There and at St. Joseph, Missouri, he consulted Republican
leaders. Throughout the summer, invitations to speak had
come to him from places as far distant as New Hampshire, New
York, Minnesota and Pennsylvania. Most of these he was obliged
to decline. But in September he made a swing through Ohio,
where Douglas had recently spoken in aid of the Democratic candidates in the fall elections. After speeches at Columbus, Dayton, Hamilton, and Cincinnati, Lincoln delivered an address at
Indianapolis on his route back home. Eight days later he was
off for Milwaukee, where he had agreed to give the annual oration at the Wisconsin State Fair.

A political speech was not appropriate to the occasion; but,
after discoursing on the possibility of improving farm machinery
and augmenting crop yields, Lincoln expounded on the oppor-

tunities for advancement offered by a system of free labor and subtly pointed out that a compliant attitude of mind toward slavery might eventually lead to the enslavement of all workingmen, white as well as black.

In a later day Lincoln himself would be regarded as the pre-eminent example of the self-made man so much admired by Americans, and already he saw himself as living proof of the chance for personal improvement offered by a system of free enterprise. If the factory system already tended to shackle the laboring man, Lincoln did not seem to be aware of it. The Northern laborer was surely better off than the Southern "mudsill" whose advancement was obstructed by slavery and the planter class. The period in which Lincoln grew up offered opportunities for self-betterment seldom equaled in American history, and among all places such opportunities were greatest in the Northwest. All about him, at home and on the circuit, Lincoln saw men who, starting life as farmhands, clerks, mechanics, or flatboat men, had become lawyers, merchants, doctors, landed farmers, and successful politicians. "There is no permanent class of hired laborers among us," he had declared in his speech at Cincinnati. "Twenty-five years ago, I was a hired laborer. The hired laborer of yesterday, labors on his own account to-day, and will hire others to labor for him to-morrow. Advancement— improvement in condition—is the order of things in a society of equals."

Lincoln believed that labor is superior to capital, "and deserves much the higher consideration. Capital has its rights, which are as worthy of protection as any other rights. Nor is it denied that there is, and probably always will be, a relation between capital and labor producing mutual benefits. The error is in assuming that the whole labor of a community exists within that relation. . . . A large majority belong to neither class."

The basic tenet of Lincoln's economic thinking was equal opportunity for all. Living part of his life in an age of craftsmanship and part of it in an age of burgeoning industrialism, with cheap land always available, he saw perseverance, thrift, and enterprise rewarded. Under a system of individualistic enterprise it seemed of first importance to him—indeed, it seemed sufficient —merely to keep the road to high attainment clear of inequitable obstructions, with government aid to projects of general benefit.

After a second speech in Milwaukee, which was unequivocally political in character, Lincoln accepted invitations to speak at Beloit and Janesville en route to Chicago, where he stopped off a few days for political consultations.

All through the hot summer days of 1859, while he wrote letters and made occasional speeches, but for the most part put in long hours with the law to build up his depleted bank balance, the Illinois Republican organization was hard at work, raising money, instructing county leaders, building local organizations to peak strength. Jesse Fell, as corresponding secretary, traveled widely throughout the state, interviewing political leaders and ordinary citizens, calculating their reactions to possible candidates. As a rule he found the people anxious to have "Abe" Lincoln as a presidential candidate; but the local party leaders, stonily unemotional, hungry for loaves and fishes, coldly calculating in their desire for a candidate most likely to bring victory, were not so sure about their native son.

*

ONE DAY in October, while Lincoln was attending court at Urbana, news flashed across the country that old John Brown, abolitionist fanatic and veteran of the Kansas troubles, with some eighteen deluded followers, had seized the Federal arsenal at Harpers Ferry, Virginia, with the purpose of instigating a slave revolt. The South was horrified; the North was shocked. The whole country hung breathless on the news as Brown and his handful of brave, foolhardy men held off Virginia militiamen and a detachment of United States Marines commanded by Colonel Robert E. Lee until all but two of the band were dead or wounded.

Extreme abolitionists applauded Brown's reckless exploit and began to make a martyr of the patriarch. Responsible Republican leaders regretted and repudiated it. In the minds of

Southerners, however, it raised the ever haunting specter of a slave revolt; this was the fruit of antislavery agitation. With the November elections impending, Democrats charged that Republicans were implicated in Brown's plot and that Brown drew his inspiration from Republican doctrine. In a parallel column with the news from Harpers Ferry, the *New York Herald* printed a year-old speech of Seward's forecasting an "irrepressible conflict." The event played into the hands of Southern radicals who were urging secession as the only recourse for the South in the event of Republican victory. Henceforward many persons both North and South would be guided by their emotions rather than their sober judgment.

*

O N A R A W day in late November, Lincoln started out at the behest of friends in Kansas to make several speeches in that territory. Having been won for freedom at long last, Kansas had adopted a constitution, elected a legislature, and was about to choose territorial officers and a delegate to Congress. As wintry winds lashed the forlorn frontier settlements and drove plainsmen to the shelter of their shanties and sod houses, Lincoln traveled from Elwood, where the largest auditorium was the hotel dining-room, to Troy, Doniphan, Atchison, and Leavenworth. On December 2, as he spoke at Atchison, John Brown went to the gallows in Charles Town, Virginia, seated imperturbably on his coffin and remarking as he gazed at the blue haze softening the outline of the mountains: "This *is* a beautiful country."

Lincoln had the old man on his mind and referred to him more than once in his Kansas speeches. Brown had shown surpassing courage and rare unselfishness. But his lawlessness was indefensible. Slavery should be dealt with at the ballot box, said Lincoln; the North could offer no objection to Brown's punishment. Opposition to slavery could never justify violence, bloodshed, and treason. Then to his proslavery auditors Lincoln declared that the South, too, must learn the lesson of John Brown. For if the South should undertake to destroy the Union, "it will be our duty to deal with you as old John Brown has been dealt with."

*

D URING the autumn Lincoln was frequently mentioned as a presidential dark horse. Two presidential hopefuls, Chase and Simon Cameron, Republican boss of Pennsylvania, indicated a desire to have him as a vice-presidential running mate. Local leaders in Illinois were coming over to him in increasing numbers; more of the Illinois hierarchy were convinced he could win. On November 1, in a letter to W. E. Frazer, of Pennsylvania, Lincoln gave the first inkling that he thought he might have a chance when he wrote: "For my single self, I have enlisted for the permanent success of the Republican cause; and, for this object, I shall labor faithfully in the ranks, unless, as I think not probable, the judgment of the party shall assign me a different position."

On December 20 Lincoln sent Jesse Fell the autobiographical sketch he had requested a year before. "There is not much of it," he explained, "for the reason, I suppose, that there is not much of me. If any thing be made out of it, I wish it to be modest, and not to go beyond the material." Fell sent it to a newspaper friend, editor of a small-town Pennsylvania journal, who made it the basis of an article used extensively by other papers. At almost the same time Lincoln was preparing this sketch, however, he wrote to Lyman Trumbull that he would rather be senator than President.

Near the end of 1859 Norman Judd made an astute move. When the Republican National Committee met in New York to select a site for the party convention, several cities favored by one or another of the prospective candidates came up for consideration. Rivalry was keen, and Judd, sharply alert but seemingly casual, suggested Chicago as a neutral place, since Illinois had no candidate of her own. The committee immediately fell in with the idea; the presidential sweepstakes would be run in Lincoln's own state.

This being the case, Lincoln, still looking primarily to another try for the Senate in 1864, concluded that his chances would be impaired unless his home-state delegates gave him a complimentary first-ballot endorsement. "I am not in a position where it would hurt much for me to not be nominated on the national ticket," he wrote to Judd, "but I am where it would hurt some for me to not get the Illinois delegates." Thus Lincoln became avowedly a candidate—not with any real hope of success, but as a means of promoting his senatorial prospects. His friends were pleased. They were more optimistic than he.

For several weeks the influential *Chicago Tribune* had been keeping Lincoln's name before its readers with extracts from his speeches and accounts of his activities. A reprint from a Milwaukee newspaper argued that Lincoln was more "available" than Seward or Chase. A long communication from "A Union Lover" protested Seward's radicalism. Joseph Medill, the *Tribune's* editor, himself journeyed to Washington to convince Republican Congressmen of Lincoln's superior chances to carry the doubtful states. On February 16, 1860 the *Tribune* came out emphatically for Lincoln.

*

B A C K I N October, Lincoln had been invited to lecture at the Reverend Henry Ward Beecher's celebrated Plymouth Church in Brooklyn. It was a high compliment. But Lincoln had tried lecturing before, without success. In several towns in Illinois he had delivered a prepared address on "Discoveries and Inventions," but it had not gone over well, and once the crowd was so small that the meeting had been called off. Lincoln realized that his forte was politics and asked the committee on arrangements if a political lecture would be acceptable. When they consented, he went to work in earnest.

He and Douglas had differed sharply on the attitude of the Founding Fathers about the extension of slavery, but neither man had adduced evidence to clinch his argument. Proposing now to do so, Lincoln embarked upon sustained historical

research, poring over Elliot's *Debates on the Federal Constitution,*
putting in hour after hour at the State Library, where he examined the *Annals of Congress* and the *Congressional Globe* and
turned interminable pages of old, dusty newspapers as he sat
hunched over a table, running his long fingers through his coarse
black hair.

Arriving in New York after a tiring two-day trip, Lincoln
learned that the Young Men's Central Republican Union of New
York City had taken over the sponsorship of his address, which
would be given at Cooper Union, in New York, instead of at
Beecher's church. Ostensibly the purpose of the Young Men's
Union was to promote a series of political lectures for the en-
lightenment of busy citizens, but actual leadership of the organization was vested in a group of veteran Republican politicians
intent on thwarting Seward's aspiration to the Presidency.

All day on February 27, 1860 Lincoln was entertained at the
Astor House as a visiting celebrity. That night, despite a snowstorm, fifteen hundred persons filed into Cooper Union, the largest
assemblage "of the intellect and culture of our city" since the
days of Clay and Webster, according to Horace Greeley. The
famous editor, once an ally of Seward and Weed but now their
avowed enemy, sat conspicuously on the platform, to which
Lincoln was conducted by the prominent New York lawyer
David Dudley Field and the celebrated literary figure William
Cullen Bryant, editor of the New York *Evening Post.* Cheers
rang out as the towering Midwesterner, known to his audience
as Douglas's most formidable antagonist, was escorted down the
aisle.

Lincoln felt nervous when he was introduced. He feared that
his Western mannerisms and quaint rural accent might be
amusing to sophisticated Easterners. He felt uncomfortably
conscious of his new broadcloth suit, which did not seem to hang
right and looked rumpled from his long trip. But his audience
were with him from the start, and he soon thought only of
convincing them.

Bringing to bear the facts he had gleaned from days of research, Lincoln proved that of the thirty-nine signers of the Constitution twenty-one, a clear majority, together with the seventy-six members of the Congress that passed the first ten amendments, "certainly understood that no proper division of local from federal authority, nor any part of the Constitution, forbade the Federal Government to control slavery in the federal territories," while all the rest of the signers of the Constitution probably shared that opinion. Consequently, he argued, quoting Douglas's own words against his rival, let all who believe that the fathers of the Republic "understood this question just as well, and even better than we do now, speak as they spoke, and act as they acted upon it."

Appealing directly to the Southern people, Lincoln took up one after another the accusations that some Democratic leaders were bringing against the Republicans. His party was not sectional, he said, except as the South made it so. It was not radical or revolutionary; it was conservative. It was the South that had rejected the old policies and in so doing caused the agitation of the slavery question. The Republicans had not instigated John Brown's raid, he said. Nor did Republican doctrines sanction such violent actions. The threat of secession in the event of Republican victory he likened to a highwayman holding a pistol to his victim's head.

Then Lincoln addressed himself to the Republicans. There must be peace. Republicans must do their part to cherish it. They must placate the South whenever possible in order to convince their Southern brethren that they did not seek to disturb them. But would they be convinced? Lincoln feared not, because nothing short of an admission of the rightfulness of slavery would satisfy them. "All they ask, we could readily grant, if we thought slavery right," Lincoln conceded; "all we ask, they could as readily grant, if they thought it wrong. Their thinking it right, and our thinking it wrong, is the precise fact upon which depends the whole controversy. Thinking it right, as they do, they are not to blame for desiring its full recognition, as being right; but thinking it wrong, as we do, can we yield to them? Can we cast our votes with their view, and against our own? In view of our moral, social, and political responsibilities, can we do this?

"If our sense of duty forbids this, then let us stand by our duty fearlessly and effectively. . . . Neither let us be slandered from our duty by false accusations against us, nor frightened from it by menaces of destruction to the Government nor of dungeons to ourselves. *Let us have faith that right makes might, and in that faith let us, to the end, dare to do our duty as we understand it.*"

As the intense figure on the rostrum uttered this stirring peroration, men and women rose to their feet, shouting, waving hats and handkerchiefs, in a long-sustained ovation. Men rushed to the platform to grasp the speaker's hand. Charged with deep emotion, the crowd was slow to disperse. Seldom had a visitor made such a profound impression on a New York audience. The next morning four New York papers printed the speech in full. Editors were lavish with praise. The *Chicago Tribune* brought out the speech in pamphlet form. Lincoln had materially enhanced his reputation in the East.

*

ONE REASON for Lincoln's agreeing to go East was that the trip would enable him to visit his son Robert, who, after failing fifteen of the sixteen entrance examinations at Harvard, was spending a year at Phillips Exeter Academy in New Hampshire in order to try again. As Lincoln's purpose to visit New Hampshire became known, delegations from cities along his route invited him to speak. The Governor of Rhode Island sat on the platform when he spoke at Providence. Large crowds turned out at Concord, Dover, and Exeter. At Manchester Lincoln was introduced as the next President.

At Hartford, where the shoemakers were on strike, Lincoln declared: "I am glad to see that a system of labor prevails in New England under which laborers *can* strike when they want to, where they are not obliged to work under all circumstances, and are not tied down and obliged to labor whether you pay them or not! I like the system which lets a man quit when he wants to, and wish it might prevail everywhere. . . . I don't believe in a law to prevent a man from getting rich; it would do more harm than good. So while we do not propose any war upon capital, we do wish to allow the humblest man an equal chance to get rich with everybody else. When one starts poor, as most do in the race of life, free society is such that he knows he can better his condition; he knows that there is no fixed condition of labor, for his whole life."

A brass band conducted Lincoln to his lodgings after a successful speech at New Haven. Meriden put on a torchlight demonstration. Woonsocket, Norwich, and Bridgeport offered gratifying crowds. His tour became a triumph as Republican admirers thronged his train to accompany him from one town to another. With little advance notice of his coming, the demonstrations were largely spontaneous.

*

W H E N L I N C O L N returned to Springfield after this dazzling Eastern trip, Milton Hay, addressing him on behalf of the local Republican Club, declared that "No inconsiderable portion of your fellow citizens in various portions of the county have expressed their preference for you as the candidate of the Republican party for the next Presidency. . . . There are those around you sir who have watched with manly interest and pride your upward march from obscurity to distinction. There are those here who know something of the obstacles which have lain in your pathway. Our history is prolific in examples of what may be achieved by ability, persevereance [*sic*] and integrity . . . but in the long list of those who have thus from humblest beginnings won their way worthily to proud distinction there is not one can take precedence of the name of Abraham Lincoln. . . .

"When in 1854 sectional strife and controversy were invited into the councils of the nation, a betrayed people began to see in your eloquent denunciations of that wanton act, and in your able vindication of the principles and policies thereby infracted, more high qualities and that true statesmanship which demonstrated their possessor to be well worthy of the highest offices and honor within their gift—well worthy the Presidency itself.

We feel well assured that we shall look in vain amongst all the high names of the Republic for the man combining in himself, in his record, and in his history more of those elements which fit the man for the time, the occasion and the place than your-self."

These assurances, added to the unmistakable evidences of popularity that had been manifested on his Eastern trip, gave Lincoln a new confidence. He no longer made light of his chances. "The taste *is* in my mouth a little," he confessed to Trumbull when the Senator asked if he was a candidate. By means of adroit letters Lincoln sought to line up delegates wherever possible without being too obvious about it.

By the time the Illinois Republican convention met at Decatur on May 9 and 10, Lincoln's self-appointed managers had their strategy well planned. Lincoln came in late and received a tumultuous ovation as he was invited to a seat on the platform. Soon afterward Dick Oglesby, one of Lincoln's firm supporters and later Governor of Illinois, announced that an old Macon County Democrat wished to offer a contribution. "Receive it," roared the delegates, by this time worked up to a high pitch of excitement. With that, Lincoln's country cousin, weather-beaten old John Hanks, assisted by a friend, marched proudly down the aisle with a curious banner, supported between two fence rails bedecked with flags and streamers, which proclaimed:

ABRAHAM LINCOLN
The Rail Candidate for President in 1860

———————

Two Rails from a Lot of 3,000 Made in 1830 by Thos. Hanks and Abe Lincoln— Whose Father was the First Pioneer of Macon County.[1]

---

[1] The sign should have read *John* Hanks; and Lincoln's father was by no means the first settler in the county.

The crowd broke loose in pandemonium. Men cheered, screamed, tossed hats and newspapers high in the air, and pommeled one another until part of the awning forming the roof of the hastily erected structure came down upon their heads. When the wreckage had been cleared away, the crowd called for Lincoln to speak. Rising slowly and pointing to the banner, he said: "I suppose I am expected to reply to that." He could not say whether he had made those rails or not, but he surely had mauled better ones. With that he sat down and the cheering broke out afresh. Thus Lincoln gained the cognomen of "Rail-Splitter," a good vote-getting nickname in that it symbolized his humble origin and kinship with the workingman.

The next day, with other business disposed of, John M. Palmer, a former Democrat, offered a resolution "That Abraham Lincoln is the choice of the Republican party of Illinois for the Presidency, and the delegates from this state are instructed to use all honorable means to secure his nomination by the Chicago Convention, and to vote as a unit for him."

Lincoln had been apprehensive lest the strong Seward sentiment in northern Illinois and the popularity in southern Illinois of Edward Bates, of Missouri, an old-line Whig, might, as he put it, squeeze him out in the middle with only slight support. But his managers had handled matters deftly. The Seward and Bates backers saw the futility of putting up a fight, and, as Palmer's resolution was unanimously adopted, Lincoln was not only certain to be put in nomination at Chicago, but could count on twenty-two votes. This was not an impressive number, but they would come from a pivotal state, whose wishes would command consideration.

*

ALMOST before the Decatur convention adjourned, the Republican host began converging on Chicago, now a city of 110,000. A robust center of trade and manufacturing, already rivaling Cincinnati as the chief location of the packing industry, Chicago still displayed a frontier lustiness. Served by fifteen railroads, its skyline stippled with the spires of fifty-six churches and the

looming bulk of numerous grain elevators, it also flaunted more
than a thousand saloons, grogshops, and weinstubes, together
with eighty ballrooms. Its plank sidewalks, following the natural
undulations of the land, rose and fell like the waves of Lake
Michigan.

Proud to be host to the Republican convention, Chicago
had prepared against its coming by erecting a rambling frame
structure, known as the Wigwam, designed to hold ten thousand
people. But even this would be too small, for besides the usual
galaxy of delegates, professional politicians, newspaper reporters,
and hangers-on, thousands of other persons planned to attend the
convention. New York sent more than two thousand men to
cheer for Seward. Pennsylvania was represented by fifteen hundred. Hundreds more came from New England. And from all
over Illinois the Lincoln men poured in, taking advantage of the
cheap railroad fares that Norman Judd had wangled.

Bands blared. Processions marched and countermarched on
the flag-bedecked streets. Men clustered in little groups with their
arms about one another, whispering supposed secrets most of
which were common knowledge, circulating rumors, speculating,
arguing, haranguing anyone who deigned to listen. Bars and
hotel lobbies were crammed. Feet were stepped on, ribs were
jabbed, occasionally a nose was punched.

Lincoln's managers set up headquarters in the Tremont
House. Their chief strategist was David Davis, of Bloomington.
An enormous man, weighing more than three hundred pounds,
rich, sagacious, indomitable, he was judge of the Eighth Circuit,
which he had traveled with Lincoln for many years, sharing his
room, roaring at his stories, sometimes chiding him for impover-
ishing the bar with his low fees, coming to appreciate his qualities
of mind and character. On hand to assist Davis was a coterie of
Lincoln's friends, many of them his associates on the circuit—
Norman Judd, Stephen T. Logan, Leonard Swett, Joseph Medill,
Jesse Fell, Republican gubernatorial nominee Richard Yates,
Orville Browning, and a score of others.

No novices in the game of politics, they knew they faced a

formidable but by no means hopeless task, for Lincoln's strength lay in his rivals' weaknesses. The acknowledged leader of the party was Seward, experienced, calculating, and somewhat cynical, a former Governor of New York, a United States Senator since 1848, and a forthright opponent of slavery extension. Backed solidly by the New York delegation, led by the smart manipulator Thurlow Weed, Seward was immensely popular. But he also had enemies, notably Horace Greeley, who, banned from the New York delegation, had contrived to be chosen a delegate from Oregon. Actually more of a compromiser than Lincoln, Seward by reason of his "higher law" and "irrepressible conflict" utterances was reputed to be a radical. Out to defeat him, besides Greeley, were Henry S. Lane, of Indiana, and Andrew G. Curtin, of Pennsylvania, both candidates for governor, who maintained that with Seward as the standard-bearer the Republicans would lose their states. The Illinois men also played upon this theme. The campaign of 1856 had demonstrated that Republican victory would hinge on Pennsylvania, Indiana, Illinois, and New Jersey; and Seward, so his antagonists alleged, could not carry a single one of them.

Salmon P. Chase, of Ohio, twice Governor and once a United States Senator, not only was more radical than Seward and far less popular, but could not even command the full support of his own state. Conservative Edward Bates, of Missouri, had antagonized the German voters by consorting with the Know-Nothings. Simon Cameron, of Pennsylvania, had an unsavory reputation and, like Chase, was opposed in his own state delegation. Colorless John McLean, of the United States Supreme Court, was seventy-five years old.

Lincoln, on the other hand, did not enjoy sufficient prominence to have been marked either as a conservative or as a radical. He had no public record he must defend. His lowly birth and self-made attributes found favor with the masses. Six weeks before the convention Lincoln correctly appraised his situation when he wrote to a friend in Ohio: "My name is new in the field; and I suppose I am not the *first* choice of a very great many.

Our policy, then, is to give no offence to others—leave them in a mood to come to us, if they shall be impelled to give up their first love."

Seating himself behind a big table in the unobtrusive Lincoln headquarters, Davis sent emissaries to visit the various delegations. Samuel C. Parks, a native of Vermont, established a liaison with the Green Mountain boys. Leonard Swett, of Maine, dropped in to talk with men from the Pine Tree State. Other New England delegations were similarly cultivated. The day before the official opening of the convention, Lincoln, waiting anxiously in Springfield, received a telegram from Nathan M. Knapp, a delegate from Winchester: "Things are working; keep a good nerve—be not surprised at any result—but I tell you that your chances are not the worst. . . . We are dealing tenderly with delegates, taking them in detail, and making no fuss. Be not too expectant, but rely upon our discretion. Again I say brace your nerves for any result."

On the eve of the convention it appeared that Indiana might be persuaded to give Lincoln her twenty-six votes on the first ballot, and that a goodly number of Pennsylvania votes might be obtained on the second ballot if Lincoln's chances appeared good. Davis was dickering with all the finesse he could command, when a telegram came from Lincoln: "I authorize no bargains and will be bound by none." Lincoln's friends were confounded. From an experienced politician such an admonition was unthinkable. Did Lincoln mean to shackle them, they wondered, or was he writing for the record? "Lincoln ain't here," the perspiring Davis grunted, "and don't know what we have to meet." Davis proceeded to clinch the Indiana delegation with a promise of the Secretaryship of the Interior to Caleb B. Smith and the Commissionership of Indian Affairs to William P. Dole.

*

INTO THE vast pine-board Wigwam on the morning of Wednesday, May 16, trooped ten thousand people, while twice as many swarmed hopefully outside. Ticket-holders took seats in the galleries, whence they looked down upon the huge platform where delegates and party leaders milled about, and in front of which, on a series of wide landings rising gradually to the rear of the building, non-ticket-holding spectators were privileged to stand, jammed in so tightly they could scarcely move. Pillars were wreathed with flags and bunting. Busts of notables stood in the corners. Portraits of statesmen and allegorical paintings of Justice, Liberty, and the like adorned the barren walls.

The first two days were devoted to routine business and the adoption of the platform. During recesses delegations met in caucus. The suspense became harrowing. The Seward men wished to ballot for President on Thursday afternoon, but the opposition effected a postponement. "There were hundreds of Pennsylvanians, Indianians and Illinoisans, who never closed their eyes that night," one participant observed. "I saw Henry S. Lane at one o'clock, pale and haggard, with cane under his arm, walking as if for a wager, from one caucus room to another, at the Tremont House." Curtin, of Pennsylvania, appeared equally agitated. Some time after midnight the Pennsylvania delegation, despite promises from Weed of tempting sums of money for campaign purposes if they would swing their strength to Seward, agreed to go for Cameron on the first ballot, McLean on the second, and Lincoln on the third. Since their first two votes were recognized as being merely complimentary, this action amounted to a commitment to Lincoln if he was still in the running when the third ballot came. In another midnight caucus the Illinoisans persuaded the New Jersey delegates to support Lincoln after a complimentary vote for William L. Dayton, their native son.

The Pennsylvanians were not won without a recompense. Davis promised Cameron a cabinet post. Recounting the history of the convention, one Pennsylvanian declared that Pennsylvania had decided for Lincoln before this promise was made, and that immediately following the decision one of Cameron's lieutenants cornered Swett and Davis and persuaded them that Cameron should be rewarded.

Conscious of the decisive part that crowd psychology

might play in the morrow's session, one member of the Illinois
delegation wished that the host of Seward shouters could be kept
out of the Wigwam. Why not? asked somebody with a flash of inspiration. Ward Hill Lamon and Jesse Fell ordered a large supply
of extra tickets printed and got them judiciously distributed
to Lincoln men, all of whom were instructed to present them
early. A Chicagoan reputedly able to shout across Lake Michigan was enlisted to take a strategic position in the hall and
bellow lustily whenever Judd took out his handkerchief. Another
man from Ottawa, equally endowed with vocal strength, was instructed to exercise his talent from another section of the Wigwam. Having done everything within their power, the weary Illinoisans snatched what sleep they could.

The convention reassembled at ten o'clock Friday morning.
The hall was packed as usual. Outside, however, some extremely
angry ticket-holders could not get in. For, while the Sewardites
paraded, Lincoln's supporters had used their bogus tickets to
advantage.

Nominations began at once, and as the name of Seward was
presented, a tremendous shout went up—not all his friends remained outside by any means. But the racket merely served to
inspire the Illinoisans. When Judd nominated Lincoln, their wild
yell, according to one witness, "made soft vesper breathings of
all that had preceded. No language can describe it. A thousand
steam whistles, ten acres of hotel gongs, a tribe of Comanches,
headed by a choice vanguard from pandemonium, might have
mingled in the scene unnoticed."

Dayton of New Jersey, Cameron, and Chase were speedily
put in nomination without the long-winded speeches of our
present-day conventions. Then, before the nominations were
finished, Caleb Smith of Indiana broke in with a second for Lincoln. It had been planned the night before. Again the Illinoisans
shrieked and howled. But they were clearly bested when Seward's
nomination was seconded, for so fiercely did the outnumbered
New Yorkers respond that many persons stopped their ears.

But another second for Lincoln came from an Ohio delegate,

and this time the Lincoln men, calling on the last full measure of their lung power, fairly made the building quiver. Many faces in the New York delegation blanched as "the Lincoln *yawp*" swelled through the building.

Bates, McLean, Cameron, and others were nominated, and the balloting commenced. After the long roll call the chairman announced the result: Seward 173½, Lincoln 102, Cameron 50½, Chase 49, Bates 48, with the remainder scattering. It looked henceforward like a two-way fight.

Seward gained only 11 votes on the second ballot, while Lincoln picked up 79 as Pennsylvania, unmindful of McLean, swung a thumping 48 additional votes to Lincoln and he gained others elsewhere. Chase and Bates trailed with 42½ and 35 respectively.

The tension became almost unbearable as a clerk called the roll again. Hundreds of pencils kept tally. Lincoln steadily picked up. His vote reached 231½; 233 would nominate him. Joseph Medill, who had seated himself quietly among the Ohio delegation, leaned over to whisper to David Cartter, chairman of the Ohioans: "If you can throw the Ohio delegation to Lincoln, Chase can have anything he wants." Cartter, a stammerer, bounded up, exclaiming excitedly: "I-I a-a-rise Mr. Chairman, to a-a-nnounce the c-ch-change of f-four votes, from Mr. Chase to Mr. Lincoln."

There was a moment's silence. Then the wildest yell of all was loosed. Men danced and jumped. Hats, handkerchiefs, banners, canes were tossed aloft. The noise lulled, only to swell again. A cannon on the roof let go with a salute. Boat whistles answered from the river. The city's bells joined in the din. Across the nation thousands of telegraph instruments commenced to chatter.

*

BACK IN Springfield, Lincoln had gone to his office in the morning. He was talking with two young law students when Edward L. Baker, coeditor of the *Journal*, burst in with the result of the first ballot. Unable to stay calmly in his office, Lincoln started for the *Journal* building with Baker. On the way they stopped at the telegraph office, but no further news had come. The crowd that waited there shouted encouragement. At the *Journal* office Lincoln slumped into a chair. Another message came—the second ballot. At last a wire notified Lincoln: "Vote just announced—whole no 466—necessary to choice 234—Lincoln 354 votes—on motion of Mr. Evarts of NY the nomination made unanimous amid intense excitement."

Lincoln learned that Hannibal Hamlin, of Maine, had been chosen as his running mate. Messages of congratulation began ticking in. "We did it. Glory to God," wired Delegate Knapp.

Lincoln, beaming, shook hands all around. Then he started home to tell his wife. That night Springfield went wild. Friends and neighbors thronged the Lincoln home.

*

THE DAY after the adjournment of the Chicago convention a group of distinguished Republican politicians got off the train at Springfield to notify Lincoln officially of his nomination. He received them in the modest parlor of his home. Only a few of them had ever seen him; several were bitterly disappointed by his victory, and some had misgivings about his ability to fulfill the duties of the nation's highest office. All of them scrutinized Lincoln closely as George Ashmun of Massachusetts, their chairman, presenting him with a letter of notification and a copy of the platform, made a short congratulatory speech.

Standing quietly before them in his ill-fitting clothes, head sunk, shoulders drooping, his huge hands clasped in front of him, and a sad, impenetrable expression on his scraggy face, Lincoln seemed embarrassed and irresolute. Ashmun finished, and the bent head lifted. The drooping body straightened to its full height. The dull eyes lighted with an intelligence that animated the whole countenance. The irresolute figure took on a calm, sure dignity.

Lincoln's words were brief—thanks for the honor done him, a recognition of the responsibility of his position, a promise to respond formally in writing when he had studied the platform. He wished to take each visitor by the hand, he said, and with that he passed from man to man, greeting each one cordially, talking easily and sometimes humorously. Governor Edwin D. Morgan of New York was somewhat startled when Lincoln, appraising his lofty stature, asked how tall he was. Refreshments were served, and the committee left.

"Why, sir, they told me he was a rough diamond," said George Boutwell, Governor of Massachusetts, to one of Lincoln's townsmen at a reception for the committee at the Chenery House. "Nothing could have been in better taste than that speech." And Judge W. D. Kelley, of Pennsylvania, turning to Carl Schurz as the committeemen walked down Eighth Street, observed: "Well, we might have done a more brilliant thing, but we could certainly not have done a better thing."

*

E v e r t h e practical politician, Lincoln reckoned his chances of election. They seemed good, even if he was accounted a sectional candidate. Studying the platform, he noted that it had been carefully framed to appeal to diversified groups. A tariff plank, designed to attract the protectionists of Pennsylvania, New Jersey, and New England without alienating the antislavery Democrats who had joined the Republican Party, conformed to Lincoln's own somewhat equivocal inclination toward "a moderate, carefully adjusted, protective tariff" which would not be "a perpetual subject of political strife, squabbles, changes, and uncertainties." A homestead plank, similar to a bill passed by the lower house of Congress but blocked in the Democratic Senate, courted those who wanted free land. River and harbor improvements appealed to the Northwest. A Pacific railroad and a daily overland mail furnished other examples of the positive economic program offered by the Republicans as opposed to Democratic traditions of laissez-faire. A pronouncement against restrictions on immigration and the granting of citizenship offered an enticement to the Germans and other foreign groups.

The platform extolled the Union, censured the Democrats for corruption and extravagance, branded the proposed reopening of the slave trade as a crime, denounced popular sovereignty, and demanded the admission of Kansas as a free state. On the general issue of slavery in the territories, however, the Republicans spoke less forthrightly than in 1856. In that year they had asserted the "imperative duty" of Congress to keep slavery out of the territories, whereas now, anxious to attract conservative votes, they simply denied the authority of Congress or a territorial legislature to give legal sanction to slavery in a territory.

Avoiding any strong pronouncement against slavery, and acknowledging the right of each state to order its own domestic institutions, the Republicans played down the moral question wherever it might lose them votes, shifting their emphasis to whatever economic issue seemed best calculated to appeal to a particular group or region.

Republican organization was thorough. The party's techniques were skilled. Speakers and campaign literature made the most of Lincoln's boyhood poverty, his pioneer background, his native genius, his rise from obscurity to fame. His nicknames, "Honest Abe" and "the Rail-Splitter," were exploited to the full. The party went into the campaign united, for Seward, suppressing the black disappointment the news from Chicago brought him, took the stump for Lincoln. Chase, Bates, and all the lesser aspirants supported him no less loyally. Pole-raisings, rallies, barbecues, songs, and speeches generated wild enthusiasm. All over the North the Republican Wide-Awakes—young men in glazed hats and capes, bearing flaming torches or lamps attached to fence rails—marched in zigzag formation simulating a rail fence.

*

W ITH T HE Republicans presenting a united front, the Democratic ranks were sorely split. The Buchanan-Douglas feud showed no abatement, and the slavery issue threatened to disrupt the Democrats as it had previously undone the Whigs. Far and away the outstanding party figure in the North, Douglas had powerful enemies among the "Buchaneers." "I do not," proclaimed Senator Jesse D. Bright of Indiana, a strong administration man, "nor shall I ever regard a set of men in this country who call themselves 'anti-Lecompton Democrats' in any other light than Abolitionists, and most of them rotten in every sense of the term. I court and defy the opposition of every one of them, from their lying, hypocritical, demagogical master Douglas, down to the sorriest puppy in the kennel."

In the South, Douglas had wide popular support, but the extremist leaders were determined to defeat him at all costs, for to them the exclusion of slavery from the territories by "unfriendly legislation" was as hateful as the Republican doctrine of Congressional prohibition. Among this group were men resolved to rule or ruin. Their last hope of keeping control of the government was to control the Democratic Party. If they failed in that, they proposed to take the South out of the Union.

One such intransigent was spade-bearded Robert Barnwell Rhett, of South Carolina, who, almost from the beginning of his political career, had preached Southern independence as preferable to Northern dominance. Another was pugnacious William Lowndes Yancey, of Alabama, all through the fifties a promoter of sectional consciousness and Southern self-sufficiency. Of like mind were Edmund Ruffin, a Virginia agriculturalist; James D. B. DeBow, New Orleans editor; and John Slidell, Louisiana politician.

On the eve of the Democratic national convention Yancey contrived to have the Alabama delegates instructed to leave the national meeting unless the platform called specifically for the free entry of slavery into all territories and its protection there by positive Federal legislation. South Carolina endorsed this "Alabama platform," as did Mississippi, Florida, Louisiana, Arkansas, and Texas. Douglas could not stand on such a platform, though he was willing again to leave the territorial question to the decision of the Supreme Court. But the fire-eaters were adamant. Douglas's policy of "unfriendly legislation" had given them a means of defeating the exponent of the strong nationalistic sentiment of the Northwest and of rallying the South behind their cause. And in their efforts to encompass the defeat of Douglas, Buchanan's train-bearers in the North would back them up.

As the national convention convened in the fervidly Southern atmosphere of Charleston, South Carolina, on April 23, three weeks before the Republicans met in Chicago, Douglas controlled enough delegates to dictate the platform but too few to obtain the presidential nomination under the Democrats' two-thirds rule. The convention considered the platform first, and Yancey, introducing the Alabama formula, blamed Douglas's type of popular sovereignty for weakening the party in the North. Advocates of Douglas's pet policy, he declared, had virtually acknowledged that slavery existed neither by the law of nature nor by that of God, but solely by popular enactment. "That was your position and it was wrong," he chided. "If you had taken the position directly that slavery was right, and therefore ought to be . . . you could have triumphed, and anti-slavery would now be dead in your midst."

Here was the moral issue, so clearly recognized by Lincoln, voiced by a Southern radical, an issue on which men of moral sensitivities both North and South could not give way. And Douglas, refusing to take a forthright moral stand, would soon find himself between the sectional millstones.

For on the issue of the platform the convention split—an unnecessary outcome because slavery's fate had been decided in almost all the national domain. What the radical forces wanted, however, was acknowledgment of the rightfulness of slavery. Defeated, they marched out of the hall, Yancey's Alabamians in the lead, followed by the entire delegations of Mississippi, Louisiana, South Carolina, Texas, and Florida, with scattering support from Arkansas, Missouri, Georgia, Virginia, and Delaware.

Under the chairman's ruling that the party's presidential

candidate must have the votes of two thirds of the delegates chosen, rather than two thirds of those who remained, Douglas could not be nominated. Neither could anyone else. So Douglas's managers, hoping that Union-loving people would replace the seceders with men of more moderate opinions, recessed the convention for six weeks to meet again on June 18 in Baltimore. Thereupon the seceders, who had adjourned to a neighboring hall, likewise recessed to meet in Richmond on June 11.

Convening in the Virginia capital, the Southern extremists marked time while a number of delegates went on to Baltimore to seek readmission to the regular convention. Some were granted seats, but withdrawals began again, until of the original 303 party representatives only $192\frac{1}{2}$ votes remained. This time the chairman ruled that two thirds of those present could select the nominee, and on the second ballot Douglas became the party's choice.

Meanwhile the Southern seceders had met in Market Hall in Baltimore, where a few die-hard Buchananites from Oregon, California, Pennsylvania, New York, and Minnesota joined them. Adopting the platform of positive protection of slavery that had been rejected at Charleston, they nominated John C. Breckinridge of Kentucky. The Richmond convention then reconvened and endorsed their action.

The situation became more complicated when a group composed mostly of elderly old-line Whigs and former Know-Nothings also met in Baltimore and formed the Constitutional Union Party. Hoping to avert disunion, they declared for "the Constitution of the country, the Union of the states, and the enforcement of the laws," and nominated John Bell, of Tennessee, and Edward Everett, of Massachusetts, as their standard-bearers. The Republicans called them "do-nothings."

Thus, with three opposition tickets in the field, the prospects favored Lincoln. In the North the contest was primarily between Lincoln and Douglas; in the South it was Douglas versus Breckinridge, with Bell also a factor in the border states.

*

IN KEEPING with the tradition that enjoined a candidate from campaigning in his own behalf, Lincoln remained quietly in Springfield. At the insistence of John Locke Scripps of the *Chicago Tribune* he wrote another autobiographical sketch, which became the basis of Scripps's campaign biography as well as others. But he issued no statement of policy, since, as he said, he had already fully defined his position and any new expression would be twisted by his enemies. His only speeches were informal greetings to paraders and well-wishers.

Lincoln's new distinction brought no change in his simple manner of life. He remained as modest, as genial, and as easily accessible as he had always been. But so many people wished to see him that neither his home nor his office would accommodate them, and the Governor's room on the second floor of the state-house was put at his disposal. Serious, systematic John George Nicolay, a German-born Pike County editor, recently in the employ of the Illinois secretary of state, became Lincoln's private secretary, with dapper, sapient John Hay as his assistant. Both of these young men, Nicolay twenty-eight and Hay twenty-two, were destined to serve Lincoln for the rest of his career.

Lincoln's office had no anteroom, but the door to the hall was seldom shut. All day visitors trooped in and out—friends, politicians, favor-seekers, reporters, profferers and seekers of advice, the merely curious—while Nicolay at his desk in a corner tried to breast the tidal wave of mail, and sometimes in another corner a portrait-painter worked on Lincoln's likeness. Lincoln never seemed hurried, never lost his patience, was always master of the situation. Questioners never drew him out against his will. He imparted only what he wished to. Orville H. Browning recorded in his diary that "Lincoln bears his honors meekly. As soon as other company had retired after I went in he fell into his old habit of telling amusing stories, and we had a free and easy talk of an hour or two." Midway of the campaign seven-year-old Tad Lincoln came down with a bad case of scarlet fever. A sore throat and a headache led Lincoln to believe he had a touch of it himself.

In October a letter from "a number of very earnest Republicans" in New York suggested that Lincoln's dignity might be enhanced with a beard, and soon afterward the same advice was proffered by eleven-year-old Grace Bedell, of Westfield, New York, who believed that since "all the ladies like whiskers" they would "tease their husbands to vote for you." Lincoln doubtless chuckled, and replied in his own handwriting: "As to the whiskers, having never worn any, do you not think people would call it a piece of silly affect[at]ion if I were to begin it now?" Soon afterward, however, he allowed his beard to grow.

If Lincoln took no public part in the campaign, his seeming inactivity was merely superficial. He followed events closely and kept a sensitive finger on the public pulse. He wrote numerous letters. Whenever a breach threatened in the Republican dike, he was quick with advice or warning. Douglas would make a supreme effort in New York, he cautioned Weed. He admonished Hannibal Hamlin, his running mate, that any show of weakness in the early-voting state of Maine might "put us on the down-hill track," and lose the state elections in Pennsylvania and Indiana and perhaps the national contest in November. While keeping close touch with the situation country-wide, Lincoln carefully stayed clear of local party squabbles and rivalries.

*

As LINCOLN measured the progress of events from Springfield, ominous news came from the South, where the extremist politicians, having disrupted the Democratic Party, now warned of the consequences of Republican victory. The protective tariff, the homestead law, and government expenditures for internal improvements were all means of plundering the South for Yankee benefit, they claimed. Slavery and the Southern way of life would be destroyed if Lincoln won.

Lincoln did not treat such bluster seriously, though he watched the situation carefully. The Southern people, he wrote to a correspondent in August, had too much common sense and good temper to break up the government rather than see it administered in the manner of those who formed it. In some respects his confidence seemed justified, for in every Southern state Unionist groups contended with the fire-eaters. Furthermore, even if the Republicans elected a President and won a majority in the House, the Democrats were sure to retain control of the Senate. How could the Republicans enact legislation destructive of Southern rights? All the presidential candidates—even Breckinridge—were committed to the Union. How could the secession peril become acute? Lincoln had often heard this threat before. It had been used effectively against Frémont. Its purpose now was to accomplish his defeat, he thought.

*

IN CONTRAST to Lincoln, Douglas threw tradition to the winds and campaigned strenuously. As the only anti-Republican candidate with a chance to carry the free states, he put everything into the fight. And despite the odds against him he still thought he might win. Knowing the Southern temper better than Lincoln, he gave more credence to Southern threats. His own election would assure peace. He must get his message to the people.

So Douglas stumped the nation, an unheard-of thing for a presidential candidate. He had been ill; his throat was bad; but he worked with superhuman energy, traveling through New England, North Carolina, and the middle states, then to the West.

In August, local elections in Vermont and Maine produced large Republican majorities. In a desperate effort to head off defeat, the anti-Republican parties attempted fusion in some Northern states. During the second week in October, however, state elections in Pennsylvania and Ohio confirmed the early trend, and Douglas, learning by telegraph of these Republican victories, remarked gravely to his secretary: "Mr. Lincoln is the next President. We must try to save the Union. I will go South."

His speeches there were fiercely Unionist. The election of a Republican offered no justification for secession, he insisted. Abolitionists and seceders alike deserved to dangle at a rope's end. Douglas appealed to the whole nation, but it was his misfortune to be accounted proslavery in the North and antislavery in the South.

*

DESPITE every effort of Douglas and the Southern Unionists, fear overspread the South. Wild rumors circulated. Abolitionists were said to be working secretly among the Negroes. Wells had been poisoned in Texas. Drought added to the despair as it threatened the cotton crop. Heavy debts to Northern banks and importers oppressed farmers and planters. The South was restless, frustrated, alarmed.

The economic loss that threatened if the Republicans should free the slaves was not the South's chief concern; only a relatively small proportion of Southerners owned slaves. What haunted everyone was the specter of savage black men roaming the country uncontrolled, or of Negroes claiming social and economic equality with the whites, attending their schools and churches, competing for their jobs, outvoting them at the polls. All classes shared these fears, because, while the planters might be badly hurt by emancipation, they could survive, whereas the poor white man faced not only destitution but degradation. For slavery gave even the meanest white man a measure of respectability; there was always the black man below him in the social scale.

What if Lincoln were elected, people asked. He had said he would not free the slaves. But how about his abolitionist cohorts? Could he hold out against them, granting that he really wished to do so? Many persons believed him to be an abolitionist regardless of his denials. And even if Lincoln made no overt move, the Republican policy of containment meant slow death to slavery. At best, the evil day would merely be deferred.

Lincoln would control the patronage. Whom would he appoint to office in the South? Mudsills? Free Negroes? Abolitionists? Republican postmasters would not censor the mails; incendiary literature would flood the country. Men wondered if some sinister purpose inspired the organization of those well-drilled Wide-Awakes. Some planters saw the election of a scion of poor whites of Kentucky as incitement to submerged Southern whites to flout planter ascendancy.

In the little crossroads stores, on the village streets, in the parlors of isolated mansions and the kitchens of lonely backwoods farmhouses, men meeting quietly gave sober utterance to their forebodings.

Cherishing an archaic institution, the South had developed a provincial philosophy. The Southern people believed they had developed a superior civilization founded on a rightful institution. It was unmarred by those sordid conflicts between capital and labor which frequently plagued the North. It provided its workers with a social security unequaled anywhere. Yet the swindling, penny-pinching Yankees, who ground the faces of their own workers in the dust and threw them on their own resources when their working days were over, these self-righteous Yankees vilified the Southern way of life, and pronounced the slaveowner evil. For too long now the North had exploited the South and held it back. More and more, especially after John Brown's raid, Southerners yielded to the belief that the old union of hearts and souls was broken, and the South should go her own way. Providing the intellectual basis for state rights and Southern independence was the political philosophy of John C. Calhoun, so universally accepted in the South that, while many persons questioned the wisdom of secession, scarcely anyone denied the right.

This feeling of "Southernism" flourished most intensely in South Carolina, where members of the ruling oligarchy were resolved to retain power. Secession appeared to be their only hope; they would sunder the old affiliations and set up a government of their own. The Gulf states were in a mood to join them. How could the money-grubbing Yankees stop the movement when they would never fight? One Southerner sneered that if a Yankee ever pointed a gun at him he would simply ask how much he would take for it. Before election day six Southern governors and virtually every Senator and Congressman from the seven states of the lower South were on record as favoring secession if Lincoln should be elected.

*

L I N C O L N spent most of election day, November 6, at his office in the statehouse. About three o'clock he walked quietly to the polls at the courthouse, where, after cutting the names of his own electors from the top of the ballot, he voted a straight ticket. A dense crowd cheered him, following him through the hall and up the stairs, then down again.

That night Lincoln sat in the telegraph office while the returns came in. The outcome did not long remain in doubt. When the tabulation was completed, Lincoln had 1,866,452 votes, Douglas 1,376,957, Breckinridge 849,781, and Bell 588,879. Douglas and Bell together had 100,000 more votes than Lincoln; his three opponents outpolled him by almost a million. Only Bell carried his home county—Sangamon went for Douglas by a narrow margin. Except for a few ballots in the border states and the Virginia panhandle, Lincoln polled not one vote in the South.

The electoral vote would shape up differently. Lincoln, carrying all the Northern states except New Jersey, whose vote he split with Douglas, would have 173 votes, Breckinridge 72, Bell 39, and Douglas 12. Yet such is the peculiarity of our electoral system that, if all the opposition votes had been united upon a single candidate, Lincoln would still have won. He would be a minority President, but there were no constitutional grounds on which to contest his election.

CHAPTER XII

Peace or a Sword

A PRESIDENT elected in November did not take office until March; Lincoln faced four months of anxious waiting. But he was not wholly powerless. While the repudiated Buchanan administration would continue to control the government, as President-elect and nominal head of his party he could influence opinion and decisions through public statements, letters, and pressure on Republican Congressmen.

The resolute intentions of the disunionists became manifest when South Carolina called a secession convention. Other Southern states followed her lead. Stocks declined sharply; some banks and business houses closed. Frightened men both North and South entreated Lincoln, as the prime cause of all the turmoil, to offer some word of reassurance to the South.

"I could say nothing which I have not already said, and which is in print and accessible to the public," he replied to an appeal from Nathaniel Paschall, editor of the *Missouri Republican*. "Please pardon me for suggesting that if the papers like yours, which heretofore have persistently garbled, and misrepresented what I have said, will now fully and fairly place it before their readers, there can be no further misunderstanding. I beg you to believe me sincere, when . . . I urge it as the true cure for any real uneasiness in the country. . . . The Republican newspapers now, and for some time past, are and have been republishing copious extracts from my many published speeches, which would at once reach the whole public if your class of papers would also publish them. I am not at liberty to shift my ground— that is out of the question. If I thought a *repetition* would do any good I would make it. But my judgment is it would do positive harm. The secessionists, *per se* believing they had alarmed me, would clamor all the louder."

As pleas for a mollifying gesture continued to pour in, Lincoln, late in November, gave way to the extent of preparing two conciliatory paragraphs for insertion in a speech by Senator Trumbull at a great Republican victory rally at Springfield. Each state would be left in control of its own affairs, promised Trumbull, speaking for the President-elect. The secessionists were in "hot haste" to get out of the Union because with them it was "now or never." Once the Republicans came to power, Southern fears would be dispelled.

But, as Lincoln had anticipated, the speech did little good. Press and politicians reacted according to their preconceived opinions. Secessionists interpreted Trumbull's remarks as threats; Democrats thought them deliberately misleading; while radical Republicans rebuked Lincoln for weakness. "These political fiends are not half sick enough yet," Lincoln complained to Henry J. Raymond, editor of the *New York Times*. " 'Party malice,' and not 'public good,' possesses them entirely. 'They seek a sign, and no sign shall be given them.' At least such is my present feeling and purpose." As time passed, Trumbull and other Republicans in Congress, convinced that Lincoln's enemies would willfully misinterpret anything he might say, endorsed his policy of silence.

While Lincoln neither made nor authorized any further public statements, he tried to reassure loyal Southerners. A Kentuckian, Duff Green, influential Democratic editor and financier, after a frank talk with him in Springfield, left in a more placid frame of mind. In letters to John A. Gilmer, a loyal North Carolinian, Lincoln reasserted his pacific purpose, making it clear, however, that he did not propose to shape his course "as if I repented for the crime of having been elected, and was anxious to apologize and beg forgiveness." Lincoln was pleased when Alexander H. Stephens, his old friend of Congressional days, defended the Union in a stirring speech before the Georgia Legislature. Commending Stephens for his patriotism, Lincoln asked if the Southern people really suspected him of wishing to disturb their institutions. If so, they were unduly alarmed. "I suppose, however, this does not meet the case," he said. "You think slavery is *right* and ought to be extended; while we think it is *wrong* and ought to be restricted. That I suppose is the rub."

Stephens, in his reply, agreed that this was so. Before long, as Vice-President of the Confederate States of America, he would declare that the foundations of this new Confederate government rested "upon the truth that the negro is not equal to the white man, that slavery—subordination to the superior race—is his natural and normal condition." Writing to Caleb Cushing of Massachusetts, Kenneth Rayner of North Carolina confirmed the correctness of Lincoln's analysis of the Southern mind. "It is not Lincoln," he explained, "—so far as he is concerned he is taken but little in account. . . . He is regarded as neither a dangerous or a bad man. We have no fears that he is going to attempt any great outrage upon us. We rather suppose his purpose will be to conciliate. But it is . . . the *fundamental idea* that underlies the whole movement of his nomination and canvass, & his election. It is the declaration of unceasing war against slavery as an institution."

*

WHEN CONGRESS met early in December, the perplexed and venerable Buchanan, fearful of secession but still sympathetic toward his Southern friends and the Southern point of view, asserted in his annual message that while a state could not lawfully secede, neither could the Federal government coerce it. He proposed to quiet Southern fears by calling a constitutional convention to frame amendments guaranteeing slavery in the states and territories, and assuring the recovery of runaway slaves.

Unmindful of the President's efforts, South Carolina seceded on December 20. Mississippi, Florida, Alabama, Georgia, and Louisiana speedily took similar action. With Texas's renunciation of the Union on February 1, 1861, revolt had swept the Gulf states. The secessionists took over Federal forts and arsenals. State flags replaced the Stars and Stripes on customhouses.

Worried Congressmen, with scant faith in Buchanan, sought for their own formula of settlement. A House Committee of Thirty-three proved ineffectual; but the Senate Committee of Thirteen, composed of capable, intelligent men of the caliber of Seward and Douglas, came up with a number of plans. Douglas again advanced the idea of popular sovereignty. Senator Crittenden of Kentucky, political heir of the famous compromiser, Henry Clay, proposed a series of permanent amendments to the Constitution whereby slavery would be guaranteed forever in the slave states and the District of Columbia, continuance of the domestic slave trade would be assured, and slaveowners would be indemnified for runaways. On the troublesome territorial question, Crittenden favored an extension of the Missouri Compromise line to the Pacific, slavery to be forever excluded north of it and guaranteed in all territory then owned or thereafter acquired to the south.

Sharing the general anxiety for the safety of the Union, a number of Republican Congressmen were disposed to be conciliatory. Several of them, notably those from Illinois, sought Lincoln's guidance. The President-elect, worn, torn, harassed by the flood of visitors and office-seekers, knew that his decision might be fateful for the Union, which he was determined to preserve at every cost. But how could this best be done—through such firmness as President Jackson had displayed in the nullification crisis of 1832, or through compromise? And would refusal to compromise mean war?

Lincoln quickly made up his mind. To all inquiries he gave essentially the same response: as to fugitive slaves, slavery in the District of Columbia, the internal slave trade, and "whatever springs of necessity from the fact that the institution is amongst us," he cared but little. But on the question of slavery in the territories he was immovable. Either popular sovereignty or toleration of slavery south of the Missouri Compromise line would, in his opinion, "put us again on the high road to a slave empire." In 1854 a restoration of the Missouri Compromise would have satisfied him. Since then, however, he had noted the eagerness of the slave power for expansion into Mexico and Central America, and for the acquisition of Cuba. Allow any sort of territorial compromise to be adopted, he warned Congressman Washburne, and "immediately filibustering and extending slavery recommences." A year would not pass, he was convinced, "till we shall have to take Cuba as a condition upon which they will stay in the Union."

Thus Lincoln took upon himself the grave responsibility of blocking compromise. "Stand firm," he admonished Senator Trumbull. "The tug has to come, & better, now than any time hereafter." "Hold firm, as with a chain of steel," he wrote to Washburne. To Lincoln, compromise did not necessarily mean peace. He had seen too many supposed compromises perverted or renounced.

But neither did Lincoln's rejection of compromise mean that he either wanted or expected war. He had supreme confidence in the sound common sense of the people. During the entire four months between his election and his assumption of office, he continued to believe that the strong Union sentiment in the Southern states would assert itself if given time. The real test would come in the more northerly slave states. If they remained under the old flag, traditions, self-interest, and inherent loyalties would soon bring the others back.

Nor did Lincoln seem to have misjudged the strength of Southern Unionism. Secession appeared to have run its course. News came from North Carolina: a decisive vote against a secession convention. Similar good tidings came from Tennessee. Arkansas and Missouri showed little disposition toward hasty action. Buchanan and his reconstructed cabinet had stiffened. Douglas was preaching loyalty. Lincoln's native state of Kentucky was resisting the efforts of her Governor to take her out. Governor Thomas H. Hicks of Maryland, where secession sentiment burned hot, staved off the disunionists by refusing to call the Legislature into session. And, most encouraging of all, Virginia, whose influence was paramount with the slave states, not only selected 122 loyalists against 30 disunionists as delegates to her state convention, but stipulated additionally that any ordinance of secession must be ratified by popular vote. Going even farther, Virginia offered her own plan of reconciliation. All the loyal slave states except Arkansas accepted her invitation to send delegates to a peace convention at Washington. With seven states out of the Union, eight showed unmistakable signs of loyalty. It seemed that the tide had turned.

With the safety of the Union hinging on the attitude of these loyal slave states, Lincoln made it his objective to maintain the national authority while avoiding any rash or provocative action. The Republicans must come to power with the government still respected, and with the slave states in a temperate mood. Tactically such a policy would demand rare skill. Signs of weakness would inspirit the hotheads and forfeit the confidence of the moderates, whereas belligerence would encourage the upper slave states to join their sister commonwealths in revolt.

It was a trying time, and already Lincoln showed the strain. Every day brought its horde of office-seekers; they descended on him in such numbers that Springfield's hotels and boarding-houses were crammed and the overflow put up in sleeping-cars. With every mail came a cascade of letters—some pleading, some counseling, others demanding, wheedling, warning, threatening, or cursing him. Lincoln's friend W. H. L. Wallace wrote to his wife: "I have seen Mr. Lincoln two or three times since I have been here, but only for a moment & he is continually surrounded by a crowd of people. He has a world of responsibility & seems to feel it & to be oppressed by it. He looks care worn & more haggard & stooped than I ever saw him."

Visits of old friends like Wallace provided brief interludes of relaxation, and Lincoln's unfailing sense of humor also helped to ease the tension under which he worked. One day, while he was talking with a newspaperman, his son Willie burst into the office demanding a quarter. "I can't let you have a quarter," Lincoln answered; "I can only spare five cents." He placed five pennies on the desk-corner, but Willie, spurning such parsimony, clattered off down the corridor. "He will be back after that in a few minutes," Lincoln observed. "As soon as he finds I will give him no more, he will come and get it." After the father and his visitor had forgotten the matter, Willie came in quietly, pocketed the money, and left without a word.

*

THE PROMISES made by Lincoln's managers at the Chicago convention caused him additional trouble. "They have gambled me all around, bought and sold me a hundred times," he complained. "I cannot begin to fill all the pledges made in my name." But if the patronage proved an annoyance, it could also serve as an effective instrument with which to cement his party. With that end in view, Lincoln began to select his cabinet.

One reason why he preferred to keep silent on the questions facing the country was the impossibility of making any statement that would not displease some faction of a political organization whose ideology ranged from political opportunism at one extreme to crusading zealotry at the other. As Lincoln faced the choice of his advisers, he planned to bring representatives of all the major elements of the Republican Party into his cabinet, trusting to his own skill and persuasiveness to reconcile their views.

Early in December, Lincoln offered Seward the portfolio of the State Department. Seward hesitated. "The wily old scarecrow," as Henry Adams described him, with his slouching, slender figure, his mussy clothes, his beaked nose and shaggy eyebrows that gave him the profile of a canny macaw, still regarded himself as the real leader of the party. Lincoln was utterly untried, Seward thought, and scarcely to be trusted with grave issues in such a perilous time. Could Seward work most effectively within or outside the cabinet? The astute New Yorker dispatched his political henchman, Thurlow Weed, to Springfield to learn more about Lincoln's opinions. On the day that South Carolina seceded, Weed and Lincoln were closeted, discussing patronage and policy, and Weed attempting to determine to what degree the inexperienced Illinoisan would accept Seward's advice.

Next on Lincoln's list came Salmon P. Chase. Tall, erect, with a finely shaped head and level blue eyes that lent a certain majesty to his appearance, Chase's sterling honesty qualified him for the Treasury. Touchy, ambitious, unbending, he was a leader of the antislavery radicals.

Long-bearded, prudent Edward Bates, of Missouri, was chosen for Attorney General. Shy, reserved, and of old-fashioned courtliness, he was a pensive, unimaginative man, slender of body, thin through the shoulders, but with a rugged face, dominated by heavy brows and prominent nose over a copious beard. An antislavery lawyer of the strict-construction school, he would speak for the border-state loyalists.

To give the critical border states a generous measure of representation, Lincoln selected shrewd, pinch-faced Montgomery Blair, of Maryland, for Postmaster General. A son of old Francis P. Blair of Andrew Jackson's celebrated "kitchen cabinet," a graduate of West Point, who, turning to law and politics, had defended Dred Scott before the Supreme Court, Montgomery Blair was prominent among the Union element in Maryland, just as his brother "Frank" Blair, Jr., once a slaveholder, was now a leader of the free-soil forces in Missouri. The Blairs—clannish, contentious, and politically adept—wielded immense influence.

Lincoln settled on Gideon Welles, of Connecticut, for Secretary of the Navy. Actually, Welles was the choice of Vice-President-elect Hannibal Hamlin, whom Lincoln consulted in Chicago regarding New England's representation in the cabinet. Testy, opinionated, and humorless, Welles affected a heavy beard and a thick, pomaded, light-brown wig that give him the appearance of Father Neptune. A former Democratic editor, an "old granny" according to his enemies, utterly inexperienced in naval matters but with the good sense to accept the expert and energetic guidance of his brilliant young assistant Gustavus Vasa Fox, Welles would prove to be a capable and conscientious administrator.

In choosing a Secretary of the Interior, Lincoln respected David Davis's pledge to Caleb B. Smith, a plodding party liegeman with influence in his own state of Indiana, but undistinguished otherwise.

Most vexatious to the harassed President-elect was the question of what to do with Simon Cameron, a rich, dominating, behind-the-scenes wire-puller to whom politics had been a profitable business. Tall and slim, with delicate features and a sort of foxy wariness, Cameron controlled a powerful faction in Pennsylvania, but was opposed by men equally strong. Soon after the election Lincoln, honoring Davis's promise, assured Cameron of a cabinet post—the Pennsylvania boss preferred the Treasury. Then, when immediate pressure was brought to bear against Cameron, and Lincoln was reminded of some of his questionable deals, the President-elect withdrew the offer. But Cameron had allowed it to reach the press; his pride and prestige would suffer if Lincoln failed to follow through. Cameron's friends and enemies hounded Lincoln week by week. At last, when the rival Pennsylvania faction became fearful that their state might be passed over altogether, and withdrew their opposition, Lincoln, perhaps against his better judgment, made Cameron Secretary of War.

Almost from the time of Lincoln's election he had known generally the men he would select, but fearing that he would be "teased to insanity to make changes," he did not tender some of the positions until he reached Washington. Meanwhile some desperate maneuvering took place, for the Seward and Cameron factions disliked Chase because of his radicalism, Welles looked upon the suave Seward as a conniver, and many party stalwarts abhorred the powerful and ofttimes mischief-making Blairs.

On the eve of Lincoln's inauguration his carefully chosen slate threatened to crash when Seward withdrew his acceptance of the Department of State, refusing to serve with Chase. "I cannot afford to let Seward take the first trick," commented the

harried Lincoln as he forced the capricious New Yorker to reconsider.

Lincoln excluded all Illinoisans from his cabinet because
he himself came from that state, but Norman Judd and many
others who had helped to promote his candidacy were rewarded
with lesser jobs. Some old-line Whigs grumbled that the three
representatives of their party—Seward, Bates, and Smith—were
outnumbered by the former Democrats—Chase, Welles, Blair,
and Cameron; but Lincoln reminded them that his own Whig
antecedents restored the balance.

The furor occasioned by Lincoln's election convinced some
of the most bitterly partisan Republicans that one cabinet post
should be offered to an out-and-out Southerner as a gesture of
good will. Lincoln did not see how any true Southerner could
serve without dishonoring his convictions, but he was willing
to try. As early as November he made overtures to James
Guthrie, of Kentucky, a Democrat and former Secretary of the
Treasury under Pierce, who pleaded age and infirmities. Lincoln's
next choice was John A. Gilmer, of North Carolina, who consulted
with Southern colleagues in Congress, turned down the President-
elect's offer, and eventually became a Confederate Congressman.
Others whom Lincoln considered proved unacceptable on one
score or another, so that he finally settled for Bates and Blair.
Outside the border states, however, their appointment did no
good; staunch Southerners considered them renegades.

For a President to select a political rival for a cabinet post
was not unprecedented; but deliberately to surround himself with
all of his disappointed antagonists seemed to be courting disaster.
It was a mark of his sincere intentions that Lincoln wanted the
advice of men as strong as himself or stronger. That he entertained no fear of being crushed or overridden by such men
revealed either surpassing naïveté or a tranquil confidence in his
powers of leadership.

*

WITH LINCOLN in Springfield, the direction of Republican
strategy in Washington fell naturally to Seward, who, because

of his influence in the Senate, his position on the Committee of
Thirteen, and his close relations with Southern Congressmen, was
well qualified as a political tactician. Weed's visit to Springfield
served to acquaint Seward with Lincoln's views, and thereafter
Lincoln and Seward kept in close touch with each other through
correspondence. Temperamentally Seward was an excellent man
to trim ship in a storm; he could play skillfully for time, his
constant smile and friendly nature helped to calm and pacify,
and he could equivocate and compromise if necessary. While he
acted generally according to Lincoln's wishes, occasional devia-
tions revealed his notion of his own superior judgment.

Most worrisome to the Republicans was the possibility that
the Buchanan administration, by its very weakness, might encourage the secessionists to strike such a vital blow at the government that the Republicans would inherit a situation beyond
saving. To guard against this possibility, Seward established a
close relationship with John A. Dix, Secretary of the Treasury,
who lived with Buchanan in the White House, and with devious,
conniving Edwin M. Stanton, a firm Unionist, who had recently
been appointed to Buchanan's cabinet. Distrustful of Southern
influence on Buchanan, and suspicious of the designs of proslavery sympathizers in Washington, Stanton secretly informed
Seward of the most intimate details of cabinet councils, so that
the Republicans could guard against surprise. Furthermore,
both Seward and Lincoln kept in close touch with wheezy,
rheumatic General Winfield Scott, three-hundred-pound, six-
foot-five general of the army, who, despite his Virginia birth and
breeding, a multitude of ailments, and the bullets that he carried
in his seventy-four-year-old body, remained loyal, vigilant, and
clear of mind.

During January near panic prevailed in Washington. Rumors
of plots to seize the city, which was surrounded by slave territory, frightened loyal citizens. By February this fear subsided,
only to give place to whisperings of Southern intentions to prevent the counting of the electoral votes, scheduled for February
13. Lincoln became apprehensive lest the Senate, still Demo-

cratic despite secessionist resignations that had given the House a Republican majority, might refuse to make his election official. The atmosphere of the capital was tense as Senate and House convened, but the count took place without disturbance. Now rumors of secessionist intentions to prevent Lincoln's inauguration and of plots to assassinate him kept Washington in turmoil.

So far, the Republicans, following the course prescribed by Lincoln, had voted down all efforts at formal compromise on slavery in the territories. Near the end of the Congressional session, however, they went as far as anyone except the most radical Southerners demanded in making concessions on this point. Whether this conciliatory action resulted from Seward's inclination toward appeasement and was taken without Lincoln's sanction is not clear. In any case, Lincoln offered no objection when Dakota, Nevada, and Colorado were organized as territories without mention of slavery. Further secessionist withdrawals had now given the Republicans control of both House and Senate, and Douglas could not suppress a note of exultation as his antagonists came over at last to the popular-sovereignty principle for which he had fought so long. "What you . . . said before the election was one thing," he said with jubilation. "What you felt it your duty as patriots to do . . . after the election is a very different thing." He referred to this in no spirit of recrimination, he declared. It was an act of patriotism.

"We talked the subject over," explained the bellicose abolitionist Ben Wade, of Ohio, "and both sides, feeling the necessity of having a territorial organization there, agreed that there should be nothing said about slavery . . . one way or the other, and the bill was framed with that in view." Not only was it ironical that after contesting for a decade Democrats and Republicans should come together on the eve of war, but it was also significant that this friendly gesture was lost on the South. Either these efforts at appeasement came too late, or Lincoln was correct in his opinion that the question of the rightfulness or wrongfulness of slavery was the insuperable obstacle to adjustment.

*

THE TIME for Lincoln's departure for Washington drew near. During the first week in February he slipped quietly away from Springfield for a farewell visit with his stepmother in Coles County. Ten miles from the railroad station he traveled by horse and buggy to exchange greetings with old friends, to recall old times, and to take into his arms the woman who had filled the place of his dead mother in his life. About to assume the highest office in the land, Lincoln put these humble people at their ease by his modesty and friendliness.

Back in Springfield, during the last week before departure, the Lincolns announced in the *Journal* that they would be pleased to receive their friends. Some seven hundred persons came to the modest house on Eighth Street, many of them waiting twenty minutes to reach the door where Lincoln stood shaking hands. In the parlor they were greeted by Mrs. Lincoln, assisted by her son Robert and three sisters. The future first lady was becomingly dressed in a gown of white moire silk with full train and a small lace collar. Afterward the Lincolns, their house already leased, sold most of their furniture, entrusted their dog to a neighbor, and took quarters at the Chenery House, where Lincoln roped their trunks with his own hands and addressed them to "A. Lincoln, The White House, Washington, D.C."

On the afternoon of Lincoln's last day in Springfield, he stopped at his office to have a final talk with Billy Herndon. Arrangements were made to complete unfinished business. Then Lincoln threw himself on the old sofa and lay gazing at the ceiling for some time. He began to reminisce. At one point he startled Herndon by asking how many times Billy had been drunk, and confided how other lawyers had tried to supplant Herndon in the partnership because of his heavy drinking. At last Lincoln rose, gathered up an armful of books, and the two men walked slowly down the stairs. Outside the street door they stopped and Lincoln looked wistfully at the "Lincoln & Herndon" sign. "Let it hang there undisturbed," he said. "Give our clients to understand that the election of a President makes no change in the firm of Lincoln and Herndon. If I live I'm coming back some time, and then we'll go right on practicing law as if nothing had ever happened." The two men parted with a firm clasp of hands. "I am sick of office-holding already," Lincoln said, "and I shudder when I think of the tasks that are still ahead."

The day of departure, February 11, was cold and drizzly. Early morning found Lincoln and his party in the waiting-room of the small, brick Great Western station. Spirits seemed depressed and gloomy as friends and neighbors gathered around him in farewell. Outside, the whistle of the stubby locomotive sounded, and the President-elect and his party climbed aboard the single passenger car, which, with engine and baggage-car, made up the special train. The crowd gathered around the rear platform, umbrellas raised against the rain. Lincoln stood for a moment at the rail, head down, an expression of tragic sadness on his face. Slowly his chin lifted and he looked into the faces of these neighbors who had come to wish him success.

A hush fell on the crowd. "My friends," said Lincoln quietly, "no one, not in my situation, can appreciate my feeling of sadness at this parting. To this place, and the kindness of these people I owe everything. Here I have lived a quarter of a century, and have passed from a young to an old man. Here my children have been born, and one is buried. I now leave, not knowing when, or whether ever, I may return, with a task before me greater than that which rested upon Washington. Without the assistance of that Divine Being who ever attended him, I cannot succeed. With that assistance I cannot fail. Trusting in Him who can go with me, and remain with you and be everywhere for good, let us confidently hope that all will yet be well. To His care commending you, as I hope in your prayers you will commend me, I bid you an affectionate farewell."

*

THE TWELVE-DAY trip to Washington was an ordeal. At last Lincoln must speak, while still reluctant to reveal his plans prematurely. In all the larger cities receptions and formal appearances had been planned. Crowds gathered at every whistle stop. The train followed a winding way in order that as many persons as possible might see and hear him. Never before or after was he required to make so many speeches in so few days.

These speeches, mostly extemporaneous, too often sounded trite. Lincoln seemed evasive and uncertain of himself. With the Confederate States of America in process of formation at Montgomery, Alabama, he assured the Ohio Legislature that nothing was going wrong. "We entertain different views upon political questions, but nobody is suffering anything." At Steubenville, Ohio, he declared that devotion to the Constitution was equally strong on both sides of the Ohio River; the difference was one of interpretation. At Cleveland, Buffalo, Pittsburgh, and Troy, Lincoln asserted that the crisis was artificial. Perhaps his greatest blunder was that he misjudged, not so much the South's affection for the Union, but its superior feeling of state loyalty. Nor did he understand to what a degree the common people of the South had come under planter dominance.

Frequently Lincoln appealed for the preservation of the Union. This was the people's task. It meant little to one man of fifty-two, he said at Indianapolis, whether the Union were shattered and the liberties of the people lost. But it meant much to the thirty millions who inhabited the United States, and to their posterity. Constantly they must bear in mind that not with politicians, not with Presidents, not with office-seekers, "but with you, is the question, 'Shall the Union and shall the liberties of this country be preserved to the latest generations.' " Cheers answered him in the hall of the New Jersey House of Representatives when he warned that if it became necessary "to put the foot down firmly," the people must support him. Again and again, however, he declared there was no need of war. The government would not use force unless force was used against it.

While the special train rolled across New York State on its way to Albany, news came that Jefferson Davis, standing on the colonnaded portico of the Alabama statehouse, had taken the oath of office as President of the Confederacy. An actress, Maggie Mitchell, had danced on the Stars and Stripes.

Lincoln became weary from the incessant round of ceremonies. Staid Easterners with slight acquaintance with the Western type marked his awkward gestures and ambling walk. His frontier pronunciation offended cultured ears. His offhand conversation and fund of homely anecdotes created the impression of a man of provincial outlook and shallow mind. New York sophisticates snickered when he appeared at the opera in black kid gloves, his huge hands hanging over the railing of his box. Playing up his every trifling social error, the hostile press dubbed him a "gorilla" and "baboon."

At intervals in a generally mediocre performance, Lincoln's earnestness welled out in eloquence. Conscious of the historical significance of his surroundings as he raised a flag at Independence Hall in Philadelphia, he declared: "I have never had a feeling politically that did not spring from the sentiments embodied in the Declaration of Independence. . . . I have often inquired of myself what great principle or idea it was that kept this Confederacy so long together. It was not the mere matter of the separation of the colonies from the mother land, but that something in the Declaration giving liberty, not alone to the people of this country, but hope to the world for all future time. It was that which gave promise that in due time the weights should be lifted from the shoulders of all men, and that *all* should have an equal chance."

The next day, at Harrisburg, Lincoln told of his inner excitement as he drew down the halyard and the flag broke out on the breeze. He had taken it for an omen. He was only an agency in sending aloft the banner of the Union. He had not provided the flag nor participated in the arrangements. He served merely as an instrument of the people who planned the ceremony. "And if I can have the same generous cooperation of the people of this nation, I think the flag of our country may yet be kept flaunting gloriously."

*

THE NIGHT before Lincoln raised the flag at Independence
Hall, a knock sounded on the door of Norman Judd, a member of
Lincoln's party, as he rested in his hotel room. Opening the
door, Judd was confronted by S. M. Felton, president of the
Philadelphia, Wilmington & Baltimore Railroad, who was accompanied by a short, bearded man with a hint of a Scotch burr in
his speech, whom Judd recognized as Allan Pinkerton, head of a
private detective agency. In the hour's conference that followed,
Pinkerton disclosed full details of a plot against Lincoln's life,
about which he had warned Judd twice before—once by letter and
once by private messenger.

Pinkerton, employed by Felton to investigate rumors that
secessionist military companies, organized in Baltimore, were
plotting to burn bridges or otherwise disrupt traffic over the
railroad to prevent troops from being sent to Washington or
points south, had sent operatives to prowl the saloons and under-
world of Baltimore, notorious not only for its intense secession
spirit but also for its gangs of lawless toughs. From the reports
of these investigators, Pinkerton became convinced of a well-
organized plot to murder Lincoln when he crossed the city to
change trains. Judd had not taken Pinkerton's previous warnings
seriously, but now, as the detective revealed his information
fully, Judd shared his alarm. He sent for Lincoln and had
Pinkerton repeat his story.

The President-elect listened calmly. He knew that feeling
in Baltimore was tense. Street-corner gossip hinted that he
would be stabbed or shot while passing through the streets,
that his train would be derailed, or that he would be abducted
and sent south on a boat lurking in the harbor. Baltimore was
the only city of any size that had made no formal preparations
to receive him and had sent no official welcome. But threats
and anonymous warnings were becoming commonplace to him.
He could not believe that anyone really wished to do him harm.

Judd and Felton, however, had become so apprehensive that

they urged Lincoln to abandon his schedule and take the train to Washington that night. He would not hear of it. He had agreed to speak to the people of Philadelphia in the morning and to the Pennsylvania Legislature at Harrisburg in the afternoon. The most he would concede was that if, when he reached Harrisburg, no welcoming delegation came to accompany him to Baltimore, he would return to Philadelphia and go on to Washington immediately.

When Lincoln returned to his room through the crowded corridors, he was accosted by Frederick Seward, son of the Senator. In Lincoln's room young Seward confided that he brought letters from his father and General Scott warning Lincoln of a plot to kill him when he passed through Baltimore. Lincoln read the letters carefully and then catechized young Seward. Convinced that Seward's information came from sources independent of Pinkerton's, Lincoln reluctantly concluded that the plot was more than rumor.

The next day, after the speech at Harrisburg, certain trusted members of Lincoln's party were told of the danger and of a plan worked out by Judd and Felton. Soon after dinner Lincoln went to his room, changed his clothes, donned an overcoat, and, with a soft wool hat stuffed into his pocket, walked inconspicuously to a waiting carriage. Burly, devoted Ward Hill Lamon, a man noted as a rough-and-tumble fighter with whom Lincoln had practiced law in partnership at Danville, armed with two pistols, two derringers, and two large knives, jumped in beside him, and immediately the carriage took off for the station, where a special train waited. As the train pulled out with its two passengers, all telegraph wires leading out of Harrisburg were cut.

Shortly after ten o'clock that night Lincoln and Lamon were met in Philadelphia by Pinkerton and a railroad superintendent, who took them in a carriage to the P., W. & B. station, where they boarded the last sleeping-car of the Baltimore train. One of Pinkerton's female operatives had reserved berths for her "in-

valid brother" and his companion. At half past three in the morning the sleeping-car was drawn through the dark and silent streets
of Baltimore to Camden Station, where it waited to be picked up
by a train from the West. Outside on the platform Lincoln heard
a drunkard singing *Dixie*. At six o'clock the President-elect
stepped off the train in Washington. As he made his way along
the platform, a man sidled up to him and said: "You can't play
that on me." Lamon drew back his massive fist, but Lincoln
caught his arm. It was Congressman Elihu Washburne, whom
Seward had informed of Lincoln's coming.

Whether an actual plot to murder Lincoln existed has never
been determined; the reports of Pinkerton's operatives are not
altogether convincing. But Lincoln did face danger. There were
no secret-service men, and his only official protection was provided by four army officers detailed to accompany him. Even in
friendly cities mishaps had been narrowly averted: Lincoln had
almost been crushed in the corridor of the statehouse at Columbus; at the Pittsburgh depot a stampede of horses in a cavalry
detachment had endangered his carriage; and at Buffalo Major
David Hunter of his suite had suffered a dislocated shoulder in a
rush of the crowd. Anything might have happened in Baltimore,
where the municipal authorities were indifferent and Lincoln's
unprotected carriage would have had to cross the city through a
surging, hostile crowd.

As soon as the manner of Lincoln's entrance into the capital
became known, ridicule was added to the hatred being vented by
the hostile press. The story of an irresponsible reporter, describing Lincoln as entering Washington disguised in a Scotch
plaid cap and long military cloak, was circulated country-wide.
Lincoln's enemies guffawed and derided his cowardice. Car-
toonists caricatured him. Lincoln himself was not proud of the
incident. Had his friends not persuaded him that his welfare and
that of the country were inseparable, he would probably have
come through Baltimore according to plan.

*

THE HEAVY clouds that lowered over Washington on the morning of March 4 broke away by noon. The city swarmed with visitors, many of them apprehensive lest the new President be violently prevented from taking office, some hoping for trouble. The outgoing Buchanan administration was alert. Strange sounds broke the quiet of the dawn—the clump of cavalry horses, the muffled, rhythmic tread of marching men, the rumble of cannon and caissons.

At noon President Buchanan called at Willard's Hotel to escort his successor to the Capitol over the historic route all Presidents have followed. As the open carriage jounced over the cobblestones of Pennsylvania Avenue, Lincoln looked into the faces of the crowd that jammed the sidewalks, baring his head to bow from time to time. Ahead rose the Capitol, still uncompleted, with the arm of a great crane swung from the dome, and a huge bronze statue of Freedom, destined to crown the edifice, recumbent on the ground.

Close about the presidential carriage marched a guard. Files of soldiers lined the streets. Cavalry guarded every intersection. Riflemen on the rooftops of the low buildings watched windows across the street. Two batteries of artillery were posted near the Capitol, which Lincoln entered through a boarded tunnel.

Onto a temporary platform on the east front of the Capitol moved the inaugural procession, Lincoln in a new black suit, black boots, and a white shirt, and carrying his tall hat and an ebony, gold-headed cane. The new President towered above the withered, bowed Buchanan as they walked behind Chief Justice Taney, old, shrunken, and shriveled like "a galvanized corpse," and the other members of the Supreme Court. On the front row close to Lincoln as the dignitaries took their seats sat Douglas, purposely conspicuous in support of the new President.

As Lincoln rose to deliver his address and saw no place to put his hat and cane, Douglas, according to an anonymous diarist who styled himself "A Public Man," reached out in a symbolic gesture to take them and hold them during the remainder of the ceremony. The diarist, who may have written long after the event, has been suspected of fabricating this incident, but at least one newspaper, the *Cincinnati Commercial*, mentioned it soon after the inaugural ceremonies.

*

UNROLLING his manuscript and adjusting his spectacles, Lincoln faced the anxious crowd. His first words offered reassurance to the South. "I have no purpose, directly or indirectly, to interfere with the institution of slavery in the states where it exists," he declared. "I believe I have no lawful right to do so, and I have no inclination to do so." Just before adjournment Congress had passed a thirteenth amendment to the Constitution, forever guaranteeing slavery in the states from Federal interference, and Lincoln, having made a last-minute insertion in his manuscript, promised his support to this amendment. Since he thought such a guarantee was already implied in the Constitution, he said, "I have no objection to its being made express, and irrevocable." He would respect the constitutional provision for the capture and return of fugitive slaves.

Having sought to quiet Southern fears, Lincoln faced squarely the question of Federal authority. "No State, upon its own mere motion, can lawfully get out of the Union," he asserted. But what of those states which already considered themselves withdrawn? "I shall take care," said he, "as the Constitution itself expressly enjoins upon me, that the laws of the Union be faithfully executed in all the States. Doing this I deem to be only a simple duty on my part; and I shall perform it, so far as practicable, unless my rightful masters, the American people, shall withhold the requisite means, or, in some authoritative manner, direct the contrary." But there need be no resort to force or bloodshed in enforcing the laws. "The power confided to me will be used to hold, occupy, and possess the property, and places belonging to the government, and to collect the duties and imposts; but beyond what may be necessary for these objects, there will be no invasion—no using of force against, or among the people anywhere."

In the original draft of the address Lincoln had expressed a purpose to *reclaim* the public places and property already seized, but on the advice of his friend Orville H. Browning he changed this to "hold, occupy, and possess" government property. In line with suggestions of Seward and experienced old Francis Preston Blair, Lincoln toned down pledges regarding the maintenance of Federal authority and stressed promises of conciliation, so that the speech in its final form was as indulgent as he could make it without renouncing his constitutional duties. Where hostility to the government was so "great and so universal" as to prevent resident citizens from administering the Federal offices, no attempt would be made to force "obnoxious strangers" upon the people, Lincoln promised. "While the strict legal right may exist in the government to enforce the exercise of these offices, the attempt to do so would be so irritating . . . that I deem it better to forego, for the time, the use of such offices." The mails would be delivered unless repelled. The customs would be collected offshore (actually no effort was made to collect them). Defiance would not be met by force. While Federal authority would be upheld in principle, every possible concession would be made, in the hope that time and an atmosphere of friendliness would compose all differences.

Physically speaking, the states could not separate, Lincoln pointed out. They must remain face to face, and commercial and political relations must continue. Would such relations be more satisfactory after separation than before? Could aliens make treaties more easily than friends could make laws? Could treaties be better enforced among aliens than laws among friends? Why should there not be a patient confidence in the ultimate justice of the people? "If the Almighty Ruler of nations, with his eternal truth and justice, be on your side of the North, or on yours of the South, that truth, and that justice, will surely prevail, by the judgment of this great tribunal, the American people." Nothing could be lost by taking time.

"In *your* hands, my dissatisfied fellow countrymen, and not in *mine*, is the momentous issue of civil war. The government will not assail *you*. You can have no conflict, without being yourselves the aggressors. *You* can have no oath registered in Heaven to destroy the government, while *I* shall have the most solemn one to 'preserve, protect and defend' it."

Lincoln had meant to close with this paragraph, but Seward suggested some final "words of affection—of calm and cheerful confidence," and offered an additional paragraph of his own phrasing. The idea met Lincoln's hearty sanction, and he transformed the Secretary's graceless sentences into a moving and exalted plea: "I am loath to close. We are not enemies, but friends. We must not be enemies. Though passion may have strained, it must not break our bonds of affection. The mystic chords of memory, stretching from every battle-field and patriot grave, to every living heart and hearth stone, all over this broad land, will yet swell the chorus of the Union, when again touched, as surely they will be, by the better angels of our nature."

Reactions to the President's address reflected the country-wide confusion of opinion, the heat of partisan passions, the incapability of forming candid judgments. It was "firm and explicit," "weak, rambling and loose-jointed." It was "the language of a man of vital common sense"; it had a "tawdry," "hard-favored" style. It was "fair to both sides, and worthy of a statesman"; it abounded in "craft and cunning." While it was almost universally denounced in the states that had seceded, it won some favorable comment in the all-important loyal slave states. Governor John Letcher of Virginia reported a growing determination among conservatives to think calmly. In the Virginia state convention Jubal A. Early spoke well of Lincoln and blamed the states that had seceded "without having consulted our views" for the perilous condition of the country. John A. Gilmer, of North Carolina, to whom Lincoln had offered a cabinet post, asked: "What more does any reasonable Southern man expect or desire?" But these views were expressed in private correspondence; the Southern newspapers, an Alabamian reported, were "one and all making it out coercive in the extreme."

*

L I N C O L N's announced intention to "hold, occupy, and possess" the places and property belonging to the government met its first test sooner than he anticipated. The day after the inauguration, word came from Major Robert Anderson, commanding Fort Sumter, in Charleston harbor, that he had only six weeks' provisions, and unless supplied within that time he must abandon the fort.

A series of dramatic events had brought the differences between North and South to a focus at Fort Sumter, a symbol of Federal authority in the crucible of secession, and the most important fort in Confederate territory still under Federal control. Three forts had been built in Charleston harbor, but at the beginning of the secession crisis only one, Fort Moultrie, was garrisoned, with Anderson, a Kentuckian whose wife came from Georgia, in command. Anderson warned Buchanan that to hold the harbor Sumter and Castle Pinckney, as well as Moultrie, must be manned. But Buchanan was not only anxious to conciliate the South Carolinians by avoiding anything in the nature of an unfriendly act; he also had few troops to spare from the small regular army of sixteen thousand men, most of whom were guarding the Western frontier from hostile Indians.

On December 26, 1860, six days after South Carolina seceded, Major Anderson moved his small garrison from their exposed position at Fort Moultrie to Fort Sumter, a brick and mortar stronghold on a sandbar near the middle of the harbor. Choosing to regard this as a hostile act, and holding herself to be an independent state, South Carolina demanded the complete evacuation of Charleston harbor. This demand Buchanan refused, and early in January sent an unarmed merchant vessel, the *Star of the West*, with reinforcements and supplies for Anderson. The South Carolina shore batteries opened fire and forced the vessel to turn back. Buchanan, instead of resisting this hostile action, decided to make no further effort at reinforcement unless the fort was attacked. The South Carolinians, having seized Fort Moultrie and Castle Pinckney, ringed the harbor with guns.

If Fort Sumter stood as a symbol of authority to the North, to South Carolina and the newly organized Confederate States of America the daily flaunting of a "foreign" flag from a fort in one of their principal harbors was reckoned a national insult. The South Carolina government at last refused to allow Anderson to purchase supplies in Charleston, an action that brought on the crisis of which Lincoln received warning on March 5. On or about April 15 Sumter must be provisioned or evacuated.

In extreme anxiety, Lincoln sought the advice of General Scott. The general thought that no less than twenty thousand men would be required to hold Charleston harbor. Lincoln called a meeting of his cabinet and certain high-ranking military and naval officers. The navy men thought they could put troops into Sumter. The army men thought such an attempt would prove disastrous. Lincoln asked for separate written opinions from his cabinet: assuming that Sumter could be provisioned, would such action be politically advisable? Blair favored it emphatically, Chase favored it with reservations; the others said no. Seward, much more inclined toward compromise than Lincoln, presented the longest argument against it.

Lincoln postponed his decision. It was an indication of innate strength of character that he would not be hurried into action; that his decision, when he made it, would be his own, based, however, on the best information and advice available to him.

*

MEANWHILE the Confederate States had appointed three commissioners to negotiate with the United States government about Fort Sumter and other points at issue. On March 12 they formally asked Seward to set a date for the presentation of their credentials to the President as the representatives of an independent nation.

To communicate with these commissioners directly would have been to recognize the Confederate claim to independence, so Seward refused to receive them. But he dealt with them unofficially through John A. Campbell, of Alabama, still a member of the United States Supreme Court despite the withdrawal of his state. Adhering to his policy of appeasement and convinced that Lincoln would adopt his views, Seward assured Campbell in mid-March that Sumter would be evacuated, and pleaded for Southern forbearance to effect a peaceful settlement. Assuming that Seward spoke for Lincoln, the Southern commissioners took his personal assurance, several times repeated, for a pledge. Later both the seceded states and those of the upper South would believe the President guilty of bad faith.

If Lincoln seemed to be following the same hesitant course that had brought such condemnation upon Buchanan, it was not with the hope of avoiding action, but of avoiding mistakes. He was studying the situation carefully. To get information on the spot he sent Gustavus Vasa Fox, later his Assistant Secretary of the Navy, to Charleston to confer with Anderson and study the possibility of supplying the fort against resistance. His trusted friend Ward Lamon, and Stephen A. Hurlbut, a lawyer friend from Illinois and a native South Carolinian, were also sent to Charleston to appraise popular sentiment.

Pondering all the elements of the problem, Lincoln thought he had an answer. He must assert Federal authority, or lose the confidence of Unionists both North and South. But why not make the demonstration at Fort Pickens, off Pensacola, Florida, where the psychological situation was less tense, rather than in the surcharged atmosphere of Charleston harbor? If he could reinforce Fort Pickens, he would assert Federal authority. That done, the evacuation of Fort Sumter might be accepted by the people as a military necessity.

Such a policy offered another advantage. The Virginia state convention, though professing loyalty to the Union, refused to adjourn so long as the Federal government showed any disposition to use force against South Carolina. And the attitude of Virginia would probably determine the course of the other loyal slave states. Believing that Virginia could be held in the Union if hostilities at Sumter were avoided, Lincoln arranged an interview with John B. Baldwin, a Unionist member of the Virginia convention, and promised confidentially that he would evacuate Fort Sumter if the Virginia convention would disband: "If you will guarantee to me the State of Virginia I shall remove the troops. A State for a fort is no bad business." But no promise was forthcoming.

*

WHILE LINCOLN grappled with the crucial problem of Fort Sumter, office-seekers beset him constantly. To many people the first Republican victory meant just one thing: the spoils of office. Pelf-seekers swarmed the White House, making ruthless demands on Lincoln's time. He felt like a man letting lodgings at one end of his house, he said, while the other end burned down. "The City is overwhelmed with a crowd of rabid, persistent office-seekers," wrote a Michigan Congressman, "—the like never was experienced before in the history of the Government." An Indiana Congressman "met at every turn a swarm of miscellaneous people, many of them looking as hungry and as fierce as wolves." Attorney General Bates reported cabinet members squabbling "about the distribution of loaves & fishes." The Congressional greed for patronage was beyond satisfying. Senator Fessenden protested that "everything in the way of offices goes west. We shall hardly get the parings of a toenail in New England and many people feel hardly about it." When Congressman William Kellogg of Illinois complained bitterly to Lincoln about a supposed slight, the distraught President replied imploringly on the back of his letter: "Mr. Kellogg does me great injustice to write in this strain. He has had more favors than any other Illinois member, not excepting, I think, Judge Trumbull. Is it really in his heart to add to my perplexities now?"

Lincoln could not shrug off these problems of patronage. The unity of his party, which was so essential to the success of any policy he might adopt, depended on his careful apportionment of Federal jobs. Grappling with some of the most serious problems ever thrust on a President, needing to learn and use the wisest statecraft, Lincoln found a large portion of each working day devoted of necessity to paltry tasks.

*

T H E   C O U N T R Y watched Lincoln's actions closely for clues to his policy. He seemed to have no policy. Many Northern editors were unfriendly. Few people had confidence in the government. As Lincoln, according to his custom, deliberately felt his way, he seemed bewildered and vacillating, especially to Seward, who found himself in a dilemma with the Southern commissioners as time passed and the garrison remained at Fort Sumter. On April 1 the Secretary of State sent Lincoln "Some Thoughts for the President's Consideration."

At the end of a month the administration had no policy, domestic or foreign, Seward declared. The delay had been unavoidable because of patronage problems, but further lack of policy would prove fatal. Local appointments should be made at once, and more important ones deferred if necessary. The issue before the country should be changed from slavery to the question of union or disunion by evacuating Sumter but holding all the other places in the South. That done, Seward would seek to unify the country in a foreign war, or at least by energetic resistance to French and English intervention in Mexico, where those nations were pressing for the collection of debts, and to Spanish interference in Santo Domingo. Whatever policy was adopted, it must be pursued and directed incessantly, either by the President or some member of the cabinet. Debate must end, "and all agree and abide. It is not in my especial province. But I neither seek to evade nor assume responsibility."

Lincoln must have been astounded. Seward was practically proposing that the President step aside and give his "prime minister" dictatorial power. The expedient of a foreign war was so desperate, and the offer to take over so presumptuous, that Seward would appear to have lost all sense of perspective under the strain. But Lincoln refused to be stampeded. In a calm, reasoned reply to Seward, he asserted that in "holding, occupying and possessing" the property and places belonging to the government he had pursued the identical domestic policy announced in his inaugural, a policy to which Seward had agreed. The course that he had followed differed in no wise from Seward's proposal except in not abandoning Fort Sumter. Lincoln scarcely mentioned Seward's warlike foreign designs. Without rancor he set the Secretary in his place. The President would conduct the government, he said, with the advice of all his cabinet.

Neither Lincoln nor Seward ever referred to this incident afterward, and no one else knew of it until Nicolay and Hay published the letters thirty-three years later. Furthermore, the fact that Lincoln's letter remains among his own papers indicates that it was never sent. Lincoln could scarcely have ignored Seward's proposal. He may have intended to reply by letter and changed his mind; if so, he probably made his position clear in a heart-to-heart talk. In any event, Lincoln evidently made sure that both letters stayed in his possession and that the incident would be hushed up. Public disclosure of such a communication as Seward's not only would have destroyed confidence in the administration at a time when it needed public support above all else, but would also have been devastating to Seward's future usefulness.

Seward took the rebuff manfully. He began to understand his chief. "Executive force and vigor are rare qualities," he wrote to Mrs. Seward two months later. "The President is the best of us."

*

MEANWHILE Lincoln ordered two expeditions made ready: one to take an additional force to Fort Pickens, where a troopship, already in the harbor, was ordered to land immediate reinforcements; the other to stand by to proceed to Fort Sumter. He planned to hold or dispatch the second expedition "according to circumstances." If the Pickens expedition succeeded, he could abandon Sumter gracefully. On April 6, however, Lincoln learned that his orders to reinforce Fort Pickens had miscarried. Buchanan had promised the Florida authorities that Pickens would not be reinforced unless attacked, and the Federal naval commander at Pensacola harbor refused to allow more troops to land.

To relieve Sumter immediately became Lincoln's only alternative; further delay would mean starvation or evacuation of the garrison. The relief expedition of troops and supplies received orders to sail, but at the same time Lincoln sent a special messenger to notify Governor Pickens of South Carolina that he proposed to supply Fort Sumter with provisions only; and that, "if such attempt be not resisted, no effort to throw in men, arms, or ammunition will be made without further notice, or in case of an attack upon the Fort."

Receiving Lincoln's notice on April 8, the day before the Sumter expedition sailed, Governor Pickens communicated immediately with the Confederate authorities at Montgomery. They did not want war; but the provisioning of Sumter meant the continued presence of Federal troops in Charleston harbor, a situation they could no longer tolerate. General P. G. T. Beauregard, Confederate commander at Charleston, was instructed to demand the evacuation of the fort.

On April 11 three officers dispatched by Beauregard demanded Anderson's surrender. He replied formally in writing that he could not in honor comply, but added orally that if not attacked he would soon be starved out. Messages flashed between Charleston and Montgomery. Anderson was asked to set a definite date for his evacuation. It would come four days later, on April 15, he replied, unless he received controlling instructions from his government or additional supplies. The conditional nature of his promise proved unsatisfactory; Beauregard's emissaries announced that the Confederate batteries would open fire in one hour.

At four thirty in the morning of April 12 a signal mortar sounded and a red ball ascended in a lazy curve to burst over the fort. With true Southern courtesy, the South Carolinians had allowed a visitor, fire-eating old Edmund Ruffin, of Virginia, the honor of firing the first gun. Cannon flashed in the red dawn. All day and into the rainy night the encircling batteries pounded at the fort. Anderson fought back. Offshore stood the relief ships, unwilling to take part in the engagement, for in a last desperate effort to avoid a clash at Fort Sumter the meddling Seward had diverted the most powerful vessel intended for the expedition to Fort Pickens.

Inside the fort Anderson's men stood grimly to their guns. One cannon burst. Others became silent under the hail of shells. Masonry crashed. Heat and smoke became intolerable as fires crept toward the powder magazine. Food was almost gone. For more than thirty hours Anderson hung on.

Beauregard offered generous terms, and Anderson surrendered. On Sunday, April 14, he marched out with the honors of war. The torn flag drooped from its mended staff as the little garrison of ninety tired, smoke-blackened men trooped to the dock, drums rattling, to board a relief ship for New York. Fifty times a defiant gun on the parapet barked in salute. The men marched with backs stiff, heads up, mute anger in their eyes. If the North had misjudged the Southern will for independence, the South equally misunderstood the North's deep reverence for the Union.

CHAPTER XIII

———◆◆———

A War for Democracy

WITH the news of Anderson's surrender, anxious visitors besieged the White House. Congressmen assured Lincoln of their loyalty and pledged the support of their states. Banks, corporations, and private citizens offered him their aid. Lincoln called a cabinet meeting and framed a proclamation calling on the states for 75,000 militia for three months' service, convening a special session of Congress on July 4, and appealing to all loyal citizens "to favor, facilitate, and aid this effort to maintain the honor, the integrity, and the existence of our National Union, and the perpetuity of popular government."

For two hours on that fateful Sunday Lincoln sat in conference with Douglas. Too ill for public business, the Little Giant had been studying the military situation, and pointed out strategic points that should be strengthened. He approved Lincoln's proclamation, except that he would have called for 200,000 men. Congressman George Ashmun, the only other person present at this interview, impressed by the former rivals' unity of views, thought that an account of their deliberations, sent out over the telegraph with Lincoln's proclamation, would rally unsure Democrats to uphold the government. So Ashmun and Douglas drove to Willard's Hotel, where Douglas prepared a statement. While he opposed the administration politically, he asserted, he would fully sustain the President in the exercise of every power to preserve the Union.

Lincoln's proclamation of April 15 brought a thundering answer from the North. Everywhere there were speeches, mass meetings, parades. Bands blared; flags flew on homes and public buildings. Twenty thousand persons attended a Union mass meeting in New York, where little Robert J. Walker, one-time Senator from Mississippi and Governor of Kansas, shouted: "Much as I love my party, I love my country infinitely more. . . . This Union must, will, and should be perpetuated, not a star shall be dimmed or a stripe erased from its banner." State legislatures, city and town councils voted money for troops and equipment. Known secessionists met rough treatment if they ventured on the streets. The *New York Times* reported one grim, determined sentiment "on every common . . . in every car, on board every ferry-boat, in every hotel, in the vestibule of every church."

Douglas labored unremittingly to encourage Union feeling. "The proposition now," he said, "is to separate these United States into little petty confederacies. First, divide them into two; and then, when either party gets beat at the next election, subdivide again, then, whenever one gets beat again, another subdivision." Fiercely unmindful of the toll on his spent body, Douglas made his way to Illinois to make a rousing speech before the Legislature. In "Egypt," where family ties and tradition linked the people with the South, his influence won supporters for the Union. All over the North men were heard to say: "I am a Democrat. I voted against Lincoln. But I will stand by my country."

Volunteers responded eagerly to Lincoln's call. Stern-faced young men formed ranks in city streets and on village greens and marched to twittering fifes and rolling drums. "How many men would Ohio furnish?" came the query. "The largest number you will receive," replied the Governor. "We will furnish you the regiments in thirty days, if you want them," Zachariah Chandler wired from Michigan, "and 50,000 men if you need them." Indiana, with a quota of 5,000, telegraphed that 10,000 had enrolled. As Governor Samuel Kirkwood of Iowa stood in a cornfield, a fagged rider on a foam-flecked horse handed him a telegram from the War Department. Reading the message, Kirkwood gazed wryly over the field of sprouting plants. "Why," he exclaimed, "the President wants a whole regiment of men!" Where could he find them? Not many days later Kirkwood wired to Washington: "For God's sake send us arms. We have the men."

Horace Greeley believed that 500,000 men would have responded if Lincoln had called for them. When the overburdened War Department felt obliged to refuse regiments because of lack of equipment, Lincoln sometimes took them anyway to please persons of influence. "With such support and such resources," declared *Harper's Weekly*, "if this war is not brought to a speedy close, and the supremacy of the Government asserted throughout the country, it will be the fault of ABRAHAM LINCOLN."

But if the attack on Sumter roused the North, Lincoln's call for troops moved the South to unified action. Union feeling all but vanished in the Gulf states. "Lincoln may bring his 75,000 troops against us," cried Alexander Stephens. "We fight for our homes, our fathers and mothers, our wives, brothers, sisters, sons and daughters! . . . We can call out a million of peoples if need be, and when they are cut down, we can call another, and still another, until the last man of the South finds a bloody grave."

Two days after Lincoln's call, the Virginia state convention passed an ordinance of secession. Without waiting for its ratification, Governor Letcher opened the state to Confederate troops. Virginia militia marched on Harpers Ferry, where several million dollars' worth of arms and ammunition were put to the torch as the small Union garrison pulled out. The Federal commander of the Gosport Navy Yard, near Norfolk, destroyed millions in government property as he abandoned the place.

On Arlington Heights the mansion of Robert E. Lee overlooked the Federal capital. General Scott rated Lee the ablest officer in the service. On the morning of Thursday, April 18, Lee rode into Washington to talk to Scott and Francis Preston Blair. Scott lectured Lee on his duty, and old man Blair, at his yellow house on Pennsylvania Avenue, spoke to him in confidence as

Lincoln's emissary. "After listening to his remarks," Lee reported, "I declined the offer he made me, to take command of the army that was to be brought into the field, stating as candidly and courteously as I could that, though opposed to secession and deprecating war, I could take no part in an invasion of the Southern states." That afternoon Lee rode silent and alone across the Long Bridge to Virginia.

Both upper and lower South regarded Lincoln as the aggressor at Fort Sumter. In calling troops to coerce those states which had exercised their natural right to secede, he had forsaken persuasion for force, they said. And had he not broken a pledge to Justice Campbell in refusing to abandon Fort Sumter? Without waiting for formal ordinances of secession, state officials in Arkansas, North Carolina, and Tennessee joined those of Virginia in arraying their states with the Confederacy.

The border slave states wrenched and twisted as the nation pulled apart. Brothers glared dourly or sorrowfully clasped hands as one went north, the other south. "Kentucky will furnish no troops for the wicked purpose of subduing her sister Southern states," wired Governor Magoffin in reply to Lincoln's call for state militia. In Louisville, Union recruits marching up one side of a street passed Confederate volunteers on the other. The same railroad train carried one car of Union volunteers and another of Confederates. Mrs. Lincoln's own family typified the situation: her eldest brother and a half-sister loyal to the Union, another brother and three half-brothers joining the Confederates, and three half-sisters married to Confederate officers. Ben Hardin Helm, husband of Mrs. Lincoln's "little sister" Emilie, West Pointer, son of a Kentucky Governor, came to the White House at Lincoln's invitation and received an offer of a commission from the President. He left undecided, but the next thing Lincoln heard of him he had joined the Confederate army.

*

ON APRIL 19 word came to Lincoln that the Sixth Massachusetts Infantry had been mobbed in Baltimore. Four soldiers had been killed and several wounded, and the mob had also suffered casualties when the troops returned their fire. At five o'clock that afternoon the weary, dirty troops reached Washington and marched to quarters in the Senate Chamber, while hacks hurried the wounded to the E Street Infirmary. The next day a Baltimore delegation appeared at the White House to urge Lincoln to bring no more troops through their city. "If I grant you this concession," Lincoln said, "you will be back here to-morrow, demanding that none shall be marched around it." Two days later a committee protested the "pollution" of Maryland's soil. "I must have troops," replied Lincoln, ". . . our men are not moles, and can't dig under the earth. They are not birds, and can't fly through the air. There is no way but to march across, and that they must do." But Lincoln knew the supreme importance of holding the border slave states. Appreciating the difficulties under which their Union men were laboring, he yielded to the practical considerations of the moment. No more troops were brought through Baltimore until the quiet but forceful Union sentiment had had time to assert itself.

Free territory almost surrounded the slave state of Delaware, and she made no move to secede. In Missouri, however, crosscurrents of opinion surged and swirled, the Unionists torn internally because of diverse views about slavery. Governor Claiborne Jackson, a fervent Southern sympathizer, set up a secessionist legislature and accepted admission to the Confederacy. But he had no capital and no archives, held no permanent territory, and controlled no taxes; and he met such bold resistance under the leadership of Captain Nathaniel Lyon and Francis P. Blair, Jr., that Missouri remained in the Union, though it suffered internal turmoil throughout the war.

Bordering the free states of Ohio, Indiana, and Illinois and extending along three fifths of the Ohio River, Kentucky held such a strategic position that Lincoln thought her decision would be fateful for the Union cause. "I think to lose Kentucky is nearly . . . to lose the whole game," he wrote. "Kentucky gone, we can not hold Missouri, nor, as I think, Maryland. These all against us, and the job on our hands is too large for us. We would as well consent to separation at once, including the surrender of this capital." With Kentucky's geographical position, her river commerce, her background and institutions all drawing her to the South, Lincoln moved watchfully and cautiously to nurture her Unionist sentiment. When Governor Magoffin refused his call for troops, he assigned Robert Anderson, a Kentuckian, promoted to brigadier general since his faithful defense of Fort Sumter, to recruiting service at Cincinnati—near, but carefully outside, Kentucky's border. Lincoln encouraged the enlistment of home guards. Through his old friend Joshua F. Speed and other trusted agents, he distributed arms to men of proved loyalty. In June, by a popular vote of 92,460 to 37,700, Kentucky elected nine Union Congressmen and only one secessionist. True, her Unionism in many cases amounted to no more than neutrality, and the situation still called for all the watchfulness that Lincoln continued to give it; but the President understood the feelings of the people of his native state and knew how to deal with them. In September the Legislature passed, over the Governor's veto, a resolution that Confederate invaders had wantonly violated the state's neutrality, and that Federal aid and protection should be sought. By December Lincoln felt able to report Kentucky "decidedly and unchangeably" ranged on the side of the Union.

*

M EANWHILE, as Lincoln sought to hold the border states, panic seized Washington. During the week after the fall of Sumter scarcely any troops had reached the city, while 15,000 Confederates were reported near Alexandria, ready to march on it. The Confederates had 8,000 men at Harpers Ferry. The *Richmond Examiner* reported "one wild shout of fierce resolve to capture Washington City, at all and every human hazard. The filthy cage of unclean birds must and will be purified by fire. . . . Our people can take it, and Scott the arch traitor, and Lincoln the Beast, combined cannot prevent it. The just indignation of an outraged and deeply injured people will teach the Illinois

Ape to retrace his journey across the borders of the Free negro States still more rapidly than he came."

Maryland secessionists had torn up railroad tracks and cut the telegraph lines from Washington. Across the Potomac, Confederate campfires lit the sky at night. Army and navy officers were deserting Washington daily. Disloyal civil workers quit by hundreds. As Washington waited, in utter isolation from the North, gloom and terror crushed the city's life.

Henry Villard, the *New York Herald* correspondent, reported that the thousand guests at Willard's had dwindled to fifty. Pennsylvania Avenue looked deserted. Many stores had closed. Barricades of flour barrels, cement, and sandbags protected public buildings, while sentries paced before their doors. Defiant Southerners flaunted secession badges on the streets. No one knew how many disloyalists waited to help overthrow the city from within. "Disaffection lurked, if it did not openly avow itself," wrote Seward, "in every department, and in every bureau, in every regiment and in every ship of war, in the postoffice and in the custom house."

Troops were reported on the way to Washington, but none arrived. Lincoln waited in an agony of suspense. If Washington were lost, the cause itself might fail; the Northern will might ebb out in despair. John Hay heard Lincoln mutter as he anxiously paced his office: "Why don't they come? Why don't they come?"

Not a train had entered Washington for four days when at noon on Thursday, April 25, the shrill whistle of a locomotive broke the stillness of the city. People rushing to the station saw the crack Seventh New York Regiment issuing from the cars. They had come by ship to Annapolis and rebuilt the railroad on their way to Washington. The men were begrimed and weary, but they marched briskly up the Avenue, flags flying and band in full performance. People relaxed in joy and cheers. Twelve hundred men of General Benjamin F. Butler's Massachusetts brigade soon followed the New Yorkers; more troops came from Pennsylvania and Rhode Island. By April 27 ten thousand soldiers had arrived, and more were on the way.

*

THE SECESSION of Virginia, Arkansas, Tennessee, and North Carolina increased the area of the Confederacy by a third and almost doubled its population and economic resources. The area of the eleven states now opposing the Union was almost double that of any European country except Russia. The Confederacy had a long coastline, with harbors snug and deep. Coastlands, mountains, and fertile plains diversified its climate. Should the South stay on the defensive, she could fight on interior lines. Railroads and long, navigable rivers afforded means for swift troop movements.

The South was better prepared than the disorganized North. From the first the seceding states had foreseen the possibility of war and had begun to amass war materials and enlist troops. The Confederacy enjoyed the best of military leadership. So many careers were open in the North that Northern officers frequently resigned from the army to enter other fields; Southerners, with fewer occupations available in civil life, more often made the army a career. From the outset the Confederacy commanded the services and West Point training of such men as Robert E. Lee, Albert Sidney Johnston, Pierre G. T. Beauregard, Joseph E. Johnston, "Stonewall" Jackson, J. E. B. Stuart, James Longstreet, and A. P. Hill. Bereft of the services of many of the army's ablest officers, Lincoln had to experiment with leadership.

A superiority in population inclined the balance toward the North; it had 20,000,000 free people against the South's 6,000,000 whites and 3,500,000 slaves. An excellent system of trunk and branch-line railroads countered the handicaps of distance. Northern wealth and industrial development far surpassed those resources in the South, which at the outset of the contest had only one establishment—the Tredegar Iron Works at Richmond—capable of producing heavy arms and armament. But the South was well supplied with arms and ammunition from Federal arsenals that she had seized. She purchased heavily abroad. She learned to use her limited resources to the best advantage. And she gained and replenished arms, clothing, and ammunition on the battlefield.

The North had great superiority in sea power. Following Lincoln's proclamation of blockade, Gideon Welles undertook the stupendous task of building up a navy capable of guarding 3,550 miles of coastline from the mouth of Chesapeake Bay to the Rio Grande. New warships were built, merchant vessels were purchased and converted, gunboats were adapted to use on Western rivers. Against this formidable armament the South resorted chiefly to privateers, and to darting blockade-runners whose venturesome forays would only be stopped with the seizure of key points along the coast.

The Northern governmental organization lent itself more readily to the demands of war than did that of the Confederate States. Although Lincoln encountered problems in his relations with state governors, the North for the most part functioned as a unit, whereas the Southern states regarded themselves as more or less independent entities associated in a common cause. President Davis often met defiance from state governors; he was frequently at loggerheads with Confederate Congressmen, who accorded prime allegiance to their states.

A far more experienced administrator than Lincoln, Davis lacked his personal warmth. The grandson of an illiterate Welsh peasant, he had won position among the most exclusive Southern planters. A formal, unbending perfectionist, he was "ambitious as Lucifer." He never whipped a slave, and never called one by a nickname. Egotistical, sensitive, and humorless, he resented contradiction and seldom welcomed advice. A graduate of West Point, he had proved his courage in the Mexican War and demonstrated administrative talents as Pierce's Secretary of War. His health was delicate; his wife described him as "a man of throbbing nerves." Notwithstanding his devotion to the Southern social system, he had doubted the wisdom of secession almost to the last. He considered himself primarily a military man, and would often clash and quarrel with generals. In his own will-power and intellect he came to see the last unfailing hope of the Confederacy. But Davis did not deceive himself regarding Northern power. Not for him the belief that one Southerner could whip ten Yankees; he had seen the Yankees fight in Mexico. He knew the contest would be grim.

The South had the advantage of an aptitude for war. Most Southern boys could ride and shoot; more Northern lads must learn those skills. The tradition of Southern chivalry fostered a spirit of defiant bravery. With slaves to do the essential work, white men could be spared to fight without disrupting the economy. In the North, however, recruits must come from field and factory; only the superior mechanical advancement of the North enabled it to recruit, equip, and maintain large armies without an economic breakdown.

The South enjoyed a great psychological advantage. Although slavery caused her to renounce the Union, with the outbreak of hostilities she fought, not for slavery, but for independence. Early victories gave her a fierce pride, a still stronger belief in the superiority of her system and in the justice of her cause. The Northern people had no such unity of purpose. Their liberty was not menaced, and they did not wish to assume the role of conquerors. When it became evident that to win they must subdue the South, many of them began to question the genuineness and utility of a Union preserved with bayonets. To bring home to the Northern people the broader meanings of the conflict, to maintain their unity of purpose, and to convince them of the nobility of a distasteful task became Lincoln's most challenging duty.

*

WITH THE safety of Washington at least temporarily assured by the end of April 1861, Lincoln planned the reorganization of the armed forces. On May 3 he called for an increase of the regular army by ten regiments of 22,714 men; for 42,034 three-year volunteers; and for the enlistment of 1,800 seamen, in order to bring the army to a total of 156,861 and the navy to

25,000. National armories went into full production. A new armory was built at Rock Island, Illinois. Private factories received orders for war equipment. Purchases in Europe were authorized. Rifles, cannon, tents, food, transportation, and uniforms must be provided. Washington became bedlam as the nation girded for war.

Lincoln's face began to reveal his inner torment as lines of travail etched his features. One need not imagine the soul-torture of this man of peaceful disposition as he launched the nation on a brothers' war; his countenance depicts his suffering. Successive photographs of Lincoln, taken throughout the war, reveal his heartache.

Yet Lincoln did not flinch from a decision for civil war; some things in life and history are worthy of death and suffering. From his boyhood he had sought the meaning of the story of America. He found it in the political philosophy of Thomas Jefferson as it extolled the rights of man.

Lincoln often let his mind dwell on Jefferson and those other earnest patriots who met at Independence Hall and brought new hope to all mankind with the avowal that "all men are created equal; that they are endowed by their Creator with certain unalienable rights; that among these are life, liberty, and the pursuit of happiness." How noble and far-seeing those men were, he thought, as they built a national structure on such foundations that if some man, some faction, or some interest in time to come should set up the doctrine that none but rich men, or none but white men, or none but Anglo-Saxons, were entitled to life, liberty, and the pursuit of happiness, their posterity might find in this great human document a source of faith and courage to keep up the fight for truth, justice, and mercy among men! Lincoln believed that in this affirmation of democracy lay the great hope of the world. America must demonstrate that in these principles mankind would find the surest way to peace, prosperity, and happiness.

One day when young John Hay brought some papers to Lincoln's office, the two men talked about the issues of the war.

"For my part," the older man explained, "I consider the central idea pervading this struggle is the necessity that is upon us of proving that popular government is not an absurdity. We must settle this question now, whether in a free government the minority have the right to break up the government whenever they choose. If we fail it will go far to prove the incapability of the people to govern themselves."

Lincoln never professed learning in world history. Yet, from the very beginning, he sensed the world significance of the American crisis. From the time of the American Revolution, Europe had looked to America as the proving-ground of democracy. Inspired by the example of that Revolution, European peoples had also striven for self-government, but despotism and autocracy had been too well entrenched. The privileged classes of Europe, who looked upon democracy as little better than mob rule, sneered at American political theories as sure to fail.

"This is essentially a People's contest," Lincoln explained to Congress when it assembled on July 4, 1861. "On the side of the Union it is a struggle for maintaining in the world, that form, and substance of government, whose leading object is, to elevate the condition of men—to lift artificial weights from all shoulders—to clear the paths of laudable pursuit for all—to afford all, an unfettered start, and a fair chance, in the race of life.

"Our popular government has often been called an experiment. Two points in it, our people have already settled—the successful *establishing* and the successful *administering* of it. One still remains—its successful *maintenance* against a formidable attempt to overthrow it. It is now for them to demonstrate to the world, that those who can fairly carry an election, can also suppress a rebellion—that ballots are the rightful, and peaceful, successors of bullets; and that when ballots have fairly, and constitutionally, decided, there can be no successful appeal, except to ballots themselves, at succeeding elections. Such will be a great lesson of peace: teaching men that what they cannot take by an election, neither can they take it by a war—teaching all, the folly of being the beginners of a war."

Lincoln's primary purpose throughout the war was to save the Union. But this was incidental to a far more important objective: for as he saw the issue in its broader aspects, upon the fate of the Union hung the fate of world democracy. He must not allow the Southern people to dissever the nation or to renounce the philosophy of human freedom and equality for the false concept of a master race.

Mindful of his own pedigree of toil, Lincoln explained to the Congress how free institutions had elevated the American people beyond any others in the world. So large an army as the government now had at its command "was never before known, without a soldier in it, but who had taken his place there of his own free choice." And there was scarcely a regiment in that army from which a president, a cabinet, a congress, and possibly a supreme court capable of administering the government could not be chosen. The same held true of the Confederate army. Whoever chose to abandon such a form of government, warned Lincoln, had best think well of what might come in place of it.

*

B Y M I D - M A Y 1861 Baltimore had been garrisoned with Union troops, Harpers Ferry had been retaken, and a military line extended along the north bank of the Ohio River and into Missouri. Thousands of troops guarded Washington. Across the Potomac at Arlington, and eight miles downriver at Alexandria, however, Lincoln could see Confederate flags. Regiments of troops from other Southern states had entered Virginia, some of them encamping and drilling almost within sight of Washington. "The people of Virginia have thus allowed this giant insurrection to make its nest within her borders," declared Lincoln, "and this government has no choice left but to deal with it, *where* it finds it." In bright moonlight at two a.m. on May 23, the day after Virginia ratified her secession ordinance, Federal troops moved quietly across the Washington bridges to fortify the hills and ridges commanding the ten-mile-square area of the capital.

Among the troops in Washington was a regiment of agile,

reckless, red-trousered Zouaves, recruited from the New York fire department by youthful Elmer E. Ellsworth, a former student in Lincoln's law office. Accompanying Lincoln to Washington, young Ellsworth had shown remarkable military aptitude. Embarking in transports, he and his Zouaves landed at Alexandria. The Confederates fell back. But the defiant Stars and Bars still floated over the hotel, and Ellsworth dashed up the stairs to cut them down. As he descended, the innkeeper jumped from a dark passage to discharge a double-barreled shotgun into Ellsworth's chest, then turned the second barrel on Corporal Francis E. Brownell, who followed close behind. But before he could pull the trigger a second time, Brownell's rifle slug burst his face, and his bayonet ripped his entrails.

Ellsworth had a White House funeral. Lincoln could not keep back the tears. "In the untimely loss of your noble son," he wrote to Ellsworth's parents, "our affliction here, is scarcely less than your own. . . . In the hope that it may be no intrusion upon the sacredness of your sorrow, I have ventured to address you this tribute to the memory of my young friend, and your brave and early fallen child. May God give you that consolation which is beyond all earthly power."

Nine days later came news of the death of Douglas at Chicago. He had worn himself into the grave in an effort to save the Union.

*

THE NORTH clamored for action. "On to Richmond!" became the cry. They would crush the South in one battle and end this irksome war. On June 29 Lincoln called his military advisers to a cabinet meeting and suggested an advance on Manassas Junction, where the Confederate army threatened Washington. General Scott opposed the plan. The troops were still too raw. He preferred to push an expedition down the Mississippi, throttle the South with a blockade, and starve her out. But Lincoln had to measure political as well as military factors; further delay might cool the Northern zeal. The army prepared to attack.

In the bright heat of Sunday, July 21, General Irvin Mc-Dowell's ill-disciplined army of thirty thousand men marched out through the rough, broken country of second-growth pine south of Washington. It was a heterogeneous array—Zouaves in red fezzes and baggy Turkish trousers, Garibaldi guards in long-plumed hats, Wisconsin boys in homespun gray, Massachusetts boys in blue, a Minnesota regiment in black felt hats, black pants, and red-checkered lumberjack shirts, with a small detachment of regulars. In the Shenandoah Valley in western Virginia, General Joseph E. Johnston, informed of the Union troop movement, threw a feint against General Robert Patterson's opposing Union force, then secretly entrained his men for Manassas Junction. With Johnston's troops Beauregard would command a force about equal to McDowell's.

Lincoln went to church that Sunday morning, as had been his custom since he came to Washington. Returning to the White House, he asked for news. The two armies had met along the rough, wooded banks of Bull Run, a tributary of the Potomac. The Union troops were gaining ground. Lincoln went to the War Department to talk to Scott and read the telegrams as they ticked off the wire. By five thirty the battle seemed won, and Lincoln took his usual afternoon drive.

At six o'clock Seward burst into the White House, his face pallid and twitchy. "Where is the President?" he asked hoarsely of Nicolay and Hay. Gone for his drive, they told him. "Have you any late news?" asked Seward. They showed him the telegrams announcing victory. "Tell no one," said Seward. "That is not true. The battle is lost. The telegraph says that McDowell is in full retreat and calls upon General Scott to save the capital. Find the President and tell him to come immediately to General Scott's."

Lincoln returned a half-hour later. He listened silently, then started quickly for the War Department. There a telegram announced: "General McDowell's army in full retreat through Centerville. The day is lost. Save Washington and the remnants of this army. . . . The routed troops will not reform."

Rain began at nightfall. Lincoln lay down on a sofa, but could not sleep. Outside, a worried crowd jammed Pennsylvania Avenue, listening fearfully for the approaching rumble of artillery or the clatter of rebel cavalry. A number of Congressmen had followed the army to view the battle. By midnight they came straggling back, haggard, angry, and frightened. Some of them came to the White House, where Lincoln listened to their stories of disaster.

By daylight shattered regiments were stumbling across the Long Bridge into the city. The British war correspondent William Howard Russell, who had returned from the battlefield sure that McDowell had matters well in hand, told how "I awoke from a deep sleep this morning, about six o'clock. The rain was falling in torrents and beat with a dull, thudding sound on the leads outside my window; but louder than all, came a strange sound, as if of the tread of men, a confused tramp and splashing, and a murmuring of voices. I got up and ran to the front room, the windows of which looked on the street, and there, to my intense surprise, I saw a steady stream of men covered with mud, soaked through with rain, who were pouring irregularly, without any semblance of order, up Pennsylvania Avenue towards the Capitol. A dense stream of vapor rose from the multitude; but looking closely at the men, I perceived they belonged to different regiments, New Yorkers, Michiganders, Rhode Islanders, Massachusetters, Minnesotans, mingled pellmell together. Many of these men were without knapsacks, crossbelts and firelocks. Some had neither great-coats nor shoes, others were covered with blankets."

Beaten soldiers dropped exhausted in the streets, slumped down on the steps of houses, or staggered on like sleepwalkers. Fagged horsemen swayed in their saddles. Women huddled on the street corners pouring hot cups of coffee. Looking out of the White House windows, Lincoln could see it all.

The President pieced together the story of the rout—coats, hats, boots, and canteens thrown aside; haversacks spilling shirts, socks, and tins of jam along the road; broken wagons, abandoned guns and rifles, the wild panic of flight.

The enemy did not pursue in the heavy rain, and by Tuesday the Union army had reintrenched on Arlington Heights. The panic had not been so widespread as reported. Many farm boys and city boys in their first encounter with gunfire had fought bravely through a long day. Some said the rout had started among the teamsters and sightseers. Others blamed the three-months volunteers whose time had expired and who thought only of getting safely home.

"Sir," said General Scott in a conference with Lincoln, "I am the greatest coward in America. . . . I deserve removal because I did not stand up, when my army was not in condition for fighting, and resist it to the last." Lincoln replied: "Your conversation seems to imply that I forced you to fight this battle." Scott hesitated, evading a direct reply. "I have never served a President who has been kinder to me than you have been," he said.

Horace Greeley wrote Lincoln that he had just passed his seventh sleepless night. What could he do to help? "If it is best for the country and for mankind that we make peace with the rebels at once and on their own terms, do not shrink even from that."

Lincoln had no thought of peace on Confederate terms, but he knew now that this war would not be won in any summer excursion. Walt Whitman, with a poet's sensitivity, understood how the catastrophe at Bull Run must have afflicted Lincoln. "But the hour, the day, the night pass'd," he wrote, "and whatever returns, a day, a night like that can never again return. The President, recovering himself, begins that very night—sternly, rapidly sets about the task of reorganizing his forces, and placing himself in position for future and surer work. If there was nothing else of Abraham Lincoln for history to stamp him with, it is enough to send him with his wreath to the memory of all future time, that he endured that hour, that day, bitterer than

gall—indeed a crucifixion day—that it did not conquer him—
that he unflinchingly stemm'd it, and resolv'd to lift himself and
the Union out of it."

The day after the battle, Lincoln called General George B.
McClellan to Washington and entrusted him with its defense.
By the following day the President had finished a "Memorandum
of Military Policy Suggested by the Bull Run Defeat." Lincoln
would hold present positions, tighten the blockade, replace the
three-months volunteers with men enrolled for longer service,
and then push expeditions simultaneously into Virginia, the loyal
region of east Tennessee, and down the Mississippi.

Despair, blame, and indignation melted into stern resolve.
Again came an outpouring from the North. Every day saw soldiers disembarking to march through the city to the camps beyond, often grounding their rifles on the White House lawn for a
word of cheer from the President. Troop shelters rose on vacant
lots in Washington. Across the river a great tent city grew.

*

To command the Union forces in the West, with headquarters
in St. Louis, Lincoln chose dashing John C. Frémont, Republican
presidential candidate in 1856. Missouri continued to be a
trouble spot, and Frémont was confronted with the discouraging
task of organizing an army with only scanty arms and equipment
in the face of a determined enemy. Frank Blair wired Lincoln
from St. Louis: "Affairs here are rather threatening but if the
Government will send Fremont a strong reenforcement & at
once he will turn the tables on the enemy & make him sorry he
left home."

But Frémont soon roused antagonisms. Renting an elegant
mansion for his headquarters, he surrounded himself with a
retinue of foreign officers in gaudy uniforms. Guards were
posted everywhere. To Lincoln came reports of arrogance, extravagance, and favoritism, of corruption in government contracts.

Rumor had Frémont planning a great expedition for the

capture of New Orleans, but he seemed less than energetic against the Confederates near at hand. While he remained desk-bound in St. Louis, the impetuous Lyon on August 10, at Wilson's Creek, attacked a Confederate force that outnumbered him two to one. Wounded in ankle and thigh, with a bullet crease in his scalp, Lyon led a desperate charge. A rifle slug found his heart. The Union defeat and Lyon's death were charged to Frémont's indifference.

Confederate guerrillas ravaged Missouri ceaselessly, and on August 30 Frémont proclaimed that the urgency of the situation demanded that the commanding general take over the administrative powers of the state. Invoking martial law, he announced the confiscation of the property of all persons in Missouri who had taken up arms against the government, and declared their slaves emancipated.

The news of this action brought fresh embarrassment to Lincoln. In the eyes of the antislavery radicals, Frémont at once took on heroic stature, but Joshua Speed wrote Lincoln from Kentucky: "I have been so much distressed since reading . . . that foolish proclamation of Fremont that I have been unable to eat or sleep. . . . So fixed is public sentiment in this state against . . . allowing negroes to be emancipated & remain among us, that you had as well attack the freedom of worship in the north or the right of a parent to teach his child to read, as to wage war in a slave state on such a principle." General Anderson reported that a company of Union volunteers had thrown down their arms and disbanded. Three Unionists wired the President from Louisville: "There is not a day to lose in disavowing emancipation or Kentucky is gone over the mill dam."

Even before these warnings came, Lincoln had hastened to explain to Frémont how his ill-timed edict would antagonize the border-state loyalists and even the great mass of Northern Democrats who would support a war for the Union but not an attack on slavery. On August 6 Congress had passed an act authorizing confiscation of property used in aid of insurrection, not arbitrarily but through customary judicial processes, and

Lincoln asked Frémont to modify his edict to make it conform to this act. "This letter is written in a spirit of caution, and not of censure," Lincoln explained. "I send it by special messenger, in order that it may certainly and speedily reach you."

Frémont considered for six days. He saw no reason to amend his proclamation. He would not "change or shade it," he decided. "It was equal to a victory in the field." If the President wished to modify it, he could issue the order himself. Jessie Benton Frémont, the general's strong-willed, devoted wife, set out to take his answer to the President.

Arriving at Willard's after two days and nights on over-crowded, tobacco-spattered railroad cars, and without even taking time to bathe, she sent a note to the White House asking when the President would see her. "Now, at once. A. Lincoln," came back a cryptic answer. The hour was almost midnight.

Lincoln did not conceal his displeasure at Frémont's reply. Mrs. Frémont became angry. It might go hard with the President, she hinted, should her husband decide to set himself up in op-position to him. Lincoln summoned all his tact and patience to avoid a quarrel. The next day he sent Frémont another tem-perate letter. He granted that the general might know more about the local situation than the President in Washington, but political decisions must be left to the President and Congress. "It is therefore ordered," declared Lincoln, "that . . . said proclama-tion be so modified . . . as to conform to . . . the act of Congress."

A storm of protest broke upon Lincoln as antislavery press, pulpit, and politicians extolled the general's act. The Germans of St. Louis, always intensely antislavery, rallied to Frémont's support. Senator Grimes described his edict as "the only noble and true thing done during this war." Lincoln now exercised the powers of a dictator, asserted Senator Sumner, "but how vain to have the power of a God and not to use it godlike." Billy Herndon wrote that the war did not go to suit him. Lincoln's friend Orville H. Browning protested from Quincy, Illinois. "Coming from you," replied Lincoln, "I confess it astonishes me." Appointed by Governor Richard Yates to fill Douglas's unexpired term in the Senate, Browning had been one of the framers of the Confiscation Act that Lincoln sought to uphold.

Matters in Missouri went from bad to worse. Crushed under a mountain of detail, Frémont seemed unable to cope with the Confederates or even to administer his department. Lincoln sent Adjutant General Lorenzo Thomas and then Secretary Cameron to investigate. Both of them reported the general unfit for his post. General Samuel R. Curtis, at St. Louis, wrote that he "lacks the intelligence, the experience, and the sagacity necessary to his command." Elihu B. Washburne, head of a Congressional investigating committee, reported stupendous graft and extravagance; Frémont refused to counsel with men of true patriotism, "while a gang of California robbers and scoundrels rule, control and direct everything." The Blair family, once Frémont's patrons, became his bitter enemies as they were convinced of his ineptitude. When Frank Blair challenged Frémont's power, the general charged him with insubordination and threw him into jail. In Washington old Francis P. Blair and his son Montgomery determined to overthrow Frémont, for the Blairs were a clannish family, and when they went in for a fight, it was said, they went in for a funeral.

But Northern sentiment was overwhelmingly on Frémont's side. O. H. Williamson warned Lincoln from St. Louis: "If you are going to have your, and the cabinet officers' time taken to investigate charges made against parties by F. P. Blair you will have your hands full. He is a mischief making, troublesome fellow, and less you have to do with the Blair family the better. *Mark that!*"

On October 26 Washburne wired Lincoln: "Things looks more & more alarming here entirely outside of contracts. In my judgment events are drifting towards resisting Government authority. This opinion concurred in by best men here. 'Forewarned fore-armed.'" John A. Gurley wrote that the government was "sleeping over a volcano"; a reign of terror threatened; there were strong indications that Frémont "does not intend to yield his command at your bidding."

Lincoln decided that Frémont must go. But to dismiss so

popular a man presented a touchy problem. What would happen if the headstrong general should defy the President, as his wife had threatened and as persons on the spot had warned that he might do?

As a precautionary measure, to allay hostile opinion, Lincoln sent Montgomery Blair to inform Governor John A. Andrew of Massachusetts, and the newspaper editors Horace Greeley and William Cullen Bryant, of the reasons why Frémont must be dismissed. Then, on October 24, 1861, he sent General Curtis a letter with two enclosures: one to Frémont, relieving him of command; the other to General Hunter, appointing him to Frémont's place. Without being informed of the nature of the message to Frémont, Curtis was instructed to take "safe, certain and suitable measures" to have it delivered to him, unless, by the time Curtis or his messenger arrived, Frémont should have fought and won a battle or be on the verge of one, in which case Curtis should wait for further orders. The enclosure to Hunter was not to be delivered until Frémont had received his dismissal. Evidently Lincoln had taken thought of the certain outcry of the antislavery radicals if Frémont should be removed after a victory or on the eve of one.

Lincoln feared real trouble from Frémont and took every precaution. He chose his trusted friend Leonard Swett to take Curtis's instructions to St. Louis. But by the time Swett reached Missouri, the intention to remove Frémont had somehow reached the New York papers. Swett met friends of Frémont's on the train, and he and Curtis, in whom he thought it best to confide, feared that these persons might have suspected the purpose of his trip. Frémont, forewarned, might refuse to admit Swett to his lines. So Curtis and Swett sent Captain Thomas J. McKenny to deliver Lincoln's order to the general.

Disguised as a farmer, McKenny arrived at Frémont's camp southwest of Springfield, Missouri, at five a.m. on November 1. Learning that there was no immediate prospect of a battle, McKenny requested to see the general. An aide asked him to state his errand. He declined, insisting that he must see the general personally. When Frémont read Lincoln's order, he exclaimed: "Sir, how did you get through my lines?" An aide caught up with McKenny as he left and asked him to tell no one of his mission. His request to leave camp was refused. About eleven o'clock that night, however, he overheard the password and escaped. In the meantime Frémont had ordered his troops to arms as though to begin a battle. But there was no enemy in the vicinity, and next day he gave up his command.

Swett reported to Lincoln that "Gen'l Fremont has talked about his signature to unlawful orders being above law & to be obeyed. The German people have talked about making him Dictator. Some of his officers in quite high standing have talked so too."

Frémont's dismissal brought another storm of protest upon Lincoln. Sumner lauded Frémont at a mass meeting in Cooper Union. Henry Ward Beecher praised him from his pulpit. "Where are you," Thaddeus Stevens asked the antislavery radicals in Congress, "that you let the hounds run down your friend Fremont?" The reaction might have been even more explosive had Montgomery Blair not made his precautionary visit to Boston and New York. Even so, such factional animosities had been aroused that hereafter Lincoln would need to exercise the wisest statesmanship to reconcile the diverse shades of opinion within his party.

*

A MATTER of grave concern to Lincoln and his cabinet was the probable attitude of foreign powers toward the Confederate States, for recognition of Southern independence might be fatal to the Union. Other nations were likely to follow England's lead. As American Minister in London, where he must have a man of tact and diplomatic skill, Lincoln chose Charles Francis Adams, whose father and grandfather had held the post before him. Adams faced a task almost as critical as Lincoln's, and under equally trying circumstances, for English upper-class sympathies were strongly for the South. English aristocrats were willing—some even eager, Adams thought—"to see the

United States go to pieces"; they feared that the pernicious doctrines of democracy might spread through their own country. Already Lord John Russell, the English Foreign Secretary, had received Confederate emissaries "unofficially."

In drawing Adams's instructions Seward had directed him to protest against any recognition of the Confederacy, official or unofficial, as an act injurious to the United States, and to "desist from all intercourse whatever . . . with the British government, so long as it shall continue intercourse of either kind with the domestic enemies of this country." The conflict, in the view of the United States, was of purely domestic concern. Fortunately, Lincoln carefully scrutinized this dispatch and toned it down. Where Seward had written that the United States was "surprised and grieved" at England's unofficial communication with Confederate emissaries, Lincoln changed the phraseology to "regrets." Where Seward called such intercourse "wrongful," Lincoln made it "hurtful." Two paragraphs reminding England of her two previous wars with the United States and threatening another were ordered struck out altogether, though when Lincoln instructed that the dispatch should be for Adams's guidance only and not for presentation to the English government, Seward left them in, as written.

On May 13, the very day that Adams arrived in London, the British cabinet decided to recognize the Confederates as belligerents. The next day Adams read in the morning papers a declaration of neutrality, granting the Confederates the rights of a state at war, entitling their flag to recognition on the high seas, and conceding their ships of war and commerce the same privileges in neutral ports as those enjoyed by Northern vessels. Actually, Great Britain had no other choice; Lincoln's proclamation of blockade was itself an official acknowledgment to the nations of the world that a state of war existed, and was later so interpreted by the United States Supreme Court. But the British action irritated Seward and caused sharp resentment in the North. If Adams's instructions had not been modified by Lincoln, and he had acted according to their original tenor, Britain's recognition of Confederate belligerency might well have led to war.

In August, President Davis appointed James M. Mason, of Virginia, as a special commissioner to England, and John Slidell, of Louisiana, as commissioner to France. Running the blockade at Charleston, Mason and Slidell proceeded to Havana, where they boarded the British mail steamer *Trent* for Southampton. As the *Trent* steamed through the Bahama Channel on November 8, the United States man-of-war *San Jacinto* overhauled her and sent a shot across her bow. Unaccustomed to such high-handed treatment, the British captain ignored this order to lay to. A shell burst close, and the *Trent* stopped her engines and drifted on the tropic sea. Three boats put off from the *San Jacinto*, and a lieutenant came aboard the *Trent* to demand the surrender of Mason, Slidell, and their two secretaries. Aboard the *San Jacinto*, Captain Charles Wilkes, a tough, iron-jawed sea-dog, watched proceedings through his glass, his guns bearing on the Britisher. Over the strong protests of the English captain, Wilkes's boats brought back the Confederates to the *San Jacinto*. Wilkes took them to Boston, where they were imprisoned in Fort Warren.

The capture of the Confederate commissioners delighted the North, especially since the United States had given the lion's tail a painful twist. New York gave Wilkes a grand reception; Boston entertained him lavishly; the House of Representatives voted him a gold medal; and Secretary Welles commended his "brave, adroit and patriotic conduct." But England quivered with indignation. Warships were conditioned for sea duty, and eight thousand British troops boarded transports for Canada. Henry Adams, who was with his father in London, wrote to his brother: "This nation means to make war. Do not doubt it."

Thurlow Weed, who had been sent to Europe to counteract Confederate propaganda, warned Seward of the highest excitement in London; if Seward could navigate safely through this peril, it would be the crowning glory of his life. "If it be not too late," Weed wrote to Lincoln, "let me beseech you to forbear—to turn if need be the other cheek, rather than smite back at present." Charles Sumner, ex-President Fillmore, and other influential persons advised caution. George Opdyke reported fear on the part of New York businessmen that England would attack their city without warning as she had struck at Copenhagen during the Napoleonic Wars.

Under international law, Wilkes had the right to search the *Trent* and, upon the discovery of contraband, to take her into port for adjudication. But he was not permitted to remove Mason and Slidell from the deck of a neutral vessel; at least, the United States had always resisted such action, even to the point of war with England in 1812. And, strangely enough, in violation of this principle of maritime law England herself had been the chief offender in the past. Traditionally, the United States would be as inconsistent in defending the unauthorized act of Captain Wilkes as was England in complaining of it.

Lincoln's legal experience had not extended to international law, but he quickly grasped the points at issue. Pleased at first by Wilkes's bold act, he soon came to doubt the validity of the American case, and did nothing to encourage the patriotic outburst. In his December message to Congress he did not mention the incident. "One war at a time," he cautioned Seward.

Still, Lincoln disliked to back down in the face of British threats, and hoped to find some face-saving solution. Anticipating the British protest, he instructed Seward to draft reasons for surrendering the Confederates. But he decided to try his own hand at a note proposing arbitration or conditional release.

On November 30 Prime Minister Palmerston and Foreign Secretary Russell drew up a virtual ultimatum threatening war, but when they presented it to Prince Albert, consort of Queen Victoria, he restrained the angry ministers. In line with his suggestions, which Queen Victoria approved, Her Majesty's government were pleased to believe that the United States had no desire to disrupt long years of friendship, that Wilkes had acted on his own initiative, and that the United States would release the two commissioners and offer a suitable apology. But England left no doubt of her intentions in case of an unsatisfactory reply: if the American government did not comply within seven days, Lord Lyons, the British Minister in Washington, was instructed to break off diplomatic relations and return to London.

Lincoln's cabinet met on Christmas Day to consider this ultimatum. Lincoln did not even present his note suggesting arbitration or conditional release; the law of nations, as the United States had always interpreted it, upheld Great Britain's case. Even so, according to Bates's account of the meeting, "there was great reluctance on the part of some of the members of the cabinet—and even the President himself—to acknowledge these obvious truths." The discussion lasted from ten o'clock in the morning until two in the afternoon with no conclusion reached. By morning, however, all eight men were of like mind. The Confederates must be released and allowed to pursue their mission.

Except for the traditionally anti-British press, the patriotic outcry was less violent than might have been expected. Lincoln's friend Richard W. Thompson wrote to him from Terre Haute: "Everybody here is satisfied with their surrender, except the secession sympathizers, who are wonderfully hurt at the idea that our national honor is tarnished."

The wisdom of the decision proved itself as the war went on, for whenever tensions, disputes, or near crises threatened, common sense and moderation dictated the decision on both sides. Although the British ruling class continued to favor the South, they dared not flout the masses who regarded the North as fighting for human liberty. Great Britain never recognized the Confederacy as an independent state. She resisted the efforts of Louis Napoleon, Emperor of France, toward joint intervention or mediation, though foreign intervention was an ever present threat for the first two years of the war. Some Confederate warships were fitted out in British ports, but the English government eventually stopped this violation of neutrality and later made reparation. By September 1863 the Confederate states became so provoked at England's carefully correct deportment that they expelled all English consuls from their cities.

CHAPTER XIV

———◆●◆———

Shadows on the White House

BESET with troubles in the West, fearful of foreign recognition of the Confederacy or even foreign intervention in the war, and striving to invigorate the uncertain Union sentiment in the border slave states, Lincoln desperately needed a military victory. Upon General George Brinton McClellan, newly appointed commander of the Army of the Potomac, rested the nation's hope. That McClellan was a Democrat did nothing to lessen his favor with the President. Intent on rallying all Northern elements in support of the war effort, Lincoln granted commissions to Republicans and Democrats alike. The President waited patiently while the general organized and trained his fighting force.

Below medium height but muscularly compact, with red hair, red mustache, and an authoritative manner, McClellan soon won the confidence of the troops, who affectionately dubbed him "Little Mac" and "the Little Napoleon." A superb horseman, he dashed through the streets of Washington, his aides pounding behind. Graduating second in his class at West Point, he had done engineering work in the Indian territory, supervised railroad construction in Oregon, installed harbor improvements in Texas, and served gallantly under Scott in the Mexican War. Versed in the classics, a keen student of military tactics, he had written a manual on the art of war, translated a French treatise on bayonet exercises, invented an improved cavalry saddle, and visited

Europe as an observer during the Crimean War. Resigning his commission, he became chief engineer and vice-president of the Illinois Central Railroad, then president of the Mississippi & Ohio Railroad, with headquarters at Cincinnati.

With the outbreak of war, McClellan accepted a major-generalship of Ohio volunteers. Then came a commission as major general in the regular army, with command of the Department of the Ohio, embracing Ohio, Indiana, Illinois, and parts of western Virginia and Pennsylvania. In this capacity he undertook a campaign that saved the northwestern mountain and Kanawha regions of Virginia to the Union.

In Confederate hands western Virginia would have been a dangerous bastion, thrusting far into the North. But the mountain people and those of the Ohio basin owned few slaves and had little in common, economically or socially, with tidewater and piedmont Virginia. After Virginia seceded they met in two successive conventions at Wheeling and set up a "reorganized" government that claimed authority throughout the state. Realizing the military significance of the area and the political importance of holding it, McClellan sent a Federal force to clear out the Confederates. His ably planned campaign was capably carried out by his subordinates; and the liberated western Virginians, renouncing all connection with Richmond, applied for admission to the Union. The Federal Constitution forbade the division of a state without its consent, and Lincoln was confronted with another knotty problem. Reluctant to disturb old forms or to violate a constitutional guarantee, even to a state in rebellion, he delayed for many months, until finally, in June 1863, under a legal circumvention whereby the "reorganized government of Virginia" gave its consent to separation, West Virginia became the thirty-fifth state.

*

M c C l e l l a n's small victories in western Virginia marked the only successes the North had enjoyed. His appointment to command the Army of the Potomac quickened the nation with new optimism. The magnetic general, only thirty-five years old, bore himself with easy confidence. With a strong sense of the theatrical, he saw his role as savior of his country—a dangerous illusion for a man disposed to vanity. Behind his assured front, however, McClellan revealed himself, in the boastfulness of letters to his wife, as essentially distrustful of his own ability.

McClellan built elaborate defenses to ensure the safety of Washington. A skillful organizer, he proceeded to improve the army's form and discipline. A perfectionist who planned to crush the rebellion in one masterful campaign, he never seemed quite satisfied that he was ready. He saw where improvement could be worked by taking time, and in such a grand design as his a few months' time meant nothing.

Shaken Congressmen and grateful citizens of Washington fawned on the young general. Scott was ready to accord his confidence. Lincoln deferred to him. As an attorney for the Illinois Central Railroad, Lincoln had personally known McClellan as an able railroad executive. "I almost think," McClellan wrote to his wife, "that were I to win some small success now I could become Dictator or anything else that might please me— but nothing of that kind would please me,—*therefore* I *won't* be a dictator. Admirable self-denial!"

From the moment McClellan assumed command he became obsessed with the notion that the Confederate army in his front outnumbered him. Knowing the need of his own troops for battle-hardening, he overlooked a similar fault in his enemy. Always wanting more troops himself, he could never understand why others should. When General William T. Sherman asked for seventy-five thousand more men in Kentucky, McClellan showed Sherman's telegram to Lincoln with disgust. "The man is crazy," he declared.

While McClellan's army drilled and paraded under the hot summer sun, the Confederates erected batteries on the south side of the Potomac to threaten Washington's outlet to the sea. Above Harpers Ferry they cut the Baltimore & Ohio Railroad, the capital's main artery to the West. While the North fumed at this Southern arrogance, McClellan's army did nothing more than pass in grand reviews.

Impatient of advice, annoyed by superior authority, McClellan became resentful of General Scott. The old general understood nothing, appreciated nothing, McClellan wrote to his wife. "Gen. Scott is the obstacle. He will not comprehend the danger. I have to fight my way against him. Tomorrow the matter will probably be decided by giving me absolute control independently of him. I suppose it will result in enmity on his part against me; but I have no choice. The people call on me to save the country. I must save it, and cannot respect anything that is in my way." He was in a desperate situation, he reported, threatened by an enemy that outnumbered him three to one.

Scott could not agree that McClellan was in the terrible predicament that he imagined; his force far outnumbered the Confederates, who were ready to retreat at his first advance. When Scott refused to accept McClellan's figures of the enemy's strength, and the administration kept the old general in supreme command in spite of his request to be relieved, McClellan became contemptuous of politicians. "I am daily more disgusted with this administration—perfectly sick of it," he confided to his wife. "There are some of the greatest geese in the Cabinet I have ever seen—enough to tax the patience of Job. . . . It is sickening in the extreme, and makes me feel heavy at heart, when I see the weakness and unfitness of the poor beings who control the destinies of this great country."

If McClellan scorned the politicians, radical antislavery senators were losing patience with him. On October 25 Senators Wade, Chandler, and Trumbull came to Washington to learn why he delayed. "Bluff Ben" Wade, of Ohio, profane, crude, and brutally sharp-witted, was mercilessly vindictive toward the South. His hard eyes, thin lips, and mastiff-like jaws marked him as the roughhewn reformer that he was. He had the narrow, sure convictions of the self-made man. Gruff, hard-drinking Zachariah Chandler, a millionaire dry-goods merchant, was the Republican boss of Michigan. A self-educated man, like Wade, gaunt, sinewy, with a long horselike face and glowering eyes, he too was vengeful toward the South.

Unswerving party men by instinct, incapable of seeing any virtue in a Democrat, Wade and Chandler had been suspicious of McClellan from the first. Lincoln's old friend and rival Lyman Trumbull seemed out of place with such men. Later he would discover his mistake. But at the moment Trumbull suspected that while Lincoln, with his integrity and patriotism, might have been a successful President in ordinary times, the present crisis was too much for him.

At the home of Montgomery Blair one night the senatorial trio pressed McClellan for three hours to launch an attack. "For God's sake, at least push back the defiant traitors," cried Wade, indignant at the Confederate flags that were visible from the Capitol. McClellan pleaded that Scott obstructed his plans. The next evening the Jacobin Club, as John Hay called the zealous Senators, visited the White House to scold the administration into battle. The conference proved stormy. The Senators demanded that the President order an advance. Lincoln, having given McClellan the responsibility of command, maintained that he must not interfere with him. Wade, Chandler, and Trumbull left in tempestuous mood.

Lincoln hastened to McClellan's headquarters. The general was irate at popular impatience, and still fretful from his own sultry session with the Senators. Lincoln sympathized with him, but explained that the Senators voiced a popular feeling that McClellan must not ignore.

The clear bright days of autumn came. Again the North cried: "On to Richmond!" McClellan made no move. Lincoln, concerned at the general's lack of fighting spirit, feared recognition of the Confederacy by foreign governments, demoralization of the Northern people, and inability to raise either men or money another season if the army should go into winter quarters with Washington threatened by the enemy. But he could not risk another crushing setback by forcing McClellan into battle as he had pressed Scott before Bull Run.

General Scott, infirm and weary, asked for the second time to be relieved of command. On November 1 Lincoln complied with fitting tribute and appointed McClellan commander in chief. The President wondered if this, added to the command of the Army of the Potomac, might be too great a task. "I can do it all," McClellan airily declared. He and his staff conducted the venerable Scott to the station at four o'clock in the morning in a drenching rain. "I feel as if several tons were taken from my shoulders," McClellan told Lincoln. "I am now in contact with you and the Secretary. I am not embarrassed by intervention." But he could no longer use Scott as a scapegoat.

Lincoln, knowing that a long war confronted him, thought he should know more about the military art than he had learned in the Black Hawk War. So he borrowed military treatises from the Library of Congress, and visited McClellan's headquarters to discuss common problems with him. But these visits bored McClellan and he hid himself away. One night Lincoln, Seward, and Hay dropped in at his house. He was attending an officer's wedding, they were told. After an hour's wait McClellan came in. A servant told him of his visitors, but he went directly upstairs. A half-hour passed. A servant, sent to remind him of his company, came down with the information that the general had gone to bed. On the way home Hay fumed at the insolence of epaulets. The President shrugged it off. This was no time for points of etiquette and personal dignity, he said. "I will hold McClellan's horse," he remarked later, "if he will only bring us success." Hay noted with satisfaction, however, that thereafter when Lincoln wished to see McClellan, he called him to the White House.

A long, lingering Indian summer kept skies clear and roads dry. "All quiet on the Potomac," at first an expression of relief, became a jeer. Horace Greeley, who at the beginning of the secession crisis would have "let the erring sisters go in peace," now led the clamor for action in the press.

McClellan ordered a small force to push across the Potomac at Ball's Bluff. A sharp fight developed. Lincoln drifted into

McClellan's headquarters that afternoon, shook hands all around, and remarked about the beauty of the day. The lines were deeper in his face. His cheeks looked sunken. A lieutenant asked the President "please to come this way"; telegraph instruments were chattering in an inner office. Five minutes later Lincoln reappeared, head sunk, breast heaving, his sallow face wet with tears. He stumbled as he stepped into the street. General McClellan came out of the telegraph office a moment later. There was not much to report, he said; the Union force had been defeated at Ball's Bluff, and Colonel Edward D. Baker, an old friend of the President's, had been killed.

In late December, General McClellan fell sick. Brigadier General R. B. Marcy, his father-in-law and chief of staff, was also ill. Military matters stood still. No one knew the tight-lipped McClellan's plans. His ailment was reported to be a cold, but there were also rumors of typhoid fever. Lincoln felt gravely disturbed. He called at McClellan's house, but was not allowed to see him.

Early in January 1862 the radical Republican Congressmen unleashed a ferocious drive against the administration. A resolution for an investigation of the disasters at Bull Run and Ball's Bluff led to the appointment of a joint Committee on the Conduct of the War, which proceeded to expose mistakes and inject vigor into the government. The driving spirit of the committee was barrel-chested Ben Wade, aided by iron-fisted Zachariah Chandler. Plain, outspoken Andrew Johnson, self-educated without a day of schooling, a leader of the Tennessee mountain people, who had denounced secession with a loaded revolver holding back his audience, was the third committee member from the Senate.

This committee became the spearhead of the radical Republican drive, an agency through which the vindictive group tried to control the war effort. Generals were haled before it and commanded to reveal their plans or explain mistakes and shortcomings. Politics governed its attitudes. Officers of radical antislavery leanings were treated with deference, while those of conservative views were scolded and broken.

Solidly behind the committee in the Senate stood pedantic Charles Sumner, the eager abolitionist, and solemn Lyman Trumbull, inclining more and more toward a harsh policy against the South. In the House it drew encouragement and support from black-wigged, clubfooted Thaddeus Stevens, chairman of the powerful Ways and Means Committee. A product of the tough Pennsylvania school of politics, the sarcastically abusive Stevens, while winning the label of "Commoner" as a supposed friend of the people, maneuvered adeptly behind the scenes for predatory business interests. These turbulent Congressmen troubled Lincoln no end. For with all their partisan ruthlessness and personal faults and blind spots, they spoke for the antislavery element in Congress, whose support he dared not forfeit.

During the first week in January the committee concluded that it had enough evidence against McClellan to lay its findings before Lincoln and asked for a cabinet interview. In cold starlight on the night of January 6 Wade clumped up the White House walk with his cohorts and demanded to know McClellan's plans. Wade attacked McClellan savagely. Why wouldn't he fight? Did he have secret leanings toward the South? Did he favor slavery? Was he conniving to bring back the Southern states peaceably and make himself president or dictator of a restored, slaveholding Union? Lincoln refused to force the general's hand. Although outwardly unruffled, he had reached the point of black despair.

The next day Lincoln sent for Quartermaster General Montgomery C. Meigs. "General," he groaned, "what shall I do? The people are impatient; Chase has no money, and tells me he can raise no more; the General of the army has typhoid fever. The bottom is out of the tub. What shall I do?" Meigs advised the President to confer with McClellan's division commanders.

Dropping in to see Lincoln about this time, Orville Browning recorded in his diary: "He told me he was thinking of taking the field himself and suggested several plans of operations." Lincoln, in desperation, did seem to be taking the direction of military affairs into his own hands. He pored over reports from the field and renewed his study of military textbooks. Many politicians with no more military knowledge than Lincoln were holding important commands, and there was strong distrust in Republican political circles of the "West Point clique." Lincoln did not share this scorn of the professional soldier, but he may have leaned toward the belief that no special training was needed for high command. In other respects, however, he was learning his military lesson fast. With his ability to master fundamentals, he recognized, sooner than most of his generals, that the North's great hope of victory lay in using its superior manpower and economic resources in sustained, co-ordinated attacks.

Such operations had been impossible at first, for political considerations had demanded that forces be deployed at many points in Missouri, Kentucky, eastern Tennessee, and western Virginia to encourage loyalist sentiment and thwart secessionist forays. Lincoln recognized the weakness of the policy of deployment from a military point of view, however, and thought he might make up for it by using every unit offensively whenever the chance afforded. To General Don Carlos Buell, commanding in Kentucky, he wrote: "I state my general idea of this war to be that we have *greater* numbers, and the enemy has the *greater* facility of concentrating forces upon points of collision; that we must fail, unless we can find some way of making *our* advantage an over-match of his; and that this can be done by menacing him with superior forces at *different* points, at the *same* time; so that we can safely attack, one, or both, if he makes no change; and if he *weakens* one to *strengthen* the other, forbear to attack the strengthened one, but seize, and hold the weakened one, gaining so much."

Watching Western operations closely, Lincoln advised General Henry W. Halleck, now commanding at St. Louis, to seize Columbus, on the Mississippi, while Buell advanced into eastern Tennessee, where Unionists were "being hanged and driven to despair." But McClellan had neglected to put Halleck and Buell in concert. Buell did nothing to relieve the loyal east Tennesseans, whose welfare had become Lincoln's special concern; Halleck was not ready to attack. "It is exceedingly discouraging," wrote Lincoln resignedly. "As everywhere else, nothing can be done." "Delay is ruining us," he wrote to Buell. The President began to recognize that without proper co-ordination at the top level the departmental commanders too often allowed themselves to be immobilized by local difficulties instead of taking the vigorous action that would have enabled them collectively to override those difficulties.

On the night of January 10, 1862 Lincoln, following Meigs's advice, called Major General Irvin McDowell and Brigadier General William B. Franklin to the White House. Three days later, at a larger meeting of cabinet and generals, McClellan unexpectedly walked in. He was properly reticent about revealing his plans before so many persons, but it developed later that he wished to abandon his position before Washington and attack Richmond by way of Urbana on the lower Rappahannock or up the Peninsula between the York and James rivers. The plan did not commend itself to Lincoln; it meant further delay. But he ordered Meigs to look into the matter of transportation by boat to the Peninsula.

*

ADDING to Lincoln's vexations came reports of graft and rascality in the War Department. Investigation by the Committee on the Conduct of the War revealed waste, favoritism, and corruption, gross greed on the part of contractors indulged by lax officials. Glued knapsacks came apart in the first rain. Uniforms could be picked to pieces with the fingers. The government had bought vast quantities of rotten blankets, tainted pork, disintegrating shoes. Cameron had not profited personally, except in using his position to pay political debts and strengthen his political position; but he was slovenly, unmethodical, and careless in choosing men with whom to deal. Against the outcry for Cameron's removal, Lincoln took into account the formidable difficulties under which the Secretary had been obliged to work in building the army from 16,000 to 500,000 men.

The subtlest of politicians, sensitive to the shifts of the political winds, Cameron tried to re-establish his position by ingratiating himself with the antislavery radicals. Without consulting Lincoln, he inserted in his annual report to Congress a long passage advocating emancipation of slaves and their employment as soldiers, both as an aid to the Union and as punishment to "rebellious traitors" who had forfeited their rights. This was in marked contrast to Lincoln's own assertion in his message to Congress that "we should not be in haste to determine that radical and extreme measures, which may reach the loyal as well as the disloyal, are indispensable."

Cameron, on his own initiative, had his report printed and mailed to postmasters for release at the same time as Lincoln's message. Learning of this action, Lincoln telegraphed orders recalling all copies and instructed Cameron to delete the unauthorized passage. But both the expurgated and unexpurgated versions reached the press, and Lincoln became more unpopular than ever with the antislavery radicals for countermanding Cameron's proposal.

Lincoln made no further reference to the matter, and Cameron accepted the implied rebuke with grace. Outwardly the two men's relations remained cordial. But when the ministry at St. Petersburg became vacant, Lincoln appointed Cameron to fill it. In conferring this new office on Cameron he expressed his "undiminished confidence" and "affectionate esteem," praised Cameron's "ability, patriotism and fidelity to public trust," and referred to "the not less important" services that he could render at St. Petersburg.

The "affectionate esteem" was not hypocrisy, for Lincoln seems to have developed a genuine fondness for the slim, genial, unassuming Pennsylvanian, in spite of his deviousness. Years later, men who were close to Lincoln during the war wrote with a sense of shock of his giving Cameron an office in the first place, of his toleration of his methods in the War Department, and of his unabated friendship when Cameron returned from Russia. Many men most intimate with Lincoln regarded it as a short-coming that, while he could judge people in the mass, his judg-ment of individuals was often too lenient. The strange fates of politics and war forced Lincoln to deal with all manner of men. And he met them as they came, seeking their good qualities and counting these more than their weaknesses.

*

O N E of Lincoln's most malicious critics had been Edwin Mc-Masters Stanton, former Attorney General in Buchanan's cabi-net, then chief legal adviser to Secretary Cameron. In the early months of Lincoln's Presidency, Stanton deplored Lincoln's "painful imbecility." To him the President was "the original gorilla," "the Illinois Ape." McClellan wrote that the most disagreeable thing about Stanton was "the extreme virulence with which he abused the President, the Administration and the Republican Party. He carried this to such an extent that I was often shocked by it." If Lincoln never learned of Stanton's scurrility, he remembered his snub at Cincinnati in the McCor-mick reaper case as one of the most crushing experiences of his life. But he saw in Stanton the qualities he needed in the War Department and, repressing any personal resentment he may have felt toward him, appointed him to Cameron's place.

A gnomelike figure, short-legged and heavy-set, with black, bushy hair and long black whiskers streaked with gray, Stanton had an explosive personality. A man of intense physical and mental vigor, he glared with menacing, nearsighted eyes through thick-lensed spectacles. The son of a widowed mother, he had worked his way through Kenyon College, clerked in a store, studied law, and, moving from Ohio to Pittsburgh, gained national eminence as a lawyer. He had saved millions for the government in an attempted California land swindle, resisting inducements and bribes. Though an unswerving Democrat, he was steadfastly loyal to the Union, and his appointment to

Buchanan's cabinet had brought firmness and new vigor to its councils.

Domineering, with an unbending will, Stanton was also sly. It was said that as Cameron's adviser he had himself written the offensive paragraphs in the annual report that led to his chief's dismissal. There was a streak of cruelty in Stanton, and a touch of personal cowardice that marks the bully. An able organizer, he drove himself and his subordinates unsparingly.

Soon after his appointment as Secretary of War, on January 12, 1862, Stanton, when he discovered that an order had been neglected, with his own hands helped drag heavy guns from the Washington arsenal and put them on the cars for Harpers Ferry. The next day the commander of the arsenal reported that he had not found it convenient to forward the guns on the preceding day, but would get them off immediately. Stanton glared at him scornfully. "The guns are now at Harpers Ferry," he roared, "and you, sir, are no longer in the service of the United States Government."

No one could make a secret deal with Stanton. Politicians, army officers, and contractors, calling at his crowded office, were required to state their requests briefly and directly, in the hearing of everyone present; Stanton gave a quick yes or no and waved them out. Scornful of rank or personal feelings, he snapped at generals and clerks alike. "As soon as I can get the machinery of the office working, the rats cleared out, and the rat holes stopped, we shall *move*," he promised an assistant secretary. "*This army has got to fight or run away . . . the champagne and oysters on the Potomac must be stopped.*" He had been a close friend of McClellan's, but he resolved to make the general fight.

Stanton's nervous gyrations around the War Department reminded Lincoln of an old Methodist preacher in the West who became so energetic in the pulpit that his parishioners talked of putting rocks in his pockets to hold him down. "We may be obliged to serve Stanton the same way," he said, "but I guess we'll let him jump a while first."

At any hour of the day or night Stanton might stump into

the White House. Lincoln dropped into the War Department at all hours. "There grew up between them," observed Nicolay and Hay, "an intimacy in which the mind and heart of each were given without reserve to the great work in which they bore such conspicuous parts." If Lincoln ever learned of the epithets that Stanton had applied to him, he gave no sign of it, and Stanton no longer spoke of Lincoln in his former vein. Lincoln interfered with Stanton only when necessary, but, like Seward, Stanton learned that Lincoln could be firm, even peremptory, when he chose.

Lincoln and Stanton, in their wide differences of personality, often canceled out each other's faults. If the War Secretary, in his tremendous efficiency, suppressed his human sympathies, victims of his petty despotism could find a ready advocate in Lincoln, whereas the gentle, tenderhearted President often needed the checkrein of Stanton's rigid sense of duty. On the other hand, Stanton's irascibility gave Lincoln a means of avoiding commitments; he seemed to encourage the impression that not even he dared cross the Secretary. And there was a quality of mystery about Stanton: once, after his usual brusque, busy hours with callers, when he had snapped out a harsh "No" many times, he had been found alone, head bowed on his desk, sobbing.

*

W H I L E Lincoln's worries multiplied, his wife had troubles, too. She came to the White House with a better education and a richer social background than many of the ladies who preceded her. But Washington "cliff dwellers," aghast at the thought of an upstart Western couple replacing the courtly Buchanan and his gracious niece Harriet Lane as leaders of the capital social hierarchy, had determined to boycott her. To this tight, aristocratic clique of wealthy residents, with their Southern Democratic sympathies, this "black Republican" woman of Kentucky birth and breeding was a traitor to her class. Republican women, on the other hand, called her "two thirds slavery and the other third secesh." They forgot that she had numerous relatives in the Union army, but chattered viciously about those in Confederate service. Rumors that Mrs. Lincoln was not only a traitor but a spy were taken with sufficient seriousness to be discussed by a Congressional investigating committee. One morning the sad-faced President came unexpectedly into one of its secret sessions to vouch for his wife's loyalty.

Mrs. Lincoln sought advice from Mrs. John J. Crittenden, who was also a Kentuckian, and Mrs. Stephen A. Douglas. But these ladies soon left Washington, and Mary Lincoln, with no real friends to lean upon, fell into designing hands. Connivers and flatterers tried to reach the President through her, and since she conceived of her position of "First Lady" as carrying with it governmental as well as social privileges, she nagged Lincoln about appointments and interfered in shaping policy. She wrote to James Gordon Bennett, editor of the *New York Herald:* "From all parties the cry for a 'change of cabinet' comes. I hold a letter just received from Governor Sprague, in my hand, who is quite as earnest as you have been on the subject. Doubtless if my good husband were here instead of being with the Army of the Potomac, both of these missives would be placed before him, accompanied by womanly suggestions, proceeding from a heart so deeply interested for our distracted country. I have a great terror of strongminded ladies, yet if a word fitly spoken in due time can be urged in a time like this, we should not withhold it."

Mary Lincoln's indiscretions were born of good intentions. When she meddled in state matters, it was not so much from any wish to play the role of Madam President as to safeguard her "good patient husband" from unscrupulous schemers and traitors. She hoped with all her heart to help make his administration a success by dutifully performing her own part as White House hostess. But she failed to appreciate the public nature of her new position and made slurring personal remarks about men in high government posts. She let Stanton know that she detested him and referred to Seward as "a dirty abolitionist sneak." Of the cabinet wives, only Mrs. Welles remained on good terms with her. She and her friend Julia Jayne Trumbull fell out over politics.

When Mrs. Lincoln went to Long Branch, New Jersey, for a vacation in the summer of 1861, Bennett put a clever special writer, Henry Wikoff, on her trail, and the *Herald* published his pryings in a daily column, "Movements of Mrs. Lincoln," which struck obliquely at Lincoln by ridiculing her. To shield herself from pitiless publicity she sometimes traveled incognito as "Mrs. Clark."

"That she should make a success here, under such circumstances, under the focalized bitterness of all possible adverse criticism was simply out of the question," a presidential secretary wrote; "but she has done vastly better than her ill-natured critics are at all willing to admit." An experienced journalist, Ben Perley Poor, thought Mrs. Lincoln may have made mistakes. "Who does not?" he asked. ". . . But I am sure that since the time Mrs. Madison presided at the White House, it has not been graced by a lady so well fitted by nature and by education to dispense its hospitalities as is Mrs. Lincoln. Her hospitality is only equalled by her charity, and her graceful deportment by her goodness of heart." Benjamin B. French, Commissioner of Public Buildings, whose many personal encounters with Mrs. Lincoln could scarcely have prejudiced him in her favor, wrote to his sister-in-law in indignation at the "vile slanders" heaped upon a kindly, well-meaning woman, mostly through political vindictiveness. "I *know* many of them to be false," he declared.

Most serious of Mary Lincoln's idiosyncrasies was a strange quirk about money. Years later, in 1867, her son Robert wrote to his fiancée: "My mother is on one subject not mentally responsible. . . . It is very hard to deal with one who is sane on all subjects but one. You could hardly believe it possible, but my mother protests to me that she is in actual want and nothing I can say or do will convince her to the contrary."

Lincoln had always earned enough to support his family in comfort, and by the time he became President he was worth some $15,000, a sum equivalent to several times as much today. If

Mrs. Lincoln had earlier been obliged to manage thriftily, now, with her husband's presidential salary of $25,000 and allowances for the upkeep of the White House, she had reason to feel financially secure. But fear of destitution never ceased to haunt her; along with this fear, strangely enough, she had a wild desire to spend. Shopping became her greatest pleasure. In keeping with her new position, she lavished money on clothes.

Nicolay described the White House as "a dirty rickety concern." Most of the shabby, antiquated furniture had been there since Madison's time, and Congress in recognition of the sorry state into which the Executive Mansion had fallen had appropriated $20,000 to refurbish it. Never had Mary Lincoln had such a princely sum at her disposal, and she gloried in spending it. Two months after the inauguration she and her cousin Elizabeth Grimsley, of Springfield, visited New York and bought an expensive dinner service embossed with the national arms, beautiful vases and mantelpieces for the Blue and Green rooms, and a seven-hundred-piece set of Bohemian cut glass. Her shopping trips became notorious as merchants sold her costly wares and importers placed orders for her in Europe. Workmen swarmed about the White House.

When the social season opened in December 1861, the place had been transformed. Old furniture had been revarnished or replaced. Chairs and sofas glittered with new satin and velvet upholstery. The East Room had been papered with Parisian velvet cloth; there was a thick, rich Glasgow carpet on the floor. White needle-wrought Swiss lace curtains decorated the long windows. French brocatelle draperies fringed with gold tassels hung from gilt cornices. The Blue Room had a new carpet and bright, fresh wallpaper. The Green Room had been redone. Costly draperies and damasks brightened the family apartment. The state guest room was resplendent with light-purple wallpaper figured with gold rose trees, and a bed canopy of purple silk trimmed with gold lace. Only the President's office escaped the transformation.

But Mrs. Lincoln had overspent the appropriation by $7,000.

Panic-stricken, she rushed to the Commissioner of Public Buildings and implored him to make good the shortage before her husband found out about it, and he took care of the unpaid bills out of an appropriation for sundry civil expenses.

Custom decreed that White House receptions should be open to the public. Headstrong Mary Lincoln caused turmoil in social circles when, in the first winter of the war, she planned a splendid private party. Social climbers scrambled for invitations, but the haughty Washington dowagers stayed at home to sneer. Nicolay reported to his fiancée that the rooms were by no means crowded and that a couple of servants, "much moved by wrath and wine," topped off the festivities with "a jolly little knockdown in the kitchen, damaging in its effects to sundry heads and champagne bottles. This last is strictly *entre nous*."

*

W H I T E H O U S E decorum suffered when the Lincolns moved in. Their eldest son, Robert, was at Harvard, but eight-year-old Tad and eleven-year-old Willie raced and shouted through the corridors, broke into the President's study in the midst of conferences, brazenly asked visitors what they came to see "paw" about, or levied tribute from them for the fairs that were held to raise money for the U.S. Sanitary Commission, forerunner of the Red Cross. Tad and Willie accumulated a small menagerie of pets—kittens, goats, rabbits, ponies, and a little dog named Jip that sat in the President's lap at mealtime, enjoying his caresses and the morsels that he slipped him now and then.

The youngsters rigged the flat roof of the White House like the deck of a ship, and sighted "enemy cruisers" through a battered spyglass. The attic became a theater for their minstrel shows. Discovering where all the bell cords came together near the roof, they sent the servants scurrying by yanking them all at once. Tad ate all the strawberries intended for a state dinner; the steward raged and tore his hair, but his mother merely asked him why he did it.

Tad and Willie had a doll named Jack, dressed in the red trousers and tight blue jacket of a Zouave, who drew a death sentence from them for sleeping on picket duty. They had prepared his grave, beneath a bush, when the gardener suggested that the President might pardon him. And a note came on Executive Mansion stationery: "The doll Jack is pardoned. By order of the President. A. Lincoln."

Mrs. Lincoln had desks and a blackboard placed in one end of the state dining-room, hired a tutor for the boys, and engaged Monsieur Alex Wolowski, a noted Polish pianist, to give them music lessons. Willie was a guileless, lovable boy, who learned quickly; but impudent, effervescent Tad, with his lisp, still had a nurse to dress him and seemed somewhat slow-witted. Tutors became discouraged and quit one after another. But the President, who had described his son Robert as "one of those rare-ripe sort that are smarter at about 5 than ever after," thought Tad would learn soon enough, while Mrs. Lincoln often said: "Let the boys have a good time."

Even the crusty Stanton succumbed to warmhearted Tad. He commissioned him a lieutenant and gave him a uniform. One night Tad mustered the household staff, dismissed the regular guard, and put cooks, doormen, and messengers on sentry duty. The President, who thought it a good joke, waited until the juvenile lieutenant fell asleep and then carried him to bed and went downstairs to dismiss the sheepish guards.

During a White House ball and reception early in 1862, Willie lay sick upstairs. Lincoln stood welcoming the guests, but his mind was on the stricken boy. Earlier in the evening he had stood at Willie's bedside, hands clasped tightly behind him, as he gazed sadly at the fevered figure on the bed. Mrs. Lincoln swept in, garbed in the height of fashion, with a low-cut dress and a long train, and the President masked his anxiety with the remark: "Whew! Our cat has a long tail tonight." His wife looked at him quizzically as he added: "Mother, it is my opinion, if some of that tail was nearer the head it would be in better style." During the evening the father and mother each slipped away several times to Willie's bedside.

Long days passed, long nights, with the anxious President treading often down the dim corridor of the White House in his old dressing-gown and flapping carpet slippers to visit Willie's room. And then at five o'clock one afternoon, when Nicolay lay half asleep on a sofa in his office, he heard the door close softly and Lincoln stood before him. The President's voice choked as he said: "Well, Nicolay, my boy is gone—he is actually gone!" He burst into tears and went into his office.

Senator Browning came in soon afterward and Nicolay told him the news. The Senator went immediately to Mrs. Lincoln, then left to bring Mrs. Browning. Nicolay later went to Lincoln's office, where he found the President lying down with Tad, trying to console the little fellow. Nicolay asked if the President wanted Browning to make arrangements for the funeral. "Yes, consult with Browning," Lincoln said.

Mrs. Lincoln became hysterical. Long vigils had exhausted her; she seemed unable to regain her mental balance. One day Lincoln gently led her to a window, put his arm around her waist, and, pointing to the asylum in the distance, pleaded: "Mother, try and control your grief, or it will drive you mad, and we may have to send you there." Perhaps Lincoln had learned something of his wife's irrational actions—of how, as a measure of economy, she had tried to abolish the position of White House steward and have his wages paid to her; of her high-handed treatment of the President's secretaries, which moved John Hay to call her "the Hell-Cat." He knew how the snubs of Washington society had hurt her, despite the brave front she assumed.

Months after Willie's death a fire broke out one night in the White House stables. A guard saw a tall, hatless man burst from a door of the Executive Mansion, dash across the lawn, and leap a boxwood hedge in a long bound. "Have the horses been taken out?" he shouted. Recognizing the President as he made a rush for the flaming stables, guards seized him and led him back to the White House—the fire might have been an assassin's ruse to lure him out. From an upper window Lincoln watched the flames die down. Tears trickled down his face. Willie's beloved pony lay in the ruins of the stable.

If many letters of sympathy came to the Lincolns after Willie's death, only a few of them remain among the President's papers. One of the tenderest of them read: "I have not felt authorized to intrude upon you personally in the midst of the deep distress I know you feel in the sad calamity that has befallen you and your family. Yet I cannot refrain from expressing to you the sincere and deep sympathy I feel for you.

"You have been a kind true friend to me in the midst of the great cares and difficulties by which we have been surrounded during the past few months. Your confidence has upheld me when I should otherwise have felt weak. I wish now only to assure you and your family that I have felt the deepest sympathy in your affliction. I am pushing to prompt completion the measures of which we have spoken, & I beg that you will not allow military affairs to give you a moments trouble. . . ." It was signed "George B. McClellan."

Lincoln found it difficult to shake off the affliction of Willie's death. From this personal bereavement and the trials of office he came to feel the need of strength beyond his own resources. More and more his official utterances and state papers breathed dependence on a Higher Power, whose existence he may have doubted in his callow years.

CHAPTER XV

McClellan in Command

M cCLELLAN still delayed. In order to force him into action, the President, on January 27, 1862, had issued General War Order Number One, commanding a concerted advance of all the armies on or before February 22. Four days later a Special War Order directed the Army of the Potomac to begin an advance on Richmond by way of Manassas Junction on or before the same date. McClellan, preferring his own plan of attack by way of Urbana or the Yorktown Peninsula, asked if he might file objections. Lincoln agreed that if he could give satisfactory answers to certain questions, he could have his own way. Would McClellan's plan require more time and money than the direct assault that Lincoln favored? How did it promise a more certain and decisive victory? In case of disaster, would withdrawal be more difficult?

McClellan had already drafted a long argument in behalf of his plan. A direct advance would mean a frontal attack on entrenched positions with lengthening supply lines in a region of bad roads and difficult terrain, he said, whereas the movement by way of the Peninsula offered the shortest land route to Richmond. Gunboats in the York and James rivers could protect the army's flanks; in case of defeat, it could fall back on Fortress Monroe; the roads on the Peninsula were passable at all seasons and the topography offered few obstacles. Events were to prove that

McClellan, an engineer officer, argued in utter ignorance of topography and roads.

*

W E L C O M E news came from the West. On February 6 General Ulysses Simpson Grant, commanding under Halleck, forced the Confederates to abandon Fort Henry on the Tennessee River, and a week later, pushing across to the Cumberland, he captured Fort Donelson, with almost fourteen thousand prisoners. The defenders had asked for terms, and Grant, with a determination that seemed so singularly lacking in Northern generals, had replied: "No terms except an unconditional and immediate surrender can be accepted. I propose to move immediately upon your works."

Grant's men were Midwesterners, and Lincoln knew a number of Grant's officers: John A. McClernand, who had practiced law in Springfield; Lew Wallace, from Indiana; popular Richard J. Oglesby; and black-haired John A. Logan, a Douglas Democrat who had enlisted troops in "Egypt." Both sides had fought bravely. The Western troops withstood cold, rain, and sleet and advanced without flinching through defenses of felled trees under a withering fire from earthworks and rifle-pits. Lincoln felt pleased that the boys from his part of the country were throwing in their weight.

The North had a new hero in "Unconditional Surrender" Grant, and Lincoln looked into the record of this stubby, whiskered, unmilitary-looking man, whose uniform, they said, was usually awry, and whose stained teeth were clamped constantly on a cigar. An Ohioan, thirty-nine years old, Grant had worked as a boy in his father's tannery and on his farm, graduated twenty-first in a West Point class of thirty-nine, and performed bravely in the Mexican War. On a lonely Pacific army post he had given way to drink and had resigned to take up farming near St. Louis. He sold wood in the city, built his family a modest house on the farm that he called Hardscrabble, then moved into the city and failed in the real-estate business. Borrowing money from his father, he had moved to Galena, Illinois, where he clerked in his brother's leather store. An offer of his services to the Adjutant General in Washington at the beginning of the war brought no reply, and Governor Yates had appointed him colonel of a raffish regiment of Illinois volunteers, whom he speedily whipped into fighting shape. His fellow townsman Congressman Washburne had got him a brigadier-generalship. Now, as a reward for these first important Union victories, Lincoln promoted him to major general. A quiet, retiring man, Grant never used profanity. He had a way with horses. He seemed to have conquered liquor. Friends said he was a devoted family man, that loneliness for his wife had caused his drinking sprees.

*

GENERAL SAMUEL R. CURTIS, also operating under Halleck, substantially ended the threat to Missouri with a victory at Pea Ridge, Arkansas. An amphibious operation under Commodore Louis M. Goldsborough and General Ambrose E. Burnside took Roanoke Island, on the North Carolina coast. But McClellan, indifferent toward even the token victory that would have stirred the North and eased the pressure on Lincoln, made no gesture against the Confederate batteries on the Potomac, no effort to break the Confederate hold on the Baltimore & Ohio Railroad. When he at last did move to eliminate this latter aggravation, the boats that he sent by way of the Chesapeake and Ohio Canal to take his troops across the Potomac proved to be six inches too wide for the canal locks.

The Committee on the Conduct of the War again called McClellan to account. He gave his usual maddening excuse: the army was not ready, his lines of retreat were not secure. Wade stormed. Stanton agreed with the committee's criticism. Again the Jacobins confronted Lincoln at the White House. Wade threatened a revolt in Congress unless Lincoln dismissed McClellan. Who could be put in McClellan's place, asked Lincoln. "Anybody!" bawled Wade. "Wade, anybody will do for you," said Lincoln quietly, "but I must have somebody."

Still doubtful about the Peninsular route to Richmond,

and concerned for the safety of Washington should the army be withdrawn from its front, Lincoln suggested that he and McClellan submit their plans to a council of generals. The council agreed with McClellan, eight to four—provided the safety of Washington was assured; and to this end they thought a covering force of not less than 25,000 men, in addition to the 30,000 troops garrisoning the forts, would be required. The next day Lincoln put this requirement in the form of an order. Otherwise McClellan was given a free hand. "Move the remainder of your force down the Potomac," instructed Stanton, "choosing a new base at Fortress Monroe, or anywhere between here and there, or, at all events, move such remainder of the army in pursuit of the enemy by some route." The instruction had the tone of a reproof.

As soon as McClellan's army showed activity, the Confederates drew off their batteries on the Potomac and fell back from their supposedly impregnable position at Manassas. McClellan ordered the army to advance and occupy the enemy's entrenchments. Then came a surprise. Many of the cannon frowning from the earthworks were logs, painted black! Senator William P. Fessenden expressed the feeling of the country in a letter to his family: "You will have heard of the wooden guns at Centerville. It is true, and we are smarting under the disgrace which this discovery has brought upon us. We shall be the scorn of the world. It is no longer doubtful that General McClellan is utterly unfit for his position. . . . And yet the President will keep him in command, and leave our destiny in his hands. . . . Well, it cannot be helped. We went for a rail-splitter, and we have got one."

Stanton and the Committee on the Conduct of the War went into a frenzy—McClellan must go! Lincoln could not afford a break with the Jacobins, so he yielded halfway, relieving McClellan as commander in chief on March 11, but leaving him in command of the Army of the Potomac. Knowing of no one fit for supreme command, Lincoln undertook to exercise over-all military control himself, aided by Stanton and veteran General Ethan Allen Hitchcock, who proved to be of little help.

*

O N S U N D A Y morning, March 9, frightening news reached the White House. In Hampton Roads, where the James River empties into Chesapeake Bay, the Confederate warship *Virginia* had steamed out from Norfolk, battered and rammed the Federal ships *Congress* and *Cumberland,* and driven the *Minnesota* aground. The Confederates had a new instrument of war: a seemingly invulnerable ironclad ship. Wooden ships were powerless against her heavy cannon and wicked ram; their shot bounced off her four-inch armor plate. The *Virginia* had formerly been the United States frigate *Merrimac.* Sunk when the Federal garrison abandoned Norfolk, she had been raised and rebuilt by the Confederates.

Lincoln called the cabinet into immediate session. It met in an atmosphere of doom. Even now the *Merrimac* might be on her way to throw shells into Washington and put the government to flight; she might disperse the blockading squadron and lay waste Northern ports; and what might she not do among McClellan's crowded transports if he tried to take his troops to the Peninsula? Seward was despondent, Chase alarmed; Stanton, almost frantic, paced the room like a caged lion, casting baleful glances at Welles as though blaming him for the disaster. Lincoln anxiously read dispatches and asked questions to get a complete picture of events.

Welles offered one hope. On the way to Hampton Roads (actually she had arrived the night before) was a new fighting ship, the *Monitor,* which might be a match for the *Merrimac.* Her low deck lay almost flush with the water, Welles explained, and her fighting equipment consisted of a revolving turret that housed two guns. Stanton looked contemptuous—two guns! The War Secretary rushed off telegrams to Northern governors and mayors, warning of the Confederate juggernaut and suggesting that they block their harbors.

Lincoln, feeling the need of professional advice, ordered his carriage and drove to the navy yard to consult Admiral John Dahlgren, an ordnance expert, and other officers. Dahlgren shared Stanton's fears, and on the Secretary's order, approved by the President, prepared to sink fifty or sixty canal boats filled with rock in the Potomac channel. When Welles heard of this encroachment on his authority, he protested vigorously against the uselessness of closing the river, since it was too shallow anyway for the *Merrimac's* heavy draft. To Stanton's utter disgust, Lincoln, realizing that the matter came within the navy's jurisdiction and that Welles was right, withdrew his approval of the order.

Evening brought news of a historic contest. The *Monitor* and the *Merrimac* had battled for two hours, neither able seriously to damage the other. The more maneuverable *Monitor* evaded the *Merrimac's* ponderous efforts to use her ram. Some of the *Merrimac's* plates buckled under the *Monitor's* pounding. Commander John L. Worden suffered temporary blindness when a shell hit the sight-slot of the *Monitor's* pilothouse. In the end the *Merrimac* furrowed back to Norfolk. Lincoln ordered the *Monitor* not to risk capture or destruction by "skylarking" up to Norfolk; she must stand by to meet the *Merrimac* should the latter venture forth again. The battle had world-wide significance; wooden ships were outmoded. They were powerless against these ironclad monsters.

*

THE RESISTLESS current of the war swept on, and Lincoln found himself insistently confronted with the troublesome slavery problem as military commanders wondered what to do with the Negroes who flocked to Northern army camps. The Confiscation Act of August 6, 1861 gave freedom to slaves used in aid of the rebellion; but what should be done with runaway Negroes of loyal owners in the border states, or with Negroes in rebellious states who escaped or were abandoned by fleeing masters? General Benjamin F. Butler, with thousands of dollars' worth of slave property within his lines at Fortress Monroe, found himself beset by arrogant slaveowners, who, having put themselves outside the Union, demanded the protection of Federal law in recovering their runaway slaves. Butler treated the Negroes as contraband, property rightfully subject to confiscation under the laws of war, and used them as laborers on fortifications.

Lincoln knew the importance of emancipation as a means of cementing the radicals to the administration, of winning liberal opinion in Europe to support the Union cause, and of forestalling European intervention or recognition of the Confederacy. But he had pledged himself not to attack slavery in the states, and Kentucky, Missouri, Maryland, and Delaware had taken him at his word. He must keep faith with them, not only in common honesty, but to sustain their loyalty. Antislavery radicals became enraged as Lincoln faithfully enforced the Fugitive Slave Law, and Washington jails filled up with runaway Negroes waiting to be claimed by masters. To mollify the antislavery faction of his party, Lincoln proposed that the United States recognize the Negro republics of Haiti and Liberia, and Congress took action to that end.

Lincoln foresaw that he could not resist the antislavery pressure much longer. Wishing to deal fairly with the border states, on March 6, 1862 he recommended that Congress pass a joint resolution offering financial aid to any state that would take measures toward gradual, compensated emancipation. He personally drafted two separate bills to effect this object in Delaware. When the border-state Congressmen remained indifferent, he called them to the White House for a long and friendly talk. His proposal set up no claim to Federal authority over slavery in the states, he pointed out; it left the subject under state control. He believed that border-state emancipation would materially shorten the war by dispelling the last hope of the Confederates that their sister slave states might join them in revolt. If the war continued, he warned, it was impossible to foresee what might come out of it; he must use every legal means to save the Union.

Soon afterward Lincoln wrote to Senator James A. McDougall, a California War Democrat, and to Henry J. Raymond of the *New York Times*, asking them to renounce their opposition to his proposal and explaining that $1,000,000, or less than one half-day's cost of the war, would buy all the slaves in Delaware at $400 per head; and that $174,000,000, or less than eighty-seven days' cost of the war, would purchase all the slaves in the border states and the District of Columbia. Would such an expenditure not shorten the war by more than eighty-seven days, he asked.

On March 10, the same day that Lincoln conferred with the border-state Congressmen, his joint resolution approving compensated emancipation came before Congress. Lacking the authority of law, it was merely a declaration of policy. Moderate Republicans and Democrats alike supported it, and even radicals like Sumner and Lovejoy raised no objections; it passed both House and Senate by large majorities. But not one favorable vote came from the border-state Democrats.

In keeping with the spirit of this resolution, Congress passed a bill providing for gradual, compensated emancipation in the District of Columbia, with voluntary colonization of freed Negroes in Haiti and Liberia. Lincoln, affixing his signature on April 16, wrote: "I have never doubted the constitutional authority of Congress to abolish slavery in this District; and I have ever desired to see the national capital freed from the institution in some satisfactory way. Hence there has never been in my mind any question upon the subject except the one of expediency, arising in view of all the circumstances. I am gratified that the two principles of compensation and colonization are both recognized and practically applied in the act."

On May 9 General David Hunter, in command of the Department of the South, proclaimed freedom for all slaves in Georgia, South Carolina, and Florida. With the first news of what Hunter had done, Chase, who had long wanted action against slavery and may even have prompted Hunter, wrote to Lincoln that "it seems to me of the highest importance . . . that this order be not revoked." Hunter was a long-time friend of Lincoln's, but the President immediately replied to Chase: "No commanding general shall do such a thing, upon *my* responsibility, without consulting me." Hunter was ordered to revoke the proclamation at once. Lincoln declared that he must reserve the right to decide himself when, if ever, such action might become necessary to preserve the government.

In revoking Hunter's proclamation, Lincoln appealed once more to the border-state Congressmen to persuade their state legislatures to accept Congress' offer of compensated emancipation. "I do not argue," he declared. "I beseech you to make the arguments for yourselves. You cannot if you would, be blind to the signs of the times. I beg of you a calm and enlarged consideration of them, ranging, it may be, far above personal and partizan politics. This proposal makes common cause for a common object, casting no reproaches upon any. It acts not the pharisee. The change it contemplates would come gently as the dews of heaven, not rending or wrecking anything. Will you not embrace it? So much good has not been done, by one effort, in all past time, as in the providence of God it is now your high privilege to do. May the vast future not have to lament that you have neglected it."

The trend of public opinion became unmistakable as Congress forbade military commanders to return slaves of disloyal owners and abolished slavery in the territories. This latter enactment, a fulfillment of a Republican platform promise, violated the Constitution as interpreted by the Supreme Court in the Dred Scott decision, but Lincoln signed it without hesitation. In May 1862 the United States and Great Britain agreed by treaty to co-operate in suppressing the slave trade.

Lincoln knew he could not much longer stay his hand against slavery. Near the end of the session he entreated the border-state Congressmen for the third time. If they had voted for the gradual emancipation resolution in March, the war would now be substantially ended, he declared with unwarranted optimism. If it continued much longer, slavery would be extinguished "by mere friction and abrasion—by the mere incidents of war." The slavery question continued to divide the North as it had divided the nation. General Hunter had been moved by conscience to issue his proclamation against slavery, Lincoln explained. Many other Northern men felt the same demands of conscience, and the President could not remain indifferent to this antislavery sentiment. The border states had it in their power to relieve the country of this disruptive pressure. "Once relieved, its form of government is saved to the world; its beloved history, and cherished memories are vindicated; and its happy future fully assured, and rendered inconceivably grand. To you, more than to any others, the privilege is given, to assure that happiness, and swell that grandeur, and to link your names therewith forever." But the border states remained unmoved.

*

N E W S came of a near-disaster in the West. After his victories at Fort Henry and Fort Donelson, Grant had moved up the Tennessee River and encamped his army at Pittsburg Landing, near the Mississippi border, with his outposts extending toward Shiloh Church. Thousands of campfires twinkled in the Sunday dawn of April 6 as sleepy soldiers squatted at their breakfasts. Suddenly the frightful rebel yell shattered the Sabbath calm. A furious attack engulfed the Union camp. Grant's Western troops formed quickly. All day the battle raged in separate combats of detached and broken units, over steep ravines, through forest thickets, swampy hollows, and small open fields, as the stubborn Union troops were forced back on the river.

Grant had been at breakfast nine miles upstream. A steamboat brought him to the field. Union gunboats belched canister in support of the hard-pressed troops. Grant fought for time; Buell and Wallace were on the way with reinforcements. They began to come in that afternoon. Massed artillery blasted the Confederate assault. The Confederate commander, Albert Sidney Johnston, fell mortally wounded. Next day Grant's reinforced army drove the Confederates from the field.

Lincoln read the appalling list of casualties: the Federals had lost 13,047 killed, wounded, and missing; the Confederates 10,694! Mute affliction gripped Midwestern homes. Alexander K.

McClure, spokesman for Pennsylvania's Republican Governor, Andrew G. Curtin, came to the White House late one night to suggest that Grant had forfeited the confidence of the country and had better be dismissed. He had not guarded against surprise. He had neglected Halleck's warning to throw up entrenchments when in the presence of the enemy. Rumor said he had been drunk again. Lincoln sat in thought for several minutes. Then came decision. "I can't spare this man," he said. "He *fights.*"

The attacks on Grant became so savage that he thought of quitting the army. In the depths of his despondency, tall, lanky General William Tecumseh Sherman slouched into his tent. The two men, both incessant smokers, chomped on their cigars. Sherman, a native of Ohio, whose father had died when William was nine, had known hardships just as Grant had. Graduating from West Point with a record better than Grant's, but with little service in the Mexican War to his credit, "Cump" Sherman too had resigned from the army to try his hand at business. He became partner in a San Francisco bank that failed; practiced law in Leavenworth, Kansas; then became principal of a military college in Louisiana. Sherman made many friends in the South, but when Louisiana seceded he moved to St. Louis to be president of a street-railway company. Then, with the outbreak of hostilities, he went back into the army. Commanding in Kentucky during the first year of the war, he had been suspected of insanity, and had borne the nastiest criticisms, confident of final vindication. Grant must not quit under fire, he pleaded with his superior; both of them would prove their worth if they stayed on.

Grant listened silently as Sherman squirmed on his camp-stool with the restless energy that always characterized him. Sherman's black felt hat slouched on his head. The multitudinous wrinkles in his face twisted and twitched as his words jerked out in quick sentences. He pulled off his hat, ran his coarse fingers through his short thatch of rusty hair, scratched his scraggly beard, and never stopped talking until Grant agreed to forget the resignation.

The second day of Shiloh saw another Union victory in the

West: as General John Pope, with the aid of gunboats, took
Island Number Ten in the Mississippi. Later that month the
ships of Commodore David G. Farragut and Commodore
David D. Porter struck at the forts and batteries guarding the
entrance to the Mississippi and ran past them in a flashing night
attack to land General Butler's troops at New Orleans. A heavy
pall of smoke burdened the city as the Confederates demolished
thousands of bales of cotton, steamboats, unfinished gunboats,
and other property before abandoning their largest seaport.

*

WHILE McClellan's transports wallowed toward the Peninsula, reports reached Lincoln that Washington lay open to attack.
Investigation revealed that instead of the 30,000 troops to
garrison the defenses and the additional covering force of 25,000
that McClellan's generals had agreed upon as being necessary,
McClellan had left behind only 19,000 untrained troops all
told, and had ordered eight regiments of these away. The general
insisted that the pressure he would put on the Confederates
opposing him would keep them fully occupied—but application of
relentless pressure had not been one of McClellan's distinguishing
traits. The headstrong general had violated a clear order. Lincoln
directed that McDowell's corps of 35,000 men at Fredericksburg
be withheld from McClellan to cover Washington.

As McClellan advanced cautiously up the Peninsula, the
small Confederate force withdrew to the fortifications at Yorktown and threw up a defensive line along the Warwick River, a
sluggish, boggy stream fringed with dense woods, which, heading
within a mile of Yorktown, flows across the Peninsula to the
James. They were prepared to retreat at the first sign of a
determined attack, but McClellan, overestimating their numbers
as well as the strength of their position, decided upon a siege.
"Do not misunderstand the apparent inaction here," he wrote to
Lincoln. "Not a day, not an hour, has been lost. Works have
been constructed that may almost be called gigantic." While
McClellan dawdled, the Confederates rushed up reinforcements.

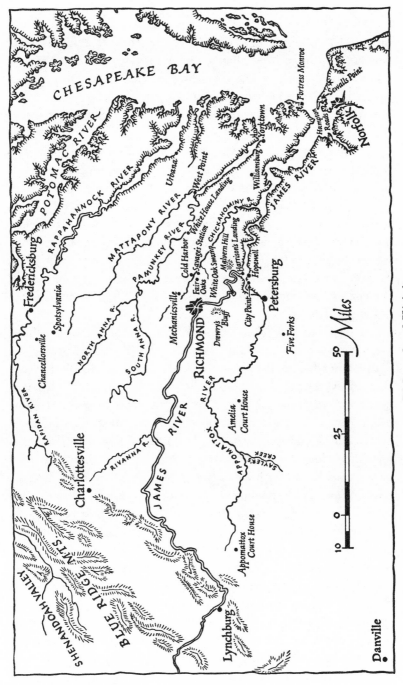

CHESAPEAKE BAY

POTOMAC RIVER

RAPPAHANNOCK RIVER

MATTAPONY RIVER

PAMUNKEY RIVER

NORTH ANNA R.

SOUTH ANNA R.

RAPIDAN RIVER

RIVANNA R.

JAMES RIVER

APPOMATTOX RIVER

SAYLER'S CREEK

JAMES RIVER

CHICKAHOMINY R.

Fredericksburg

Spotsylvania

Chancellorsville

Charlottesville

BLUE RIDGE MTS.

SHENANDOAH VALLEY

Lynchburg

Appomattox
Court House

Amelia
Court House

RICHMOND

Mechanicsville

Drewry's
Bluff

White Oak Swamp

Fair
Oaks

Savage's Station

Cold Harbor

White House Landing

Urbana

West Point

Malvern Hill

Harrison's Landing

City Point

Hopewell

Petersburg

Five Forks

Williamsburg

Yorktown

Hampton
Roads

Fortress Monroe

Sewall's Point

NORFOLK

JAMES RIVER

Danville

Miles

10   0   25   50

Richmond and Vicinity

Joseph E. Johnston arrived to take command. Still his force was far inferior to McClellan's, and John Hay wrote to Nicolay: "The little Napoleon sits trembling before the handful of men at Yorktown, afraid either to fight or run. Stanton feels devilish about it. He would like to remove him if he thought it would do."

McClellan seized on the retention of McDowell's corps as further reason for caution. "I am now of the opinion that I shall have to fight all of the available force of the rebels not far from here," he telegraphed the President. "Do not force me to do so with diminished numbers." Lincoln wired back that McClellan had better break the enemy's Warwick River line at once: "They will probably use time as advantageously as you can." McClellan reconnoitered from a balloon and pushed small forces out to feel the enemy. He complained to Lincoln that the government was not supporting him.

In reply to McClellan's repeated complaints and accusations, Lincoln asked if he really thought the President would be justified in allowing the direct line from Richmond to Washington through Manassas Junction to lie open to attack? "This is a question," declared Lincoln, "which the country will not allow me to evade." And there was a curious mystery about the number of McClellan's troops. The general's own returns of a few days before showed 108,000 with him or en route to him. Now he declared he would have only 85,000 when all en route had arrived. What had happened to the remaining 23,000? "And, once more," concluded Lincoln, "let me tell you, it is indispensable to *you* that you strike a blow. *I* am powerless to help this. You will do me the justice to remember I always insisted, that going down the Bay in search of a field, instead of fighting at or near Manassas, was only shifting, and not surmounting, a difficulty—that we would find the same enemy, and the same, or equal intrenchments, at either place. The country will not fail to note—is now noting—that the present hesitation to move upon an entrenched enemy is but the story of Manassas repeated."

Rains came. The supposedly all-weather roads of the Peninsula churned into sticky bogs. McClellan asked for a certain type of heavy gun from Washington, and Lincoln replied: "Your call for Parrott guns from Washington alarms me—chiefly because it argues indefinite procrastination. Is anything to be done?" On May 4, with McClellan at last ready to bring Yorktown under bombardment, it was discovered that the Confederates had evacuated the place the night before. "I shall push the enemy to the wall," McClellan boldly wired Stanton, who hopefully took him at his word and replied: "I hope soon to hail your arrival in Richmond." Johnston checked McClellan's pursuit at Williamsburg and then withdrew again.

That night, May 6, Lincoln, Stanton, and Chase arrived at Fortress Monroe. The President and the Secretaries conferred with Commander Goldsborough of the naval forces and quizzed high-ranking officers. They visited camps and near-by points of interest.

McClellan had done nothing to remove the menace of the *Merrimac*, still lurking at Norfolk across the bay. Lincoln slammed his hat on the floor. On May 8 he ordered gunboats to attack the Confederate batteries at Sewall's Point, while others demonstrated up the James. Transports pushed across behind the gunboats to land troops for an attack on Norfolk if such a move proved feasible. The *Merrimac* came out during the bombardment. The wooden ships drew off, but the *Monitor* held her position. The Confederate leviathan turned back.

A landing at Sewall's Point seemed hazardous, and Chase, aboard a revenue cutter, reconnoitered another prospective spot. Returning to Fortress Monroe, he found Lincoln talking to a pilot and studying a chart. Convinced that he had found a suitable landing-place, Lincoln boarded a tug with Stanton to investigate it. Chase followed in the revenue cutter. Lincoln went ashore and walked along the beach, but the spot that Chase had found seemed better. Two days later, troops landed there and marched on Norfolk, which surrendered, with 6,000 men. A dull boom shook the city as the defenders blew up the *Merrimac*. Union gunboats, relieved of this peril, steamed up the James River as far as the fortifications at Drewry's Bluff. "So has ended a brilliant week's campaign of the President," recorded Chase; "for I think it quite certain that if we had not come down, Norfolk would still have been in possession of the enemy, and the *Merrimac* as grim and defiant and as much a terror as ever. The whole coast is now virtually ours."

McClellan continued his slow advance to within five miles of Richmond. But he was astride the Chickahominy River, a languid stream flowing through a broad, marshy flood plain and liable to swift rise in case of rain. Forced to keep a large part of his force north of the river in order to protect his base at White House Landing on the Pamunkey, a tributary of the York, McClellan busied himself building bridges.

In response to McClellan's urgent calls for troops, Franklin's division of McDowell's corps was sent from Fredericksburg to join him, while the troops of James Shields, Lincoln's old dueling antagonist, were ordered back from General Nathaniel P. Banks's command in the Shenandoah Valley to replace Franklin's division. On May 17 Stanton ordered McDowell to advance on Richmond from the north as soon as Shields should arrive, and to link up with McClellan's right wing. Visiting McDowell on the 24th, Lincoln reported to McClellan that Shields's troops had come, but needed rest. If McClellan could strike behind the Confederate force opposing McDowell, he would not only hasten McDowell's advance, but perhaps cut off part of the enemy's force and save some of the railroad bridges they would otherwise destroy in their retreat. "Can you not do this almost as well as not," asked Lincoln, "while you are building the Chickahomany [*sic*] bridges?"

The general situation looked good, reported Lincoln, except that at Front Royal a surprise attack and defeat of the small Union garrison had put General Banks's 6,000 men at Strasburg in some peril. This was a harbinger of trouble, for, as Lincoln would soon discover, rawboned, black-bearded General Thomas Jonathan "Stonewall" Jackson, his well-thumbed Bible in his mess kit, was on a foray down the Shenandoah Valley.

*

H A U N T I N G the War Department telegraph office as messages ticked in from the Valley, Lincoln tried to find out what was happening. How large was Jackson's force? Where was he now? Had he been reinforced from Richmond? Was his movement merely a diversion, or was he headed for Washington by way of Harpers Ferry? What Union forces were available to oppose him?

The self-willed Frémont had been placed in command in West Virginia; Banks, a Massachusetts politician of unproved military competence, was at or near Strasburg in the Valley; McDowell's corps was still on the Rappahannock at Fredericksburg. Should these forces be thrown against Jackson; and, if so, how and where? Jackson had struck first at units of Frémont's command at McDowell, West Virginia; disappearing, he turned up at Front Royal, which had been weakened when Shields joined McDowell. This movement threatened Banks's rear and forced him to move hastily down the Valley to save his army. Jackson raced him to Winchester, where Banks almost suffered disaster before freeing his command from Jackson's trap. Banks retreated toward Harpers Ferry with Jackson close behind.

May 24 became a day of vital decision for Lincoln, now exercising supreme command in person. Should he send McDowell to the Valley, or push him against Richmond on the chance that Johnston had weakened his force in order to reinforce Jackson? If McClellan could have been counted on to make the most of his chance, Lincoln might have sent McDowell to join him. Instead he decided to try to cut off Jackson. "In consequence of Gen. Banks' critical position I have been compelled to suspend Gen. McDowell's movement to join you," Lincoln wired McClellan. "The enemy are making a desperate push upon Harpers Ferry, and we are trying to throw Fremont's force & part of General McDowell's in their rear."

Lincoln ordered Frémont to move with all speed to Harrisonburg. To McDowell went a telegram to rush 20,000 men to the Valley to capture Jackson in co-operation with Frémont, or, "in case want of supplies or of transportation interferes with his

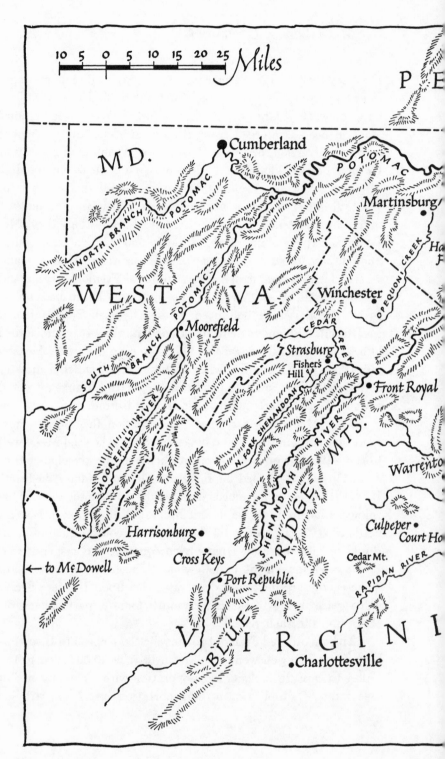

Washington

and Vicinity

movement, it is believed that the force with which you move will be sufficient to accomplish the object alone." McDowell immediately put Shields in motion for the Valley.

Washington cowered under possible attack, and Lincoln has been described as panic-stricken. Actually he worked with dogged resolution to bring victory out of the turmoil. He took all the railroads under government control and rushed troops and armament to Harpers Ferry. If Frémont could get in Jackson's rear, and Shields could close his eastern escape routes from the Valley, while Banks turned on him with the aid of reinforcements from Harpers Ferry, Jackson might be destroyed.

On May 27 Lincoln discovered that Frémont was at Moorefield, far north of Harrisonburg, where he had been ordered to go. Shields's troops were approaching Front Royal, and Jackson had turned back up the Valley to escape the Union pincers. Lincoln ordered Frémont to get to Strasburg in all haste, while Shields closed in at Front Royal. It was "a matter of legs," Lincoln implored. "Put on all the speed you can." But Frémont arrived at Strasburg just as Jackson's footsore rear guard hurried through.

On June 8 and 9 the elusive Jackson defeated Frémont and Shields successively at Cross Keys and Port Republic, then slipped away. Lincoln saw the futility of further effort, and ordered Shields's detachments back to Fredericksburg.

Although a faulty disposition of Union forces in the Valley made Jackson's operation possible, Lincoln countered him skillfully. If Frémont had gone to Harrisonburg as ordered, he would have blocked Jackson's retreat; but lack of food forced him to go to Moorefield in order to meet a supply train. Shields performed his assignments well. The rejuvenated Banks failed to press Jackson's rear as vigorously as he might have, and torrential rains delayed troop movements. Nor should Jackson's genius for swift, confusing strokes be underestimated. In a month's campaign he had marched 245 miles, won five battles, always with superior numbers against dispersed Union forces, and kept important reinforcements from McClellan. Now he suddenly turned up on the Peninsula.

*

THE SAME rainstorms that impeded Union troop movements in the Shenandoah Valley swept away most of McClellan's bridges. On May 31, in the Battle of Fair Oaks or Seven Pines, Johnston suddenly smashed at that part of McClellan's force south of the Chickahominy. The Federals held on desperately. Some of McClellan's own generals thought he would use the opportunity to counterattack north of the river, where the enemy was weak, and perhaps sweep into Richmond; but he failed to do so. A few days later McClellan learned that Johnston had been wounded, and that grave, courtly Robert E. Lee now commanded the Army of Northern Virginia. "I prefer Lee to Johnston," McClellan informed Lincoln, "—the former is *too* cautious & weak under grave responsibility—personally brave & energetic to a fault, he yet is wanting in moral firmness when pressed by heavy responsibility & is likely to be timid and irresolute in action." McClellan's appraisal would prove to be a classic in misjudgment.

With the Valley campaign ended, Lincoln and Stanton rushed McCall's division of McDowell's corps, ten regiments from Fortress Monroe, and a number of new units to McClellan. "I am glad that you are pressing forward reinforcements so vigorously," McClellan replied when Stanton asked if he could now push on to Richmond. "I shall be in perfect readiness to move forward and take Richmond the moment McCall reaches here and the ground will admit the passage of artillery." Already McClellan had another reason for delay: steady rains had again made those "all-weather" roads impassable. Noting that the Confederates had attacked regardless of bad weather, Lincoln observed that McClellan, in defiance of Scripture, seemed to think that Heaven sent its rain only on the just and not the unjust.

With McClellan almost ready to attack, Lee beat him to the punch with a drive north of the Chickahominy, aimed at the Federal base at White House Landing. A seven days' battle developed. McClellan beat off the first attack at Mechanicsville. At Gaines' Mill, on the second day, Lee won a costly victory that shook McClellan's nerves. "Have had a terrible contest," he wired Stanton. "Attacked by greatly superior numbers in all directions on this side, we still hold our own, though a very heavy fire is still kept up on the left back of the Chickahominy. The odds have been immense. . . . Had I 20,000 fresh and good troops we would be sure of a splendid victory tomorrow. My troops have fought magnificently." Although at the point of attack on the north side of the river McClellan had been out-numbered two to one, on the south side his force exceeded Lee's by three to one. But McClellan never brought these 60,000 troops into the action.

Some time that evening McClellan decided to concentrate his army south of the Chickahominy, changing his base from White House Landing to Harrison's Landing on the James. Shortly after midnight an operator handed E. S. Sanford, super-visor of military telegrams in Washington, a message from McClellan to Stanton. "I feel too earnestly tonight," it read; "I have seen too many dead and wounded comrades to feel otherwise than that the Government has not sustained this army. If you do not do so now the game is lost. If I save this army now, I tell you plainly that I owe no thanks to you or to any other person in Washington. You have done your best to sacrifice this army." Sanford read the hysterical words with shock. This was rank insubordination. He ordered the last two sentences deleted from the copy he gave to Stanton.

The change of base was a hazardous maneuver, involving the movement of enormous trains and heavy cannon over treacherous ground. The army moved by night and fought by day while Lee attacked relentlessly. Huge stores of supplies were given over to the flames as the army abandoned its base at White

House Landing. Communication with Washington was severed. McClellan fought sharp rear-guard engagements at White Oak Swamp and Sawyer's Station. A hot fight took place at Frayser's Farm. Massed Union artillery devastated the Confederates at Malvern Hill. Then, well based at Harrison's Landing, under the protection of gunboats, the Union army nursed its wounds.

The country learned of the hard fighting, the dreadful casualties, of the army thrown back from Richmond despite its courageous resistance. McClellan's failure brought new outcries from the radicals. Governor Israel Washburn of Maine warned that unless the war brought better results the people would turn out the Republican Party. Senator Fessenden called McClellan a moral and physical coward; Seward's meddling and Lincoln's weakness were bringing ruin upon the country. Senator Browning came into the White House library late one night. Lincoln sat writing at a desk. He had a weary, careworn look. Browning expressed concern about the President's health; he was under fearful pressure and needed rest. "Browning," Lincoln replied as though it scarcely mattered, "I must die sometime."

Lincoln feared to ask the country for more troops; people might fly into panic, thinking the situation more desperate than it was. So he delegated Seward to communicate confidentially with Northern governors. "I expect to maintain this contest until successful," Lincoln assured them, "or till I die, or am conquered, or my term expires, or Congress or the country forsake me." Seward conferred with some governors in person and communicated with the rest by wire. Assured that favorable responses would be forthcoming, Lincoln—ostensibly at the governors' suggestion—asked for 300,000 volunteers.

On July 1 McClellan wired that he would need 50,000 more men, "and with them I will retrieve our fortunes." Lincoln replied with gentle patience to a general who, whatever his faults, had been through hard battles under heavy strain, that he had no troops to send. He might have brought them from the West, but he was unwilling to sacrifice gains elsewhere to bring more troops to the Peninsula. "I am satisfied that yourself, officers, and men have done the best you could," he wired McClellan. "All accounts say better fighting was never done. Ten thousand thanks for it."

Under terrific pressure to change commanders, the President visited Harrison's Landing to appraise McClellan's situation for himself. He and Stanton reviewed the troops. They seemed in excellent spirits. One soldier wrote: "I have seldom witnessed a more ludicrous sight than our worthy Chief Magistrate presented on horseback yesterday. . . . McClellan was beside him, stout, short, and stiffly erect, sitting his horse like a dragoon, and the contrast was perfect. It did seem as though every moment the President's legs would become entangled with those of the horse he rode and both come down together, while his arms were apparently subject to similar mishaps. . . . That arm with which he drew the rein, in its angles and position resembled the hind leg of a grasshopper—the hand before—the elbow away back over the horse's tail. The removal of his hat before each regiment was also a source of laughter in the style of its execution—the quick trot of the horse making it a feat of some difficulty, while from the same cause, his hold on it, while off, seemed very precarious.

"But the boys liked him, in fact his popularity with the army is and has been universal. Most of our rulers and leaders fall into odium, but all have faith in Lincoln. 'When he finds out,' they say, 'it will be stopped.' . . . His benign smile as he passed us by was a real reflection of his honest, kindly heart, but deeper, under the surface of that marked and not all uncomely face were the signs of care and anxiety. God bless the man and give answer to the prayers for guidance I am sure he offers."

Lincoln quizzed McClellan and his corps commanders in the manner of a cross-examining lawyer, inquiring about the location of the enemy, the size of the Federal force, the health of the troops in their malarial encampments. And he also asked: "If it were desired to get the army away from here, could it be safely effected?"

As Lincoln boarded a steamboat for Washington, McClellan

handed him a long letter explaining his ideas on general policy. However much surprised Lincoln may have been at this unsolicited advice, he merely thanked the general and pocketed the letter. When he opened it, he must have wondered how McClellan, burdened with military duties, could devote so much thought to politics. The general prided himself on waging a gentlemanly war, and in this so-called Harrison's Bar letter he commended this manner of warfare to the President. The idea of subjugation should be dismissed; the rights of private property, including property in slaves, should be scrupulously respected. To turn the war against slavery would mean the disintegration of the Union army.

Lincoln felt baffled about McClellan. General John Pope had been made commander of the troops in and around Washington and in the Shenandoah Valley by regrouping them into the Army of Virginia, and Lincoln debated whether to give McClellan another chance against Richmond or to transfer his troops to Pope.

Feeling the need of professional military advice, the President slipped away to West Point for a conference with General Scott. On July 11 he appointed General Halleck to command all the land forces of the United States and ordered him to report to Washington. He arrived on the 23rd, and Lincoln noted his stooped posture, flabby cheeks, ample paunch, and large head with heavy features and bulging eyes. Halleck smoked cigars incessantly and scratched his elbows while he thought. Well versed in technical and theoretical matters, the author and translator of military manuals, "Old Brains," as his soldiers called him, was more at home in the study than in the camp. The campaigns under his direction in the West, after victories by subordinates, faltered when he took the field himself. But he seemed well qualified for top command behind the lines.

Halleck immediately visited McClellan's army. McClellan was eager to advance, if reinforced. But Halleck's trained eyes could hardly fail to see the same things that the surgeon of the Eighth New Hampshire Infantry was writing home about—

"the barefooted boys, the sallow men, the threadbare officers
and seedy generals, the diarrhea and dysentery, the yellow eyes
and malarious faces, the beds upon the bare earth in the mud, the
mist and the rain." A few days after his visit, Halleck ordered
McClellan to begin the embarkation of his sick and wounded,
then to move his whole force to Aquia Creek, south of Bull Run
and close to Washington.

McClellan protested that this would be disastrous. "Here is
the true defense of Washington," he pleaded. "It is here on the
banks of the James River that the fate of the Union should be
decided." On August 7 Halleck telegraphed: "I must beg of you,
general, to hurry along this movement. Your reputation as well
as mine may be involved in its rapid execution." Pope would be
in grave danger until McClellan's forces reached him. Already
Jackson had lashed Pope viciously at Cedar Mountain. McClellan's army was needed elsewhere. The Peninsular campaign
must be called off.

*

IN FAIRNESS to McClellan it must be admitted that he met
the Confederacy at its high tide, before the prime of its manhood and its store of brilliant field officers had suffered the
wastage of war. His defeats were never disasters, and always
left the enemy badly hurt. His choice of the Peninsular route to
Richmond had much to recommend it.

McClellan maintained, as do his defenders, that most of his
difficulties originated in interference from Washington. He was
obliged, for example, to keep his right wing exposed north of the
Chickahominy to make contact with McDowell, who never did
link up with him; and this put him in a situation of which Lee
took full advantage. There is merit in this complaint. But
Lincoln's interference came almost without exception from
political considerations that McClellan failed to comprehend.
Lincoln knew he must hold Washington, for it was a symbol of
Federal authority both to the North and to Europe. A more
determined fighter, one more relentless in attack, might have

defended it on the Peninsula, but on McClellan's record Lincoln could not trust him. Similarly, the President's demand for action resulted from political necessities to which the general was blithely indifferent.

McClellan had no zest for battle; he lacked a fighting heart. Lincoln, as head of the government, must share the blame with Stanton for the inexcusable blunder of closing the recruiting offices early in April, about the time the Confederacy began conscripting men, so that when the crisis came, Lincoln had no more troops to send to McClellan, whereas the Confederates, far outnumbered in the beginning, steadily built up their fighting force. But McClellan was never outnumbered. When Lee attacked, the Confederate force was still inferior. And when McClellan asked for 100,000 new troops to renew his campaign against Richmond, Lincoln observed that if he got them he would immediately complain that the enemy had 400,000 men. Sending troops to McClellan, said the President, was like shoveling fleas across a barnyard—so few of them seemed to get there.

While Lincoln's experiences with McClellan were sorely exasperating, they taught him invaluable lessons for the future conduct of the war. It did not take him long to realize the absurdity of McClellan's notion of "gentlemanly war," or the ineffectiveness of a war of mere maneuver. Lincoln knew that he could not fight on the defensive, as President Davis could, and as McClellan preferred to do; he must wage a war of conquest, no matter how unpleasant such a task might be to him. For victory over such a powerful and determined enemy as the South could be achieved only by destroying her army, wasting her economic resources, and crushing her will to win.

McClellan's almost total neglect of operations in the West convinced Lincoln that no general, however competent, could supervise the vast field of operations from the Atlantic to beyond the Mississippi and at the same time personally command one of the armies. A conflict of such magnitude called for co-ordinated planning at the center to weld the nation's armed forces, its politics, economy, and the psychology of its people into an irresistible instrument of war. This must be the President's role.

Lincoln also recognized, when he brought Halleck to Washington, that lack of time and professional training forbade his exercising personally those functions of commander in chief which the Constitution granted him, and that he must have as his right arm a general with a solid background of military learning and experience. Halleck's performance would prove disappointing because he failed to understand the true nature of his job and was unwilling to assume responsibility. Chase appraised Halleck with a fair degree of accuracy as a man "with an immense brain, clear, powerful intellect, full knowledge of his work, but cold as a stone, caring not one penny for the work only as a professional performance; no more heart in it than a shoemaker who pegs away at his last."

Out of Halleck's inadequacies, and those of other generals, Lincoln would learn that what he needed was a man with the killer instinct, who thought not in terms of winning battles but of destroying the enemy, and who, when necessary, would throw away the military textbooks and resort to daring tactics just as Lee did. He must also be a man without political ambition or designs, who recognized that the true function of an army in a democracy is to carry out the policies of the civil government.

Lincoln's chief military problem would be to find a general of this caliber. By the end of the Peninsular campaign, however, it had been borne in upon him that too many men of supposed military competence actually knew so little about their business that his own judgment was as good as theirs or better; so that while he did not minimize his own shortcomings in military affairs, still, in matters where he was better posted to see and appreciate all sides, neither did he hesitate to interpose. Until time and trial brought forth the man he needed, the very force of circumstances obliged him to plan grand strategy himself. And his plans were invariably sound—failure came from faulty execution by his generals. In averting disaster until he found a general he could trust, Lincoln became a master of the art of war.

*

L I N C O L N had reached a solemn decision, unknown to anyone outside the cabinet. He had shaped his policies to command the united support of Republicans, war Democrats, and loyal border-state slave owners. But he could resist the antislavery Republicans no longer and still command the support he must have to win the war. They represented the largest group numerically, and the trend of public opinion favored them. Lincoln had waited as long as possible for the border states to take measures toward compensated emancipation. He must take into account the opinion of European liberal groups.

Notwithstanding Lincoln's personal dislike of slavery, he was constrained by his campaign pledges, by his oath to uphold the Constitution, and even by his own inclinations from molesting it in the states. But his oath also pledged him to preserve the Constitution, the government, and the nation with every means at his command. He must not imperil the nation through blind loyalty to governmental forms. "By general law," he reasoned, "life *and* limb must be protected; yet often a limb must be amputated to save a life; but a life is never wisely given to save a limb." He believed that measures otherwise unconstitutional might become lawful when the nation was imperiled. He could not feel that he had tried to preserve the Constitution to the best of his ability if, to save slavery, he should permit the nation to go down.

In the delicate balance of events, Lincoln doubted if the Union could survive without some drastic measure. His armies had failed. But the abolition of slavery would paralyze the economic system of the enemy. Such action would be justified as a war measure. He must not lose the game with any card unplayed. He would not act from malice—what he dealt with was too vast for malicious dealing—and he would respect the rights of the loyal border states. His sole purpose was to weaken the enemy.

At a cabinet meeting on July 22, Lincoln read a document he had prepared—a proclamation freeing all slaves in the rebellious states. He did not wish advice on the main point, he said;

he had made up his mind on that. But he would gladly hear suggestions as to details. Except for Seward and Welles, to whom Lincoln had confided his intentions, the cabinet members sat in blank astonishment. Then various suggestions were put forward.

Seward, ever conservative, had been turning over the matter in his mind. He did not oppose the policy, he said, but he thought the time unpropitious because of the unfavorable military situation. With the public mind oppressed by defeat, such an announcement would seem like an admission of exhaustion—an act of desperation—a cry for help—"the last *shriek* on our retreat . . . the government stretching forth its hands to Ethiopia, instead of Ethiopia stretching forth her hands to the government." Everyone realized the force of Seward's argument. Lincoln put the document in his pocket. From time to time he would amend it verbally. It would be ready when the right time came.

CHAPTER XVI

"The Occasion is Piled High with Difficulty"

LINCOLN endured anxious days as McClellan's troops withdrew from the Peninsula, for Lee, anticipating the Union movement, hurried on interior lines to strike Pope with superior numbers before the Union armies joined. But Pope, maneuvering skillfully along the north bank of the Rappahannock, foiled Lee's repeated efforts to force a crossing.

Lincoln knew both John Pope and his father personally. The young officer, West Point '42, an experienced engineer, promoted on the field for valor in Mexico, had been detailed to accompany the President-elect on his journey to Washington; and Judge Nathaniel Pope, presiding over the United States District Court for Illinois, had tried many of Lincoln's cases.

When Pope's operations under Halleck opened the Mississippi River south to Memphis, and influential Illinois politicians urged Lincoln to reward him with high rank, the badgered President had reminded them in characteristic phrase that major-generalships in the regular army "are not as plenty as blackberries." Lincoln seems to have had misgivings about John Pope, but now the handsome, sharp-bearded general was to have his chance, and Lincoln hoped he might prove worthy of it.

Pope had the aggressiveness that McClellan lacked, but showed the same vainglory. One of his first acts on taking command of the Army of Virginia was to issue a proclamation contrasting the achievements and fighting qualities of the Eastern and Western armies, and boasting that thenceforth attack and not defense would be the order of the day. His headquarters would be in the saddle, he declared. Contemptuous of McClellan's policy of gentlemanly war, he ordered stern measures against the civil population of Virginia. Pope's proclamation had been intended to infuse new spirit in the army. Instead it brought sly jeers from the ranks, antagonized officers who were loyal to McClellan, and caused Lincoln grave concern; too often military bombast had foretold defeat.

Balked at the Rappahannock, but eager to attack before McClellan's troops joined Pope in force, Lee determined on a daring movement. Dividing his army, he sent Jackson on a wide swing around Pope's right flank. In a maneuver similar to a modern airborne operation, but accomplished with foot soldiers, Jackson struck with his usual suddenness, severing Pope's communications and capturing his supply depot at Manassas Junction. Ragged Confederate soldiers feasted on lobster salad and Rhine wine from the Union commissary, and stuffed their empty haversacks, before setting fire to enormous stores of food, ammunition, and equipment. Confusion swept the Union army.

Lincoln slept scarcely at all night after night as he tried to locate divisions and follow the fast-moving tide of battle. "Any news from Gen. Pope?" he wired to General Ambrose E. Burnside at Newport News. "What news from direction of Manassas Junction? What generally?" he telegraphed McClellan, who had moved his headquarters to Alexandria. "Is the railroad bridge over Bull Run destroyed?" the perplexed President inquired of General Herman Haupt, his chief of railway transportation. Halleck ordered McClellan to rush his veteran regiments to the battle area as rapidly as they arrived from the Peninsula. All furloughs in Pope's army were revoked.

Having wreaked havoc behind the Union lines, Jackson retreated northwestward, fighting off pursuers to give Lee time to join him. On August 29 Pope launched costly attacks against a railroad embankment sheltering Jackson's troops. Instead of attacking he should have been seeking a position for defense, for while he hammered futilely at Jackson, Confederate General James Longstreet circled west of the Bull Run Mountains, forced the virtually undefended Thoroughfare Gap, and massed on Pope's left flank.

All through the ensuing desperate two-day battle near the old field of Bull Run, while Pope groped blindly for the enemy and failed to bring his full force into the fight, McClellan dallied in sending forward reinforcements. As Pope's situation became desperate, McClellan advised Lincoln either to concentrate all available forces to open communication with Pope, or to leave that general "to get out of his scrape" as best he could and provide for the safety of the capital. No middle ground would do, McClellan said; Lincoln should define McClellan's authority and instruct him what to do.

During the Peninsular campaign McClellan had shown small concern for Washington; now its safety seemed of first importance to him. For days Lincoln and Halleck had begged him to hasten troops to Pope; now he asked the President what to do. Stanton denounced McClellan's treachery. Lincoln thought Pope could still be saved, but he would leave the decision to Halleck, "aided by your counsels," he told McClellan.

Late on August 31, with the fighting virtually over and with demoralized Union troops straggling into Washington, Halleck, weary and petulant, sought McClellan's advice. McClellan replied promptly that Pope seemed utterly beaten; the whole army should be withdrawn to the fortifications surrounding Washington. The next night brought a report from Pope complaining of the unsoldierly conduct of many of the units that had served under McClellan, of ill-feeling on the part of high-ranking officers, and of their lack of co-operation. In view of the poor spirit of the army, Pope, too, advised withdrawal.

Three thousand convalescent soldiers were moved from Washington to Philadelphia to make room for new casualties. Hospital cots lined rooms in the Capitol and the Patent Office.

The War Department wired for surgeons, lint, bandages. Street signs appealed for male nurses. Stragglers and ragged Negro fugitives from Virginia crowded Washington's streets. An ominous silence hung over the city, broken by the clatter of ambulances and the mournful hoot of river steamers bringing back the wounded. Once again, as after First Bull Run, Lincoln saw a Union army badly beaten, a general's reputation shattered, Washington menaced by the enemy.

The President could not blame Pope too much. If he had shown poor generalship, even more deplorable were McClellan's smug complacency and the insubordination of some of his high-ranking friends, one of whom, General S. D. Sturgis, had been heard to remark at the height of the battle: "I don't give a pinch of owl dung for John Pope." Justly or unjustly, Pope would have to go; Lincoln's first concern must be the morale of the army. But to whom could the President turn?

On September 1, two days after Pope's defeat, Lincoln and Halleck dropped in on McClellan at breakfast. Appealing to the general to persuade his friends to place the welfare of the nation above army jealousies, Lincoln appointed McClellan to command the defenses of Washington and take charge of Pope's demoralized troops as they returned.

Welles reported the greatest consternation he had ever witnessed when the President told the cabinet what he had done. Only Blair backed up his chief's decision. Lincoln himself showed great distress, but he risked the disfavor of his cabinet and rose above personal feeling to take the safest course in an emergency. To John Hay he confided that McClellan had acted despicably toward Pope—"he really wanted him to fail"—but no one else could restore the morale of the army. The political situation must also be considered; with the Democrats threatening to withdraw their support of the war, McClellan's reappointment might quiet unrest on the home front. Stanton refused to accept responsibility for what might happen with McClellan again in command. Chase, foreseeing calamity, agreed that Lincoln had no other choice. "It is indeed humiliating," he recorded, "but prompted, I believe, by a sincere desire to serve the country, and a fear that should he supersede McClellan by any other commander, no advantage would be gained in leadership, but much harm in the disaffection of officers and troops."

*

L E E, reluctant to assault the formidable defenses of Washington, moved his army into Maryland. The crops lay ripe for harvest; his footsore troops might find new shoes in small-town stores; and the coming of his army might encourage the people of slaveholding Maryland to throw off the "foreign yoke." Across the wide Atlantic, British Prime Minister Palmerston and Foreign Secretary Russell kept close watch on the military situation in America. Lincoln correctly suspected that in the event of a Southern victory they were prepared to intervene for peace on the basis of Confederate independence.

As Lee moved northward, the Army of the Potomac hovered on his flank, safeguarding Washington. McClellan sent a portion of his provost guard to protect the White House. The Army of Virginia passed out of existence as all units became part of the Army of the Potomac. Lincoln noted gratefully that McClellan was "working like a beaver," freshening the spirit of the troops, issuing new equipment, putting detachments on the march. A hard, seasoned, loose-swinging army moved north out of Washington as McClellan performed a marvel of reorganization.

While McClellan followed Lee closely and tried to fathom his intentions, Lincoln inquired repeatedly by telegraph: "How does it look now?" "How about Harper's Ferry?" "Please do not let him get off without being hurt." One of his telegrams bore the stamp of four a.m.

The lonely man in the White House had time for meditation while he waited for news night after night. With his strong sense of fatalism, he felt a Power beyond himself shaping the nation's destiny, and in an hour of anxiety he solemnly penned his thoughts. "The will of God prevails," he wrote. "In great contests each party claims to act in accordance with the will of

God. Both *may* be, and one *must* be wrong. God can not be *for*, and *against*, the same thing at the same time. In the present civil war it is quite possible that God's purpose is something different from the purpose of either party—and yet the human instrumentalities, working just as they do, are of the best adaptation to effect His purpose. I am almost ready to say this is probably true—that God wills this contest, and wills that it shall not end yet. By his mere quiet power on the minds of the now contestants, He could have either *saved* or *destroyed* the Union without a human contest. Yet the contest began. And having begun He could give the final victory to either side any day. Yet the contest proceeds."

To what end, the President asked himself. With Lee's army at Frederick, Maryland, Lincoln, with a conviction that he controlled events much less than they controlled him, promised himself, and, as he said in telling it, his Maker, that if Lee were driven out of Maryland he would issue the Emancipation Proclamation that he had been withholding since July.

On September 13 Lee's entire plan of operations fell into McClellan's hands when an Indiana private found a copy of an order wrapped around three cigars. Lee was dividing his force, sending Jackson to Harpers Ferry in order to protect his communications, while the remainder of his troops moved toward Boonsboro and Hagerstown, where he could threaten Harrisburg and other Pennsylvania towns. With Lee's army widely dispersed, here was a chance to destroy it in detail. McClellan moved with unaccustomed speed for him, but still with extreme caution. With some 100,000 troops at his disposal, he thought Lee, whose whole strength did not amount to 50,000, must surely outnumber him.

While Lee's hungry, tattered soldiers replenished themselves on Maryland's bounty, word came to Lincoln from Kentucky that the Confederate General Braxton Bragg had evaded Buell, captured Lexington, and driven the State Legislature out of Frankfort. Bragg's destination might be Louisville, Cincinnati, or the East. "Do you know . . . where Gen. Bragg is?" the careworn Lincoln wired Buell. "What degree of certainty have you, that Bragg, with his command, is not now in the valley of the Shenandoah, Virginia?"

Harpers Ferry fell to Jackson with 11,000 prisoners. At Carlisle, Pennsylvania, where the Confederate General Ewell attended church, the loyal pastor asked his permission to offer the usual prayer for the President of the United States. "I'm sure he needs it," Ewell commented dryly as he granted the request.

September 14 brought news of vicious fighting at Turner's Gap and Crampton's Gap, as Lee tried to hold off McClellan at the mountain passes while he brought his forces together again at Sharpsburg. On September 16 McClellan reported to Lincoln that his army faced the enemy along Antietam Creek and he was waiting for a heavy fog to rise. Knowing that time was all-important, Lincoln lingered at the telegraph office for news of the attack, but McClellan put it off until next day.

Lincoln scanned the decoded messages as the reports came in. Direct communication was broken, but messages from Harrisburg and Frederick told of heavy fighting. McClellan was reported to have trapped the enemy between Antietam Creek and the Potomac River; he had given Lee twenty-four hours to surrender or suffer annihilation. Reopening of the direct wire brought more reliable news. Two days after the battle McClellan informed Halleck: "Our victory was complete. The enemy is driven back into Virginia. Maryland and Pennsylvania are safe."

As Lincoln studied details of the battle, it became evident to him that McClellan's habitual hesitancy, the uncoordinated nature of his attacks, and reluctance to commit his reserve troops had probably cost him the opportunity to annihilate or desperately cripple Lee's army. But he had parried the threat to the North. Lincoln confided to his friend Ward Hill Lamon: "I suppose our victory at Antietam will condone my offense in reappointing McClellan. If the battle had gone against us poor McClellan and I, too, would be in a bad row of stumps." Thankful for victory, he still hoped for a knockout blow. As Lee prepared to recross the Potomac, Lincoln wired McClellan: "God bless you and all with you. Destroy the rebel army if possible."

*

A L L through the troublous summer, while Lincoln waited for a victory in order to issue the Emancipation Proclamation, he and his cabinet had kept his intention secret. When a delegation of church leaders brought the President a memorial for emancipation adopted at a great meeting in Chicago, he asked them what good a proclamation could accomplish. Would it not be as ineffective as the Pope's bull against the comet? How could he free slaves in areas where he could not even enforce the Constitution? What about the effect of such a step on the border states? With the Emancipation Proclamation in his desk drawer, it was as though Lincoln sought the opinions of others on questions he had already answered for himself. "Do not misunderstand me," he said at the end of an hour's conference; ". . . I have not decided against a proclamation of liberty to the slaves, but hold the matter under advisement. And I can assure you that the subject is on my mind, by day and night, more than any other."

Horace Greeley lashed out at Lincoln in the *Tribune* for the "preposterous and futile" notion of trying to put down a rebellion while upholding the evil that caused it. In an editorial entitled "The Prayer of Twenty Millions," the mercurial editor informed Lincoln that the controlling majority of loyal voters demanded that he strike out boldly at slavery. Lincoln, anticipating that both proslavery and antislavery extremists would be dissatisfied with the emancipation edict when it came—the former because it touched slavery at all, and the latter because it would not free the slaves in loyal states—used Greeley's outburst to prepare the people for what was coming.

"My paramount object in this struggle *is* to save the Union," he replied to the impatient editor, "and is *not* either to save or destroy slavery. If I could save the Union without freeing *any* slave I would do it, and if I could save it by freeing *all* the slaves I would do it; and if I could save it by freeing some and leaving others alone I would also do that. What I do about slavery and the colored race, I do because I believe it helps to save the Union; and what I forbear, I forbear because I do *not* believe it would help to save the Union. I shall do *less* whenever I shall believe what I am doing hurts the cause, and I shall do *more* whenever I shall believe doing more will help the cause. I shall try to correct errors when shown to be errors, and I shall adopt new views so fast as they shall appear to be true views." This was his purpose with respect to his official duty, Lincoln concluded, "and I intend no modification of my oft-expressed *personal* wish that all men every where could be free."

Senators Charles Sumner and Henry Wilson of Massachusetts and relentless Thaddeus Stevens likewise gave Lincoln no peace. The President told a visitor how they came singly, in pairs, and all together to argue for a forthright assault on slavery. With that, Lincoln stepped to a window, and there, to be sure, were the three legislators, hastening up the White House walk. Lincoln's sense of humor steeled him against their attack. He was reminded of the boy in Sunday school who, chosen to read the story of the three Hebrew children in the fiery furnace, stumbled miserably over the names of Shadrach, Meshach, and Abednego. In pained embarrassment the boy read on, when his eye, traveling down the page, lighted again on the three names, and he cried out in anguish: "Look! Look there! Here comes them same three damn fellers again!"

After the long days of waiting, Antietam gave Lincoln the chance to carry out the silent promise he had made when Lee entered Maryland. He gave the Emancipation Proclamation some final literary touches, and called a cabinet meeting for Saturday, September 21. When his advisers had taken seats, the President opened the session by reading a chapter from the humorist Artemus Ward's "A High Handed Outrage at Utica." The President had a good chuckle. But Chase's smile looked sickly, and Stanton's expression was glum. They did not understand that Lincoln, about to take a step of enormous consequence not only to the immediate military and political situation, but also to the social and economic pattern of the nation for all time to come, sought a moment of relief in time of trial.

His mental tautness eased, Lincoln reminded the cabinet members of the decision he had made two months before. He would have preferred a more decisive victory than Antietam with which to herald emancipation, but at least the military outlook had improved. The morning papers of September 23 printed Lincoln's warning that in one hundred days, on January 1, 1863, all slaves in any state still in rebellion, or in any part of such a state that the President might designate, would be declared free, and that the military power of the United States would be used to assure the freedom of such persons. The fact that a state should, on that day, be represented in good faith in Congress by members chosen at elections in which a majority of the qualified voters had participated would "be deemed conclusive evidence that such state, and the people thereof, are not then in rebellion against the United States." As heretofore, Lincoln explained, the purpose of the war would be to restore the Union. And at the next meeting of Congress he would recommend Federal grants-in-aid to any state adopting some plan for the immediate or gradual abolition of slavery.

Lincoln's new policy met a swift test of public opinion in the elections in October and November. The result proved ominous. Radical Republicans, resentful of Lincoln's tolerance of McClellan and dissatisfied with the limited nature of his proclamation, campaigned halfheartedly, while the determined Democrats harped bitterly on the unwisdom and unconstitutionality of emancipation, and denounced the administration for arbitrary arrests of suspected disloyalists. The failure of the Peninsular campaign and Buell's fumbling opposition to Bragg's thrust into Kentucky were only partially offset by Antietam. The Democrats swept New York, Pennsylvania, Ohio, Indiana, and Illinois, all of which had gone for Lincoln in 1860, carried New Jersey, and won an evenly divided delegation from Wisconsin to increase their representation in Congress from 44 to 75. They elected Horatio Seymour Governor of New York. The

Republican Governors of Indiana and Illinois would now have to deal with Democratic legislatures. In Lincoln's home district John T. Stuart, his old friend and law partner, campaigning against Lincoln's presidential policies, beat Leonard Swett, the President's avowed champion. The newly elected Illinois Legislature would replace Senator Browning with a Democrat.

Trying to analyze the meaning of this setback, Lincoln felt like a boy who had stubbed his toe. He was too big to cry, he said, and it hurt too much to laugh.

*

A F T E R Antietam, as days passed in inactivity, Lincoln visited the army to urge McClellan to attack. Lee was in the Shenandoah Valley, far from Richmond and insecurely based. Viewing the battlefield and the camps and noting the renewed spirit of the troops, Lincoln chided McClellan for overcautiousness. The general offered numerous reasons for delay. Lincoln remained unconvinced. Back in Washington once more, he ordered McClellan, through Halleck, to "cross the Potomac and give battle to the enemy or drive him south." McClellan, replying that he was pushing preparations as fast as possible, found time to write a long message to his army apologizing for the Emancipation Proclamation. While conceding that the army was subordinate to the civil government, he explained that political errors could be remedied at the polls. Shortly before this, he had written significantly to his wife that his countrymen should open their eyes and remove the difficulties from his path.

When McClellan showed no disposition to attack and denied the charge of overcautiousness, Lincoln wrote him a long, patient letter. "Are you not over-cautious," he asked, "when you assume that you can not do what the enemy is constantly doing? . . . Change positions with the enemy, and think you not he would break your communications with Richmond within the next twentyfour hours? . . . If he should . . . move towards Richmond, I would press closely to him, and at least, try to beat him to Richmond on the inside track. . . . If we can not beat the enemy where he now is, we never can, he again being within the entrenchments of Richmond." At McClellan's next excuse—that his horses were sore-tongued and tired—Lincoln could not restrain a burst of exasperation. "Will you pardon me for asking what the horses of your army have done since the battle of Antietam that fatigues anything?" he inquired. Repenting quickly, however, Lincoln sent a soothing letter to a commander who, after all, had won a crucial battle.

From St. Paul, Minnesota, where he had been sent to guard the Indian frontier, General Pope wrote to Lincoln's old friend Governor Yates of Illinois that the nation was in greater danger of destruction with McClellan victorious than if he should be defeated. "Unless you had been present in Washington and had seen and knew what I did, you can scarcely realize the condition of things. The Praetorian system is as fully developed and in active operation in Washington as it ever was in ancient Rome. . . . Already this Potomac Army clique talk openly of Lincoln's weakness and the necessity of replacing him by some stronger man; of shooting Wilson, Sumner, Chase etc. . . . You would be surprised and alarmed to see how openly these things are talked of by the very officers of the Potomac Army who now by their mutinous clamor control the Administration."

Whether Pope's protestations reached the President we do not know, nor how much credence Lincoln gave them if they did. About this time, however, a report that circulated in the army was brought to his notice—it was "not the game," so it was said, to destroy the rebel army, but to bring about a compromise settlement that would assure the continuance of slavery. Lincoln traced the story to Major John J. Key and dismissed him from the service.

These rumors, however ill-founded, could not fail to impress Lincoln. Could it be that McClellan had no desire to inflict a decisive defeat upon the enemy? The President determined on a test. If McClellan allowed Lee to cross the Blue Ridge Mountains and put his army between the Army of the Potomac and Richmond, Lincoln would remove him once and for all.

Almost six weeks after Antietam, McClellan began to push across the Potomac. He took nine days to cross. Lincoln asked the whereabouts of the enemy. Reports were conflicting, the general replied. He complained of lack of supplies of one sort or another, while his chief quartermaster was reporting that "no army was ever more perfectly supplied than this one has been as a general rule."

With McClellan massing near Warrenton, Lee moved without opposition to Culpeper Court House, between the Federal army and Richmond. On November 5, the day after the disastrous state elections, Lincoln signed the order for McClellan's removal. He could not "bore with an auger too dull to take hold," he complained. McClellan had not only amply demonstrated his temperamental unfitness for the sort of warfare that would bring the South to terms, but had also confirmed the President's conviction that he could no longer repose confidence in a general who allowed his own political conceptions to determine his strategy.

In a raw, blustery snowstorm Brigadier General C. P. Buckingham, a confidential assistant to the Secretary of War, arrived at army headquarters from Washington by special train to order General Burnside to take command. Some of McClellan's high-ranking friends expressed resentment. Mutterings of a march on Washington were heard. But Lincoln believed that he now stood higher than McClellan in the estimation of most officers and of the troops. They knew McClellan had let the fruits of victory spoil.

Meanwhile, in Kentucky, Buell and Bragg, after marching and countermarching, clashed on October 8, 1862 in a hard battle at Perryville. Bragg withdrew to Nashville, and it seemed to Lincoln that at last he might push an army into eastern Tennessee. When Buell voiced objections, Halleck wrote to him, at Lincoln's direction: "You say it is the heart of the enemy's resources, make it the heart of yours. . . . Your army must enter East Tennessee this fall . . . while the roads are passable." The President could not understand, Halleck declared, "why we cannot march as the enemy marches, live as he lives, and fight as he fights, unless we admit the inferiority of our troops, and of our generals."

Lincoln would not admit the inferiority of the Union troops. It grieved him that such brave soldiers lacked competent leadership. When Buell, a Democratic crony of McClellan's, continued to offer reasons for delay, Lincoln replaced him with General William S. Rosecrans. Buell, like his friend McClellan, lacked the aggressive qualities required for total victory.

*

EVENTS were to prove General Ambrose E. Burnside a poor choice for command, but to the desperate President he seemed the best man available. A graduate of West Point, thirty-eight years old, the new commander had a genial, pleasing manner and an imposing presence, enhanced by lush side-whiskers. Entering the regular army too late to see much service in the Mexican War, he had resigned in 1853 to engage in the manufacture of small arms. When this business venture failed, he took charge of land sales for the Illinois Central Railroad, eventually became treasurer of that company, and struck up a warm friendship with McClellan, its vice-president.

Re-entering the army at the outbreak of the war, Burnside conducted a successful amphibious operation on the North Carolina coast, and later performed capably as a corps commander under McClellan. Ranking second to McClellan, he retained his friendship while holding himself aloof from army politics. Having twice rejected an offer of the command of the Army of the Potomac, he assumed it with misgivings, as a duty. An honest, conscientious soldier, mindful of his own limitations, and often suffering from dysentery, he told brother officers that he was not up to this job. His acceptability to the McClellan clique aroused the immediate suspicion of the Jacobins.

With Longstreet's corps near Culpeper and Jackson's in the Shenandoah Valley, Burnside proposed to strike straight south through Fredericksburg for Richmond. Lincoln preferred that he make the Confederate army his objective, but finally, on November 14, Halleck wired the new commander: "The President has just assented to your plan. He thinks that it will succeed if you move rapidly; otherwise not."

But pontoons for crossing the Rappahannock River failed to arrive on time; while Burnside waited impatiently, Lee collected his forces on the heights behind Fredericksburg. With some 72,000 troops at his disposal against Burnside's 113,000, he occupied a position almost impregnable against a frontal attack, with his left flank resting on the river and his lines extending along low hills behind the town. To reach Marye's Heights, the key to his position, the Union troops must not only cross the river, but advance up open slopes, across a drainage ditch, against a stone fence bordering a sunken road. In case of defeat the river would be at their backs.

Lincoln became uneasy and on November 25 telegraphed Burnside: "If I should be in a Boat off Aquia Creek, at dark tomorrow (wednesday) evening, could you, without inconvenience, meet me & spend an hour or two with me?" Details of this and other conferences are lacking, but a letter from Halleck to Burnside, dated January 7, 1863, proves that Lincoln consented to an attack solely on condition that it be accompanied by diversionary movements at the fords above the town.

Burnside began building pontoon bridges on December 10. Sharpshooters harassed his engineers. The Union commander, after trying to clear the town with a bombardment, put skirmishers across in pontoon boats. A friendly fog shrouded the river. When it lifted, the Confederates on the ridge saw two of the three Grand Divisions of the Federal army drawn up on the plain below them. Lincoln waited with foreboding for news of the assault; there were no indications of the diversionary movements he had ordered.

At eleven o'clock on the 13th the telegraph reported a heavy artillery duel. Later messages told of a terrific fight; "Cannot tell from this point who has the best of it," the operator wired. At 3.50 p.m. he reported: "The battle rages furiously. Can hardly

hear my instrument. . . . Wounded are arriving every minute."
At 6 p.m. a message said: "The roar of musketry is almost deaf-
ening. Cannonading still kept up. Nothing definite in regard to
the progress of the fight." At last, a few minutes later: "The firing
has ceased."

A dispatch from Burnside at four o'clock next morning
scarcely hinted at the horror of the disaster he had suffered. "I
have just returned from the field," he wired. "Our troops are all
over the River and hold the first ridge outside the town & three
miles below. We hope to carry the crest today. Our loss is heavy
say five thousand."

Actually, as Lincoln learned next day, the battle had been a
slaughter as Burnside threw his troops head-on against Lee's
strong position. The Union casualties would reach 10,000, the
enemy's no more than one fifth as many. Burnside's division
commanders dissuaded him from another reckless assault. The
Union army withdrew across the river.

Lincoln, out of the depths of his own misery, offered consolation to the troops: "The courage with which you in an open field
maintained the contest against an entrenched foe and the consummate skill and success with which you crossed and recrossed
the river in the face of the enemy, show that you possess all the
qualities of a great army, which will yet give victory to the cause
of the country and of popular government."

The army needed encouragement; it had been stunned by the
disaster. Campfire gossip reproached Burnside for the futile loss
of life. Desertions became alarming. Disgruntled officers resigned. Some regiments seemed on the verge of mutiny. A
breakdown on the home front threatened Lincoln as people read
the long roll of the dead. The faint-hearted abandoned hope of
victory and demanded a negotiated peace. Not a few critics of the
administration clamored for a dictator. War-weariness oppressed
the stricken nation.

*

AMID trials and reverses Lincoln found consolation in the
companionship of Seward. Both men had wit and discernment

and saw eye to eye politically. The easygoing, cigar-smoking Secretary, after his defeat in 1860, came to appreciate Lincoln's sound common sense, and renounced his own ambitions in loyalty to his chief. They even had their little friendly bets; once when the Union navy was trying desperately to close in on the Confederate blockade-runner *Nashville*, Hiram Barney, port collector at New York, wired Lincoln: "You have won the quart of hazlenuts from the Secretary of State. The Nashville is not destroyed—but is actively at work."

Seward, like Lincoln, had become less the partisan and more the statesman under the stress of war; but in the minds of the radical Republican malcontents he was responsible for restraining Lincoln from an uncurbed antislavery policy that would bring a quick end to the conflict.

This hostility to Seward was subtly encouraged by Chase. The Secretary of the Treasury, a competent administrator who performed financial wizardry in raising money to support the war, regarded himself as the ablest member of the cabinet and felt resentful that his advice on matters of policy was not more frequently sought. Ever ready to listen to criticism of the President, Chase seldom defended him. "I am not responsible for the management of the war," he said, implying that it might go better if he were, "and have no voice in it, except that I am not forbidden to make suggestions."

Driven by ambition, yet with a smug sense of rectitude, Chase sought to ingratiate himself with the radical Republican politicians. To all talk of Seward's sinister influence on Lincoln he lent a sympathetic ear, not only encouraging but even inspiring complaints. For if Seward could be removed from the cabinet, the heads of the other conservative members might also roll; and in a new cabinet of radical complexion Chase might be the spokesman and the power behind the throne.

Lincoln was fully aware of Chase's attitude; the Secretary wrote and talked too freely to keep his conniving a secret. But Lincoln, with his fondness for Seward, also respected Chase. The two men gave balance to his cabinet, and each did his own work well. "Seward comforts him," wrote Welles, "Chase he deems a necessity."

The defeat at Fredericksburg brought matters to a head. Even such a loyal friend of Lincoln's as Joseph Medill of the *Chicago Tribune* wrote: "Seward must be got out of the Cabinet. He is Lincoln's evil genius. He has been the President *de facto*, and has kept a sponge saturated with chloroform to Uncle Abe's nose all the while. . . . Smith is a cipher on the right hand of Seward's integer. . . . Bates is a fossil . . . and should never have been quarried from the rocks in which he was imbedded. . . . Seward, Smith and Bates must go out."

On December 16 and 17, Republican senators held long, heated caucuses. Criticism of Seward was freely voiced. Wade wanted a Republican to head the armies. There was talk of asking Lincoln to resign. Cooler heads prevented the passage of resolutions denouncing Seward by name. The caucus finally decided to ask Lincoln to reorganize the cabinet, and chose a committee of nine senators to present their grievances.

Seward learned of the outcome of the caucus and, wishing to relieve Lincoln of embarrassment, tendered his resignation. Joshua F. Speed, calling at the White House, found his old friend toilworn and worried. The President felt no concern for himself; he had already told the cabinet that he would gladly step aside in favor of anyone with the right attitude toward the war who commanded more of the nation's confidence than he; but knowing of no such person, he must continue to serve. In serving, he must exercise real leadership; to give way to the Jacobins would be to forfeit all power to lead. Yet Lincoln could not afford to lose the radicals' support. Escape from this dilemma would require all the political sagacity he had learned in the Illinois Legislature and in Congress, all the statecraft he had thus far mastered in the White House.

At an evening session on December 18 Lincoln listened patiently while the senatorial spokesmen charged Seward with lukewarm conduct of affairs, with being only mildly opposed to slavery, and with exercising undue influence on the President. They demanded an end to the all-parties policy, more frequent cabinet meetings, and by implication a larger voice in policy for Chase. Lincoln asked them to return the following night.

The next morning he called an emergency meeting of his cabinet. Seward did not attend. The President told how the senators' complaints had shocked and grieved him. If he called fewer cabinet meetings than his critics thought he should, it was a mark of increasing self-assurance that he knew when he did and did not want advice. In so far as administrative matters were concerned, he followed all departmental policies carefully. He seldom interfered with Chase's management of finances, or with Welles's and Fox's direction of naval matters; but his supervision of the War Department was constant, and he consulted with Seward regularly on foreign affairs.

Lincoln was not an efficient administrator in the usual sense of the term. He disliked set procedures and frequently cut red tape. Welles complained to his diary that "the want of system and free communication among all as equals prevented that concert and comity which is really strength to an administration." Yet, as all members of the cabinet admitted when Lincoln put the question to them, there had seldom been disagreement on fundamental policies.

When the senators returned to the White House that night, they were surprised to find all the cabinet except Seward already on hand. Lincoln wanted all matters in dispute cleared up, he said. No one must be able to say thereafter that anything remained unexplained. As the President defended his failure to call more frequent cabinet meetings on the plea of lack of time, and asserted that the cabinet acted harmoniously in all major matters of policy and that Seward made no vital decisions without his consent, Chase found himself embarrassed by the turn of events. He could scarcely deny the truth of Lincoln's statements in the presence of his cabinet colleagues, and to show sympathy for the senators would mark him as the originator of the uprising. Senators to whom he had spoken so critically of Seward and the President regarded him quizzically. His reticence and evasion were leaving them on shaky ground.

Lincoln, as moderator, kept the meeting well in hand.

Throughout he was conciliatory but firm, and he left no doubt that he regarded the cabinet as his own affair and was not in the least disposed to submit to senatorial dictation.

Toward the end of a five-hour session the senators' mood had calmed. When Lincoln asked how many of them still thought Seward should be replaced, only four voted aye. As the meeting broke up, Senator Trumbull turned back at the door to tell Lincoln privately that Chase's tone had been quite different before. Senator Fessenden said afterward that the meeting accomplished nothing except "to unmask some selfish cowards."

Lincoln had not accepted Seward's resignation. The next morning he sent him a hasty note: "Please do not go out of town." Chase, visiting the White House, where Stanton and Welles were in consultation with the President, said he had been so pained by the events of the previous night that he had prepared his resignation. "Where is it?" asked Lincoln. "I brought it with me," Chase replied, holding a letter in his hand. "Let me have it," demanded Lincoln, reaching out his long arm. Seemingly loath to part with the letter, Chase was on the point of saying more, but Lincoln, snatching the missive, eagerly unfolded it as a smile brightened his face. "This," he said, "cuts the Gordian knot." Stanton offered his resignation, too, but Lincoln waved him aside. "I don't want yours," he said. When Senator Ira Harris of New York came in a few minutes later, he found Lincoln alone. Explaining what had happened, the President was reminded of his boyhood on the farm. "I can ride now," he said joyfully, "I've got a pumpkin in each end of my bag."

Lincoln sent Chase and Seward identical notes, stating that the public interest forbade his accepting their resignations, and asking each man to resume his office. Seward immediately complied. Chase, mindful of Lincoln's gratification at his resignation, sensing that the President had outwitted him, and with sorely wounded pride, asked for time to consider. But when he learned that Seward had withdrawn his resignation, he speedily came around.

Everyone except Chase was in a better mood. Lincoln had

cleared up misunderstandings with the senators and enhanced his own prestige. He had retained two valued advisers in his cabinet and maintained its factional balance. If he had allowed the senators to have their way, he said, "the thing would all have slumped over one way, and we should have been left with a scanty handful of supporters." Thereafter the radical senators would use greater circumspection in their dealings with the subtle President.

One cabinet change did follow the meeting, though it had no relation to it, when Lincoln appointed Caleb B. Smith to a judgeship in Indiana and chose as his successor at the head of the Interior Department John Palmer Usher, former assistant secretary, a loyal but inconspicuous Republican whom he had known as a Hoosier lawyer.

*

J A N U A R Y 1, 1863 drew near, and people wondered if Lincoln would adhere to his resolution to free the slaves, especially since he had referred to it only casually in his December message to Congress. Compensated emancipation seemed uppermost in his mind, and he had recommended in his message the adoption of a constitutional amendment providing, first, for remuneration in the form of government bonds to all states abolishing slavery before the year 1900; second, guaranteeing freedom to all slaves liberated by the war, with compensation to loyal masters; and third, authorizing Congress to provide for colonization of freed Negroes.

Lincoln continued to believe that emancipation by the border states would speed the end of the war. The most eloquent passages of his message entreated Congress to support his proposed amendment. "The dogmas of the quiet past," he said, "are inadequate to the stormy present. The occasion is piled high with difficulty, and we must rise—with the occasion. As our case is new, so we must think anew, and act anew. We must disenthrall ourselves, and then we shall save our country.

"Fellow-citizens," he continued, "_we_ cannot escape history.

We of this Congress and this administration, will be remembered
in spite of ourselves. No personal significance, or insignificance,
can spare one or another of us. The fiery trial through which we
pass, will light us down, in honor or dishonor, to the latest
generation. We *say* we are for the Union. The world will not
forget that we say this. We know how to save the Union. The
world knows we do know how to save it. We—*even we here*—hold
the power, and bear the responsibility. In *giving freedom* to the
slave, we *assure* freedom to the *free*—honorable alike in what we
give, and what we preserve. We shall nobly save, or meanly lose,
the last best, hope of earth. Other means may succeed; this could
not fail. The way is plain, peaceful, generous, just—a way which,
if followed, the world will forever applaud, and God must forever
bless."

Lincoln did not exclude the rebellious slave states from the
benefits of the proposed amendment; he had never considered
them as other than still in the Union. Besides, ratification of the
amendment would require an affirmative vote of three fourths of
the states, an impossibility unless some Southern slave states
voted for it.

In the preliminary Proclamation of Emancipation Lincoln
had stated that representation in Congress would be taken as
proof of renewed allegiance to the Union, and that states, or
parts of states, so represented would be exempt from the emancipation edict. Eager to make it easy for the seceded states to
return, he stood ready to assist wherever the Southern people
seemed disposed to heed his warning. To the White House came
John Edmund Bouligny, of New Orleans, the only representative
from the deep South who had remained in Congress. An invalid,
he could scarcely mount the stairs to Lincoln's office. He came to
ask the President to give the renascent Union sentiment in
Louisiana a chance to assert itself.

Through Bouligny, Lincoln sent confidential letters to
General Butler, commander of the Department of the Gulf, and
to General George F. Shepley, military governor of Louisiana,
asking them to aid Bouligny and all others wishing to elect

representatives to Congress. If some legal circumvention proved necessary in order to hold an election before January 1, 1863, he thought such action would be justified. Where no state authority could act, the military authorities should do so. The largest possible number of people should be encouraged to vote. Candidates should be men of character, willing to support the Constitution, and above suspicion of duplicity. Having determined on this policy, Lincoln sent similar letters to General Grant in Mississippi, to Andrew Johnson, now military governor of Tennessee, and to commanders in Tennessee and Arkansas.

With the prospect of an election in Louisiana, political night-crawlers began to issue from their holes. Lincoln heard rumors that Federal officers, not citizens of the state, proposed to run for Congress. This must not be tolerated; it would defeat his purpose of proving that respectable local citizens were willing to vote in a Federal election and serve in the Federal legislature. "To send a parcel of Northern men here as representatives," he warned Governor Shepley, "elected as would be understood (and perhaps really so,) at the point of the bayonet, would be disgusting and outrageous, and were I a member of Congress here I would vote against admitting any such man to a seat."

But many Republican Congressmen lacked Lincoln's forgiving spirit. They wished to punish the rebellious states and, in so doing, assure the Republican Party of ascendancy for years to come. A Yankee colonel in the South expressed their views: "The thing we seek is *permanent* dominion & what instance is there of permanent dominion without changing, revolutionizing, absorbing, the institutions, life, and manners of the conquered peoples? . . . They think we mean to take their *Slaves.* Bah! We must take their *ports,* their *mines,* their *water power,* the *very soil* they plough, and develop them by the hands of our *artisan* armies. . . . We are a regenerating, colonizing power, or we are to be whipped. Schoolmasters, with howitzers, must instruct our Southern brethren that they are a set of d—d fools in everything that relates to . . . modern civilization. . . . *This army must not come back.* Settlement, migration must put the seal on battle, or we gain nothing." Already a vicious contest over reconstruction of the South was shaping up.

On December 3, 1862, however, Governor Shepley, following Lincoln's instructions, caused orderly elections to be held in the First and Second Louisiana Congressional districts, which embraced the city of New Orleans and outlying areas within the Union lines. Only Louisiana men were candidates, and Benjamin F. Flanders and Michael Hahn, both antisecessionists, were the winners. About half the usual number of citizens cast ballots.

*

LINCOLN's merely casual reference to the Emancipation Proclamation in his December message, and his seeming preoccupation with compensated emancipation, induced some persons to believe he had experienced a change of heart. Friends of the Negro prayed that the President might prove steadfast to his purpose, and for the nation and the army to sustain him. John Murray Forbes, a Boston businessman, wrote to Senator Sumner: "The first of January is near at hand, and we see no signs of any measure for carrying into effect the Proclamation." But those closest to the President had learned that while he came to his decisions slowly, once made he seldom reversed them. On Christmas Day, Sumner replied to Forbes: "The President is occupied on the Proclamation. He will stand firm."

On New Year's Day the Proclamation came, decreeing that all slaves in the rebellious areas should be forever free. But Lincoln acted as leniently as he could. Exempted from the provisions of the edict were the Louisiana parishes that had elected Congressmen, though Congress had not yet consented to seat their representatives; the state of Tennessee, where Governor Johnson had brought about a restoration of civil government; two counties on the Eastern Shore of Virginia; others around Norfolk and Fortress Monroe, where the Union army exercised control; and those counties of western Virginia soon to be admitted as a state.

Although a slave revolt would have paralyzed the Confederacy and might have ended the war, Lincoln took care that no such barbarism should scourge the South. He enjoined the black men to abstain from unnecessary violence and to labor faithfully for wages. Such as chose to serve would be received into the armed forces of the United States. And upon this act, believed to be one of justice, warranted by the Constitution upon military necessity, Lincoln invoked "the considerate judgment of mankind, and the gracious favor of Almighty God."

Except for this final sentence, which had been suggested by Chase, the proclamation was a prosaic document, void of moral preachment or propagandist appeal. Lincoln had signed it with scant ceremony. The usual New Year's reception had been held at the White House on that muddy, dismal day. From eleven o'clock in the morning until two o'clock in the afternoon he had shaken hands with an unbroken line of callers. He had copied the proclamation the day before, the names of the exempted counties and parishes had been inserted that morning, and it lacked only his signature. When he came to his office in midafternoon, his right hand felt limp and swollen. Those cabinet members and prominent officials who happened to be in the White House gathered in his office. There were less than a dozen in all. When Lincoln dipped his pen and held it poised, his hand shook with fatigue. He hesitated. He had never been more certain of doing right, he said, but he feared that a trembling signature might be taken as showing compunction. "But anyway it is going to be done!" Slowly and carefully he signed his full name to the document.

The public reaction was mixed. Many persons experienced a bewilderment of joy, but sullen notes intruded. As Lincoln had anticipated, abolitionist extremists expressed dissatisfaction at a halfway measure. Some persons in the border states predicted a social cataclysm. Proslavery Northern Democrats saw Lincoln's perfidy unmasked; after wheedling them into supporting a war for the Union, he had turned it against slavery. Secession leaders claimed they had been right about the intentions of Lincoln and the Republican Party from the first; there could be no reconciliation now, the South must fight to the bitter end to preserve its social system.

Charles Francis Adams reported from London that Lincoln's proclamation was exercising a decisive influence in England, if not in America. "It has rallied all the sympathies of the working classes," Adams wrote, "and has produced meetings the like of which, I am told, have not been seen since the days of the corn laws." From many of these meetings came resolutions of commendation to the President. In reply to one such resolution from Manchester, where the closing of the cotton mills because of the Federal blockade had brought thousands of workers to the verge of destitution, Lincoln praised the understanding of the working people. Their loyalty to the ideals of free government in the face of severe suffering furnished an instance of sublime Christian heroism, "which has not been surpassed in any age or country." Writing similarly to the workingmen of London, Lincoln thanked them for their "exalted and humane sentiments" in support of free institutions throughout the world. The President felt grateful that reports from France, Spain, and other European countries told of a popular approval of his action that autocratic rulers would scarcely dare ignore.

In so far as practical results were concerned, Lincoln's proclamation had little immediate effect. Applying only in areas where he exercised no authority, it left slavery undisturbed where he could control it. Moreover, Congress by the second Confiscation Act, of July 17, 1862, which freed all slaves of persons adhering to the rebellion, and through other legislative measures, had largely anticipated Lincoln's action. And while its enactments had been unenforceable except in limited areas, Lincoln's was a paper edict, too.

No slave insurrections followed the President's action. While some slaves welcomed "Lincum's" proclamation with wild rejoicing, others, especially in the deep South, shared their masters' fear and hatred of Yankees. Most slaves in the interior regions of the Confederacy continued to work faithfully for the white family that fed and clothed them. But wherever the Union armies penetrated, this situation changed. In areas

under military occupation the slaves, deserted by their masters
or fleeing from the plantations, flocked to Union encampments
as havens of refuge. Thus, over the long term, the effect of
Lincoln's edict would depend on the outcome of the war. A
Confederate triumph would render it a dead letter; a Union victory would give it life.

When Chase suggested some time later that Lincoln should
bring the excepted areas in Virginia and Louisiana within the
authority of the proclamation, the President showed how carefully he kept within the bounds of legality. "The original proclamation has no constitutional or legal justification, except as a
military measure," he explained. "The exemptions were made
because the military necessity did not apply to the exempted
localities. Nor does that necessity apply to them now any more
than it did then. If I take the step must I not do so, without the
argument of military necessity, and so without any argument
except the one that I think the measure politically expedient, and
morally right? Would I not thus give up all footing upon Constitution or law? Would I not thus be in the boundless field of
absolutism? Could this pass unnoticed, or unresisted? Could it
fail to be perceived that without any further stretch, I might do
the same in Delaware, Maryland, Kentucky, Tennessee, and
Missouri, and even change any law in any state?"

*

ALTHOUGH Lincoln announced the proposed use of colored
troops in the Emancipation Proclamation, he had not come easily
to that decision. The act of July 17, 1862 gave him complete
discretion in the employment of Negroes for any purpose what-
soever, but he had shrunk from using black men to kill white
men. To deprive the South of the services of her slaves was
a legitimate and necessary war measure. To use colored men
as teamsters and laborers in the Union army would release white
men for combat. But to put weapons in the hands of black men,
some of whom might become frenzied with the flush of new-found
freedom, was a matter of most serious consequence.

Understanding how the race problem transcended the question of slavery and made slavery so difficult to deal with, Lincoln, from the time he decided upon an emancipation proclamation, had pondered the problems of race relationship that were certain to result from it. The more he thought about it, the more he became confirmed in the conviction that the white race and the black race would be better off apart—that in view of inherited prejudices it would be best to remove the Negroes from the country. But while Lincoln thought it best that the Negroes should go to some land of their own, he would not force them into exile. Their departure must be voluntary.

While waiting to issue the preliminary edict of emancipation, Lincoln called certain intelligent free colored men to confer with him. It was the first time that a Negro group had been invited to the White House. Lincoln spoke to them frankly. There were certain ineradicable differences between the races, he declared. Freedom would improve the Negro's chances of self-betterment, but it would not assure him equality, and the President could not change this if he would. Except for the presence of the Negro in the United States there would have been no war, though many men on each side cared not at all about the black man.

Lincoln appealed to the free Negroes to make sacrifices for themselves and for mankind. In the Chiriquí region of Central America, near the Isthmus of Panama, in the Republic of New Granada, were rich coal mines, and ports on two oceans. Certain capitalists with investments in that region were willing to sponsor a venture. If the President could induce some intelligent Negroes to go there and make a start, others could be persuaded to follow them. The place might provide a new homeland for the Negro. The President promised to see that the migrants were fairly treated. In seeking to promote colonization Lincoln followed a policy deplored by abolitionist believers in Negro equality, but favored by liberal Southerners.

The President clung tenaciously to the idea. When scientific tests proved the supposedly rich coal deposits in Chiriquí to be worthless, and a territorial dispute developed between New

Granada and Costa Rica, he abandoned the Central American project in favor of a Negro colony on Isle 'a Vache, a possession of the Negro Republic of Haiti. A certain Bernard Koch, who had obtained a concession on Isle 'a Vache, agreed to colonize 5,000 Negroes at fifty dollars a head, and to provide them with housing, food, medicine, churches, schools, and employment. More than four hundred Negroes were sent to Isle 'a Vache at government expense before the project failed, owing to poor planning, Haitian opposition, and the selfishness of the promoters. In March 1864 a government vessel brought back the survivors of the enterprise.

Although colonization had been an integral part of Lincoln's emancipation plan, long before the failure of the Isle 'a Vache experiment he had reluctantly concluded that colonization was impracticable and that he must reconcile himself to a program of racial adjustment within the United States. Whites and blacks must learn to live together as free men. Helping to bring Lincoln to this conclusion was a growing conviction that the use of the Negro as a soldier was the only resource left to him to tip the scale of battle. And as a soldier, rather than a mere menial laborer for the army, the Negro could not only help to win the war and his own freedom, but also prove his bravery and intelligence.

While the abolitionists and radical Republicans would applaud the use of black soldiers, they were only a portion of the people. Lincoln must move cautiously lest the nation as a whole repudiate his plans for Negro self-betterment. While seeking to guide public opinion, he must not move too far in advance of it. In the preliminary Emancipation Proclamation he had not mentioned the use of Negro soldiers. The final emancipation edict offered Negroes the chance to fight. Already some Union commanders in the South had begun to instruct black men in the use of arms. In March 1863 their enrollment was systematized, and Adjutant General Lorenzo Thomas went to Mississippi to superintend enlistments. The following May the poet Henry Wadsworth Longfellow saw the Fifty-fourth Massachusetts, the first full regiment of colored troops to be enlisted in the North, marching through the streets of Boston, bound for the battlefield. "An imposing sight," he wrote, "with something wild and strange about it, like a dream. At last the North consents to let the Negro fight for freedom." By the end of the war some 186,000 colored troops had been enrolled in the Union army.

*

THE NEW YEAR'S DAY of the Emancipation Proclamation brought no surcease of military worries. Lincoln had held an imperative conference with Burnside in the morning. Throughout the day he wondered what was happening at Murfreesboro, Tennessee, where Bragg had smashed at Rosecrans's Army of the Cumberland the day before. The news on New Year's Eve had been alarming; Bragg's furious attack had rolled back the Union right until the battle line extended at right angles to the original position. Apparitions of dead and mutilated soldiers, of battle-spent men lying on cold ground soaked by a winter rain, tortured the President's sleep. For two more days the battle raged; the Union losses mounted to almost 13,000, the Confederate to more than 11,000, out of 41,000 and 34,000 troops respectively engaged. But Rosecrans's regrouped divisions crumpled the attack as General George H. Thomas, a Virginian loyal to the Union, held on the left flank, and the name of young Phil Sheridan, a fighting Irishman, began to appear in news dispatches. The Confederate army drew off sullenly toward Chattanooga.

The New Year's conference with Burnside placed Lincoln in a dilemma. After his annoying experiences with McClellan the President had sought an aggressive general. The determined Burnside showed no lack of energy, but his resolution was so untempered with discretion that it was said of him that he waged war as some folk play the fiddle, "by main strength and awkwardness." Immediately after the Fredericksburg disaster Burnside proposed to attack again, above or below Fredericksburg. His division commanders protested. And when General John Newton, a loyal Virginian, and General John Cochran, a former New York

Congressman, came secretly to warn Lincoln of the demoralization of the army and of probable disaster in the event of another
battle, the President hastily wired Burnside: "I have good reason
for saying you must not make a general movement of the army
without letting me know."

In the New Year's consultation at the White House, Burnside urged the necessity of keeping the troops occupied rather
than leaving them to grumble in the boredom of winter quarters.
Lincoln asked Halleck to decide. "If in such a difficulty . . . you
do not help," he told the reluctant commander in chief, "you
fail me precisely in the point for which I sought your assistance."
Lincoln wanted Halleck to study the ground of Burnside's
proposed attack, to weigh the chances of victory, and to recommend the proper course to be taken. "Your military skill is useless to me, if you will not do this," he implored.

Resentful of the implied criticism, Halleck resigned in a
huff. To mollify him, the President withdrew his letter. Burnside
renewed his request for permission to advance. Halleck favored
action, but thought Burnside should decide the time, place, and
manner of the attack, since conditions changed from day to day.
With a note of caution, Lincoln authorized Burnside to proceed.
The army broke camp in a cold winter rain and marched north
to cross the Rappahannock. The ground became impassable.
Wagons and cannon bogged down. Men and horses slogged in
deep mud to pull them out. Burnside persisted, using his cavalry
mounts as pack-horses. But Nature proved too formidable an
antagonist. The disgruntled army returned to winter quarters.

Burnside made a night ride to Washington. He proposed to
relieve Joseph E. Hooker, Newton, Cochran, and six other
complaining generals of their commands. Unless Lincoln approved he would resign. Burnside returned hastily to the army,
leaving the President to ponder his ultimatum. The decision
respecting Burnside was not difficult; he had utterly lost the
confidence of the army. Stanton and Halleck favored Rosecrans
as his successor, but Lincoln made the somewhat startling choice
of Hooker, Burnside's most persistent critic, and the general

who, after Fredericksburg, had clamored most loudly for a dictator.

Lincoln was aware of Hooker's weaknesses—his blunt loquacity, promoted perhaps by steady drinking, his resentment of superior authority, his braggadocio. But the florid, curly-headed Hooker, whose weak chin marred his robust handsomeness, had soldierly qualities, too. A West Point graduate and a veteran of the Mexican War, he had taken part in all the important engagements on the Eastern front and earned the nickname "Fighting Joe." His dashing valor endeared him to the troops. Nicolay and Hay had heard Lincoln say, appraising his generals: "Now there is Joe Hooker. He can fight . . . but whether he can 'keep tavern' for a large army is another matter."

Late in January 1863 Halleck telegraphed Hooker that the President wished to see him at the White House. The general took away from the interview a forthright letter that reveals the tenor of the conversation. "I have placed you at the head of the Army of the Potomac," wrote the President. "Of course I have done this upon what appear to me to be sufficient reasons. And yet I think it best for you to know that there are some things in regard to which, I am not quite satisfied with you. I believe you to be a brave and skilful soldier, which, of course, I like. I also believe you do not mix politics with your profession, in which you are right. You have confidence in yourself, which is a valuable, if not an indispensable quality. You are ambitious, which, within reasonable bounds, does good rather than harm. But I think that during Gen. Burnside's command of the Army, you have taken counsel of your ambition, and thwarted him as much as you could, in which you did a great wrong to the country, and to a most meritorious and honorable brother officer. I have heard, in such way as to believe it, of your recently saying that both the Army and the Government needed a Dictator. Of course it was not for this, but in spite of it, that I have given you the command. Only those generals who gain successes, can set up dictators. What I now ask of you is military success, and I will risk the dictatorship. The government will support you to the utmost of it's [sic] ability, which is neither more nor less than it has done, and will do for all commanders. I much fear that the spirit which you have aided to infuse into the Army, of criticising their commander, and withholding confidence from him, will now turn upon you. I shall assist you as far as I can, to put it down. Neither you, nor Napoleon, if he were alive again, could get any good out of an army, while such a spirit prevails in it.

"And now, beware of rashness. Beware of rashness, but with energy, and sleepless vigilance, go forward, and give us victories."

*

IN EARLY April, Lincoln, accompanied by Tad and a few friends, spent a week with the Army of the Potomac; these visits to the army were almost his sole vacations, though he usually went with some purpose. Peering through field glasses, he could see the town of Fredericksburg across the river with scarcely a building free from battle scars. Walls lay in ruins. Loose sheets of tin fluttered from the steeple of a church. Smoke trailed from a blackened chimney that rose alone close to the riverbank where two gray-backed pickets had built a fire on the hearth for relief from the early-morning chill.

Riding over the rough campground in an ambulance drawn by six mules, the President marveled at the driver's proficiency in a soldier's manner of speaking to a mule. "Pardon me," said he, tapping the driver on the shoulder, "but are you an Episcopalian?" The blasphemous driver professed to be a Methodist. "Well, I thought you must be an Episcopalian," observed the President, "because you swear just like Governor Seward, who is a churchwarden."

Lincoln noted that Hooker had restored the army's spirit. What seemed like interminable lines of infantry swung past the chief of state in a grand review. Lincoln, mindful of the welfare of the troops, asked Hooker if the gaudy uniforms of the Zouaves did not make them conspicuous targets. Mud flew in all directions when the cavalry and artillery clattered by. Out on the edge of a cavalry column rode little Tad in the charge of a mounted orderly, "his gray cloak flying in the gusty wind like the plume of Henry of Navarre." Lincoln visited a hospital and stopped for a few words at every cot.

Hooker declared that he commanded the finest army on the planet. With 100,000 troops against Lee's 60,000, he was eager to try conclusions with the enemy. In the next fight, Lincoln cautioned, he should make certain to put in all his men. Too often the Union superiority in numbers had been wasted by faulty tactics. Lincoln's old friend Dr. Anson G. Henry, a member of the President's party, wrote to his wife: "We are all more hopeful than we ever have been—Genl Hooker has a most exalted opinion of Mr. Lincoln's sound judgement & practical sense, and will act in accordance with his suggestions in good faith for the reason that they meet his own views in the main—This has never been the case before—McClellan seemed to try to go counter in every particular to the Presidents suggestions."

The plan worked out by Lincoln and Hooker involved essentially the same strategy that the President had expected Burnside to employ. Sending General Stoneman with his cavalry on a widespread raid to ravage the Confederate communications and threaten Richmond, Hooker left General Sedgwick with 40,000 men to cross the Rappahannock at Fredericksburg, after he had marched the remainder of his army up the river to force Lee to leave his entrenchments.

Crossing the Rappahannock and the Rapidan, Hooker reached Chancellorsville on April 30. The next day his advance encountered new Confederate works, and in a sudden fit of indecision he drew back on Chancellorsville. Lee seized the initiative. On May 2 he undertook his favorite maneuver of swinging Jackson out to strike Hooker's exposed right wing. Warned of heavy troop movements to the west, Hooker thought Lee was retreating.

Jackson's surprise blow caught the Federal troops preparing supper. Their first warning was a dash of deer, rabbits, and other small game through their camp. Close behind came Jackson's men, three columns deep. The battle raged in a wilderness so dense that brambly thickets tore the clothing from the men. Regiments disappeared in the thick undergrowth. Union headquarters lost contact with the troops. Artillery finally slowed Jackson's advance. Darkness averted a rout of Hooker's army.

Meanwhile Sedgwick had crossed the river to take Lee in the rear. Lee drove him back and pressed pincers on Hooker. During May 3, the second day of swirling battle, Hooker clamped on a censorship and little news came into Washington until 2.45 p.m., when a wire from General Butterfield, his chief of staff, informed the President: "The battle has been most fierce and terrible. Loss heavy on both sides. General Hooker slightly, but not at all seriously wounded. . . . You may expect his dispatch in a few hours, which will give you the result."

At four o'clock a telegram from Hooker stated: "We have had a desperate fight yesterday & today which has resulted in no success for us having lost a position of two lines which had been selected for our defence. It is now 1.30 & there is still some firing of artillery. We may have another turn at it this p.m. I do not despair of success. If Sedgwick could have gotten up there could have been but one result. As it is impossible for me to know the exact position of Sedgwick as regards his ability to advance & take part in the engagement, I cannot tell when it will end."

Lincoln had read too many military dispatches to miss the note of doubt in this one. "Where is Hooker?" he wired anxiously to Butterfield. "Where is Sedgwick? Where is Stoneman?"

Little information came through the next day. By Wednesday, May 6, Lincoln felt certain that Hooker had been whipped. Fragmentary messages confirmed his suspicions that Hooker and Sedgwick had not co-ordinated their attacks; that Hooker, outmaneuvered, had brought only part of his army into the battle. At 1.35 p.m. came news that the Army of the Potomac, badly battered, had withdrawn across the Rappahannock. Noah Brooks, a reporter for the *Sacramento Union*, who was in the White House when this news came in, observed that the President's face turned ashen; he had never appeared so broken and dispirited.

Head bent, hands tightly clasped behind his back, he paced his office, groaning: "My God! My God! What will the country say? What *will* the country say?"

A few moments later Brooks heard a carriage draw up at the entrance to the White House. Lincoln darted into it and drove to Halleck's office. Soon he was off to Hooker's head-quarters.

Taking counsel of the situation, however, Lincoln rebounded quickly. A heavy rain had raised the Rappahannock and rendered the Union army safe from attack; and Richmond papers, coming through the Union lines, told of severe Confederate losses among high-ranking officers—Stonewall Jackson was reported seriously wounded—and of Stoneman's cavalry having spread destruction to within five miles of Richmond. Later it developed that the intrepid Jackson, returning from a night reconnaissance, had been shot by his own men; the Confederacy suffered a disaster in his death a few days later.

At army headquarters Lincoln put his thoughts on paper. "What next?" he inquired of Hooker. "If possible I would be very glad of another movement early enough to give us some benefit from the fact of the enemies [*sic*] communications being broken. But neither for this reason or any other, do I wish any-thing done in desperation or rashness. An early movement would also help to supersede the bad moral effect of the recent one, which is sure to be considerably injurious. Have you already in your mind a plan wholly or partially formed? If you have, prosecute it without interference from me. If you have not, please inform me, so that I, incompetent as I may be, can try [to] assist in the formation of some plan for the Army."

*

A F T E R numerous frustrations the situation in the West held greater promise. With Halleck's promotion to supreme command, Grant had succeeded to the command of the Army of the Ten-nessee, and the Federals, advancing from both north and south, had won control of the Mississippi River except for some 250

The Mississippi Theater

miles between Vicksburg and Port Hudson. The retention of this
stretch of river by the Confederates not only closed the great
waterway as an outlet for produce from the Northwestern states,
but also provided the Confederacy with its sole means of overland
communication with the outside world. For across the river
through this entryway came droves of cattle from Texas, hogs
and foodstuffs from Arkansas and western Louisiana, arms,
munitions, drugs, and other sorely needed manufactured products of European origin that were consigned to Mexican ports
and transshipped by wagon or mule train.

Vicksburg, the key to this stretch of river, was a natural
citadel. Situated on a commanding bluff, two hundred feet above
the water, it was protected in the rear by rough terrain. The
few roads followed the heavily timbered ridges, and a rank
growth of vines and canebrakes made the ravines impenetrable.
Stagnant pools of water breathed miasma. The Confederates had
lined the riverbank with heavy guns. Redoubts surrounded the
city.

In November 1862, when Grant marched south from Memphis to attack, the enemy had cut his rail communications and
destroyed his supply depot at Holly Springs. Twice Sherman was
repulsed with heavy loss at Chickasaw Bluffs, and Grant, deciding that Vicksburg must be taken from the south, but fearing
to run his transports past the heavy batteries, cut loose from
his base and crossed to the west bank of the Mississippi. Here
he tried to bypass the city by digging a canal across a great
bend in the stream; but mud, mosquitoes, and swamp fever
plagued his tough Midwestern troops as Confederate batteries on
the waterfront harassed them.

Rumors came to Washington that Grant was drinking again.
Murat Halstead, of the *Cincinnati Commercial*, wrote to Chase:
"You do once in a while, don't you, say a word to the President,
or Stanton, or Halleck, about the conduct of the War?

"Well, now, for God's sake say that Genl Grant, entrusted
with our greatest army, is a jackass in the original package.
He is a poor drunken imbecile. He is a poor stick sober, and he is

most of the time more than half drunk, and much of the time idiotically drunk. . . .

"I know precisely what I am writing about and the meaning of the language I use.

"Now are our Western heroes to be sacrificed by the ten thousand by this poor devil?

"Grant will fail miserably, hopelessly, eternally. You may look for and calculate his failures, in every position in which he may be placed, as a perfect certainty.

"Don't say I am grumbling. Alas! I know too well I am but feebly outlining the truth. . . ."

The prim Chase sent Halstead's letter to Lincoln with the comment that the *Cincinnati Commercial* was an influential paper, and that such reports about Grant were becoming too common to overlook.

Lincoln sent Congressman Washburne, Governor Richard Yates of Illinois, and Adjutant General Lorenzo Thomas to investigate Grant's conduct. Washburne was Grant's fellow townsman from Galena; he and Yates had been Grant's most active sponsors; the investigators reported the general and his command in excellent order. Charles A. Dana, whom Stanton sent to Mississippi as an observer, likewise found nothing to complain about. When a delegation came to Lincoln to demand Grant's dismissal, the President used a jest to stall them off. "If I knew what kind of liquor Grant drinks," he said, "I would send a barrel or so to some other generals." But the attacks on Grant became so persistent and so bitter that Lincoln confided to Nicolay: "I think Grant has hardly a friend left, except myself."

Thwarted for three months by terrain, Grant decided to risk the scowling batteries above the river. Moving his army down a series of bayous and streams west of the Mississippi to a point some fifty miles below Vicksburg, he ordered Rear Admiral Porter to run his ironclads, steamers, and barges past the city. In pitch-darkness on the night of April 16, Porter's flotilla cut loose from its anchorage and drifted silently downstream, fires banked and lights extinguished. The flash of a heavy cannon split the night. Guns roared along the bluff as the Confederates discovered Porter's ships. The gunboats thundered back. The Union vessels hugged the shadows of the shore as the Confederates set fire to houses on the riverbank to light the stream. Smoke-stacks trailed sparks and flame as the flotilla, full steam ahead, churned on down the river with slight damage. Porter ferried Grant's troops to the east bank. By the end of April 1863 Grant had his army south of Vicksburg and was ready to attack.

General John C. Pemberton commanded some 35,000 Confederate troops in Vicksburg and along the railroad south of it. General Joseph E. Johnston, in command of all the Confederate forces in the West, had almost as many more around Jackson, the capital of Mississippi. Grant had superiority in numbers, but, bereft of communication with the North, he must live off the hostile country. Behind him flowed the broad river, commanded above and below him by the enemy. A serious defeat might mean the annihilation or surrender of his army.

On May 11 Grant cut loose from his base and telegraphed Halleck: "You may not hear from me for several days." Except for an occasional report from General Stephen A. Hurlbut at Memphis, Lincoln's chief knowledge of Grant's movements for the next two weeks came from items in Southern newspapers that were acquired by capture or exchange, and from Confederate semaphore messages intercepted by Army of the Potomac signal-men, who had broken the Confederate code.

At last, on May 25, a report forwarded by Hurlbut from General John A. Rawlins, Grant's chief of staff, brought Lincoln official information that Grant had fought and won five battles in three weeks, capturing the town of Jackson, forcing General Johnston to draw off, and driving Pemberton behind the Vicks-burg redoubts. Admiral Porter telegraphed by way of Cairo: "There has never been a case during the whole war where the Rebels have been as successfully beaten at all points. . . . It is a mere question of a few hours & then with the exception of Pt. Hudson which will follow Vicksburg the Mississippi will be open its entire length."

Victory did not come that easily, however, for Pemberton had been ordered to hold Vicksburg at all costs. Two frontal attacks failed, and Grant settled down to a siege. Night and day his batteries pounded the city, while Porter's gunboats shelled it from the river. Citizens and soldiers burrowed into the hillsides as Grant pushed ever closer with saps and mines. Gaunt hunger stalked the city streets. Grant had Vicksburg in his clutch unless Johnston could bring troops to raise the siege.

Then Grant, whatever his conduct may have been before, went on a roaring spree. Sylvanus Cadwallader, correspondent of the *Chicago Times*, encountered him on a river boat deep in his cups. Cadwallader got him to his cabin, pulled off his pants and boots, fanned him to sleep. Grant sobered up and sought more liquor on a sutler's boat. Mounting his horse, he dashed wildly back toward camp, outdistancing his frantic escort, scattering campfires and wrathful troops, who luckily failed to recognize the wild night rider. The faithful Cadwallader caught up, persuaded the general to dismount, and when he fell asleep summoned an ambulance. At headquarters Grant "shrugged his shoulders, pulled down his vest, shook himself together as one just risen from a nap," and, seeing the ever suspicious General Rawlins and other officers evidently waiting for him, bade them good-night "in a natural tone and manner, and started to his tent as steadily as he ever walked in his life."

The incident earned Grant's lasting confidence for Cadwallader, who was accorded rare privileges during the rest of Grant's campaigns, when he wrote for the *New York Herald*. Cadwallader's conclusion, based on close observation, was that Grant was not a habitual drinker—he might go for months without a drop—but he could not drink moderately.

Whatever Lincoln's conclusions about Grant's drinking may have been, he recognized his fighting qualities and resolved to make the most of them. Always Grant sought for a death-grip; shaken off, he dashed in to claw and crunch again.

CHAPTER XVII

The Signs Look Better

LINCOLN'S bipartisan policy threatened to break down. From the beginning he had favored loyal Democrats with important positions and commands, both as a means to national unity and because he welcomed the services of every loyal man regardless of his politics. This policy had proved especially effective in helping to hold the border states and in encouraging a Union spirit in those southern counties of Illinois, Indiana, and Ohio which had shown strong Southern sympathies. Some Democratic leaders like Stanton, Ben Butler of Massachusetts, and John A. Logan of Illinois became outright Republicans. Others tried to co-operate in a nonpartisan spirit. But this very situation offered ambitious Democratic politicians of minor stature a welcome opportunity. The Democratic Party came under the leadership of men of narrow vision or doubtful loyalty who were incapable of resisting the chance to reap political profit from the government's embarrassments.

The first serious Democratic defections came when Lincoln issued his preliminary Emancipation Proclamation. Many Democrats who had previously supported, or at least refrained from opposing, a war to save the Union, now became more critical in their allegiance; others became furtive or open enemies of the government. Throughout the North—but especially in those counties of the Midwest where the majority of the people were of southern antecedents—secret societies, known variously as Knights of the Golden Circle, the Order of American Knights, and the Sons of Liberty, enrolling thousands of members, spoke openly in favor of the Southern cause, and committed acts of violence against the government.

Recruiting officers were found murdered. Lonely countrysides were terrorized. Union agents reported a maze of plots and conspiracies, one to seize prison camps and arm Confederate prisoners; another, inspired by Confederate agents in Canada, to set up a Northwestern Confederacy. These seditionists were known as Copperheads, because of their practice of cutting the head of the Goddess of Liberty from a copper penny to wear in their coat lapels, and from the venomous snake of that name.

With the outbreak of armed conflict, Lincoln had dealt sternly with "the enemy in the rear." On April 22, 1861, acting under an opinion from Attorney General Bates, he authorized General Scott or any officer in command to suspend the writ of *habeas corpus*, in case of necessity, along the railroad line from Washington to Philadelphia. As suspected seditionists were hustled off to military custody, legalistic old Chief Justice Taney, taking the position that only Congress was empowered to suspend the privilege of *habeas corpus*, offered a blistering opinion on Lincoln's usurpation of power and warned him not to violate the laws he had sworn to uphold.

"Are all the laws, *but one* to go unexecuted," Lincoln replied, "and the government itself go to pieces, lest that one be violated?" But no law had been violated, he maintained, because the Constitution does not specify whether Congress or the President shall judge of the necessity of suspending the privilege of *habeas corpus*. Lincoln declared that he would consider himself faithless to his oath of office "if the government should be overthrown, when it was believed that disregarding the single law, would tend to preserve it."

Arbitrary arrests continued to be made, and in the autumn of 1862 Lincoln denied the privilege of *habeas corpus* to all persons imprisoned by military order. The next year, on authority granted by Congress, he suspended it throughout the Union when state courts obstructed the draft law.

Soon after Stanton became Secretary of War, jurisdiction of political prisoners passed from Seward's State Department to the War Department. Stanton exercised his power ruthlessly, arresting more than thirteen thousand persons for disloyalty. Since most of them were Democrats, arrested frequently in anticipation of seditious actions rather than for anything they had done, Lincoln's political opponents accused him of attempting a political purge. The Constitution "can not be enlarged or abridged to meet supposed exigencies at the caprice or will of the officers under it," declared the *Cincinnati Inquirer*. ". . . Exigencies and necessities will always arise in the minds of ambitious men, anxious to usurp power—they are the tyrant's pleas, by which liberty and constitutional law, in all ages, have been overthrown."

Faced by the paradox that always confronts a democratic government in time of war—the necessity of curbing civil liberties as a means of ultimately preserving them—Lincoln took the position that the people had entrusted him to preserve the democratic government they had reared, and that to be faithful to that trust he must use any power, not clearly illegal, which would enable him to cope with the emergency.

But the policy of arbitrary arrests, the Emancipation Proclamation, the prolongation of the war with mounting casualties, the threat of a draft of manpower, and the general war-weariness of the people, all offered tempting targets to the Democrats. Some Democratic newspapers openly justified desertion from the army on the ground that Lincoln had deliberately deceived the nation as to the real purpose of the war. Joseph Medill noted that "the leaders of the Democratic Party are fast swinging that powerful organization into an attitude of serious hostility to the Government." As so-called "Peace Democrats" added to the Northern discouragement by declaring the South to be unbeatable, and clamoring for a negotiated peace—heedless of the fact that the Confederacy had shown no disposition whatever to negotiate except on terms of Southern independence—a spirit of defeatism spread through the Northern people and the Union army.

After Hooker's promotion to the command of the Army of the Potomac, Burnside had been put in charge of the Military Department of the Ohio, which embraced the Midwestern states. In the southernmost areas of his command, dislike of slavery carried with it an inborn hatred of the Negro and fear that emancipation would permit him to migrate northward. Burnside encountered such open opposition to the government in that area that on April 13, 1863 he ordered that all persons within his lines who expressed sympathy for the enemy should be arrested, tried by court martial, and, if found guilty, sent "into the lines of their friends." More serious offenses would be punished by death. "It must be distinctly understood," the general warned, "that treason, express or implied, will not be tolerated in this department."

Most venomous of the Democratic malcontents was tall, bearded Clement L. Vallandigham, a member of Congress who had been defeated for re-election by a Republican gerrymander of his district. As a "lame duck" Congressman, the defiant, austere Vallandigham upbraided the administration for a useless sacrifice of blood and money. "Defeat, debt, taxation, sepulchres, are your trophies," he declaimed to a packed session of the House of Representatives. "In vain the people gave you treasure, and the soldier yielded up his life. War for the Union has been abandoned and war for the slave begun. With what success? Let the dead at Fredericksburg and Vicksburg answer. Ought this war to continue? I answer no—not a day, not an hour. What then? Shall we separate? Again I answer no, no, no. Stop fighting. Make an armistice. Accept at once foreign mediation."

In meetings throughout Ohio, Vallandigham spoke violently against the war and the despotism of the Lincoln government. Its purpose, he said, was to free the slaves and enslave the whites; to allow the war to continue would mean the end of civil liberties. He spat upon Burnside's obnoxious order. With the government about to draw the first names in a draft, he declared that free men who would tolerate conscription deserved to lose their freedom.

At Mount Vernon, Ohio, where the agitator held forth with extreme rancor, an officer in civilian dress, dispatched from Burnside's headquarters, slouched against the platform, jotting down choice samples of invective. Three days later Union soldiers took Vallandigham from his home at night and brought him to a military prison in Cincinnati. Despite his indignant professions of loyalty, a military commission sentenced him to confinement for the duration of the war. Burnside approved the sentence. A Federal judge denied a motion for a writ of *habeas corpus.*

The arrest took Lincoln by surprise. Had he known of Burnside's intention, he would probably have disapproved, though he appreciated the knotty problems faced by his commanders and did not wish to weaken their authority. But he also recognized the danger of playing into the hands of Peace Democrats and Copperheads by making a martyr of Vallandigham. Taking a cue from Burnside's order, and probably with appreciation of the wry humor of his action, on May 26 he commuted Vallandigham's sentence to banishment within the Confederate lines. A cavalry detachment conducted the agitator to a point near Murfreesboro, Tennessee, where it turned him over to a puzzled Confederate outpost.

The Democratic press played up the incident as typical Republican tyranny. Speakers denounced the President. Mass meetings adopted scarehead resolutions. Was all criticism of the government forbidden? Had the people lost the cherished right of free speech?

In a long reply to one set of hostile resolutions, adopted by the Ohio Democratic state convention, Lincoln conceded that denunciation would be justified if the government had acted merely to promote its political prospects. But Vallandigham's outbursts, by impeding enlistments and encouraging desertion, were damaging the army, the mainstay of the nation's existence. "Must I shoot a simple-minded soldier boy who deserts," asked

Lincoln, "while I must not touch a hair of the wiley [*sic*] agitator who induces him to desert? This is none the less injurious when effected by getting a father, or brother, or friend, into a public meeting, and there working upon his feelings, till he is persuaded to write the soldier boy, that he is fighting in a bad cause, for a wicked administration of a contemptible government, too weak to arrest and punish him if he shall desert. I think that in such a case, to silence the agitator, and save the boy, is not only constitutional, but, withal a great mercy."

*

A L L spring the hostile armies had faced each other across the Rappahannock. On June 5, 1863 Hooker telegraphed Lincoln that the Confederates were breaking up their camp. Expecting Lee to cross the river north of Fredericksburg, Hooker proposed to move directly on Richmond; but Lincoln warned: "I would not take any risk of being entangled upon the river, like an ox jumped half over a fence and liable to be torn by dogs front and rear without a fair chance to gore one way or kick the other." Lee's army, not Richmond, should be Hooker's objective.

On Sunday, June 14, Washington heard scary rumors that Lee was moving northward. Going to the War Department in the late afternoon, Secretary Welles found Lincoln at the telegraph office in serious consultation with Halleck and Stanton. Welles asked what Hooker was doing—if Lee's army was spread out in marching columns, here might be Hooker's chance for a decisive stroke. Lincoln, with the same thought, had already wired Hooker: "If the head of Lee's army is at Martinsburg and the tail of it on the plank road between Fredericksburg and Chancellorsville, the animal must be very slim somewhere. Could you not break him?"

Monday brought news that General Milroy's force at Winchester had been wiped out. Martinsburg was isolated. Confederate troops were reported as far north as Chambersburg in Pennsylvania. No one knew Lee's destination. It might be Washington, Harrisburg, Baltimore, or Philadelphia.

As the Army of the Potomac moved northward to counter the Confederate threat, a long, slow-burning animosity between Hooker and Halleck flared. For some time Hooker had bypassed Halleck and communicated directly with the President. Halleck protested that such action threatened the efficiency of the army. "To remove all misunderstanding," Lincoln wired Hooker, "I now place you in the strict military relation to Gen. Halleck, of a commander of one of the armies, to the General-in-Chief of all the armies. I have not intended differently, but as it seems to be differently understood, I shall direct him to give you orders, and you to obey them." In a letter of explanation Lincoln assured Hooker of his support, as well as Halleck's, and pleaded for the same frankness between the two generals that he showed toward each of them. "I need and must have the professional skill of both," he urged, "and yet these suspicions tend to deprive me of both. . . . Now, all I ask is that you will be in such mood that we can get into our action the best cordial judgment of yourself and General Halleck, with my poor mite added, if indeed he and you shall think it entitled to any consideration at all."

A fog of rumor settled over Washington as Jeb Stuart's hard-riding Southern cavalry skirted south and east of Hooker's columns. Proud, devil-may-care Stuart, smarting under a recent defeat by General Alfred Pleasonton at Brandy Station, was out to recover lost éclat with a wide-swinging raid around the Union army—an exploit he had twice performed against McClellan. His raid was to prove costly to Lee by depriving him of intelligence of Federal movements; but it spread panic through the North. The Confederates were reported at Leesburg, at Carlisle, at York; western Maryland and southern Pennsylvania seemed overrun with them.

With the Confederates thrusting ever deeper into Pennsylvania, and with the North in fright, Lincoln faced the breakdown of his high command. As Hooker approached Frederick, Maryland, he demanded that the garrison at Maryland Heights, overlooking Harpers Ferry, be sent to join him. Halleck refused—he thought the important railroad bridge at Harpers Ferry should be defended as long as possible. Hooker asked to be relieved of command.

This action forced a showdown. Either Hooker or Halleck must be replaced. Except for his lapse at Chancellorsville, the tart-tongued Hooker had done well. But might he not show the same indecision in a crisis as before? Could the President trust a general who resigned on the eve of battle? Lincoln decided in favor of "Old Brains." He had received numerous telegrams imploring him to restore McClellan to command, but on Sunday morning, June 28, he informed the cabinet that General George Gordon Meade would replace Hooker.

Only Stanton and Seward had been consulted beforehand. Most of the cabinet knew little about the solemn, modest, quick-tempered Meade, the fifth general to command the Eastern army within a year. A West Point product, like his predecessors, a veteran of the Army of the Potomac who was still bothered by two bullet wounds taken at Frayser's Farm, Meade was a steady, hard-working general who had avoided aligning himself with army cliques. Tall and spare, with a full beard and thinning hair well streaked with gray, he had a Roman cast of countenance. His troops knew "the damned old goggle-eyed snapping turtle" as a careful, dogged fighter. If they never learned to love him, they respected and trusted him.

*

TRAMPING the hot turnpikes of southern Pennsylvania, the lean marchers from the South moved through pleasant, fertile valleys creased by rocky hills. It was a land of broad-backed horses and heavy-uddered cows, of big red barns and neat stone houses. One of Lee's purposes was to carry the war away from the ravaged regions of Virginia to this unspoiled land of plenty.

Fumbling toward each other like a pair of sidling crabs, the two great armies approached the quiet little town of Gettysburg, where a number of roads converged. Believing that a battle was imminent, Lincoln canceled the cabinet meeting scheduled for June 30 and spent the day with Stanton and Halleck.

July 1 brought news of heavy fighting. Heth's division of A. P. Hill's corps, hoping to find new shoes in Gettysburg, had encountered Buford's cavalry northwest of the town. The dismounted Union troopers held on grimly, while both sides rushed up reinforcements. Sharp fighting, with heavy casualties, lasted throughout the day. By late afternoon the Union troops were overmatched, and retreated grudgingly through the town to encamp on a fishhook ridge just south of it, some regiments bivouacking among the tombstones in the village cemetery.

Both armies lumbered up throughout the night. Union troops, coming in at daybreak, were oppressed by the sultry heat. Along the ridge that ran south from the Gettysburg cemetery, regiments and batteries moved into position. Men loomed like tall specters in the mist; the guns of the frowning batteries looked gigantic. Lee had not meant to bring on a major engagement, but now he determined to fight it out.

Stubborn "Dutch" Longstreet, distrustful of Lee's plan of battle, was slow to get his troops in motion against the Union left; the Federal troops waiting on Cemetery Ridge began to think the day might pass without a battle. But shortly after two o'clock Longstreet's massed cannon spoke. Desperate fighting lasted throughout the remainder of the day. Thrown back at some positions, the Confederates clung tenaciously to part of the ground they had won.

That night, as the rattle of ambulances broke the stillness of the battlefield, and men with flickering lanterns sought the wounded, Lincoln trudged wearily to the White House from his long vigil at the War Department. Deep lines furrowed his melancholy face.

July 3 dawned terrifically hot. Lincoln came to the War Department as soon as he awoke. At seven o'clock a dispatch from Chief Quartermaster Rufus Ingalls, sent at eight thirty the night before but somehow delayed in transmission, reported: "at this moment the battle is raging as fiercely as ever. . . . The loss has been great on both sides. All our forces have been, and still are in action, and we shall be compelled to stand and fight it out."

Only fragmentary information came over the wire throughout the day as the two great armies locked in bloody grip.

Meade, having called a council of war the preceding evening, decided to hold his position and let the Confederates attack. Over in the Confederate camp on Seminary Ridge, Longstreet judged that this was what Meade wanted and argued strongly against it. But Lee's fighting blood was up. Furthermore, it seemed less dangerous to attack than to retreat. Lee planned his crucial effort against the Union center—pierced momentarily the day before, but now reinforced, entrenched, and bristling with heavy guns.

The concussion of a hundred cannon heralded the assault. A hoarse roar shook the shallow valley that lay between the armies as Meade's guns replied, searching out Confederate batteries, probing for the assaulting columns forming in the woods across the way. On the crest of Cemetery Ridge the Union infantry hugged the ground and suffered little damage, but the Confederate fire took heavy toll among the sweating gunners. Branches crashed down from splintered trees. Cannon swerved and slumped on shattered wheels. Exploded limberboxes threw fire and tearing fragments all around them. Shells found corrals of battery horses; they pulled and reared and screamed in tortured fright. Bleeding men stumbled toward the rear. For two hours the blazing tongues of heavy guns spat death across the valley in a bombardment such as the world had never known. The sun peered luridly through smoke and sulphur fumes.

The firing lulled. Federal soldiers gripped their muskets tighter as dull gray masses surged from the woods a mile away. Horsemen galloped among the forming regiments. A forest of slanting rifles caught the sunlight. Red flags rippled above the columns. Lee was throwing fifteen thousand men into a massed assault—nine thousand in the first wave, six thousand in support, Pettigrew's North Carolinians, Pickett's Virginians, the flower of the Army of Northern Virginia.

Federal skirmishers in the valley dropped back with a spattering fire. The guns bellowed again. As the range shortened, the Federal artillerymen changed to shrapnel, then to canister. The guns jumped and jolted like things alive as the grimy gunners rammed home the charge, stood by, rushed to reload, while officers pleaded: "Feed it to them! Feed it to them!"

The torn ranks of the Confederates closed up. Pettigrew's men hesitated, but still came on. The Virginians never faltered. The column paused to re-form in a swale. Ahead lay the last two hundred yards of fire-swept slope.

Union breastworks flamed with rifle fire. The gray horde stopped—to pour in one raking volley. Then all was wild disorder on the crest. Blue and gray swirled in a fighting mass. Sharp yells and shrieks cut through the murmuring growl. The issue hung in balance for a moment, but the Confederate strength had been spent. The gray wave broke. The backwash drifted down the slope and eddied back across the crimsoned valley. The Union guns smashed into it again.

Late in the afternoon Lincoln read a telegram from General Robert C. Schenck in Baltimore: "I learn that the suffering near the battlefield at Gettysburg and beyond is terrible, in the want of sufficient medical attendance, food, and other help."

*

AT MIDNIGHT Lincoln, still watchfully waiting at the War Department, remained uncertain of the outcome, but the news seemed good. Throughout Independence Day he analyzed dispatches and wondered if the battle would be resumed. The following day brought news of Lee's retreat. A wagon train of wounded had started toward Chambersburg.

Reports of casualties came in. The Union loss would reach 23,000 out of 93,000 engaged, the Confederate probably 30,000 out of 70,000. Pickett's division had lost 3,392 of its 4,500 men, including all commanders of brigades and regiments.

The War Department rushed 20,000 fresh troops to Meade. Lincoln urged him to follow up his victory with another stunning blow before Lee crossed the Potomac. But three days passed with nothing more than skirmishing.

At a cabinet meeting on July 7 Lincoln looked despondent. In response to a serenade that night he said: "These are trying occasions, not only in success, but for the want of success." A telegram from Meade the next morning depressed him further. Lee had reached the Potomac and, finding it swollen by heavy rains, with all the fords impassable, had thrown up entrenchments. "I expect to find the enemy in a strong position," warned Meade, "well covered with artillery, and I do not desire to imitate his example at Gettysburg and assault a position where the chances are greatly against success. I wish in advance to moderate the expectations of those who in ignorance of the difficulties to be encountered may expect too much."

That afternoon an aide handed Gideon Welles a telegram from Admiral Porter. Welles read the message and almost jumped for joy. Vicksburg had surrendered to General Grant! Welles hurried to the White House on pumping legs. Lincoln was sitting at a table tracing certain of Grant's movements on a map for Chase and three or four others. He leaped up at the news and, throwing his arms around the stocky Welles, exclaimed: "What can we do for the Secretary of the Navy for this glorious intelligence? He is always giving us good news. I cannot in words tell you of my joy over this result. It is great, Mr. Welles! It is great!"

At Lincoln's direction Halleck immediately wired Meade: "We have certain information that Vicksburg surrendered to General Grant on the Fourth of July. Now, if General Meade can complete his work so gloriously prosecuted thus far, by the literal or substantial destruction of Lee's army, the rebellion will be over."

Further news from Vicksburg told of Grant's having taken 31,600 prisoners and 172 guns. On July 9 the roll of prisoners increased to almost 38,000, when Port Hudson, the last Confederate stronghold on the Mississippi, surrendered to General Banks.

The news of two great victories put the North in a transport of joy. Bells pealed in cities, towns, and villages. Cannon boomed salutes. A wave of optimism forced down the price of gold in terms of greenback paper money. Lincoln sent a letter of congratulation to General Grant: "I do not remember that you and I have ever met personally. I write this now as a grateful acknowledgment for the almost inestimable service you have done the country. I wish to say a word further. When you first reached the vicinity of Vicksburg, I thought you should do, what you finally did—march the troops across the neck, run the batteries with the transports, and thus go below; and I never had any faith, except a general hope that you knew better than I, that the Yazoo Pass expedition, and the like, would succeed. When you got below, and took Port-Gibson, Grand Gulf, and vicinity, I thought you should go down the river and join Gen. Banks, and when you turned Northward, East of the Big Black, I feared it was a mistake. I now wish to make the personal acknowledgment that you were right and I was wrong."

*

LINCOLN and Halleck continued to urge Meade to attack. But a reconnaissance on the morning of July 13 revealed that Lee had crossed the river in the night. When Lincoln learned that Meade had congratulated his army on "driving the enemy from our soil," he shook his head in discouragement. "This is a dreadful reminiscence of McClellan," he complained; "it is the same spirit that moved him to claim a great victory because 'Pennsylvania and Maryland were safe.' Will our generals never get that idea out of their heads? The whole country is our soil."

Halleck telegraphed Meade: "I need hardly say to you that the escape of Lee's army without another battle has created great dissatisfaction in the mind of the President." Meade asked to be relieved of his command. Lincoln wrote him a long letter of explanation: he was grateful for Meade's "magnificent success," and sorry to cause him the slightest pain, but he was in such deep distress himself that he could not restrain some expression of it. Meade had fought and beaten the enemy. Losses had been equally severe. Lee's retreat had been halted by a flood. Meade had been reinforced, while Lee could not possibly have received a single new recruit; yet Meade had waited for the river to subside, for bridges to be built, and for Lee to withdraw at his leisure. "Again, my dear general," wrote the President, "I do not believe you appreciate the magnitude of the misfortune involved in Lee's escape. He was within your easy grasp, and to have closed upon him would, in connection with our other late successes, have ended the war. As it is, the war will be prolonged indefinitely. If you could not safely attack Lee last monday, how can you possibly do so South of the river, when you can take with you very few more than two thirds of the force you then had in hand? It would be unreasonable to expect, and I do not expect you can now effect much. Your golden opportunity is gone, and I am distressed immeasurably because of it.

"I beg you will not consider this a prossecution [*sic*] or persecution of yourself. As you had learned that I was dissatisfied, I have thought it best to kindly tell you why."

Then Lincoln thought of Meade's magnificent fight at Gettysburg, and of how the general had dutifully taken command at a critical time. Perhaps the President remembered that there is no such thing as certainty in war—that it was too much to say that an attack was sure to succeed. His letter would probably cost the services of a conscientious general. Lincoln folded it and placed it in an envelope on which he wrote: "To Gen. Meade, never sent or signed."

But the lesson of Gettysburg and Vicksburg was not lost on the President; the contrast in commanders confirmed his judgment of Grant. Meade had fought magnificently in a battle forced upon him. But Grant had seized and kept the initiative in the face of grave discouragements, and had been satisfied with nothing less than the annihilation of his foe. Grant had another quality that Lincoln deemed essential in a general: he recognized the subordination of the army to the civil government. When Lincoln ordered him to assist General Lorenzo Thomas in recruiting Negro troops in Mississippi, Grant, who favored such enlistments, had replied: "You may rely upon it I will give him all the aid in my power. I would do this whether the arming the negro seemed to me a wise policy or not, because it is an order that I am bound to obey and I do not feel that in my position I have a right to question any policy of the government."

Here was the sort of general Lincoln sought for top command. But he could not yet be spared in the West.

*

THE UNION victories at Gettysburg and Vicksburg marked a turning-point in the war. Never again would the Confederacy command sufficient power to invade the North in force or to impose peace through military victory. The blockade squeezed more tightly as Union amphibious operations sealed off seaports one by one. Federal command of the Mississippi split off Texas, Arkansas, and western Louisiana and largely ended Confederate foreign trade through Mexico.

But the South was far from defeated. Determined attacks on Charleston had all failed. Sleek, black-hulled blockade-runners crept in and out at Mobile, Savannah, and Wilmington. Confederate forces west of the Mississippi, resorting to guerrilla tactics when too weak to fight pitched battles, kept large Federal forces occupied.

Heavy losses of field officers were beginning to handicap Lee, but the Confederacy still had reserves of manpower. Georgia, Alabama, and the Carolinas, relatively untouched by war, provided ample food supplies. Village forges and foundries throughout the South pounded out guns, shot, and shell casings to supplement the output of converted factories and the Tredegar Iron Works at Richmond. By remaining on the defensive the South could still win victories, make the North pay dearly for every small success, and perhaps exhaust the Northern will to win. Lincoln's paramount problem now would be to convince the Northern people of the worth of further sacrifices.

The most pressing Northern need was increased manpower. Some states, unable to meet their quotas otherwise, had already resorted to conscription. An act of March 3, 1863 put the draft on a national basis.

The law had numerous faults. Provisions whereby any drafted man could escape service by hiring a substitute or paying three hundred dollars commutation justified complaints that it was "a rich man's war and a poor man's fight." Lincoln disliked the commutation feature of the law, and on June 8, 1864 recommended its repeal, but Congress failed to change it.

Since volunteers were credited against a district's quota, states, cities, and counties, to escape the compulsion of the draft, offered bounties to volunteers. Some communities raised money for mass exemptions, and recruiting agents invaded the conquered areas of the South to fill state quotas with Negroes. But the practice of offering cash rewards encouraged "bounty-jumping"—men would enlist, collect their bounties, desert, and enlist again, sometimes repeating the process many times.

Although the draft produced only about 46,000 conscripts and 118,000 substitutes, it served its real purpose of inducing large enlistments; during the time that the various draft laws were in effect, more than a million persons volunteered.

With the first spin of the conscription wheels, however, a wave of opposition swept the North. Resistance was encountered in Illinois, Ohio, Wisconsin, Indiana, Missouri, Kentucky, and the hard-coal region of Pennsylvania. Riots broke out in Boston, Troy, and Newark.

Most of these disturbances were quickly quelled, but in New York City a mob smashed into one draft office, broke the wheel, fired the building, and went raging through the streets. Overpowering the police, the rioters wrecked other draft offices and looted saloons, jewelry stores, and groceries. Race hatred leered; Negroes were lynched and beaten; the mob set fire to a colored orphanage. On July 14, the second day of rioting, Lincoln wired his son Robert, who was stopping at the Fifth Avenue Hotel: "Why do I hear no more from you?" For four days the mob controlled the city. Estimates of the dead ranged from 500 to

1,200. More than a million dollars' worth of property was destroyed. Sailors from a gunboat in the harbor, a company of cadets from West Point, and troops rushed from Meade's army helped the police to restore order.

Tall, dark-eyed Governor Seymour, who had made a spineless plea to the rioters from the steps of City Hall, urged Lincoln to suspend the draft until the Supreme Court could decide on its validity. Seymour, as a leader of those Democrats who claimed to be loyal to the Union but resisted Lincoln's alleged seizure of unconstitutional powers, had opposed the Emancipation Proclamation, denounced Vallandigham's arrest, and disapproved of the Conscription Act as unconstitutional, unfair, and unnecessary. Greeley and other Republican editors reviled Seymour as a Copperhead, but Lincoln treated his opposition as born of honest conviction. He would welcome an opinion from the Supreme Court, he replied to the Governor, but he could not wait for it. He must have soldiers, for the enemy was driving every able-bodied man into the ranks "very much as a butcher drives bullocks into a slaughter-pen." He would give New York all possible credits for enlistments, but the draft must go on.

Lincoln was not responsible for the deficiencies of the draft law; he was obliged to administer it as Congress had framed it. But much of his time had to be spent in explanation and adjustment of various governors' complaints. "My purpose," he wrote to Seymour, "is to be . . . just and constitutional; and yet practical, in performing the important duty, with which I am charged, of maintaining the unity, and free principles of our common country." About a month later the draft was quietly resumed in New York City.

*

FOR six months, while Grant clawed and crunched at Vicksburg, Rosecrans remained encamped near Murfreesboro. Lincoln pleaded with him to advance into East Tennessee to prevent Johnston's relieving Vicksburg, but Rosecrans found numerous reasons for inactivity—poor roads, bad weather, lack of essential supplies.

When Rosecrans at last advanced toward Chattanooga late in July, Lincoln questioned the likelihood of success, now that large Confederate detachments were free to concentrate against him. "Do not misunderstand," he wrote; "I am not casting blame upon you. I rather think by great exertion, you can get to East Tennessee. But a very important question is, Can you stay there? . . . And now, be assured once more, that I think of you in all kindness and confidence; and that I am not watching you with an evil-eye."

By September 9 Rosecrans, maneuvering skillfully through the mountains, forced Bragg to evacuate Chattanooga, the entryway to Georgia and an important railroad junction. But from Charles A. Dana, whom Stanton had dispatched to Rosecrans in his usual role of observer, came disquieting reports of the rumored arrival of Longstreet with 20,000 men from the Army of Northern Virginia, and of other Confederate reinforcements sent to Bragg by Johnston. Two hundred miles to the northeast, however, the Union outlook was better; General Burnside, in another movement into East Tennessee, had driven the Confederates from Knoxville. Lincoln read Dana's warnings and ordered Burnside to rush troops to Rosecrans's aid.

On the night of Sunday, September 20, John Hay rode to the Soldiers' Home, outside of Washington, where Lincoln often slept during the hot summer, to bring the President to a conference called by Stanton. Lincoln felt extremely worried; it was the first time Stanton had ever summoned him from his sleep. Seward and Chase were already at the War Department when Lincoln arrived. Halleck and other officials soon came in. Dispatches from Dana told of a terrible battle along Chickamauga Creek. The whole Union right had seemed to melt away in a rout reminiscent of Bull Run. Dana had seen the road to Chattanooga choked with baggage wagons, artillery, ambulances, loose mules, and frightened men. Rosecrans admitted "a serious disaster, extent not yet ascertained."

Lincoln remained in Washington all night. The next day's reports were less discouraging. General George H. Thomas, posting his 25,000 men along a horseshoe crest, had repulsed repeated attacks with heavy slaughter. One of his brigades had flung itself on the enemy with bayonets when ammunition failed. The Union army had withdrawn to Chattanooga, but Rosecrans warned: "We have no certainty of holding our position here. If Burnside could come immediately it would be well."

Stanton asked Halleck the number of men available at Knoxville. Had Burnside sent help to Rosecrans as ordered? When it developed that Burnside had been occupied in pursuing a party of guerrillas, Lincoln wrote: "It makes me doubt whether I am awake or dreaming. I have been struggling for ten days, first through Gen. Halleck, and then directly, to get you to go to assist Gen. Rosecrans in an extremity, and you have repeatedly declared you would do it, and yet you steadily move the contrary way." Lincoln endorsed the note: "Not sent," but ordered Burnside: "Go to Rosecrans with your force without a moment's delay."

Hooker was detached from the Army of the Potomac and rushed to Chattanooga with 30,000 men. Dana reported that the Confederates had occupied Missionary Ridge and Lookout Mountain. Their batteries controlled the Tennessee River and the road from Bridgeport, Alabama, where the railroad from Nashville had been cut. The back roads into Chattanooga were bottomless mud. Forage and supplies in the vicinity of the city became exhausted. The troops went on half-rations.

Lincoln wired Rosecrans to hold on; Burnside and Grant were both sending help. Chattanooga held such strategic importance, he declared in a note to Halleck, that if Rosecrans could maintain his position "without more, this rebellion can only eke out a short and feeble existence, as an animal sometimes may with a thorn in its vitals." Lincoln's chief concern was Rosecrans's state of mind; Dana reported that the general seemed to be losing his grip; Lincoln told Hay that he acted "stunned, like a duck hit on the head."

Fortunately for Rosecrans, President Davis intervened about this time. Visiting Bragg's army, he proposed that Longstreet be sent to destroy Burnside. At this very juncture Lincoln telegraphed Rosecrans: "I now think the enemy will not attack Chattanooga; and I think you will have to look out for his making a concentrated drive at Burnside. You and Burnside now have him by the throat; and he must break your hold, or perish. . . . Sherman *is* coming to you, though gaps in the telegraph prevent our knowing how far he is advanced. He and Hooker will so support you on the West & North-West, as to enable you to look East & North East."

On October 17 General Grant, at Cairo, received an order to proceed to the Galt House, in Louisville, Kentucky, where an officer from the War Department would meet him with instructions. Within an hour Grant was on his way by rail via Indianapolis. There, just as his train pulled out, a messenger came hurrying to stop it; the Secretary of War had that minute arrived by special train and wished to see General Grant. The two men had never met.

Stanton accompanied Grant to Louisville. Soon after the train started, he handed the general two orders from Lincoln, of which Grant could take his choice. Both created the Military Division of the Mississippi, composed of the Departments of the Ohio, the Cumberland, and the Tennessee and embracing all the area between the Alleghenies and the Mississippi except the territory occupied by Banks in the Southwest. Both put Grant in command of this division. The only particular in which the orders differed was that one left the department commanders as they were, while the other assigned Thomas to Rosecrans's place. Grant accepted the second order.

That evening at Louisville, Stanton received a dispatch from Dana informing him that Rosecrans planned to retreat. Grant immediately wired Thomas to assume command and to hold Chattanooga at all hazards. A reply came back: "We will hold Chattanooga till we starve."

Grant arrived at the Bridgeport railhead on October 21.

From there he must travel fifty-five miles on horseback over gullied mountain roads. An injury sustained in a fall from his horse had put him on crutches, and he had to be carried over washouts in the road. On the 23rd, six days after he received the message at Cairo, the stubby, persistent general rode into Chattanooga and took command. Within a week he had gained control of the Tennessee River and opened the road from Bridgeport. Within another week Grant's supply lines were secure and his troops were back on full rations.

*

MEANWHILE, with the off-year elections approaching, the Democrats were laboring to their utmost. Lincoln, knowing that he could not maintain the war without the support of the people, watched developments closely. The critical area was the Midwest, where the arrest of Vallandigham and the activities of the secret societies brought discontent to a dangerous pitch. The Ohio Democratic convention at Columbus on June 11 showed to what extremes the party of Douglas had drifted when it nominated Vallandigham for governor. Disappointed in his reception at the South, the agitator had removed to Canada, whence he issued provocative addresses to the voters. The South could never be defeated, he declared; the administration should negotiate a peace. He denounced Lincoln's "tyranny." The Democrats held rousing meetings. A few riots took place. In the President's own city of Springfield, Illinois, a huge mass meeting on June 17 listened to furious oratory and adopted peace resolutions.

The Republicans, appealing to loyal Democrats to join them, campaigned as the National Union Party. In Springfield they planned a record-breaking turnout on September 3 to counteract the influence of the previous Copperhead meeting. All persons unconditionally devoted to the Union were invited to attend, and the committee on arrangements asked Lincoln to come and speak. Business kept him in Washington, but he took advantage of the occasion to put his views before the country in a long letter addressed to his old friend James C. Conkling, chairman of the committee.

Lincoln expressed gratitude for the support of all true Union men—all those "whom no partisan malice or partisan hope can make false to the nation's life." Some persons were dissatisfied with him, he said, because they wanted peace and blamed him for not bringing it. But peace could be attained in only one of three ways: first, by suppressing the rebellion, which he was earnestly trying to do; second, by giving up the Union, which he would never do; and third, through some sort of compromise, which he believed impossible except on terms of Southern independence. If the South should offer any peace proposals contemplating the maintenance of the Union, Lincoln would neither reject them nor keep them secret.

Besides those persons who were dissatisfied that he did not bring peace, Lincoln continued, there were others who disapproved of his actions respecting the Negro. Many declared that they would not fight for the Negro. Lincoln did not ask them to, he said; he asked them to fight for the Union. But the Negro, to whatever extent he could aid the Union cause, left so much the less that white soldiers must do. Some military commanders believed that emancipation was the heaviest blow yet dealt to the rebellion. The nation required the Negroes' help; but they, like other persons, acted from motives. They must be given an incentive. "Why should they do any thing for us, if we will do nothing for them? If they stake their lives for us, they must be prompted by the strongest motive—even the promise of freedom. And the promise being made, must be kept."

The signs looked better, Lincoln declared. "The Father of Waters again goes unvexed to the sea. . . . And while those who have cleared the great river may well be proud, even that is not all. It is hard to say that anything has been more bravely, and well done than at Antietam, Murfreesboro, Gettysburg, and on many fields of lesser note. Nor must Uncle Sam's Web-feet be forgotten. . . . Not only on the deep sea, the broad bay, and the rapid river; but also up the narrow muddy bayou, and wherever the ground was a little damp, they have been, and made their tracks. Thanks to all. For the great republic—for the principle it lives by, and keeps alive—for man's vast future— thanks to all.

"Peace does not appear so distant as it did. I hope it will come soon, and come to stay; and so come as to be worth the keeping in all future time. It will then have been proved that, among free men, there can be no successful appeal from the ballot to the bullet. . . . And then, there will be some black men who can remember that, with silent tongue, and clenched teeth, and steady eye, and well-poised bayonet, they have helped mankind on to this great consummation; while I fear there will be some white ones, unable to forget that, with malignant heart, and deceitful speech, they have strove to hinder it.

"Still, let us not be over-sanguine of a speedy final triumph. Let us be quite sober. Let us diligently apply the means, never doubting that a just God, in his own good time, will give us the rightful result."

Picturesquely eloquent, Lincoln's letter revealed a man chastened by responsibility, trusting in the intelligence of the people, and in God. The *New York Times* rated it a masterpiece: "Even the Copperhead gnaws upon it as vainly as a viper upon a file. The most consummate rhetorician never used language more pat and to the purpose, and still there is not a word not familiar to the plainest plowman. He 'hits the nail upon the head.' In spite of all the hard trials and the hard words to which he has been exposed, Abraham Lincoln is today the most popular man in the Republic. All the denunciation and all the arts of the demagogue are perfectly powerless to wean the people from their faith in him." But to the Democratic New York *World* the President's letter exhibited only a "homely untutored shrewdness," that sort of "vulgar honesty" which prevails in every country town.

Ohio and Pennsylvania balloted on October 14. Lincoln confided to Welles that he felt more anxious than when he had been a candidate himself in 1860. Early returns from Ohio showed

John Brough, the Union candidate for governor, leading Vallandigham in an election that would measure the people's loyalty. About ten o'clock Lincoln telegraphed to Columbus: "Where is John Brough?" He was in the telegraph office, came the answer. "Brough, what is your majority now?" wired Lincoln. "Over 30,000." At midnight Brough reported "over 50,000"; at five next morning, "over 100,000." "Glory to God in the highest," wired Lincoln, "Ohio has saved the Nation."

The Pennsylvania returns were equally encouraging. Loyal Governor Andrew G. Curtin won handsomely over Judge G. W. Woodward, who in 1861 had said: "If the Union is to be divided, I want the line of separation to run north of Pennsylvania."

The elections in November showed the same favorable trend. The Union ticket carried every Northern state except New Jersey. Several emancipationist candidates won in the border states. Springfield went Unionist by 138 votes, with a gain of 440 over 1862. *Harper's Weekly* credited the outcome to the President, who had stood above party to command the loyalty of Union-loving people. Sumner declared that Lincoln's "true and noble" letter to Conkling had proved unanswerable. Sardonic Zach Chandler confessed that, while Lincoln moved more slowly than some persons wished, "when he puts his foot down, he is there."

*

S o o n after the Battle of Gettysburg the Governors of eighteen Northern states had appointed trustees to establish a new cemetery where the hastily buried dead might be reinterred. The dedication was scheduled for Thursday, November 19. Edward Everett, the celebrated Massachusetts orator, had consented to be the speaker of the occasion. David Wills, chairman of the cemetery board, acting on behalf of Governor Curtin, sent invitations to the President, his cabinet, the members of Congress, the diplomatic corps, and numerous state dignitaries, and asked the President to make a few appropriate remarks. Not many of these persons were expected to attend, however, and it was assumed that the crowd would be essentially local.

The pressure of business obliged Lincoln to decline most invitations to public functions, but late in September Charles Sumner had brought him a letter from John Murray Forbes, the prominent Boston businessman, in which Forbes asserted that the President's letter to Conkling had proved so effective in bringing people to a correct attitude on the Negro question that he should now set the public mind aright on the true issue of the war. "People at a distance have discovered this better than most of us who are in the midst of it," Forbes declared. "Our friends abroad see it! John Bright and his glorious band of European Republicans see that we are fighting for Democracy or (to get rid of the technical name) for liberal institutions. The Democrats and liberals of the old world are as much and as heartily with us as any supporters we have on this side.

"Our enemies too see it in the same light. The Aristocrats and the Despots of the old world see that our quarrel is that of the People against an Aristocracy. . . .

"My suggestion then is that you should seize an early opportunity and any subsequent chance to teach your great audience of *plain people* that the war is not North against South but *the People against the Aristocrats.* If you can place this in the same strong light that you have the Negro question you will settle it in men's minds as you have that."

Forbes's letter had nothing to do with shaping Lincoln's opinions—he had entertained a similar view of the war from the beginning. But it may have induced him to accept the invitation to Gettysburg. At any rate, the cabinet members were surprised when he announced that he would go. He had little time for preparation, but before leaving Washington he had written a first draft of his remarks, one sheet in ink and a second in pencil.

The simple artistry of Lincoln's language and the impressive earnestness of his appeal indicate the depths of emotion under which he wrote. Perhaps he pictured the setting in his mind—the blue haze softening the outline of the hills where two great armies had locked in stubborn combat for three days; the valley across which brave men, who fought for the right as it was given them to see the right, had swept to death against the Union guns; the ridge where the Union boys hung on with such grim resolution, meeting those brave men with equal bravery.

In that valley, quiet once again, and on those rocky ridges, the President knew he would see thousands of wooden crosses, marking the temporary graves of both Northern and Southern boys, for whom this cemetery would provide a final resting-place. There would be no exultation in his message—Lincoln had never had it in his heart to condemn the South. His thoughts went back to the Founding Fathers, then forward into the far reach of time.

On November 18 Tad Lincoln was gravely ill, and Mrs. Lincoln, remembering Willie, was tense and nervous. But the President felt obliged to keep his appointment, and with his party boarded a special train, which arrived at Gettysburg at sundown.

Lincoln was the guest of Mr. Wills, whose house fronted on the public square. Thousands of people had already gathered in the town, and more were arriving constantly. A military band blared in the square. Serenaders roamed the streets under a harvest moon. Lincoln answered their calls with a brief greeting, then retired to his room about ten o'clock. Telegrams from Stanton reported quiet on all fighting fronts, and relayed a message from Mrs. Lincoln that Tad felt better. Lincoln made some minor revisions in his address. Next morning he recopied it.

The straggling official procession wended toward the cemetery, the President looking ungainly on a horse too small for him. At least fifteen thousand persons were on hand. Souvenir-hunters were gleaning the battlefield for bullets, buttons, and shell fragments. Those who ventured to more distant areas found the skeletons of horses still unburied. Coffins lay scattered here and there.

For two hours Everett's rich mellow voice rose and fell as he rendered his memorized oration. His gestures were faultless. He had mastered all the arts of eloquence. When he finished, Ward Hill Lamon introduced the President. Lincoln rose, put on his spectacles, and unfolded his single sheet of manuscript.

He did not read from it closely, but merely glanced at it from time to time.

"Four score and seven years ago," he said, "our fathers brought forth upon this continent, a new nation, conceived in Liberty, and dedicated to the proposition that all men are created equal.

"Now we are engaged in a great civil war, testing whether that nation, or any nation so conceived, and so dedicated, can long endure. We are met on a great battle-field of that war. We have come to dedicate a portion of it, as a final resting place for those who here gave their lives that that nation might live. It is altogether fitting and proper that we should do this.

"But in a larger sense we can not dedicate—we can not consecrate—we can not hallow this ground. The brave men, living and dead, who struggled here, have consecrated it far above our poor power to add or detract. The world will little note, nor long remember, what we say here, but it can never forget what they did here. It is for us, the living, rather to be dedicated here to the unfinished work which they have, thus far, so nobly advanced. It is rather for us to be here dedicated to the great task remaining before us—that from these honored dead we take increased devotion to that cause for which they here gave the last full measure of devotion—that we here highly resolve that these dead shall not have died in vain; that this nation under God shall have a new birth of freedom; and that government of the people, by the people, for the people, shall not perish from the earth."

The words "under God" do not appear in either the first or second draft of Lincoln's address. They came to him while he spoke. He included them in all three of the copies he made at later dates.

Lincoln had finished almost before the crowd realized he had begun. The applause came tardily. A photographer was still fussing with his tripod when the President sat down.

Reports of the audience's reception of Lincoln's words vary almost as strikingly as the newspaper appraisals of his remarks. The big dailies printed Lincoln's speech, but most of them inconspicuously, as an appendage to Everett's remarks. Country weeklies found it well suited to their limited space and generally gave it a prominent place. Editorial comment followed political alignments. To Democratic editors it fell short of the demands of the occasion. "The cheek of every American must tingle with shame," observed the *Chicago Times*, "as he reads the silly, flat and dishwatery utterances of the man who has to be pointed out to intelligent foreigners as the President of the United States." Republican editors, however, invariably praised the address, if they commented at all. The *Springfield* (Massachusetts) *Republican* thought it "a perfect gem, deep in feeling, compact in thought and expression."

Time has immortalized what Lincoln called his "little speech." In 268 well-chosen words he gave America a chart and compass for the days and years ahead. Demonstrating that our nation's strength lies in rededication to those beliefs to which it was committed at its birth, pleading for steadfastness to democratic principles as the best hope of peace, prosperity, and happiness among mankind, his appeal comes as a strong, clear call to every generation of Americans.

*

W I T H I N a week of his return from Gettysburg, Lincoln lay ill in his high-ceilinged White House bedroom. Physicians diagnosed his ailment as varioloid, a mild form of smallpox. The White House became silent as office-seekers shunned the place. The President remarked ironically that he now had something he could give to everybody.

Propped up with pillows, Lincoln read telegrams from Chattanooga, where Grant, joined at last by Sherman, was ready to attack. Bragg had been weakened by the dispatch of Longstreet's 20,000 men to Knoxville, but his remaining troops were strongly posted on Missionary Ridge and Lookout Mountain. Soon after supper on November 23 Hay brought Lincoln a dispatch from Grant, stating that he had gained a position in the valley between these heights, and a critical battle was imminent. "The President, who had been a little despondent ab[ou]t Grant," recorded Hay, "took heart again." Next day's reports were encouraging: Sherman had a foothold on Missionary Ridge; Hooker's men had carried the point of Lookout Mountain. Grant's casualties were light.

At ten o'clock the night of the 25th a telegram from Grant announced: "Although the battle lasted from early dawn to dark this evening, I believe I am not premature in announcing a complete victory over Bragg. Lookout Mountain Top, all the rifle pits in Chattanooga Valley, and Missionary Ridge entire, have been carried and now held by us. I have no idea of finding Bragg here tomorrow."

A telegram from Dana next morning gave details of the battle. "The storming of the Ridge by our troops was one of the greatest miracles in military history," he reported. "No man who climbs the ascent, by any of the roads that climb along its front, can believe that eighteen thousand men were moved up its broken and crumbling face, unless it was his fortune to witness the deed." Neither Grant nor Thomas had ordered such a charge. Their orders were to take the rifle-pits at the base of the cliff. But the troops, having overrun this first line of entrenchments, had gone on up the mountainside, close on the heels of the Confederates, to capture the batteries on the crest and turn them on the enemy. For the first time in the war a Confederate army had broken in panic.

Early morning of the 27th brought a telegram from Grant: "I am just in from the front. The rout of the enemy is most complete. . . . The pursuit will continue to Red Clay in the morning, for which place I shall start in a few hours."

Grant halted his pursuit to send Sherman to relieve Burnside at Knoxville, where Longstreet, anticipating such a move as soon as he learned of Bragg's defeat, had attacked at once, only to be beaten off with heavy losses. On December 7 Lincoln learned that Sherman had reached Knoxville and that Longstreet was in full retreat toward Virginia. Next day he sent a telegram to Grant: "Understanding that your lodgment at Chattanooga and Knoxville is now secure, I wish to tender you, and all under your command, my more than thanks—my profoundest gratitude—for the skill, courage and perseverance, with which you and they, over so great difficulties, have effected that important object. God bless you all."

Lincoln indicated in a confidential talk with Nicolay that Grant would soon be made commander in chief.

*

LINCOLN wanted to achieve a peace worth keeping, not the sort that breeds another war. He realized the necessity of careful planning—the terms of peace must be thought out, and perhaps applied, in time of war. From the beginning of the conflict he had seized every opportunity, however small, to bring disaffected areas and individuals within the Union fold again. His terms were not exacting: it was enough for him that persons in rebellion should repent. During the first six months of 1862 he had established military governments in Louisiana, Arkansas, and Tennessee, not as a means of suppression, but to bring order so that loyal state governments could be organized.

The chief obstacle to such a program was not the vanquished. Lincoln's problem, as has been the case with other wartime Presidents, was to win acceptance of his terms at home. The radical leaders of his party, wishing to impose stiff penalties on the conquered South, had so far balked his plans. Pontifical Charles Sumner raised the question of Lincoln's authority to deal with the conquered states at all. "So far as I understand Mr. Sumner," Lincoln told John Hay, "he seems in favor of Congress taking from the Executive the power it at present exercises over insurrectionary districts, and assuming it to itself. But when the vital question arises as to the right and privilege of the people of these States to govern themselves, I apprehend there will be little difference among loyal men. . . . The practical matter for discussion is how to keep the rebellious population from overwhelming and outvoting the loyal minority."

In October 1863 General Rosecrans had asked Lincoln, if military affairs progressed favorably and the elections turned out right, "would it not be well to offer a general amnesty to all officers and soldiers in the Rebellion? It would give us moral strength and weaken them very much." Lincoln replied: "I intend doing something like what you suggest whenever the case shall appear ripe enough to have it accepted in the true understanding rather than as a confession of weakness and fear." Anticipating that Lincoln might be contemplating some such conciliatory gesture, Zach Chandler wrote to him from Detroit that only a tough policy would whip the South and win the next election. "Conservatives and traitors are buried together," he declared, "for God's sake don't exhume them. . . . They will smell worse than Lazarus did after he had been buried three days."

With the assembling of Congress in December 1863, however, Lincoln believed the time had come to offer a general plan of reconciliation to the South. He supplemented his annual message with a proclamation guaranteeing a full pardon to persons implicated in the rebellion—except a few major offenders—who would take an oath of loyalty to the Constitution, and swear to support the Emancipation Proclamation, together with all acts of Congress dealing with slaves. The proclamation further promised that when, in any rebellious state, a number of citizens equal to one tenth of the voters in the election of 1860 should reestablish a democratic government, in conformity with the oath of allegiance, it should be recognized as the true government of the state and receive Federal protection.

Lincoln offered no threats if the Southern states rejected his plan. He contemplated no reprisals, no wholesale hangings of "traitors," no transformation of the South into a "desert," no imposition of vengeful military rule. He sought for a genuine reconciliation without retribution or revenge.

In a letter to General Banks in Louisiana four months before, Lincoln had expressed the hope that the people, in establishing a new state government, would adopt some practical system whereby whites and blacks "could gradually live themselves out of their old relation to each other, and both come out better prepared for the new. Education for young blacks should be included in the plan." As a man of Southern origins, Lincoln understood that racial adjustments would take time and careful planning. Inherited and deep-seated prejudices must be acknowledged as realities to be dealt with, because "a universal feeling, whether well or ill-founded," he once said, "cannot be safely disregarded." The important thing was to make a start. If a new state government would recognize the permanent freedom of the Negroes and take measures to prepare them for their new status, Lincoln would not object to temporary restrictions made necessary by "their present condition as a laboring, landless, and homeless class." Provided certain overriding principles were respected, he would allow the Southern people to solve their own race problem.

In March 1864, when Louisiana prepared to draw up a new state constitution in accordance with Lincoln's plan, the President wrote to Michael Hahn, the newly elected Governor: "I congratulate you on having fixed your name in history as the first freestate Governor of Louisiana. Now you are about to have a Convention, which among other things, will probably define the elective franchise. I barely suggest for your private consideration, whether some of the colored people may not be let in—as, for instance, the very intelligent, and especially those who have fought gallantly in our ranks. They will probably help in some trying time to come, to keep the jewel of liberty within the family of freedom. But this is only a suggestion, not to the public, but to you alone."

Lincoln knew that the respective houses of Congress could control the reconstruction process if they chose; through their right to determine the qualifications of their own members they could exclude representatives of restored Southern states. In presenting his plan of reconciliation he did not mean to rule out other plans. While he remained President, he promised, he would neither modify the Emancipation Proclamation nor reenslave any person freed by it or by any act of Congress.

In offering pardon and amnesty Lincoln had not usurped any Congressional prerogative, for the act of July 17, 1862 had granted him that power. All factions of his party seemed to approve his plan: Wade, Chandler, Sumner, and Lovejoy all visited the White House to congratulate him, and Horace Greeley called the program "devilish good." The Democrats seemed satisfied with it.

As the hectic year of 1863 closed on a note of hopefulness and party harmony, long months of hard thought, cautious advance, and sometimes fruitless experiment seemed to offer results at last. Out of the turmoil and the heartache of the war Lincoln was emerging as a strong, sure leader. Fumbling and uncertain at the start, and still plagued by problems of deficient military leadership that deferred the peace for which he yearned, he was showing more markedly than ever his capacity to grow in mind and character. The qualities of patience, tolerance, and forgiveness, with which hard experience, domestic trials, and personal affliction had endowed him, proved wonderfully helpful to him now. The long practical training in politics, which acquainted him with the ways and wiles of politicians, made it difficult to outmaneuver or outwit him. Knowledge of the people gave him faith in their basic virtues and a sure sense of when to coax, when to demand, when and how far he could lead, when he must wait or forbear.

John Hay saw Lincoln sitting like a backwoods Jupiter, hurling the thunderbolts of war and guiding the machinery of government with a firm, steady hand. His powers were constantly expanding. He was managing the war, the draft, and foreign relations and planning a reconstruction of the Union, all at once. Hay had never known anyone so wise, so gentle, and so strong. He seemed called of God for his place.

CHAPTER XVIII

"There Are No Lincoln Men"

THE PARTY nominating conventions were only a few months off. Already the political kettle bubbled noisily. While Lincoln seemed to have reached a turning of the road, he knew that long months of struggle, bloodshed, and patient planning lay ahead, and that the tasks he wished to finish would outlast his term of office. In a letter to Elihu Washburne, in October 1863, he had confided: "A second term would be a great honor and a great labor, which together, perhaps I would not decline if tendered." His renomination and re-election would assure the continuance of the war to total victory, and would commit the people to his lenient terms of peace.

But a single term had become almost traditional; no President since Jackson had served a second term, and Lincoln gave no public indication of an intention to run again. Perhaps his keen sense of public opinion told him he did not need to, for he had so won the people's confidence that there was no question of their wish to have him serve another term.

The people's trust in Lincoln had been born of his faith in them, for whenever a strong opposition developed in any quarter, he had explained in a public letter what he sought to do and why. His letter to Horace Greeley in August 1862 had set forth his views on emancipation and its relation to the war. His replies to protests of Ohio and New York Democrats against the arrest of Vallandigham defended his severity against seditionists. His

letter of August 1863 to James C. Conkling explained his views
on peace, emancipation, and the use of colored troops. In these
remarkable state papers he manifested that capacity to understand an opponent's point of view, and to present his own case
clearly and simply, which he had so painstakingly acquired as a
circuit lawyer. His straightforward arguments, void of partisan
deceptions, cutting through nonessentials to the nub of the
matter, and presented in plain language clarified by homely
analogies, had proved as effective with the people of the nation as
they had with the humble jurymen of the Eighth Circuit.

But the people's trust in Lincoln was not shared by the
politicians. Many of them still doubted his ability and looked
for an abler man. Lyman Trumbull wrote to Henry G. McPike, of
Alton: "The feeling for Mr. Lincoln's re-election *seems* to be
very general, but much of it I discover is only on the surface.
You would be surprised, in talking with public men we meet here,
to find how few, when you come to get at their real sentiment,
are for Mr. Lincoln's re-election. There is a distrust and fear
that he is too undecided and inefficient to put down the rebellion.
You need not be surprised if a reaction sets in before the nomination, in favor of some man supposed to possess more energy and
less inclination to trust our brave boys in the hands and under
the leadership of generals who have no heart in the war. The
opposition to Mr. L. may not show itself at all, but if it ever breaks
out there will be more of it than now appears."

The radical Republicans, while at first offering lip-service
to Lincoln's Amnesty Proclamation, had no intention of allowing
the Southern states to re-enter the Union unpunished, or of
renouncing the political profits of the war. By imposing conditions of readmission that would impoverish the planter aristocracy and force Negro suffrage on the vanquished population,
they planned to assure Republican dominance for years to come.
Lincoln was a stumbling-block to such designs. David Davis,
manager of Lincoln's nomination in 1860, who had been rewarded with a seat on the Supreme Court, wrote: "The politicians
in and out of Congress, it is the current belief, would put Mr.

Lincoln aside if they dared." The correspondent of the *Detroit Free Press* reported: "Not a single Senator can be named as favorable to Lincoln's renomination for President."

The crabbed Polish exile Count Adam Gurowski, a close observer of people and events in Washington, recorded in his diary: "The radicals, the purest men in Congress, begin to cave in, and to be reconciled to the idea of accepting the re-election of Lincoln as an inevitable necessity. They say that the outward pressure is very great. The masses are taken in by Lincoln's *apparent* simplicity and good-naturedness, by his awkwardness, by his vulgar jokes, and in the people's belief, the great shifter is earnest and honest. The stern and clear-sighted radicals expect to be able to bind Lincoln by pledges to change his Cabinet and his entourage."

The sole hope of the radicals lay in an adverse turn of events. They chose to play for time. Already there was talk of postponing the Republican national convention till late summer. Edward Bates reported that Lincoln knew full well that the radicals would strike him down if they dared, but they feared to fall under his power "as beaten enemies."

With practically all the malcontent Republicans disposed to act with prudence, the colossal egotism of Salmon P. Chase blinded him to the signs of the times. Few men found it so easy to delude themselves as the Secretary of the Treasury. In the letters that poured incessantly from his pen he pictured himself as wholly unselfish, anxious solely for the public good, and averse to self-promotion. Yet he seldom failed to relate how influential men lauded his qualifications for the Presidency and pleaded with him not to shirk his duty. Convinced of Lincoln's inadequacy, Chase never missed a chance to undermine his chief. His beautiful and restlessly ambitious daughter, Kate Chase Sprague, spread charm in her father's behalf.

Chase controlled some ten thousand jobs in the Treasury Department. The celebrated Philadelphia banking firm of his friend Jay Cooke, which served as fiscal agent in marketing government bonds, employed twenty-five hundred salesmen who

penetrated all parts of the country. Treasury advertising could
exert a potent influence on newspaper policies. As early as
October 17, 1863, Attorney General Bates commented that
"Mr. Chase's head is turned by his eagerness in pursuit of the
presidency. For a long time back he has been filling all the offices
in his vast patronage with extreme partizans and contrives also
to fill many vacancies, properly belonging to other departments."
Welles noted that port collectors and revenue agents were
organizing Chase clubs throughout the country. Reports came to
Lincoln that Treasury officials were "remorselessly decapitating
every subordinate believed or suspected of being in the least
tainted with Lincolnism." More often now Chase stayed away
from cabinet meetings; he seemed reluctant to meet Lincoln
face to face.

Lincoln had full knowledge of Chase's intrigues. The Secretary had never ceased trying to make personal capital out of the
President's troubles. "I suppose," Lincoln told Hay, "he will,
like the bluebottle fly, lay his eggs in every rotten spot he can
find." But Lincoln appeared to be more amused than concerned
at Chase's tactics. "I have determined to shut my eyes, so far as
possible, to everything of the sort," he told the young secretary.
"Mr. Chase makes a good Secretary, and I shall keep him where
he is. If he becomes President, all right. I hope we shall never
have a worse man. . . . I am entirely indifferent as to his success
or failure in these schemes so long as he does his duty at the head
of the Treasury Department."

Lincoln was not wholly selfless in his attitude toward Chase.
An open break would not only force the Secretary out of the cabinet into more vigorous opposition, but also mean the breakdown of that party unity which had always claimed priority in
the President's thinking and was more than ever essential in an
election year. Congressman George Ashmun wrote to General
Banks, after a visit at the White House, that there would be a
showdown with Chase; but Lincoln wanted it to come about
through some circumstance in which Chase was clearly in the
wrong. "He thinks that Mr. C. will sufficiently soon force the

question, in the mean time, I think, he is wise in waiting till the pear is ripe. . . . I have had little conversation with him *directly* on the subject," Ashmun confessed, "but Mrs. L. keeps me thoroughly informed of everything, & you may rely upon the existence of the ripest state of inflammation between Mr. L. and Mr. C."

Early in February 1864, Chase's "brain-trusters," in an effort to influence various state conventions that were soon to convene, distributed a "strictly private" circular, signed by Senator Samuel C. Pomeroy of Kansas, chief manager of Chase's campaign, to numerous editors and individuals throughout the country. Asserting that the renomination of Lincoln was not only undesirable but impossible, that the honor of the nation and the cause of liberty and union would suffer by his re-election, and that the one-term principle was an essential safeguard of republican institutions, it declared that Salmon P. Chase possessed more of the qualifications of a President in that critical time than any other man in public life. "When it becomes evident that party machinery and official influence are being used to secure the perpetuation of the present Administration," said Pomeroy, in reference to certain state conventions that had already endorsed Lincoln, "those who conscientiously believe that the interests of the country and of freedom demand a change in favor of vigor and purity and nationality, have no choice but to appeal at once to the people, before it shall be too late to secure a fair discussion of principles." A Chase central organization, with connections in all the states, had been formed, Pomeroy explained, in order to enable the Secretary's friends "most effectually to promote his elevation to the Presidency."

Pomeroy's "strictly private" circular became public knowledge at once. On February 6 Ward H. Lamon wrote Lincoln from New York that H. G. Fant, a banker, had received that morning, under the frank of Congressman Ashley of Ohio, "a most scurrilous and abominable pamphlet about you, your administration and the succession." Many other copies fell into the hands of Lincoln's friends.

When the *National Intelligencer* printed the full text of the circular on February 22, Chase wrote to Lincoln disclaiming responsibility for it and offering his resignation. "If there is anything in my action or position which in your judgment will prejudice the public interests under my charge, I beg you to say so," he implored. "I do not wish to administer the Treasury Department one day without your entire confidence."

Lincoln unhesitatingly accepted Chase's disavowal. He had not read the circular, he replied, "and I think I shall not. I was not shocked, or surprised by the appearance of the letter, because I had had knowledge of Mr. Pomeroy's Committee, and of secret issues which I supposed came from it, and of secret agents who I supposed were sent out by it, for several weeks. I have known just as little of these things as my friends have allowed me to know. . . . I do not inquire for more." Lincoln intimated that since he knew so much of what was going on, Chase must have known about it, too. But the President agreed that neither of them should be held responsible for the unauthorized acts of their friends. "Whether you shall remain at the head of the Treasury Department," he concluded, "is a question which I will not allow myself to consider from any stand-point other than my judgment of the public service; and in that view, I do not perceive occasion for a change."

The chief effect of the circular was to rally Lincoln's supporters. More state conventions and numerous Union League committees endorsed his renomination. The Republican National Committee, meeting in Washington, virtually named him as the candidate and called the national convention to meet in Baltimore on June 7.

With Chase on the verge of a knockout, Frank Blair dealt the lethal blow. Soon after the outbreak of the war, the pride of the Blair clan had obtained a commission in the army, where he made an excellent record. In the recent elections he had won a seat in Congress, but as a brigadier general he was forbidden by law to serve. Lincoln thought that Blair as Speaker of the House could render greater assistance to the Union cause than in the army, though as an ordinary member he could better be spared for the field. So he suggested that Blair deliver to him his commission and take his seat in Congress. Should Blair be elected Speaker, Lincoln would accept his resignation from the army; otherwise he would return the commission. Schuyler Colfax had been chosen Speaker before Blair arrived in Washington, but nevertheless Blair lingered on in Congress.

On February 27, the belligerent Missourian, his tall, wiry frame aquiver and his gray eyes shooting fire, attacked Chase viciously from the floor, charging political favoritism in the Treasury Department's system of granting permits to bring cotton out of the subjugated areas of the South. The great red beard that Blair had cultivated in the army wagged with indignation as he shouted: "I say here in my place and upon my responsibility as a Representative that a more profligate administration of the Treasury Department never existed under any government, that the whole Mississippi Valley is rank and fetid with the frauds and corruptions of its agents . . . that these permits to buy cotton are brought to St. Louis and other western cities by politicians and favorites from all parts of the country and are sold on 'change to the highest bidder, whether he be a secessionist or not, and that too, at a time when the best Union men in those cities are denied permits." Treasury agents known to be guilty of the grossest practices were still employed, Blair charged. Some of them, he supposed, busied themselves in distributing that "strictly private circular that came to light the other day" and in promoting the organization of Chase clubs. Blair demanded that Congress investigate this scandal.

Montgomery Blair wrote to the Reverend W. B. Sprague almost two years later that Lincoln understood very well the probable effect of such an attack as Blair's, and "shouldered all the responsibility of allowing my brother to go into Congress & back again into the army for the purpose of enabling him to make it." But this claim is open to question, for when Blair assailed Chase a second time a few weeks later, and certain Ohio Congressmen protested to Lincoln, the President disclaimed responsibility for Blair's attacks on the Secretary and deplored his having "kicked over another bee-hive." Immediately after his second outburst Blair took back his commission from Lincoln and returned to Sherman's army.

Early in March an Ohio party worker, E. Perkins, of Cleveland, wrote to Pomeroy: "We are united in both measures and men. We are in entire harmony with the great popular current which points so unmistakably to Abraham Lincoln as the Union nominee in 1864. In my judgment there are not a dozen Union men in this city who are not unequivocally for Honest Abe." Chase's hopes were dashed the next day when a Republican legislative caucus at Columbus passed him over and came out for Lincoln, leaving Chase a candidate without the endorsement of his own state, just as he had been in 1860. "What is the matter?" George B. Lincoln gleefully wired the President. "Friend Pomeroy's yeast don't make the Chase pudding rise."

On March 5 Chase wrote to James C. Hall, an influential Ohio politician, that the action of the Ohio caucus indicated such a preference for Lincoln that Chase hoped no further consideration would be given his name. But cynical politicians gave scant credence to Chase's withdrawal. Bates thought it proved only that Lincoln's "*present* prospects" were too good to be openly resisted. James Gordon Bennett editorialized in the *New York Herald:* "The Salmon is a queer fish, very wary, often appearing to avoid the bait just before gulping it down." And David Davis wrote to Thurlow Weed on March 21: "Mr. Chase's declination is a mere sham, and very ungraceful at that. The plan is to get up a great opposition to Lincoln, use Frémont and others, and represent, when the Convention meets, the necessity of united effort, that anybody can unite except Lincoln, etc., etc. and then to present Chase." Davis asserted as proof of Chase's unquenchable aspirations that a meeting of his supporters—mostly Treasury officials—had been held in Washington the night before.

With the Chase boom seemingly deflated, the proposal to postpone the national convention came to the fore again. Horace Greeley wrote hopefully to a friend that Lincoln was "not out of the woods. I shall keep up a quiet but steady opposition and, if we shall meantime have bad luck in the war, I guess we shall back them out."

*

G R A N T's victories at Chattanooga made him the hero of the North. Here at last was the man the nation needed for over-all command. Congressman Washburne, who often spoke for Lincoln, introduced a bill to revive the grade of lieutenant general, a rank previously enjoyed only by Washington, and conferred by brevet on Winfield Scott. As approved by Congress on February 22, 1864, the bill authorized the President to appoint, with the advice and consent of the Senate, a lieutenant general from those officers "most distinguished for courage, skill and ability" to command the armies of the United States. Lincoln immediately appointed Grant and directed him to report to Washington.

Grant reached the capital on the evening of March 8. He might have avoided the White House had he known this was the night of the weekly reception, for when he entered, about half past nine, the place was thronged. Secretary Welles, standing near the center of the reception room, heard a buzz and stir where Lincoln stood welcoming the guests. Men in uniform stood at the entrance, and one of them, a short, dark-haired man with light-brown whiskers and tarnished epaulets, was shaking hands with the President. Charles A. Dana, whose attention had also been attracted, thought Grant had a somewhat seedy look as the gangling President bent down to talk with him.

Grant became plainly embarrassed as people crowded around. Seward, hastening over, led him to Mrs. Lincoln, then guided him to the East Room. Dana noted Grant's awkward gait—he did not "march, nor quite walk, but pitches along, as if the next step would bring him on his nose." Grant was obliged to mount a red plush sofa to escape the crush. Cheer after cheer rang out; men climbed on chairs and sofas for a better view. At last the uneasy general made his escape to where Lincoln waited for him.

Two typical Americans sat down together in a small White

House room—the lanky, dark-visaged President slumping as usual in his chair, encumbered by his uncommonly long legs; the short, hard-knit general sitting stiffly, ill at ease. Both were plain, somewhat plodding Westerners; both possessed the frontier qualities of pluck, persistence, and hard common sense; each had the quiet modesty of the man who knows his job.

Lincoln explained that Grant's commission would be formally presented the next day. The President would deliver a short speech—just four sentences—which he read to Grant, and would read again at the ceremony so that Grant, who was probably not accustomed to public speaking, could also read his reply.

The formal presentation took place at one o'clock in the afternoon, in the presence of the cabinet, General Halleck, and officers of Grant's staff. "General Grant," Lincoln read, "the nation's appreciation of what you have done, and it's [*sic*] reliance upon you for what remains to do, in the existing great struggle, are now presented with this commission, constituting you Lieutenant General in the Army of the United States. With this high honor devolves upon you also, a corresponding responsibility. As the country herein trusts you, so, under God, it will sustain you. I scarcely need to add that with what I here speak for the nation goes my own hearty personal concurrence."

Grant read from a hastily penciled scrawl on a half-sheet of notepaper. Visibly uncomfortable, he found his own writing hard to decipher. "Mr. President," he said, "I accept this commission with gratitude for the high honor conferred. With the aid of the noble armies that have fought on so many fields for our common country, it will be my earnest endeavor not to disappoint your expectations. I feel the full weight of the responsibilities now devolving on me and know that if they are met, it will be due to those armies, and above all to the favor of that Providence which leads both nations and men."

Two days later Grant was on his way back to the West. Sherman had pleaded with him to shun Washington with its shams and ostentation, and Grant had thought of still leading the armies of the West. But he knew now that his place was in the

East—in the camp, however, rather than in the capital. Near the end of March he established headquarters near Culpeper Court House.

Grant's plan of operations was simple and direct. He had originally suggested a movement upon Richmond from the North Carolina coast, but it would seem that Lincoln persuaded him that this was impractical. His strategy, as modified, conformed to Lincoln's ideas. His prime purpose now would be to obliterate the power of Lee's army. Without that, not even the capture of Richmond would end the war. While Grant was hammering continuously at Lee, Banks was to finish his Louisiana campaign and move against Mobile, while Sherman, succeeding Grant as commander of the armies in the West, attacked Joseph E. Johnston, Bragg's successor, with the heart of Georgia as his goal. General Franz Sigel, in command in western Virginia, was to move in two columns, one up the Shenandoah Valley and the other upon the railroads running southwest out of Richmond, while Butler would advance up the James River from Fortress Monroe against Richmond and Petersburg. Meade would remain in command of the Army of the Potomac. Halleck would act as chief of staff in Washington.

Grant made several visits to Washington while preparations went forward. Both Stanton and Halleck cautioned him about revealing details of his plans to Lincoln; the President found it so difficult to refuse any request that some friend would learn all he knew. Grant need not have worried on this score, for Lincoln modestly explained to him that he had never professed to be a military man and had never wanted to interfere in army matters; the procrastination of his generals in the face of popular impatience, and especially the constant pressure from Congress, had forced him to interpose. He knew he had sometimes been wrong. All he had ever wanted was someone who would act, while he used the vast power of the government to provide supplies and manpower.

Grant's *Memoirs*, written long after the war, along with Lincoln's modesty, give the impression that Lincoln was still naïve in military matters. Actually, however, the final strategy was as much his as Grant's. Satisfied to know that at last there was to be that concert of action that he had urged on Grant's predecessors as the only means of utilizing the Union superiority in numbers with decisive effect, Lincoln, for the most part, would allow Grant a free hand. But even with Grant he would continue to watch military movements closely and to exert decisive influence at crucial times. When Grant explained how he proposed to exert unrelenting pressure at all points while wearing Lee into submission, Lincoln claimed no credit for prior discernment, but simply nodded his agreement. "Those not skinning," he said, "can hold a leg." Neither Grant nor Lincoln expected an easy victory. But neither of them conceived of the long, bloody months that lay ahead.

On April 30 Lincoln sent Grant his farewell. "Not expecting to see you again before the Spring campaign opens," he wrote, "I wish to express, in this way, my entire satisfaction with what you have done up to this time, so far as I understand it. The particulars of your plans I neither know or seek to know. You are vigilant and self-reliant; and, pleased with this, I wish not to obtrude any constraints or restraints upon you. While I am very anxious that any great disaster, or the capture of our men in great numbers shall be avoided, I know these points are less likely to escape your attention than they would be mine. If there is anything wanting which is within my power to give, do not fail to let me know it. And now with a brave army, and a just cause, may God sustain you."

Promptly at the time appointed, soon after midnight on May 4, the Army of the Potomac broke camp to cross the Rapidan. Grant had 122,000 troops—a numerical superiority of two to one over Lee's 62,000. His army was well fed, well clothed, with abundant ammunition. Lee had terrain on his side, and the might of his own genius. His ill-clad, ofttimes hungry, battle-hardened troops were dogged fighters. His strategy would be to hold Grant off, inflicting such losses that the North would despair of victory.

Lee did not oppose Grant at the Rapidan. He preferred to fight him in the Wilderness, a dense forest of scrub oak, dwarf pines, and hazel thickets, crisscrossed by marshy streams and threaded by roads that were little more than winding trails. Here the Federal advantage in numbers and artillery would count least. Here Hooker had suffered disaster just a year before.

May 5 saw the beginning of a blind death-wrestle in the gloomy, tangled woods. Artillery proved useless; it was a battle of detached brigades and regiments fighting at close quarters. Vicious rifle-flashes split through the murky thickets. The heavy woods deadened the roll of musketry. Grant's troops fought with such vigor that Lee dashed up in person to rally his wavering lines. Longstreet was wounded by his own men, as Jackson had been at Chancellorsville. In two days of fearful combat both sides suffered heavily. "More desperate fighting has not been witnessed on this continent," Grant wrote. Night brought an end to the confusion, but not to the suffering. Fires crackled through the woods. Dense smoke choked friend and foe. From the thickets came the shrill cries of the wounded, pleading for rescue from the flames. The battlefield became a holocaust.

For weeks regiments had moved through Washington headed for the front. Everyone knew that something big was happening. But the Confederate cavalry controlled a wide strip of country in Grant's rear, and for three days little news came through. The artist Francis B. Carpenter, working at the White House on a picture of the signing of the Emancipation Proclamation, saw Lincoln pacing the corridor in a long morning wrapper, hands clasped behind him, head bent low on his breast, with great black rings under his eyes from loss of sleep.

Sunday, May 8, brought rumors of vicious fighting. Grant's first dispatches arrived that afternoon. Stanton announced a victory. That night a cheering crowd beset the White House. Lincoln made a short speech. His tone was confident but wary. Much more remained to be done, he said. To John Hay he was less reticent. The significant fact was that the Federal army had not waited to be attacked, but had taken the initiative. With any other commander than Grant, it would probably have retired after the battle. Lincoln liked a story that came in: Meade had said to Grant that the enemy seemed disposed to make a Kilkenny-cat fight out of the affair, to which the laconic Grant replied: "Our cat has the longest tail."

Unable to thrust straight forward against Lee, Grant moved by the left flank toward Spotsylvania Court House, an approach to Hanover Junction, where the Virginia Central and the Fredericksburg & Potomac railroads joined. But Lee fathomed his intentions, got his troops there first, and threw up hasty entrenchments. His position was unusually strong. Heavy brush concealed his works. His artillery commanded the broken ground over which Grant must advance. A salient, known later as the "bloody angle," jutting out almost a mile from his main line, offered a point of attack.

Hard-driving General Winfield Scott Hancock opened the assault. The blue-clad troops moved forward in thick fog and heavy showers to sweep over the breastworks of earth and logs and drive through the dripping woods almost a mile. Once again Lee rallied his men in person. The Confederates held on grimly at the base of the bulge. Fierce countercharges drove the Federals back to the works at the apex of the salient. The troops fought furiously across the barricade. Bayonets thrust viciously between the logs. Bayoneted rifles hurtled through the air like spears. Men were pulled savagely over the breastworks to be killed or made prisoners. Rifle bullets flew so thickly that tree trunks were dissevered. The dead piled up in layers along the barricade. For sixteen hours the battle raged. But Grant's men held the salient.

After eight days of fighting came a lull. Grant had bogged down in the mud. Lee was fighting behind breastworks and would not be coaxed out. Day after day the people of the North awoke to the same headlines—heavy, desperate fighting, terrible casualties. Grant had lost a third of his army, but on the 13th he telegraphed: "I propose to fight it out on this line if it takes all summer." Lincoln read the message to a crowd. The words echoed through the nation. Here was a new spirit in the army.

But the losses were appalling. All day the mournful whistles hooted as steamers landed at the Sixth Street wharf in Washington. Sheeted forms lay in the bows. Stretcher cases came off by the thousands. All night the work went on as the murky water shimmered in the torchlight. Ambulances rumbled over the Long Bridge. Hearses rolled through the streets. The city became an overburdened hospital, and fresh graves scarred the earth at Arlington. At twilight Lincoln's carriage took him slowly toward the Soldiers' Home. As he stopped at a street corner for a word with Congressman Isaac N. Arnold, a line of wounded men filed by. The President caught his breath. "Look yonder at those poor fellows," he said. "I cannot bear it. This suffering, this loss of life is dreadful."

*

N o t only had Grant's advance been checked; his plan of concerted movement had broken down. Butler had been defeated at Drewry's Bluff and sealed up between the Appomattox and the James "as in a bottle tightly corked"; Sigel had been roughly handled in the Shenandoah Valley; Banks had narrowly escaped disaster on the Red River and was in no condition to assail Mobile. Sherman was still moving toward Atlanta, but his progress seemed discouragingly slow.

With Lee's position at Spotsylvania too strong to attack again, Grant moved once more by the left flank, only to be checkmated at the North Anna River. Again Grant slid around Lee's flank, always moving southward. On June 1 the armies faced each other at Cold Harbor, a road hub north of the Chickahominy. Grant recognized the strength of Lee's position, but determined on a final effort to destroy him.

Grant expected heavy losses. They proved to be murderous. As the blue ranks came on in waves, Lee's men in their entrenchments mowed them down in windrows in a slaughter worse than Fredericksburg. Grant lost ten thousand men, the pride of his army. The Union dead covered five acres of ground as thickly as they could have lain. Many Northern officers thought it a wanton sacrifice. The stench of rotting corpses became nauseating as Grant refused to ask a truce to bury the slain.

The wave of Northern optimism ebbed. Welles recorded: "There is intense anxiety in relation to the Army of the Potomac. . . . The immense slaughter of our brave men chills and sickens us all. The hospitals are crowded with the thousands of mutilated and dying heroes who have poured out their blood in the Union cause." After a month of horrible carnage Grant was no closer to Richmond than McClellan had been in 1862. Resentment centered on Lincoln for putting a stolid butcher in command. And the Republican national convention was only a few days off.

*

RADICAL antagonism to Lincoln's renomination had not ceased with Chase's ostensible withdrawal from the race; but the sullen, taciturn radicals could find no candidate who struck fire. Mention of Ben Butler fell on heedless ears. The efforts of James Gordon Bennett's *New York Herald* in behalf of Grant found the general uninterested. The most outspoken opponents of the President were the antislavery Germans, whose chief strength lay in Missouri, and the New England abolitionists of the Wendell Phillips school. Their candidate was the supposedly maligned John C. Frémont, now engaged in railroad promotion in New York.

As early as February 6, 1864, Congressman Ashmun had written to General Banks: "The friends of Fremont seem determined to run him at all events. But he has no real strength, & is to a great extent an object of contempt rather than alarm, and yet he can do some mischief." On March 19 the Frémont movement broke into the open with a meeting in New York. William Cullen Bryant, of the New York *Evening Post*, seemed friendly to it; Governor Andrew of Massachusetts offered guarded encouragement; and Horace Greeley stalked into the meeting to announce that, while he expected to support the regular Republican nominee, he entertained the greatest respect for General

Frémont and his views. Acknowledging that they lacked the strength to dominate the regular Republican convention, the Frémont men called a convention of their own to meet at Cleveland one week earlier, on May 31.

Lincoln's friends regarded Frémont as a stalking-horse for Chase. "Nobody is simple enough to believe that the distinguished Secretary has really retired from the canvass," Frank Blair declared in his second attack on Chase in Congress. ". . . The work is now being done in Fremont's name and that poor creature is unconscious of being made a cat's paw to accomplish the objects of his intriguing rival. His program is to hold a convention of Jacobins and red Republican revolutionary Germans at Cleveland . . . which will say to the Union Convention to be held at Baltimore, 'if you insist on the nomination of Lincoln we will nominate Fremont against him as an independent candidate.' In this way if the delegates who have been instructed to vote for Lincoln can be bought with greenbacks or frightened by the Jacobin hobgoblin, it is expected that Chase, who has so magnanimously declined to be a candidate, will then be taken up as a compromise candidate."

Whatever may have been the underlying purpose of the Cleveland convention, it turned out to be a farce. Influential politicians took care to stay away. Postmaster Edwin Cowles of Cleveland wired Montgomery Blair: "Convention tremendous fizzle. Less than two hundred from abroad consisting of disappointed contractors, sore-head governors and copperheads." S. Newton Pettis telegraphed Lincoln that "it is the most perfect failure, the most magnificent fizzle I ever looked in upon. . . . Take from the body assembled Gen. John Cochrane of New York and ex-Gov. Johnson of Pennsylvania and in my opinion a motion to be in mourning would be perfectly in order."

The platform called for uncompromising prosecution of the war, a constitutional amendment prohibiting slavery, free speech and a free press, a one-term presidency, reconstruction of the South by Congress, confiscation of rebel property and its division among the veterans of the Union army. The new party took

the name "Radical Democracy," nominated Frémont by acclamation, and, in ignorance of the constitutional provision that the
President and Vice President must come from different states,
chose General Cochrane as Frémont's running mate. Frémont, in
accepting the nomination, declared that should the Republican
convention select "any man whose past life justifies a well-
grounded confidence in his fidelity to our cardinal principles, there
is no reason why there should be any division among the really
patriotic men of the country. To any such I shall be most happy
to give a cordial and active support. . . . But if Mr. Lincoln
should be nominated—as I believe it would be fatal to the country
to endorse a policy and renew a power which has cost us the
lives of thousands of men, and needlessly put the country on the
road to bankruptcy—there will remain no other alternative but
to organize against him every element of conscientious opposition
with a view to prevent the misfortune of his reelection." Thus the
Republican convention was forewarned.

The proceedings at Cleveland caused indignation among
Lincoln's friends. Welles complained that these separatists would
hazard the Union cause to gratify their spite against the President; in the same breath they blamed him for lethargy and
despotism, for being too gentle toward the rebels and for being
tyrannical and intolerant. "There is no doubt he has a difficult
part to perform," thought Welles, "in order to satisfy all and do
right."

Democratic and Copperhead papers tried to give significance
to the Republican split, but few others took it seriously. Lincoln
seemed to be amused. When a friend told him that, instead of the
thousands who had been expected at the Cleveland convention,
only about four hundred persons had been present, he was struck
by the number. Reaching for the Bible that lay handy on his desk,
he thumbed through it to I Samuel xxii, 2 and read: "And every
one that was in distress, and every one that was in debt, and every
one that was discontented, gathered themselves unto him; and
he became a captain over them: and there were with him about
four hundred men."

*

DELEGATES en route to the national convention called on Lincoln to learn his views. He had already suggested to ex-Governor Edwin D. Morgan of New York, now a Senator and chairman of the Republican National Committee, that the platform should advocate a thirteenth amendment to the Constitution, abolishing slavery. Such an amendment not only would safeguard the emancipation measures already taken by himself and by Congress against possible revocation by the Supreme Court, but would also mark the doom of slavery by ending it in the border states. These states were largely reconciled to such a proposal, and it would be a concession to the radicals. Otherwise Lincoln resolved to keep hands off the convention. With the will of the people so clearly manifest, his own renomination was assured; none of his radical antagonists dared to oppose him openly.

They could and did, however, express their rankling hostility by striking him through his cabinet, whose most vulnerable member was Montgomery Blair, symbol of the Blair influence in the government. Frank Blair's attacks on Chase and his relentless opposition to the radicals in Missouri had not been forgotten. Montgomery Blair had made himself equally obnoxious to the Maryland radicals. And old man Blair, by reason of his frequent visits to the White House in his role of elder statesman, was thought to be Lincoln's evil genius.

Missouri sent rival delegations to Baltimore. When the convention voted 440 to 4 to seat the anti-Blair radicals, it served notice on the President that it wanted no more of the Blairs. And it underlined this warning when it inserted a plank in the platform, at the behest of the Missourians, to the effect that a cabinet change would be in order, though this ultimatum was adroitly worded to preserve the appearance of harmony. Other planks endorsed Lincoln's proposed Thirteenth Amendment, called for unrelenting prosecution of the war, and commended the practical wisdom and unselfish patriotism of the President. But in almost the same breath with which they praised Lincoln the radicals openly rebuked him with a resolution that "rebels" and "traitors" should receive "the punishment due their crimes."

The Missourians rifted the lute of harmony again when, on the first ballot, they cast their 22 votes for Grant. All other 484 votes went to Lincoln, and his nomination was then made unanimous. The usual cheers roared forth. Men shouted, danced, and capered as the big band broke into *Hail, Columbia!*

The race for the vice-presidential nomination proved to be more exciting. The Republicans, as in previous elections, tried to attract loyal Democrats by campaigning as a Union party, and it was believed that the ticket would be strengthened by nominating a War Democrat to run with Lincoln. Most prominent of the eligible Democrats were Daniel S. Dickinson and General John A. Dix, of New York, Judge Advocate General Joseph Holt, of Kentucky, and Andrew Johnson, military governor of Tennessee. Incumbent Vice President Hannibal Hamlin, who had left the Democratic Party over the repeal of the Missouri Compromise, was also a candidate.

During the early hours of the convention Lincoln's friend Leonard Swett came out for Holt. Nicolay, on hand as an observer, wrote to Hay at the instance of Chairman Burton C. Cook of the Illinois delegation: "Cook wants to know confidentially whether Swett is all right; whether in urging Holt for Vice-President he reflects the President's wishes; whether the President has any preference, either personal or on the score of policy; or whether he wishes not even to interfere by a confidential intimation." Lincoln endorsed on the letter: "Swett is unquestionably all right. Mr. Holt is a good man, but I had not heard or thought of him for V.P. Wish not to interfere about V.P. Can not interfere about platform. Convention must judge for itself."

The platform resolution demanding a reorganization of the cabinet had been directed against Seward as well as Blair; and Seward's enemies, believing that Lincoln could scarcely keep two men from the same state in his official family, rallied behind the candidacy of the New Yorker Dickinson, with the slogan:

"Dickinson in, Seward out." Holt and Dix dropped out of the running early. The Weed-Seward faction in New York, throwing their strength behind Hamlin in order to head off Dickinson, split the New York delegation so irreparably that Dickinson's chances dimmed. Then, as Hamlin's hopes began to dwindle in the face of the demand for a War Democrat, the Sewardites swung their support to Johnson, who polled 200 votes on the first ballot, to Hamlin's 150 and Dickinson's 108. On the second ballot Johnson gained 31 votes, to come within 28 of a majority. With that the stampede started, and Johnson's nomination was made unanimous.

Lincoln had no part in the outcome, as some self-styled insiders claimed in after years. Though he had been somewhat disappointed in Hamlin, who usually sided with the radicals, the President did nothing to help defeat him; it was Seward, or Seward's New York machine, that brought about Johnson's victory. And it may have been a sense of obligation to Seward that induced Johnson, originally a radical, to adopt a moderate policy when he succeeded Lincoln as President.

The President showed no elation at his renomination. He supposed, he told a delegation from the National Union League who came to congratulate him, that the convention had simply concluded "that it is not best to swap horses while crossing the river, and have further concluded that I am not so poor a horse that they might not make a botch of it trying to swap." Bates grumbled that the convention "did indeed nominate Mr. Lincoln, but in a manner and with attendant circumstances as if the object was to defeat their own nomination." Adam Gurowski believed that "many, many have not made up their minds to go for him, and what is still worse, to go for his Sewards and Blairs." The grumpy Count thought it not improbable that before election day another convention might be called and a new nominee put forward.

Immediately after the convention Montgomery Blair tendered his resignation. Lincoln refused to accept it; he was still disinclined to be dictated to in the choice of his advisers. But Blair

knew his retirement could only be a matter of time, and placed
an undated resignation in Lincoln's hands, with the injunction to
use it whenever the radical pressure became irresistible.

*

S H O R T L Y after the convention Lincoln reached the breaking-
point with Chase. The Secretary, with his conviction of self-
righteousness, had obstinately refused to heed the President's
wishes respecting appointments in the Treasury Department.
Lincoln was as concerned as Chase about the honesty and competence of men in public office; but he also respected the custom, so
essential to party unity, that officeholders have the approval of
the senators and representatives of their state or district. Twice
already Chase had submitted his resignation in protest over
Lincoln's alleged interference, and each time he had been allowed
to have his way. But relations between the Secretary and the
President had reached a point where they communicated with
each other chiefly by written notes.

In June 1864, when Chase nominated Maunsell B. Field as
assistant treasurer in New York, Lincoln wrote to him: "I can
not, without much embarrassment, make this appointment, prin-
cipally because of Senator Morgan's very firm opposition to it."
Morgan had suggested three other men to the Secretary, and the
President urged: "It will really oblige me if you will make choice
among these three, or any other man that Senators Morgan and
Harris will be satisfied with, and send me a nomination for him."

Chase asked for a private interview. Lincoln refused it, an
uncommon thing for him, "because the difficulty does not . . .
lie within the range of a conversation between you and me.
. . . I do not think Mr. Field a very proper man for the place."
Chase resigned once more, and this time, on June 30, Lincoln
wrote: "Your resignation of the office of Secretary of the Treasury, sent me yesterday, is accepted. Of all I have said in commendation of your ability and fidelity, I have nothing to unsay; and
yet you and I have reached a point of mutual embarrassment in

our official relation which it seems can not be overcome, or longer sustained, consistently with the public service."

Chase was utterly surprised; he thought Lincoln would surrender as he had done before. "It was still within his power," he wrote aggrievedly to W. T. Coggeshall, an Ohio editor, "to send [for] me for public talks, and agree on what was best to be done." Chase wrote in hurt tones to Greeley that there had been no response in Lincoln's letter "to the sentiments of respect and esteem that mine contained."

When ex-Governor David Tod of Ohio declined to serve as Chase's successor, Lincoln appointed William P. Fessenden, of Maine, chairman of the Senate Finance Committee.

*

C O N S T A N T fighting continued in Virginia as Grant tried to wear Lee down. Every day saw its stream of dead and wounded coming into Washington, while fresh troops moved to the front. On June 5 Grant telegraphed to Halleck: "I now find, after thirty days of trial, the enemy deems it of first importance to run no risks with the armies they now have. They act purely on the defensive behind breastworks, or feebly on the offensive immediately in front of then, and where in case of repulse they can instantly retire behind them. Without a greater sacrifice of human life than I am willing to make, all cannot be accomplished that I had designed outside the city."

Grant decided to cross the James, swing southward around Richmond, and work on Lee's supply lines. For four days he pounded at Petersburg, and lost ten thousand men. Such casualties could not be sustained, and Grant settled down to a siege. Long lines of earthworks, buttressed by forts at frequent intervals, enveloped Richmond on the east and south. Each side elaborated its defenses. Grant pushed his lines steadily toward the west, reaching for Lee's communications, forcing the Confederates to extend their thinner lines. Reconnaissances, probing actions, and small-scale battles occurred constantly along the front; Grant never relaxed the pressure.

A week after the Baltimore convention Lincoln had hinted that more men would be needed. In an address at a sanitary fair in Philadelphia he had asked: "If I shall discover that General Grant and the noble officers and men under him can be greatly facilitated in their work by a sudden pouring forward of men and assistance, will you give them to me?" Cries of "Yes" answered him. "Then, I say stand ready," he replied, "for I am watching for the chance."

A few days later Lincoln visited the front. All signs pointed to the necessity of another draft call. His friends urged him to avoid it. Every day the North was sinking deeper in despair as hope of a speedy victory vanished; another draft would arouse the opposition and endanger Republican prospects. On July 19, however, Lincoln called for 500,000 men to be drafted on September 5.

All the submerged discontent broke into open clamor. The awful losses of the last few weeks had horrified the nation. The thought of further bloodshed brought revulsion. Radical Republicans again cried out against Lincoln's mismanagement of the war. Democrats denounced the draft as the act of a heartless despot. "Lincoln has called for *five hundred thousand more victims!*" raged the La Crosse (Wisconsin) *Democrat.* ". . . Let the women buy mourning goods now. . . . Only half a million more! Oh that is nothing. We are bound to free the niggers or die. . . . Continue this administration in power and we can all go to war, Canada, or to hell before 1868."

*

G E N E R A L   D A V I D   H U N T E R, replacing Sigel in the Shenandoah Valley, resorted to ruthless destruction. Sweeping up the Valley, he burned mills, iron furnaces, and barns, fired the Virginia Military Institute and Washington College at Lexington, then moved on Lynchburg, the key to Lee's communications with the West. Lee dispatched stout, stoop-shouldered Jubal Early with 17,000 men, with orders to take Hunter in the rear, move down the Valley, and threaten Washington. "I still think it is our policy," Lee wrote to Jefferson Davis, "to draw the attention of the enemy to his own territory." Lee hoped that a movement against Washington would goad Grant into a reckless counterattack.

On July 2 Sigel telegraphed Halleck from Harpers Ferry that the enemy was moving down the Valley. Hunter retreated westward down the Kanawha River, leaving the way to Washington unbarred. The telegraph line to Harpers Ferry went dead. Boatmen coming down the Chesapeake and Ohio Canal to Washington brought news that the upper fords of the Potomac swarmed with "graybacks," some of them less than thirty miles above the capital. Welles recorded: "The President has been a good deal incredulous about a very large army on the upper Potomac, yet he begins to manifest anxiety."

News came that Early had laid Hagerstown under heavy requisition on penalty of burning the town. Frederick had to pay $200,000 to escape destruction. Grant dispatched General James B. Ricketts's division of the Sixth Corps to Baltimore, where it arrived on July 8.

General Lew Wallace led all the troops available at Baltimore to oppose Early at the Monocacy River. They could delay him only a day. "The Rebels are upon us," Welles recorded. "Having visited upper Maryland, they are turning their attention hitherward. General Wallace has been defeated."

Reports from the Monocacy threw Washington into panic. With all available troops dispatched to Grant, the city was only lightly guarded by a small force of hundred-day men, a veteran reserve corps, District militia, and a few dismounted cavalry. Mails stopped. No newspapers came in. Telegraph lines were severed. Early cut the railroad to the north.

Convalescent veterans and undisciplined recruits trudged to the forts. Government clerks drilled frantically on vacant lots. Quartermaster General Meigs hastily organized the men of his department into fighting units. Refugees, streaming into the city with household goods stacked high on creaking wagons, reported the country alive with gray uniforms. Stanton wrote hastily to Lincoln: "A fact that has just been reported by the watchman of the Department, viz. that your carriage was followed by a horseman not one of your escort and dressed in uniform unlike that used by our troops induces me to advise you that your guard be on the *alert* tonight." Next evening, when Lincoln departed as usual to sleep at the Soldiers' Home, Stanton summoned him back.

All through the day on July 11 the rumble of gunfire could be plainly heard at the White House. "At three o'clock P.M.," wrote Hay, "the President came in bringing the news that the enemy's advance was at Fort Stevens on the 7th Street road. He was in the Fort when it was first attacked, standing upon the parapet." Looking northward, Hay could see two columns of smoke in the brassy summer sky. Word came that the Confederates had set fire to Montgomery Blair's home at Silver Spring. Detachments from Grant's army had arrived in the nick of time that day, and the panic in the city had subsided. Hay reported Lincoln in excellent spirits: "He seems not the least concerned about the safety of Washington. With him the only concern seems to be whether we can bag or destroy the force in our front."

A number of civilian officials rode out to Fort Stevens the next day. Lincoln stood watching from the fort as the Union troops marched out to drive off Early's skirmishers. An officer fell within three feet of him. Twenty-three-year-old Captain Oliver Wendell Holmes of General Horatio G. Wright's staff— later to be Associate Justice of the Supreme Court of the United States—looking up to see a tall civilian in a high silk hat heedlessly exposed above the parapet, shouted: "Get down, you damn fool, before you get shot!" General Wright, recognizing the President, asked him more politely to take cover. When Welles came up soon afterward, he saw Lincoln sitting in the shade, his back against the parapet. Welles watched the Confederates take to flight as two of Wright's regiments charged. "We could see them running across the fields," he wrote, "seeking the woods on the brow of the opposite hills." Stretcher-bearers began to carry in the wounded. Early got safely away during the night.

*

T H E S L O W passage of the hot summer months brought no rift in Northern gloom. Commodore Farragut closed in at Mobile. Grant remained stalled at Petersburg. Down in Georgia two skillful fighters fenced as Sherman tried to break through Johnston's guard. Grant had drawn Sherman's orders in the most general terms: "You I propose to move against Johnston's army, to break it up and get into the interior of the enemy's country as far as you can, inflicting all the damage you can against their war resources." Sherman's army was one claw of a great pair of pincers, Grant's the other.

Sherman made Atlanta his destination. A railroad center, distant one hundred and twenty miles from Chattanooga over rugged, mountainous country, it was a strategic military depot, with factories, foundries, and rolling-mills ceaselessly engaged in war work.

Sherman and Johnston were both resourceful fighters. Whenever Sherman gained an advantage of position, Johnston withdrew; when Johnston got his army strongly posted, Sherman forced him to draw back by moving around his flank. Both armies dug in wherever they stopped, for both North and South had learned the value of entrenchments. Twice Sherman brought Johnston to battle—on Johnston's terms. Twice he was repulsed. As Sherman moved ever deeper into Georgia, he was obliged to leave detachments to guard the single-track railroad that brought his supplies. His original force of 98,000 shrank, while Johnston, picking up more troops as he fell back, increased his strength from 45,000 to 62,000. After ten weeks of fluid warfare Sherman could see the steeples of Atlanta.

President Davis, dissatisfied with Johnston's tactics, replaced him with John B. Hood. A reckless, slashing fighter, Hood attacked at Peach Tree Creek. Beaten off in hand-to-hand encounter, he attacked again, but Sherman forced him back to his entrenchments. Sherman, unable to take Atlanta by assault, probed for Hood's communications. Hood countered with cavalry raids.

*

NONE of the Union military undertakings seemed to promise success. The country's war-weariness and disappointment centered on Lincoln, and blamed him for not making more serious efforts for peace. No man craved peace more than the President, but he knew the Southern leaders would reject all overtures that denied them independence.

Most clamorous of the would-be peacemakers was the cherubic busybody Horace Greeley. Word came to him early in July that Confederate emissaries waited on the Canadian side of Niagara Falls with full powers to treat for peace. Lincoln put no faith in such reports, but a long, hysterical letter from Greeley placed him in a position where he must investigate them. "If you can find any person anywhere professing to have any proposition of Jefferson Davis in writing, for peace, embracing the restoration of the Union and abandonment of slavery," he replied to Greeley, "what ever else it embraces, say to him he may come to me with you. . . . The same, if there be two or more persons."

Greeley had not counted on being drawn into the matter in such an active way; he preferred to remain a watcher while Lincoln encountered the worries. Four days after receiving Lincoln's authorization he sent another letter of advice. "I was not expecting you to *send* me a letter," Lincoln wired him, "but to *bring* me a man, or men." In a covering letter delivered by John Hay, Lincoln asserted: "I not only intend a sincere effort for peace, but I intend that you shall be a personal witness that it is made."

Hay accompanied the reluctant Greeley to Niagara Falls. But nothing came of their efforts. The Confederates had no power to negotiate, and were in Canada primarily to try to influence the outcome of the approaching elections. But Greeley's course had put Lincoln in a bad light before the country. Such mystery surrounded what went on at Niagara Falls that again the cry arose that Lincoln would not listen to peace proposals. To set the matter straight before the people, Lincoln asked Greeley's permission to publish their correspondence with the omission

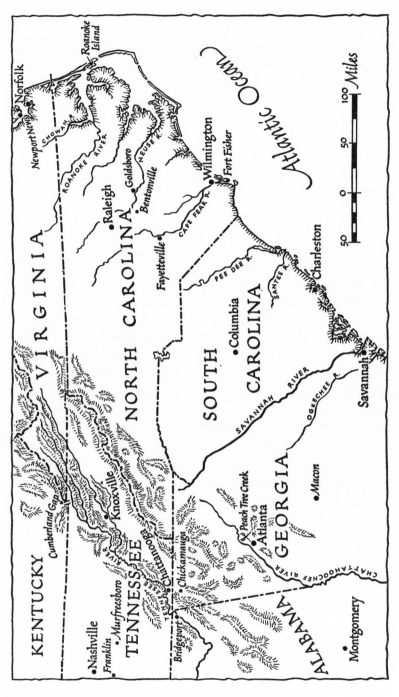

The Southeastern Theater

of one or two passages in which Greeley had spoken of a bankrupt country and had prophesied awful calamities. The testy editor replied that he could consent to no suppression; if the President chose to publish the letters, the country should read them entire. Lincoln decided to let the matter drop. He explained to the cabinet that while Greeley's stubborn attitude allowed the people to blame him for continuing the war, it was better to bear this accusation and withhold the letters rather than "to subject the country to the consequences of publishing their discouraging and injurious parts."

*

A f e w weeks after the issuance of the Amnesty Proclamation, Lincoln sent General Daniel E. Sickles on a tour of observation in the South. "Please ascertain at each place," read Sickles's instructions, "what is being done, if anything, for re-construction; how the Amnesty Proclamation works, if at all—what practical hitches, if any, there are about it—whether deserters come in from the enemy . . . since the Amnesty, and whether the ratio of their arrival is any greater *since* than before the Amnesty; what deserters report generally, and particularly whether, and to what extent, the Amnesty is known within the rebel lines."

Under Lincoln's careful nurture Louisiana and Arkansas had already organized provisional governments, and with Tennessee taking steps to the same end, the apprehensive radicals decided that they must take counteraction. Sardonic Ben Wade headed the resistance to Lincoln's reconstruction efforts in the Senate, while vehement, ambitious Henry Winter Davis, a cousin of Lincoln's friend David Davis and an implacable rival of Montgomery Blair in Maryland politics, emerged as the House spokesman for the radicals. Abetted by Chandler and Sumner in the Senate, and by Stevens and abolitionist George W. Julian in the House, these men became the sponsors of a bill sharply at odds with Lincoln's lenient plan of reconstruction.

Known as the Wade-Davis bill, it required for the formation of state governments a pledge of loyalty, not of a mere one tenth of the voting population, but of a majority. All persons who had held state or Confederate offices, or who had voluntarily borne arms against the United States, were forbidden to vote for delegates to state constitutional conventions or to serve as delegates. Slavery was prohibited in any restored state; the "rebel" debt was to be repudiated; and no officer under the "usurping governments" should be eligible for membership in a state legislature or for a governorship.

This bill still did not represent the full measure of the radicals' vengeful designs. If they could force Lincoln to recognize Congress as the rightful agency of reconstruction, they could formulate a stronger policy later. "In getting up this law," Welles wrote, "it was as much an object of Mr. Henry Winter Davis and some others to pull down the Administration as to reconstruct the Union. I think they had the former more directly in view than the latter."

The measure passed on July 2, the last day of the session. Less than an hour before adjournment, as Lincoln sat signing bills in the President's room at the Capitol, this one was thrust before him. He put it aside and went on with the others. Chandler, Sumner, and other radical senators stood watching what he would do. Chandler asked if Lincoln intended to approve the Wade-Davis bill. The President said it was too important "to be swallowed in that way"; he wanted time to study it. Chandler angrily replied: "If it is vetoed, it will damage us fearfully in the Northwest. The important point is the one prohibiting slavery in the reconstructed states." Lincoln calmly remarked: "That is the point on which I doubt the authority of Congress to act."

Lincoln had never swerved from the conviction that Congress had no power over slavery in the states, and that he as President could never have interfered with it except as a necessity of war. He did not veto the bill, but simply refused to approve it, and took his case to the people by means of a proclamation. While willing to acknowledge the Wade-Davis bill as offering one means of restoration, Lincoln explained, he was unwilling to commit himself to any single plan, to set aside the free-state constitutions and governments already established in Louisiana and Arkansas, or to acknowledge the power of Congress to abolish slavery in the states. The radicals raged. "What an infamous proclamation!" stormed Stevens. ". . . The idea of pocketing a bill & then issuing a proclamation as to how far he will conform to it."

The radicals published their answer in the *New York Tribune* of August 5. Papers all over the North reprinted it. Known as the Wade-Davis Manifesto, it was the most savage attack ever directed against a President by men of his own party. Addressed to "the Supporters of the Government," it declared that all good Republicans owed allegiance to a cause rather than to a usurper of authority. Lincoln persisted in recognizing those "shadows of governments" in Arkansas and Louisana, it charged, because he hoped to obtain their electoral votes to assure his re-election. The President's proclamation was the most "studied outrage on the legislative authority of the people" that had ever been perpetrated.

Lincoln refused to read the manifesto. From what he heard of it, he told Welles, he had no desire to see it, or to be provoked into malicious bickering. "To be wounded in the house of one's friends," he said to Noah Brooks, "is perhaps the most grievous affliction that can befall a man."

*

M E N friendly to the Union cause remembered July and August 1864 as the darkest days of the war. Earlier setbacks had tried the nation's faith, but the reverses of this hot, dry summer fell with greater oppressiveness because high hopes had been dashed. No joyful tidings came from the army now. Confusion reigned in politics. Peace appeared to be a distant dream.

Grant failed in an effort to break through north of the James. Inner military and official circles entertained great expectations of an enormous mine, burrowed beneath the Confederate lines, with which Grant planned to blast a way to Petersburg. But Burnside bungled the assault. The Union troops could never penetrate beyond the crater, where they suffered horrible losses. Lincoln hastened to consult with Grant to learn the cause of failure. Welles reported apprehension that Grant was not up to his job.

Early's Confederates, after retiring from Washington, had turned back down the Shenandoah Valley, raided through Maryland and Pennsylvania, and burned the town of Chambersburg. Grant sent Phil Sheridan to the Valley with orders "to put himself south of the enemy and follow him to the death." But the short, tough-faced, hard-riding Sheridan needed a larger force in order to cope with Early. In mid-August, Grant informed Halleck that he thought of leading reinforcements to Sheridan in person, but disliked easing the pressure on Lee. Grant also resisted appeals that troops from his army be sent to deal with Copperhead disturbances in the North, and Lincoln wired him on the 17th: "I have seen your dispatch expressing your unwillingness to break your hold where you are. Neither am I willing. Hold on with a bull-dog grip and chew & choke, as much as possible."

With Sherman blocked before Atlanta, a victory by Farragut in Mobile Bay did little to lift the gloom. Welles wrote in his diary: "There is no doubt a wide discouragement prevails."

*

D ESPA I R over the coming elections brought a movement to force Lincoln to withdraw as a candidate. Secret correspondence between dejected Republican politicians and newspapermen led to a meeting at the home of ex-Mayor George Opdyke, a leader of the anti-Seward faction in New York. Most prominent among the endorsers of this scheme were David Dudley Field, the eminent lawyer, whose brother, Stephen T. Field, Lincoln had lately appointed to the Supreme Court; Roscoe Conkling, Speaker of the House; Henry Winter Davis, and Daniel S. Dickinson. Horace Greeley, Parke Godwin of the New York *Evening Post*, Theodore Tilton of the *Independent*, and Whitelaw Reid of the *Cincinnati Gazette* promised editorial support. Chase guardedly expressed good will, and devious Ben Butler lent encouragement in the hope of superseding Lincoln as the Republican candidate. But Wade and Sumner held aloof—Wade because he preferred to wait until the Democrats had picked their candidate, and Sumner because he favored asking Lincoln to withdraw voluntarily.

This and other consultations resulted in a call for a convention to meet at Cincinnati on September 28 "to consider the state of the nation and to concentrate the Union strength on some candidate who commands the confidence of the country, even by a new nomination if necessary." Greeley wrote to Opdyke: "Mr. Lincoln is already beaten. He cannot be elected. And we must have another ticket to save us from overthrow. If we had such a ticket as could be made by naming Grant, Butler or Sherman for President, and Farragut for Vice, we could make a fight yet. And such a ticket we ought to have anyhow, with or without a convention."

Even Lincoln's most devoted supporters despaired of his success. On August 22 Henry J. Raymond, editor of the *New York Times* and chairman of the Republican National Committee, wrote to Lincoln: "I feel compelled to drop you a line concerning the political condition of the country as it strikes me. I am in active correspondence with your staunchest friends in every State and from them all I hear but one report. The tide is setting strongly against us. Hon. E. B. Washburne writes that 'were an election to be held now in Illinois we should be beaten.' Mr. Cameron writes that Pennsylvania is against us. Governor Morton writes that nothing but the most strenuous efforts can carry Indiana. . . . And so the rest. Nothing but the most resolute action, on the part of the Government and its friends, can save the country from falling into hostile hands."

Raymond attributed the public dissatisfaction, first, to military failures, and second, to an impression in some minds, and a fear or suspicion in others, that the administration would entertain no terms of peace until slavery had been abolished. "In some way or other," explained Raymond, "the suspicion is widely diffused that we can have peace with Union if we would.

It is idle to reason with this belief—still more idle to denounce it. It can only be expelled by some authoritative act, at once bold enough to fix attention and distinct enough to defy incredulity and challenge respect." Raymond suggested that a peace commission be appointed to negotiate with Davis on the sole question of acknowledgment of the supremacy of the Constitution, all other questions to be settled by a convention of the reunited people.

Confirmation of Raymond's dismal prophecies came from various sources. A Union worker in New York wrote to Welles: "There are no Lincoln men. . . . We know not which way to turn." Congressman Julian asserted that the President was a burden to the cause. Lincoln's close friend Orville H. Browning confided to Senator Edgar Cowan of Pennsylvania that, while personally attached to the President, he had long suspected that he could not measure up to his position. "Still, I thought he might get through, as many a boy has got through college, without disgrace, and without knowledge; but I fear he is a failure."

In the solitude of his study, Lincoln reconciled himself to probable defeat. What would be his duty when it came? Taking a sheet of Executive Mansion stationery, he wrote: "This morning, as for some days past, it seems exceedingly probable that this administration will not be re-elected. Then it will be my duty to so co-operate with the President elect, as to save the Union between the election and the inaugeration [*sic*]; as he will have secured his election on such ground that he can not possibly save it afterwards." Lincoln carefully signed his name, and folded and sealed the paper. At the cabinet meeting later in the day he asked each member, without telling them what the paper contained, to sign it on the back. The promise, thus attested, he put carefully in his desk.

Two days later the executive committee of the Republican National Committee met in special session at the White House. "Hell is to pay," Nicolay wrote to Hay, who was on a vacation in Illinois. "Everything is darkness and doubt and discouragement."

Raymond pushed his plan for a commission to Richmond as "the only salt to save us." Lincoln, who at first had been disposed to go along with Raymond's scheme and had drawn up instructions appointing him an emissary to Richmond, on further thought insisted that such a course would be worse than defeat, it would be to surrender the contest in advance. Seward, Stanton, and Fessenden sided staunchly with Lincoln, who presented such a bold front, despite his inner discouragement, that Nicolay thought: if he "can infect R. and his committee with some of his own patience and pluck, we are saved." The committee members left in a more hopeful mood.

*

I N T O the same Wigwam in Chicago where Lincoln had triumphed so spectacularly in 1860 trooped the emboldened Democrats on August 29, 1864. Some, like Vallandigham, the master mind of the convention, had felt the hard hand of the government, though it had made no effort to hinder his recent return from Canada. Some entertained sincere fears of the loss of cherished civil rights if Lincoln remained in office four more years. Most of them professed to be loyal Unionists. Some harbored secret sympathies for the South. All wanted peace— some of them at any price. Noah Brooks attended, at Lincoln's "express wish," and kept the President advised of what went on.

Governor Seymour declared in his keynote speech: "The administration cannot save the Union. We can. Mr. Lincoln views many things above the Union. We put the Union first of all. He thinks a proclamation worth more than peace. We think the blood of our people more precious than edicts of the President."

Brooks informed Lincoln that General George B. McClellan's nomination was a certainty from the first. The party could extol him as a victim of Republican persecution, as a man who had accomplished much and might have done a great deal more except for partisan obstruction. Always politically minded, and assured of his capacity to guide the country through its crises, McClellan, since his retirement, had avoided doing anything that might impair his availability. George H. Pendleton, of Ohio, was chosen for second place on the ticket.

The platform proved an embarrassment to McClellan. Framed by Vallandigham, it declared the war a failure and called for immediate peace. "I could not look in the face of my gallant comrades of the army and navy who have survived so many bloody battles," said McClellan in accepting the nomination, "and tell them that their labors and the sacrifices of so many of our slain and wounded brethren had been in vain, that we had abandoned that Union for which we have so often periled our lives . . . no peace can be permanent without Union."

Although McClellan thus virtually repudiated peace on terms of disunion, his nomination and the Democratic platform brought new hope and new determination to the South. The Confederate leaders had despaired of victory; but they still hoped for independence through foreign intervention or by a revulsion against Lincoln that would bring the Peace Democrats to power. General Stephen D. Ramseur, of North Carolina, wrote to his wife: "You will know before this reaches you that McClellan & Pendleton are the nominees of the Chicago Convention. Their platform is ingeniously contrived to mean either war or peace—so as to catch all of the opponents of the Lincoln administration—& to be governed by events between now & the election. If our armies can hold their own, suffer no crushing disaster before the next election, we may reasonably expect a termination of this war." Five days later, on September 11, Ramseur wrote again: "We learn from gentlemen recently from the North that the Peace party is growing rapidly—that McClellan will be elected & that his election will bring peace, *provided always* that we continue to *hold our own* against the Yankee Armies."

Hardly had the Democratic delegates reached their homes when the situation underwent a startling change. The telegraph chattered a message from Sherman: "Atlanta is ours and fairly won." Joy flashed across the North. Lincoln, as though in answer to the Democratic platform, called for a day of thanksgiving for the signal successes vouchsafed by Providence at Mobile and Atlanta. Grant ordered a salute with shotted guns from every battery bearing on the enemy. The *Charleston Courier* announced Sherman's victory with the comment: "All of us perceive the intimate connection existing between the armies of the Confederacy and the peace men in the United States. These constitute two immense forces that are working together for the procurement of peace. . . . Our success in battle assures the success of McClellan. Our failure will inevitably lead to his defeat."

*

On September 12 Lincoln telegraphed Grant: "Sheridan and Early are facing each other at a dead-lock. Could we not pick up a regiment here and there, to the number of say ten thousand men, and quietly, but suddenly concentrate them at Sheridan's camp and enable him to make a strike?" A week later the broad-chested young Irishman launched a smashing campaign up the Shenandoah Valley. His one-two punch at Opequon Creek and Fisher's Hill sent Early reeling southward. Grant was determined that Lee should never again use the Valley either as a corridor to the North or as a storehouse of supplies. "Nothing should be left to invite the enemy to return," he instructed Sheridan. "Take all provisions, forage, and stock wanted for the use of your command; such as cannot be consumed destroy. . . . The people should be informed that so long as an army can subsist among them recurrences of these raids must be expected, and we are determined to stop them at all hazards."

On October 10 General Ramseur wrote dolefully to his wife: "This beautiful & fertile valley has been totally destroyed. Sheridan had some of the houses, *all* of the mills and barns, every straw stack & wheat stack burned. We have to haul our supplies from far up the valley."

While Sheridan despoiled the Valley, Lee quietly sent reinforcements to enable Early to regain the offensive. With that uncanny foresight that he so often manifested, Lincoln telegraphed Grant: "I hope it will lay no constraint on you, nor do harm any way, for me to say I am a little afraid lest Lee sends re-enforcements to Early, and enables him to turn upon Sheridan." On October 19 Early surprised the Union troops at Cedar Creek. Sheridan, returning from a conference at Washington, heard the rumble of the battle at Winchester, twenty miles north of it. Dashing toward the battlefront, he met a routed army, rallied it, and turned disaster into a victory that made him a major general and a hero to the North.

With Early decisively beaten, Sheridan resumed his task of wholesale destruction. Houses stood in lonely desolation, barns and fences burned and livestock driven off. Blackened chimneys pointed forlornly heavenward. Little remained in the Valley to sustain man or beast.

*

T H E   F A V O R A B L E   turn of military events brought a scurry for the Lincoln bandwagon. Chase made a peace mission to the White House, then took the stump for Lincoln. Henry Winter Davis toured Maryland in his behalf. Greeley ceased trumpeting for a negotiated peace and declared that the only effective peace commissioners were Grant, Sherman, Sheridan, and Farragut. "I shall fight like a savage in this campaign," he promised Nicolay. "I hate McClellan." At a great Lincoln meeting in New York several leaders of the "Lincoln withdrawal" movement occupied conspicuous places on the platform.

Radical Senator Henry Wilson wrote from Massachusetts that New England Republicans, who had been very much cast down, were at last getting to work. But there was still much discontent. "One scolds about the Cabinet, another finds fault with something else. Our merchants are down on Welles. Stanton is not loved, nor I am sure at all appreciated. Blair everyone hates,— tens of thousands of men will be lost to you or will give a reluctant vote on account of the Blairs. . . . Let us not throw away any help. If we are beaten our friends will cast the blame on you for they believe they can carry the country easy with another candidate. You must lose no time in the work of putting all our friends in the fight. You will think I have written you a very strange letter. I have written it as a friend of our cause and a friend of your election. Read it and then *destroy it*."

The administration swung its power behind Lincoln's candidacy. Patronage and contracts were awarded in a manner to gain votes. Stanton kept careful watch on the political attitudes of government employees and dismissed a quartermaster for betting against the party.

Lincoln refused to modify the draft, despite pleas from fearful politicians. "What is the Presidency to me," he asked an Ohio committee, "if I have no country?" But he promised to appoint James Gordon Bennett minister to France to obtain the support of the *New York Herald*. And he yielded at last to the clamor against Montgomery Blair.

Denunciations of "the Blair tribe" had burdened Lincoln's mail. "They never had anything to do with any one," one correspondent complained, "unless they left their sting. I am afraid you will find this out too late. If you will kick them out of your presence you will be our next President and otherwise you will not." The retention of Blair, with Chase out of the cabinet, had upset the party equilibrium and nettled Chase's friends. And the Republican national convention, the party's court of last resort, had forcefully repudiated the provocative Postmaster General.

Blair's caustic disposition had not improved. Cabinet colleagues and party leaders found it increasingly difficult to get along with him. When Early's raiders burned his home at Silver Spring, Blair blamed the "poltroons and cowards" in the War Department. Stanton and Halleck had demanded that Lincoln dismiss "the slanderer," but the President replied: "I do not consider what may have been hastily said in a moment of vexation at so severe a loss is sufficient ground for so grave a step." Lincoln used the occasion to reprove backbiting in the cabinet; he must continue to be the judge, he said, of when any man should be removed. For any of his advisers publicly to disparage another would be wrongful to him and to the public; he wanted nothing of the sort to happen again.

In late September, however, Lincoln at last gave way before the pressure. Zach Chandler took credit for arranging a bargain whereby Frémont withdrew from the presidential race in return for Blair's dismissal from the cabinet, and there is evidence that he did so; or rather that he obtained Lincoln's assent to such a bargain; for in a letter to his wife he wrote: "The President was most reluctant to come to terms *but came.*" Chandler's subsequent negotiations with Frémont have never been completely clarified, but Frémont apparently would have no part of the bargain. On September 22 he renounced his candidacy, however, and Lincoln accepted Blair's resignation the next day.

Frémont's tone was most ungracious. He had come to his decision, he asserted, not because he approved of Lincoln's policies, but because McClellan had declared, in effect, for the restoration of the Union with slavery and must be defeated at all costs. Lincoln was simply the lesser of two evils. "I consider," Frémont stated, "that the administration has been politically, militarily, and financially a failure, and that its necessary continuance is a cause of regret for the country."

Lincoln appointed ex-Governor William Dennison of Ohio, a man of high character and gracious manner, as Blair's successor. "Sheridan's victory is glorious," a party worker wrote to Lincoln, "but it is excelled by the removal of Blair." Another asserted: "The change will be worth thousands of votes to you and our country's cause." Welles thought Lincoln's election was now assured, but that the radicals, having had their way with Blair, would be encouraged to take further steps to gain control of the party. Wade threw his influence behind the President, though his speeches condemned the Democrats much more than they praised Lincoln. "To save the nation," he wrote to Chandler, "I am doing all for *him* that I could possibly do for a better man."

*

O h i o, Pennsylvania, and Indiana held state elections in October. The outcome would be important to the party and as a forecast of results in November. Ohio and Pennsylvania allowed soldiers to cast ballots in the field, but Indiana, with twenty-nine regiments and two batteries serving with Sherman, had made no provision for the soldier vote. So Lincoln sent a letter to Sherman by special messenger, suggesting: "Any thing you can safely do to let her soldiers, or any part of them, go home and vote at the State election will be greatly in point. They need not remain for the Presidential election, but may return to you at once." Sherman granted wholesale furloughs to his Hoosier troops. Generals Frank Blair and John A. Logan, on Lincoln's authority, made speeches in Indiana.

The day after the state elections Lincoln telegraphed Grant: "Pennsylvania very close, and still in doubt on home vote. Ohio largely for us, with all the members of congress but two or three. Indiana largely for us—Governor, it is said by 15,000, and 8 of the eleven members of congress. Send us what you may know of your army vote." Soldier ballots swelled the Republican pluralities, and *Harper's Weekly* commented: "The October elections show that unless all human foresight fails, the election of Abraham Lincoln and Andrew Johnson is assured."

There were the usual campaign smears. One Democratic paper accused Lincoln of drawing his salary in gold while the soldiers received their pay in depreciated greenbacks. Actually Lincoln was paid by salary warrants, payable in greenbacks, which he often failed to cash for months. The estate of some $15,000 that he had accumulated as a lawyer had grown considerably, but preoccupation with public matters left him little time for personal affairs. One day in June 1864 he made a list of his personal holdings, pocketed everything at hand, walked over to the Treasury, and dumped the contents of his pockets on Chase's desk, with the request that everything be invested in one type of government bonds. George Harrington, an assistant secretary, to whom Chase turned over the confused mass on his desk, counted $50,381.40 in government obligations of one sort or another, $4,044.67 in unredeemed salary warrants, $89 in greenbacks, and a bag of gold amounting to $883.30—a total of $55,-398.37. The estate of some $90,000 that Lincoln had accumulated by the time he died increased under the skillful administration of David Davis to $110,974.62.

Both Lincoln and McClellan followed custom in refraining from formal speechmaking during the campaign. But in informal talks to soldiers passing through Washington the President never failed to remind them of the issues the country faced. "I almost always feel inclined," he said to the 166th Ohio Regiment, "when I happen to say anything to soldiers, to impress upon them, in a few brief remarks, the importance of success in this contest. It is not merely for to-day, but for all time to come, that we should perpetuate for our children's children that great and free government which we have enjoyed all our lives. I beg you to remember this, not merely for my sake, but for yours. I happen, temporarily, to occupy this White House. I am a living witness that any one of your children may look to come here as my father's child has. It is in order that each of you may have, through this free government which we have enjoyed, an open field and a fair chance for your industry, enterprise and intelligence; that you all may have equal privileges in the race of life, with all its desirable human aspirations. It is for this the struggle should be maintained, that we may not lose our birthright. . . . The nation is worth fighting for, to secure such an inestimable jewel."

Lincoln knew that "practical" means were being used in his behalf. The Union executive committee assessed each member of the cabinet $250 and levied five per cent on the salaries of all workers in the War, Treasury, and Post Office departments. Virtuous old Gideon Welles refused to condone such methods among his employees. "To a great extent the money so raised is misused, misapplied, and perverted and prostituted," he complained. "A set of harpies and adventurers pocket a large portion of the money extorted." At the Brooklyn Navy Yard, however, workmen who voiced sympathy for McClellan walked the plank by scores.

Two days before the election Thurlow Weed wrote to the President from New York City: "All has been done that *can* be done here. Every Ward—here and in Brooklyn—and every

Election District, is abundantly supplied with 'material aid.' "
The outlook was promising, Weed thought, though he was "sorry
to see so many returning soldiers against us. They obtained
furloughs under false pretenses."

*

ELECTION day, November 8, found Washington quiet. Many
persons had gone home to vote. A cold rain with wintry gusts
kept people off the streets. Noah Brooks stopped at the White
House and found Lincoln alone. The President felt gravely uncertain as the people registered their will.

"It is singular," Lincoln observed to John Hay later in the
day, "that I, who am not a vindictive man, should always, except
once, have been before the people in canvasses marked by great
bitterness. When I came to Congress it was a quiet time, but
always, except that, the contests in which I have been prominent
have been marked with great rancor."

About seven o'clock in the evening Lincoln and Hay splashed
across the White House grounds to the side door of the War
Department. A soaked and steaming sentry huddled against the
wall. Few persons except the telegraph clerks remained in the
building. Stanton was sick with chills and fever.

A dispatch from Indiana showed Lincoln well ahead. Philadelphia Republicans reported 10,000 plurality. Party leaders
in Baltimore claimed the city by 15,000, and the state by 5,000.
The Union ticket led in Massachusetts. The heavy storm delayed
dispatches from distant states, but the trend continued to be
favorable. McClellan led in New York City by 35,000, Lincoln in
the state by 40,000. The President sent these first returns to
Mrs. Lincoln. "She is more anxious than I," he said.

Gustavus Fox exulted over news that Henry Winter Davis
had been defeated in Maryland. "You have more of that feeling of
personal resentment than I," Lincoln replied. "Perhaps I have
too little of it, but I never thought it paid. A man has no time
to spend half his life in quarrels. If any man ceases to attack
me I never remember the past against him."

Toward midnight Major Thomas T. Eckert provided supper. Lincoln awkwardly dished out the oysters. About half past two in the morning a band played under the window. In the course of the evening Lincoln, who was in a reminiscent mood, had told how, after the election of 1860, he went home utterly tired and threw himself down on a sofa. Opposite where he lay, a large mirror hung over a bureau. Looking in the glass, he saw himself nearly at full length, but his face had two distinct images, one nearly superimposed on the other. Perplexed and somewhat startled, he got up to study his reflection, but the illusion vanished. When he lay down again, however, it reappeared, plainer than before, and he noticed that one face looked paler than the other. Again, when he rose, the vision disappeared. The phenomenon troubled him, and he had told his wife about it. Mrs. Lincoln had taken it for a sign—her husband would be elected for two terms, but the pale face signified that he would not live through the second one.

The complete election tally a few days later gave Lincoln 2,203,831 ballots to McClellan's 1,797,019—more than 400,000 plurality. With Lincoln carrying every state except Kentucky, Delaware, and New Jersey, the electoral vote would be 212 to 21. The soldier vote was an important factor in his triumph.

*

T H E N I G H T after the election a crowd with banners, lanterns, and transparencies marched to the White House to cheer the President. Lincoln read a speech from a window, with Brooks holding a candle to light his manuscript. The country had been sorely tested by days of hate, mistrust, and bitterness. "If the loyal people, *united* were put to the utmost of their strength by the rebellion, must they not fail when *divided* and partially paralized [*sic*], by a political war among themselves?" Lincoln inquired. "But the election was a necessity. We can not have free government without elections; and if the rebellion could force us to forego, or postpone a national election, it might fairly claim to have already conquered and ruined us. . . . But the election, along with its incidental, and undesirable strife, has done us good too. It has demonstrated that a people's government can sustain a national election, in the midst of a great civil war. Until now it has not been known to the world that this was a possibility."

At a cabinet meeting next day Lincoln asked the members if they recalled the sealed paper he had asked them to sign in late August. Then he had Hay remove the seals and read it to them. "You will remember that this was written at a time (6 days before the Chicago nominating Convention)," the President said, "when as yet we had no adversary and seemed to have no friends. I then solemnly resolved on the course of action indicated above. I resolved, in case of the election of McClellan, being certain that he would be the candidate, that I would see him and talk matters over with him. I would say, General, the election has demonstrated that you are stronger, have more influence with the American people than I. Now let us together, you with your influence and I with all the executive power of the Government, try to save the country. You raise as many troops as you possibly can for this final trial, and I will devote all my energies to assisting and finishing the war."

Seward grinned wryly. McClellan would have answered: "Yes, yes," he thought, and done nothing. And again it would have been "Yes, yes," and nothing done.

"At least," Lincoln responded, "I should have done my duty and have stood clear before my own conscience."

*

LINCOLN's story of his dream on election night brought new forebodings to the mind of Ward Hill Lamon. Since Lincoln's nomination to the Presidency the devoted Lamon, whom Lincoln had appointed marshal of the District of Columbia, had feared for his friend's safety and acted as a self-appointed bodyguard. Possibly only he and Lincoln knew that one night in the autumn of 1862, as the President rode alone to the Soldiers' Home, a rifle bullet had whined through the darkness and knocked Lincoln's hat into the ditch. Lamon knew the vile hatreds that had been born of civil strife. He warned the President that there were cranks, villains, and misguided Southern patriots who would welcome a chance to kill him.

Now, with Lincoln elected for another four-year term, Lamon knew that these hatreds would be intensified; cold fear gripped the burly marshal as Lincoln told about his dream. When the President left for home, Lamon accompanied him to the White House in the dark early-morning hours, saw him safely to his bedroom, and then, without Lincoln's knowledge, curled up on a blanket in the corridor outside his door, where he slept till daybreak.

Stanton also feared for Lincoln's safety and had cautioned him to take care. While the President continued to take solitary walks to the War Department in the dead of night, as he had done since the beginning of the war, Stanton ordered that he must never leave alone. An Ohio company had been detailed to guard the White House, and a cavalry detachment was stationed at the Soldiers' Home.

These precautions annoyed Lincoln, not because he failed to realize his danger—scarcely a week passed without a threatening letter—but because he believed that no safeguards would prove effective if anyone wishing to kill him dared to risk his own life. He thought it unbecoming in a President to surround himself with armed guards, like some pompous emperor; and he considered it important "that the people know I come among them without fear."

CHAPTER XIX

Profile of a President

A PRESIDENT'S life is wearying and worrisome at best, but in Lincoln's case all the vast problems of the war were added to the normal tasks of office. Nicolay and Hay comprised his secretarial staff until William O. Stoddard was brought in to assist them midway of the war. Edward D. Neill succeeded Stoddard when the latter became ill, and was in turn succeeded by Charles Philbrick. These young men scrutinized and questioned visitors, prepared a daily digest of news and military information, read and sorted the mail, and took care of whatever other details happened to call for attention. They had rooms at the White House, but walked to Willard's for their meals.

Lincoln started his workday early, for he was a light and fitful sleeper, and sometimes walked alone across the White House lawn in the gray dawn to summon a newsboy. By eight o'clock, when breakfast was announced, he had already been at work for an hour or more. His morning meal consisted of an egg and a cup of coffee; he was so little concerned about eating that Mrs. Lincoln sometimes invited guests to breakfast to make sure he would come. After breakfast he put in another hour of work before his door opened to visitors.

Except for the hot summer months, when they lived at the Soldiers' Home, the Lincoln family occupied the west wing of the second floor of the White House. The east wing was devoted to

business. Lincoln's office was a large room on the south, next
to Nicolay's office in the southeast corner. Its furnishings were
simple—a large oak table covered with cloth, around which
the cabinet met; another table between the two long windows, at
which Lincoln usually wrote, seated in a large armchair; a tall
desk with pigeonholes for papers against the south wall; a few
straight-back chairs, and two plain, hair-covered sofas. A
marble mantel surmounted the fireplace with its high brass fender
and brass andirons. Glass-globed gas jets hung from the ceiling.
The only wall adornments were an old discolored engraving of
President Jackson above the mantel, a photograph of John Bright,
the English liberal leader, and numerous military maps in wooden
frames. One door opened into Nicolay's office and another into
the hall, where a messenger sat to bring in the cards of visitors.
A bell cord hung near the President's desk.

At first Lincoln refused to limit the visiting-hours. "They
do not want much," he said of the throng waiting to see him, "and
they get very little. . . . I know how I would feel in their place."
So people began coming before breakfast, and some still remained
late at night. Lincoln realized at last that something must be
done to conserve his time, and agreed to restrict the visiting-
period from ten o'clock in the morning till three in the afternoon.
But his other work continued to pile up, and the hours were again
shortened, from ten till one.

Priority was granted to cabinet members, senators, and
representatives in that order; finally, if any time remained,
ordinary citizens were admitted. Army officers, many of whom
had made nuisances of themselves with requests for promotion or
demands for redress from supposed injustices, were forbidden to
come to Washington without special permission.

Notwithstanding Lincoln's wish to keep himself accessible,
it was not easy to see him. His friend Dr. Anson G. Henry, who
was a house guest at the White House in February 1863, noted
that "nine times out of ten not half the Senators get in unless
several go in to-gether & this is very often done, and they can
take in with them as many of their friends and constituents as

they please. It is no uncommon thing for Senators to try for
ten days before they get a private interview."

Many persons, after waiting unsuccessfully for several days,
went home and made their wishes known by letter. Joseph Medill,
of the *Chicago Tribune*, wrote to Lincoln: "Not having either time
or inclination to hang round waiting rooms among a wolfish crowd
seeking admission to your presence for office or contracts or
personal favors, I prefer stating in writing the substance of what
I would say verbally."

With only Edward Moran, a short, thin, humorous Irishman,
who had served since President Taylor's time, stationed at the
front door, and Louis Bargdorf, another White House veteran,
posted in the upstairs corridor, the throng enjoyed access to all
the public rooms and trooped about unhindered. Lamon warned
Lincoln that eavesdroppers and traitors lurked among the crowd,
and suggested that Allan Pinkerton or some other shrewd detective be employed to ferret them out. At least everyone should be
kept downstairs until his name was called, he thought. But not
until November 1864 were four District of Columbia policemen
in plain clothes detailed to the White House. A secretary gave
each visitor a final scrutiny, but even so, unworthy persons often
managed to intrude upon the President.

Once a visitor had passed the outer barriers and entered
Lincoln's office, he encountered no further formality. The
President never effused: "I am delighted to see you," unless he
meant it; he simply said: "How do you do?" or "What can I do
for you?" with a pleasant nod and smile. Lincoln wore no outward signs of greatness. He inspired no awe or embarrassment.
He had no pomp, no wish to impress. But along with his awkward
angularity he had an innate poise and casual unaffected dignity.
Meeting all sorts of people, he shaped his response to their
approach. He was lowly to the meek, dignified to the pompous,
flippant or stern with the presumptuous, and courteous to everyone, even his foes, when they came to him in good faith. He
respected the views of others and listened while they talked, for

he knew that in some matters they might see truth more clearly than he, and that men arrive at truth by free discussion. His usual attitude while listening was to cross his long legs and lean forward, hands clasped around his knee, or with one elbow on his knee to support his arm while he stroked his chin.

Samuel R. Suddarth, Quartermaster General of Kentucky, observed after an interview: "His conversational powers are fine—and his custom of interspersing conversation with incidents, anecdotes and witticisms are well calculated to impress his hearers with the kindheartedness of the man. And they are so adroitly and delicately mingled in the thread of his discourse that one hardly notices the digression. His language is good though not select. . . . He is dignified in his manners without austerity." Suddarth was one of very few persons who heard Lincoln use profanity; "He is a damned rascal," the President said of a certain politician, and then added hastily, as though surprised: "God knows I do not know when I have sworn before."

Nicolay always rejoiced when Congress adjourned. The members presented countless trivial demands that kept the President vexed and anxious and troubled him no end. Many private citizens were scarcely less considerate of Lincoln's time. "Going into his room this morning to announce the Secretary of War," Nicolay confided to his fiancée, "I found a little party of Quakers holding a prayer-meeting around him, and he was compelled to bear the affliction until the 'spirit' moved them to stop. Isn't it strange that so many and such intelligent people often have so little common sense?"

Nicolay and Hay noted that through all the stirring days of war Lincoln almost invariably remained assured and steady on the surface no matter how afflicted he might be within. One caller observed the same fund of anecdote in Lincoln, but not the old free, lingering laugh. Another remarked about "the two-fold working of the two-fold nature of the man: Lincoln the Westerner, slightly humorous but thoroughly practical and sagacious. . . . Lincoln the President and statesman . . . seen in those abstract and serious eyes, which seemed withdrawn to an inner sanctuary of thought, sitting in judgment on the scene and feeling its far reach into the future."

*

IT ALWAYS gave Lincoln pleasure to be able to grant a request. But the glibbest talkers could not back him down. He seldom gave an outright "No." He was more likely to make the necessity of saying it so obvious that refusal became unnecessary. Or he would turn the conversation with a story or a jest; when petitioners found themselves back in the hall, they wondered how he had got rid of them. Men of the strongest personalities felt Lincoln's quiet dominance. Thurlow Weed went home after a talk with him and wrote: "I do not, when with you, say half I intend, partly because I do not like to 'crank,' and partly because you talk me out of my convictions and apprehensions. So bear with me, please, now, till I free my mind."

Lincoln gave way to annoyance at times. "Now go away!" he told one visitor. "Go away! I cannot attend to all these details. I could as easily bail out the Potomac with a teaspoon!" He replied sharply to a lady who sent him a long, demanding letter that "the bare reading of a letter of that length requires more than any person's share of my time."

Usually, however, he kept his temper under tight control. "If I do get up a little temper," he wrote, "I have no sufficient time to keep it up." He refused to quarrel himself, and tried to keep others from quarreling. He wrote to Senator Pomeroy about a senatorial dispute over an appointment: "I wish you and Lane would make an effort to get out of the mood you are in— It does neither of you any good—it gives you the means of tormenting my life out of me, and nothing else."

One time it became the President's duty to administer a rebuke to a young captain, James Madison Cutts, a brother-in-law of Stephen A. Douglas, who became involved in quarrels with brother officers. Evidently Lincoln drew up a memorandum of what he wished to say, for among his papers is a document which reads: "Although what I am now to say is to be, in form, a reprimand, it is not intended to add a pang to what you have already suffered upon the subject to which it relates. You have too much of life yet before you, and have shown too much of promise as an officer, for your future to be lightly surrendered. . . . The advice of a father to his son, 'Beware of entrance to a quarrel, but being in, bear it that the opposed may beware of thee,' is good, and yet not the best. Quarrel not at all. No man resolved to make the most of himself, can spare time for personal contention. Still less can he afford to take all the consequences, including the vitiating of his temper, and the loss of self-control."

Lincoln had come a long way in charity and self-discipline from the satirical young politician of 1842, who goaded an opponent to challenge him to a duel, when he could say in November 1864: "So long as I have been here I have not willingly planted a thorn in any man's bosom."

He owed not a little of this self-mastery to the irrepressible sense of humor that enabled him to recognize the ridiculous and to hold things in true perspective. In addition to quarreling, Captain Cutts also faced the charge of taking a valise or portmanteau from his room at the Burnet House, in Cincinnati, and "placing himself thereon" in a corridor to look through a transom at a lady while she undressed. In reprimanding Cutts, Lincoln referred to this offense as "not of great enormity, and yet greatly to be avoided," and one which he felt sure that Cutts would not repeat. But as he remitted Cutts's sentence of dismissal from the army, he commented privately to Hay that the young man should be elevated to the "peerage" with the title of Count Peeper—a cognomen suggested to him by the name of the Swedish Minister, Edward Count Piper.

*

W I T H government officials and men of influence so often turned away from Lincoln's office, it is remarkable that so many humble people managed to get in. But if he learned that some anxious old lady or worried wife, or a young soldier in a private's uniform had been waiting patiently from day to day to see him, he would arrange an appointment and if necessary overstay his time to hear his story. His secretaries estimated that he spent at least three quarters of his time in meeting people, despite their efforts to shield him from annoyance. It was as though he tried to make himself the nation's burden-bearer; and when his door swung shut at last, he was often near exhaustion.

While these daily sessions wore on him physically, they refreshed his mind and spirit. Through them he measured the pulse-beat of the people and learned to key his actions to its changing throb, using caution when it slowed, moving boldly when he felt it quicken. He called them his "public opinion baths," but they were more than that, for they also enabled him to curb the undue harshness of subordinates, and to override bureaucratic arrogance and indifference.

Time and again, after listening to someone's woes, the President would send him to Stanton, Welles, Seward, or some other person in authority with a brief but precious missive: "Mr. Secretary, please see and hear this man"; "Please give this matter your immediate attention"; "Can this man be accommodated?" "Has the Sec. of the Navy any knowledge of this case? and if any, what?" "There is a mistake somewhere in this case. . . . Will the Secretary of War please have the matter corrected? or explain to me wherein the hitch is?" "Mr. Defrees—Please see this girl who works in your office, and find out about her brother, and come and tell me." To Surgeon General William A. Hammond, Lincoln wrote: "A Baltimore committee called on me this morning, saying that city is full of straggling soldiers, half-sick, half well, who profess to have been turned from the hospitals with no definite directions where to go. Is this true? Are men turned from the hospitals without knowing where to go?"

An "influence peddler," who gave his name as Captain Parker, claimed to know Judge Advocate General Joseph Holt, and promised a Mrs. Anna S. King that for three hundred dollars he would obtain a pardon for her husband. It was all the money the poor woman had; and John Hay, when he heard her story,

took her to the President. After listening to her, Lincoln telegraphed to General Meade: "An intelligent woman in deep distress
called this morning, saying her husband, a Lieutenant in the A.P.
was to be shot next morning for desertion." She had left without
giving her name or that of her husband, but the President made
sure that Meade would delay all executions, ran down the man's
identity, and commuted his sentence to imprisonment. The doors
of military prisons opened for untold numbers of repentent
Confederates at the behest of Lincoln's terse endorsement: "Let
this man take the oath and be discharged."

Times almost innumerable the President sent petitioners
joyfully on their way to a department head with a brief but
authoritative note: "Let this woman have her son out of Old
Capital Prison"; "Attorney-General, please make out and send
me a pardon in this case"; "Injustice has probably been done in
this case, Sec. of War please examine it"; or a brief statement of a
request followed by: "Let it be done." It would be difficult to
estimate how many tired, scared, or homesick boys in the Union
army who fell asleep on picket duty, ran away in battle, or slipped
off without leave to visit wives or parents were spared from the
death sentence by a terse telegram from Lincoln: "Suspend
sentence of execution and forward record of trial for examination,"
or "Let him fight instead of being shot."

Lincoln's orders to Stanton often display sly humor. The
crabbed Secretary must have snorted with disgust when he read
Lincoln's order: "Please have the adjutant general ascertain
whether second Lieutenant of Company D, 2nd infantry, Alexander E. Drake, is entitled to promotion. His wife thinks he is.
Please have this looked into." Stanton had learned that he could
oppose the President up to a point; but to go beyond that point
might bring him a rebuff such as: "I personally wish Jacob R.
Freese, of New Jersey, to be appointed a Colonel of a colored
regiment—and this regardless of whether he can tell the exact
shade of Julius Caesar's hair." On August 23, 1862 Lincoln
wrote, either to Stanton or as a memorandum for himself: "To-
day, Mrs. Major Paul of the Regular Army calls and urges the

appointment of her husband as Brig-Genl. She is a saucy woman
and I am afraid she will keep tormenting me till I have to do it."
Less than two weeks later, Major Gabriel R. Paul was commissioned a brigadier general.

Many of Lincoln's instructions were subtly philosophical.
"This man wants to work," he wrote, "so uncommon a want that
I think it ought to be gratified." His most commonplace writings
bear the stamp of individuality. "You request my autograph.
Well here it is"—or "here 'tis. A. Lincoln," he scribbled many
times.

*

T H I S sort of work filled Lincoln's mornings. At one o'clock, or
some time afterward, he made his way to the living-quarters
through the still-crowded corridor. His passage gave the more
intrusive callers an opportunity to intercept him, for his informal
habits made him prone to stop and talk. In 1864 a door cut from
his office gave direct access to the family apartment.

The visiting time ended early on Tuesdays and Fridays, when
the cabinet met regularly at noon. On Mondays, when the President held a reception from one to two, he usually missed his
lunch. This was of small concern to him, however, for he normally
ate only a biscuit, with perhaps some fruit in season, and drank
a glass of milk.

After lunch Lincoln might sprawl in a big armchair by the
window in the family sitting-room to read for a few minutes, one
leg crossed over the other and bouncing up and down as though
to music. Corns bothered him—he wrote a testimonial for a
Jewish chiropodist who also performed confidential missions for
him: "Dr. Zacharie has operated on my feet with good success,
and considerable addition to my comfort"—so he often slipped
off his shoes and sat in his stocking feet, until Mrs. Lincoln
noticed it and sent a servant for his slippers. Some time during
the day a servant shaved his upper lip and trimmed his beard, and
had been seen to shake the towel out the White House window.

*

E A R L Y afternoon found Lincoln again at work. With the expansion of the army, thousands of commissions must be signed; later these became less numerous, but in their place came batches of court-martial sentences, amounting to thirty thousand in a year, for him to modify or approve. Those involving the death penalty received his closest attention, but none escaped his notice. John Hay told of six hours spent in such work on a humid July day and noted how eagerly Lincoln seized on any possible excuse to save a soldier's life. Only cases of meanness or cruelty failed to evoke his sympathy. He was especially averse to approving the death penalty for cowardice—"leg cases" he called those in which a soldier ran away in battle—and as he remitted sentence he said wryly: "It would frighten the poor fellows too terribly to kill them."

But while his impulse was always toward forgiveness, he could be hard when military discipline called for sternness. In the case of five bounty-jumpers sentenced to death for desertion, he wrote to General Meade: "I understand these are very flagrant cases and that you deem their punishment as being indispensable to the service. If I am not mistaken in this, please let them know at once that their appeal is denied."

Some time during the morning the secretaries had sorted the mail. Correspondence arrived in torrents: resolutions and petitions written in copperplate scroll, letters carefully composed, and almost illegible scrawls. Threatening or abusive letters were usually tossed into the wastebasket. Those of a routine nature went to various departments. Only a relatively small number reached the President's desk, usually with a secretarial notation— "Personal," "Political," or a brief summary of their contents written on the back.

Even after careful sifting they made a formidable pile. Lincoln snatched what time he could to read them, but many suffered the same fate as that of Dr. Henry P. Tappan, chancellor of the University of Michigan. The well-meaning educator sent Lincoln fifteen pages of advice, routing his letter by way of David Davis to make sure Lincoln would read it. Davis endorsed

it: "This letter is an elaborate one, written in good temper &
from the Christian character of the author entitled to be read."
But even such a testimonial was not enough; Lincoln wrote on the
back of the letter: "Mr. Nicolay, please run over this & tell me
what is in it."

John Hay answered some of Lincoln's mail, usually with the
introduction: "In reply to your letter, the President directs me
to say—" But in most cases where an answer was required,
Lincoln penned it in longhand, and frequently took the trouble
of making a copy for his files. He employed the same rudimentary
filing system that he had used as a country lawyer; the pigeonholes of his tall desk were marked alphabetically, with a few of
the apertures assigned to individuals. Each cabinet member and a
number of generals had pigeonholes of their own. So did Horace
Greeley. One compartment marked "W. & W." aroused the
interest of Frank B. Carpenter, the artist, and Lincoln explained:
"That's Weed and Wood—Thurlow and Fernandy." "That's a
pair of 'em," he chuckled.

*

THE PRESIDENT endured a great deal of pestering at the
hands of well-meaning friends, who could scarcely appreciate how
much the kindly, simple man they knew had grown. His old
Illinois colleagues Governor Richard Yates, Ozias M. Hatch, and
Jesse K. Dubois often took it upon themselves to tell him what to
do, especially in matters affecting Illinois. Usually they acted as
a team and signed their letters jointly. Joseph Medill continually
sent Lincoln letters of advice; when he failed to heed or answer
them, Medill at last wrote a long list of admonitions to Commissioner of Indian Affairs William P. Dole, with instructions to
bring them to Lincoln's attention. He would not have bothered
Dole, he explained, "if I had any influence with the President."

When Congressman Isaac N. Arnold pressed his ideas of
military matters upon Lincoln, the President replied sharply:
"I am compelled to take a more practical and unprejudiced view
of things. Without claiming to be your superior, which I do not,

my position enables me to understand my duty in all these matters better than you possibly can, and I hope you do not yet doubt my integrity." Lincoln had no false pride in little things. But he likewise had no false modesty. He would not be bullied, even by his friends, John Hay observed.

Lincoln had been generous in appointing friends to office. Some of them added to his worries by getting into trouble. He had rewarded "Uncle Jimmy" Short, who came to his aid at New Salem by purchasing his surveying instruments at sheriff's sale and returning them to him, with a job at the Round Valley Indian Reservation in California at a salary of $1,800 a year. And Uncle Jimmy wrote that he had been discharged for "gambling with the Indians and cohabiting with a squaw." He offered proof of innocence: the squaw was merely a housekeeper, and he had done no gambling. The real reason for his discharge was that a swindling supervisor wanted him out of the way.

Yates, Hatch, and Dubois warned Lincoln that his brother-in-law Ninian W. Edwards, who had been in straightened circumstances until Lincoln appointed him a quartermaster, was now living well beyond his $1,800 salary and bragging about his wealth. Edwards and John A. Bailhache, coeditor of the *Illinois State Journal*, whom Lincoln had made a commissary, were giving all the jobs at their disposal to enemies of the administration. Street gossip said they were in league with corrupt contractors, and that the chief beneficiary of their purchases for the government was ex-Governor Joel A. Matteson, a Democratic stalwart. Edwards came to Washington to protest his innocence. Lincoln evidently believed him. But he transferred him to Chicago and sent Bailhache to New York.

Another of Lincoln's brothers-in-law, Clark M. Smith of Springfield, wrote to him on February 7, 1864 to ask "a very small favor." Smith had started out in life just as Lincoln had, he said, "a poor Boy without Friends money or influence" and was now worth $125,000. Much of this was in the form of high-priced goods in his three stores, and "If you could at the proper time give me a little notice or a hint that things was likely to be brought to a close in our troubles," Smith could unload before a drop in prices came. He would keep the information strictly confidential, since to divulge it would defeat his plans. A letter would reach him in care of George Bliss & Company, 340 Broadway, New York, and "no one Will ever Know but what it would be a family letter if they should see that the letter was from Washington."

No reply from Lincoln is extant, but later letters from Smith indicate that he had felt the sting of rebuke.

*

THE WARTIME afflictions of friends and acquaintances never failed to touch Lincoln deeply. When Lieutenant Colonel William McCullough, of Bloomington, met death in the Vicksburg campaign, Lincoln learned that one of McCullough's daughters had become inconsolable. And just before Christmas in 1862 a letter came to young Fanny McCullough from a busy President: "It is with deep grief that I learn of the death of your kind and brave Father; and especially, that it is affecting your young heart beyond what is common in such cases. In this sad world of ours, sorrow comes to all; and, to the young, it comes with bitterest agony, because it takes them unawares. The older have learned to ever expect it. I am anxious to afford some alleviation of your present distress. Perfect relief is not possible, except with time. You can not now realize that you will ever feel better. Is not this so? And yet it is a mistake. You are sure to be happy again. . . . The memory of your dear Father, instead of an agony, will yet be a sad sweet feeling in your heart, of a purer, and holier sort than you have known before."

With his own son Willie not long dead, Lincoln understood the feelings of Congressman William Kellogg when his son resigned from West Point under demerit that would have led to his dismissal. Lincoln defied the rules of the Academy and reappointed young Kellogg. The case came upon him in the most painful manner, he explained: "Hon. William Kellogg, the father, is not only a member of Congress from my state, but he is my personal friend of more than twenty years' standing, and of whom I had many personal kindnesses. This matter touches him very deeply—the feelings of a father for a child—as he thinks, all the future of his child. I can not be the instrument to crush his heart."

Lincoln's deep human sympathy reached beyond his acquaintances and made him kin to all. "I have been shown in the files of the War Department," he wrote to Lydia Bixby, a Boston widow, "a statement of the Adjutant General of Massachusetts that you are the mother of five sons who have died gloriously on the field of battle. I feel how weak and fruitless must be any word of mine which should attempt to beguile you from the grief of a loss so overwhelming. But I cannot refrain from tendering to you the consolation that may be found in the thanks of the republic they died to save. I pray that our heavenly Father may assuage the anguish of your bereavement, and leave you only the cherished memory of the loved and lost, and the solemn pride that must be yours to have laid so costly a sacrifice upon the altar of freedom."

Lincoln had been misinformed: Mrs. Bixby had only two sons killed; of the other three, two deserted and one was honorably discharged. But that he wrote under a misconception detracts in no wise from the nobility of his motives, nor from the beauty of his tribute to democratic motherhood.

*

NUMEROUS inventors were to be found among the White House throng, each sure that his idea would win the war. Lincoln grasped mechanical principles quickly, and had a faculty for finding flaws in their devices. But if a new explosive or gun model offered promise, the President made sure that it reached the attention of the proper authorities. The new breech-loading rifles interested him keenly, and early morning might find him on the marsh south of the White House watching while they were tried, or perhaps taking a rifle to fire a few rounds himself. A rustic observer at one such experiment afforded him much merriment with the comment that "a good piece of audience hadn't ought to rekyle," and if it did, it should "rekyle a leetle forrid." Lincoln also visited the navy yard to watch tests of naval ordnance. He saw to it that a young chemist was detached from the Department of Agriculture to help Isaac Diller, a Springfield druggist who had sold the Lincolns their cough syrup and calomel, in experiments with a new gunpowder that Diller was trying to perfect.

Lincoln wrote his own speeches and prepared his own state papers in the midst of trivial duties that crowded his working day. Seward arranged for ceremonial introductions and formal interviews with foreign ministers and wrote the brief remarks Lincoln made on such occasions. The President had to receive various delegations and respond to them; parades must be reviewed, and serenaders greeted in the night.

Lincoln had been threatened with tuberculosis during his circuit days, and Mrs. Lincoln insisted that he have fresh air. So almost every day at four o'clock, unless bad weather interfered, the coachman brought a carriage to the White House portico, and the President and his wife went for a drive. They often stopped at some hospital, where Lincoln walked from cot to cot, taking the wan hands in friendly grip, joking with the convalescents, and offering cheer and comfort to those with more serious hurts. He was especially solicitous to the friendless Southern boys.

During the early years of his Presidency Lincoln sometimes rode horseback in the late afternoon. Lamon once sent him a note stating that his wife, "Puss," had been suffering from neuralgia in her face and thought a ride might do her good. Lamon wanted to know "if you are going to ride this evening, if not, please loan her 'George'—your roan horse as he is the only one in the city I would like to trust her with.— If you design taking a ride yourself dont allow us to interfere with it.—for I am sure no one needs such exercise more than you do (and you ought to have it every day)."

*

T H E   L I N C O L N S dined at six o'clock, unless a state function had been planned, and again the President ate sparingly of one or two courses. Military uniforms sometimes lent splendor to the White House dining-room. The artist Carpenter remembered a dinner attended by twelve officers; another time two generals and two colonels, captured at Bull Run and Seven Pines and recently exchanged, were honored guests. There was a splendid dinner for Prince Napoleon Jerome Bonaparte when he visited the United States during the summer of 1861, and another for officers of the Russian navy in 1863. Grant, Meade, and other officers were dinner guests soon after Grant's appointment as commander in chief.

A memorandum furnished by the State Department for the President's social guidance decreed that state dinners should begin at seven thirty o'clock. Correct dress for gentlemen was a black dress coat or one of blue with bright buttons—one should never wear a frock coat. Protocol determined those officials who must be invited to various functions, and the proper seating arrangement. The Lincolns followed the custom of serving wine at official dinners.

Once a week, except in summer, the President held an evening reception or levee. People came by thousands to shake his hand and perhaps steal an opportunity to ask a favor of him. Mrs. Lincoln offered a striking contrast to her husband as she stood beside him elegantly gowned, with a sprig or wreath of flowers in her carefully dressed hair, and jewels at her wrists and throat; for while she saw to it that he wore good clothes and kept them brushed and pressed, they never seemed to hang right on his tall, stooped frame. The white gloves that were the fashion at receptions made his big hands look enormous; once when his glove burst with a loud pop under an especially strong handclasp, he held it up ruefully and laughed.

Carpenter thought these functions must be a torment to the careworn President. But whenever anyone tried to sympathize with Lincoln, he would parry with a jest, and remark that the tug at his hand was much easier to bear than the pull upon his

heartstrings when people asked him for favors that were beyond
his power to grant. As the artist bade good-night, Lincoln asked
in his homely way: "Well, Carpenter, you have seen one day's
run—what is your opinion of it?"

Most evenings when no formal function had been planned,
found Lincoln back at his desk. Nicolay wrote that it was
"impossible to portray by any adequate words, the labor, the
thought, the responsibility, the strain of intellect and the anguish
of soul" that he endured. Carpenter came into Lincoln's office at
eleven o'clock one night and found him seated alone at his long
table with a pile of military commissions before him. They were
made of heavy, oily parchment, very hard to handle or sign, but
he went about his labor with patient industry. "I do not, as you
see, pretend to read over these documents," he said to Carpenter
as the artist sat down beside him. "I see that Stanton has signed
them so I conclude they are alright." He paused to read one.
"John Williams is hereby appointed adjutant-general with the
rank of captain, etc. E. M. Stanton, Secretary of War." "There,"
he said, adding his own signature, "That fixes him out." He
went on chatting and writing till he reached the bottom of the
stack. Then rising and stretching his long arms above his head,
he remarked: "Well, I have that job *husked out;* now I guess I'll
go over to the War Department before I go to bed and see if there
is any news."

A visit to the War Department telegraph office was usually
his last chore. The operators left copies of all military telegrams
in a pile in a desk drawer for him, with the last dispatch on top.
They noticed that as he read them he sat far forward on the edge
of his chair with one knee almost touching the floor. When he had
worked through the pile to the messages he had read before, he
put all of them back and said: "Well, I have got down to raisins."

The curiosity of the young operators got the better of them
at last, and one of them asked the President what he meant by
that remark. He told them he had known a little girl back home
who once gorged herself with a stupendous meal of soup, chicken,
ham, salad, potatoes and sundry other vegetables, ice cream and

cake, and at last a handful of raisins. Things began coming up; and after she had been busily occupied for some time, she looked at her mother and said reassuringly: "I am all right now. I have got down to the raisins."

Lincoln usually read a little before he went to bed. The telegraph operators noticed that he often carried a worn copy of *Macbeth* or *The Merry Wives of Windsor* under his arm when he made his last visit to their office. And John Hay told how at midnight, when he sat writing in his diary, the President came into the office laughing to read him and Nicolay a funny story by Thomas Hood, "seemingly utterly unconscious that he with his short shirt hanging about his long legs, and setting out behind like the tail feathers of an enormous ostrich, was infinitely funnier than anything in the book he was laughing at."

"What a man it is!" thought Hay. "Occupied all day with matters of vast moment, deeply anxious about the fate of the greatest army in the world, with his own plans and future hanging on the events of the passing hour, he yet has such a wealth of simple *bon hommie* and good fellowship that he gets out of bed and perambulates the house in his shirt to find us that we may share with him the fun of poor Hood's queer little conceits."

Mrs. Lincoln's days were busy, too. "I consider myself fortunate," she wrote to Mrs. James C. Conkling, "if at eleven o'clock, I once more find myself, in my pleasant room & very especially, if my tired & weary husband, is *there*, resting in the lounge to receive me—to chat over the occurrences of the day."

*

OCCASIONALLY in the evening Lincoln listened to music in the White House drawing-room. The massive Lamon had a deep, rich voice, and Lincoln loved to hear him sing. One of his special favorites was *The Blue-Tailed Fly*, and Lamon recalled how "he often called for that buzzing ballad when we were alone and he wanted to throw off the weight of public or private cares. . . . But while he had a great fondness for witty or mirth-provoking ballads, our grand old patriotic airs and songs of the tender and sentimental kind afforded him the deepest pleasure." The simple melodies of Stephen Foster never failed to move him deeply.

Lincoln enjoyed the Marine Band; it played twice weekly during the summer months on the south lawn of the White House. But the President was more of an attraction than the musicians, and Carpenter recalled how, when he appeared on the portico, the crowd loudly applauded and called for a speech. Lincoln bowed his thanks, stepped back into the parlor, and slumped down on a sofa. "I wish they would let me sit out there quietly, and enjoy the music," he said wistfully.

Henry C. Whitney, who had traveled the circuit with Lincoln, remembered how he often went alone to any sort of little show or concert and even slipped away one time to attend a magic-lantern show intended for children. Residence in Washington gave him his first chance to hear opera. He became very fond of it, as well as concert music, and as the war took a turn for the better, he attended the theater, opera, or concerts whenever he could, usually with Mrs. Lincoln or a party of friends. Among the operas that he heard were Gounod's *Faust*, Verdi's *Ballo in maschera* and Boïeldieu's *La Dame blanche*. John W. Forney, of the *Philadelphia Press*, recalled an evening at the opera during which the President sat in a corner of his box the entire time, wrapped in a shawl, "either enjoying the music or communing with himself." A vicious battle was raging and Lincoln remarked afterward that he supposed some people would think it indiscreet of him to seek amusement at such a time. "But the truth is," he declared, "I must have a change of some sort or die."

Marshal Lamon never ceased worrying when Lincoln went to public functions without guards. On December 15, 1864 he wrote to Nicolay from New York that he had good reason to fear for the President's safety—"See that he dont go out alone either in the day or night time." Soon afterward, when Lamon made his customary inspection of the White House and found that the President had gone out, he left a note of warning on his desk: "Tonight, as you have done on several previous occasions, you went unattended to the theater. When I say unattended I mean you went alone with Charles Sumner and a foreign minister, neither of whom could defend himself against an assault from any able-bodied woman in this city."

*

"'F o r one of my age," Lincoln wrote to the Shakespearean actor James H. Hackett on August 17, 1863, "I have seen very little of the Drama. The first presentation of Falstaff, I ever saw, was yours here, last winter or spring. . . . Some of Shakespeare's plays I have never read; while others I have gone over perhaps as frequently as any unprofessional reader. Among the latter are Lear, Richard Third, Henry Eighth, Hamlet and especially Macbeth. I think nothing equals Macbeth. It is wonderful. Unlike you gentlemen of the profession, I think the soliloquy in Hamlet commencing 'Oh my offense is rank' surpasses that commencing 'to be or not to be.' But pardon this small attempt at criticism. I should like to hear you pronounce the opening speech of Richard the Third. Will you not soon visit Washington again? If you do, please call and let me make your personal acquaintance."

The President's letter fell into the hands of the press, and when hostile papers used it to deride his literary tastes, Hackett wrote to apologize. Lincoln told him not to worry. "I have endured a great deal of ridicule without much malice, and have received a great deal of kindness, not quite free from ridicule. I am used to it," he wrote. After attending a number of plays, Lincoln concluded that Shakespeare's comedies were most enjoyable when acted on the stage, but he preferred to read the tragedies at home.

While Lincoln derived much pleasure from concerts and the theater, he spent most of his leisure evenings in his office, swapping yarns with friends who happened in. Such sessions found him at his best, according to John Hay, who remembered that "his wit and rich humor had free play, he was once more the Lincoln of the Eighth Circuit, the cheeriest of talkers, the riskiest of story tellers," as a long leg dangled over his chair arm or his ample feet adorned a desk. Seward, Senators Browning, Ira

Harris, and James Harlan, Marshal Lamon, Congressmen Washburne of Illinois and W. D. Kelley of Pennsylvania, and Indian Commissioner Dole were among his most frequent evening visitors. Old friends from Illinois were usually present whenever they came to Washington, and witty Sam Galloway, of Ohio, was always a welcome guest.

Courtly, polished Charles Sumner came so often that Harlan said: "Ah, Sumner, we are sure of finding you here." The fastidious Sumner with his elegantly tailored brown coat, maroon vest, and lavender pantaloons made a strange companion for the easygoing President, whose garb on these informal evenings was likely to be a faded, long-skirted dressing-gown, belted around the waist, and an old, worn pair of carpet slippers. Lincoln's and Sumner's sharp disagreement over reconstruction policies never dampened their personal friendship. Mrs. Lincoln was also fond of Sumner and often invited him to drive with her and the President and to attend their theater parties. But whenever Lincoln, at ease in his office, heard Sumner's gold-headed cane thumping down the White House corridor, he deferred to the Senator's pompous dignity by dropping his feet to the floor.

If only one or two persons were with Lincoln in the evening, he liked to read aloud from Shakespeare, Robert Burns, or the works of the contemporary humorists Artemus Ward, Orpheus C. Kerr, or Petroleum V. Nasby. Bryant and Whittier also ranked among his favorites, and he never tired of Oliver Wendell Holmes's "The Last Leaf." Novels had no appeal for him; he had never been able to finish *Ivanhoe*.

While Lincoln derived much pleasure from these informal evening gatherings, none of those whom Zach Chandler referred to as his "*particular* friends, those who drop in & chat with him of evenings & who have his confidence," became really intimate with him; for he seldom fully opened his heart to anyone.

In summer the evening sessions in Lincoln's office must have resounded with slaps, for the White House windows had no screens or netting. Nicolay complained to his fiancée: "My usual trouble in this room (my office) is from . . . 'big bugs'—

(oftener humbugs)—but at this present writing (10 o'clock p.m. Sunday night) the thing is quite reversed, and *little bugs* are the pest. The gas lights over my desk are burning brightly and the windows of the room are open, and all bugdom outside seems to have organized a storming party to take the gas lights, in numbers that seem to exceed the contending hosts at Richmond. The air is swarming with them, they are on the ceilings, the walls and the furniture in countless numbers, they are buzzing about the room, and butting their heads against the window panes, they are on my clothes, in my hair, and on the sheet I am writing on."

*

LINCOLN had a questing mind. He sometimes went to the Observatory to study the moon and stars, and it gave him unusual satisfaction to talk with men of broad intellect. Louis Agassiz, the scientist, and Dr. Joseph Henry, curator of the Smithsonian Institution, both marveled at his intellectual grasp. It must have delighted a man of his meager educational opportunities when Princeton (then known as the College of New Jersey), Columbia, and Knox College, in Illinois, saw fit to honor him with degrees of Doctor of Laws, and when Lincoln College, in Illinois, was named for him, as the town where it was located had been.

But while Lincoln relished and appreciated the cultural side of life, he was no less keenly interested when Herman the Magician came to the White House and performed his tricks in slow motion to show how they were done. And there were certain things of beauty to which he seemed obtuse. When Mrs. Ninian W. Edwards, his sister-in-law, admired the flowers as he took her on a tour of the White House conservatory, in the spring of 1862, he confessed it was the first time he had been there.

During the Edwardses' visit Lincoln suggested that Mrs. Edwards make up a party of Springfield folk for a visit to Mount Vernon. So next morning the President and Mrs. Lincoln, Marshal and Mrs. Lamon and Lamon's brother, Robert, Mrs. Milton Hay, who was visiting the capital, Mr. and Mrs. Edwards, and one or two others met at the navy yard at ten o'clock and

boarded a government steamer. Passing the arsenal and Fort
Washington, they arrived at Mount Vernon about twelve thirty
and spent a delightful hour and a half visiting Washington's
tomb and wandering through the mansion and the gardens. Mrs.
Hay reported to her husband: "The President looks much as he
did when he left Springfield and tells jokes yet. I had the happiness of sitting by him and conversing with him for some
time—but, did not know how to flatter him as some ᵇothers
did."

One of the Lincolns' receptions honored Tom Thumb, the
midget, and his tiny bride. A guest noted the great respect
with which the little pair looked into the gaunt face that towered
far above them, the gentleness with which the President took
their fragile hands in his gnarled fist, and the grave courtesy with
which he presented them to Mrs. Lincoln. He carefully saw to it
that their chairs were high enough at dinner, and he watched
them with a sort of amused sympathy throughout the evening.

Mrs. Lincoln regularly attended Sunday morning service at
the New York Avenue Presbyterian Church of Dr. Phineas D.
Gurley, and Lincoln went with her when he could. Sometimes
they took the boys, but they were more likely to be found at the
Fourth Presbyterian Church, where they attended Sunday
school with their playmates Bud and Holly Taft. Browning
remembered seeing Lincoln read the Bible in the White House,
but he did not say grace before meals.

*

W ILLIE's death was the hardest blow that Lincoln ever
suffered, but his sense of public duty gave him strength to carry
on. To Mrs. Lincoln, however, it came as a stunning shock. The
defiant courage with which she had faced the gibes of society and
the cruel spotlight of a hostile press wilted at the loss of a second
child. She never again entered the guest room where Willie
died, or the Green Room, where his body had been embalmed.
All except the most necessary White House social functions
stopped. Mrs. Milton Hay wrote home to her husband on April

13, 1862: "This morning we went to Mr. Gurly's church and had the honor of sitting just behind Mr. & Mrs. President. He evidently got very tired—and she was so hid behind an immense black veil—and very deep black flounces—that one could scarcely tell she was there."

For almost three years Mrs. Lincoln had lived in virtual seclusion and it became the fate of the overburdened President to walk alone, haunted by fear that his distraught wife might go insane. Few persons came to see her, for most of those who came she turned away. Mrs. Elizabeth Keckley, her colored seamstress, became her closest confidante, although Dr. Henry, who had been the Lincolns' family physician in Springfield, managed to draw her out. He wrote to Mrs. Henry, on February 18, 1863: "Mrs. Lincoln has told me all about her troubles, and especially the cause of the breach between herself and her own family friends in Springfield. . . . I think Mary is right, & that they were the aggressors. . . . Mary & Julia [Trumbull] have both made me their confidant telling me their grievances, and both think the other *all* to blame. I am trying to make peace between them. It is as I told you. Mr. Trumbull was jealous of Col. Baker's influence with Mr. Lincoln, and this was the cause of the family rupture."

Spiritualism had become a Washington fad and Browning recorded in his diary: "Mrs. Lincoln told me she had been, the night before . . . out to Georgetown, to see a Mrs. Laury, a spiritualist and she had made wonderful revelations to her about her little son Willie. . . . Among other things she revealed that the cabinet were all enemies of the President, working for themselves, and that they would have to be dismissed, and others called to his aid before he had success." A medium named Colchester, who preyed on Mrs. Lincoln by pretending to bring her messages from Willie, was warned to get out of town by Noah Brooks.

At last Mary Lincoln sought to lose herself in serving others. She made almost daily visits to the hospitals and convalescent camps to dispense motherly sympathy and little gifts of fruit and flowers. Otherwise she scarcely left the White House except to go to church or to accompany her husband on drives. But her errands of mercy had to be discontinued in the summer of 1863, when she was thrown from her carriage in a runaway and struck her head on a stone. Lincoln wired Robert: "Don't be uneasy. Your mother only slightly hurt in her fall." But she suffered severely from shock.

The same Washington society that had criticized her wartime social activities callously denounced her for neglecting her social duties when she discontinued White House functions after Willie's death. Her cancellation of the Marine Band concerts on the lawn brought such an outcry that the President ordered them to be resumed in Lafayette Square. Mrs. Keckley told how tenderly the President watched over his wife, and how she, after a tirade, would tearfully beg his forgiveness. Both of them suffered from her malady.

November 1862 brought news of the death of Mrs. Lincoln's brother David Todd; she suppressed her grief for fear of being thought disloyal. In August 1863 her youngest brother, Alec, was killed in a skirmish near Baton Rouge, and again she locked her grief inside herself. She and Tad went to New York in September, and the President sent word that Ben Hardin Helm, husband of her favorite sister, Emilie, had been killed at Chickamauga. When Mrs. Helm visited the White House at her sister's invitation, Lincoln begged her to stay with Mary through the summer. "It is good for her to have you with her," he explained. "I feel worried about Mary, her nerves have gone to pieces; she cannot hide from me that the stress she has been under has been too much for her mental as well as her physical health."

The President's attitude became almost fatherly as sorrows bore Mary down. Emilie Helm confided to her diary during her White House visit: "Sister and I cannot open our hearts to each other as freely as we would like. This frightful war comes between us like a barrier of granite closing our lips but not our hearts, for though our tongues are tied, we weep over our dead together and express through our clasped hands the sympathy we feel for each other in our mutual grief."

On November 20, 1864 Mrs. Lincoln wrote to a former Springfield neighbor, Mrs. John Henry Shearer, who had just lost her only son: "Now, in this, the hour of *your* deep grief, with all my *own wounds* bleeding afresh, I find myself, writing to you, to express, my deepest sympathy, *well knowing* how unavailing words, are, when we are broken hearted. . . . I know, *you are* better prepared than I was, to pass through the fiery furnace of affliction. I had become, so wrapped up in the world, so devoted to our own political advancement that I thought of little else besides. Our Heavenly Father sees fit, oftentimes to visit us, at such times, for our worldliness."

Mary Lincoln bravely tried to keep her heartbreak from her husband. Emilie Helm noticed that she always brightened when she heard his footsteps in the hall. But one time after he left she held out her arms and cried: "Kiss me, Emilie, and tell me that you love me! I seem to be the scapegoat for both North and South."

The President had been overjoyed on New Year's Day of 1865 when Mrs. Lincoln laid aside her heavy mourning and resumed her social duties. But grief had left deep scars. Unexpected noises frightened her; she worried constantly lest something happen to her husband or her son Robert. She was as stubborn and erratic as before.

A cabinet dinner had been planned, and Nicolay, who addressed the invitations, discovered that Mrs. Lincoln had omitted the names of Chase and his son-in-law and daughter, Governor and Mrs. William Sprague. Foreseeing the social crisis that was certain to result, Nicolay took up the matter with Lincoln, who declared that Chase and the Spragues must be invited. "Whereat," wrote Nicolay, "there rose such a rampage as the House hasn't seen in a year." Young Stoddard "fairly cowered at the volume of the storm, and I think for the first time begins to appreciate the awful sublimities of nature."

Mrs. Lincoln backed down and apologized to Nicolay. But she never forgave him. Dr. Henry, on a second visit to the White House, wrote to his wife on March 13, 1865: "I have been

working ever since I have been here with Mrs. Lincoln to get
Nicolay out as private secretary and Mr. Brooks in his place.
Mr. Lincoln had never intimated what he would do. . . . But
to our happy surprise it was officially announced yesterday
morning that Mr. Nicolay had been confirmed as consul to Paris.
. . . Mr. Nicolay will remain two or three weeks yet, & we dont
want it known that Mr. Brooks expects his place, but by the
time this reaches you it will be disposed of." Nicolay had already
asked to be relieved, and Lincoln was probably glad to oblige
him, for the situation had become intolerable.

*

A F T E R Willie's death, Tad and his father turned to each other
in mutual loneliness. Tad was never happier than when he was
with his father; the President found his greatest comfort in the
whimsical small boy. No matter who was with him or how
important his work, he never rebuked the impetuous little fellow
when he burst excitedly into the office with a flood of scarcely
intelligible words or flung himself into his lap, but always listened
to him gravely or cuddled him in his arms. Evening visitors often
found the two together, the father with a book open on his knee,
and the boy standing beside him, listening while he explained the
pictures, or gazing rapturously into his face.

The President humored Tad's childish self-importance by
entrusting him with small errands. One day the boy hurried to
one of his favorite haunts, the headquarters of a fire company
a few blocks from the White House, with a card signed by the
President: "Will Mr. Dickson, Chief Engineer of Hibernia, please
pump the water out of a certain well which Tad will show?"

Tad knew he could always find a champion in his father when
his pranks got him into trouble; the President's office provided
sanctuary from his unpredictable mother and the vengeance of
outraged servants. The father knew how to manage the boy when
everyone else despaired. One day a secretary interrupted a
conference to whisper in Lincoln's ear. The President excused
himself and left the room. Tad had been ill and his nurse stood

in the hallway. "Mrs. Lincoln insists that I see you," she said apologetically. "Tad won't take his medicine." They walked to the boy's room. "You stay here," the father said outside the door, "and I'll see what I can do." He soon came out with a grin. "It's all right. Tad and I have fixed things up," he announced.

Tad was smiling happily from his pillow when the nurse walked into the room. She had no further trouble about his medicine. For his small hand clutched a check that read: "Pay to 'Tad' (when he is well enough to present) Five Dollars." It bore the signature: "A. Lincoln."

The President had singular ways with checks. He once drew another for five dollars payable to "colored man with one leg," a sufficient identification for the most careful teller at the meticulous Riggs Bank.

Lincoln was never too busy to make Tad's concerns his own. He wrote to Mrs. Lincoln at New York on August 8, 1863: "Tell dear Tad, poor 'Nanny Goat' is lost, and Mrs. Cuthbert & I are in distress about it. The day you left Nanny was found resting herself, and chewing her little cud, on the middle of Tad's bed. But now she is gone! The gardener kept complaining that she destroyed the flowers till it was concluded to bring her down to the White House. This was done, and the second day she had disappeared and has not been heard of since. This is the last we know of poor Nanny."

"I especially like my little friends," Lincoln wrote to two small girls who made an afghan for him. His affection embraced children generally, not merely his own. Sixteen-year-old Julia Taft remembered him as a "good, uncle-like person," smiling and kind, who called her a flibbertygibbet. When she asked what a flibbertygibbet was, he described it as a small, slim thing with curls and a white dress and a blue sash that flies instead of walking. The grandchildren of Francis Preston Blair recalled years afterward how the President once visited Silver Spring and played with them on the lawn, his long coat-tails flying out behind him as he ran.

Children in trouble always gained his sympathy. On the

reverse side of an expired pass that had been issued to a twelve-year-old boy, he wrote: "They say that by the destruction of a bridge the boy has been unable to pass on this. Might it not be renewed for the little fellow." And on a packet of letters covering a particular case, he asked: "What possible injury can this lad work upon the cause of this great Union? I say let him go."

*

AS THE war bore heavily upon the South, the White House became a haven for Mrs. Lincoln's proslavery relatives—Mrs. Helm, Mrs. Charles Kellogg (Margaret Todd) of Cincinnati, and Mrs. Clement White (Martha Todd) of Selma, Alabama. Lincoln gave Mrs. White a pass to Richmond, and a story got about that she had filled her trunk with quinine, a contraband article badly needed in the Confederacy, and, flourishing the President's pass under the noses of the customs officers, had defied them to stop her. The story was untrue, but Lincoln had to take time to investigate it.

Of the President's own lowly relatives, only Dennis Hanks dared to visit him at the White House. He brought with him requests for favors from his sons-in-law, W. F. Schriver and Allison C. Poorman. Schriver wanted a permit to trade within the army lines "in all kinds of merchandize—Liquor excepted"; Poorman asked for the much coveted privilege of bringing cotton and hides out of the South. Lincoln approved both requests.

In early April 1864 Hanks reported to Lincoln about his stepmother and other relatives in Coles County.

Dear Abe [he wrote], I Received your Little check for 50.00 I shoed it to Mother   She cried like a Child   Abe she is mity Childish heep of trouble to us   Betsy is very feble and has to wait on her which ort to have sum person to wait on her we are getting old   We have a great many to wait on of our Connections they will come to see us wile we Live   Abe Charles has Reinlisted a gain for three years or during the war   This is hard on his mother. . . . Abe I Received a Letter from Sophia Lynch now John Lagrand is her last husband   She wants to Know whether you are that Abe Lincoln her cousin or not is this not

strange to you it was to me. . . . Abe you have never seen as
Strong a young Boy as Charles Hanks   I am mity fraid that
Theophilus will go into the army with Charles he is 15 years Old
a very Stout Boy he can shoot almost as well as I can   Abe
Remember My Boys if you can   I dont want any thing   how
is Your family   Nothing More   Drop me a few Lines if you feel
Like it

Yours Respectfully
D. F. Hanks

About six months later Lincoln received tidings of a different
nature about his stepmother from his nephew John Hall:

This leaves us all well but Grand Mother she is quite poor.
I write to inform you that Grand Mother has not and does not
receive one cent of the money you send her Dennis & Chapman
[Dennis's son-in-law] keep all the money you send her, she now
needs clothes and shoes, they have the money in their Pockett,
& Uncle Dennis is cussing you all the time and abusing me & your
best Friends for supporten you they make you believe they are
takeing Care of her which is not the case. I & Mother are now
takeing care of her and have for the past four years—If you wish
her to have any thing send it by check here to the bank at Charleston or send some [to] her I tell you upon the honor of a Man she
does not get it & he and Dennis has threatened to put her on the
county. . . .

So to the President's big worries were added a multitude
of little ones, no less harassing to him. It must have been with
great relief that he read letters of good will like that from William
Florville, a colored barber whom he had known at New Salem and
Springfield:

Tell Taddy that his (and Willys) Dog is alive and Kicking doing
well, he stays Mostly at John E Rolls with his Boys Who are
about the age now that Tad & Willie Were when they left for
Washington. . . . Your Residence here is kept in good order.
Mr. Tilton has no children to ruin things. . . .

And then there was a time in early March 1865 when a
beautiful tribute came from Hamilton, Massachusetts, dated on
Inauguration Day.

Dear Sir [it began]. I only wish to thank you for being so good—and to say how sorry we all are that you must have four years more of this terrible toil. But remember what a triumph it is for the right, what a blessing to the country—and then your rest shall be glorious when it does come!

You cant tell anything about it in Washington where they make a noise on the slightest provocation—

But if you had been in this little speck of a village this morning and heard the soft, sweet music of unseen bells rippling through the morning silence from every quarter of the far-off horison, you would have better known what your name is to this nation.

May God help you in the future as he has helped you in the past; and a people's love and gratitude will be but a small portion of your exceeding great reward.

Most respectfully
Mary A. Dodge

The letter bears only a formal secretarial endorsement; perhaps Lincoln never saw it. But one may hope he did.

———•••———

CHAPTER XX

To Bind Up the Nation's Wounds

DEEP in the interior of the Confederacy, Sherman found it difficult to feed his army as the bold cavalry chieftains Forrest and Wheeler harassed his supply lines. Hood himself turned west and north to draw Sherman out of Atlanta, but the lean, grizzled Ohioan, refusing to relax his grip, sent Thomas to hold Tennessee. It was useless to pursue Hood, Sherman instructed the stolid Thomas, for he could "twist and turn like a fox and wear out any army in pursuit."

Sherman asked Grant to allow him to destroy the railroad from Chattanooga, which the Confederates raided constantly, and bring his troops to the sea. To march a well-appointed army through the heart of the enemy's country would demonstrate the invincibility of Union arms and bring the South to terms. Sherman could accomplish this march, he pleaded, "and make Georgia howl!" He would devastate the country. Personally warmhearted and friendly toward the Southern people, Sherman proposed to teach them the awfulness of war.

Grant questioned Thomas's ability to cope with Hood. He doubted that Sherman could sustain so large an army on a long march through hostile country with an enemy in his rear. Lincoln, too, had grave misgivings, and Stanton informed Grant: "The President feels much solicitude in respect to General Sherman's proposed movement and hopes that it will be maturely considered.

The objections stated in your telegram of last night impressed him with much force, and a misstep by General Sherman might be fatal to his army."

Already, however, Grant had been convinced. "I say then, go on, as you propose," he wired to Sherman. Grant assured Lincoln that an army such as Sherman's, with a commander of his resourcefulness, would be difficult to corner or capture.

Lincoln accepted the decision of his military chiefs. Within three hours of the arrival of Grant's telegram Stanton wired Sherman the President's approval of his plan. "Whatever the result," he promised, "you have the confidence and support of the Government." Halleck wired that a fleet would meet Sherman at Savannah with supplies.

Sherman issued orders for the destruction of all military installations at Atlanta. All public buildings, arsenals, depots, and machine shops must be burned. Nothing useful to the enemy should be left behind. The sick and wounded were sent to Chattanooga and Nashville, along with every pound of baggage not absolutely needed. The railroad and the telegraph were severed.

Promptly at seven o'clock on the morning of November 16, Sherman's hard, healthy, hearty army of 62,000 men, mostly Midwesterners, swung off on the march, banners flying and troops chorusing *John Brown's Body* to the rhythm of blaring bands. Smoke from the ruins of Atlanta trailed skyward in their rear. Gun barrels gleamed in the sun. White-topped wagons stretched for miles along the red clay roads. The army moved in three columns with skirmishers in advance. Cavalry patrolled its flanks. Fighting cocks rode proudly on artillery caissons, for many regiments had their feathered champions. The pace was fifteen miles a day.

Winter nipped the air at night. The days were clear and cool. Each morning foragers left early to work ahead of the columns. Few plantations or farms escaped their vigilance. Usually they would find a wagon or a fashionable family carriage, which by evening, when the regiments caught up, would sag under a burden of bacon, cornmeal, pigs, turkeys, and ducks. Mules, horses, sheep, and cattle were rounded up in droves. The troops feasted on the plenty of the land.

Sherman authorized this foraging, while forbidding pillage and robbery. But there were rough men in his army and men with revenge in their hearts. Feather beds were ripped open in search of family treasures. Wardrobes and chests were ransacked. Preserves, quilts, heirlooms, and other furnishings were carted off. As the army swung into one little Georgia town, a forager greeted his comrades in an ancient militia uniform found in some family attic. Enormous epaulets adorned his shoulders. Mounted on a rawboned horse, with a piece of carpet for a saddle, he rode with gracious dignity, his plumed hat raised in salute. Behind him came a carriage laden with yams and hams, drawn by two horses, a mule, and a cow, the two latter ridden by uniformed postilions from a Hoosier regiment. To the resentful, terror-stricken people Sherman said: "We don't want your Negroes, or your horses, or your houses, or your lands, or any thing you have, but we do want and will have a just obedience to the laws of the United States. That we will have, and if it involves the destruction of your improvements, we cannot help it. . . . I want peace, and . . . I will ever conduct war with a view to perfect and early success."

The army moved in utter isolation. For thirty-two days all that Washington knew of it came from the Southern press, which insisted that it was starving and demoralized. The Northern people became anxious. Lincoln showed concern. But Grant assured him that Sherman would turn up safely in due time. In his annual message Lincoln said: "The most remarkable feature in the military operations of the year is General Sherman's attempted march of three hundred miles directly through the insurgent region. It tends to show a great increase in our relative strength that our General-in-chief should feel able to confront, and hold in check every active force of the enemy, and yet to detach a well appointed large army to move on such an expedition. The result not yet being known, conjecture in regard to it is not here indulged."

Behind Sherman's army lay a long strip of silent wasteland.

Naked chimneys marked the sites of mansions. Bridges, trestles, ties, water tanks, and woodsheds smoldered in charred ruin along the railroad grades. Rails had been heated and twisted around trees. Not a haystack or a corncrib was left standing. Every bale of cotton had been burned. Not a mule was left to plow the trampled fields. Rotting carcasses of pigs, cattle, and sheep littered abandoned campsites. "The destruction could hardly have been worse," one commentator wrote, "if Atlanta had been a volcano in eruption, and the molten lava had flowed in a stream sixty miles wide and five times as long."

Meanwhile Hood had reorganized his army at Florence, Alabama. On November 19 he started north to capture or destroy Thomas's army and either draw Sherman back from Georgia or go on to reinforce Lee. Checked by Schofield in a bloody fight at Franklin, Tennessee, Hood pushed on against Thomas at Nashville. The cool, deliberate Thomas, outnumbering the Confederates two to one, waited to mount and equip his cavalry. He planned to destroy when he struck. Then icy weather intervened, and Grant came near removing the loyal Virginian for delaying his attack.

On December 15, in a heavy fog, Thomas threw his army forward through a sea of mire. Hood's left cracked like an egg-shell. His entire army gave way in rout. News of Thomas's victory reached the War Department late at night. Major Eckert jumped into an ambulance to take the telegram to Stanton. Together they rode to the White House to rouse Lincoln from his sleep. Eckert thought he would never forget the tall, ghostly form of the President as he received the news in his nightshirt at the head of the stairs, a lighted candle held above his head.

Next day Lincoln sent Thomas his own and the nation's thanks. "You made a magnificent beginning," read his telegram. "A good consummation is within your easy reach. Do not let it slip." Thomas did not need the admonition. A drenching rain slowed his pursuit, but at the end of a week he had so slashed and torn at Hood's retreating troops that they would never again be useful as an organized fighting force.

Christmas evening brought Lincoln a telegram from Sherman dated three days before: "I beg to present you as a Christmas gift the city of Savannah, with 150 heavy guns and plenty of ammunition; also about 25,000 bales of cotton." Sherman had taken the city almost without a fight, to make contact with the Union fleet.

The news sent pandemonium through the North. The dull boom of salutes shook Washington as Lincoln penned his thanks to Sherman. "When you were about leaving Atlanta for the Atlantic coast," he wrote, "I was anxious, if not fearful; but feeling that you were the better judge, and remembering that 'nothing risked, nothing gained,' I did not interfere. Now, the undertaking being a success, the honor is all yours; for I believe none of us went further than to acquiesce. And taking the work of Gen. Thomas into the count, as it should be taken, it is indeed a great success. Not only does it afford the obvious and immediate military advantages, but, in showing to the world that your army could be divided, putting the stronger part to an important new service, and yet leaving enough to vanquish the old opposing force of the whole—Hood's army—it brings those who sat in darkness to see a great light. But what next? I suppose it will be safer if I leave Gen. Grant and yourself to decide."

*

O n O c t o b e r 13, 1864 John Hay recorded in his diary: "Last night Chief Justice Taney went home to his fathers. The elections carried him off. . . . Already (before his old clay is cold) they are beginning to canvass vigorously for his successor. Chase men say the place is promised to their *magnifico.*"

The eighty-seven-year-old Taney had outlived the spirit of his age. His death seemed to many persons like the removal of a barrier to progress. Chase had long been regarded as Taney's logical successor; while his preoccupation with politics had kept him from that eminence he might have attained as a lawyer, his intellectual powers were unquestioned, and as a former member of the administration his views on such issues growing out of the war as emancipation, arrests, and various financial measures, all of which would be subjected to the severest legal tests, were expected to accord with government policies.

Chase had often told intimates of his aspiration to the Supreme Court—as its head, of course. And Lincoln had expressed a willingness to appoint him, should the vacancy occur. But Associate Justice Noah H. Swayne and the New York lawyer William M. Evarts were also strongly recommended, and, in view of recent strained relations, persons in inner circles wondered if Lincoln might have changed his mind about Chase's fitness.

Weeks passed and Lincoln gave no indication of his choice. To Sumner, Stanton, Fessenden, and other radicals who pleaded the merits of Chase, Lincoln, to use his own expression, kept "very shut pan" about it. When Chase wrote him a friendly letter, Lincoln chuckled and told Nicolay: "File it with his other recommendations." Yet when Richard Henry Dana and Judge E. R. Hoar of Massachusetts came to the White House to voice protests against Chase, Lincoln replied: "Mr. Chase is a very able man. He is a very ambitious man and I think on the subject of the presidency a little insane. He has not always behaved very well lately and people say to me, 'Now is the time to *crush him out.*' Well, I'm not in favor of crushing anybody out! If there is anything that a man can do and do it well, I say let him do it. Give him a chance."

Actually, Lincoln had pretty well settled on Chase, for he was favored by a majority of the party. His only misgiving was that Chase's political ambition might influence his conduct as a judge. He even contemplated pledging Chase to renounce any further presidential aspirations, but Senator Sumner pointed out that the President's enemies might charge him with using unfair means against a rival. On December 6 Lincoln wrote Chase's nomination in his own hand and sent it to the Senate for confirmation, thus honoring his most troublesome antagonist with the highest office he could bestow.

Lincoln also made two new appointments to his cabinet

about this time. James Speed, brother of his old friend Joshua Speed, an accomplished lawyer who had helped to hold Kentucky in the Union, became Attorney General when Bates retired because of age; and Hugh McCulloch, of Indiana, Comptroller of the Currency, became Secretary of the Treasury when Fessenden returned to the Senate.

*

B Y T H E end of January 1865, Arkansas, Louisiana, Maryland, and Missouri had abolished slavery. Tennessee and Kentucky were moving unmistakably toward similar action. On April 8, 1864 the Senate had passed a Thirteenth Amendment to the Constitution, prohibiting slavery throughout the United States, but the House had failed to approve it by the necessary two-thirds vote. Lincoln, in his annual message of December 6, asked the House to reconsider it. The abstract question had not changed, he said, but the intervening election showed unmistakably that the next Congress would pass the amendment if this one failed to do so. And to pass it now would put it sooner before the states for ratification. Lincoln made no claim that the election had imposed a duty on members to change their views or their votes. But for the first time the voice of the people had been heard on this matter.

The amendment, duly reintroduced, came up for passage on January 31. Spectators crammed the galleries. The lobbies were crowded. Many senators watched from the House floor. Lincoln himself had done some quiet maneuvering. Knowing that the vote would be extremely close, he had enlisted Congressman James M. Ashley of Ohio as his emissary in obtaining two or three doubtful Democratic votes. One Democratic Congressman was promised a Federal appointment for his brother in New York; another, whose seat had been contested, gained assurance of support; and a third, attorney for a railroad that faced a threat of adverse legislation, was assured of friendly votes. The art of logrolling, so masterfully employed by Lincoln in the Illinois Legislature, proved equally effective now. Charles A. Dana, to whom the President had entrusted the same sort of mission when votes were needed for the admission of Nevada as a state, admired the President's astuteness. "Lincoln was a supreme politician," he observed. "He understood politics because he understood human nature. . . . There was no flabby philanthropy about Abraham Lincoln. He was all solid, hard, keen intelligence combined with goodness."

The roll call on the amendment began at four in the afternoon. Cheers broke out when Democrats voted aye. The clerk whispered the tally to Speaker Colfax: ayes 119, nays 56, not voting 8; the amendment had just three votes to spare. Colfax asked to be called and voted aye, then announced that the measure had passed. Hysteria shook the galleries and the halls. Staid Congressmen jumped and whooped. Outside a battery let go with a one-hundred-gun salute. Except for secession, a Thirteenth Amendment forever guaranteeing slavery in the states might well have been enacted after Lincoln's inauguration. Now the Thirteenth Amendment dealt slavery its death stroke.

The day after the passage of the amendment, a procession with music marched to the White House and called loudly for the President. Lincoln came out on a balcony. He thanked Congress for its action. The work of ratification still lay ahead, he said, but he felt proud that his own state of Illinois had been the first to approve the amendment that very day, and that a former slave state, Maryland, had followed close behind. He wished the Union of the states to be perfected and the cause of their strife blotted out. The amendment would consummate emancipation. His proclamation had been a beginning, but it might have been held invalid by the courts—and it left vestiges of slavery undisturbed. Now the whole evil would be eradicated. He congratulated himself, the country, and the world on this great moral victory.

So by early 1865 the United States was well on its way to becoming a free nation. And the military prospects assured its unity. Victory could not be far off, for the Confederacy was suffering its death throes. On January 15, 1865 a formidable armada of sixty war vessels under Porter, with 8,500 troops commanded by General Alfred H. Terry, retrieved a failure of General Butler's by taking Fort Fisher by bombardment and assault to close the port of Wilmington. Only far-off Galveston remained open to Confederate blockade-runners. Lee's troops in the lines around Richmond became destitute of blankets and overcoats. Some of them were barefoot. Rations were short. During the harsh winter months men came off picket duty whimpering like children from the cold.

Desertion sapped Lee's strength. After Christmas, when Sherman's army started northward and every mail brought woeful news from wives and families of the approach of his marauders, more and more men from the Carolinas slipped off in the night, taking their arms along. State rights, the cornerstone of the Confederacy, became its basic weakness when governors whose states were threatened with invasion refused to send their troops away from home. Governor Joseph E. Brown of Georgia resisted Confederate authority within his state. Peace movements smoldered underground in Arkansas and Alabama and broke into the open in North Carolina. Governmentally as well as militarily the Confederacy was coming apart at the seams.

*

LINCOLN had been the imponderable factor that frustrated the South. Her troops had fought with matchless courage under inspired leadership. Her people had shown heroic fortitude. With a less determined leader in the White House they might well have achieved their goal. But Lincoln, with unwavering faith in the nation's destiny, had infused his own unconquerable spirit into the Northern people. On July 6, 1862 Frederick Law Olmsted, later to become the famous landscape architect, at that time secretary of the U.S. Sanitary Commission, had written to him: "In the general gloom, there are two points of consolation and hope which grow brighter and brighter. . . . One is the trustworthy patriotic devotion of the solid, industrious, home keeping people of the country; the other, the love and confidence constantly growing stronger, between these people and their president.

"Here is the key to a vast reserved strength, and in this rests our last hope for our country."

Lincoln had drawn deeply on this wholesome reservoir. Aware from the beginning that the chaotic tumult of opinion called for careful, cautious guidance rather than a headstrong type of leadership, he had probed forward through all obstacles along a course of justice and good sense. He had made the principles of democracy his daily guide, not consciously perhaps, or with any predetermined purpose to do so, but because his dedication to democracy's ideals had made them a component of his nature.

His faith in the people had survived the harshest trials; for war brings out the worst as well as the best in human nature. Lincoln hated its corruption, its questionable profits, the manner in which "every foul bird" and "every dirty reptile" gorged on its filth. Through his door had come swindlers, hypocrites, liars, charlatans, and bootlickers. He knew man's imperfections. The writings of humorists appealed to him because they unmasked the pretenses, the vanities, and the pomposities that he encountered every day. Knowing the faults and frailties of men, he understood that the ideals of democracy might never be fully achieved, that they are goals to be approximated, but that men gain strength in striving for them.

Lincoln's human dealings had given him fixity of purpose. Time and again, in one crisis after another, he had seen the judgments of supposedly great minds turn out to be so utterly mistaken that they would have brought ruin beyond retrieving if he had followed them. The people's composite wisdom and moral rectitude had proved to be surer guides, and he had deferred to mass opinion, firm in the conviction that the people were trustworthy, when informed. He had appealed to reason rather than emotion, while remembering that the mind is best reached through the heart. "Plain common sense, a kindly disposition, a straight forward purpose, and a shrewd perception of the ins and outs of poor, weak human nature," observed the *New York Herald*, "have enabled him to master difficulties which would have swamped any other man."

So deft had been Lincoln's leadership that people often failed to recognize it. Few persons thought him great. His strength was flexible, like fine-spun wire, sensitive to every need and pressure, yielding but never breaking. Forced to adopt hard measures, he had tempered them with clemency. He exercised stern powers leniently, with regard for personal feelings and respect for human rights.

Some had thought him weak because he did not ram things through; others thought him dull and obstinate because they could not move him. Essentially he had embodied the easygoing, sentimental, kindly spirit of America, which revolts at extreme measures but moves steadily, if sometimes haltingly, toward lofty goals. His conduct had been essentially Christian. He conformed to the teachings of the Golden Rule and the Sermon on the Mount, not self-righteously or sanctimoniously, but because he learned that Christian virtues are democratic virtues, too, in offering men a means of living together in dignity, equality, and mutual respect.

The exercise of power and the pressure of responsibility endowed him with new strength. He had grown with his task. Horace Greeley, no admirer of Lincoln in his lifetime, wrote in after years: "He was not a born king of men . . . but a child of the people, who made himself a great persuader, therefore a leader, by dint of firm resolve, patient effort and dogged perseverance. He slowly won his way to eminence and fame by doing the work that lay next to him—doing it with all his growing might—doing it as well as he could, and learning by his failure, when failure was encountered, how to do it better. . . . He was open to all impressions and influences, and gladly profited by the teachings of events and circumstances, no matter how adverse or unwelcome. There was probably no year of his life when he was not a wiser, cooler and better man than he had been the year preceding."

Plain people, baffled by the constitutional issues of the war or incapable of comprehending Lincoln's broad democratic conception of it, could understand the simple, homespun President. They trusted "Father Abraham," and accepted his decisions because he epitomized their hopes. His life story proved that democracy gives the humblest man his chance; his exercise of power showed government of, by, and for the people working at its best. The notion that the people were incapable of governing themselves could scarcely be defended in the face of such a fact as Lincoln's life.

Tough, shrewd, and canny in his younger years, the man who was bringing the nation through to victory had become strong, merciful, and wise. Success had come to him, and to the nation that he served, because he had lived and governed according to its ideals.

*

P o l i t i c s is the drive shaft of democratic government, the means by which the people make their will effective. And Lincoln had proved himself to be a consummate politician. Except for a few years of retirement, politics had been his life. He had come to his task much better prepared than most people had realized. For during his years in Illinois we have seen him devoting hour upon hour to caucuses, conventions, and legislative sessions, to writing party circulars and making party speeches, to considering requests and weighing recommendations, to devising party strategy and formulating party policies.

In too many politicians such a background makes for a narrow, selfish outlook and partisan pettiness. These were no parts of Lincoln's nature, or if he had been tainted with them in his early years, he had learned to overmaster them when high principles were at stake. The practice of managing people in the mass developed traits of subtle manipulation and long-sighted calculation which were vastly congenial to him; he used these skills as President, but he used them honorably.

He would have been more than human if, in the contemporary climate of spoils politics, he had not bestowed favors on his friends and relatives. But, more often than not, he gave them not necessarily what they desired but what he thought them fitted for. He made mistakes. Yet he acted so circumspectly in this matter that later more than one close friend charged him with ingratitude. Campaign funds and offices were his indispensable tools; but he had scorned the insidious instruments of falsehood and deceit. To hold together in wartime a party made up of abolitionists and Negro-haters, high- and low-tariff men, hard- and soft-money men, former Whigs and erstwhile Democrats, Maine law prohibitionists and German beer-drinkers, Know-Nothings and immigrants was a task almost beyond accomplishment. But if he did not always hold them loyal to himself, he held them steadfast to his major purpose.

He never forgot that democratic politics is the art of the possible, that to insist on the unattainable would merely bring his downfall. He recognized that the present has deep tap-roots in the past, and that to hew recklessly at those tap-roots, even the cankerous ones, might be calamitous.

His own slow advancement had taught him the virtues of patience. Knowing the supremacy of the popular will, he had waited until popular conviction or the current of events enabled him to move effectively. He consolidated each new position before advancing to the next one.

Realizing that the function of a political leader in a democracy is not to impose his will, but to help the people to decide wisely for themselves, he constantly pointed out to them how man serves himself best in the long run by being fair and generous toward others. He defined the cause of the Union in terms of human betterment throughout the world.

With a sense of the continuity and slow tide of human progress, he moved toward new horizons from a firm foothold in the past. "Mystic chords of memory" had been a lifeline for him.

In a time of change and danger he sought wisdom from generations gone before. The ideals of the Founding Fathers had been
his beacon in the storm.

"Reason, cold, calculating, unimpassioned reason," he had
said as a young man, "must furnish all the materials for our
future support and defence." And, in accord with this maxim,
logic had shaped his actions. But the cold reason that controlled
his mind had never chilled his heart.

Mastery of language may have been that ultimate factor
without which he would have failed. For the self-taught man who
once would have given all he owned and gone in debt for the gift
of lyric utterance had touched the summits of eloquence. Yet
this, like his other achievements, had not come by mere chance.
Patient self-training, informed reflection, profound study of a few
great works of English literature, esteem for the rhythmic beauty
that may be coaxed from language, all these had endowed him
with the faculty to write well and to speak well, so that at last,
when profound emotions deep within him had felt the impulse of
new-born nobility of purpose, they had welled forth—and would
well forth once more—in imperishable words.

*

NOTWITHSTANDING the rapid deterioration of the Confederacy, Lincoln doubted that peace overtures would accomplish
any good; President Davis had stubbornly determined to fight on
to defeat. "He would accept nothing short of severance of the
Union," Lincoln said in his annual message of December 1864,
"—precisely what we will not and cannot give. His declarations
to this effect are explicit and oft repeated. He does not attempt to
deceive us. He affords us no excuse to deceive ourselves."

While most thinking persons of the North agreed with Lincoln that negotiations would be fruitless, some advocates of
peace still nagged the President, assured that emissaries could
arrive at an agreement. Most optimistic and persistent of these
peace men was the elder statesman Francis P. Blair, who, in
mid-December, sought Lincoln's permission to visit Davis in

Richmond. "Come to me after Savannah falls," replied the President, and immediately after Christmas Blair renewed his plea. On December 28 Lincoln handed him a pass: "Allow the bearer, F. P. Blair, Senr. to pass our lines, go South and return." Blair's lengthy conversations with Davis brought forth a promise that if Lincoln would receive peace commissioners, Davis would appoint such emissaries at once "with a view to secure peace to the two countries."

Lincoln caught the significance of Davis's final phrase. As he had expected, the Confederate President insisted on recognition of Southern independence. But Lincoln wished to overlook no chance for peace. Blair returned to Richmond with a letter from Lincoln stating: "You having shown me Mr. Davis' letter to you of the 12th inst., you may say to him that I have constantly been, am now, and shall continue, ready to receive any agent whom he, or any other influential person now resisting the national authority, may informally send me with the view of securing peace to the people of our one common country."

There was no mistaking the intent of Lincoln's letter. He had repeatedly asserted that his sole condition for peace was cessation of hostilities and submission to the national authority under the Constitution. Either in a forlorn hope or to put the blame for further bloodshed upon Lincoln, Davis appointed three peace commissioners: Alexander H. Stephens of Georgia, Vice President of the Confederacy; Judge John A. Campbell of Alabama, with whom Seward had negotiated for the surrender of Fort Sumter; and R. M. T. Hunter of Virginia. "In conformity with the letter of Mr. Lincoln, of which the foregoing is a copy," their instructions stated, "you are requested to proceed to Washington City for informal conferences with him upon the issues involved in the existing war and for the purpose of securing peace to the two countries." Since such instructions were at cross-purposes with Lincoln's letter, negotiations were foredoomed.

Lincoln sent Major Eckert to meet the commissioners at Grant's headquarters. One look at their instructions was enough for Eckert, and he broke off all dealings with them. But the commissioners had convinced Grant of their good intentions, and he appealed to Lincoln to confer with them. Lincoln wired immediately that he and Seward would meet them at Hampton Roads.

On February 3 Lincoln and Seward sat down with the three Confederates in the cabin of the *River Queen* under the guns of Fortress Monroe. Frail Alexander H. Stephens, for whom Lincoln had entertained a genuine fondness and admiration since their days in Congress, arrived bundled in a tremendous overcoat with numerous scarves and vestments. The President watched him good-humoredly as he unwrapped his puny body, and remarked later to Grant that it was the smallest nubbin for so much shucking that he had ever seen.

For four hours there was a swift interplay of acute minds across the council table. Lincoln would make no bargain with an enemy in arms. When Hunter retorted that Charles I had negotiated with persons in arms against his government, the President replied that he was not posted on history; all that he distinctly remembered about the matter was that Charles had lost his head. Hunter said he understood that Lincoln looked upon the leaders of the Confederacy as traitors. Lincoln granted that was "about the size of it." There was a moment's silence. Then Hunter smiled. "Well, Mr. Lincoln," he observed, "we have about concluded that we shall not be hanged as long as you are President—if we behave ourselves."

Lincoln let it be known that he still favored compensation to owners of emancipated slaves. It had never been his intention to interfere with slavery in the states; he had been driven to it by necessity, he explained. He believed that the people of the North and South were equally responsible for slavery, and if hostilities should cease and the states would voluntarily abolish slavery, he thought the government should indemnify the owners—to the extent, possibly, of $400,000,000.

The conference came to nothing. Two days later, however, Lincoln read his cabinet a proposal to appropriate $400,000,000 for reimbursement to slaveowners, provided hostilities stopped by April 1. With victory imminent, it was the ultimate in magnanimity. But the cabinet unanimously disapproved this generous gesture, and Lincoln regretfully abandoned the idea. He had hoped that it might be a means of avoiding further bloodshed and desolation and of dissolving sectional hatreds. "You are all opposed to me," he said sadly, and it would be best to say nothing of his proposal to anyone outside the cabinet.

Early in March, Lee, with the approval of Davis, tried to draw Grant into negotiations for an adjustment "of the present unhappy difficulties by means of a military convention." Lincoln learned of this overture at the Capitol, where he sat signing bills, when Stanton brought him a telegram from Grant. Reading it through, Lincoln took his pen and wrote: "The President directs me to say to you that he wishes you to have no conference with General Lee unless it be for the capitulation of Gen. Lee's army, or on some minor, and purely, military matter. He instructs me to say that you are not to decide, discuss, or confer upon any political question. Such questions the President holds in his own hands; and will submit them to no military conferences or conventions. Meantime you are to press to the utmost, your military advantages."

*

M A R C H 4 was reminiscent of inauguration day four years before. Low clouds scudded swiftly before heavy gusts of wind. The short inaugural procession churned through thick mud on Pennsylvania Avenue. The bronze statue of Freedom crowned the Capitol dome at last. A mighty crowd greeted the official party as it emerged on the portico.

A hush fell as Lincoln rose and read: "Fellow-countrymen: At this second appearing to take the oath of the presidential office, there is less occasion for an extended address than there was at the first. . . . The progress of our arms, upon which all else chiefly depends, is as well known to the public as to myself; and it is, I trust, reasonably satisfactory and encouraging to all. With high hope for the future, no prediction in regard to it is ventured. . . .

"Neither party expected for the war, the magnitude, or the duration, which it has already attained. Neither anticipated that the *cause* of the conflict might cease with, or even before, the conflict itself should cease. Each looked for an easier triumph, and a result less fundamental and astounding. Both read the same Bible, and pray to the same God; and each invokes His aid against the other. . . . The prayers of both could not be answered; that of neither has been answered fully. . . . If we shall suppose that American Slavery is one of those offences which, in the providence of God, must needs come, but which, having continued through his appointed time, He now wills to remove, and that He gives to both North and South, this terrible war, as the woe due to those by whom the offence came, shall we discern therein any departure from those divine attributes which the believers in a Living God always ascribe to Him? Fondly do we hope—fervently do we pray—that this mighty scourge of war may speedily pass away. Yet, if God wills that it continue, until all the wealth piled by the bond-man's two hundred and fifty years of unrequited toil shall be sunk, and until every drop of blood drawn with the lash, shall be paid by another drawn with the sword, as was said three thousand years ago, so still it must be said 'The judgments of the Lord are true and righteous altogether.'

"With malice toward none; with charity for all; with firmness in the right, as God gives us to see the right, let us strive on to finish the work we are in; to bind up the nation's wounds; to care for him who shall have borne the battle, and for his widow and his orphan—to do all which may achieve and cherish a just and lasting peace, among ourselves, and with all nations."

Chief Justice Chase administered the oath of office. Lincoln kissed the Bible, bowed, and retired from the platform.

*

PRIOR to the capture of Savannah, Grant had planned to bring Sherman's army north by sea, leaving only a force sufficient to hold Georgia in submission. But Sherman had persuaded Grant to allow him to march northward and unite with Grant by land. He spent a month refitting in Savannah. Late January found him on the march. His route led through a lowland country laced with streams and swamps. Few maps were available, and the roads, mere quaking causeways through the mud, must almost all be corduroyed.

Sherman's boys hit South Carolina like a horde of avenging Goths. The crucible of secession gave off no hot bluster now; the once haughty South Carolinians cowered before their conquerors. Sherman entered Columbia on February 17. That night the city burned. Charleston was abandoned the next day. Major James Austin Connolly wrote to his wife in Ohio: "The army burned everything it came near in the State of South Carolina, not under orders, but in spite of orders. The men 'had it in' for the State and they took it out in their own way. Our track through the State is a desert waste. Since entering North Carolina the wanton destruction has stopped."

Troops from General Terry's command, flushed with their capture of Wilmington, joined Sherman at Fayetteville. Behind the Union army trailed a throng of Negro refugees, afoot or riding in carts, tumbledown wagons, or carriages piled with their meager possessions. Sherman crossed the Cape Fear River in mid-March. Johnston had been restored to command to oppose him. Skirmishing became sharper along the Union front. Johnston offered battle in pine woods and swampy thickets near Bentonville. But Sherman now had almost 90,000 men to Johnston's 35,000. He brushed past and moved toward Raleigh.

Lee hung on courageously as the Union pincers closed. Grant was ready for his final drive; he had spent the winter seasoning new troops. His army waited, snug and cozy in its huts and tents. Food, clothing, guns, and ammunition came to it in abundance. More troops would be coming, too, for in January Lincoln had ordered another draft of 300,000 men. The country had responded with a lilt, as "We are coming, Father Abraham, three hundred thousand strong," became a favorite war song.

Lee's situation was so desperate that he must move or starve. More often the wagons he sent out for food and forage returned empty or half-filled. Richmond faced destitution. Every day the red flags of the auctioneers, displayed on houses, announced that the residents were selling their possessions to buy food. Flour soared to $1,500 a barrel. A Negro slave would bring $10,000 in Confederate money and $100 in gold. Mrs. Jefferson Davis sold her cherished carriage horses.

For several weeks Grant's chief concern had been that Lee might slip off in the night to join Johnston, and force Grant to undertake a long pursuit far from his base. "I was afraid every morning," the Union commander wrote, "that I would awake from my sleep to hear that Lee had gone, and that nothing was left but a picket line."

*

On March 20, Grant invited the President and Mrs. Lincoln to visit his headquarters. Lincoln accepted, for he needed to escape his grinding toil. Greeley noted after an interview with Lincoln that "his face was haggard with care and seamed with thought and trouble. It looked care-ploughed, tempest-tossed and weatherbeaten." The last seven weeks had been exhausting: Lincoln had guided the passage of the Thirteenth Amendment, matched wits with the Confederate commissioners at Hampton Roads, kept careful watch on the activities of Grant, Sherman, and Sheridan, called for new troops and searched for means to raise more money, selected two new cabinet members, and drafted his second inaugural, all in addition to his usual daily tasks. On March 14, for the first time, he held a cabinet meeting in his bedroom, so utterly worn physically and mentally that he must have a day of rest.

Welles recorded in his diary on March 23: "The President has gone to the front. . . . There is no doubt he is much worn down; besides he wishes the war terminated, and to this end, that severe terms should not be exacted of the Rebels."

The *River Queen*, with the President, Mrs. Lincoln, and Tad aboard, pulled away from the Sixth Street wharf at one o'clock in the afternoon. Next evening after sundown it tied up in the

James River at City Point. To the north lay the flats of Bermuda
Hundred, with a light flashing from a lookout tower. Beyond lay
Harrison's Landing, where McClellan's army had encamped.
Giant warehouses loomed like great shadows in the night. In the
dark silence to the westward, 130,000 well-clad, well-fed Union
soldiers faced 50,000 ragged, hungry Confederates. Steamers,
transports, and gunboats stirred the river constantly, unloading
men and supplies, carrying away the wounded and the prisoners.
Grant, his wife, and staff had quarters in comfortable huts along
the riverbank.

Captain Robert Lincoln arrived next morning in time for
breakfast. He was serving on Grant's staff. The President's eldest
son had posed a problem. Graduating from college, he wished to
join the army, and Lincoln agreed that he should serve. But the
thought of the loss of another son made Mrs. Lincoln frantic, and
the matter demanded tactful handling. On January 19 Lincoln
had written to Grant: "Please read and answer this letter as
though I was not President, but only a friend. My son, now in his
twenty-second year, having graduated at Harvard, wishes to see
something of the war before it ends. I do not wish to put him in the
ranks, nor yet to give him a commission, to which those who have
already served long, are better entitled, and better qualified to
hold. Could he, without embarrassment to you, or detriment to
the service, go into your military family with some nominal rank,
I, and not the public, furnishing his necessary means? If no, say
so without the least hesitation, because I am as anxious, and as
deeply interested, that you shall not be encumbered as you can be
yourself."

Captain Lincoln reported a brisk fight that morning in the
frosty dawn. Lee had tried to break through the Union lines at
Fort Stedman, near Meade's Station, an important supply depot.
His desperate attack had carried the fort, but a counterattack
threw him back. Lincoln told Grant he would like to see something of the fight, but Grant thought it too risky. Later, with confirmation of the news that Lee had been repulsed, he allowed
Lincoln to go. The President rode in a jolting coach behind a

slow-moving locomotive over rough tracks behind the lines. From
an embankment he looked out upon the battlefield, still strewn
with dead and wounded.

Sherman arrived from North Carolina on March 27. Next
morning Lincoln, Grant, and Sherman sat down together in the
cabin of the *River Queen*: two warriors and a man of peace who
was using their talents to attain what he hoped would be an ever-
lasting harmony within the great American Republic. All three
were Midwesterners, though Lincoln came of Southern origin.
None of them could have come to the top except in America. War
had made them comrades of a sort; each trusted the others to do
their job. There had been no bickering between any two of them,
no suspicions of secret purposes or unrevealed designs, no fears of
dictatorial intentions. The generals had let Lincoln define policies
and manage affairs on the home front; they had used the armies
to further his purposes. Admiral Porter also attended the conference.

Grant and Sherman agreed that one or the other of them
must fight one more bloody battle. Lincoln asked if it might not
be avoided, but he supposed events must decide. The President
seemed disturbed that Johnston might break away in Sherman's
absence, but Sherman assured him that Schofield would keep
matters well in hand. Sherman asked what should be done with
the defeated rebel armies, with Jeff Davis and other political
leaders. Lincoln said he hoped to get the troops back to their
homes, at work on their farms and in their shops as speedily as
possible. As for Davis, he could not say it openly, but he hoped he
would escape "unbeknownst to me," and he told how an old
Illinois drunkard who had taken the temperance pledge used that
expression in trying to beguile a bartender into "spiking" his
lemonade with whisky. Sherman, who had been unfavorably
impressed with Lincoln when they met once before the war, now
came to realize the depths of his compassion and kindliness. "In
the language of his second inaugural," the general wrote, "he
seemed to have 'Charity for all, malice toward none,' and

above all, an absolute faith in the courage, manliness and integrity of the armies in the field."

From the dark deck of the *River Queen* that night, Lincoln perhaps reflected that the next few days would prove decisive. Grant and Sherman were both ready to deliver the final stroke. Their success would mark the end of the bloodletting. But if either Lee or Johnston got away, it might mean long months of harrowing guerrilla warfare. Would there be peace, quiet, and rest under a restored democracy, or a long, racking, bloody spasm?

*

ON MARCH 26 Lee notified President Davis that Richmond must be abandoned. He would try to hold on at Petersburg a few days longer to gather supplies for flight, but his position was becoming extremely shaky as Grant pushed his lines westward to threaten Lee's right and rear. Sheridan had joined Grant from the Valley, and on the 29th Grant ordered him to Five Forks, a strategic road hub, whose seizure would threaten Lee's escape route.

Rain set in that night and lasted all the next day. The wooded, swampy ground became a sea of quicksand. Horses sank to their bellies. Wagons went down to their beds. Someone asked Sheridan: "How do you propose to supply your command with forage if this weather lasts?" "Forage?" Sheridan replied. "I'll get all the forage I want. I'll haul it out if I have to set every man in the command to corduroying roads. . . . I tell you I'm ready to strike out tomorrow and go to smashing things." That night Lincoln wired Stanton from City Point: "I begin to feel that I ought to be home and yet I dislike to leave without seeing nearer to the end of General Grant's present movement. . . . Last night at 10:15 p.m. when it was dark as a rainy night without a moon could be, a furious cannonade soon joined in by a heavy musketry fire opened near Petersburg and lasted about two hours. The sound was very distinct here as also were the flashes of the guns up in the clouds."

Late in the afternoon of April 1 Grant telegraphed Lincoln that Sheridan had carried everything before him, capturing three brigades of infantry, several batteries, and a train of wagons. Lincoln forwarded the news to Stanton, who announced it to the country.

Still later that afternoon, war correspondent Cadwallader came to Grant's field headquarters from the front. He was tired, muddy, and hungry. Grant, commenting that his staff were all away on duty, asked if Cadwallader felt equal to a ride to City Point; Sheridan had just forwarded a number of Confederate battle flags that Grant wished to send to the President with his compliments and as evidence of the good work done at Five Forks.

Picking his way along the boggy roads, Cadwallader arrived at City Point near sundown. Lincoln, who had been notified of his coming by telegraph, sent a tug to meet him at the wharf and greeted him with outstretched arms on the deck of the *River Queen*. "Here is something material," said the President as he unfurled the battle flags, "something I can see, feel, and understand. This means victory. This *is* victory." In the cabin of the *River Queen* Lincoln had Cadwallader repeat the reports from Grant, and asked the correspondent to relate what he had personally witnessed at the front. The President's face showed the joy of a schoolboy at each bit of encouraging news. Every table in the cabin was covered with large maps on which Lincoln had marked the lines of the armies with red- and black-headed pins. Cadwallader spent more than an hour with him, moving pins to the latest known positions of the troops.

Hundreds of guns opened all along Grant's front at quarter of five next morning. Grant sent reports to Lincoln hour by hour, and Lincoln relayed them to Washington. Point after point gave way as Lee's resistance crumbled; he was fighting a delaying action to enable the Confederate government to make its escape from Richmond. That night Lee abandoned Petersburg and slipped off toward the west. Before dawn the Union troops were in the town. Grant entered it at nine o'clock and telegraphed

Lincoln to join him. Not long afterward Union officers on the porch of the comfortable brick house where Grant had set up headquarters saw the President swing down from a horse and stride rapidly up the walk, leading Tad by the hand. His face glowed as he shook hands with Grant. For an hour and a half the two men talked, chiefly about the civil complications that would result from Lee's defeat. Again the President made it plain that he wanted a merciful peace.

Grant had hoped for news from Richmond, but none arrived. Since dawn the noise of heavy explosions had come from that direction, and columns of smoke filled the sky. Lincoln, on his return to City Point, learned that the city had surrendered to General Weitzel. "It is certain now that Richmond is in our hands," he wired Stanton, "and I think I will go there to-morrow." Stanton warned him of peril in the enemy's capital. "Thanks for your caution," Lincoln replied. ". . . I will take care of myself."

Early next morning the *River Queen* churned up the James toward Richmond, preceded by a tug. Admiral Porter followed in his flagship, and the transport *Columbus* carried ambulances and a cavalry escort for the convenience and safety of the presidential party. The Confederates had blocked the channel a few miles above Drewry's Bluff, and Lincoln was obliged to transfer to a barge rowed by twelve husky sailors.

Lincoln, Porter, and three other officers, entering Richmond with an escort of ten seamen armed with carbines, trudged two miles through the streets to General Weitzel's headquarters. A large section of the city had been burned by the Confederates. Three high-arched bridges sagged in ruin. Scuttled gunboats slumped along the waterfront. Tottering walls and chimneys marked the sites of warehouses and arsenals. Shattered glass littered the sidewalks. Smoldering cotton bales sent off a heavy stench to mingle with the smell of burnt tobacco.

A Union officer saw a great crowd pushing up the street. It was a throng of bowing, worshipful Negroes, following the President, who swung along in his flat-footed, shambling stride,

interestedly taking in everything about him. As news of his
arrival spread, the sidewalks became crammed. Heads jammed
every window. Men hung from tree-boxes and climbed telegraph
poles. Blank silence greeted Lincoln in the midst of his sailor
escort; no yells of defiance and no cheers came from the crowd.
Only the Negroes capered joyously. The onlookers seemed
stunned. Lincoln walked with a set face, like one performing a
duty. He gave no sign of fear.

General Weitzel had set up headquarters in President Davis's
house. Lincoln arrived there sweaty, dusty, and tired. "I wonder
if I could get a glass of water," he asked as he sank into a chair.
Lincoln curiously examined the place where Davis had lived. A
cavalry escort took him to the burned district, to Libby Prison
and Castle Thunder, Confederate military prisons. Evidence of
how Union prisoners had suffered moved an officer to exclaim that
Jefferson Davis should be hanged. Lincoln answered softly:
"Judge not, that ye be not judged." When General Weitzel
questioned him about the treatment of Richmond's conquered
people, Lincoln said: "If I were in your place, I'd let 'em up easy,
let 'em up easy."

Back at headquarters, Judge John A. Campbell waited to
consult with the President about Virginia's future course. If
Lincoln would promise mercy and forgo further confiscation of
property, Campbell believed that the Old Dominion would
abandon the fight. Lincoln agreed to allow the Virginia Legislature to assemble in Richmond to repeal the ordinance of secession
and withdraw her troops from the war. He could scarcely pardon
Jefferson Davis, he explained, but few other secessionists need
fear punishment at his hands.

*

L I N C O L N waited anxiously at City Point while Lee played his
last card—Lee's sole remaining hope lay in fast movement. If he
could reach the railroad at Danville, southwest of Petersburg, he
might join forces with Johnston.

Lee ordered supplies to be forwarded to Amelia Court House,

but none had come when he arrived there. The two days he was obliged to spend in foraging not only provided little food but enabled Sheridan's cavalry to outdistance him and seize the Danville Railroad. Lee changed direction and headed west in an effort to reach Lynchburg. On April 6 Sheridan's troopers and detachments of Meade's infantry caught Ewell's corps at Sayler's Creek. Lee lost half of his army and most of his wagon train. Sheridan wired Grant that Lee's situation was desperate: "If the thing is pressed, I think that Lee will surrender." Grant sent the message to Lincoln and got back a reply: "Let the *thing* be pressed."

Hunger became Grant's ally now; Lee's men marched on short rations. Their horses had no forage. Ammunition was desperately low. Here at last were the slow fruits of the policy of wearing down the Confederacy. Sheridan's destruction in the Valley, Sherman's devastations in the deep South, the strangling grip of the blockade, and Grant's incessant pounding, all born of the patient determination of the leader in the White House, had exacted their inexorable toll, beating down the dogged Southern will, whittling, wearing, and sapping until Lee commanded only a shadow of that dauntless army which had terrified Pennsylvania not quite two years before.

*

W O R D came that Secretary Seward had fallen from his carriage and suffered severe injuries. Lincoln started back to Washington at once. The *River Queen* docked early in the evening of Palm Sunday, April 9. The President hurried to Seward's bedside to find his friend in racking pain with a broken jaw and arm. Seward whispered through the iron frame and bandages that swathed his face: "You are back from Richmond." "Yes," replied Lincoln, "and I think we are near the end at last."

Before Lincoln retired that night, a telegram came from Grant: "General Lee surrendered the Army of Northern Virginia this morning on terms proposed by myself. The accompanying additional correspondence will show the conditions fully." The surrender had taken place at Appomattox Court House. Lee's officers and men would be paroled and permitted to go home. Officers could keep their sidearms, and the men their horses for plowing. Grant had acted generously in the spirit of Lincoln's instructions.

Booming salutes shook Washington at dawn, tumbling people out of bed and shattering windowpanes. The morning papers blazoned the glad news. Bells pealed. Flags broke out on homes and public buildings. Lincoln scribbled a hasty note to Stanton: "Tad wants some flags. Can he be accommodated." All business houses closed. Great crowds milled through the streets to congregate at the White House. Lincoln appeared briefly at a window while Tad wildly waved a captured Confederate flag. The President looked joyful, but so tired. He promised to make a speech the following night. He had developed a great fondness for the rebel war song *Dixie*. The Union had now rightfully captured it, he said, and he asked the band to play it.

Washington prepared to give the President a mighty ovation when he made his promised speech. An immense crowd overflowed the White House lawn and blocked traffic on the Avenue. The White House blazed with lights as the tall, gaunt President, an expression of deep seriousness on his face, looked out upon a sea of faces stretching into far-off misty darkness. There was no triumph in his voice. For weeks he had waited for the end, looking to the time when he could discard the ways of war and reunite the people in a firm and lasting peace. His worn body yearned for rest. There was a tired spot, deep inside, he said, that seemed beyond all restoration.

More and more, with peace assured, his thoughts had turned to tranquil themes. On the voyage from City Point to Washington he had read feelingly from *Macbeth*:

> *Duncan is in his grave;*
> *After life's fitful fever he sleeps well;*
> *Treason has done his worst: nor steel, nor poison,*
> *Malice domestic, foreign levy, nothing,*
> *Can touch him further.*

It distressed the President that men of his own party sought revenge upon the South. Representatives of none of the restored state governments had been allowed to take seats in Congress. The Wade-Davis bill had been reintroduced at the last session, and though it had been decisively defeated, there was much talk of ruthless confiscation, of mass disfranchisement of Southern citizens, of treating the Southern states as conquered provinces.

So Lincoln appealed now to the people to act with forgiveness. "We all agree that the seceded States, so called," he said, "are out of their proper practical relation with the Union; and that the sole object of the government, civil and military, in regard to those States is to again get them into that proper practical relation. I believe it is not only possible, but in fact, easier to do this, without deciding, or even considering, whether these states have ever been out of the Union, than with it. Finding themselves safely at home, it would be utterly immaterial whether they had ever been abroad. Let us all join in doing the acts necessary to restoring the proper practical relations between these states and the Union, and each forever after, innocently indulge his own opinion whether, in doing the acts, he brought the States from without into the Union, or only gave them proper assistance, they never having been out of it."

Lincoln made a forceful plea. But it was not the sort of thing his audience wanted at the high tide of victory. The crowd became a little bored and wandered off with dampened ardor.

The speech sounded a warning to the radicals, who planned quick counteraction. "I find Stanton much excited," Sumner wrote to Chase. "He had a full & candid talk with the Prest. last eve & insisted that the proposed meeting [of the Legislature] at Richmond should be forbidden. He thinks that we are in a crisis more trying than any before with the chance of losing the fruits of our victory. He asks if it was not Grant who surrendered to Lee, instead of Lee to Grant. He is sure that Richmond is beginning to govern Washington." Sumner reported Lincoln "very anxious" because his speech had fallen dead.

*

Good Friday, April 14, was a glorious spring day. Lincoln rose early, according to his custom, went to his office about seven o'clock, left instructions for Frederick Seward to call a cabinet meeting at eleven, and wrote a note inviting Grant to attend—the general had arrived in town the day before. The President had his usual light breakfast with Mrs. Lincoln and Tad; when Robert arrived, before they finished, the family was reunited. A few callers had already gathered in the reception room, and Lincoln began his customary round of conferences.

Schuyler Colfax, Speaker of the House, came to protest against the President's allowing the insurgent Virginia Legislature to assemble at Richmond. Lincoln admitted that his action may have been injudicious; but his purpose had been to add to the demoralization of Lee's army through a legislative order recalling the Virginia troops, and he had been careful to avoid recognition of the Legislature as a rightful body by referring to it as "the gentlemen who have acted as the legislature of Virginia in support of the rebellion." The President explained, however, that Lee's surrender had accomplished the purpose he had in mind, and he had already revoked his authorization for the secessionists to meet.

The President made a hasty trip to the War Department for the latest news from Sherman. None had come, and he returned to his office, where Grant and the cabinet waited. Grant recounted incidents of his final drive and gave particulars of Lee's surrender. He expected to hear hourly from Sherman, he declared, for Johnston's capitulation could be only a matter of time. Lincoln said it would come soon, because last night he had a dream—one that had come to him several times on the eve of an important happening, usually a Union victory. It was a vision of a phantom ship, moving very rapidly toward a dark, indefinite shore. It had come to him before Antietam, Murfreesboro, Gettysburg, and Vicksburg. The matter-of-fact Grant observed that Murfreesboro had been no victory; but Lincoln, not to be denied a sign of peace, asserted that this time the dream must foretell the awaited news from Sherman.

The discussion turned to the future dealings with the Southern people. Lincoln spoke kindly of Lee and other officers and especially of the enlisted men in the Confederate army who had fought so bravely in a cause they held dear. Stanton presented a plan of reconstruction which would have wiped out old state boundaries, but Lincoln did not favor it. He was glad that Congress was not in session, for he hoped to have friendly relations re-established before it met. "There are men in Congress," he observed, ". . . who possess feelings of hate and vindictiveness in which I do not sympathize and can not participate." He hoped there would be no persecutions, "no bloody work"; enough blood had been shed. No one need expect him to take part in vengeful dealings, even toward the worst of the secessionists. "Frighten them out of the country," he said, "open the gates, let down the bars, scare them off"—he waved his great hands as though shooing sheep out of a lot.

Grant remained after the meeting to explain why he and Mrs. Grant felt obliged to decline the President's invitation to attend Laura Keene's performance of *Our American Cousin* at Ford's Theater that evening; they were anxious to catch the afternoon train to Philadelphia in order to see their sons at Long Branch, New Jersey.

Lincoln had a scanty lunch and returned to his office. He signed the pardon of a deserter with the comment: "Well, I think the boy can do us more good above ground than under ground." He revoked the death sentence of a Confederate spy, and put his signature to other documents. Afternoon had brought the usual medley of callers, but by four o'clock Lincoln escaped from his office for a quiet drive with Mrs. Lincoln.

In spite of everything the President did to calm and restore his wife, her recent temperamental outbursts had embarrassed him more and more. The loss of Willie made her cling to him with desperate possessiveness; she resented his showing even ordinary courtesies to other women. Lincoln had suffered painfully at City Point when she publicly accused Mrs. Grant of scheming to succeed her in the White House, and at her jealous tirades at the wives of two generals, Mrs. Edward O. C. Ord and Mrs. Charles Griffin, because they rode beside the President at reviews. Even Lincoln did not know all, however; his secretaries spared him what they could. He would have been horrified to learn that his wife had indulged in such an orgy of spending in New York and Philadelphia stores that her debts amounted to many thousands of dollars.

Lincoln bore these new trials patiently and sympathetically, along with all the others, and as the Lincolns rode together on that Good Friday afternoon, they talked about the life ahead of them. "We must *both* be more cheerful in the future," Lincoln said, "—between the war & the loss of our darling Willie—we have both been very miserable."

Returning from the drive shortly after five o'clock, Lincoln found Governor Richard J. Oglesby of Illinois and General Isham N. Haynie about to leave the White House. He called them back and took them to the reception room, where he read four chapters of the humorist Petroleum V. Nasby's "Letters" and talked so long that he kept dinner waiting.

Afterward he made another quick trip to the War Department. More visitors arrived. It was nearly quarter past eight before he and Mrs. Lincoln started for the residence of Senator Ira Harris, whose stepson, Major H. R. Rathbone, and daughter Clara had accepted the Lincolns' invitation to the theater after several others, whom they had invited when the Grants declined, had been unable to go. The beautiful weather of the morning had given way to fog as the presidential carriage turned out of the White House gates. Gas jets on the street corners glimmered faintly through the mist. The sodden air muffled the horses' hoofbeats. At half past eight Charles Forbes, the White House coachman, drew rein in front of Ford's Theater.

The play stopped and cheers resounded as an usher conducted the party to a flag-draped box. Major Rathbone and Miss Harris took seats toward the front. Mrs. Lincoln sat farther back, and the President, after acknowledging the ovation, slumped wearily into a haircloth rocking-chair near the rear of the box.

John F. Parker, a White House guard who had been assigned to protect the President, sought a seat where he might watch the play. No one noticed that a small peephole had been bored in the door of the box, or that two inches of plaster had been chipped out of the brick wall of the narrow corridor to hold a prop against the door.

Less than a block away, at the time the President's party entered the theater, four men sat at a table in the Herndon House, at Ninth and F streets, talking in conspiratorial tones. Leader of the group was John Wilkes Booth, a handsome actor with smooth, pallid skin, silky black hair and mustache, and gleaming, fevered eyes. A member of a Maryland family that had won distinction on the stage, Booth had brilliant talents which had failed of full development. A superb gymnast and swordsman, a skilled horseman, and a crack pistol-shot, the vain, twenty-six-year-old tragedian was subject to fits of temper. Too domineering and impatient for hard study, he had won celebrity with theatergoers by his romantic personal attractions, his impassioned gestures, and his bounding leaps upon the stage. A sentimental lover of the South, he had let others fight for her, but with the imminence of Northern victory a restless conscience impelled him to some drastic deed that might redeem a lost cause. His first wild scheme had been to kidnap Lincoln and spirit him off to the South as a hostage for the release of Confederate prisoners whom Grant refused to exchange. That project failing, Booth formed a mad design—he would assassinate the President.

Booth's winsome personality enlisted others in his plot, but a number of them drew off from him when murder became his purpose. Around the table with Booth now sat Lewis Payne, a brawny, low-browed young giant; George Atzerodt, small, sinewy, and villainous; and Davy Herold, a dark youth with a low, receding forehead, scanty hair and beard, and a slack mouth.

The group broke up. Booth led his gray mare up the alley behind Ford's Theater, passed through the building to the street, entered Taltuvall's saloon, and ordered whisky.

*

THE PLAY went into the third act. Lincoln was enjoying it immensely. Mrs. Lincoln reached out to him possessively. Scarcely anyone observed the dark man who sauntered unconcernedly down the aisle of the dress circle, surveyed the stage and the audience, and handed a note to Forbes, the coachman, who sat on the aisle near the door to the President's box. Forbes allowed him to go in.

A muffled shot and sounds of a scuffle broke in upon the play. A man hurtled from the President's box and crouched on the stage. Smoke drifted from the shadows that concealed the President—a piercing scream came from the box. Booth rose painfully from the stage, brandished a knife, and shouted something that sounded like "*Sic semper tyrannis*," the motto of Virginia. "Stop that man!" someone shouted. Booth hurried off the stage by a rear exit, his right leg dragging clumsily.

There was a moment of stunned paralysis. Then the theater became bedlam as word spread that the President had been shot. Aisles, stage, and galleries filled with shouting, frenzied men. Seats were wrenched from their fastenings in a tumult of disorder.

Soldiers hurried to clear the building and force a passageway across the street, through which men carried the unconscious President to the modest house of William Peterson, a tailor. Tenderly they bore him up the high front steps and through a narrow corridor to a rear room, where they placed him upon a bed, diagonally because of his great height. His breath came in long gasps. Examination showed that the bullet had entered the back of the head toward the left side and lodged near his right eye. The wound bled very little.

Surgeons, cabinet members, Congressmen, and other officials thronged the little room. News came that Secretary Seward had been critically stabbed, that his sons Frederick and Augustus had been wounded, perhaps fatally, by a desperado who had forced his way into their house. Rumors said that Vice President Johnson and General Grant had also been attacked. Terror spread through

Washington under the spectral shroud of night. Measured foot-falls sounded as hastily posted sentries paced the streets.

Secretary Welles, gazing pitifully at the President where he lay partially undressed across the bed, marveled at the great muscles of his arms. Mrs. Lincoln sobbed in a front room. Stanton hurried in and out as he signed and dispatched orders. And always from the bedroom came the moan of that labored breathing.

Throughout the night the watchers at the bedside main-tained their hopeless vigil. From time to time the doctors gave the President stimulants and removed blood clots to relieve the pressure on the brain. Beyond that, there was nothing they could do. Dawn brought cold rain from a heavy, sullen sky, but the silent, stricken crowd still filled the street. The end came slowly. The President seemed to cling tenaciously to life. At last, however, the tortured breathing slowed. It became faint. At 7.22 in the morning of April 15, 1865 Abraham Lincoln gained peace—and immortality.

*

F o r in the days that followed, while Lincoln's body lay in state in the White House, then while a sable-shrouded funeral car took him, along the same winding way that he had followed on his journey to Washington, back to the prairie soil from which he came, while a nation sorrowed, a Lincoln legend grew throughout the land.

Even during Lincoln's lifetime, qualities of the folk hero had been attributed to him. Two political campaigns had made by-words of "Honest Abe" and "the Rail-Splitter." Joke books of "Old Abe's" stories had met a ready sale. The title "the Great Emancipator" made him a symbol of freedom. Simple folk had called him "Father Abraham."

Now it was with reverence that men pronounced these names, along with "Martyr" and "Savior of the Union." People looked upon Lincoln as embodying the nation's commendable traits. He came to be regarded as the true American.

But only with the slow march of time would it be given to most of his countrymen to understand the supreme meaning of his life. Only with that national soul-searching which is born of trial and challenge would they begin to share his vision of man's vast future, and to know their proper part in shaping it.

Because to him the American people were the leaders of an awakening of plain people the world over. Out of the revolution in America which heralded that awakening had come a declaration of freedom and equality foreshadowing "the progressive improvement in the condition of all men everywhere."

Lincoln saw his countrymen as inheritors of a trust. To them it had been given to make democracy succeed, to cleanse it of the hypocrisies that deprive it "of its just example in the world." For in democracy, made genuine, he saw our "last, best hope" of frustrating any tyrant who seeks to regiment or debase or mislead any people, anywhere, and of achieving peace on earth and good will among men through "the universal liberty of mankind."

Lincoln Literature

Jay Monaghan's *Lincoln Bibliography, 1830–1939* (2 vols., 1945) lists 3,958 books and pamphlets written about Lincoln, and the output has shown no diminution since the period it covers. As might be expected, many of these books were trivial or worthless to begin with. Others have been outmoded. The essential parts of still others are available in works of later vintage. The pamphlets need concern only the specialist, the collector, or the bibliophile, because whatever worth-while matter they contain soon becomes incorporated in books. The same thing is true of the thousands of Lincoln articles in newspapers and periodicals.

Paul M. Angle's *A Shelf of Lincoln Books* (1946), an attempt to "winnow the permanent from the inconsequential" in Lincoln literature, contains critical appraisals of eighty-one books that the author deemed of current value. A recent check list of important Lincoln books prepared by Ralph G. Newman, of the Abraham Lincoln Book Shop, includes one hundred titles.

The significance of the important Lincoln books will be explained here, first by discussing the full-length biographies or books planned as full-length biographies, together with those devoted to the entire Lincoln theme. Then books dealing with special topics will be appraised under the relevant chapter headings of this book. Articles will be mentioned only if they have unusual pertinence or have been published too recently to have

gained currency in books. I shall venture into that almost boundless littoral of diaries, biographies of Lincoln's contemporaries,
general, state, and local histories, reminiscences, the whole vast
literature of the Civil War—in all of which important information about Lincoln is sometimes found—only to mention books
that have been especially useful or enlightening to me.

*

THE LINCOLN beginner, or the person who can allocate only
a small portion of his time to learning about Lincoln, looks first
for an accurate, readable one-volume biography. As I stated in the
preface, my hope and purpose is to supply one with this book;
for no satisfactory life of Lincoln within the covers of a single
volume has been published since Godfrey Rathbone Benson,
Lord Charnwood's, in 1917. That is still an excellent book, particularly in its delineation of Lincoln's character and its analysis
of the reasons for his actions. But it antedates all the modern
scholarly research on Lincoln. The same holds true of Nathaniel W. Stephenson's *Lincoln* (1922), which has grave defects
besides, and of John G. Nicolay's *A Short History of Lincoln*
(1902). The recent one-volume *Abraham Lincoln and the United
States* (1949) by another Englishman, K. C. Wheare, deserves
high praise; but it is too brief to touch more than the high-lights.
Paul M. Angle's *The Lincoln Reader* (1947) serves well as an
anthology, but is not biography.

Josiah G. Holland's *The Life of Abraham Lincoln* (1866) is
interesting historically. In presenting the Mid-Victorian conception of Lincoln as a model youth, who forged to the top through
sheer merit and the force of high ideals, it set a pattern that
was followed by conventional biographers for fifty years or more.
Some of the reminiscent material that Holland gathered proved
unreliable; the rest of it is available in better books. His emphasis
on Lincoln as an orthodox Christian touched off a lively controversy.

With Lincoln's death, perhaps even earlier, William H.
Herndon began to gather facts for a biography. But the need of

making a living kept him from writing the book until, in discouragement, he sold copies of his material to Ward Hill Lamon. Lamon's *The Life of Abraham Lincoln* appeared in 1872, ghostwritten by Chauncey F. Black, son of Buchanan's Attorney General. Based on Herndon's material and personal information supplied by Herndon, it depicted Lincoln with sometimes shocking realism: his mother was born out of wedlock, and he probably was too; Thomas Lincoln was a lazy vagabond; Mrs. Lincoln was a shrew; Lincoln had run off and left her waiting at the altar the first time they planned to be married; Lincoln loved smutty stories; he was an opportunist and an infidel; Ann Rutledge was the only woman he ever loved. Black handled political questions with a partisan bias that enraged good Republicans. Still the book had a solid core of fact. It offered more than had ever been known about Lincoln's early life. But it was far from a true picture of its subject.

None of its contents is attributable to Lamon, who had firsthand knowledge of Lincoln that his ghostwriter lacked. But in 1896 Lamon's daughter, Dorothy Lamon Teillard, published *Recollections of Abraham Lincoln, 1847–1865, by Ward Hill Lamon* from notes and memoranda left by her father when he died.

Feathers ruffled by the Black-Lamon biography were smoothed by Isaac N. Arnold's *The Life of Abraham Lincoln*, published in 1885, a book that still has interest because the author knew Lincoln intimately for twenty-five years, though he handled personal matters with restraint.

Turmoil broke out again when *Herndon's Lincoln: The True Story of a Great Life* appeared at last in 1889. It was written by Jesse W. Weik, but Herndon furnished the materials and approved the text. Herndon did not mean to disparage Lincoln; he wanted the world to know him as he was. Matters that he relates from personal knowledge are usually reliable. But he was incapable of balancing conflicting evidence and indulged a belief in his own clairvoyance. Most of Lamon's allegations were repeated in Herndon's book: the illegitimacy of Lincoln's mother, the Ann Rutledge romance, Lincoln's desertion of his prospective bride, the domestic hell that he endured, his lack of orthodox religious faith.

Herndon is the most controversial figure in Lincoln literature, yet to him, more than to any other writer, we owe our knowledge of Lincoln the man—how he looked and walked, his love of fun, his melancholy, the way he thought, his personal habits and idiosyncrasies. A failure at the time of its publication, *Herndon's Lincoln* has been republished several times. The most useful edition, because of the introduction and notes by Angle, was brought out by Charles and Albert Boni in 1930 and reprinted by the World Publishing Company in 1949.

Part of the mass of material collected by Herndon, which is now in the Library of Congress, was published by Emanuel Hertz in *The Hidden Lincoln, From the Letters and Papers of William H. Herndon* (1938).

The year 1890 saw the publication of a monumental work on which John George Nicolay and John Hay had been at work for twenty years: *Abraham Lincoln: A History*, in ten volumes. It was based primarily on Lincoln's personal papers, owned by Robert Todd Lincoln, to which no one else would have access until 1947. The authors also did exhaustive research in official records and sought to keep abreast of the flood of Civil War books and reminiscences that were pouring from the presses. Hay had kept a diary during his White House days, and Nicolay made notes. They interviewed participants in the events they wrote about.

They were "Lincoln men all through" and avowed Republican partisans. Robert Lincoln censored what they wrote as a condition of their using his father's manuscripts. Their Lincoln is conventional. Yet many intimate details of his life are treated with surprising frankness. They depended mostly on Lamon for Lincoln's early years; their treatment of Lincoln as a national figure is warped by partisan bias; and in dealing with his Presidency they sometimes lost him in the confusion of the war. Herndon complained that they omitted or slurred over much that they could have told. But their work has living merit.

Ida M. Tarbell discovered a great deal of new material bearing on Lincoln's life. This has been incorporated in more recent books, but her *The Life of Abraham Lincoln* (1900 and subsequent editions) is still worth reading because she understood Lincoln the man. While she liked to think the best of him, she had an open mind, a quality, singularly lacking in earlier biographers, that foretold and helped to make possible the work of modern writers.

William E. Barton was the first of this modern school. A great admirer of Lincoln, he did not think Lincoln must be perfect. It could not harm a man of such surpassing stature to acknowledge his faults; his human frailties gave ordinary people a feeling of kinship with him. So Barton sought the facts and grounded his work solidly in documents. His most important writings were monographs, which will be discussed in connection with particular chapters of this book. His *The Life of Lincoln* (2 vols., 1925) is superficial except for those portions based on his own research. He did his soundest work in Lincoln genealogy.

Albert J. Beveridge was the first biographer to apply the techniques of the trained historian to Lincoln research, though he was not a professionally trained historian. He conceived of his work as more than biography; it was a constitutional interpretation of America woven about great figures. He had approached his *Life of John Marshall* from this angle, and patterned his Lincoln along the same lines. Thus one of the chief merits of his *Abraham Lincoln, 1809–1858* (2 vols., 1928) lay in its bringing Lincoln scholarship out of the sheltered eddy, where it had been circling rather aimlessly, back into the full current of the historical stream.

Beveridge's passion for new facts led him to investigate such obvious but hitherto neglected sources as the *Journal of the Illinois House of Representatives*, the *Journals of Congress* and the *Congressional Globe*. He worked through masses of newspapers. He checked his conclusions with the best professional historians. He always portrayed his hero against a fully detailed background of events and personalities. As a politician, he understood practical politics and Lincoln's reactions to political pressures. He achieved a great admiration for Douglas—temperamentally he was closer to him than to Lincoln—and rightfully gave him the center of the stage throughout the 1850's. He depended too much on Herndon in some controversial matters. In a reaction from early sectional bias, he sometimes leaned to the South. Death ended his labors just at the point where Lincoln's true greatness begins.

James G. Randall's *Lincoln the President: Springfield to Gettysburg* (2 vols., 1945) is the work of a thoroughly trained and unusually competent historian. The scope of the book is larger than the title indicates, because Randall gives a rather full treatment of Lincoln's pre-presidential life in order to show the influences that had played upon him and the sort of man he was when he entered the White House. Thoroughly documented, the book not only gives the results of the author's years of study but also incorporates the work of other scholars. Randall's approach is critical but sympathetic. He weighs the evidence carefully and is justifiably suspicious of unvalidated reminiscences. Yet Lincoln emerges from his scrutiny as essentially the same powerful, compelling human figure that people have learned to know. Randall's *Civil War and Reconstruction* (1937) is also a basic book.

Carl Sandburg's *Abraham Lincoln: The Prairie Years* (2 vols., 1926 and other editions) and *Abraham Lincoln: The War Years* (4 vols., 1939) are Lincoln classics. Sandburg has become so intimate with Lincoln through long study that the man and his era come alive in his mind. Sandburg recaptures the past. And his power with words enables him to bring it to the reader. He sees Lincoln as the product of American influences. His books are crammed with details, some of them seemingly irrelevant until one realizes that he is building up a background "on which the life of Lincoln moved, had its rise and flow, and was moulder and moulded." It is panamora through minutiæ. Interpretation comes through subtle suggestion. Some of his passages are almost poetry. It is a unique way to write history, but a powerfully effective one.

In *The Prairie Years* Sandburg used his imagination to put thoughts in Lincoln's head, and he allowed too many errors to creep in. These faults were corrected in *The War Years.* The latter book is more authentic history, the former more lyrical.

There have been bitter controversies among Lincoln students in their search for truth. My own *Portrait for Posterity: Lincoln and His Biographers* (1947), which is based primarily on personal letters of various biographers, reveals the feuds and intrigues behind the Lincoln books.

On July 26, 1947, new vistas opened before Lincoln students when the seals were broken on Lincoln's personal papers that Robert Todd Lincoln had deposited in the Library of Congress. Students have already delved extensively into the 18,000 manuscripts in 194 folio volumes, but this is the first full-length biography since Nicolay and Hay's in which they have been used. They contain much new material in Lincoln's handwriting, but the great bulk of the collection consists of letters to Lincoln. Through them we can feel the pressures put upon him as we never could before. They clarify letters that he wrote and explain some of his actions. And we can understand, in reading some of them, why Robert Lincoln kept them under seal. David C. Mearns brought out *The Lincoln Papers: The Story of the Collection with Selections to July 4, 1861* (2 vols., 1948), but his work contains only a fragment of what is to be found there.

The Nicolay Papers in the Library of Congress have also been opened to students and have been extensively used in this book.

The opening of the Robert Todd Lincoln Collection has made possible the preparation of what will become the greatest primary source of knowledge about Lincoln: the *Collected Works of Abraham Lincoln*, prepared by the Abraham Lincoln Association of Springfield, Illinois, under the editorship of Roy P. Basler, and soon to be published by the Rutgers University Press. This will supersede the older printed collections—Nicolay and Hay: *Complete Works of Abraham Lincoln* (2 vols., 1894; Tandy edition, 12 vols., 1905); Arthur Brooks Lapsley: *Writings of Abraham*

Lincoln (8 vols., 1905); Gilbert A. Tracy: *Uncollected Letters of Abraham Lincoln* (1917); Angle: *New Letters and Papers of Lincoln* (1930); and Hertz: *Abraham Lincoln: A New Portrait* (1931). All the Lincoln letters and speeches in those books will appear in the new *Collected Works*, along with a wealth of letters, documents, and speeches hitherto unpublished. More than a fourth of the items are new, and full editorial annotation is provided. As an editorial adviser, I have been privileged to use these volumes before their publication.

For those who may find the *Collected Works* too large or too specialized, there are two excellent books containing selections from Lincoln's writings: Basler's *Abraham Lincoln: His Speeches and Writings* (1946) and Philip Van Doren Stern's *The Life and Writings of Abraham Lincoln* (1940). Stern's volume contains an interesting biographical sketch of Lincoln. Basler's has an introduction dealing with him as a literary craftsman. Basler's text is the more reliable of the two, because it is based on original manuscripts, photostats, or the best authenticated printed versions of the letters and speeches used.

For ready reference to what Lincoln said on particular subjects we have two books, neither of them, unfortunately, as reliable as they should be. Archer H. Shaw's *The Lincoln Encyclopedia: The Spoken and Written Words of A. Lincoln, Arranged for Ready Reference* (1950) not only quotes inaccurately but includes a number of known forgeries. Caroline Thomas Harnsberger's *The Lincoln Treasury* (1950), which also prints forgeries but labels them as suspect, contains too many items that may represent Lincoln's thinking but are not his own words. Both books must be used with a discrimination that few persons possess.

Through the late Oliver R. Barrett's generosity to Lincoln students, all the Lincoln letters in his collection have been published, or will be, in the *Collected Works;* but collateral material will be found in Carl Sandburg's *Lincoln Collector: The Story of Oliver R. Barrett's Great Private Collection* (1949).

Two magazines are devoted to Lincoln study: the scholarly *Abraham Lincoln Quarterly*, published by the Abraham Lincoln

Association, and the *Lincoln Herald*, which leans somewhat more to the popular, published by Lincoln Memorial University at Harrogate, Tennessee. The Lincoln National Life Foundation at Fort Wayne, Indiana, issues a periodical leaflet, *Lincoln Lore*.

Most of the known photographs of Lincoln may be found in *The Photographs of Abraham Lincoln* (1944) by Frederick Hill Meserve and Carl Sandburg. This book also contains pictures of Lincoln's family and friends, government officials, and army officers. The text is reliable. Stefan Lorant's *Lincoln, His Life in Photographs* (1941) is a pictorial history of Lincoln and his times. The pictures are sharp and clear but there is no known picture of Thomas Lincoln, nor any known facsimile of the Bixby letter, the original of which is lost, though both will be found in this book. Roy Meredith's *Mr. Lincoln's Camera Man: Mathew B. Brady* (1946) and *Mr. Lincoln's Contemporaries* (1951) are exquisite pictorial histories. Albert Shaw's *Abraham Lincoln: A Cartoon History* (2 vols., 1929) suffers from a tedious text and ends with Lincoln's accession to the Presidency.

I. *"The Short and Simple Annals of the Poor"*

Louis A. Warren's *Lincoln's Parentage and Childhood* (1926) is the most thoroughly documented study of the Lincolns' Kentucky years. Warren is chiefly responsible for our more favorable view of Thomas Lincoln. Reliable books on Lincoln's ancestry, besides Warren's, are Waldo Lincoln: *History of the Lincoln Family* (1923) and Barton: *The Lineage of Lincoln* (1929). Barton's *The Paternity of Lincoln* (1929) deals with various allegations reflecting on Lincoln's legitimacy, which were current not so long ago, and by exhaustive critical analysis establishes Thomas Lincoln as Abraham's father in wedlock beyond a reasonable doubt.

Warren attempted to refute Herndon's claim that Nancy Hanks was illegitimate by proving that her mother, Lucy Hanks, was a widow when she married Henry Sparrow, after Nancy's birth. Barton vehemently disagreed and the resulting controversy is described in *Portrait for Posterity*. The truth remains in doubt, but the preponderance of evidence favors Herndon and Barton. Warren published many of his genealogical findings in *The Lincoln Kinsman*, which appeared from August 1938 to December 1942. Roy Hays arrives at a negative conclusion in "Is the Lincoln Birthplace Cabin Authentic?" in the *Abraham Lincoln Quarterly* (September 1948).

Beveridge gives the most trustworthy account of Lincoln's Indiana years. Lamon's account, based on Herndon's manuscripts, is more vivid than Herndon's. Warren's "The Environs of Lincoln's Youth," in the *Abraham Lincoln Association Papers* for 1932, is based on careful research. Tarbell's *The Life of Abraham Lincoln* and *In the Footsteps of the Lincolns* (1924) show the author's fine feeling for places, and are also literary landmarks, since Miss Tarbell was the first biographer to recognize the wholesome features of pioneer life and what the frontier did in fashioning Lincoln.

For meticulous information on Lincoln's early life one may consult Harry E. Pratt's *Lincoln, 1809–1839*, one of four volumes published by the Abraham Lincoln Association to give a day-by-day account of Lincoln's activities, so far as they can be determined, from his birth to his Presidency. Pratt compiled the first two volumes, Thomas the third, and Angle the fourth. In addition to the factual material, each volume has an explanatory introduction. Taken together, these introductions are in themselves a factual life of Lincoln to the time he became President.

II. *Young Man on His Own*

Lincoln's life at New Salem, the history of the village, and its restoration by the state of Illinois are described in Thomas's *Lincoln's New Salem* (1934 and subsequent printings). Thomas P. Reep's *Lincoln at New Salem* (1927) contains biographical sketches of New Salem settlers. Pratt's authoritative *The Personal Finances of Abraham Lincoln* (1943) shows that Lincoln overcame his financial difficulties in a relatively short time. His *Lincoln,*

1809–1839 gives a reliable concise account of Lincoln in the Black Hawk War.

The discovery of a copy of William Dean Howells's campaign biography, *Life of Abraham Lincoln* (1860), corrected by Lincoln with marginal notations, enables us to treat many traditional incidents of his early life with certainty; for Lincoln's corrections are so meticulous that the book takes on the nature of an autobiography. The Abraham Lincoln Association republished it in facsimile, showing Lincoln's corrections, in 1938.

William H. Townsend's *Lincoln and Liquor* (1934) is an authentic treatment. See also Angle: "Lincoln and Liquor" in *Bulletins of the Abraham Lincoln Association* (June and September 1932). *Berry and Lincoln, Frontier Merchants* (1947), by Zarel C. Spears and Robert S. Barton, attempts to rehabilitate Berry and must be used with caution.

III. *Frontier Legislator: His Love Affairs*

Lincoln's campaigns for the Legislature and the record of his votes at various elections are treated by Thomas: "Lincoln: Voter and Candidate, 1831–1849" in *Bulletins of the Abraham Lincoln Association* (September and December 1934). William E. Baringer's *Lincoln's Vandalia* (1949) is the best history of the early Illinois capital, its environmental influence on Lincoln, and his activities in the Illinois Legislature. Beveridge's account of Lincoln as a legislator is excellent. Pratt's *Lincoln, 1809–1839* and *Lincoln, 1840–1846* add enlightening detail.

The best critical analysis of Lincoln's relations with Ann Rutledge is in the appendix to Volume II of Randall's *Lincoln the President*, where all previous studies of the incident are cited. The discovery of the article in the *Menard Axis* is related by Jay Monaghan: "New Light on the Lincoln-Rutledge Romance" in the *Abraham Lincoln Quarterly* (September 1944).

All the standard biographies treat the Mary Owens incident. *Lincoln's Other Mary* (1946) by Olive Carruthers and R. Gerald

McMurtry resorts to fictionalized conversation, but does not distort the facts, and has an appendix of all the relevant documents.

R. Carlyle Buley's *The Old Northwest* (2 vols., 1951) gives the best and most complete treatment of the Northwestern frontier. Charnwood points out the possible effect of Lincoln's oddity on his character.

Albert A. Woldman's *Lawyer Lincoln* (1936) describes Lincoln's law studies and his admission to the bar. See also Pratt: "The Genesis of Lincoln the Lawyer," *Bulletin of the Abraham Lincoln Association* (September 1939). Lincoln's partnership with Stuart is discussed in Angle's *One Hundred Years of Law: An Account of the Law Office Which John T. Stuart Founded in Springfield, Illinois, a Century Ago* (1928).

Angle's *"Here I Have Lived": A History of Lincoln's Springfield, 1821–1865* (1935) is an authentic and well-written description of the growth of the Illinois capital and its influence on Lincoln.

iv. *Courtship and Marriage*

All the standard biographies describe Lincoln's near-duel. Angle gives one of the best accounts of it in *"Here I Have Lived."* "The Authorship of the Rebecca Letters" by Basler is in the *Abraham Lincoln Quarterly* (June 1942).

Townsend's *Lincoln and His Wife's Home Town* (1929), a perceptive account of Mary Todd's ancestral and environmental background, also discusses Lincoln's first-hand contacts with slavery during his visits to Lexington, and the Southern influences brought to bear upon him there and by his wife. William A. Evans's *Mrs. Abraham Lincoln* (1932) is a physician's analysis of Mary Lincoln's health and personality. Sandburg and Angle's *Mary Lincoln, Wife and Widow* (1932) is a well-documented, short biography. The appendix by Angle gives an account of Lincoln's courtship and marriage that puts Herndon's story in the realm of fiction. Ruth Painter Randall displays unusual understanding of Mrs. Lincoln in "Mary Lincoln: Judgment Appealed" in the *Abraham Lincoln Quarterly* (September 1949). See also Robert L. Kincaid: *Joshua Fry Speed: Lincoln's Most Intimate Friend* (1943).

Milton H. Shute's *Lincoln and the Doctors* (1933) is a medical biography. William F. Peterson's *Lincoln-Douglas: The Weather as Destiny* (1943) advances some interesting hypotheses regarding Lincoln's changing moods. Leon Pierce Clark's *Lincoln, A Psycho-Biography* (1933) psychoanalyzes Lincoln. See also Pratt: "Dr. Anson G. Henry, Lincoln's Physician and Friend" in the *Lincoln Herald*, Vol. XLV, Nos. 3 and 4.

v. *Lawyer—Politician*

Woldman's is the best available treatment of Lincoln the lawyer, but persons specially interested in his earlier practice may consult Thomas: "Lincoln's Earlier Practice in the Federal Courts, 1839–1854" and "The Eighth Judicial Circuit" in *Bulletins of the Abraham Lincoln Association* (June and September 1935); and Angle: "Where Lincoln Practiced Law" and "Abraham Lincoln Circuit Lawyer" in the *Abraham Lincoln Association Papers* for 1927 and 1928. David Donald's *Lincoln's Herndon* (1948), an outstanding biography, describes the Lincoln-Herndon partnership and appraises Herndon's biographical work. See also *Portrait for Posterity*, where the lively controversies in which Herndon was a central figure are described. Joseph Fort Newton's *Lincoln and Herndon* (1910) contains illuminating letters between Herndon and Theodore Parker.

Donald W. Riddle's *Lincoln Runs for Congress* (1948) is accurate and thorough. Pratt's *Lincoln, 1840–1846* gives daily details of this period.

Barton's *The Soul of Abraham Lincoln* (1920) is still the best objective analysis of Lincoln's religious beliefs. Newton's "The Spiritual Life of Lincoln" in the *Abraham Lincoln Association Papers* for 1933 emphasizes the depth of his faith. Edgar DeWitt Jones's *Lincoln and the Preachers* (1948) describes his relations with ministers. In reading any book on Lincoln's religion, it must be borne in mind that religion was too personal a thing with him to be treated dogmatically.

vi. *The Gentleman from Illinois*

The most detailed accounts of Lincoln as a Congressman will be found in Beveridge and the introduction to Thomas's *Lincoln, 1847–1853.* The national background is portrayed by Allan Nevins in *Ordeal of the Union* (2 vols., 1947). Roy D. Packard's *The Lincoln of the Thirtieth Congress* (1950) is a good short treatment. Charles S. Sydnor's *The Development of Southern Sectionalism, 1819–1848* (1948) helps one to understand this period.

vii. *Echoes of National Conflict*

Beveridge, and Thomas: *Lincoln, 1847–1853* offer the most detailed treatments of the period of Lincoln's retirement from politics. Nevins writes stirringly of national events in *Ordeal of the Union.*

Herndon and Randall are excellent for Lincoln's personality. Sandburg's account is colorful. Isaac N. Phillips: *Abraham Lincoln by Some Men Who Knew Him* (1910) portrays Lincoln as he appeared to Illinois friends. A new edition with a foreword and notes by Angle was published in 1950. Jesse W. Weik's *The Real Lincoln* (1922) is a reworking of Herndon's materials.

George Fort Milton's *The Eve of Conflict: Stephen A. Douglas and the Needless War* (1934) treats the period vividly and with sympathy toward Douglas. See also Allen Johnson's *Stephen A. Douglas: A Study in American Politics* (1908).

viii. *Lincoln Re-enters Politics*

Nevins, Beveridge, and Milton give excellent descriptions of the condition of party flux during this period. Arthur C. Cole's *The Era of the Civil War* (1919) tells about the formation of the

Republican Party in Illinois. Angle's *Lincoln, 1854–1861* describes Lincoln's re-entry into politics and traces his activities day by day. Granville D. Davis's "Douglas and the Chicago Mob," *American Historical Review* (April 1949), disproves the oft-repeated story of Douglas's leaving the platform at Chicago with the words: "It is now Sunday morning; I'll go to church, and you may go to hell!" James C. Malin's *John Brown and the Legend of Fifty-Six* (1942), a profound study of events in Kansas, is hard but rewarding reading.

Lincoln's later law practice is described by Woldman and Beveridge. Valuable information is contained in Angle's "Lincoln and the United States Courts, 1855–1860," *Bulletin of the Abraham Lincoln Association* (September 1927), and Thomas's "Lincoln and the Courts, 1854–1861," *Abraham Lincoln Association Papers* for 1933. Henry C. Whitney's *Life on the Circuit with Lincoln* (1892) gives colorful first-hand observations, though the author sometimes wanders far afield. The edition published by the Caxton Printers (Caldwell, Idaho, 1940) is the most useful because of the introduction and notes by Angle.

Law cases to which Lincoln was a party are treated by Townsend in *Lincoln the Litigant* (1925) and *Abraham Lincoln, Defendant* (1924).

ix. *A Political Plunge*

See the first paragraph under Chapter viii.

x. *Defeated for the Senate*

Nevins's *The Emergence of Lincoln* (2 vols., 1950) depicts the rivalry of Lincoln and Douglas against a graphic national background. An appendix sheds new light on the Dred Scott decision. For Lincoln's attitude toward the United States Supreme Court, see also Angle: "Lincoln and the United States Supreme Court," *Bulletins of the Abraham Lincoln Association* (June and September 1937). William E. Baringer's *Lincoln's Rise to Power* (1937) is accurate and written in lively style. Roy Franklin Nichols's *The*

Disruption of American Democracy (1948) is a scholarly study of
the rifts within the Democratic Party. Don E. Fehrenbacher:
"The Nomination of Lincoln in 1858," *Abraham Lincoln Quarterly*
(March 1950), is an original treatment of the resistance of Illinois
Republican leaders to Eastern efforts to have Douglas head their
ticket.

Edwin Earle Sparks: *The Lincoln-Douglas Debates of 1858*
(1908) conveys the excitement of the times through contemporary
newspaper accounts. Angle's *Lincoln, 1854–1861* gives Lincoln's
itinerary during the campaign. Randall's *Lincoln the President*
ably analyzes Lincoln's and Douglas's arguments. Beveridge's and
Sandburg's accounts are well worth reading.

XI. *The Making of a President*

Sherman D. Wakefield: *How Lincoln Became President* (1936)
stresses the part played by Jesse Fell and other Bloomington
residents in making Lincoln President. Barton discovered Lincoln's purchase of the *Illinois Staats-Anzeiger* and describes it in
his *Life of Lincoln*. Richard Hofstadter's chapter on Lincoln in
The American Political Tradition and the Men Who Made It (1948)
analyzes his political and economic thinking. Nevins's *The
Emergence of Lincoln* contains new material on John Brown and
relates Lincoln's nomination and election to the politics of the
times. Reinhard H. Luthin: *The First Lincoln Campaign* (1944)
is a critical study of the origins, growth, and triumph of the Republican Party, with emphasis on economic factors. Nichols traces
the downfall of the Democratic Party and analyzes the Southern
state of mind. Milton describes Douglas's campaign and his efforts
to hold the South in line. Baringer's account is highly readable.

Editorial comment on Lincoln during the campaign may be
found in Dwight L. Dumond: *Southern Editorials on Secession*
(1931) and *The Secession Movement, 1860–1861* (1931), and
Howard C. Perkins: *Northern Editorials on Secession* (1942).

Mearns's *The Lincoln Papers* contains messages to Lincoln
from persons at Chicago. Murat Halstead's *Caucuses of 1860: A*

History of the National Conventions of the Current Presidential Campaigns (1860) is a colorful contemporary account. *The Memoirs of Gustave Koerner, 1809–1896* (2 vols., 1909) look backstage at Chicago and are revealing throughout. See also *The Reminiscences of Carl Schurz* (3 vols., 1908). Pratt's "David Davis, 1815–1886," in *Transactions of the Illinois State Historical Society* (1930), is the only thing in the nature of a biography of Davis.

Milton Hay's address to Lincoln, a new discovery, is in the Illinois State Historical Library.

XII. *Peace or a Sword*

Angle gives a calendar of Lincoln's daily activities as President-elect in *Lincoln, 1854–1861*. David M. Potter's *Lincoln and His Party in the Secession Crisis* (1942), based on exhaustive research, probes Lincoln's intentions. *Lincoln on the Eve of '61*, edited by Harold G. and Oswald Garrison Villard (1941), gives the observations of a journalist, Henry Villard, who covered Lincoln in Springfield as President-elect. See also *Memoirs of Henry Villard, Journalist and Financier, 1835–1900* (2 vols., 1934). General W. H. L. Wallace's letter to his wife is in the Illinois State Historical Library.

Kenneth M. Stampp: *And the War Came* (1950) studies the North's reaction to secession. The author concludes that there was no hope of harmony between the sections as long as slavery existed and that most of the compromise proposals left the root of the trouble untouched. Randall thinks war was avoidable, though Lincoln was powerless to prevent it. Avery Craven in *The Coming of the Civil War* (1942) attempts to discover how war came in the face of so many factors making for peace. Nevins thinks the race problem that would result from emancipation was more important than slavery in inducing the South to secede. On why war came, see also Cole: *The Irrepressible Conflict, 1850–1865* (1934) and Dumond: *The Antislavery Origins of the Civil War* (1939).

Lincoln and the Baltimore Plot, 1861 (1949), by Norma B. Cuthbert, based on the Pinkerton and other records, supersedes all earlier accounts. Frank Maloy Anderson's *The Mystery of 'A Public Man'* (1948) is a fascinating historical detective story that falls just short of conviction. Many efforts have been made to identify the "Public Man" and to verify his observations about Lincoln, but never with complete success. The Abraham Lincoln Book Shop published the *Diary* in 1945 with a foreword by Sandburg and an introduction by F. Lauriston Bullard.

Burton J. Hendrick: *Lincoln's War Cabinet* (1946) and Baringer: *A House Dividing: Lincoln as President-Elect* (1945) are the best accounts of the selection of the cabinet and the personal and factional hostilities within it. See also Pratt's "Simon Cameron's Fight for a Place in Lincoln's Cabinet," *Bulletin of the Abraham Lincoln Association* (September 1947).

Whether or not Lincoln promised to abandon Fort Sumter if the Virginia secession convention would adjourn, which has long been a point of controversy, is settled by two letters in the Robert Todd Lincoln Collection. On January 9, 1863 George Plumer Smith of Philadelphia wrote to John Hay that a few days after the Virginia convention passed the secession ordinance, he went to the White House with a delegation to procure arms. During the interview Lincoln told them confidentially of having called Baldwin to the White House and of making the promise. Smith asked Hay to have Lincoln verify Smith's recollection of what he had heard Lincoln say. Hay replied on January 10 that the President had stated that Smith's recollection was substantially correct, but he asked him still to keep the matter confidential. See also John Minor Botts's letter of July 2, 1866 to Nicolay, and other material in the Nicolay Papers.

Lincoln and the Patronage (1943) by Harry J. Carman and Reinhard H. Luthin is a work of tremendous research dealing with Lincoln's appointments to a host of government jobs.

Randall's treatment of the Fort Sumter incident in *Lincoln the President* is convincing. He deals with it in greater detail in "When the War Came in 1861," *Abraham Lincoln Quarterly*

(March 1940). For the view that Lincoln jockeyed the South into firing the first shot, see Charles W. Ramsdell: "Lincoln and Fort Sumter," *Journal of Southern History* (August 1937). John Shipley Tilley's *Lincoln Takes Command* (1941) is also highly critical of Lincoln.

XIII. *A War for Democracy*

Milton describes Douglas's efforts to save the Union. Sandburg catches the excitement of the first days of war. E. Merton Coulter's *The Confederate States of America, 1861–1865* (1950) is the best study of the Confederate home front. The offer of the Union command to Lee is fully discussed by Douglas Southall Freeman in an appendix to the first volume of his *R. E. Lee: A Biography* (4 vols., 1947, 1949). Randall makes a careful analysis of Lincoln's border-state policy in *Lincoln the President*. See also his *Lincoln and the South* (1946). Nicolay and Hay's biography takes on increased importance with Lincoln's assumption of office. Hay's *Diary* is indispensable. Its most significant parts are available in Tyler Dennett's *Lincoln and the Civil War in the Diary and Letters of John Hay* (1939). The *Diary of Orville Hickman Browning* (2 vols., 1927, 1933), edited by Randall and Theodore Calvin Pease; the *Diary of Gideon Welles* (3 vols., 1911), edited by John T. Morse, Jr.; the *Diary and Correspondence of Salmon P. Chase* (1903) and the *Diary of Edward Bates, 1859–1866* (1933), edited by Howard K. Beale, contain invaluable material.

Lincoln's relations with state governors are analyzed by William B. Hesseltine: *Lincoln and the War Governors* (1948); Coulter discusses Davis's troubles with Southern governors. William Howard Russell's account of Bull Run in *My Diary North and South* (2 vols., 1863) is a classic. Nicolay described Seward's coming to the White House with the news of Bull Run in a letter of July 21, 1861 to his fiancée, Therena Bates (Nicolay Papers).

The Robert Todd Lincoln Collection yields much new material on Lincoln's difficulties with Frémont. See also Nevins:

Frémont, Pathfinder of the West (1939) and William E. Smith: *The Francis Preston Blair Family in Politics* (2 vols., 1933). A. Howard Meneeley: *The War Department, 1861* (1928) deals with Cameron's mismanagement.

Jay Monaghan's lively *Diplomat in Carpet Slippers* (1945) describes Lincoln's part in directing foreign relations, but should be balanced by Henry W. Temple's estimate of Seward as the more important factor in this field, in *American Secretaries of State and Their Diplomacy* (10 vols., 1927–9), edited by Samuel F. Bemis. Ephraim Douglass Adams's *Great Britain and the American Civil War* (2 vols., 1925) is a standard work. Frank L. Owsley's *King Cotton Diplomacy* (1931) presents the Confederate side. Worthington C. Ford: *A Cycle of Adams Letters, 1861-1865* (2 vols., 1920) describes English sentiment. For European opinion, see also Donaldson Jordan and Edwin J. Pratt: *Europe and the American Civil War* (1931). Thurlow Weed's letters to Lincoln and Seward are in the Robert Todd Lincoln Collection.

xiv. *Shadows on the White House*

McClellan's Own Story (1887) is enlightening, especially the letters to his wife. T. Harry Williams's *Lincoln and the Radicals* (1941) reveals the sordid factionalism within the Republican Party. Kenneth P. Williams's *Lincoln Finds a General* (2 vols., 1949), actually a military history, is merciless to McClellan. Randall defends McClellan as an outstanding general who was ruined by the radicals. William Starr Myers: *A Study in Personality: General George Brinton McClellan* (1934) is sympathetic. Bruce Catton's *Mr. Lincoln's Army* (1951), a history of the Army of the Potomac under McClellan, is written with understanding.

Margaret Leech presents a delightful study of the wartime capital in *Reveille in Washington* (1941). For the Lincolns' advent to Washington and its reaction to them, see also the references to Mrs. Lincoln under Chapters iv and xix. Nicolay recorded Lincoln's grief at Willie's death in a notebook that he kept during part of February 1862 (Nicolay Papers).

xv. *McClellan in Command*

T. Harry Williams's *Lincoln and His Generals* (1952) is the most recent and most penetrating study of Lincoln as a military strategist. Colin R. Ballard's *The Military Genius of Abraham Lincoln* (1926), along with John M. Palmer's *Washington, Lincoln, Wilson: Three War Statesmen* (1930) and Sir Frederick Maurice's *Statesmen and Soldiers of the Civil War* (1926) changed the general attitude toward Lincoln's military leadership from blame to praise. For Lincoln's instigation of the capture of Norfolk, see Baringer: "On Enemy Soil: President Lincoln's Norfolk Campaign," *Abraham Lincoln Quarterly* (March 1952). See also the books on military matters cited under Chapter xiv.

Bell Irvin Wiley's "Billy Yank and Abraham Lincoln" in the *Abraham Lincoln Quarterly* (June 1950) describes the common soldier's feelings toward the President. McClellan's opinion of Lee, and Chase's letter to Lincoln about General Hunter's proclamation, are in the Robert Todd Lincoln Collection.

xvi. *"The Occasion is Piled High with Difficulty"*

For military affairs, see the books cited under Chapters xiv and xv. Otto Eisenschiml's *The Celebrated Case of Fitz John Porter* (1950) defends McClellan at Second Bull Run.

All the standard biographies describe the cabinet crisis. T. Harry Williams and Hendrick are especially good. Randall analyzes the Emancipation Proclamation and its effects. See also Wiley: *Southern Negroes, 1861–1865* (1938). "Lincoln and Negro Colonization in Central America," by Warren A. Beck, is in the *Abraham Lincoln Quarterly* (September 1950).

Lincoln's visit to Hooker's army is described by Noah Brooks in *Washington in Lincoln's Time* (1895) and in Dr. Henry's letter to his wife, in the *Abraham Lincoln Quarterly* (March 1942).

Pope's letter to Yates is in the Chicago Historical Society. Telegraphic reports from Antietam, Fredericksburg, Chancellorsville, and Vicksburg, Hiram Barney's telegram to Lincoln, a copy

of Halleck's letter to Burnside about the strategy at Fredericksburg, and a copy of Murat Halstead's letter about Grant are in
the Robert Todd Lincoln Collection. The unpublished reminiscences of Sylvanus Cadwallader are in the Illinois State Historical
Library.

xvii. *The Signs Look Better*

Wood Gray: *The Hidden Civil War* (1942) and Milton's *Abraham
Lincoln and the Fifth Column* (1942) deal with Lincoln's troubles
with Northern seditionists. Randall's scholarly *Constitutional
Problems under Lincoln* (revised edition, 1950) is the basic book
on the subject. See also John M. Zane: "Lincoln, the Constitutional Lawyer," *Abraham Lincoln Association Papers* for 1932, and
Andrew C. McLaughlin: "Lincoln, the Constitution and Democracy," ibid., 1936. Robert S. Harper's *Lincoln and the Press*
(1951) is an encyclopedic treatment of the Lincoln administration's suppression of newspapers and of editorial opinion about
Lincoln.

The draft laws are explained in Fred A. Shannon's *The
Organization and Administration of the Union Army, 1861–1865*
(2 vols., 1928). Barton's *Lincoln at Gettysburg* (1930, 1950) and
Bullard's *"A Few Appropriate Remarks": Lincoln's Gettysburg
Address* (1944) fully cover the subject. Luther E. Robinson's
Abraham Lincoln as a Man of Letters (1918) and Daniel Kilham
Dodge's *Abraham Lincoln, Master of Words* (1924) are incisive
studies of Lincoln's literary artistry.

Grant's letter to Lincoln about colored troops, the reports
from Chattanooga, Rosecrans's and Zach Chandler's letters to
Lincoln about an amnesty, and John Murray Forbes's letter to
Lincoln are in the Robert Todd Lincoln Collection.

xviii. *"There Are No Lincoln Men"*

Much new material for this chapter came from the Robert Todd
Lincoln Collection. George Ashmun's letter to General Banks is

from *Concerning Mr. Lincoln* (1944), a book revealing Lincoln as contemporary letter-writers saw him, compiled by Pratt. Montgomery Blair's letter to the Reverend W. B. Sprague is in the Illinois State Historical Library.

James F. Glonek's "Lincoln, Johnson and the Baltimore Ticket" in the *Abraham Lincoln Quarterly* (March 1951) disproves Lincoln's alleged participation in the nomination of Andrew Johnson for Vice President, once a subject of sharp controversy between Nicolay and Alexander K. McClure (see the appendix to McClure's *Abraham Lincoln and Men of War Time* (1892) and *Portrait for Posterity*). Nicolay describes the meeting of the Republican executive committee at the White House in letters to Hay and Therena Bates, dated August 25 and 28, 1864 (Nicolay Papers). Republican campaign tactics are described in Francis Brown's *Raymond of the Times* (1951).

T. Harry Williams in *Lincoln and his Generals* shows that Grant's plans had undergone such modifications through Lincoln's influence that the final strategy was as much Lincoln's as Grant's, though the President allowed the general to take the credit for it. John Henry Cramer has made the most searching study of the Fort Stevens incident in *Lincoln under Enemy Fire* (1948). General Ramseur's letters to his wife are in Henry Steele Commager's *The Blue and the Gray* (2 vols., 1950), from originals at the University of North Carolina. Lincoln's relations with James Gordon Bennett are the subject of David Quentin Voigt's " 'Too Pitchy to Touch'—President Lincoln and Editor Bennett" in the *Abraham Lincoln Quarterly* (September 1950).

For Lincoln's alleged bargain with Frémont to dismiss Montgomery Blair, see Nevins's *Fremont, Pathfinder of the West;* Winfred A. Harbison's "Zachariah Chandler's Part in the Reelection of Abraham Lincoln," *Mississippi Valley Historical Review* (September 1935); and Charles R. Wilson's "New Light on the Lincoln-Blair-Fremont Bargain" in the *American Historical Review* (October 1936).

Pratt's *The Personal Finances of Abraham Lincoln* tells about the accumulation and administration of Lincoln's estate.

Charles H. McCarthy: *Lincoln's Plan of Reconstruction* (1901), and Williams: *Lincoln and the Radicals* make excellent companion studies on Lincoln's efforts to restore the South. Randall handles the subject ably in *Lincoln the President* and *Lincoln and the South.*

XIX. *Profile of a President*

The Robert Todd Lincoln Collection and the Nicolay Papers yielded new material for this chapter. John Hay's "Life in the White House in the Time of Lincoln," *Century Magazine* (November 1890); Helen Nicolay's *Personal Traits of Abraham Lincoln* (1912), her *Lincoln's Secretary* (1949), and William O. Stoddard's *Inside the White House in War Times* (1890) portray Lincoln as his secretaries saw him. Hay confided many incidents of White House life to his *Diary.* David H. Bates's *Lincoln in the Telegraph Office* (1907) gives the young operators' impressions of Lincoln during his nightly visits.

Pratt's *Concerning Mr. Lincoln* contains first-hand accounts of interviews with Lincoln. Julia Taft Bayne: *Tad Lincoln's Father* (1931) and Katherine Helm: *True Story of Mary, Wife of Lincoln* (1928) describe intimate scenes. Francis B. Carpenter recorded his observations in *The Inner Life of Abraham Lincoln: Six Months at the White House* (1866, 1883). Elizabeth Keckley's *Behind the Scenes* (1868), the work of a ghostwriter, must be used critically. See also Elizabeth Todd Grimsley: "Six Months in the White House," in *Journal of the Illinois State Historical Society* (October 1926); Virginia Kinnaird: "Mrs. Lincoln as a White House Hostess," in *Papers in Illinois History* (1938); Townsend: "Lincoln's 'Rebel' niece—Katherine Helm, Artist and Author," in the *Lincoln Herald* (February 1945), and the references to Mrs. Lincoln under Chapter iv.

David Rankin Barbee's "The Musical Mr. Lincoln," *Abraham Lincoln Quarterly* (December 1949) is an original study. Noah Brooks's *Washington in Lincoln's Time* is the outgrowth of contemporary articles for a newspaper. Ten previously unpublished letters of Mary Lincoln to Mrs. John Henry Shearer are quoted by Charles V. Darrin in "Your Truly Attached Friend, Mary Lincoln," *Journal of the Illinois State Historical Society* (Spring 1951). Bullard describes touching family scenes in *Tad and His Father* (1915). Francis Fisher Browne's *The Every-Day Life of Abraham Lincoln* (1886, 1913) is based mainly on eye-witness testimony. See also John E. Washington: *They Knew Lincoln* (1942); Allen Thorndike Rice: *Reminiscences of Abraham Lincoln by Distinguished Men of His Time* (1886); McClure's *Abraham Lincoln and Men of War-Time;* Rufus Rockwell Wilson: *Lincoln among His Friends* (1942) and *Intimate Memories of Lincoln* (1945); and Lucius E. Chittenden: *Recollections of President Lincoln and His Administration* (1891).

Barton's *A Beautiful Blunder: The True Story of Lincoln's Letter to Mrs. Lydia A. Bixby* (1926), Bullard's *Abraham Lincoln and the Widow Bixby* (1946) and his "Again, The Bixby Letter," in the *Lincoln Herald* (Summer 1951) treat the subject fully.

Facets of Lincoln's personality are described by Thomas in "The Individuality of Lincoln as Revealed in His Writings," *Abraham Lincoln Association Bulletin* (September 1933) and "Lincoln's Humor: An Analysis" in *Abraham Lincoln Association Papers* for 1933. Sandburg's *War Years* is replete with incidents revealing Lincoln's human side.

The quoted letters of Dr. Henry, Mrs. Ninian W. Edwards, and Mrs. Milton Hay are in the Illinois State Historical Library.

xx. *To Bind Up the Nation's Wounds*

Leech depicts the excitement in Washington as the war drew to a close. Lincoln's maneuvers in behalf of the Thirteenth Amendment are revealed in Albert Gallatin Riddle's *Recollections of War Times* (1895). See also Bullard: "Abraham Lincoln and the Statehood of Nevada," *American Bar Association Journal* (1940). Coulter's *The Confederate States of America* and Freeman's *Lee* describe the breakdown of the Confederacy and the last throes of Lee's army.

T. V. Smith: *Abraham Lincoln and the Spiritual Life* (1951) is a philosopher's view of Lincoln's moral nature. In Randall's *Lincoln the Liberal Statesman* (1947) and "Lincoln and the Governance of Men," in the *Abraham Lincoln Quarterly* (June 1951) we see a very human ruler. Lincoln's many-sidedness is exemplified by the fact that Randall considers him a liberal, while Stanley Pargellis in "Lincoln's Political Philosophy," the *Abraham Lincoln Quarterly* (June 1945), sees him as a conservative.

John W. Starr's *Lincoln's Last Day* (1922) is based on faithful searching. George S. Bryan: *The Great American Myth* (1940) gives the best-balanced account of the assassination. Eisenschiml's *Why Was Lincoln Murdered?* (1937) brings forth much new material, with startling implications about men in high position, especially Stanton. David Miller DeWitt's *The Assassination of Abraham Lincoln* (1909), a careful study, also presents some puzzles.

Sumner's letter to Chase deploring Lincoln's softness toward the South is in the Illinois State Historical Library.

INDEX